FIFTY BILLION DOLLARS

My Thirteen Years with the RFC

(1932–1945)

THE MACMILLAN COMPANY
NEW YORK · BOSTON · CHICAGO
DALLAS · ATLANTA · SAN FRANCISCO

MACMILLAN AND CO., LIMITED
LONDON · BOMBAY · CALCUTTA
MADRAS · MELBOURNE

**THE MACMILLAN COMPANY
OF CANADA, LIMITED**
TORONTO

FIFTY BILLION DOLLARS

——————— ☼ ———————

My Thirteen Years with the RFC

(1932-1945)

By JESSE H. JONES

with EDWARD ANGLY

THE MACMILLAN COMPANY

——————— ☼ ———————

NEW YORK : 1951

17837

DEDICATION

I dedicate this story to the memory of my father, William Hasque Jones, from whom I received the precepts which have guided my life, and to the men and women of the Reconstruction Finance Corporation who rendered a great service to our generation in the depression of the early 1930's and in World War II.

JESSE H. JONES

"Things nearly always get better if you give them time. That is particularly true with collateral and properties and people."

—JESSE H. JONES, before Subcommittee of Committee on Appropriations, House of Representatives, Dec. 18, 1939.

FOREWORD

The purpose of this book is to record in narrative form some of the principal accomplishments of the Reconstruction Finance Corporation between its inception in 1932 and my departure from government service in 1945. It has been my endeavor to show what was done and could be done again by government in overcoming economic adversities in a businesslike way when the operation is carried on by men experienced in business and finance who are prompted by proper motives and are not influenced by politics.

I wish here to render unto the taxpayers of the United States of America an accounting of the $50,000,000,000 of their money of which the RFC authorized the expenditure while I was in its service.

Throughout that entire period we received in a manner probably unique in the history of federal agencies the complete cooperation and confidence of each successive Congress. Not a single request that I made of Congress during those thirteen years was refused. On the other hand, Congress increased and broadened our powers from year to year.

I wish also to acknowledge here the generous cooperation which the Corporation received during both the depression and the Second World War from American business, industry, and banking.

The material for this book was gathered and woven together by Edward Angly, who has devoted himself entirely to the project for three years. He has interviewed hundreds of people, and, of course, examined countless records.

JESSE H. JONES

Houston, June, 1951

Any royalties accruing to Mr. Jones from the publication of this book will go to Houston Endowment, Inc., a philanthropic enterprise established by Mr. and Mrs. Jones many years ago.

THE GENESIS OF THE RFC

——————————— ☼ ———————————

President Hoover to Congress in his message of December 7, 1931:

"In order that the public may be absolutely assured and that the Government may be in position to meet any public necessity, I recommend that an emergency Reconstruction Corporation of the nature of the former War Finance Corporation should be established. It may not be necessary to use such an instrumentality very extensively. The very existence of such a bulwark will strengthen confidence. The Treasury should be authorized to subscribe a reasonable capital to it, and it should be given authority to issue its own debentures. It should be placed in liquidation at the end of two years. Its purpose is by strengthening the weak spots to thus liberate the full strength of the Nation's resources. It should be in position to facilitate exports by American agencies; make advances to agricultural credit agencies where necessary to protect and aid the agricultural industry; to make temporary advances upon proper securities to established industries, railways and financial institutions which cannot otherwise secure credit, and where such advances will protect the credit structure and stimulate employment."

Statement issued by President Hoover upon signing the RFC Act, January 22, 1932:

"I have signed the Reconstruction Finance Corporation Act.

"It brings into being a powerful organization with adequate resources, able to strengthen weaknesses that may develop in our credit, banking and railway structure, in order to permit business and industry to carry on normal activities free from the fear of unexpected shocks and retarding influences.

"Its purpose is to stop deflation in agriculture and industry and thus to increase employment by the restoration of men to their normal jobs. It is not created for the aid of big industries or big banks. Such institutions are amply able to take care of themselves. It is created for the support of the smaller banks and financial institutions, and through rendering their resources liquid to give renewed support to business, industry, and agriculture. It should give opportunity to mobilize the gigantic strength of our country for recovery.

"In attaching my signature to this extremely important legislation, I wish to pay tribute to the patriotism of the men in both Houses of Congress who have given proof of their devotion to the welfare of the country irrespective of political affiliation."

CONTENTS

PART II
PREPAREDNESS AND WAR

ILLUSTRATIONS

PART I

Whipping the Depression

1

---- ☼ ----

UP FROM THE BOTTOM—

THIRTEEN YEARS IN PEACE AND WAR

FROM 1929 through 1945, our world was racked by devastating forces which lowered some of the living standards and wrenched the well-being of almost every inhabitant of the earth. The first of these frightening forces became known as the Great Depression. The other was the Second World War, which started in 1939 with Hitler's blitz on Poland and continued until the unconditional surrender of Germany and Japan in 1945.

In January, 1932, the Reconstruction Finance Corporation was created to combat the ravishing elements of deflation and despair in our own country. Farm products had fallen to a starvation level, and the stocks of many banks, railroads, and industrial corporations had dropped to less than 10 per cent of their previous market value; some as low as 1 per cent. Eight years later, with the coming of the war, the immense resources and well trained capacities of the RFC were turned to strengthening America's arsenal and military might.

In these two roles, as a corporate combatant, the RFC loaned and spent, invested and gave away a total of more than thirty-five billion dollars ($35,000,000,000) and authorized many billions more that were not finally used. It grew to be America's largest corporation and the world's biggest and most varied banking organization.

This story which I am setting out to tell cannot be adequately put down. But in its telling I shall try as best I can to give an account of the many billions of dollars granted to the RFC by Congress, with almost unlimited authority to use it, first, in fighting the depression, and, later, for defense and war purposes. In the struggle against the depression the Corporation used approximately ten and one-half billion dollars ($10,500,000,000) without loss to the taxpayers. To the contrary, that money was all returned to the Federal Treasury with approximately $500,000,000 profits, after paying the Corporation's operating expenses and a fair rate of interest on the money which it borrowed to finance this phase of its operations.

In the war effort the Corporation authorized expenditures of more than $34,000,000,000, of which $22,439,000,000 was actually disbursed on behalf of the country's defense and salvation. Of this vast outlay $9,313,736,531 was unrecoverable. That loss, which was foreseen and specifically authorized by Congress, was but a small part of the measureless price of victory in the costliest of human conflicts. After the war, by Public Law 860, approved June 30, 1948, Congress directed the Secretary of the Treasury to cancel RFC notes given it for this $9,313,736,531 war loss.

Similarly ten years before, at our request and after reviewing the Corporation's record in the fight against the depression, Congress authorized the Secretary of the Treasury to cancel RFC notes to the extent of $2,785,867,007, representing relief funds which the RFC had been ordered by Congress to give to the Federal Emergency Relief Administration and other government agencies, with no provision for its repayment to the RFC. There was a disposition on the part of President Roosevelt to use the RFC as a sort of grab bag or catchall in his spending programs, but I insisted on its being operated on a business basis with proper accounting methods, and that when Congress gave the RFC's money away the Federal Treasury should replace it.

Amid the prosperity which now suffuses the country, the bleak conditions which blighted the lives of millions of Americans in the early 1930's have almost been forgotten. They certainly have been by the younger generation. The then agonizing days and nights of fear and insecurity now seem a bad dream, but dimly remembered. In those dire days, between ten and fifteen million employable Americans disconsolately walked about without a means of livelihood. Other millions, whose incomes had been reduced, worked in daily dread of being dismissed or furloughed, or of having to suffer still another cut in the necessities of life. The national income had fallen from eighty billion dollars in 1929 to forty billion in 1932. This meant very simply that the income of every individual in the United States, every farmer, businessman, industrialist, clerk, wage earner, or whatever, on the average had been cut in half. But many had no income at all because they had no work, and, in countless cases, family savings had been swept away in the collapse.

When the $40,000,000,000 national income of 1932 is compared to the more than $240,000,000,000 of 1950, the distress of the early thirties may be better realized and understood.

During the depression many of the big boys suffered as well as the little ones.

Their predicament and that of millions of other people may aptly be illustrated by two stories which concerned my friend Will Rogers, the humorist. One day in the spring of 1934 Will told in his syndicated newspaper column of attending a dinner of the United States Chamber of Commerce.

"It is the caviar of big business," he wrote. "Last time they met I happened to be in Washington and was the guest of Jesse Jones (head of the Reconstruction Finance) at their dinner. Now the whole constitution, by-laws and secret ritual of that Orchid Club is to 'keep the government out of business.' Well, that's all right for every organization must have a purpose but here was the joke, they introduced all the big financiers, the head of this, that and the other. As each stood up Jesse would write on the back of the menu card just what he had loaned him from the RFC (I've got that menu card yet) yet they said 'keep the government out of business.' " *

Bill Costello, who was assistant to the chairman of our Board, likes to relate the story of a day when Will Rogers phoned to ask if he might see me right away. Our switchboard operator immediately spread the news around the offices, and as soon as Will entered the building he was surrounded by employees of the Corporation. Costello tried to usher him into my office, but Rogers balked. "Wait a minute," he said. "I want to commiserate with these folks here."

One of them pointed to the aged, bulging brief case Will was carrying and asked, "What have you got there, Mr. Rogers?" Will motioned them all in close and said: "I'll let you in on a little secret. I am going to see Jesse about getting a little money, and I brought along my frozen assets."

* Reproduced by courtesy of The McNaught Syndicate, Inc.

HEIGH-HO! HEIGH-HO!

Jim Berryman in the Washington Evening Star.

The seven dwarfs (left to right):

Senator Alben Barkley; Representative William B. Bankhead; Harold L. Ickes, Public Works Administrator; Jesse H. Jones; Harry L. Hopkins, Works Progress Administrator; Henry Morgenthau, Secretary of the Treasury; and President Roosevelt.

In its ministrations to the nation's sorely stricken people and their economy, the RFC gave aid and comfort at first hand, or indirectly, to every person in the United States. Let us try for a few moments to visualize the distressful situation of those days.

Five thousand banks had failed, and but for the aid of the RFC seven thousand others would have had to close—if not, indeed, all the rest of them. In rescuing our financial institutions, the Corporation loaned and invested nearly $4,000,000,000. About one-third of these disbursements were loans to pay depositors some part of their deposits in banks which had closed. Another third were loans to help other banks remain open. The remaining third were employed to lay a new and solid foundation for the whole commercial banking structure by investing government money in the preferred capital of banks, trust companies, and insurance companies.

During the Great Depression one-third of America's railway mileage fell into receivership or bankruptcy even after help from the RFC, and more than another third would have done so but for RFC help —more than a billion dollars of it.

When Congress brought the Corporation into being in January, 1932, at the behest of a harassed and unhappy President, Herbert

Hoover—the depression's political victim No. 1—the business, industry, and agriculture of the American people were all about as low as the proverbial toad. For durable goods—the sinews of heavy industry —the market had almost disappeared. For consumer goods the public demand had shriveled almost to the minimum required to keep body and soul together. Farmers were being paid as little as 12 cents a bushel for their corn, 40 cents a bushel for wheat, and, in some places, less than a nickel a pound for their cotton—not enough to cover the cost of production. Their children, like those of many an urban worker, often had not enough to eat or to wear.

The situation can be better understood when compared to prices of today: corn at nearly $1.50 a bushel, cotton above 40 cents per pound, wheat more than $2.00 a bushel, and other things in proportion.

To help the farmer and push upward the prices paid for his products, the Corporation made loans approximating $1,500,000,000, about half of which was disbursed through the Commodity Credit Corporation, one of the earliest offspring of the RFC. With the lifting of land values and commodity prices, most of these loans were repaid and occasioned no loss to the taxpayer.

No form of investment escaped the terrible grinding of the Great Depression. Even some United States Government bonds sold below 83 cents on the dollar in January, 1932, the month Congress created the RFC. The market for real estate mortgages—the largest single form of investment for the savings of the American people—was frozen stiff for a period of several years. To thaw it out the RFC finally established two subsidiaries—the RFC Mortgage Company and the Federal National Mortgage Association. In capitalizing and financing these two subsidiaries and in its direct loans to private mortgage companies, the RFC disbursed more than $500,000,000. We loaned to insurance companies, which were large investors in real estate and railroad securities, more than $125,000,000. We disbursed almost as much to building and loan associations that were limping along the financial wayside. With the return of better times, these loans too were repaid.

Our country is dotted today with thousands of public works— bridges, aqueducts, tunnels, dormitories, toll highways, recreation centers, water and sewer systems, and sundry other improvements— which were financed by the RFC during the depths of the depression as self-liquidating work projects. These constructions provided tens of thousands of jobs on the projects themselves, while indirectly creating employment in the supplying and transportation companies which manufactured the required materials or moved them to sites chosen for their utilization.

Government credit, much of it supplied through the RFC, saved from foreclosure a million urban homes and half a million farms. It built several hundred thousand new homes and repaired and modernized a million and a half other dwellings throughout the land.

The RFC established the Export-Import Bank of Washington to stimulate the sales of the American exporter and American manufacturer to foreign markets. It created the Disaster Loan Corporation to aid the victims of sudden catastrophes, such as floods, hurricanes, and tornadoes. It financed the Rural Electrification Administration through the years of its infancy to make it possible for people in thinly populated areas to enjoy the boon of electricity. It took under its roof the Electric Home and Farm Authority, which enabled hundreds of thousands of people to buy stoves, pumps, refrigerators, vacuum cleaners, cream separators, and other useful machines on easy payments in areas which private finance companies engaged in extending such credits had been unable to accommodate. The bolstering arm of the RFC was extended not only to individuals, farms, and urban corporations, but also to states and cities which found themselves short of funds and of tax collections at a time when part of their population was standing in line to ask for relief.

By 1935 the nation's banks were out of the woods; but the real estate market was still a melancholy one, and for many of the railroads no light was yet visible at the end of the long dark tunnel of deficit operations. In general, however, most of the many facets making up the nation's economy began to sparkle with a brighter luster in the later 1930's, so much so that in 1936, 1937, and 1938 the RFC's collections exceeded its disbursements. Repayments during those three years topped outgo by more than a billion dollars.

The little businessman, who in his tens of thousands makes up the backbone of the nation's economy, was not forgotten in the busy offices of the RFC. During the 1930's the Corporation's directors and other executives worked harder to persuade banks to make loans to small businesses and industries than they did at any other of their various undertakings. The prewar advances by the Corporation to business and industry involved more than nine thousand loans, aggregating about half a billion dollars. The majority of these loans ranged between $500 and $10,000 each, with commercial banks participating in about fifteen hundred of them.

The job of pulling the country out of the depression had been substantially accomplished before the autumn of 1939. By 1940 the national income had climbed to $78,000,000,000, almost double that of 1932 and close to the previous all-time peak of $80,000,000,000. The return of better times would have been far longer delayed but for the billions pumped into the bloodstream of our economy by the RFC against the overpowering forces of the depression.

THE WORLD'S BIGGEST BUSINESS

Then came the war. In the June week of 1940, when France fell and the world of free men stood dazed and full of dread, Congress, with a grant of perhaps the broadest powers ever conferred upon a single government agency, authorized the RFC to help the United States gird itself for whatever military perils might befall. Under this almost limitless power the RFC could do practically anything the defense and war-making authorities thought best for the nation's safety and the prosecution of the war. The Corporation set up subsidiaries to devote themselves exclusively, first, to strengthening the country's ramparts and, after Pearl Harbor, to the waging of total war. The law provided that these wide powers should be exercised in each instance only upon my request, as Federal Loan Administrator, with the approval of the President.

When the Amendment to the RFC Act granting us these unprecedented powers was being discussed in the Senate in June, 1940, one of the Senators called attention to the fact that under the amendment "that fellow," meaning me, "could lend any amount of money for any length of time at any rate of interest to anyone he chose." To this objection Senator Carter Glass of Virginia, who was in charge of steering the amendment through the Senate, replied: "Yes, but he won't."

We began our preparedness program by making contracts to purchase for stockpiling purposes all the tin and rubber available to an American buyer anywhere on earth. These contracts we worked out while the legislation giving us authority to make them was under consideration. Three days after the President signed the legislation, we executed contracts with the British and the Dutch for rubber and tin.

Later on—months before Pearl Harbor—scores and scores of other materials designated as critical and strategic by the President were added to these purchases. Billions of dollars were poured out to procure them or to build plants in which to make them. Through one of its subsidiaries the Corporation loaned or invested more than $9,000,000,000 in building or equipping more than two thousand industrial plants. Among these were fifty-one plants which gave the nation its new synthetic rubber industry and the only tin smelter in the Western Hemisphere.

On the day the United States was bombed into the Second World War, the RFC and its subsidiaries were already conducting the most gigantic single business enterprise, or series of enterprises, the world has ever known. We were engaged in literally hundreds of separate businesses which, individually and collectively, affected the entire economy of our nation and stimulated the economy of many foreign countries in which we were making purchases of materials or helping to establish plants or mines.

Wartime loans and investments by the Corporation helped to bring a 10 per cent increase in the country's steel-making capacity. They helped to build airplanes by the tens of thousands and to fuel them with billions of dollars' worth of gasoline. They constructed and operated pipe lines for gasoline and petroleum transportation. They brought about enormous expansion in the production of magnesium and aluminum, and set up competition in both of those formerly monopolistic industries.

While the Corporation's spectacular plant investments and material purchases, running into the billions, attracted public notice, its directors during the war quietly made nearly thirteen thousand loans to small businesses and industries, mostly to enable them to engage in war work as subcontractors, or feeders, to the big war plants. These small business loans in wartime aggregated almost $2,000,000,000, with local banks participating in many of the transactions, encouraged by a take-out agreement by the RFC.

One RFC subsidiary engaged in preemptive buying in Latin America and the neutral countries of Europe to keep essential war materials out of the grasp of the Axis powers. This was begun even before Pearl Harbor. Another subsidiary subsidized mining and farming to stimulate defense and war production. With other cash subsidies, which ran into hundreds of millions of dollars, the RFC, by direction of the President, helped to hold down the cost of living during the war, particularly the price of meat, bread, and butter.

The Corporation cooperated with the State Department in driving the Nazi air lines out of South America and provided funds to train Latin American pilots and technicians to replace the Germans. Outside the United States it made loans to China and Russia in exchange for needed materials, and, through the Export-Import Bank, advanced money to various other foreign countries to enable their nationals to arrange long-term purchases of American goods and services. Each day the Corporation had a thousand and one things to do at home and abroad. Its loyal personnel accomplished most of these assignments with high competence.

Here let us tell the story of some of those countless human contacts made by the Corporation through its executives and employees with hundreds and hundreds of businesses, with Americans and foreigners of all sorts—bank presidents and one-mule farmers, Senators and sewer commissioners, railroaders and real estate operators, steel corporation executives and stockmen. To the Corporation's door came scores of the nation's most prominent industrialists and thousands of its "little business" men. Always we were in close touch with President Roosevelt, and, during the war, in almost daily contact with the top men of the war agencies, the Army, Navy, Maritime Commission, War Production Board, and the rest.

Always we were pressed. Always we were busy. Each day there was a new problem, first in trying to roll back the devastating forces of the depression, later in pushing forward the war effort. Running day and night under forced draft and dealing in hundreds of thousands, millions, and billions, the Corporation's bookkeeping was simple but accurate. There were no irregularities. Although at the peak the Corporation's personnel exceeded twelve thousand men and women, there was not a single instance of fraud in the entire organization from its inception in 1932 until I left it in 1945. I had been with it from its first day, and its chief for twelve of those thirteen years.

It took more than just a lot of money to do all that the RFC accomplished. It took courage and determination, coupled with business and financial experience on the part of those doing the job. Most of the time it also demanded prodigious enterprise and extra-long working hours, seven days a week. We had to learn as we went along.

During the depression, as during the war, the tasks to which the RFC set itself required not only patriotism, but endurance. No one in the organization ever refused to work long hours or to be at his desk on Sunday. Men representing business and industry seemed ever willing to labor with us for the common good and the country's cause, ofttimes at considerable personal and financial sacrifice. The job required intelligent planning, diligence, probity, and a constant willingness to put country above self.

Looking back, I don't see how we accomplished all the myriad things that we did.

2

---- ☼ ----

AID TO BANKS

*The Breakdown Began in Boom Times—The Crash and
Blackout of 1933—My Suggestion to J. P. Morgan that
He Help—On Trial at the White House—Preferred Stock
Solves the Problem—Wall Street Joins the Program—
Morgenthau Learns a Fact of Banking Life—Cities That
Suffered the Most—FDR Opposes Deposit Insurance—
$150,000,000 to Save Three Banks*

THE breakdown of the American banking system, which came to a
complete ten-day stop in the nation-wide moratorium of March,
1933, was not a sudden catastrophe. Ugly signs and warnings of the
disintegration had continually cropped out in one spot after another
on the nation's map long before the depression crept across the
country in the wake of the stock-market break of October, 1929.
A chance-taking, expanding, and optimistic people, we Americans had
always had more than our share of bank failures, in good times as
in bad. From 1904 through 1920 some 1,170 banks failed. Between
1921 and the end of 1929 there were 5,642 suspensions.

The general depression accelerated both the pace—3,635 failures
in 1930–1931—and the size of the average loss to depositors,
creditors, and stockholders. Deposits affected by the failures in those
two years totaled $2,624,000,000, or about $900,000,000 more than
all the deposits in all the banks that failed in the entire decade of the
1920's.

Nearly all the banks that went broke during the ten boom years
of the twenties were small. Only 12 per cent had a capitalization
above $100,000, and 40 per cent were village establishments started
with less than $25,000. Most of these never should have been opened,

[13]

for the capital investments were too small. With the shrinkage of all values—real estate, commodities, and everything else—which followed the stock-market break of 1929, middle-sized banks began to show up alarmingly in the ever lengthening roll of business failures. Before the snowball stopped rolling downhill in 1933, it had taken with it to destruction some banks capitalized in the millions.

Between January, 1921, and September 30, 1932, more than ten thousand banks in the United States went out of existence—a truly shameful record for the richest country on earth. Many of these crashes were caused by poor management. Other banks were too weak to stand up against even a passing local squall, such as a poor crop or a sudden drop in commodity prices. Still others drowned because they tried to ride the high wave of the stock market and real estate financing in the latter 1920's.

The first centralized effort to block the snowball path of failures was made in October, 1931, when a group of bankers called to a White House conference by President Hoover formed the National Credit Corporation. This hastily assembled financial pulmotor had $500,000,000 of available funds voluntarily made accessible by some of the stronger banks. The National Credit Corporation's purpose was to make loans to weakened banks on their frozen securities. Thus it was able, but only for a few weeks, to lower the financial fever in a few communities. The germs of disaster continued to spread. In December, President Hoover recommended to Congress, among other measures, creation of the RFC in order that the situation might be met with federal funds. He anticipated that the RFC would be needed no longer than a year or two.

The American people had only themselves to blame for many of their bank failures. Some of the ill winds, however, had blown in upon them from across the Atlantic. England's decision to go off the gold standard in September, 1931, following the collapse of the exchanges in Central Europe, set off a tremendous testing of our own gold position. Foreign owners of American securities began throwing them on the markets and withdrawing their dollar balances from this country. These waves of selling sent stock and bond prices tumbling to such low levels that the investment and collateral portfolios of banks, insurance companies, and fiduciary agencies, already shrunken by our many domestic difficulties since 1929, dwindled toward the border line of solvency—and, in some cases, went over the brink.

Foreign holdings dumped on our exchanges were frequently converted into gold. The gold was then transferred abroad in such quantities that our metallic reserve—the backbone of the dollar—decreased to the lowest point in a decade. During the six weeks immediately following Great Britain's abandonment of the gold standard, 15 per cent of the monetary gold in the United States was loaded into ships and sent overseas, a movement without precedent. Among the more frightened of our people, rich, poor, and in-between, the hoarding of currency spread infectiously.

On the February day when the RFC opened its doors—and its big new but inadequate purse—all these destructive forces, and others equally pernicious, had drained the combined reserves of the Federal Reserve member banks to within $50,000,000 of the lowest amount allowed by law. In the last half of 1931 total bank deposits had dropped nearly $6,000,000,000, or about 12 per cent. This decline was further accelerated by increased hoarding in the early weeks of 1932.

The extent of hoarding at that time was exemplified in a story told to us by John W. Slacks, who subsequently became president of the RFC Mortgage Company. By his account, one of the surviving banks in South Dakota which had foreclosed on a large farm advertised it for sale at $12,000. A man and his wife who had read the advertisement went to the bank and had the banker take them out to see the farm. They said they would buy it for $12,000 and make settlement in a few days.

Two days later they showed up at the bank with a large tin can filled with money, and handed it to the banker. When he had counted the money the banker said, "There is only $10,000 here."

The man looked at his wife in puzzlement and said: "Mamma, that can't be right. You count it."

She did, and said, "That's right, there's only $10,000 here."

With a look of disgust the husband remarked, "Well, Mamma, I guess you brought the wrong can."

Even the bankers began to hoard. They called in loans. They declined to make new loans. In the spreading fright the aim of many of the bankers was simply to get their institutions into a more and more liquid position, to convert everything possible into cash and let the business of extending credit—the lifeblood of commerce and industry—take shelter until the dark skies had cleared.

During our first weeks of operating the RFC, several sudden blows, here and abroad, sent the groggy public confidence reeling around the ring. A few days after the RFC authorized its first loans to bolster the economic structure, Ivar Kreuger, the "Swedish match king," committed suicide in Paris and toppled over an international pyramid of financial and industrial enterprises which he had built on a foundation almost as flimsy as the matchstick that first made him famous.

In March the Insull utilities "empire" dissolved, carrying down with it the savings of tens of thousands of small investors scattered over the country, and weakening many other institutions, including Chicago's largest bank.

By midsummer of 1932 the sorry situation changed somewhat for the better, partly because of the swelling streams of money poured by the RFC into distressed banks, insurance companies, mortgage loan companies, building and loan associations, railroads, and the pockets of a million farmers—some of whom had got out shotguns to prevent foreclosure sales. For the first time since the 1929 crash, new and resumed deposits began to exceed in the weekly reports the sum of the deposits tied up by bank suspensions.

The Glass-Steagall Act of February 27, 1932, had also been helpful to the banks. It authorized the Federal Reserve to use United States bonds instead of eligible commercial paper as security for currency notes. This made it easier to meet the growing demand for currency. It enabled the banks to increase their reserves and breathe a bit more easily. Most industrial indices, such as railroad car loadings, unfilled steel orders, electric power production, and corporation earnings, were showing improvements. The index of business failures was falling off. Between the bear-market low of July 8, 1932, and mid-October of that year the aggregate value of all common and preferred securities listed on the New York Stock Exchange nearly doubled. During that troubled summer gold had begun to return from abroad—some $100,-000,000 worth of it in July and August. Farm prices also started upward. We began to take hope.

But we were far from being out of the woods. In the autumn farm prices and securities started to slip downward again. New bank troubles broke out, like fires, in many spots. We took to employing firehouse similes in discussing our work in the RFC. Like a fire department we were on call all around the clock. When a particularly acute banking difficulty in one locality or another required us to send an examiner to the spot, we spoke of him as going there to "put out a fire."

Some blazes, such as the one in Chicago, which we first doused with the "Dawes Loan" of $90,000,000, and others to which we subsequently rushed our help in Baltimore, Newark, New Orleans, Detroit, and Cleveland, were extensive enough to light up distant skies and create nation-wide attention—and dread. Meanwhile hundreds of banks burned out in small towns, their dying embers ignored, for the most part, by all except near neighbors. But in our headquarters we heard about them, night and day, including Sundays and holidays. Many times we saved a bank between midnight and the opening of its doors at nine A.M.

In October, 1932, Nevada declared a state-wide banking moratorium; but there were only twenty banks in that thinly populated state. Eleven of those ignored the proclamation and remained open. East of the Rockies little heed was paid to Nevada's financial troubles. Yet all through the autumn and early winter the inhabitants of seven Nevada towns had to get along on a cash basis without any local banking facilities.

THE CRASH AND BLACKOUT OF 1933

As Christmas approached, sporadic runs troubled country banks in various parts of the Midwest and in Pennsylvania. In January this epidemic spread to some of the larger cities—Memphis, Little Rock, Mobile, Chattanooga, Cleveland, St. Louis. By early February the fever had appeared in Baltimore, Nashville, San Francisco, New Orleans, and Kansas City. On February 9 we were informed that the banking situation in Detroit, which we previously had aided with loans, was critical. Dried out of liquid assets, the larger Detroit banks were tinder for a conflagration that soon got beyond control in a manner I shall later describe in detail.

The debacle in Michigan soon affected the entire country. In one state after another the lights of finance flickered and faded so that it became necessary to declare a nation-wide bank holiday until government help could be arranged. In this task the RFC was called upon for long labors and hurried loans and investments of unprecedented magnitude. All the banks in Michigan had been closed by Governor William A. Comstock on February 14. On the 24th Governor Albert

C. Ritchie proclaimed a three-day holiday in Maryland: withdrawals from banks and trust companies in Baltimore had drained some large institutions to the danger point.

On the day Maryland's bank moratorium began, Charles E. Mitchell resigned as chairman of the National City Bank of New York and its affiliates. Three days later the seven member banks of the Cleveland Clearing House Association limited withdrawals from their 103 branches. Similar restrictions were imposed in Akron and Indianapolis. That same day Samuel Insull and 116 others were indicted by a federal grand jury in Chicago on charges of using the mails to defraud. Public confidence in banks and bankers and in most securities was rapidly evaporating.

Before the following dawn the legislatures in Ohio, Pennsylvania, and Delaware amended their banking laws to empower the state banking authorities to control withdrawals by depositors. By the last day of February, 1933, the hoarding fever had swollen the money in circulation—though not the money in banks—to six and one-half billion dollars, an increase of more than $900,000,000 in four weeks. Gold coin and bullion in the public's hands had jumped to $571,-000,000, almost the equivalent of a $5 gold piece for every man, woman, and child in the country. President Hoover pondered whether he could evoke an old wartime law to make hoarding a criminal offense.

On March 1 bank holidays were declared in Alabama, Louisiana, and Oklahoma. The next day all banks were ordered shut in seven other states—Texas, Oregon, Arizona, Idaho, Nevada, Washington, and Utah. Visitors arriving in Washington for the inauguration of President Roosevelt found notices in their hotel rooms that no checks on out-of-town banks would be honored. On March 3 the Ford interests abandoned their plans to start two new banks in prostrate Detroit. Four more states—Missouri, Wisconsin, Georgia, and New Mexico—declared holidays. After midnight, a few hours before the sunrise of Inauguration Day, state moratoriums were declared in New York and Illinois. That was the knockout blow. By breakfast time every state that still had any banks in operation ordered them closed.

On that unforgettable Saturday morning, as Herbert Hoover and Franklin D. Roosevelt rode together to the Capitol for the great moment of a presidential succession, the economic sun was in total eclipse over all the United States.

The time had now come to build a new foundation for the financial structure and to make permanent improvements.

Under the Act which created the RFC our original repair work had been limited to making loans "fully and adequately secured." Each day it had become increasingly clear to some of us that the banks needed something which we had no authority to provide—fresh investment capital, not loans.

Despite the restraint enforced by law, and the initial reluctance of bankers to ask our help, we had pumped loans, during our first seven months of operation, into almost one out of every four banks in the country. Most of these early borrowers were small-town banks, approximately 70 per cent of them in communities of less than 5,000 population. Towns and cities below 50,000 accounted for 90 per cent of our early loans. We figured these loans directly helped about ten million rural and small-town depositors and borrowers and, indirectly, gave aid to many millions more.

The first application from a bank for an RFC loan came in February, 1932, from the Bank of America National Trust & Savings Association, San Francisco, which had more than four hundred branches covering the whole state of California. For some weeks previously a bitter fight for control of that institution had been waged between A. P. Giannini, its founder, and Elisha Walker, a New York banker who had gotten control away from Mr. Giannini two years before. Their 1932 fight, occurring at a time when the whole banking structure was under public suspicion, gave considerable worry to the Hoover administration. In the struggle both sides held public meetings in a campaign for proxies.

Emerging victorious, Mr. Giannini was elected president and chairman of the bank on February 15. That same day, we formally approved the $15,000,000 loan to his bank which our Board had conditionally authorized at its first meeting on the morning we opened our offices, February 2. Between then and the following July 15 we lent Mr. Giannini's bank $64,488,644. These loans were well secured, for the most part by real estate installment mortgages against homes. The loans were entirely repaid by June 28, 1933, $30,000,000 of the $64,488,644 being transferred to a related mortgage-loan company.

We then lent that company another $30,000,000, which it used in buying mortgages from the bank. The $30,000,000 loan was entirely repaid by February 4, 1934.

Under Mr. Giannini's aggressive leadership the Bank of America later became the largest bank in the world.

By August 25, 1932, we had approved loans aggregating $1,331,-724,000 to 5,520 financial institutions. Of these, 4,865 were banks and trust companies. We had helped reorganize or liquidate 386 other banks which either had sunk or seemed about to go under.

Despite all these efforts, as fast as one situation was improved, several others got worse. It became increasingly evident to us that loans were not an adequate medicine to fight the epidemic. What the ailing banks required was a stronger capital structure.

Obviously, a distressed country could not support an unsound banking system, but a sound banking system could support a distressed country. It was not, however, until the nation-wide collapse of 1933 made drastic measures necessary that Congress became convinced that a new, sound foundation should be put under America's credit structure.

On March 9, 1933, five days after President Roosevelt's inauguration and the fourth day of the nation-wide bank moratorium, a bill authorizing the RFC to invest in the preferred stock or capital notes of commercial banks and trust companies was rushed through the special session of Congress which had assembled only that morning. This Act, revolutionary in our economy, was promptly signed by the new President. He then told the people, in a memorable broadcast, that only sound banks would be permitted to reopen.

In one stroke Congress had turned the tide toward recovery. But it took many months of hard work and much persuasion for us to convince the banking fraternity that this was so.

What constituted sufficient soundness to permit a bank to open was not left to the determination of the men who managed it. The decisions were made by the Comptroller's office, the Treasury, the banking departments of the forty-eight states, and the RFC. Our work week became one of seven days and seven nights. At RFC headquarters Saturday nights were sometimes left free for relaxation; but many of us were back on the job every Sunday morning, particularly through the spring, summer, and autumn of 1933.

President Roosevelt began his second week in the White House by announcing that bank reopenings would commence on March 13 in the Federal Reserve cities, on the following day in the two hundred fifty other cities having recognized clearinghouse associations, and on March 15 in the rest of the country.

In literally thousands of cases, in those feverish days and nights, it was difficult to decide whether a bank was truly sound. The plunge in values, particularly market values, made one man's guess as good, or bad, as another's in assessing the probable worth of many a bank's portfolio. Mistakes were inevitable. A great many unsound banks were allowed to resume business. Judged by the panic prices then prevailing, four thousand of the banks which were allowed to open after the moratorium were unsound. Most of these were originally permitted to resume operations only on a limited withdrawal basis. It was then up to us in the RFC to make them sound with additional capital.

Hundreds of banks were placed in the hands of conservators, a title akin to receiver but less harsh on the public ear.

The legislation providing for conservators, known as the Bank Conservation Act, was passed by Congress March 9, 1933, the same day the RFC Act was amended to permit us to invest in the capital of banks. The conservator of a national bank was in effect a receiver appointed by the Comptroller of the Currency.

Under a conservator a bank could continue to accept new deposits to be kept segregated and paid out on demand. It might also pay old depositors on a parity basis a certain percentage of the money they had on deposit at the time the bank was closed—whatever percentage the conservator deemed the bank could safely pay out. This new method helped keep banks open and on an even keel until the turbulent economic conditions could quiet down. The idea, which was justified, was to stave off creditors long enough to rehabilitate a bank rather than let it go into receivership.

Both the amendment authorizing the RFC to invest in banks and the Conservation Act were the outgrowth of many conferences held during the weeks immediately prior to President Roosevelt's inauguration. These were attended by representative groups of the RFC, the Treasury, and the Federal Reserve. The conferees included Arthur A. Ballantine, Under Secretary of the Treasury; Francis G. Awalt, Acting Comptroller of the Currency; James B. Alley, RFC Counsel in charge of bank reorganizations; Francis T. P. Plimpton, our General Solicitor; Stanley Reed, our General Counsel; Secretary of the Treasury Mills and his successor Secretary Woodin, and myself.

Mr. Reed and I realized, as did various others, that some drastic new legislation would be necessary to take care of bank closings, which were beginning to occur in woeful wholesale lots. Immediately after the big banks at Detroit went under, sundry drafts of proposed bills were whipped into form. During the national bank holiday these were carefully studied and reconsidered. There emerged from these conferences the Bank Conservation Act and the preferred stock amendment. Both were put into final form for submission to Congress by Walter Wyatt, General Counsel of the Board of Governors of the Federal Reserve System. Chosen for this task by Acting Comptroller Awalt, Mr. Wyatt and his staff began working on the Bank Conservation Act on the Sunday immediately following President Roosevelt's inauguration. Mr. Wyatt finished writing the preferred stock amendment about half past eleven on the night of March 8, the eve of the reassembling of Congress, which passed it unanimously after about thirty-five minutes' discussion. Not a copy of the bill was in the hands of any member. With cries of "Vote, vote" the chamber howled down the efforts of several speakers to be heard, and the measure was approved by acclamation. It was an unprecedented expression of confidence in the new administration to go forward with the program of revival.

The Comptroller's office was primarily concerned with national banks. The Federal Reserve was concerned with banks which were members of its system. The RFC and the Treasury were concerned with both national and state banks, either within or without the Federal Reserve. Secretary Woodin found the situation a little confusing, and asked me to make all arrangements for naming the first conservators.

During the arduous days and nights of the bank holiday, all national banks were classified into three categories; i.e., A, B, and C banks. The A banks were those whose capital was considered sound. The B banks were those whose capital had largely disappeared, but which had assets considered sufficient to pay the depositors in full. The C banks were those in which the capital was completely gone and there was an indicated loss to depositors. The various state banking commissioners followed a somewhat similar classification in respect to state banks.

A banks were reopened immediately the holiday ended. B banks were opened as quickly as they could be got into shape. C banks were placed in the hands of conservators, for reorganization with RFC assistance, or for ultimate liquidation, as later developments should determine.

The Comptroller of the Currency's first appointments of conservators were made March 13, 1933, affecting nine banks of which the most important were:

The First Wayne National Bank, Detroit, Michigan, with $25,000,-000 capital and total deposits of $373,000,000;

The Guardian National Bank of Commerce, Detroit, with $10,-000,000 capital and total deposits exceeding $108,000,000;

The Harriman National Bank & Trust Company of New York, with $2,000,000 capital and total deposits exceeding $22,000,000;

The Fidelity National Bank & Trust Company, Kansas City, Missouri, with capital of $4,000,000 and total deposits exceeding $18,000,000.

MY SUGGESTION TO J. P. MORGAN THAT HE HELP

Some days after the Harriman National Bank had failed to open, I went to New York and called on J. P. Morgan, head of the famous firm at 23 Wall Street which bears his name. Mindful that when we had had bank trouble in Houston in October, 1931, I had made it my business to get the bankers and industrialists together and raise enough money to save two failing banks, I suggested to Mr. Morgan that he take it upon himself to see that the depositors of the Harriman Bank received their money in full. It had deposits of only a little more than $22,000,000—a small bank for Fifth Avenue, New York City.

In effect, I stated to Mr. Morgan that country bankers looked to the city bankers for leadership, especially to the New York City bankers; that the leading banker in New York City—and at that time probably the leading banker in the world—was Mr. Morgan; that, with what RFC could do, it would require only $5,000,000 or $6,000,-000 to pay the Harriman Bank depositors, and that might not all be a loss. And I suggested that he write his personal check or his firm's check, for a substantial sum; that he get the other principal bankers in New York, all of them within a stone's throw of his own door, to chip in and raise five or six million dollars and join with the RFC in paying the depositors of the Harriman Bank—he would never have an opportunity to render a greater service to his country, at little cost.

Mr. Morgan told me that it was not his business to tell people what to do with their money. He said he had no responsibility to the depositors of the Harriman National Bank. I replied to Mr. Morgan that it was probably not my business to tell him what to do with his money, but that it was my business and responsibility to save bank depositors where possible over the country. I told him in effect that I thought the small amount of money required to pay the depositors in full of the only New York bank that was closed would be a good investment on the part of the banks of New York. One of his partners joined him soon after I went in, and a little later another partner, who made the statement that there was not even a moral obligation on their part to do what I had suggested.

I then reminded him that the Clearing House Banks of New York City had run a page advertisement in a New York newspaper recently, before the Harriman Bank closed, stating that no depositor of any bank which was a member of the New York Clearing House had ever lost a dollar of his deposit. And the Harriman National Bank was a member of the Clearing House.

I then asked the gentleman the purpose of the advertisement. Was it to induce depositors to leave their money in failing banks and lose it? There was no answer; but Mr. Morgan did not adopt my suggestion, repeating that it was not his business.

Even President Roosevelt, at my suggestion, used his influence in our fruitless efforts to have the New York bankers see to it the depositors in the Harriman National Bank should be paid in full. The President penciled a blunt note on cheap lined tablet paper, such as a third-grade child might use, to James H. Perkins, chairman of the National City Bank, which read:

JIM PERKINS:

I am greatly concerned by the refusal of Judge Proskauer to approve arbitration in Clearing House Banks liability, for full amount necessary for remaining 50% payment. Either a thing is

THE FATHER OF THE RFC

President Hoover in 1931, the year he asked Congress to create the Corporation.

THE FIRST PRESIDENT OF THE RFC

Brigadier General Charles G. Dawes.

right or it is wrong. To attempt to set a limit of $6,000,000 is as I view it either pretty sharp practice or a compromise with right.

If he insists on this course I shall in all probability express my personal opinion of it.

Please do all you can to have this moral obligation lived up to—I have already said this in effect to Geo. Whitney.

F. D. R.

Mr. Whitney was a senior partner in J. P. Morgan & Company.

Conservators were appointed for the remaining unopened national banks on March 16, and on subsequent dates. Meanwhile, the RFC went about the business of strengthening the capital structure of thousands of reopened banks.

During the first three days following the bank holiday, 4,510 national banks with deposits of $16,222,583,000 (based on the December 31, 1932, call for reports on condition) were licensed to reopen. On March 16 there were 1,400 national banks unlicensed, the deposits totaling nearly $2,000,000,000. Conservators were appointed for all of them, as well as for ten state banks in the District of Columbia.

Several score of the banks placed in the hands of conservators in March had, by the end of 1933, been placed in receivership or otherwise put into liquidation. Meanwhile, the RFC made loans to closed banks to enable them to pay off their depositors in whole or in part, as quickly as seemed safely possible. By mid-April, 12,817 banks with deposits exceeding $31,000,000,000 were opened. As 1933 came to a close 14,440 commercial banks were doing business in the United States.

A new banking measure, known as the Glass Act, had been enacted on June 16 to provide for the separation of investment from commercial banking, for tighter control over loans and speculative credit, and for the beginning of federal deposit insurance on January 1, 1934.

The RFC proceeded to invest $1,171,411,111.56 in the capital structure of 6,104 banks. We authorized the investment of many millions more in approximately 1,000 other banks; but, as conditions improved, they were able to proceed without our proffered help.

In national banks and in state banks permitted to issue such securities, we bought preferred stock. From state banks which could not issue preferred stock under their state laws, we bought debentures and capital notes, the effect being the same. Two-thirds of the banks in which we invested were state banks; the others, national banks.

This program of putting capital into banks prevented the failure of our whole credit system. It was carried out without loss to the government or the taxpayer. On the contrary, it has shown profit through interest and dividends. In the fifteen years from the program's inception in March, 1933, through March 31, 1948, the RFC realized interest and dividends on its purchases of bank capital in the approximate amount of $205,600,000, which more than covered the cost of the money to the Corporation. The losses incurred through charge-offs of bank investments during that period totaled only $13,660,000. Of the 6,104 banks in which we invested, only 206 were later compelled to close. From some of these we recovered our entire investment. In the others our losses were relatively small, as the figures above have shown.

Getting the banks to cooperate in the preferred stock program was unexpectedly difficult. In April, 1933, when a large number of newspaper editors and publishers were in Washington on their way to the annual Associated Press meeting in New York, I met with perhaps forty or fifty of them at the National Press Club and discussed in confidence the banking situation. I told them something of the reluctance of the banks to take help from the government. I knew newspapermen could be trusted even in large groups. I was frank with them in seeking their help in discouraging the bankers' fears.

Nevertheless, as the weeks went by, bankers, in general, remained reluctant to ask the government for help. Our preferred stock program moved at a very slow pace. So, in late August, I asked the American Bankers Association for time to address their convention, which was to be held in September in Chicago. They granted my request.

*   *   *

My speech to the convention—in which I advised the bankers to "be smart, for once," and without stint to go partners with the government—was not well received. I was followed on the program by Eugene R. Black, Sr., who had but recently resigned his membership of the Federal Reserve Board to resume his old post as Governor of the Federal Reserve Bank in Atlanta. A good part of his time was devoted to apologizing for my speech.

That evening the Reserve city bankers gave their usual convention-week party. It took the form of a dinner and floor show, held in one of the Chicago hotels. When the show was over, the food eaten and the liquor drunk, Mr. Black was introduced. He made a very entertaining speech for practically an hour. He was one of the most delightful after-dinner speakers I ever heard.

When he had finished I was called upon, but declined. The crowd insisted, and I finally arose. As best I can recall, I said "off the record" that I had addressed them once that day, and that they had not liked my speech. I added that all I had to say on this second appearance was that more than half the banks represented at the gathering in front of me were insolvent, and no one knew it as well as the men in our banqueting room. I then sat down.

That blast started the rush into the preferred stock program. From then on until the end of the year we often processed and authorized purchase of capital in as many as one hundred banks in a day. Yet the job was not perfunctorily done. To help the regular force we borrowed junior bank officers from all over the country. The directors of the RFC, however, passed on each application.

When the President authorized banks to open for business after the bank holiday, he stated in a nation-wide broadcast on March 12, 1933, that only banks that were sound would be allowed to open. This naturally gave people confidence, but it developed that probably no fewer than 5,000 of these banks required considerable added capital to make them sound. In approaching the bank repair job, I discussed it freely with the President and recommended that we should not be too open-handed or too quick about the government putting in all the needed capital, because if we did so the government would soon own the control of too many banks. I told him we should try to interest people in the various communities in reestablishing the banks by putting some of their own money in the stock. He agreed, and we decided that we would be liberal in valuing the assets of the banks.

It was our job in the RFC to see that sufficient new capital was forthcoming to make the banks sound. Because of the uncertainty of values we determined upon a policy of putting capital into those banks whose assets appeared to equal 90 per cent of their total deposits and other liabilities exclusive of capital. We adopted this plan in order to give us time to put pressure on the banks' stockholders and customers and the people in their vicinities to get them interested in putting capital in and owning their own banks.

Such banks as could not measure up to our 90 per cent formula we laid aside in what we called the "hospital." By mid-December, 1933, there were more than two thousand of these "patients," and they had combined deposits of approximately $8,000,000,000. They included national banks, state member banks, and state banks that were not members of the Federal Reserve System.

The situation was serious. On December 15, a fortnight before the dead line, I asked the Senate Banking and Currency Committee, of which Senator Duncan U. Fletcher of Florida was chairman, to let me appear before the Committee in an executive session. I wanted to discuss the situation confidentially. All members of the Committee assembled, and I reported in detail. The session continued for more than two hours. I explained what we were doing, that we had saved or would save all the banks whose assets appraised at 90 per cent of the deposits and other liabilities of the bank exclusive of capital, but that upon the average the assets of the two thousand banks in mind would probably not appraise at more than 75 per cent of the deposits and other liabilities, exclusive of capital.

There was nothing the Committee could do about it, but I wanted to lay the matter before them and get any suggestions that they might care to make. I guess I just wanted them to hold our hands.

After much discussion Chairman Fletcher asked the Committee what was its pleasure. Some Senator started to offer a resolution, but Senator Carter Glass, father of the Federal Reserve System and the wisest of them all, especially in banking matters, interrupted cryptically, as was his custom.

"You fool," he said, "it's Jones' responsibility—not the responsibility of this Committee. We passed the law; it is his job to administer it."

I have never seen a body of men so relieved. The meeting broke up then and there.

Senator Glass had given exactly the answer I hoped for; but I wanted this Senate Committee to know what we were doing and to give them a chance to offer suggestions, for we, the directors of the RFC, were taking upon ourselves a grave responsibility and were stretching the law, in our efforts to save banks by the thousands.

I told the Committee I would come back on the 28th or 29th of December for another conference before deposit insurance went into effect. I went back on the 28th by appointment, but there were only three Senators in the committee room. It was plain the Committee agreed with Senator Glass that this was not their problem child, and that they were mighty glad it wasn't.

Bear in mind that the two thousand impaired banks in our hospital about which I had told the committee were all still open. In October, 1933, the President had mentioned in a broadcast that federal bank deposit insurance would go into effect on January 1, and had added, "We are now engaged in seeing to it that on or before that date the banking capital structure will be built up by the government to the point that the banks will be in sound condition when the insurance goes into effect."

As I left the December 28 meeting on the Hill, we had only two or three days left in which to make good the President's promise. The federal deposit provisions of the Glass Act, which were about to go into effect, contained a clause that the deposits of no bank should be insured until the Secretary of the Treasury certified, on January 1, 1934, that the bank was solvent. With that date only a few hours away, administration officials who were more or less in the know feared another bank debacle would occur if, suddenly, it had to be made known to the public that some two thousand banks could not qualify for deposit insurance.

It could easily be charged, and properly so, that a fraud was practiced on the public when the President proclaimed during the bank holiday broadcast that only sound banks would be permitted to reopen. It was not until the late spring of 1934, nearly fourteen months afterwards, that all the banks doing business could be regarded as solvent. At the time he made his broadcast, the President, of course, thought he was making a correct statement; but the deeper we delved into the condition of banks after the holiday, more and more of them showed up to be insolvent. However, we had the power to make most of them solvent. It is perhaps fortunate that we did not know in March, 1933, the true condition of several thousand of the banks that were allowed to open after the moratorium.

Following my December 28 appearance before the Senate Banking and Currency Committee, I explained the situation to Secretary of the Treasury Morgenthau. I told him there was a way to avoid fresh bank troubles if he would cooperate with us. I proposed that the RFC make an agreement with him which would provide that, if he would certify as solvent the banks in our hospital group, the RFC would make them solvent within six months. Mr. Morgenthau readily agreed. He really had no choice. We put the agreement into writing and were able to keep those banks open.

Carefully we listed the amount of additional capital each of the banks required. Having six months in which to conclude individual deals with them, their officers and directors, we set out to interest them in raising at home some of the additional capital they needed. We wanted their institutions to belong to them and their neighbors rather than to the RFC. In the entire program we succeeded in getting private subscriptions for approximately $180,000,000 of new bank capital. We put up the remainder that was required, and the local private capital was subordinated to the RFC's investment.

ON TRIAL AT THE WHITE HOUSE

The RFC was one of the first of the alphabetical agencies created to meet the depression with money to spend. When the Democrats took over in March, 1933, Washington was soon alive with New Dealers hatching fresh schemes every day to spend money. Soon the National Recovery Administration was created with money to spend. While Buckskin Britches Hugh Johnson rode herd on that, it fell to our lot in the RFC to have to listen to many smart boys about some new scheme or another to save the world. We could not brush them off too ruthlessly because most of them had access to the White House. The unhappy condition of the country lay very heavily on the President's chest. Now and then we had calls and suggestions from capable men as interested as any of us in wanting to lend a helping hand.

About the middle of October, 1933, when we were wrestling with the problem of putting capital into insolvent banks so that they could qualify for federal deposit insurance on January 1, 1934, I had a call from the White House, asking me to meet with the President and some other gentlemen. When I arrived I found in the President's company Eugene Black, then governor of the Federal Reserve Board, Lewis W. Douglas, Director of the Budget, and Henry Bruère, president of the Bowery Savings Bank of New York, a close friend of the President. They were discussing the bank situation and the repair work we were doing in putting new capital in banks. They inquired as to how we were getting along, etc., and we had quite some discussion about it. Certainly if any three men in the country after the President had a right to be concerned about the public, it was these three men in his office that day—the governor of the Federal Reserve Board, the Director of the Budget and the head of the largest savings bank in the country.

A day of two later we met again with the President in his office. The President opened the meeting by asking Mr. Douglas to speak, then Mr. Black, and finally Mr. Bruère. Each in turn criticized the way we in the RFC were handling the job. They were frank and vigorous and predicted that we should have another bank debacle on January 1st when a great many banks would not be able to qualify for federal deposit insurance.

They told the President that it would take $600,000,000 to make solvent all the banks that were open. They said the RFC would be unable to complete the job in anything like the time necessary to avoid more trouble. It was not until these men started talking that I realized I was on trial, the President being the trial judge and my three friends the prosecuting attorneys. When they had finished the President said, "Well, Jess, what have you got to say?"

By this time my ire was up a bit, principally because they had been criticizing me to the President without having the decency to come and talk to me about it. I did not claim that we in the RFC had all the answers, or that we were infallible; but it was our job to do, and it was their place as associates in government work to come to me without trying to horn in on the job by going to the President.

I answered the President about as follows: "These gentlemen have told you that it would require $600,000,000 to make the questionable banks sound enough to qualify for deposit insurance, and that I could not get the job done. I tell you that it will take more than double $600,000,000 to do the job, and that we in the RFC can do it within the required time. Furthermore, these three gentlemen all put together could not possibly do it!"

The President then said, "Boys, I am going to back Jess." Then he added, "Henry, you and Lew and Jess get together and work out a plan."

My plans were already in operation; that is, we in the RFC were getting on with the job. However, from the President's desk I accompanied Messrs. Bruère and Douglas to another room in the Executive Offices. They suggested getting together next morning at breakfast at the Mayflower, saying that, in the interval, they would work out some suggestions.

After they left I went back in to see the President.

"I would like for you to make me a promise," I said.

"What is it?" he inquired.

"Promise me that you will forget that there is a bank in the United States, and I promise you there will be no more bank trouble."

I met with Douglas and Bruère the following morning at breakfast. They presented a long program of five or six pages covering procedure. I started reading it. The first page was all right but contained only a lot of platitudes. Page 2 started out with a plan to set up an organization with a New York banker at the head of it. That was as far as we got. I told them that the job would remain in the RFC, and that there would be no New York banker at the head of it. That ended the meeting.

We completed the job within the time required, and all the banks in the country that were open January 1, 1934, automatically had their deposits insured under the law. They had all been certified by the Secretary of the Treasury as solvent. Incidentally, it required $1,350,-000,000 to do the job instead of the $600,000,000 that Messrs. Bruère, Black, and Douglas told the President it would take.

Messrs. Bruère, Black, and Douglas were all very able men and were well intentioned in interjecting themselves into this problem; but it was our job and we were not turning it over to someone else. They were not the only men who tried to horn in on our RFC operations in the thirteen years of my association with it. We had a big bowl of sugar that a lot of do-gooders would have liked to help give away.

If the RFC had been authorized to invest in the capital stock of banks when it was first organized, or even when its powers were first enlarged in July, 1932, the big Detroit and Cleveland banks which later failed could have been saved. So could thousands of others that went broke all over the country. And the rescue could have been accomplished with little, if any, loss to the government.

PREFERRED STOCK SOLVES THE PROBLEM

We were at least a year late in obtaining the proper implement to fight the depression. Even then, many of those in trouble were reluctant to ask for help. Although there were a few bankers in our waiting room eager to sell us preferred stock the moment Congress authorized us to buy it, the banking community as a whole, and the big-city bankers in particular, balked at accepting the new idea.

To fix the genesis of the preferred stock idea, I have cudgeled my memory and questioned many of my former colleagues without precise success. My earliest recollection of it is a remark made to me in June, 1932, in Chicago, by Melvin A. Traylor, one of that city's foremost financiers. During one of our many conversations that week he remarked, "Our banks don't need loans; they need more capital." He was correct, but our hands were tied during that galling summer and for months thereafter, by the original law which had created the RFC to be strictly a lending agency.

Opponents of the preferred stock program fanned a fear that the Federal Government as part of the New Deal plans was reaching out for control of the nation's banking structure. Not a few thoughtless and selfish bank officers began boasting that their institutions did not need, never had needed, and never would need assistance from Washington.

Our first investment in preferred stock was $2,000,000 in the American National Bank of St. Paul, Minnesota. We authorized it on March 13, 1933, less than four days after receiving our new powers from Congress. That same day, our directors voted to buy $2,000,000 preferred stock in the Baltimore Trust Company, which had first repaired its own capital back in 1931. Unhappily, that bank could not be got into condition to reopen after the national holiday, and our authorization was canceled. Later in the year the Baltimore Trust was reorganized as the Baltimore National Bank. We then put $1,500,000 into its preferred stock.

Our second investment, authorized on March 21, was $12,500,000 in the newly organized National Bank of Detroit. The next two were $32,500 in the stock of the First National Bank of Park City, Utah, and $150,000 in the First National Bank of Paris, Texas. Such was the extent of the program's slow progress during the first three weeks.

At the start we requested the clearinghouses in some of the larger cities to endorse our plan. We also asked some of the stronger banks which did not actually need new capital to participate by selling us a modest amount of preferred stock or capital notes. We had no authority to require anybody to take our preferred stock money. Our motive in asking the stronger banks to cooperate was to take the curse off the many weaker banks which did need new capital.

Officers of the weaker banks were apprehensive that their stronger brothers would point the finger of scorn at them, thereby hurting their business, disturbing their depositors and their stockholders. As a matter of fact, most of the sturdier brethren in the banking fraternity were not as strong as they thought themselves. If the system as a whole had not been assisted by injections of a large amount of new capital into about one-half of all the banks in the country, the collapse would have become so widespread that few, if any, banks could have continued operating.

Looking back on it in later years in the light of the whole experience, we in the RFC concluded that fewer than twenty of the more than six thousand banks into which we put capital actually had no need of it. Of the fifty-five hundred banks which suspended operations shortly before the general bank moratorium of March, 1933, a great proportion had to do so because they lacked sufficient capital and liquidity to weather the storm.

Without new supplementary capital, most of the banks in which we invested would also have succumbed to the shrinkage of values. In a crash of such magnitude it is doubtful if any bank, however sound, could long have continued a going concern.

To get the bigger banks to realize that fact was difficult. I devoted a good deal of effort to persuading the New York banks to join in the preferred stock program. Publicly their argument was that they had more cash than they knew what to do with and, therefore, would simply be paying us interest for money they did not need. This was true with some of them; but, in private, others expressed themselves differently.

WALL STREET JOINS THE PROGRAM

The first crack in the New York situation came October 28, 1933, when we put $25,000,000 new capital into the Manufacturers Trust Company. The other New York banks were holding back, but Harvey D. Gibson, the Manufacturers' president, and Thomas L. Chadbourne, its attorney, admitted the desperateness of their situation and came begging for help.

Shortly thereafter, I had two meetings with groups of other New York bankers, with many of whom I had previously had individual talks. I tried to sell them the idea that, if the big banks of New York would cooperate with our program by selling us preferred stock or capital notes, the banks in the country would follow.

During our second group meeting, they requested me to ask President Roosevelt to receive a committee of three of their number. I agreed. What they wanted, I suppose, was to have the President himself ask their cooperation. Their committee was James H. Perkins, chairman of the National City Bank, William C. Potter, head of the Guaranty Trust Company, and Percy Johnston, president of the Chemical Bank & Trust Company.

I arranged an appointment with the President to see us, but suggested to him that he not ask them to do anything, that it was a bank problem and one in which they should determine what they should do.

I have forgotten whether Mr. Potter or Mr. Johnston first spoke for the committee. Anyway, the President replied to him just as I had suggested. Mr. Perkins then immediately said, "Mr. President, to be perfectly frank, I would like very much to have $50,000,000 new capital for our bank."

That broke the ice. Their cooperation had the effect I thought it would and was very helpful. Eleven state banks in New York soon entered the program to the extent of $43,700,000 in capital notes, $20,000,000 of these being issued by the Guaranty Trust Company, which did not need the capital. Mr. Perkins' National City Bank overhauled its capital structure. It cut the common stock from $124,-000,000 to $77,500,000 to take care of losses by reducing the par value from $20 to $12.50 a share, and it sold $50,000,000 preferred stock to the RFC. The Chase National, under the leadership of

Winthrop W. Aldrich, also issued $50,000,000 in preferred stock, of which $46,000,000 was taken by the RFC, the other $4,000,000 being subscribed for by the bank's common-stock holders. Simultaneously, Chase also overhauled its capital structure, cutting the common stock from $148,000,000 to just above $100,000,000 to take care of losses. These rearrangements by the two biggest banks in the United States were overwhelmingly approved by their stockholders and were helpful to us in getting banks all over the country to acknowledge their true situations and ask our assistance.

By July, 1934, most of the New York banks felt their entrance into the preferred stock program had served its purpose. At that time fourteen of them repaid their capital notes which we held, these amounting to more than $50,000,000. A few years later both the Chase and the National City retired their preferred stock from earnings and recoveries without the necessity of replacing it with new capital.

My advice to most bankers was not to be in too big a hurry to retire their preferred stock. I like to see banks have plenty of capital. By March, 1951, all but 392 of the 6,104 banks in which the RFC put capital had completely retired the preferred stock, capital notes, and debentures held by the Corporation. By then the RFC's investments in banks had been reduced to $92,728,685.05, or less than 10 per cent of the peak total.

At the start of our program our interest charges and dividend rates on capital notes and preferred stock were set at 5 per cent. This we soon reduced to 4 per cent, then to 3½ per cent. Delegates to the bankers' convention in San Francisco in 1936 asked that we reduce the rate to 3 per cent. I agreed that beginning October 1, 1936, all banks which paid promptly according to agreement would get a 3 per cent rate.

Our contract with banks provided for payment of dividends on the preferred stock, and interest on capital notes, at specified dates, the money to be deposited to our credit in the Federal Reserve Banks. A great many banks would be anywhere from ten to sixty days late in making their payments. Giving the reduced rate only on condition of prompt payments had a good effect. At first quite a number of banks would still be anywhere from ten to thirty days late, and would expect the 3 per cent rate; but they didn't get it. After a few months that lesson soaked in, and the money was in the Federal Reserve to our credit the day it was due.

Our purpose was to encourage good housekeeping and punctuality. The 3 per cent rule for good housekeeping is still in effect except that mandatory retirements have not been required since 1942.

Many banks had a ratio of deposits out of proportion to their capital. Because they couldn't lend profitably, they were inclined to retire their RFC capital without replacing it with private capital. To retard that movement we agreed, late in 1936, to accept interest-bearing United States Government bonds at par and accrued interest from banks in retirement of their RFC capital whenever the retirement should take place. Thus a bank could earmark long-term government bonds against its RFC capital, and, if the bonds bore 2½ per cent interest the capital would cost the bank only ½ of 1 per cent a year, which is cheap capital.

The last of the big banks to issue preferred stock was the Bank of America N.T. & S.A. As I have related, A. P. Giannini, the astute and sturdy founder of that expanding chain of western banks, was not in control of his institution on the day the RFC began business; but he recaptured the steering wheel in a proxy battle twelve days later. We made him a loan the following day. He believed that eastern financial interests, and later on some men highly placed in the Roosevelt administration, had designs upon his institution.

MORGENTHAU LEARNS A FACT OF BANKING LIFE

There was a twenty-four-hour delay in licensing the Bank of America to reopen after the holiday of March, 1933. Mr. Giannini asked the two California Senators, William Gibbs McAdoo, who had previously been the bank's lawyer, and Hiram Johnson, to get his bank open. The Governor of the Twelfth Federal Reserve district hadn't included his bank among those to be opened. He got his license to open on Tuesday rather than Monday, as also did a competitive chain, the Anglo California National Bank.

As time went on, there was no love lost between Mr. Giannini and Secretary Morgenthau of the Treasury. One day in 1938 Secretary Morgenthau told a group he had called to his office that the Bank of America had "defied" the Comptroller of the Currency by paying dividends after he had instructed the bank not to do so.

Attending that meeting in Mr. Morgenthau's office were Marriner S. Eccles of the Federal Reserve Board, Leo T. Crowley, chairman of the Federal Deposit Insurance Corporation; Marshall Diggs, Acting Comptroller of the Currency, William P. Folger, chief national bank examiner; and, from the RFC, Sam Husbands and myself.

After seeming to question the soundness of Mr. Giannini's bank, Mr. Morgenthau said he thought he should withdraw from it the government's deposit of several million dollars. I reminded him that all government deposits were secured by government bonds. The Secretary said he didn't know that the Treasury's deposits in commercial banks were secured by government bonds. He turned to Mr. Folger who, of course, confirmed that fact for him.

Some months later Mr. Giannini decided to improve the appearance of his balance sheet in the Treasury's eyes by increasing his capital. He issued $30,000,000 in preferred stock. Individuals subscribed for $2,500,000 of this new stock, and the remainder was purchased by the banks' holding company, Transamerica Corporation, which borrowed the money from the RFC, putting up the preferred stock as collateral. The loan was soon paid.

Six years later I received from Mr. Giannini a letter graciously attributing much of the latter-day success of his institution to the faith we placed in it in 1938. His letter follows:

May 25, 1944

Dear Jesse:

You don't know how delighted I was to receive that nice letter of yours of May 18.

I heartily agree with you that this is the only country where success comparable to that achieved by Bank of America is possible, and I want you to know, Jesse, that the stockholders, myself, and the management of the institution are very much indebted to you for having arrived where we are today. Had it not been for the faith you had in us in 1938 we would, I am quite confident, have found ourselves out of this picture and a part of some other institution in control of the very fellows who today are cornering most of the important business of the country.

You have been a most loyal and true friend, Jesse, and I want you to know that Mario and I and the other members of our

Managing Committee will ever bear in mind your having voluntarily undertaken to sponsor us at the time we were unjustly attacked by certain governmental agencies.

With sentiments of high esteem, I am, with warmest personal
regards,

Yours sincerely,

A. P.

Honorable Jesse H. Jones
c/o Reconstruction Finance Corporation
Washington, D.C.

In carrying out our preferred stock program we held to the conviction that, given a stable banking system in which public confidence
had been restored, the banks would earn the money to pay for and
retire their preferred stock within twenty years without, meantime,
depriving their common stockholders of dividends. With that idea in
mind, our agreements in buying preferred stock provided that after
dividends upon it had been paid, a part of the bank's net earnings
should be set aside each year to retire the RFC's investment. This
plan worked out better and far faster than we had anticipated.

One of the reforms born of the depression was the repeal of the
law subjecting owners of bank stock to double liability. The purpose
of making bank stock subject to assessment equal to the par value
of the stock, in the event of the bank's failure, was to insure careful
and prudent management. The idea worked rather well until the big
depression, when the banks failed by the thousands and the investors in bank stocks went broke individually by the tens of
thousands. Without the removal of the double liability clause bank
stocks would have become a less desirable investment during the
country's period of recovery.

As collateral on our loans to closed banks the RFC accepted their
slow and frozen assets. This made at least a part of the depositor's
balance available to him, pending liquidation. It also prevented forced
liquidation by individual concerns which had borrowed from the
banks and were in straitened circumstances because their deposits
had been locked up. The government could afford to wait; often the
individual could not.

To closed banks we endeavored to lend up to the probable liquidating value of their assets. Thus, with the country's continued improve-

ment, there would be further equities for the depositors. The law, as amended by the Seventy-third Congress, authorized us to buy assets in closed banks as well as to lend upon them, so that receiverships could be wound up. As a practical matter, however, it seemed in the interest of the depositors to lend upon this paper rather than buy it.

The RFC's loans to all banks, open and closed—not including capital stock, capital notes, and debentures—totaled just above $2,-000,000,000 distributed among 7,343 banks. There were no balances outstanding on January 1, 1950. The losses and charge-offs resulting from loans to banks were relatively small, about 1 per cent of the amount disbursed. The Corporation had to take over and liquidate collateral securing a number of the loans and, of course, did not always recover the full amount of the original advance.

The loans were helpful, as medicines are helpful; but I should like to emphasize again that it was our investments in the preferred stock of banks that immunized them against a recurrence of their previous troubles.

CITIES THAT SUFFERED THE MOST

The most painfully punished of all the big cities afflicted by bank runs and bank failures were Chicago, Detroit, and Cleveland. In each of the three, the casualties among depositors were counted in the hundreds of thousands; and the wreckage, in dollar values, ran into the hundreds of millions. Those three tragic situations were of such scope and so acutely dramatic that I have treated them in separate chapters.

Among lesser centers grievously struck by bank failures were Akron, Toledo, Youngstown, New Orleans, and Baltimore. Perhaps the heaviest percentage of deposit losses occurred in Atlantic City. At one time that resort had not a single bank left open. Most of its building and loan associations and other lending and promotional agencies also went to the wall.

At the end of the bank holiday of March, 1933, only one commercial bank remained open in Akron, a city of more than 250,000 population where, in 1930, there had been nine banks. The lone survivor was the Firestone Park Trust & Savings Bank, which Harvey

S. Firestone had established principally for the convenience of the employees of his tire and rubber plants.

Toledo's banks were reduced by the depression from thirteen to six, Youngstown's from nine to six, Baltimore's from forty to twenty-six and Chicago's from more than two hundred to fewer than sixty

In New Orleans, where nine banks had bloomed before the depression, three of the larger ones, despite our previous loans to them totaling nearly $75,000,000, withered so badly that they could not reopen after the national holiday. Into the reorganization of two of these the RFC put an additional $1,500,000 each in preferred stock in May, 1933. The third bank and its title guarantee affiliate, operated by two brothers who were friends of spectacular Senator Huey Long of Louisiana, father of the present Senator Russell B. Long, were beyond salvation. We discovered that their institutions had been broke when they came to us for loans. So we foreclosed. Slowly, through orderly liquidation, the RFC got back nearly all it had advanced to those institutions.

Depositors in the closed banks of New Orleans had to wait longer for their money than those in most of the other large cities. Through the slow sieves of liquidation it was not until the latter 1940's that the old Canal Bank & Trust Company was able to trickle down the last installment due to its depositors. The $48,298,000 lent that bank by the RFC was fully repaid by July 28, 1947.

More than fifteen years after the shutdown, depositors in the old Hibernia Bank & Trust Company were still waiting for a good part of their money. The liquidators by then had reimbursed the RFC for nearly all the $24,120,000 of its loans.

The courts held the New Orleans depositors were entitled to interest, but the old stockholders in the closed banks were not required to put up double indemnity. The largest bank in New Orleans, the Whitney, with twice the assets of its nearest competitor, rode out the hurricane successfully. It required no aid from the RFC

One of the larger Memphis institutions, the Bank of Commerce & Trust Company, closed but had plenty of assets; and with RFC assistance a new bank, the National Bank of Commerce, was organized to take its place. It has prospered. Though we bolstered it temporarily to the extent of $14,300,000 and it had enough cash on hand to meet every deposit, a clerical oversight in the Federal Reserve Bank, whose responsibility it was to notify banks to open after the holiday, almost prevented its opening. At three o'clock on the first morning that banks were to open, a telephone call from two of the directors, Phil Canale and A. L. Pritchard, reached me in the Treasury Building in Washington, where we were all still at work. They said their bank hadn't received instructions to open. I knew the bank's condition, and while it was not my job to say which banks should open I took the responsibility of telling them to open, which they did at nine o'clock. I mention this only to indicate the excitement and tension everywhere prevalent at that time. Every bank naturally wanted to open the first day.

*　　*　　*

The backaches of Baltimore's banks began in 1931 when the Baltimore Trust Company, to keep solvent, was obliged to raise $7,750,000 over a week end and repair its capital. This was accomplished by having some of the bigger depositors subordinate their claims. After the holiday of 1933, neither the Baltimore Trust nor its big neighbor, the Union Trust Company, was able to open. Maryland's financial malady was further complicated by the many millions of dollars in losses sustained by two large casualty companies with headquarters in Baltimore, which had been gravely weakened by guaranteeing real estate mortgage bonds. It took $50,-000,000 of RFC money in loans and preferred stock to save one of them, the Maryland Casualty Company. We helped protect the other, the United States Fidelity & Guaranty Company, with smaller loans.

The situation was so alarming that the then Governor of Maryland, Albert C. Ritchie, had come to Washington and appealed to the RFC Board to save those companies. He feared the effect of their collapse would be so widespread it might wreck almost everything in Maryland. While helping the casualty companies, we also shored up Maryland's badly damaged building and loan structure.

In the Far West the banks grouped together by Crawford Moore of Boise, Idaho, were among the depression's earlier casualties. They held many loans on livestock when the bottom fell out of the market for cattle and sheep. The chain of Nevada banks dominated by George Wingfield of Reno was broken by the plight of the stockmen. To the Wingfield banks the RFC made several loans; but finally the time came when they had no more available collateral. Under the law requiring us to have full and adequate security, we could render no further help; and we had to watch the banks go to the wall. Mr. Wingfield—and the western stockmen in general—later made a comeback. The RFC didn't lose a dime on those loans.

Two RFC offspring—the Regional Agricultural Credit Corporations and the Commodity Credit Corporation—were helpful in tiding the stockmen over their crisis, as were the generous appraisals we used in setting a schedule of loan values on livestock. This part of our work was directed by one of our original directors, Wilson McCarthy, of Salt Lake City. He received courageous assistance from Ford Hovey of the Stockmen's National Bank of South Omaha and also the help of Mr. Moore of Boise and Elbert G. Bennett, now president of the First Security Corporation of Ogden, Utah. Had the livestock industry not been bolstered up by loans from Washington, a great many more banks throughout the West would have failed.

In Denver not one major bank went under. In the Los Angeles metropolitan area the only large bank to close was the United States National.

About 80 per cent of California's banks sought help from the RFC, with loans or new capital, or with both. All the larger San Francisco banks weathered the storm, some of them without any direct assistance from Washington; but there were periods when not all of them were in really sound condition.

Month after month through this era, we nursed along most of the 1,417 unlicensed national banks which had been placed in conservatorship following the holiday of 1933. On the licensed banks which were in an impaired condition I conferred frequently, either in short conferences or by telephone, with Leo T. Crowley, chairman of the Federal Deposit Insurance Corporation. We kept looking for ways and means to rehabilitate those institutions, constantly whittling down the list of doubtful ones, until finally there were only a few banks that simply couldn't be salvaged. By the middle of 1935 not one of the unlicensed national banks placed in conservatorship in 1933 remained in that embarrassing condition.

As I was preparing to leave government service in 1945, I received, among many letters from public officials, the following from Mr. Crowley:

FEDERAL DEPOSIT INSURANCE CORPORATION
WASHINGTON

Office of the Chairman

February 14, 1945

Dear Jesse:

As your retirement from public life draws near, I vividly recall the month of December of 1933. It was then that I came here from Wisconsin as the representative of 385 small Wisconsin banks which sought federal aid so that they might qualify for deposit insurance. I was deeply impressed at that time with your sympathetic and constructive approach to the problems of these small banks and I marvelled at the great courage with which you made commitments which enabled them to rebuild their capital structures and qualify for FDIC membership. Without your courageous assistance, but few of these small institutions would have survived. I shall never forget how overjoyed I was to be able to go back home and report that every one of these banks had been accepted for deposit insurance. Little did I realize then that I was soon to become Chairman of the Federal Deposit Insurance Corporation.

In the succeeding years of '34, '35 and '36, during which I worked constantly with your organization rehabilitating thousands of banks throughout the country, I was reminded daily of the magnificent job you were doing for the nation and I became acutely aware of your deep concern for the welfare of the small independent banking unit. This awareness meant a great deal to me because it meant that in you I had a friend who shared my own sincere belief that the small bank is the real backbone of the nation's financial structure and that its survival must go hand in hand with the welfare of small business.

Thus from the very beginning up to these present days, my relationship with you and your associates has been most pleasant and it is a source of deep regret to me that soon you will no longer be available for counsel on the tremendous problems that confront us.

With warmest personal regards, I am

Faithfully yours,
LEO

Financial crashes in the larger cities were spectacular, but it was in the small towns, all over the Union, that we did most of our bank repair work day after day, month after month, in some places with only a few thousand dollars. Little country bankers were given as careful attention as the big fellow who required millions to get back on his feet. In large cities as in villages, our principal concern was always the small depositor.

FDR OPPOSES DEPOSIT INSURANCE

In thinking of the little fellow, I had shared the conviction of Speaker Garner that provision for federal deposit insurance was a necessary prelude to a full restoration of public confidence in the banks. An attempt to establish it toward the close of the Hoover administration was abandoned because Governor Roosevelt, who had become President elect, opposed it.

A deposit insurance bill, inspired by Speaker Garner and prepared by Chairman Steagall of the House Banking and Currency Committee, had been passed by the House on May 25, 1932. After Mr. Roosevelt's sentiments became known, it was allowed to expire in the Senate.

On the day before their inaugurations as President and Vice President, with most of the nation's banks already closed through state moratoriums, Mr. Garner called on Mr. Roosevelt at the Mayflower Hotel and again tried to swing him over in favor of deposit insurance.

The President elect was amiable but adamant. He insisted that it wouldn't work. He cited the fact that it had been a failure in Mr. Garner's Texas and in the other states which had tried it, with the weak banks draining the strong. Mr. Garner was sure that a federal guarantee would be successful. He offered to have Tom Love, former Texas State Bank Commissioner, hurry to Washington to explain why it hadn't worked as merely a state-wide proposition. Messrs. Love and Roosevelt had both been in the Woodrow Wilson administration, the former as Assistant Secretary of the Treasury, the latter as Assistant Secretary of the Navy. But Mr. Roosevelt's mind was made up.

Later a Republican introduced in the first New Deal Congress the legislation which brought about federal deposit insurance. In the late spring of 1933, Senator Arthur H. Vandenberg of Michigan tacked a bank deposit guarantee amendment onto the Glass-Steagall banking bill. President Roosevelt wrote the Senate and House conferees asking them to reject this amendment *in toto,* but they left it in. The Act was passed, and the President signed it on June 16. A success from the start, the Federal Deposit Insurance Corporation began by guaranteeing all deposits up to $2,500, this sum later being raised to $5,000, and more recently to $10,000. Some years afterwards, President Roosevelt publicly cited the deposit insurance as one of the fine achievements of his administration.

*   *   *

The conception of the RFC, for which credit must be accorded President Hoover, had been good, but it was a year too late. Even when it started, its Board, for a time, was entirely too timid and slow to save the country from the disasters of 1932 and 1933. And the funds available to it—$500,000,000 capital and $1,500,000,000 borrowing authority—were far too small.

A few billion dollars boldly but judiciously lent and invested by such a government agency as the RFC in 1931 and 1932 would have prevented the failure of thousands of banks and averted the complete breakdown in business, agriculture, and industry—and in private charity. It would have made unnecessary a large part of the government lending and spending for relief that we had to do in later years. It would have saved the fortunes as well as the morale and self-respect of thousands of Americans who had never before bowed their heads in adversity or had to acknowledge themselves unable to carry on without aid from their government.

The amendment to our Act in August, 1932, gave us limited authority for financing public works, but Congress made the conditions so restrictive that not a great deal could be accomplished. Anyway, there was not time enough left before the change in the administration to avert the complete crash which culminated in the bank holiday in March, 1933.

It will be recalled that President Roosevelt's first act was to close all the banks until a law could be passed giving us authority to save them.

When the curtain rose the following week, many banks were organized on the foundations of old ones by a process of having the common stocks subscribed for by depositors of the old banks. The RFC began matching them, dollar for dollar, in purchasing preferred stock. But that ratio wouldn't work in many places. So we added whatever more capital was necessary to make the bank sound. Sometimes old banks were reorganized by freezing a percentage of the deposits to provide new capital. Often we would buy a bank's preferred stock with one hand and make it a loan with the other. To provide extra liquidity, these loans were sometimes made on frozen assets.

FIFTY MILLIONS TO SAVE ONE CHICAGO BANK

Our subscriptions for preferred stock varied from $12,500 in some small country banks to the $50,000,000 investments in each of two banks—the National City in New York and the Continental Illinois National Bank & Trust Company, in Chicago, and $46,000,000 in the Chase National in New York.

The Continental Illinois was one of the relatively few large banks in which we required a strengthening of the management. Our controlling stock ownership and the bank's previous management justified these requirements.

Created by the Reynolds brothers, George and Arthur, the Continental Illinois had suffered heavy losses in the collapse of the Insull enterprises and was sorely in need of a tonic. It was the first really big bank to come to us for new capital. In October, 1933, by which time the Messrs. Reynolds had passed from its scene, we bought $50,000,000 of its preferred stock on the understanding that, to offset losses, the outstanding common stock would be reduced from $75,000,000 to $25,000,000.

The Continental's losses had been staggering. The bank had been obliged to write off $50,000,000 of potential losses in 1932 and $60,-000,000 more in 1933. The depression had drained its deposits from a sum above $1,000,000,000 down to about $450,000,000. It was a great correspondent bank—a bankers' bank—in which a large proportion of the country banks of the Middle West and many in the South and Southwest kept accounts. Had it collapsed, the effect would have been frighteningly felt in fields and towns and cities over a large area of the country.

The bank had been put together in a series of amalgamations in

March, 1929. As often happens when banks are merged, there ensued a noticeable lack of harmony in the upper circles of its management. The bank's chairmanship had not been filled since the retirement of George Reynolds. When we put in $50,000,000 capital, it was with the understanding that at the following January meeting we would agree upon a new chairman. Both George Reynolds and his brother Arthur, who had been the president, were heavily in debt to the bank. That fact and the far-reaching effect of the Insull collapse prompted extreme care and concern on our part as to who would be the new top boss.

I had suggested to Sewell L. Avery, head of Montgomery Ward & Company, that he accept the chairmanship of the bank, but he declined. I had seen a good deal of Walter J. Cummings, then executive assistant to the Secretary of the Treasury, and had formed a good opinion of him. It occurred to me he might make a good chairman for the Continental Illinois. He was a substantial businessman and a car builder in Chicago, where he had been associated with William H. Woodin, who was Secretary of the Treasury at the time of the bank's crisis and, as such, an ex-officio member of the RFC Board.

Secretary Woodin and I had become close friends. While considering his former associate for the bank chairmanship, I frankly asked Mr. Woodin if Walter Cummings was broke. After the Insull collapse I didn't know who in Chicago was broke and who wasn't. I didn't want anyone as head of the Continental Illinois who would in any way be handicapped by former associates or who was in debt or otherwise obligated to any interest or individual.

Mr. Woodin commended Mr. Cummings to me as a solid and solvent citizen and a good executive. I then got word passed to a few of the Continental's directors that he might make a good choice. The directors were not disposed to accept Mr. Cummings. They sent a committee of directors to Washington to see me. This group included L. A. Downs, then president of the Illinois Central Railroad; Alfred Cowles, the economist; Chauncey B. Borland, a prominent real estate operator; Colonel Albert A. Sprague, one of the country's foremost wholesale grocers; James R. Leavell, who had succeeded Arthur Reynolds as the bank's president, and Herman Waldeck, a vice president.

The directors who came to Washington finally acquiesced in our point of view, and on January 9, 1934, Mr. Cummings was elected their chairman. Of the twenty-five directors on the bank's new board we concurred in the selection of seventeen from the old board.

On the day the RFC invested $50,000,000 in the Continental, the bank's common stock was selling at $25 a share. These shares four years later, with stock dividends, were selling at approximately $225. In market value this ninefold increase amounted to about $150,000,-000. The bank continued to prosper. By December, 1939, it had retired the last of the RFC's preferred stock.

When we felt a bank was well run we did not raise our voice as to its management, even though our investments were sufficient to afford effective control. A few days after Mr. Cummings took charge of the Continental Illinois, the next largest Chicago bank, the First National, lost its chief executive through the death of Melvin A. Traylor. The RFC had $25,000,000 invested in the First National's preferred stock, but we took no part in the selection of his successor. We felt the bank was in good hands. From its executive staff Edward Eagle Brown, an excellent banker of broad and sagacious views, was elected to succeed Mr. Traylor.

I received a letter from Mr. Brown, dated April 10, 1936, which read:

Dear Jesse:

I want to again say, in writing and more formally, that I feel that not only I and the other officers of the First National Bank of Chicago but all its stockholders owe a debt of gratitude to you and the Reconstruction Finance Corporation for the attitude you have consistently taken towards us; and that the present market value of the First National Bank stock is primarily due to the fact that we did take preferred stock from the R.F.C. in January of 1934.

In the cases of a few of the many banks that we saved, as with some of the railroads, we placed an RFC official on the bank's board of directors to keep an eye on the management. An instance of this was the Anglo California National Bank of San Francisco. One of our directors, Sam H. Husbands, represented the RFC on the board of that bank.

*   *   *

One rather ticklish reconstruction job was the First National Bank at Amarillo, Texas, which was owned by W. H. Fuqua. Mr. Fuqua had been successful in his general section of the Southwest for more than fifty years. He once boasted to me that he owned every share of the capital stock of his bank; that even the directors' qualifying shares were endorsed and in his safe. He dealt in cattle and ranches and was regarded as the big man of his region. His private operations had drawn heavily on his bank, and it was in a failing condition. Its collapse would have carried with it many smaller banks in the Panhandle of Texas and adjacent territory in Oklahoma, Colorado, and New Mexico. While his bank required only a few hundred thousand dollars, more than $3,000,000 was needed to save Mr. Fuqua from failure, a failure which would have carried his bank down and several others. The situation required a new president and a new management for the bank, to free it from Mr. Fuqua's domination.

Mr. Fuqua came to Washington to negotiate for a loan. I explained that we would require new management for the bank and also for the preservation of his own estate, in the interest of the bank, since we were lending his company more than $3,000,000, the then full probable value of the available collateral. To find a man qualified for the job at Amarillo, I was considering three of our best examiners in the Washington office. Before final approval of the loan, I had these three men sit with Mr. Fuqua for the better part of an afternoon going over his situation. I had not mentioned to our three men what I really had in mind—that one of them would be chosen to go to Amarillo.

I had known Mr. Fuqua a long time. I told him in confidence that in all probability one of the men who would interview him would be sent to Amarillo to run the bank and take charge of his general situation, and that after his interview with them he might indicate to me which one of the three he would prefer.

Tully Garner, son of Vice President Garner, was president of the Production Credit Corporation of Houston, a part of the Farm Credit Administration handling government loans in South Texas, and happened to be in Washington at the time.

After Mr. Fuqua had had his séance with our three Washington examiners, he came into my office and told me which of the three he preferred. I told him all right, he could have him, but about that time my secretary came in, announcing that Tully Garner was waiting. I had Tully come in and interviewed him in the presence of Mr. Fuqua about his experience as a government lender, how he was getting along, how his loans were working out, et cetera. We visited for some fifteen or twenty minutes. When Tully left, Mr. Fuqua said to me, "That is the man I want"; and so Tully was selected. But I first had to get the consent of the Vice President. So that evening I dropped in on Mr. and Mrs. Garner. I explained to Mr. Garner the situation and asked his consent. Mrs. Garner promptly said, "Mr. Jones, if you want Tully you can have him." The Vice President said nothing.

Taking charge of the Amarillo situation on January 31, 1937, as president of the bank and also president of Mr. Fuqua's holding company, Tully Garner handled the whole business for nearly six years and did an excellent job; and the Fuqua account to the RFC was fully paid. On November 22, 1942, Stone & Webster, Inc., for a price around $2,000,000, acquired the Fuqua interests by purchasing the West Texas Mortgage Loan Company, which then owned the First National Bank of Amarillo, the Fuqua ranches, and a few other corporations. Tully Garner then returned to Uvalde, leaving behind him a substantial situation in a prospering Panhandle of Texas, and Mr. Fuqua with a substantial fortune. Without RFC help he would have gone bankrupt and his bank would have busted. Tully Garner's salary in Amarillo was $5,000 a year.

*　　*　　*

I have told of requesting permission to address the convention of the American Bankers Association in 1933 and have recalled that they didn't like the speech. Nevertheless, in each of the next three years the A.B.A. asked me to address the annual gatherings, and each time I accepted. Long before the last of these little lectures was given, quite a few bankers came to regard me as something of a scold. Yet it was my lot, meanwhile, to have the free-spending, Santa Claus school of government reformers belabor me for possessing what they described as a "banker mentality."

It was patent that if the bankers didn't provide credit to accommodate agriculture, commerce, and industry based on a going country, the government would have to. No community can prosper if its banks fail to supply local credit. Yet during that period bankers, scared by what they had been through, went to extremes on keeping liquid. A few even solicited deposits with the boast that they were 75 per cent liquid. One bank, which had amassed an un-commonly large surplus, bragged of being 110 per cent liquid.

Some banks of excessive liquidity strove for even higher liquidity. They called loans, thereby forcing liquidation by the borrowers. This was breaking men's hearts, destroying values, sometimes snuffing out a lifetime's savings. And it was creating more unemployment.

In 1934, with deposit insurance in operation, there was no longer any valid excuse for a bank to cram its vault with idle cash which borrowers could be using with profit all around. The cheapest deposit insurance, it seemed to me, was ample capital, and the government was offering to provide it by purchasing preferred stock. By the autumn of that year, when the A.B.A. convened again, the preferred stock program was well on its way to completion, and the banks were clearly out of the woods.

Real estate mortgages had replaced the banks as our Problem No. 1. But the absence of bank credit to commercial and industrial bor-rowers was still holding back the recovery movement. Credit simply had to flow more freely, and be extended in a normal way, if our relief rolls were to recede.

To get things moving again, long-term credit was essential—credit running two, three, or possibly up to five years. Much of it could properly have been furnished by banks. We believed the investment market would return, though nobody could say when. To stimulate recovery the banks had been given the right to discount long-term paper with the Federal Reserve and to borrow from the Federal Reserve on all kinds of collateral. The RFC was ready to lend on favorable terms or to furnish capital. Under the new legislation practically any loan the RFC could make might quite properly be shared in or made by any bank. The RFC urged the bankers to work together with the Corporation and the Federal Reserve in making industrial loans. Putting that idea across was a long crusade with only moderate success.

Over the past forty years I have at various times been a vice president, president or chairman of several banks in Houston. I have never occupied a desk in a bank. Until recent years, furthermore, I had always been a borrower from banks. It is the borrower who employs people, buys materials, and makes for prosperity.

*   *   *

So far this chronicle has been concerned almost exclusively with our aid to commercial banks. We also helped mutual savings banks, although the law creating the RFC had made no specific provision for our doing so. Much of our aid in that field was indirect. Since the mutual savings banks had no capital stock they could not issue capital notes or sell us preferred stock. Our directors believed, however, that Congress intended all banks to be treated alike. So we made them loans, payable only out of a part of their earnings and from assets in excess of whatever the law required.

We obliged them to reduce their interest or dividends to their depositors and to use a part of these economies to repay the RFC.

In 1932 and 1933 many savings banks, particularly in New York State and in New England, found it necessary to restrict withdrawals to a certain sum during stated periods. In New York City alone, savings banks' deposits were declining early in 1933 at an estimated rate of $2,000,000 a day. Part of this was due to the necessity of furloughed or unemployed people to tap their savings to pay the landlord and the grocer; but much of it was sheer fright—the spread of hoarding. To allay depositors' fears and provide the savings bank a means of meeting withdrawals without forcing loan collections or selling securities in a depressed market, more than a hundred of the mutuals got together in July, 1933, and organized the Savings Banks Trust Company and the Institutional Securities Corporation. The RFC agreed to buy $50,000,000 capital notes in the former, and agreed to lend the latter $100,000,000 on mortgages that it would acquire from savings banks which had to raise cash.

The mere announcement of these plans dispelled public fears. Withdrawals declined so rapidly that within a few weeks all restrictions on them were removed. The Savings Banks Trust Company did not have to call on us for any part of the promised $50,000,000 capital. Of the $100,000,000 earmarked for the Institutional Securities Corporation we were called on for only $14,312,567, a loan soon repaid.

Indirectly we helped almost every savings bank by our aid to railroads, in whose securities they are investors, and by our part in restoring a market for real estate mortgage bonds.

3

☼

THE DEBACLE IN DETROIT

*President Hoover Tries to Save the Situation—Jim Couzens
Makes a Threat—How Henry Ford Said No—The Lights
Go Out in Michigan—We Arrange to Pay 700,000 Small
Depositors—The Collapse in Cleveland*

IN NO other large city was the drama of the banking crisis so prolonged or so tense as in Detroit. The closing of all banks in the motor capital on February 14, 1933, by proclamation of the Governor of Michigan, was the principal prelude to the collapse, during the next three weeks, of the nation's entire financial system. In reviews of that period Detroit is often likened to a domino whose fall sends the whole stack tumbling down.

Into the earlier efforts to keep the Detroit domino from tottering, President Hoover thrust his hand. He made repeated personal appeals to such old friends as Henry Ford. He exerted the official influence of his high office on other industrialists, bankers, Senators, and government officials, including the RFC's board of directors. Yet, three weeks before his term expired, every bank in Michigan was tightly shut.

Ten days after the Roosevelt inaugural, at the lifting of the national blanket moratorium, as sound banks began reopening all over the country, Detroit had to swallow still another bitter pill. Neither of the bigger bank units in the two largest groups of banks, whose dominance in Michigan spread from the motor center to the smaller cities of the state, was granted a license to resume operations. During the month-long Michigan shutdown their depositors had been allowed to draw only 5 per cent of their balances.

These unfortunate people numbered more than eight hundred thousand individuals and firms. Many of them suffered severe privations. It was only with the help of loans from the RFC—one of these being the largest single bank loan we ever made—that more than seven hundred thousand of the smaller depositors were enabled to get out the rest of their money in full; the larger depositors patriotically consented to wait the slow process of liquidation.

Detroit's banking collapse may have been inevitable, the situation in the sorely stricken automobile industry being what it was, and the laws being what they were at the time; but the circumstances would have been less painful, the personal tragedies fewer, had not insurmountable difficulties been created by personal, industrial, and political hostilities at almost every step of our approach to the problem in February, 1933.

The survivors of the early competitive struggles in the automobile industry are a particularly tough and sometimes stubborn breed. We ran head on into granitelike obstacles in two of the city's most powerful and wealthiest men, Henry Ford and United States Senator James Couzens.

As young pioneers in founding the Ford Motor Company, they had been closely bound in friendship; but in middle age their ways had parted. To the Ford Company's modest start in 1903 with a capital of $49,000 in cash and notes, Couzens, as one of twelve stockholders, had contributed $1,000 in cash and a note for $1,500 for which he received twenty-five shares. In its first year the company paid dividends of 68 per cent. At the outset Couzens was assigned the title of business manager with a salary of $2,500 a year, with Ford drawing $3,600 as president. Later Couzens bought eighty-five more shares of the capital stock. One year the company declared a stock dividend of 1,900 per cent.

In 1915, by which time Couzens' salary was $150,000 a year, the two pioneers had a disagreement. Couzens then retired from the management; but he held onto his 2,180 shares until 1919, when Henry Ford and his son, Edsel Ford, bought out the other stockholders and converted their great enterprise into a strictly family affair. Couzens demanded—and got—more per share than the other retiring stockholders. The others sold for $12,500 a share; Couzens successfully held out for $13,444.

To buy his stock, Ford sent Couzens a check for $29,308,857.80. Over the preceding sixteen years the company's total dividends had exceeded $96,000,000, out of which, of course, Couzens, owning 11 per cent of the stock, had received his pro rata portion, which amounted to several millions.

After leaving the Ford Company's offices Couzens entered both banking and politics. So, in some degree, did Ford. The two men had differed over military preparedness in 1915, Ford then being a pacifist. After the First World War the prohibition issue widened the breach. Ford was an outspoken dry, Couzens an advocate of repeal. In 1924, in the weeks before Calvin Coolidge was nominated for the Presidency by the Republicans and John W. Davis was chosen as a compromise candidate by the Democrats, there had been a brief "Ford for President" campaign. Couzens openly opposed it. In 1918 Ford had sought a seat in the United States Senate, and it was denied him. Couzens, after being Mayor of Detroit, was elected to the Senate. Upon entering the banking business he had refused to let his bank, the Bank of Detroit, join the Detroit Clearing House Association. Over this and other differences, his relations with some of the Detroit bankers became chillier and chillier.

Ford retained a lingering suspicion that "Wall Street" was forever plotting to get its hands on his immense motor-making enterprise.

Couzens also had had a long drawn-out feud with Andrew W. Mellon, Secretary of the Treasury in the Harding, Coolidge, and Hoover administrations. Their quarrel arose in part from the tax which the Treasury had slapped on the sale of the Couzens stock in the Ford Motor Company.

At the time when the Detroit bankers began their first knockings on the RFC's door, Couzens was the senior Senator from Michigan. He was an influential member of the Senate Banking and Currency Committee before which all legislation relating to the RFC originated.

Against the pleas and arguments and plans of President Hoover to provide a large loan as part of a pool to ease the situation in Detroit's banks, Senator Couzens hurled the threat that he would publicly denounce any such loan if it were a dime above the then depressed value of the collateral which the tottering banks and trust companies could scrape together to secure it.

Before reviewing the clash of personalities and judgments which stymied the early rescue program for Detroit's banks, let us glance at the backdrop against which the action of the drama unfolded. As

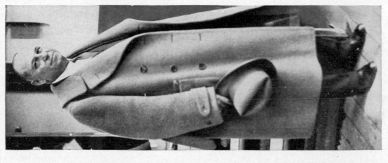

THE BIG THREE OF THE AUTOMOBILE INDUSTRY IN 1933, WHEN
DETROIT LAY ECONOMICALLY PROSTRATE

Henry Ford, Alfred P. Sloan, Jr., Walter P. Chrysler (International News Photos).

THREE LEADING FIGURES IN THE CONFERENCES ON
THE DETROIT BANKING CRISIS

Above: Edward Eagle Brown of the First National Bank of Chicago. Below: John K. McKee (left), chief examiner of the RFC, with Senator James Couzens, of Michigan.

the core of the motor industry, Detroit was particularly sensitive to the rise or fall of the public's buying power in any part of the country. In the easy-riding era of the 1920's, as the automobile became the accustomed vehicle of all but the poorest of the American people, the city enjoyed extensive and exuberant expansion. Scores of new factories and plants and tens of thousands of new homes were built. To provide shelter for the legion of workmen attracted from farms and communities all over the country by the motor industry's high wages, the banks of Detroit and their affiliated trust companies financed the making of tens of thousands of mortgages. Then, when the depression sliced the income of almost everyone and made it impossible for millions of people to buy the new cars they craved, Detroit was harder hit than any other American metropolis.

Many a laid-off worker returned to the farm or the Main Street from which he had come. Back home, he believed, he could at least find enough to eat and perhaps get credit from old neighbors. He might even be able to swap a squirrel dog for a stove or some flour, corn meal, or beans. Trade by old-fashioned barter became fairly common in those days of five-cent cotton and fifteen-cent corn.

The mortgage many a discouraged homebound workman left behind him in Detroit froze and became unsalable. Often the departing worker, as well as the unemployed or part-time mechanic who remained on in the big city, had to leave his taxes unpaid. The City of Detroit was forced to default on its municipal bonds. The streets no longer roared with motor traffic. Shopkeepers grew increasingly reluctant to let customers have charge accounts. Many a small merchant went broke when his little suburban bank froze to death. Economic stagnation set in.

Common stocks of the big automobile corporations had become popular investments even among pedestrians. Their share certificates formed the security for numerous loans made by the Detroit banks. By February, 1932, the forces of the depression had pushed General Motors stock down to $10 a share and Chrysler to $7.75.

Earlier in the depression, as security prices slipped lower and lower from their boom time peaks, many an investor and speculator, deciding the decline had run its course, began buying stocks. About that time—it was before the RFC was created—I encountered on Main Street in Houston one morning an old cattleman friend, Dick Coon.

"Dick," I said, "why don't we buy some of these cheap stocks?"

"Hell, no," he said. "Never rope a steer going down hill; he'll kill you every time."

* * *

Both of Detroit's two large banking groups were topped by holding companies whose stock also was widely distributed in the area. These securities also slid down the toboggan. Each day the unemployment picture grew darker. Fear of rioting by desperate men spread from street to street.

The RFC's first major contact with Detroit's difficulties was effected during the Fourth of July week end in 1932, only a few days after we had granted the "Dawes Loan" to palliate the Chicago situation. During the Independence Day lull the leading officials of one of the two big Michigan banking structures came to Washington. Their group included the Union Guardian Trust Company and the Guardian National Bank of Commerce. They told the RFC board that they regarded their local banking situation as having reached a critical stage. The trust company, they said, was the weakest stone in their particular pyramid.

The Fords were directly and rather heavily interested in the Guardian group. Edsel Ford was a director both of the holding company and of the trust company. When these concerns encountered their first troubles in 1930, he had loaned them $1,000,000 in cash and $5,000,000 in securities. The next year he had given his personal credit as security for a larger loan which the group obtained in Chicago. A few months later the Ford Motor Company had loaned the group $3,500,000 to enable it to lift out some of the trust company's assets which the bank examiners had criticized.

After reviewing this situation with the Detroit delegation the RFC directors, on July 5, 1932, authorized a six-month loan of $8,733,000 to the trust company as temporary relief and promised that more money would be forthcoming later. It was expected the Fords would work out a rescue plan in a short time.

In the Guardian group were twenty-one banks, located in Detroit and its suburbs and in other cities in Michigan. Except for the directors' qualifying shares, all the capital stock of these banks had been put into the holding company. This holding company had been established a few years previously as a rival to the Detroit Bankers Company, a group headed by the First National Bank of Detroit, which had amalgamated since then with one of the largest savings-bank consolidations in the country, the Peoples Wayne County Bank. This latter bank had more than half a million depositors. It held more than fifty thousand separate mortgages, nearly all of them on homes in Detroit's metropolitan area. The average mortgage was a little less than $3,000, so that the bank's holdings in this slow paper totaled about $150,000,000. As more and more of these mortgages defaulted, the bank's liquidity gradually disappeared.

Before the storm clouds gathered over Detroit's proud sky line, the lightning had struck scores of Michigan's little one-story and two-story country banks. Between January 1, 1931, and January 25, 1933, there were 195 bank failures in the state. Scarcely a county escaped.

During that angry period the crusading radio voice of the Rev. Charles E. Coughlin was much in vogue. In his Sunday-afternoon broadcasts he took to berating what he called the "Banksters." As regularly as Monday morning business hours followed these Sunday afternoon orations, the Michigan bankers noticed an increasing amount of withdrawal by small depositors.

Later on, bigger depositors began transferring funds from Detroit to New York and Chicago. With increasing frequency the Detroit bankers communicated with the Treasury, the RFC, and even the White House to recount their worries and their woes. Early in February, 1933, the Guardian group asked for an additional loan of $50,000,000, the earlier loan having been renewed a few weeks previously. We had already dispatched our chief examiner in charge of bank reorganization, John Keown McKee, to Detroit. At the panic prices then prevailing, he and his assistants were unable to sift enough good collateral out of the bank's portfolios to supply $50,000,000 worth of "full and adequate security" which was required for RFC loans.

JIM COUZENS MAKES A THREAT

As a way out of the difficulty, it was proposed that our loan be part of a pool to which the big motor companies and other large interests in Detroit should contribute new money while subordinating their old deposits. President Hoover sent for Senator Couzens to tell him about this plan and ask his cooperation. As Mr. Hoover later recalled it, he first reviewed the situation, telling the Senator there were more than a million depositors, mostly small people, who had money in the Detroit banks, and that the Senator's entire home town would suffer if the banks went under. He explained the plan to form a pool in which the government would take part and probably lose some money.

Mr. Hoover remarked that if his home town, San Francisco, were threatened with such a catastrophe, he would do all in his power as an individual of some means in the community to contribute to its salvation, though his own fortune was very much smaller than the Senator's. He suggested bluntly that Senator Couzens put part of his personal fortune into the proposed pool. As Mr. Hoover has since described it, the Senator "ranted all over the room and said much worse things" than the oft quoted remark that he would denounce the proposed loan from the housetops unless the loan was secured to the last dime.

The next day President Hoover sent for Senator Couzens again, and also for his colleague from Michigan, Senator Arthur H. Vandenberg. In the meantime the President had telephoned Mr. Ford, a personal friend of long standing and a supporter of his administration. The President told Mr. Ford about the plan for a pool and said: "The Guardian group owes you several million dollars. Will you subordinate that?" When Mr. Ford replied, "It's done," the President asked if he would join in a pool with General Motors and Chrysler, and Mr. Ford said he would. Senator Vandenberg was agreeable to the plan, but he was at that time junior Senator. His senior, Senator Couzens, remained adamant. Later on, as we shall see, Mr. Ford changed his mind about joining the pool or subordinating his claims on the banks.

After his first talk with the two Senators, President Hoover called them once more to the White House on February 9. This meeting also was attended by Charles A. Miller, who had succeeded General Dawes as president of the RFC, by Ogden L. Mills, Secretary of the Treasury, and Roy D. Chapin, a former Detroit industrialist who was then the Secretary of Commerce. Senator Couzens held his ground. The next day Secretary Chapin and Arthur A. Ballantine, Under Secretary of the Treasury, went to Detroit on behalf of the administration and the RFC to see what could be done on the spot. Mr. Ballantine, as Under Secretary, represented Secretary Ogden Mills as an ex-officio member of our RFC Board.

Senator Couzens called several times at my office, though I was not then the chairman. He said he was not in favor of trying to save any banks that were not sound and solvent.

Lincoln's Birthday was to fall on the following Sunday, and the holiday would be celebrated on Monday. Thus the banks would be closed from Saturday noon until Tuesday morning. This, we hoped, would give the various interests concerned time to work out an acceptable rescue program. General Motors and Chrysler said they would go along with this program provided Mr. Ford joined in.

The Union Guardian Trust Company, which had already borrowed about $15,000,000 from the RFC, had deposit liabilities of $20,-500,000. Its assets, other than those already pledged against our previous loans, had a borrowing value which did not exceed $5,-000,000. The plan was to have the Guardian group put assets of $3,600,000 into the trust company so that we could make it a new loan of $8,600,000, this to be a part of a larger loan of about $23,000,000 to other units in the group. It was in order to fill up the gap between what this plan would supply and what was needed that the larger deposits were to be subordinated and fresh capital of about $4,000,000 raised by the big depositors. At that time the Ford interests had $32,500,000 on deposit in the Guardian units and nearly $25,000,000 more in the First Wayne National.

HOW HENRY FORD SAID NO

On Saturday morning, about the time Secretary Chapin and Under Secretary Ballantine reached Detroit, President Hoover had as his breakfast guests at the White House table Walter P. Chrysler, head of the Chrysler Corporation, Alfred P. Sloan, Jr., president of General Motors, Secretary Mills, and Mr. Miller of the RFC. They all felt a suspension of the Union Guardian might precipitate a general panic in Detroit. They recommended, among other measures, that the RFC undertake additional direct relief in Detroit to help the city meet the pay rolls for teachers, firemen, police, and other employees.

Through the speeding hours of the week end, efforts were stimulated to soften Senator Couzens and to obtain Mr. Ford's cooperation. Once I persuaded Senator Couzens to call Mr. Ford from my office while, with the Senator's permission, I listened in. Those two old roosters were scrupulously polite to each other, but frigid. On

Sunday, just before midnight, President Hoover telephoned Mr. Ford, who then agreed to see Messrs. Chapin and Ballantine on Monday morning and hear their explanation of the rescue plan.

They explained it at length, but Mr. Ford refused to put his chips into the kitty. He said he would not subordinate his deposits in the Union Guardian Trust Company. Furthermore, he said that if the trust company should fail to open for business on Tuesday morning he would immediately send his treasurer down to the First Wayne National and draw out the twenty-odd million he had on deposit there.

Messrs. Ballantine and Chapin told him that if he refrained from cooperating with the Guardian rescue program the Guardian group could not survive. And, they added, if he withdrew his fat account from the First Wayne National, it would be very difficult to preserve that bank; and if it went under they did not see how any banks anywhere in Michigan could be kept open. The general distress, they predicted, would then spread to neighboring states.

"All right, then," said Mr. Ford, "let us have it that way; let the crash come."

If everything went down the chute there would be a cleaning-up process, he said, and everybody would then have to get to work. Whatever happened, he said he was sure he could again build up a business, as he still felt young.

Mr. Ford was host at lunch to another worried caller, Wilson W. Mills, chairman of the board of the First Wayne National, which was then the sixth largest bank in the country. Mr. Mills was a close friend of President Hoover. Some months previously, the President had asked him to consider accepting the presidency of the RFC.

It was only on the Saturday, two days before his call on Mr. Ford, that Mr. Mills learned of the rival Union Guardian's request for another loan from the RFC. He had then telephoned to President Hoover, to Senator Couzens, and to our headquarters. From us, too, he sought a loan, and from Senator Couzens assurance that he would not oppose it. The Senator told him he was not going to have "the United States Government lend money to bail out Henry Ford." Mr. Mills told me, and also Senator Couzens, that he was fearful that if the Union Guardian collapsed the First Wayne National would fall unless he could "placate" Mr. Ford and persuade him to leave his deposits untouched. It was with this idea in mind that he arranged to lunch with Mr. Ford on that critical Monday. There was no third chair at their table.

As Mr. Mills later recalled the conversation, he asked Mr. Ford if he would subordinate his deposits and the reply was: "No, no, there is no reason why I should. There is no reason why the government should make me the goat. And there isn't any reason why I should tie up several million to keep Senator Couzens from shouting from the housetops. And there isn't any reason why I, the largest individual taxpayer in the country, should bail the government out of its loans to banks."

That night Mr. Mills called some of his other large' depositors, and he also telephoned us in Washington. He said his directors had decided to open the bank as usual the next day, provided they could get $100,000,000 from the RFC. But by then it was clear to us that the jig was up. An eleventh-hour loan couldn't save the impending collapse. It would merely favor a few depositors who would draw out their money.

The unyielding stances taken by Mr. Ford and Senator Couzens had already blocked the plan to bail out the Guardian group. All through the afternoon and evening momentous meetings droned on in Detroit, the local bankers and the government representatives having been joined there by several distinguished out-of-town financiers. From Chicago had arrived on Saturday night Melvin A. Traylor, chairman, and Edward Eagle Brown, executive vice president, of the First National Bank of Chicago, and Abner J. Stilwell, vice-president of the Continental Illinois National Bank & Trust Company. From New York had come E. A. Potter, Jr., vice president of the Guaranty Trust Company, S. Sloan Colt, president of the Bankers Trust Company, George W. Davison, chairman of the Central Hanover Bank & Trust Company, and Donaldson Brown, then vice president and chairman of the finance committee of General Motors. B. E. Hutchinson joined the first day's conferences as representative of the Chrysler Corporation. On Sunday Mr. Chrysler entered the meetings, having returned to Detroit overnight from his White House conference with President Hoover and Mr. Sloan of General Motors.

About midnight on Sunday a bomb exploded in the meeting room in the form of the next morning's issue of the Detroit *Free Press,* its front page peppered with an interview in which Senator Couzens advocated letting the weak banks of the country perish. He suggested a general moratorium from which only strong, sound banks would be resurrected. Clifford B. Longley, the Ford Motor Company's counsel and president of the Union Guardian Trust Company, left the meeting to telephone the substance of the interview to Mr. Ford. Upon returning he reported Mr. Ford as having commented:

"For once in his life, Jim Couzens is right."

This fell upon the burdened brethren like the last straw on the camel's back. In the deepening gloom they decided to go to their homes and hotel rooms and get some sleep, agreeing to meet again on Monday morning. Then, the Mountain having refused to come to the Mohammeds, Messrs. Chapin and Ballantine drove out to Dearborn to call on the Mountain. At midday, when they got back and made their disappointing report on Mr. Ford's "Let the crash come" position, they and the other out-of-town participants decided to hold a separate meeting in another room away from the gathering of Detroit bankers.

Once again the assets and liabilities of the distressed banks were reviewed. The consensus of the out-of-town advisers was that the Union Guardian could not long withstand the withdrawals that were certain to be resumed if it reopened the next morning, and that, once it had to close, the First Wayne National could survive only a few hours.

The repercussions of these closings, they foresaw, would soon be felt in Cleveland and other Ohio cities. They feared that if a moratorium then had to be proclaimed in Ohio, neither Chicago nor New York nor any other center could avoid unbearably heavy drains.

There were also the country banks of Michigan to consider. A state law required non-member banks to keep half of their reserves in some bank within the state, which in practice meant a bank in Detroit. Mr. Traylor asked Messrs. Chapin and Ballantine whether Mr. Ford realized that banks over a wide area might have to go on a clearinghouse certificate basis and that such a situation would react adversely on the automobile business. Mr. Ballantine then telephoned E. G. Liebold and urged him to make that possibility clear to Mr. Ford. Late in the afternoon, Mr. Liebold telephoned back that there was no change in Mr. Ford's position in any respect.

LIGHTS OUT IN MICHIGAN

Reluctantly, in another room, the Union Guardian directors came to the inevitable conclusion that they would not be able to open the tellers' windows the next morning. The out-of-town bankers and examiners suggested to them that the wisest course would be a state-wide bank holiday for a few days. Otherwise there would be wild runs the next morning.

Governor William A. Comstock was sent for. He drove to Detroit from Lansing, the capital. Over a period of several hours, the entire situation was again reviewed for his information.

About nine P.M., President Hoover again telephoned to Mr. Ford and, as he recently recalled it, talked to him for about an hour. The President went to bed believing he had "got Ford back on the track." Mr. Hoover was shocked and completely surprised to learn, when he arose on Tuesday morning, that Governor Comstock had declared an eight-day bank holiday for all of Michigan.

The proclamation had been drawn late in the night and was not made public until the early hours of the morning. It ordered the banks of Michigan to remain closed for eight days, which would terminate on Washington's Birthday. As the out-of-town conferees broke up their meeting, the sad but generally held view among them was that by Washington's Birthday a national moratorium would be necessary. They were only slightly overpessimistic. Less than a fortnight after Washington's Birthday, not a bank in the United States was open.

In the interval Michigan had been without banking facilities for three awkward, agonizing weeks. On Washington's Birthday the Michigan banks were in no better shape than they had been on Lincoln's Birthday to reopen the following morning, so Governor Comstock simply extended the holiday. Four days later, on Sunday February 26, the RFC announced a $54,000,000 loan to the First Wayne National Bank of Detroit and a $24,000,000 loan to the Guardian National Bank of Commerce. We also agreed to lend out-of-state banks $20,000,000 against the deposits they had on balance in Michigan banks. The next day we made an emergency relief loan of $1,432,734 to the City of Detroit to help care for the increasing distress.

With the lifting, in mid-March, of the nation-wide moratorium only four of Detroit's banks were immediately licensed to reopen. These four, the Detroit Savings Bank, the Commonwealth State Bank, the United Savings Bank, and the Industrial Morris Plan Bank, all were comparatively small. The two big giants still lay prostrate. Both the Union Guardian and the First Wayne National were ordered into liquidation. During the second week of the Michigan holiday their depositors had been permitted to draw out 5 per cent of their balances. To enable the small depositors to obtain the remainder of their money, the RFC eventually authorized loans of more than $214,-000,000 to the conservator of the First Wayne National, of which $177,000,000 was disbursed, and $16,000,000 to the conservator of the Guardian National.

WE ARRANGE TO PAY 700,000 SMALL DEPOSITORS

I went to Detroit to advise with the local bankers and industrialists on a program to permit the small depositors to get all their money while the larger depositors stood aside. In this program we received the generous cooperation of all the major industrialists of the city, including the Fords. To meet their pay rolls in a bankless city, some of the automobile companies had been hauling currency into Detroit by truck. Smaller firms sent trusted agents to Chicago or New York with empty suitcases which were filled with greenbacks for the return trip. The Chrysler Corporation opened a temporary bank to cash the checks of its employees.

Soon after reaching Detroit I met with a group of bankers and businessmen. I outlined what we proposed to do to open the paying tellers' windows in their larger shut-down banks and how we would do it. I had a feeling that those fellows looked askance at us Democrats, so I addressed my remarks largely to one man in the audience, a tough, hard-headed Republican, Edward Douglas Stair. As these lines are being written he is approaching his ninety-second birthday,* still active in business. At the time of the bank crisis he was seventy-four. Among other interests, he was then publisher of the Detroit *Free Press,* chairman of the Detroit Bankers Company (holding company of the First Wayne National group), and a director of the Wabash.

* Mr. Stair died May 22, 1951.

"You're the man," I told him, "to lead us out of the wilderness in Detroit." He accepted the challenge.

Under the plan we worked out together, all deposit accounts up to $300 in the First Wayne National group (there were nearly 600,000 of these little accounts) and all up to $1,000 in the Union Guardian (these numbered 116,000) were paid off in full with the money the RFC advanced. To make the payments possible, we lent over $190,000,000 to the conservators and receivers of the two banks. When the better times of later years increased the value of the collateral in the liquidating banks, all remaining depositors received every cent coming to them, plus 5 per cent interest, so that they, too, were rewarded for their admirable patience and generosity. Since then, the stockholders of both the First Wayne National and the Guardian National have received a substantial recovery on the assessments imposed on them when the banks failed.

Making the small depositor's money available to him, so that he could meet his bills and pay his taxes, was only one part of the banking problem that had to be faced in Detroit when the national moratorium was lifted. New banks had to be launched to replace those which had sunk. With the disappearance of the Guardian and the First Wayne National, there were not enough surviving banking facilities to meet the community's requirements.

Within a few weeks two new banks were opened, one backed by General Motors, the other by the Fords. Both have flourished; but at the time they were put afloat no amount of salesmanship could persuade the bank-shy public to invest in their stock.

It was no easy matter to persuade General Motors to assume the responsibility of a bank in Detroit and put $12,500,000 capital in its common stock to match the $12,500,000 preferred stock subscribed for by the RFC. I first approached Mr. Sloan with respect to that matter on March 20, 1933. He sent his corporation's general counsel, John Thomas Smith, and the chairman of the finance committee, Donaldson Brown, to continue the discussions with me. After two or three meetings we reached an agreement to go fifty-fifty in capitalizing a bank.

The new bank, called the National Bank of Detroit, was organized on March 31. As owner of all its common stock, General Motors was responsible for its management and naturally wanted to name its president; but, because the situation in Detroit was so serious and failures so far-reaching, I felt somewhat about Detroit as I did with respect to selecting a new head for the Continental Illinois National Bank in Chicago. The General Motors officials wanted a banker from New York to head the new institution in Detroit, but I suggested the selection of someone from the Middle West. In a few days they gave me two or three names, including that of Walter S. McLucas, a banker in Kansas City whom I knew well. I recommended his selection, as president. Later he became chairman of the board. Mr. McLucas proved very satisfactory, not only to General Motors, but also to Detroit.

At its opening the new bank took over the more liquid assets of both the First Wayne National and the Guardian National Bank of Commerce, paying the conservators nearly $120,000,000 for this paper.

General Motors offered the public any or all of the 500,000 shares of common stock in the new bank at $25 each, the price they paid for it. Except for the Chrysler interests, which bought about 20,000 shares, there were no large purchasers and very few small ones. When the subscription books were closed in May, 1933, General Motors was holding nine-tenths of the common shares. During its first seven months the bank's deposits increased from $29,000,000 to $163,000,000 and the number of accounts from a cautious 4,386 to a confident and encouraging 90,000.

As the Detroit area recovered from the depression a market blossomed for the bank's stock. General Motors gradually reduced its ownership to 51 per cent by 1940. The corporation then decided to hold this control until all its stock could be disposed of at a stroke, which would enable the motor company to get out of the banking business. General Motors' stock in the bank was offered to the public in the spring of 1945, along with an issue of new shares. The entire offering was readily absorbed. With ample new capital on hand, the bank retired the preferred stock in January, 1947, and the RFC stepped out of that particular enterprise with principal and interest in full.

Detroit's second new bank, the Manufacturers National, was entirely underwritten by the Ford interests. It opened in August, 1933, a few months after I had persuaded General Motors to set up and daddy the National Bank of Detroit. During the preceding winter, when Detroit lay stifling under the debris of the collapse, the Fords had proposed to organize two new banks, one to take over the First Wayne National's assets, the other to be built on the old Guardian foundation. Their plan did not progress beyond the blueprints, which had fixed March 2 for the opening date.

Later, in organizing the Manufacturers National, the Fords, like General Motors before them, offered to sell their bank's stock to the public; but investors were still shy, so they decided to keep all the stock. Until his death Edsel Ford controlled the bank. He would not accept RFC participation in its capital structure. As public confidence increased, the Ford interests slowly disposed of a majority of the shares to the public. The bank's deposits increased nearly fifteenfold—from $36,000,000 to $538,000,000—in seventeen years.

Whatever their rivalries in the automotive field, the Big Three auto companies had no ambition to compete with one another, or anyone else, as bankers. Of that fact I had tried, as early as July 13, 1933, to reassure the public, with a statement which said:

"The Ford interests, General Motors, and Mr. Walter P. Chrysler have made it clear that they have no desire to engage in the banking business. They have made these investments for the sole and only purpose of giving to Detroit proper banking facilities and to relieve as much as possible of the deposits in closed banks."

In that purpose they succeeded splendidly, and are entitled to credit.

THE COLLAPSE IN CLEVELAND

Infection from Michigan's banking sores in the winter of 1932–1933 spread swiftly into adjacent states. The bankers of near-by Cleveland already had troubles enough of their own. Like all industrial centers, their city was suffering severely from the ills of unemployment. When the banks of Michigan closed, there began a heavy drain of millions of dollars a day out of the Cleveland banks. Some of this was the shifting of "smart money" to New York and Chicago; much of the rest of it went into hoarding.

By February 27 Cleveland's Union Trust Company had seen its deposits drop from a normal $300,000,000 to $143,000,000 while the Guardian Trust Company's shrank from above $150,000,000 to $81,000,000. On that date, both these banks and all but one of the

Cleveland banks went on a restricted withdrawal basis. Guardian depositors were allowed to check out only 1 per cent of their balances and the Union's depositors 5 per cent.

After the holiday neither of these banks was able to reopen. To bolster Cleveland's other banks, the RFC invested in their preferred stock: $15,000,000 in the Cleveland Trust Company, $12,000,000 in the Central National, $4,000,000 in the National City Bank, and $2,000,000 in the Society for Savings.

Mismanagement and overoptimistic acceptance of the perpetual prosperity myth of the 1920's had contributed to Cleveland's financial difficulties. In the clean-up after the crash, two of the city's prominent bank executives were sent to prison. Into the reopened Cleveland banks it seemed advisable to inject new blood as well as fresh money. The RFC, as a preferred stockholder, helped change the top names on the letterheads of several Cleveland banks. As president of the National City Bank of Cleveland, which succeeded another institution, we installed Sidney B. Congdon. He had been chief of our examining division. Later we arranged for Loring L. Gelbach, another RFC executive, to be president of the Central National Bank of Cleveland. Both of these banks have done well.

In addition to homemade difficulties and the repercussions of the Michigan moratorium, Cleveland, as central city of the Fourth Federal Reserve District, was slapped by the backwash from banking disturbances in Akron, Youngstown, Toledo, and other Ohio cities.

Of all the larger communities in Ohio, Cincinnati alone escaped the severer forms of the infection; partly, perhaps, because in its old-fashioned conservatism that mellowed city had not very noticeably contracted the promotion fever and booster spirit which prevailed in so many other parts of the country during the earlier boom. But no city was immune to the epidemic of fear and hoarding in 1932–1933. The Cincinnati banks felt it prudent to put deposit withdrawals on a restricted basis the same day Cleveland banks hoisted similar storm warnings.

As real estate, stock market securities, and other values rose out of the mire, the liquidators of the two big Cleveland trust companies that were closed paid off the depositors. Those who had money in the Union got all of it back by March, 1943. A little later the Guardian's depositors were fully repaid, after a wait of eleven years.

In the general recovery even the stockholders of the closed institutions fared less badly than they had anticipated in the darker days. Those who elected to hold on to their Union Trust stock recovered their entire investments before the summer of 1948. By then the Guardian's stockholders, upon whom assessments had been levied, had got back 80 per cent. In thawing out slow assets of the closed banks and trust companies, the Home Owners' Loan Corporation, which took over the slow mortgages, aided Cleveland's recovery as it did that of many other cities.

Of the thousands of banks the RFC helped to bail out, hundreds gave good examples of how an alert, diligent banker, by cooperating with government agencies while raising fresh capital among his neighbors, could restore a crippled institution to good health. Let me give one example—Harry Nicholl, now president of the National Bank of Lorain, Ohio, a steel town. He was the bank's cashier when it went down the chute in 1933.

Our examinations at that time convinced us that with new capital the bank could be usefully reorganized. Our Cleveland agency advised Mr. Nicholl to go out and try to raise some money, promising that we would match the local citizens, dollar for dollar, by taking preferred stock. He reorganized the bank on the waiver plan, by old depositors waiving part of their deposits to establish new capital. The bank examiners estimated the liquid assets on hand would permit a 30 per cent payment on old deposits when the bank reopened. Mr. Nicholl, by moving his slower mortgage paper into HOLC and taking government obligations for it, so increased the liquidity that he was able to declare an initial dividend of 50 per cent to the depositors. Ultimately they got 100 per cent plus interest. The old stockholders, at last accounts, had received $140 a share and expected this to jump to $160 as soon as two pieces of real estate could be profitably sold.

4

☼

THE DAWES BANK LOAN

*An All-Day, All-Night Conference—How the $90,000,000
Was Repaid*

OF ALL the hundreds of thousands of transactions handled by the
RFC and its subsidiaries, the one which stirred up the most and
longest public interest and evoked the keenest controversy in Congress
and out was the so-called Dawes Loan.

Even now, eighteen years later, my associates of those disastrous
days tell me that frequent inquiry is made at RFC headquarters as to
"how the Dawes loan has panned out." Though there were times
during the middle 1930's when I thought we might have a substantial
loss, the loan has panned out very well. The RFC has collected the
entire $90,000,000 loan plus more than $10,000,000 interest, in
addition to several millions of expenses in connection with the
liquidation.

The acute circumstances under which this loan was made gathered
quickly about our heads. General Charles G. Dawes, though bearing
the title of "Honorary Chairman" of the Central Republic Bank, had
not been in its management for the previous seven years.

During that period he had served four years as Vice President of
the United States and three years as Ambassador to the Court of
St. James's, rendering distinguished public service. In February, 1932,
when the RFC was created, he was made President of the RFC by
President Hoover. Early in the following June he suddenly resigned.
Just ten minutes before boarding a train in Washington on June 15,
he publicly announced that he was returning to Chicago to take
charge of his bank, though he was neither a director nor an active
officer.

I had no intimation that his bank was threatened with trouble. I am sure that the other two Democratic members of our board, Harvey Couch and Wilson McCarthy, were also ignorant of that fact. Neither Eugene Meyer, our chairman, nor Ogden Mills, who as Secretary of the Treasury was an ex-officio member of our board, had yet learned the desirability of taking us three country-boy Democratic members into their confidence and counsel. Apparently they expected us blindly to do their bidding. I hated to see General Dawes leave our Corporation. He had a broad and sympathetic appreciation of our whole economic situation.

On the morning of Saturday June 25, ten days after the General left us, I arrived in Chicago as a delegate to the 1932 Democratic National Convention which was to convene there the following Monday. This was the convention that nominated Franklin D. Roosevelt for his first term as President.

From my hotel, that ominous Saturday morning, I walked through the Loop and watched the tail end of the week's terrible runs on the big downtown banks. Thousands of frantic, rumor-spreading depositors were still milling about every bank entrance in La Salle, Clark, and Dearborn streets. Bank lobbies swarmed with nervous customers. Many of these disturbed people had already lost heavily in the collapse of several outlying neighborhood banks which had dotted almost the entire city. Others, during the two previous months, had seen part of their savings disappear when the Insull empire of "customer-ownership" public utilities crashed into insolvent splinters.

Furthermore, during the previous three weeks twenty-five of Chicago's outlying banks had closed. On the Wednesday preceding my arrival the bank-run fever had spread into the Loop, where Chicago's five big banks were located, among these being the two largest banks in the Middle West, the First National and the Continental Illinois. On Thursday the Carroll chain of seven banks had failed to open. On Friday eight more of the smaller "corner banks" were piled up onto the week's wreckage. Alarming rumors fanned the fears of the city's millions, of whom hundreds of thousands, being unemployed, had only their dwindling savings on which to exist and could not afford to lose their deposits or have them tied up.

At eleven o'clock that Saturday morning, Melvin A. Traylor, the chief executive officer of the First National Bank, breasted the wave of fearful depositors sweeping through his banking house. Stepping up on the pedestal of a marble pillar in the savings department he calmly addressed the crowd. He said he did not blame them for worrying or for what they were doing, after all that had happened to the banking business in Cook County; but he wished to assure them that if they would talk to people who knew the facts, they would learn that the First National, which had been in business for seventy years, was sound and in a position to pay all its depositors their money. Mr. Traylor was regarded as a possible presidential nominee of the Democratic convention that was to open its sessions two days later. He was placed in nomination by the Illinois delegation.

Saturday night General Dawes, whose bank had seen its deposits slip within a year from $240,000,000 to half that amount, made a decision which, as he later explained to one of his friends, so relieved his anxious mind that, for the first time in the ten nights since his return to Chicago, he was able to get several hours of untroubled sleep. His decision was not to open his bank on Monday morning.

He arose very early on Sunday and assembled in his office his principal associates and also a few leading officials of the other larger banks. Mr. Traylor, after his first conversation that morning with General Dawes, got in touch with Edward Eagle Brown, the executive vice president of the First National, and asked him to call other officials and directors of the First National to a second meeting, in their bank. He told Mr. Brown that, in his opinion, the General meant what he said about not opening Monday.

Later that morning Mr. Traylor came to my hotel room and asked me to go with him to a meeting of bankers. He did not tell me the purpose of the meeting or where it was to be held, but his demeanor manifested that it was serious and urgent. He took me to the Central Republic. We got there a little before noon. Gathered in the board room were thirty or forty of Chicago's leading bankers, businessmen, and industrialists. It was obvious that they had been awaiting our arrival, and that I was to be, as the saying goes, the fall guy.

GENERAL DAWES DECIDES TO CLOSE HIS BANK

Quietly but with a firm jaw and an attitude that carried conviction, General Dawes told us he had called the meeting to inform the other banks in Chicago, and me, as a government official, that he did not intend to open his bank the following morning, Monday. He gave as his reason that, while he thought the bank was solvent, the "smart" money was being withdrawn through the clearinghouse, as well as over the counter, at the rate of more than $2,000,000 a day, and he did not intend to sit idly by and allow frightened depositors to get all the ready cash the bank had available to meet current demands while friendly, trusting depositors and those who were not in the know might be forced to wait for their money until the bank could be liquidated.

He made it clear that he was not asking for assistance, but said that he wanted to inform the other bankers of his purpose not to open his bank, so that they might take such steps as they could to meet their own requirements when his bank did not open the following morning. It must have been apparent to all those present, as it certainly was to me, that a renewal or continuation of the bank runs and clearinghouse withdrawals would force all the banks in the Chicago area to close. The General was the coolest man in the room. The situation was dramatic in the extreme.

We sent out for sandwiches, peeled off our coats, and got down quickly to the business of seeing what could be done. It was nearly sixteen hours later, just before Monday's dawn, that we put on our coats again and left the bank to go to bed.

Early in the discussions I was advised that during the previous week Loop banks had paid out more than $100,000,000 in currency over the counter and had lost many more millions of deposit through clearinghouse withdrawals to other cities. One of the comparatively large banks had been but recently rescued by the clearinghouse and absorbed by the First National.

Mr. Traylor, who took the lead for all the Chicago bankers, requested that I telephone President Hoover and recommend that the government take steps to keep the Dawes bank open. I explained to the meeting that I did not have enough information to make such a recommendation to the President, but that if I could have a few hours to go into the affairs of the bank, and the situation generally, I would then call the President and give him my views.

Obviously neither I nor any other outsider could examine a large bank in a few hours. But, for several months prior to that direful Sunday, I had had a great deal to do with banks in trouble. In little more than four months of operation the RFC had already authorized some forty-one hundred bank loans aggregating hundreds of millions of dollars. From my experiences in making these loans I had found that a fairly adequate appraisal of the condition of a bank could be achieved in a sort of thumbnail-sketch fashion which would prove to be about as accurate for general purposes as a detailed analysis of its assets supported by credit information.

Skimming the bank's condition with several Chicago financiers and the RFC staff stationed in that city, whom we had called into conferences, I concluded there could not be any great loss to the creditors of the bank on its liquidation, if it came to that—which it later did. It was clear to me that the bank should not be allowed to close. Having reached that conclusion, I called President Hoover. As best I could by telephone I explained the situation to him. I told him I thought it much too dangerous to the country to allow the bank to close. The President said he would consult the Secretary of the Treasury and some of his advisers and would then call me back. I told the President that I was willing to take the responsibility of making the loan. I figured that the bank's $14,000,000 capital with surplus and undivided profits of $12,000,000 and a stockholders' liability of $14,000,000 if the bank failed would, together with the assets of the bank, be sufficient security for a $90,000,000 loan. I also felt certain that, if the bank closed, all Chicago banks would have to close, and that would soon mean a closing of all banks in the country. Of one thing I am sure, that if we had not saved the Chicago bank situation through making the loan, President Hoover would very shortly have had to close all banks until Congress could pass a law guaranteeing all bank deposits—which, as we look back, might have been a cheap price to pay.

General Dawes also talked with Mr. Hoover. When the President called me back he told me to make as good a trade with the other banks as possible, that is, get them to take as much participation as they could, but to save the Dawes bank.

AN ALL-DAY, ALL-NIGHT CONFERENCE

Meanwhile a number of other bankers and directors had been summoned into our huddles or to another meeting at the First National by the simple process of collaring them and turning them back to town as rapidly as their cars reached a suburban country club where a pre-convention garden party was being given in honor of Mrs.

Woodrow Wilson, who was the guest of Mrs. Jones and me at the convention. Surely never before had so many well known men been seen on a Sunday afternoon going in and coming out of banks in Chicago's Loop, a fact which quickly gave rise to speculation in alert newspaper offices. We succeeded, however, in keeping secret through the day the nature of our business, partly, perhaps, because one of the more influential bankers in Chicago had the delicate task of telephoning the leading Chicago publishers and letting them in on it.

After President Hoover had called me back to the telephone, I suggested to the assembled bankers that they take $10,000,000 of the required loan, and that the RFC would put up as much as $85,000,000. Two days before, the Dawes bank had applied to the RFC for a loan of $16,000,000 which our board had authorized on Saturday, after I had left for the convention; but this loan had not yet been consummated. In the hours which had since elapsed General Dawes had reached his decision not to open the bank on Monday.

During our meetings that Sunday there was much telephoning back and forth between Chicago and the East. I had found that both Secretary Mills and Eugene Meyer were in New York. With Mortimer Buckner, then head of the New York Clearing House, they got a group of New York bankers together to see what aid they could render the situation in Chicago. At five o'clock in the afternoon a telephone circuit linked their meeting in New York, ours in Chicago, President Hoover, the offices of the Treasury and the RFC in Washington. General Dawes talked to the President, Mr. Traylor and I to Secretary Mills, Mr. Brown and I to Mr. Buckner.

It was tentatively arranged that a group of interested New York banks would make a loan of $10,000,000 with the Chicago banks putting up $5,000,000 and the RFC $80,000,000.

General Dawes insisted, however, that the commitment of the New York banks be put into writing. It being a Sunday, those attending the meeting at New York were not able to reach all the bankers they proposed to commit to the loan. Eighteen months before, on another gloomy Sunday in the December of 1930, Mr. Buckner had sought to commit a group of New York banks, through the Clearing House, to go to the rescue of the failing Bank of United States in New York; but when he returned to Wall Street on Monday morning the brethren who had been absent from the Sunday conference refused to be considered as committed. General Dawes was taking no such chance.

So we had to set off on another tack, for the situation would not wait. By then I had been joined at the bank by another RFC director, Mr. McCarthy, who also had arrived in Chicago to attend the Democratic convention. He and our examiners quickly thumbed through the bank's collateral. About two o'clock in the morning, with New York removed from the picture, the Chicago bankers said that $3,000,000 would be about as much of the loan as they would take, whereupon I suggested we might as well go to bed and let events take their course. I knew we couldn't do that, but I thought they were able to take and should take a larger share of the loan.

At that moment something in Mr. Traylor's voice and attitude convinced me that maybe these banks had stood about all they could, and that we shouldn't press them further. So I reduced our requirement to $5,000,000, the Chicago banks to lend that sum against the foreign securities of the Central Republic (the RFC being permitted to lend only on domestic collateral). Mr. McCarthy and I then agreed that the Corporation would authorize a loan up to $90,000,000. By then the clock hands were edging close to four A.M.

In making loans it was the procedure of the RFC to set up an advisory committee wherever there was a Federal Reserve Bank. Our loans were made only on the recommendations of our agency managers and examiners and these local advisory committees. The chairman of the Chicago committee was George M. Reynolds, then the head of the city's largest bank, the Continental Illinois. Melvin Traylor was the vice chairman of the advisory committee. Mr. Reynolds had been with us through most of the long day and the night. Now that the culminating hour had arrived, we could not find him to certify that in his opinion the loan would be fully and adequately secured. We began looking for him all over the bank. I happened to open the door of a large clothes closet. There, flat on his back, loudly, peacefully snoring, lay Mr. Reynolds.

He got up, and with Mr. Traylor signed the recommendation. Other signatories were Howard Preston, then manager of our Chicago agency and later First Vice President of the Chicago Federal Reserve Bank; Ralph Buss and W. R. Milford, examiners from our Washington office. They certified that the security for the loan in their opinion was sufficient to assure its repayment. Without their certification neither I nor Mr. McCarthy could have approved the loan. Messrs. Buss and Milford later became officials of Federal Reserve Branch Banks, the former in Detroit, the latter in Baltimore.

I have related how the Dawes loan was made. How it was repaid and what happened to the bank itself are stories too long to be told here in other than a sketchy manner.

Five hours after the loan was arranged the bank opened for Monday's business. On the markets its stock, which on Saturday had been quoted at $47 bid—$49 asked—quickly plunged as low as $1 bid —$4 asked. General Dawes announced to the public that loans arranged over the week end had made the bank's position impregnable. The fact that the RFC had put up most of this money soon leaked out.

That day, and during the next two days, the RFC moved $40,-000,000 of its commitment into the bank's vault. To secure these advances the bank deposited with the RFC nearly all of its assets except cash on hand. Our loan acted as oil on extremely stormy and dangerous waters. It lessened the turbulence, but could not stop the storm. Though the runs on the downtown banks ceased, withdrawals from the Central Republic continued to exceed deposits. Within a few weeks General Dawes decided that voluntary liquidation would be the wiser course.

Despairing of any other method of protecting his depositors, he submitted to us on August 1, only five weeks after the loan was made, a plan for the organization of a new bank to take over the deposits of the old one, which had dropped a further $35,000,000 since the loan was made. He proposed beginning with $3,000,000 capital. We approved the plan with the proviso that the capital be increased to $5,000,000. The new bank was named the City National Bank & Trust Company.

HOW THE $90,000,000 WAS REPAID

From its inception General Dawes became its active chairman, while the old Central Republic went into receivership.

When we made the $90,000,000 loan General Dawes told me that if stockholders' assessments were necessary to pay the bank's debts it would cost Dawes Brothers, Inc., about $1,000,000. In considering the security for the loan he had told me we could rely on stockholders' liability of at least $7,000,000, which was fifty cents on the dollar of the bank's $14,000,000 capital stock.

In November, 1936, United States District Judge Wilkerson ruled in Chicago that the stockholders were liable for assessments on their stock. General Dawes then assured me that Dawes Brothers, Inc., would pay their assessment as soon as the Court's decree was entered. He was more than good for his word. The decree was entered and became effective Saturday May 1, 1937, but Judge Wilkerson imposed the condition that executions should not be levied for six months. Yet on the following Monday, May 3, Dawes Brothers, Inc., paid the receiver of the bank $1,027,000, for that part of their assessment covered by the decree. The General had paid his personal assessment of $5,200 as soon as the suit was brought.

When the Central Republic came on evil days General Dawes was neither an officer nor a director of the institution. He had, however, been the founder of the Central Trust Company of Illinois back in 1902 and was its chief executive officer until becoming Vice President of the United States in 1925. The Central Trust Company had amalgamated in 1931 with the National Bank of the Republic to form the Central Republic. This consolidated bank had become known to Chicagoans and to the nation's financial fraternity as "the Dawes bank." When it got into trouble, it was typical of General Dawes' character that he should simply, swiftly, silently go back home to take the moral and personal responsibility for whatever might happen.

As this chapter is being written, General Dawes, in his middle eighties, is still going to his office every day and remains active in many of the affairs of the community to whose upbuilding he greatly contributed.*

In bringing about the famous "Dawes Loan" it could, in the parlance of bridge, be said of him that he played his hand well. It should also be said that probably twenty million depositors in other banks throughout the country suffered a greater loss on their accounts in closed banks than they would have suffered had their banks not remained open too long, thus allowing the frightened or "smart" money to skip out, leaving unsuspecting and more loyal depositors to hold the bag.

* General Dawes died April 23, 1951.

Though the Dawes family interests willingly paid their assessments in full in the liquidation of their bank, we had to go to court to collect from some of the Central Republic's other 4,000 stockholders. Out of the $14,000,000 total due, the RFC collected as stockholders' liabilities approximately $11,000,000, or $4,000,000 more than General Dawes told me we could rely on. Thus the $90,000,000 loan was paid out in full with about 2 per cent interest.

5

CONTROVERSY OVER PUBLICITY FOR LOANS

Bankers Shy from Publicity—We Keep the Public In-formed—Saving the Situation in Houston—Maine Sets a Good Example

SOME bankers whose banks failed in 1932 and 1933 felt they could have weathered the storm if it had not been made public that they were getting help from the RFC. It is doubtful if any of them were right.

The original RFC Act provided that we should make quarterly reports to the President and Congress of the aggregate amount lent, by states, to each class of borrower: banks, insurance companies, railroads, et cetera. It did not call for giving the names of the borrowers or the amount lent to each.

Shortly after the Dawes Loan became common knowledge, the RFC Act was amended to require that henceforth we should make monthly reports of all loans. Debate in Congress was bitter. On the vote the House divided evenly, 169 to 169. Mr. Garner, as Speaker, had to break the tie. He voted in favor of the amendment. It became law on July 17, 1932. The amendment required the RFC to make monthly reports on all loans granted the previous month. The reports were to be made to the President of the United States, the Senate and the House of Representatives (or the Secretary of the Senate and the Clerk of the House of Representatives, if these bodies were not in session).

The new law did not specifically provide that the loans should be publicized. But when we sent up our first report, in August, Mr. Garner instructed the Clerk of the House to make it public—and the cat was out of the bag.

Immediately the subject Congress had debated—whether loans should be made public—spread as a controversy to almost every community where there was a bank.

It was quite some time before bankers became reconciled to the fact that it was better to admit the truth and take RFC help than to continue trying to put up a bold front which was not justified by the circumstances.

Beginning in August, 1932, we sent current monthly reports to Congress and the President; but the amendment to the Act requiring publicity did not include loans made prior to that date, and they were not made public. When Congress reassembled in December, 1932, some of the Democrats in the House sponsored a resolution demanding publication of all these early loans. Henry B. Steagall, then chairman of the House Banking and Currency Committee, sided with Speaker Garner in favoring full dissemination.

"The funds being lent by the RFC belong to all the people and they are entitled to know what is being done," Mr. Steagall said during the debate. The following February, on the day the Michigan bank holiday began, Speaker Garner, who happened also to be a director of two Texas banks, gave out one of his rare statements for publication. It was characteristically brief, candid, and pungent.

"There is no place now under the flag," he wrote, "where a man can deposit $100,000 to check against and be sure he can get it. The banks are afraid to make loans, even on adequate security. I have contended consistently that there has been too much secrecy about what has been going on in the last twelve months. If the truth scares people, let it come. Let the people know all about everything the government does."

His statement ignited another fiery debate in the House. One Representative wailed that Congress, wittingly or unwittingly, had already "broken a thousand banks." Another critic said publication of RFC loans had been an "engine of destruction which crushed the life out of numerous institutions." But the bill was passed, and the early loans were made public.

Undoubtedly the fact that our loans were to be made public prevented many bankers from applying for help that was sorely needed. Probably a combination of pride and fear influenced them.

WE KEEP THE PUBLIC INFORMED

Unfortunately, neither Eugene Meyer, our first RFC board chairman, nor Atlee Pomerene, who succeeded him in July, 1932, and served until the Roosevelt inauguration, was in favor either of boldly making credit available on all fronts in an effort to stop the downward trend in our whole economy, or of emphasizing what we were doing and were prepared to do.

Neither of these men can necessarily be censured, for it is only fair to say that the country was in a situation that it had never experienced before. Few members of Congress probably thought that the government could afford to put its credit behind our whole economy, which we later did under Roosevelt.

During Mr. Meyer's chairmanship and Mr. Pomerene's, newspapermen were not especially welcome at RFC headquarters. When I became chairman of the board in May, 1933, I felt that if the RFC was to perform effectively the services for which it had been created it must have public confidence, and fear of borrowing from it must be dispelled.

I began holding press conferences, usually two a week, submitting myself to the freest possible questioning by correspondents. Often I would be questioned about specific situations, and there were plenty of them. I always told the press correspondents the truth, but sometimes asked them not to use a particular item, for it might be hurtful. I had the best possible cooperation from the correspondents. They were really helpful in dispelling fear.

I put it to them on the basis that we were all working to a common purpose—to save the country. While I could not ask them to color news, I could ask them not to use information when it would hurt.

I tried to get it over to the country that the RFC wanted to help everyone it was authorized to help, and on generous but business-like terms. I continually preached the doctrine that it was the duty of heads of institutions which needed help to come ask for it. We spent a lot of time and effort trying to rebuild shattered morale, as well as weakened balance sheets.

A great many banks which went under could have been saved if bankers and business leaders in local communities had worked together and tried hard enough to avert trouble. As examples I will cite two cases.

The first one was in my own home town, Houston, in October, 1931, before the banking situation had become so grave, and before there was an RFC. Two of our seven banks—they were national banks—came to grief Saturday October 24. I had been expecting it for several months and had not left the city all summer. Sunday morning, October 25, I called all the bankers of the city to meet in my office at two o'clock. We spent the entire afternoon, evening, and night until six o'clock Monday morning, going over the situation. We sent out for food. No one left the meeting. When we adjourned the group directed me, acting for all our banks, to furnish the two troubled banks with such funds as they might need on Monday. We agreed to meet again Monday after banking hours.

Monday afternoon at five o'clock we met again in my office on the thirty-third floor of the Gulf Building, which seemed to be the safest place all the bankers could get together on a Sunday and through two all-night sessions without knowledge of their meetings becoming too widespread. We completed our program just before Tuesday's dawn. To absorb the losses of the two troubled banks, we raised a fund by assessing the remaining banks a certain percentage of their capital and surplus. We also got substantial contributions from the public utilities—the light and power company, the local gas company, and the telephone company—and one cotton firm. At our request, the morning newspaper delayed its final Tuesday morning edition until after six o'clock so as to carry the news that the banking situation had been cleared up. With all our care and precautions, it had not been possible for all the leading bankers in town to hold two all-night meetings without a considerable number of people knowing of it and wondering what it was all about.

I arranged for immediate publication of two announcements. One was that my own bank, the National Bank of Commerce, then one of the youngest and smallest in town, had taken over the assets and assumed the deposit liabilities of one of the troubled institutions, the Public National Bank & Trust Company, and that we would liquidate it.

The second announcement was that control of the Houston National, the other bank in trouble, had been bought by the family of Joseph F. Meyer, Sr. Pioneers in the Houston business world, the Meyer family were widely known to be both wealthy and conservative. We anticipated that their ownership would inspire confidence and the bank would continue. It worked out that way.

MAINE SETS A GOOD EXAMPLE

Now for the other case I mentioned. Early in 1933 the Merrill Trust Company of Bangor, the largest bank in Maine, with eleven branches in three adjoining counties, found itself in trouble. Like many other banks, it was continuing to accept deposits while insolvent. One day early in April, 1933, the Governor of the State, Louis J. Brann, a Democrat who had been elected with the Roosevelt landslide, came to my office with a delegation of a dozen directors of the bank. I never saw a finer or more substantial-looking set of men. The spokesman stated that the bank was in trouble, and that they wanted to borrow $1,000,000. We in the RFC knew what their situation was; it was our business to know. I replied to the gentlemen that they needed not $1,000,000 but $4,000,000, and if they would raise $2,000,000 the RFC would put in $2,000,000 preferred capital stock. When anyone telephoned us for an appointment, say by tomorrow, we immediately got busy orienting ourselves about their situation and general conditions in their vicinity. When Governor Brann telephoned me for the appointment, I immediately put our boys to work getting together as much information as we could about the situation they were coming to discuss. That is the reason I was prepared to tell the gentlemen they needed $4,000,000 instead of $1,000,000.

The spokesman for the group replied that they could not raise any money. I thought they could if they would try. I then said to them: "In that case, you gentlemen had better consult your Governor." What I meant, of course, was that it is a violation of the law for a bank to accept deposits when its officers and directors know it to be insolvent, and the punishment is severe. Governor Brann, a lawyer by profession, understood what I meant. He said: "Gentlemen, we will go back home, and see Mr. Jones later."

What they did proved again that if you tell the American people the truth they can stand anything—and take it. They formed a civic committee and launched a drive to "save our banks." They conducted the campaign much in the manner of the Liberty Loan drives during the First World War. They held public meetings. They ran advertisements in the newspapers. They put out placards and all the rest. They told the truth.

Nobody got frightened or drew his money out of the banks except in current operations. The depositors pledged $1,800,000 to the "Save Our Banks" fund, the stockholders put up $900,000 and other citizens, $300,000. About five thousand people contributed to this $3,000,000 fund of fresh capital. The RFC put in $2,000,000 preferred stock, and made a loan on some rejected assets. The bank was saved.

By not stampeding when they learned their banks were in trouble, the citizens of that section of Maine demonstrated what might have been accomplished in many other places, had there been leadership by men willing to put their heads, hearts, and pocketbooks together, cooperating willingly and unselfishly for the common good and to avert disaster.

Yes, the truth can hurt, but not as badly as uncertainty and fear.

6

AID TO AGRICULTURE

Lending on Cotton—Deluged with Bumper Crops—
Helping the Corn and Wheat Farmers—Butter, and Naval
Stores—Tobacco, Goobers, Prunes, and Firewater

ONE afternoon in 1933, President Roosevelt called me to the White House and, as soon as I entered his office, said: "Jess, I want you to lend 10 cents a pound on cotton."

Cotton was then selling around 9 cents. The law which created the RFC stated clearly that we should lend only on "full and adequate security." Therefore, to lend 10 cents a pound on cotton when it was selling at 9 and less, was not easy. I did not tell the President we could not do it. I took it to be my job to find a way to do it because I thought cotton was worth more than 10¢ and that to lend that amount on it would be very helpful and entail no loss to the government.

That is how the RFC took its first really deep plunge into agriculture. Before we had finished helping the farmer, the job had become second only to our bank rescue program. We loaned money to millions of farmers. We raised the price of farm commodities and came out ahead on the books.

But for the billions of federal dollars loaned to farmers to enable them to sell their crops in an orderly manner rather than rush them into distressed markets at harvest time, the whole agricultural economy of the country would have collapsed. It almost did in 1932.

For long periods we carried a large paper loss on our farm-aid program. Eventually, however, as this story will relate, the piled up mountains of cotton, wheat, and many other commodities were disposed of at a profit to both the farmer and the government.

Upon returning to my office after the President asked me to lend

10 cents on cotton, I discussed the matter with our general counsel, Stanley Reed, now Associate Justice of the Supreme Court. We decided to organize the Commodity Credit Corporation and have the RFC provide it with money to make the loans. To capitalize the Commodity Credit Corporation, we found $3,000,000 unexpended balance from funds Congress had authorized the President to allocate for aid to agriculture. I knew, of course, that $3,000,000 would not cover all the cotton loans we would make, but reasoned that when we offered to lend 10 cents a pound on cotton, with no recourse to the borrower, that its value would soon be established at no less than that figure.

So, with the $3,000,000 furnished by the President, we organized the Commodity Credit Corporation, and the RFC loaned it the money to lend on cotton. Its operations have run into billions, with Congress finally, in 1938, giving it direct authority to borrow for its requirements with government guarantee and without going through the RFC. From cotton, its operations were rapidly extended to corn, wheat, and other farm commodities.

I am told that Oscar Johnston of Mississippi put the 10 cent cotton loan idea in the President's head. The New Deal's Secretary of Agriculture, Henry A. Wallace, at that time was hatching his scheme to offer rewards to farmers who would plow under every third row they had planted in the spring.

It was suggested to the President by some of the promoters of the idea that the Regional Agricultural Credit Corporations, then under the directorship of Henry Morgenthau, Jr., be authorized to make the loans. But that plan was abandoned, and the President sent for me.

On October 16, 1933, creation of the Commodity Credit was authorized by Executive Order No. 6340. Incorporated the next day under the laws of Delaware, Commodity Credit promptly set up offices in RFC headquarters.

At the request of the President, Secretary Wallace was put on the board. The Corporation was operated for its first six years under the direction of the RFC. By then it had got to be a highly successful operation, and Mr. Wallace's mouth began to water to have it put into his Department of Agriculture. Finally, in 1939, the President transferred it there. By that time its work had become routine procedure.

ONE LITTLE PIG HE ISN'T GOING TO PLOW UNDER!

Talburt for Scripps-Howard newspapers.

While Commodity Credit was in the RFC, Lynn P. Talley, special assistant to the RFC directors, was its president and John D. Goodloe its vice president, general manager, and general counsel. Mr. Talley had formerly been a banker in Texas, and was familiar with lending on cotton. Mr. Goodloe, a Kentucky-bred attorney then only twenty-five years old, had come to the RFC legal department in 1932 from the Federal Farm Board. Early in the Roosevelt regime he had gone over to the Farm Credit Administration to help operate the Regional Agricultural Credit Corporations—known as the "Regionals." When we started Commodity Credit we needed a lawyer acquainted with government operations in the agricultural field. Mr. Reed, recalling Mr. Goodloe's abilities, asked him to request a thirty-day leave of absence from the Farm Credit Administration. This leave lasted many years. After Mr. Talley's health failed in July, 1935, Mr. Goodloe became the operating head of Commodity Credit and did an excellent job for the following four years.

He afterwards became general counsel of the RFC, later a director, and finally chairman of the board. He resigned the chairmanship in the spring of 1948 to accept a prominent place in the Coca-Cola Company at Atlanta, of which he is now vice president. The president of Coca-Cola is another RFC alumnus, William J. Hobbs.

Mr. Hobbs was one of our young lawyers in Washington when we sent him to Atlanta as general counsel of our agency there. Edgar Dunlap, his predecessor in the RFC's Atlanta agency, was a close friend of United States Senator Walter F. George and had resigned because of President Roosevelt's angry effort in 1938 to "purge" the Georgia Senator. Senator George was reelected by an overwhelming vote, notwithstanding President Roosevelt's determined effort to defeat him. We sent Bill Hobbs, a North Carolinian, to Atlanta to succeed Attorney Dunlap because we did not want to select a Georgian on account of the political situation. We tried to stay out of politics, though in this situation our sympathies were with Senator George.

The RFC's helping hand was first extended to the farmers during the Hoover administration; but it was a new venture, and Congress was timid about it. Cotton had been selling on the farms at 6 cents a pound and less, corn for 15 to 25 cents a bushel, and wheat for 40 or 50 cents. In addition to the many hundreds of millions invested later, through the Commodity Credit Corporation, in the farmer and his products, the RFC advanced almost $2,000,000,000 through various other agencies, private and governmental, in aid to agriculture.

Of that money, nearly $400,000,000 went in loans to federal land banks, all of which was repaid by August, 1938. We put more than $600,000,000 into the program of rural rehabilitation, conducted by the Department of Agriculture. That debt was entirely repaid by March, 1947.

At the very bottom of the depression, in 1932, the RFC through the Regional Agricultural Credit Corporations made loans of nearly $175,000,000 to farmers and stockmen in every state of the Union —from the potato fields of northern Maine to the citrus groves of California, Texas, and Florida. We even loaned money on a drove of reindeer in Alaska. Happily we collected that loan, for we might never have been able to corral the collateral.

To assist the orderly marketing in foreign countries of American farm surpluses, we loaned more than $50,000,000 without loss.

In all these programs the RFC directors had the responsibility of deciding to whom to lend and how much. In addition to these discretionary loans, we allocated nearly $426,000,000 by direction of Congress for aid to agriculture without the privilege of employing our own judgment. We simply passed the money along, as directed, to other government agencies.

Between February and June of 1932 we estimated the RFC had directly aided at least one million farmers, cattlemen, and sheepmen.

While under RFC direction, Regional Agricultural Credit Corporations paid out from five to six million dollars each week. A fifth of their loans were for less than $250. The largest single class of loans was in the $500 to $1,000 category, but there were quite a few really large ones, thirty-seven being above $100,000 each. To the famous King Ranch on the coastal plains of Texas the RFC, in cooperation with the Federal Intermediate Credit Bank of Houston and the National Finance Credit Corporation of Forth Worth, made loans of nearly $2,000,000 in 1932 and 1933. These were repaid in the autumn of 1933.

Our miscellaneous aids to farmers and stockmen were helpful, but what really saved the whole country from disaster, in my view, was the work of the Commodity Credit Corporation. When Commodity Credit was organized the failure of the plow-under program Secretary Wallace had instituted lay heavily on the markets. Despite his payments to cotton farmers to destroy "every third row," they had brought to the gins an even larger crop than that of the previous year, an appalling crop of nearly 13,100,000 bales. In the face of this situation, our problem was to offer the farmer something sufficiently attractive for him to accept instead of selling his newly ginned cotton immediately and thus further depressing a market already overburdened with a surplus of millions of bales carried over from previous years. We arranged it in those first weeks so that the farmer wishing to borrow on his cotton could go to his customary bank or warehouse and pledge his cotton as security for Commodity Credit loans. The bank could tender the note to the nearest RFC loan agency and get its face value, plus 4 per cent interest, through Federal Reserve channels, or, if it wished to carry the paper, the bank could keep 3 per cent interest and send the remaining 1 per cent to us for our commitment to take over the note without recourse at any time.

After a few months we decided to cut down the take allowed to banks for making and servicing the loans. An income of 3 per cent on what amounted to a government-guaranteed obligation was such an attractive plum that the city banks in the cotton belt were eager to discount the paper from the country banks which originated the loans. The New York banks, in turn, sought it from the portfolios of the secondary banks. After a few months we cut the rate. While continuing to allow 3 per cent to the originating country banks, we sliced the yield to the secondary banks to 2½ per cent. Whatever the season, whatever the size of the crop or the loan, the interest rate to the farmer remained the same—4 per cent—for several years. Then it was reduced to 3 per cent.

Only a small portion of the 1933 cotton crop—some $103,000,000 worth—was pledged under our original 10-cent program. When the 1934 crop was ready to be picked, President Roosevelt decided to jump the loan price to 12 cents. Of that crop 4,500,000 bales came into the program on 1,198,055 separate loans.

In the spring of 1935 producers were moving their bales into the 12-cent-loan warehouses instead of taking them to market. Mill owners and merchants began besieging the government to make available some of the cotton tied up as security for the loans. We looked around for an alternative to calling the loans, taking the cotton, having it classed in even lots, and selling it. The alternative which the Commodity Credit board selected was ingenuous. We announced that until further notice any farmer or his designee might redeem his pledged cotton for the average price of the ten spot markets on the previous day, less 25 points, or $1.25 a bale, irrespective of whether this amount would pay off his note.

Thus, instead of a huge sale by one holder—the government—which would have driven prices downward, all the normal forces of competition in a free market were put into play. The buyer took the cotton from the individual grower at the warehouse nearest its origin, and it moved on through normal channels. Instead of one agency selling cotton, several hundred thousand farmers were selling. In this way the Commodity Credit Corporation encouraged the movement of about 2,000,000 bales in one hundred and twenty days and *on a rising market*.

When the 1935 crop came in, the President reduced the loan to 9 cents a pound but guaranteed the farmer 12 cents for his cotton. The Department of Agriculture agreed to make him a gift of the difference between the market price and 12 cents. With these gifts, Commodity Credit was not directly concerned.

We continued to pursue, as much as possible, our theory that the farmer is the best salesman of his own product. To encourage him to keep moving bales out of the loan program and into the market we continued to grant him 25 points. Under that system, another million bales were sold during the summer of 1936. While this orderly movement was proceeding a great drought began blistering the cotton belt. A short crop was soon indicated. We then stopped our release program in order not to interfere with the marketing of the 1936 cotton.

We should, of course, have liked to liquidate our cotton at the beginning of 1936, if it could have been done in an orderly way a little at a time. As it was, the interest charges, insurance, and storage had, by then, carried the cost to us on our 12-cent-loan cotton to 13½ cents—and cotton wouldn't bring that price. There was nothing to do but hold on and hope. We figured then, and so informed Congress, that it would take five years, at least, to get the government out of the cotton business. Against that background the position of the Commodity Credit Corporation was this: By then the Corporation owed something over $300,000,000 on three per cent loans from the RFC, of which about $286,000,000 was on cotton, $11,-

000,000 on corn, and the remainder on tobacco and naval stores. In little more than two years and three months of operation the Commodity Credit had disbursed on commodity loans about $628,-000,000, of which $308,000,000 had been repaid. The balance due came to $320,000,000, and there was great pressure to have the cotton loans extended again.

The Commodity Credit Corporation was in no condition to go into the open market and borrow from the banks. To get it into such a condition, I suggested to President Roosevelt, in a letter written February 4, 1936, that we ask Congress to authorize an increase in the Commodity Credit's capital stock to $100,000,000.

We could then margin our own loans and go into the market and borrow on the cotton at a low rate.

When we asked authority from Congress to increase the Commodity Credit Corporation's capital from $3,000,000 to $100,000,000, sharp criticism of the administration's commodity loan program was expressed by some of the members of the Senate Committee on Banking and Currency.

At one hearing I remarked that the RFC could borrow like anybody ought to borrow, and I happened to add "like the farmer should have borrowed, but we loaned him 12 cents." When I let slip that remark, the day's session was quickly brought to a close with the following colloquy:

Senator William Gibbs McAdoo, of California—Why did we loan him 12 cents to begin with? Who determined that?

Mr. Jones—Well, who determined most of the questions during the last three years?

Senator McAdoo—Well, I don't know. Do you?

Senator James Couzens, of Michigan—The President.

Mr. Jones—Well, all right.

Senator Couzens—Mr. Chairman, let us adjourn.

Of the $97,000,000 which Congress directed the RFC to supply to the Commodity Credit Corporation as new capital, we borrowed $73,000,000 from banks at less than 1 per cent interest. On our loans from the Treasury at that time, we were paying $2\frac{3}{4}$ per cent interest —so we made a considerable saving.

On the 1935 crop we loaned 10 cents a pound; but cotton during the winter and autumn which followed that harvest could be sold at 11 to 12 cents, so the farmers did not borrow to any great extent from the Commodity Credit at that time. On the short drought-year crop of 1936 we had no demand for loans and made none. The government agencies refrained from pushing any of the old cotton into the market, and the new crop brought a price—12 to as high as 14 cents—which the farmer preferred to our loan.

DELUGED WITH BUMPER CROPS

Cotton stored against Commodity Credit loans was being gradually reduced when the gigantic 19,000,000-bale crop of 1937 threw our hopes—and our balance sheet—completely out of joint. We had to take under our umbrella every bale that was offered because Congress had amended the Agricultural Adjustment Act so as to require us to make loans on cotton, corn, and wheat whenever those commodities reached a fixed price set by the Secretary of Agriculture.

Then came the deluge. We were swamped with bumper crops. The loan program was covering 11,000,000 bales, and our losses on cotton had risen to $90,000,000. Commodity Credit had no more loanable funds. It had put out against the notes on cotton and corn growers and other farmers its entire capital of $100,000,000 and all the $500,000,000 it had been authorized to borrow. And a new borrower—the wheat farmer—was knocking at the door.

The corn coming in was at a low enough price to entitle the grower to mandatory loans under the law, and so was wheat. But the cotton farmer, whose crop had come in first, had used up all of Commodity Credit's money, so we had nothing for the wheat farmer to tap.

Congress was not in session. The President was out of pocket. We had to do something. I suggested to our general counsel, Mr. Reed, that the RFC buy $150,000,000 worth of farmers' cotton notes from the Commodity Credit Corporation to provide it with funds to lend on corn and wheat. Mr. Reed looked into the matter and advised me that we could not do it, that the law did not give us the authority. I then asked him what would be the penalty if we did it anyway. He said that I could be fired. I asked him if he were sure that was the only penalty. He assured me that it was. So I had the RFC buy $150,000,000 of the cotton farmers' notes from Commodity Credit Corporation. This gave Commodity Credit money to lend on corn and wheat.

While there was no special provision in the law for Commodity

Credit to sell the farmers' notes, it was clear to me that it had the right to do so, and also that RFC had the right to buy them since it was all in compliance with the spirit of the laws that we were administering. Furthermore, I felt sure the Congress would approve it.

In January, 1939, I prepared a letter for the President's signature, and explained to him that we needed additional funds for lending on farm commodities. He promptly signed it, and I asked the Congress for the authority, which was granted. The letter follows:

THE WHITE HOUSE
WASHINGTON

January 25, 1939

Dear Jesse:

I suggest you ask Congress to extend the lending life of the RFC, Commodity Credit Corporation, Export-Import Bank, and the Electric Home and Farm Authority to January 15, 1941, and that the borrowing limit of the Commodity Credit Corporation with Treasury guaranty be increased from $500,000,000 to $900,-000,000.

This would give the Corporation a lending fund of $1,000,-000,000.

Sincerely,
FRANKLIN D. ROOSEVELT

Honorable Jesse H. Jones
Reconstruction Finance Corporation
Washington, D.C.

During my testimony to get the increase before the Senate Banking and Currency Committee, what we had done to get the money to lend on corn and wheat the previous summer and fall came out through a series of questions and much discussion. A prominent member of the Committee, after asking me many questions, said, "Mr. Jones, you have violated the law."

I replied: "No, Senator, I haven't violated the law. I construed the law and administered the law as I thought the Congress intended it, and I think you will agree that, under the circumstances, we were right."

In testifying for the increase, I told the Committee that undoubtedly there would be some ultimate losses in our loans on commodities, but expressed the opinion that any such losses would not be a drop in the bucket compared to what the nation's loss would have been had we not made the loans.

It turned out, with the passing years, the demands of wartime, and the soaring prices, that most of the commodities we had sheltered so long were sold at a profit.

HELPING THE CORN AND WHEAT FARMERS

Loans on corn were inaugurated in November, 1933. Corn was selling on farms as low as 15 to 25 cents a bushel—a price so far under the cost of production that much of the crop was being allowed to rot in the fields.

This program was launched at a White House conference to which the President summoned Secretary Wallace, George N. Peek, the Agricultural Adjustment Administrator, and me. The President and Mr. Wallace favored lending 40 cents a bushel in the crib; Mr. Peek, 45 cents; and, to be consistent, I favored a 35-cent loan, hoping to trade out for 40 cents. But Mr. Peek finally had his way, and the loan was 45 cents.

When the meeting was over I explained to the President that we would need more capital. He told me to arrange for it. When I went back to my office I prepared the following letter, which he promptly signed, and which I used as a basis for making the corn loan:

THE WHITE HOUSE
WASHINGTON

November 7, 1933

Dear Mr. Chairman:

Confirming our conversation today during which Secretary Wallace and Mr. George N. Peek strongly urged that loans to farmers in the corn belt at the rate of 45 cents per bushel be made by the Commodity Credit Corporation, secured by corn on the farm, beg to advise that, in my opinion, this should be done. The economic situation in the corn belt is very bad, and furthermore, I think loans on corn at this rate are good.

For the purpose of better enabling the Commodity Credit Corporation to meet its obligations on corn loans, and such other loans as it may have made, or may yet be called upon to make on commodities, I shall ask Congress to provide such additional capital as may be necessary. This will greatly strengthen the corporation to which your loans will be made.

In the meantime, I suggest that your board make funds available, through loans to the Commodity Credit Corporation, to be secured by loans to farmers in the corn belt on corn at 45 cents a bushel, upon the condition that the borrowers agree to an acreage reduction in the 1934–5 corn hog crop as may be outlined by the Department of Agriculture.

Yours very truly,
FRANKLIN D. ROOSEVELT

Honorable Jesse H. Jones
Chairman
Reconstruction Finance Corporation
Washington, D.C.

While the President's letter was not law, I knew perfectly well that the Congress would grant the request whenever we made it, because it was in the interest of the farmer, and of course it did.

When we launched the corn loans, lending on unshelled corn sealed in cribs on the farm was largely unknown. Normally only about 15 per cent of the corn raised each year in the United States goes to market as a grain. About 80 per cent of the crop reaches the buyer "on the hoof" in the form of hogs, cattle, mules, poultry, and other livestock to which the corn is fed. The shelled corn that does not go back into the earth as seed reaches the ultimate consumer in many forms—from packaged breakfast foods to bottled nightcaps.

We brought to Washington a busted farmer and a country banker from the Middle West to tell us their experiences in arranging loans on corn in the crib.

Most of the corn-growing states had laws providing for such security for loans, but this device had rarely been employed. It involved putting a state inspector's seal on the crib after determining the cubic space occupied by the corn. The certificate would be filed with the county recorder. A duplicate of it had the effect of a chattel mortgage.

Corn which normally enters the cash markets and is dealt with on the grain exchanges is shelled corn measured exactly in bushels. But there is no precise way of determining how many cubic feet and inches of corn remaining on the ear will shell out into a bushel. The customary approximations entail such variables as the corn's quality.

We made the early loans on the basis that 2½ cubic feet of crib space would contain a bushel. Later, to avoid losses, we increased the size of a "bushel" of unshelled corn from 2½ to 3 cubic feet, thereby obtaining more security.

Unlike the cotton loans, of which so many had to be renewed from year to year, all the 225,000 separate loans made on the 1933 corn crop in 1933, 1934, and 1935 were repaid with interest before the end of 1936. The whole situation was well handled throughout the country. Whoever bought the corn paid our loan first, and the balance of the purchase price went to the farmer. On the 1934 crop we loaned 55 cents a bushel; but in 1935 we dropped back to 45 cents.

These 1935 loans, which kept the surplus corn on the farm, turned out to be a godsend in 1936 when a calamitous drought cut the crop so severely that tens of thousands of farmers were not able to grow enough corn to feed their own livestock. But for the existence of so many convenient cribs filled with the corn of the previous years, the government would have had to buy much larger quantities than it did of shelled corn in the market to ship from the milling and storage centers back to the farms for distribution in the relief program. As it was many farmers simply reacquired their own corn by paying their notes, then took it from the unsealed cribs to feed their livestock, or to sell to their neighbors.

In 1937 there was another good-sized crop. On it we lent 50 cents a bushel. Against these loans, about 15,000,000 bushels remained in sealed cribs on the day the Commodity Credit Corporation moved out of the RFC and into the Department of Agriculture.

Our experience with wheat was brief and not bad. The wheat farmer did not come to us until 1938, when we made 47,867 loans aggregating $46,300,700. The next year we had made only eighteen loans on the new wheat crop before Commodity Credit was transferred to the Department of Agriculture.

At that juncture the book loss on wheat loans was about half a million dollars. Depending on location these loans had run from 81 cents down to 50 cents a bushel. The average loan on the 69,-

000,000 bushels remaining pledged on the day of the transfer was about 59 cents, and the wheat market was below that figure.

Three years later, wheat had climbed above $1 a bushel, and Commodity Credit was well in the black on that commodity. As prices soared up to $2 and then to $3 the loan program prospered accordingly. The agency's cumulative balance on wheat rose by June 30, 1947, to a profit of $22,710,000, almost enough to offset the loss, up to that date, on corn.

BUTTER, AND NAVAL STORES

The housewife who had to keep on friendly terms with her grocer or delicatessen counterman to enjoy the privilege of being allowed to get any butter at all in 1946 and who, later, when supplies were more plentiful, winced at paying $1 a pound for it, may have yearned, as she did so, for a return of the good old prewar days. But the dairy farmer didn't. Among other things he may have remembered were the cheerless churning days when Commodity Credit loans made the difference between 15-cent butter and 25-cent butter. Large surpluses accumulated during the depression years had driven prices below his cost of production. To raise and help stabilize butter prices the Corporation loaned $31,000,000 in 1938 and 1939 to cooperative associations in California, Illinois, Michigan, Minnesota, Missouri, Nebraska, New Jersey, New York, Ohio, Oregon, Pennsylvania, and Washington. Butter quickly came to fourth rank, after cotton, corn, and wheat, in our tally of loans on farm products. The butter loans were all repaid without loss to the government.

In fifth place came the $20,000,000 lent on naval stores—that is, turpentine and resin—made in six southern states, Alabama, Georgia, Florida, Louisiana, Mississippi, and South Carolina. To produce gum naval stores, the pine tree is scarified, the gum flowing into cups hung on the tree.

The immediate object of our program for gum naval stores, begun in 1934, was to support prices which had dropped distressingly low. In Savannah, the principal market place, vines and weeds half covered some of the thousands of flimsy wooden barrels containing resin. Some of these had rotted and collapsed. Softened by the hot Georgia sun, the resin had flowed over the ground and formed a crust often a foot thick. Mr. Talley, then the president of the Commodity Credit Corporation, had the country banker's penchant for taking a look at the collateral put up for his loans. One raw winter day in Washington, he decided the balmier climate of Savannah made the moment propitious for sizing up the naval stores. On his return from Savannah, he shook his head sadly and said it was "the damnedest worst-looking collateral" he'd ever seen.

Only small quantities of naval stores, a few barrels at a time, were being traded in from day to day on the Savannah Board of Trade. Yet these few transactions seemed to fix the price throughout the world. We had a hunch, which soon grew into a conviction, that the market was being rigged downward at harvest time, upward later on. We decided to do a little rigging ourselves and to reverse the seasonal practice. After contracting to make future deliveries we would buy naval stores, on rising offers, through a Savannah broker. There was so little trading that the scheme worked, although we had allocated only $5,000 for the first experiment.

The loans were terminated July 31, 1935, when marketing controls lapsed after a Supreme Court decision had killed the National Recovery Administration. Our holdings of resin were later disposed of at a profit of $645,000 over all costs, including interest. Turpentine stocks were liquidated slowly and at a loss of $1,778,000.

TOBACCO, GOOBERS, PRUNES, AND FIREWATER

We began making tobacco loans in 1936 and advanced $10,000,000 during the following three years, mostly to growers' associations in Tennessee, Kentucky, and Virginia. When Europe went to war in 1939 a really major emergency arose for flue-cured tobacco. Commodity Credit went to the rescue. Ever since Sir Walter Raleigh acquired the smoking habit, a large percentage of American tobacco growth had always gone to England. But after the British declared war on Hitler they felt the dollars they had available in the exchange markets could be better employed in buying other American products. These, too, might go up in smoke—but it would be the smoke of battle.

Whitehall forbade further purchases of American tobacco, and British buyers withdrew from our auction sheds. With their departure American tobacco growers faced ruinously low prices. The flue-cured tobacco markets were closed. Within a few days of their closing, however, a program was developed through which the Commodity Credit Corporation supplied funds necessary to carry tobacco inventories over the emergency period. The markets then reopened, and the farmers were able to sell their 1939 crop at prices substantially the same as those which prevailed before the British withdrew. After the war was over, when Europe had to husband its dollars for more essential purposes, tobacco became for the Commodity Credit Corporation the headache which cotton had been.

On many a red hill in the South is a farmer who, in the days when cotton was his only cash crop, got along with one mule and existed in an unpainted shack, and who now lives in an attractive cottage with built-on garage, electricity, butane gas, and labor-saving gadgets. If you ask him to explain, in a word, his improved status the word is likely to be peanuts. The great depression, which did not spare gilt-edged securities, also put its blight on the humble goober. Peanuts dropped to less than 3 cents a pound. To tide the growers over that dip, we loaned $12,000,000 on peanuts in seven southern states. Since then the American peanut acreage has greatly increased, and the price of peanuts has tripled. Our peanut loans turned in a profit.

We lent generously on many other commodities—on pecans in Georgia, prunes in California, hops in the state of Washington, and wool and mohair in seventeen states from Massachusetts to the Pacific coast. Under the law we were instructed to lend on any commodity designated by the President and recommended to us by the Secretary of Agriculture.

When the grape growers of California felt the pinch of hard times, they, like almost everyone else, hollered for help in Washington. Secretary Wallace, a teetotaler, seemed indisposed to assist anything that smacked of connection with the cup that cheers. The only part of the grape-growing industry he chose to recommend as eligible for Commodity Credit loans was that whose products were converted to raisins. Through the Pro-ration Raisin Association of Fresno, $3,685,000 was loaned on raisin grapes.

On wine grapes we arranged for the loans to be made, not by the Commodity Credit Corporation, but by the RFC—which did not need to be concerned with the scruples of Mr. Wallace. A goodly proportion of the wine grapes on which the RFC made direct loans, in which the Bank of America participated, was used in the distillation of brandy. It mellowed into exceedingly smooth collateral. When the war put a stop to whisky distilling, the resulting shortages of rye and bourbon created an increased demand, and higher prices, for domestic brandies. The brandy stocks pledged to the RFC were sold at a stimulating profit.

7

------------------ ☼ ------------------

HELPING RAILROADS

*One-Third of the Nation's Mileage Goes into Bankruptcy
—Limiting Salaries of Borrowing Railroads—Rescuing the
Great Northern—Saving the Southern—Tilting with the
Van Sweringens—How the Frisco Was Treated—Rebuild-
ing the Rock Island—Lightening the Load on the Boston &
Maine—Harold Vanderbilt and His Bankers—Bolstering
the B. & O.—Letting the Erie Sink*

OF THE 250,000 miles of railroad which interlace the United
States, more than a third went into receivership or bankruptcy
during the 1930's, and another third would have except for loans from
the RFC. Under the law we could lend to a railroad only if and when
the Interstate Commerce Commission certified that the company was
not in need of reorganization; i.e., if the Commission thought with our
help the road would be able to meet its charges and stay out of trouble.
We worked very close with Division 4 of the Commission and in large
measure they shared the responsibility of our loans to railroads.

We loaned more than a billion dollars to eighty-nine railroad companies. Taken together, they owned two-thirds of the nation's total
trackage. In making these loans, we tried to get security that would
bring the money back when the country recovered its economic
health, even if in the meantime a road were forced to receivership;
and it worked out that way. By 1949 all but sixteen of the borrowing
lines had fully repaid their obligations. Only two of the railway debts
then outstanding—those of the Baltimore & Ohio and of the Colorado
& Southern—were still above $10,000,000. The $80,000,000 loan
to the B. & O. is now secured by bonds having a current market
value of approximately two to one.

On behalf of the board I assumed personal charge of practically all the RFC's negotiations in the railroad field. With so many irons to watch, each director more or less had specialties; but the board approved all loans.

The $1,054,016,375 we put into the railroads created tens of thousands of jobs in trying times of unemployment and frequent furloughs. Some of the money encouraged the borrowers to improve run-down properties and buy new equipment. Much of it went to meet maturing obligations and to prevent bankruptcies. Not a little was used to pay taxes. In many a community the railroad is the largest taxpayer.

Indirectly our railroad loans benefited every American who had an insurance policy or an account in a savings bank. Doubtless they alleviated considerable worry not only among individual holders of railway securities but also in the minds of the learned guardians of many a college or university endowment fund. Of the eleven billions in railroad bonds which were in the hands of the public ten years ago, about seven billions were held by insurance companies, savings banks, and other fiduciary institutions and in educational and religious endowment funds.

In helping the distressed roads we sometimes clashed with their bankers. I had long felt that the men who operated our railroads were required to spend entirely too much time traveling back and forth to New York for conferences with and instructions from their bankers, and that the bankers all too often dictated the policies of the roads, and not always wisely. In a few instances the railroads appeared to be manipulated for the profit of the promoters and bankers.

Another thought I had long had about the operation of our railroads was that too many of them maintained their top offices in New York. That, of course, was directly traceable to their bankers. I do not mean the commercial banks in which they carried their current accounts. I refer to the private banking institutions that distributed their securities. They should have been called not bankers but brokers and promoters, for that, so far as their relations with the railroads went, was what they were.

In the case of the great Southern Pacific system, the three top executive officers all lived in New York City, and operated the properties from there: the chairman, Hale Holden; the vice chairman,

Paul Shoup; and the president, Angus McDonald; and their necessary forces. The properties of the railroad extended from New Orleans through Houston to Los Angeles, and on up to San Francisco and Portland, about as far away from New York as they could possibly get and still be in the United States.

When we made our first loan to the Southern Pacific, I began discussing this situation with these gentlemen. After a few years Mr. McDonald, president of the road, came to see me at Washington for the sole purpose of telling me that he was moving his offices to San Francisco and would operate the railroad from there, and also that Chairman Holden and Vice Chairman Shoup had resigned their positions and that these would not be filled. The place for a man to run a railroad is on the line.

In the case of the M-K-T, which extends from St. Louis through Missouri, Kansas, Oklahoma, and Texas, its president, Matthew S. Sloan, lived in New York City. I fussed at him about that, and am glad to say that the chairman of that railroad now lives in Dallas and the president in St. Louis. In other words, they are living on the property they are managing, just as the president of the Southern Pacific railroad is living on the property he manages. In granting our second loan to the M-K-T, we made it a condition that the president spend at least one-half of his time on the system.

Originally our loans to railroads bore 5 per cent interest; but we soon established the policy of accepting 4 per cent when the roads made their payments promptly when due. And we made no underwriting charges. We encouraged roads to buy new equipment with RFC loans on liberal terms. All this was very helpful to the roads in meeting their great tasks during the war, and it created work.

While saving the financial structure of several of our most important railroads from a trip to the wringer, we assisted in reorganizing others which, despite our earlier help, could not be kept out of bankruptcy. As a matter of fact, the plight of our railroads was as much the cause of the RFC being created as that of the banks. And the railroads bore the brunt of the early discussions in Congress.

A railroad, unlike most other corporate enterprises, has to keep on doing business whether it is prosperous or impoverished, solvent or broke. A bankrupt railroad cannot cut bait; it has to keep on fishing. Though its revenues may fall below expenses, it must go on running trains, hauling passengers and freight, and serving the communities touched by its rails. It cannot establish wage scales or freight or passenger rates to suit itself; nor may it abandon a mile of track, however unprofitable, without permission of the Interstate Commerce Commission, which often requires a long time to obtain.

It is a curious fact that the chief operating man of a railroad may feel a sense of relief in seeing his line put into receivership, for then he doesn't have to worry about meeting the fixed charges on its securities. Railroads which go broke are often able to keep their properties in better shape than those which remain out of receivership. I think it safe to say that some roads sought the shelter of the courts.

Collectively the railroads had been the largest industry in the country. In 1932 they probably still were the largest, for the manufacturing end of the automobile industry, which was challenging their primacy, was then wallowing in the doldrums. Normally the railroads employed about 1,500,000 workers. In a multitude of markets, from the Christmas calendar trade to the builders of bridges, the railroads were regarded as the best of all customers.

Similarly esteemed, by the local merchants of every roundhouse town, was the trade of the railroader and his family. In the early years of the depression, whole regiments of these railroadmen were laid off for long stretches, or put on part-time employment. Their painful lack of spending money made a bad situation worse in every section of the land. The farmer felt it when the family of a furloughed brakeman, car knocker, or gandy dancer couldn't buy their accustomed portions of beef, pork, eggs, and dairy products. Steel plants and numerous manufacturers felt it when the railroads stopped buying new rolling stock and reduced their orders for other materials and supplies.

To cut expenses the roads closed repair shops and eliminated much of the usual maintenance. Some of them allowed their roadbeds, cars, and locomotives to run down close to the danger point, or even beyond it. New investments in additions and betterments by Class I and Class II railways dropped from $596,000,000 in 1930 to $137,000,000 in 1931. While these slices were being made, interest rates and banker commissions for handling railroad finances continued high.

There wasn't enough revenue to provide for proper maintenance, let alone improvements. Between 1929 and 1932 the total operating revenues of Class I railways fell almost by half—from $6,112,000,000 to $3,117,000,000. Car loadings declined in about the same ratio.

In some instances it was from the railroad bankers that orders went out to railway presidents to lay off men, close down repair shops, and take other measures to reduce operating expenses; and, in one of two I shall touch upon, the banking influence exerted against expenditures on the property also saw to it that the road's directors declared the usual dividends. Sometimes when two or more lines were interlocked, financial manipulators took from Peter to give to Paul so that Paul would look attractive to investors. The opportunity to employ such tactics not infrequently occurred because almost one-third of the capital stock of our railroads was held by other railroads.

Such, in rough outline, was the transportation situation when the RFC embarked upon its rescue mission as directed by Congress. We found several railway presidents already on our doorstep. Some of their roads had security issues about to mature and not enough money to meet them. Nor could they borrow any more from their bankers, or find a market for their bonds.

During the first three quarters of 1932 exactly 122 Class I railroads failed to earn their fixed charges. A distinguished group of Americans, which included Calvin Coolidge, Bernard M. Baruch, Alfred E. Smith, Clark Howell, and Alexander Legge, had been at work as the National Transportation Committee studying the illnesses of the roads in order to recommend remedial measures. Their report was not issued until February, 1933, just as the banks of the country were skidding into the national moratorium. Because of that coincidence the study received less than its due of attention.

By that time, in the words of Joseph B. Eastman, then a prominent member of the Interstate Commerce Commission, only the extensive emergency relief provided during 1932 by the RFC had prevented an epidemic of railroad receiverships.

In our first year we had loaned more than one-third of a billion dollars to sixty-two railroads. Of that money 30 per cent went to meet maturing funded debt, more than 20 per cent to keep up interest on bonds, and another 15 per cent to pay off loans that had to be met to avoid receivership. Many roads that were in need of help were unable to qualify for RFC loans because they lacked sufficient security.

In dealing with loan applications our first rule was that we must be convinced that the road had been unable to obtain funds upon reasonable terms through banking channels or from the investing public. Next the ICC had to certify that the road was not in need of reorganization.

LIMITING SALARIES OF BORROWING RAILROADS

Furthermore Congress amended the RFC Act so as to require RFC directors to certify to the appropriateness of salaries paid by any corporation borrowing from it. For top railroad executives large salaries had become the custom. They ranged as high as $150,000 a year. Hale Holden, chairman of the Southern Pacific, had been paid that figure; General W. W. Atterbury, president of the Pennsylvania, received $135,000; and Daniel Willard, president of the Baltimore & Ohio, got $120,000. The Southern Pacific paid Paul Shoup, vice chairman, $100,000 and A. D. McDonald, president, $85,000.

The railroad situation was becoming more critical each day, and we were receiving applications for help from some of the larger lines, among them the Southern Pacific. In conferring with President Roosevelt one day about some current matters soon after Congress had amended the law under which we operated with respect to salaries of borrowers, I brought up the question of salaries to railroad executives. Offhand the President said $25,000 should be a top salary for a railroad president. When Congress was considering that particular amendment to our Act, Senator James Couzens mentioned that insurance companies to which we made loans should not pay their top officials more than $25,000 a year. The Senator was inclined to be tough, so I countered by saying to him that he and I were working for $10,000 a year. We split the difference and inserted into the bill a provision that the largest pay for executives of insurance companies borrowing from the RFC should be $17,500.

When the President mentioned that $25,000 should be a top salary for railroad presidents I made no immediate comment because I needed time to think about it and to reason out what would be proper under the circumstances.

To begin with, I knew that most men who had been accustomed to drawing $100,000 a year salary usually lived it up, and that to cut them to $25,000 would be too severe, particularly since nearly everybody was in debt, regardless of his bracket. I figured railroad officials were probably no exception.

In the meantime, while we were considering the Southern Pacific loan, I told the officials of that road what the President's view was as to salaries. Naturally, they were none too happy about it.

At a subsequent meeting, I told the President that I had adopted a formula for salaries to railroad executives: to wit, salaries which had been $150,000 be cut 60 per cent, or to $60,000; those which had been $100,000 be cut 50 per cent, and the others be graded down accordingly. The President agreed that it was a good formula and was probably severe enough. What it did was to fix a maximum salary of $60,000 to any official of a railroad which borrowed from the RFC.

Other railroad salaries which had been high—$90,000 and up— included those of John J. Pelley of the New Haven, which later went into receivership, L. A. Downs of the Illinois Central, which but for our help would have gone into receivership, and L. F. Loree of the Delaware & Hudson. Carl Gray of the Union Pacific was also drawing good pay, but his road was operating at a profit and needed no assistance from the RFC.

The day our board approved the Southern Pacific loan, all three of the top officials, Messrs. Holden, Shoup, and McDonald, were in my reception room waiting for our action. When I told them the loan had been granted and their salaries limited to the formula above mentioned, which still allowed Mr. Holden $60,000, Mr. Shoup $50,000, and Mr. McDonald $42,500, their faces broke into smiles of obvious relief. They had been having bad dreams about our carving knife. It was not necessary that I discuss such items with the President; but I kept him posted as well as I could about our operations, which made for better cooperation.

A few days later, on May 28, 1933, I made public the salary conditions laid down in granting the Southern Pacific loan, and announced that it would be the policy of the RFC to impose similar salary limitations in all future loans to railroads and other corporations asking our help.

About a year before his death, Daniel Willard, then eighty, president of the Baltimore & Ohio, our heaviest railroad borrower, wanted to employ Roy B. White, president of the Western Union Telegraph Company, to take the presidency of the B. & O. Mr. White had formerly been with the B. & O. and had left it some dozen years before to go with the Western Union. As president of the Western Union his compensation was $88,000 a year. Mr. Willard felt he could not ask Mr. White to come back to the B. & O. at $60,000. On the second and last time he came to see me about it, tears were actually in his eyes. He told me he did not want to pass on without leaving the road in good hands, and pleaded with me to make an exception with respect to the $60,000 limit on salaries. I liked Mr. Willard very much, first because he was one of the finest men I ever knew, and next because I had been working with him for several years to keep his road out of receivership. He had come up from a locomotive engineer to the top job of our oldest railroad. I said to Mr. Willard that we could not very well make an exception, but that I would guarantee him that Mr. White would accept $60,000. I did not know Mr. White personally, but I have never known a railroad man who was satisfied at any other job. I felt sure Mr. White would come back to the B. & O. for $60,000, and he did. He has done an excellent job with the road.

The law with respect to salaries paid by our borrowers included lawyers' fees. It provided the borrowers should only pay salaries and lawyers' fees which in the opinion of our board of directors were appropriate to the circumstances.

RESCUING THE GREAT NORTHERN FROM ITS BANKERS

An interesting case that came to us was the Great Northern Railway.

The Great Northern is one of our best systems, running through a rich section of the country. In its fifty-seven years of existence it had never once defaulted. Until the depression dragged down its earnings it had never missed paying a regular dividend. Among its fixed charges were 7 per cent interest payments on a $120,000,000 bond issue, of which a balance of $105,850,000 was still outstanding. The road had sold its 7 per cent bonds to its bankers in 1921 at 91½ cents on the dollar, a discount of probably $10,000,000. The bonds were maturing July 1, 1936.

Fearing that he would not be able to get the money from the bankers to pay the bonds when they matured, W. P. Kenney, then president of the road, came to see me to learn whether we could help him. I told him we could, but would like to do it in cooperation with his bankers. We did not want to replace bankers, but were trying to help railroads get their money requirements at a more reasonable rate of interest than they had formerly been required to pay. He told me the bankers were working on a new loan or bond issue at 5 per cent interest at a discount.

I then wrote Mr. Kenney a letter offering to take $50,000,000 of a $100,000,000 issue at 4½ per cent if the bankers would take the other half at the same time and price. I also proposed that, after the bankers had sold their $50,000,000, they could have ours at the same price. This the bankers said they could not do.

I felt that the Great Northern, with its excellent record, should not have to pay a high rate for its money. To do so would affect our whole program of helping railroads. The second time Mr. Kenney came to see me he brought his banker, who criticized us for offering to lend the road money when it could get the money elsewhere. I replied that his rate and charges were not reasonable, and the law said we should lend when the money was "not otherwise obtainable on reasonable terms."

Mr. Kenney came back some time later and told me the bankers would lend him the money at 5 per cent interest, with an underwriting fee of $1,000,000 plus 1 per cent additional on any bonds they themselves might buy. I thought the rate and the charges were too high.

Mr. Kenney asked me to write a letter expressing my thoughts about his railroad's situation and our offer to take over the financing, and to make it public, so that his bankers would not punish him should he need them again at a time when there might be no RFC to help him. So on December 18, 1935, I made public the following letter:

December 15, 1935

Dear Mr. Kenney:

Your letter of the 13th has been given due consideration by our Directors, and we feel that you will be paying entirely too much for the money under the plan proposed, especially in view of prevailing interest rates.

I have repeatedly stated that I am as anxious as anyone to get the government out of the lending business, but I have also stated that it should not get out too soon; by which I mean until money is available from private sources, at fair interest rates and on fair terms.

In my recent address before the American Bankers Association at New Orleans, I stated that one way the government could assist railroads was to help them get their money cheaper.

The Great Northern is one of our best systems, has never been in receivership, and as I recall, you told me the other day had never missed paying dividends until 1931 or '32.

You should not have to pay more than 4 per cent for ten-year money, and if you wish to issue ten-year bonds to meet your $100,000,000 maturity July 1, 1936, convertible as provided in your letter, and offer the bonds to your stockholders, to present holders of your 7 per cent bonds, or the public, at par and accrued interest, this Corporation will, subject to prior approval by the Interstate Commerce Commission, take any that are not sold, on that basis, July 1, 1936. There will be no underwriting charge.

We should like to have you notify us by April 1st, if convenient, the amount of bonds that you would likely call upon us to take. We would want to approve as reasonable and fair any expense, incident to distribution of the bonds, that you may be put to. Also, if practicable, a sinking fund should be provided that would amortize 15 per cent or 20 per cent of the issue at maturity.

We appreciate your efforts and those of your bankers to provide this money without coming to the government, but feel that in offering to pay such a high rate you will be hurting all railroad financing, and unnecessarily penalizing your own security holders. Four per cent is a fair yield, a good rate in this market, and we think you should not be required to pay more.

We have no desire to supplant your bankers, but would like to cooperate with them and the railroads to the end that railroad financing can be done at much less cost to the roads.

Sincerely yours,
JESSE H. JONES, *Chairman*

Mr. W. P. Kenney, President
Great Northern Railroad
2 Wall Street
New York City

Mr. Kenney issued the bonds and sold them all to the public—saving his road $14,000,000.

SAVING THE SOUTHERN RAILWAY

One of the first railways to seek our assistance was the Southern. Its directors had followed an improvident policy. In 1931 they had paid three quarterly dividends at full 1929 rates and four dividends on their noncumulative preferred stock, though the road had lost money for the year equal to $6.87 per share of common stock.

Here was another case of banker domination paying extra dividends when the road was losing money. After that, as business kept falling off, the Southern couldn't raise a dollar in any bank in the country. It was earning only a little more than one-third of its fixed charges. Its president was Fairfax Harrison. He was a proud old man and resented having to come to the RFC for money, but he had no choice. He was in our offices by orders of his bankers almost as soon as we opened them.

Our first loan to the Southern, for $7,500,000, was granted on February 29, 1932. We made the road three more loans that year and two additional advances in 1936, the latter to meet bond maturities and save the system from bankruptcy. All together we lent the Southern $31,405,000 at 4 per cent interest, and bought $18,852,000 of its equipment trust certificates—a total help of $50,257,000.

As the situation with the Southern grew more serious, John J. Pelley, president of the Association of American Railroads, asked me to have lunch with him and Mr. Harrison in his apartment at the Mayflower. During the lunch Mr. Harrison told me he had asked for the conference to tell me his road would have to seek the protection of the courts (receivership). I replied that we would be glad to lend the Southern more money. He said he had no further collateral. I then told him we would increase his loan on the existing collateral, which we already held, if the ICC would approve. I felt sure they would not or could not authorize another loan. I also believed the Southern could get along without any more money. My guess was right. I did not want the road to go into receivership.

Ernest E. Norris, who soon succeeded Mr. Harrison as president of the Southern, came to see me and told me he'd pay us every cent he owed us if he had to do it with dollar bills. The Southern completed its payments May 15, 1941, before the wartime boom got started. Mr. Norris is no leather-chair railroader. His office is in Washington, but he spends most of his time on the road, getting acquainted with his customers, "ringing doorbells," as he calls it, and keeping in direct touch with shippers on his properties.

One afternoon in 1938, still in debt to us, he came in with a new proposition.

"Jesse," he said, "I owe you about thirty millions. We haven't bought a freight car in eight years, and we can't get any money anywhere else. Half the car-making plants of the country are shut down. The only men they've got at work are the guards at the gates. We badly need some new freight cars. I'd like to order about eight or nine thousand of them. I can save enough on rent that I'm paying other roads for the use of their cars to pay for the new ones."

I asked him how much the cars would cost and how much he could pay down. He said that they would cost about $20,000,000, but that he couldn't pay anything down.

I said, "O.K., Ernest, issue equipment trust certificates at 4 per cent, and we'll buy them."

Our rate on equipment trust notes was 2½ to 3 per cent with a 20 per cash payment; but with no down payment we charged more.

The whole conversation arranging that deal lasted less than twenty minutes. The result was that many men were put to work building the cars and we helped the railroad at the same time. The payments were met promptly as the certificates matured, and these were sold by the RFC at a substantial profit.

An equipment trust is a device which enables railroads to buy new cars and locomotives on the installment plan. Until payment is completed title to the equipment is vested in a trustee for the benefit of the security holders. It was not until the spring of 1938 that Congress, at my suggestion, amended the RFC Act to permit us to buy equipment trust obligations without certification from the ICC that the railroad issuing the certificates was not in need of reorganization.

At that time, following the so-called recession of 1937, the railroads had got down about as low as it seemed to me they could go. They had been laying off men at a painful rate, 100,000 since the previous autumn. Many of the lines were becoming badly undermanned and poorly maintained. In the eight years since the start of the depression ninety-eight railroads had gone into receivership or bankruptcy.

Web. Brown in Akron Beacon Journal.

Fewer than half a dozen roads were still able to pay dividends. Most of the lines were not earning their fixed charges. Some were hardly taking in enough money to meet operating expenses.

In their efforts to stay out of receivership the roads were cutting employment and maintenance to the quick, and postponing the purchase of needed supplies. Almost one-third of the freight engines had become unserviceable. Maintenance-of-way expenditures had been chopped from two billion a year to one billion, supply purchases from a billion and a half to about six hundred million dollars. Every reduction meant less work for somebody.

Seeing so many men laid off whose only experience was in railroading, I felt there should be a national remedy for the situation better than having them turn to "made jobs" of the Works Progress Administration, the Harry Hopkins operation. It seemed to me they would be of more service to the country working on the railroads, which really belonged to the public. I thought the RFC might as well invest some government money that otherwise Harry Hopkins would ladle out through the WPA, particularly since we should get most of the money back and the railroads, their employees and the country would benefit.

In offering this new help we made two requirements of the roads: first, they would repay us before they paid any dividends to stockholders; and, second, in accepting the "work loans" they would agree to spend 75 per cent of the money in rehiring furloughed labor. Our legal division framed the bill which we presented to Congress to provide for that. The new amendment permitted us to make these work loans without regard to the security offered.

We fixed the percentage of the loan that had to go to labor because in railroad shop work about 75 per cent of the cost is labor, and 25 per cent materials. Many roads had new rails, ties, and other supplies on hand which they were not installing because they didn't have the money to pay the workmen. In maintenance-of-way improvements, labor accounts for about half the cost.

At the time we began making these "work loans" the listed values of railroad bonds and securities which we held as collateral for earlier loans had fallen by between one-half and two-thirds during the previous year or eighteen months. As an illustration of what was happening, take the New York Central Railroad. Its indebtedness together with the value of leased properties came to about $1,050,000,000. And its securities in May, 1938, when we got our lending act amended, were selling at from 30 to 80 cents on the dollar. The stock of the New York Central, which had sold in 1929 as high as $256.50 a share, had gone as low as $8.75 a share in 1932, and was still around $10 in 1938.

I figured we might say to such a road, "Put five thousand men back to work, and we will lend you the money on a different basis. You need not pay us back tomorrow or next week or next year, but pay that debt before you pay any more dividends."

I had discussed the matter at a meeting held in my office on April 26, 1938, which was attended by John J. Pelley and Robert Fletcher representing the railroads, George Harrison representing the railroad unions and brotherhoods, Judge Felter representing the federal courts, Charles D. Mahaffie of the Interstate Commerce Commission, United States Senators Harry S Truman and Burton K. Wheeler and Representative Clarence F. Lea, chairman of the House Committee on Interstate Commerce.

We agreed to adopt a recommendation made by an ICC committee which President Roosevelt had appointed to study the railroad situation. They had suggested that the RFC be permitted to lend for the purchase of equipment, taking the equipment as security, and that we also be empowered to make "work loans" to the carriers regardless of the appearance of their balance sheets.

*   *   *

The equipment trust certificates which we bought from Mr. Norris of the Southern without a down payment were among the first we purchased. Mr. Norris got his nine thousand new freight cars, and we made $800,000 on the deal.

By the time the United States entered the war Ernest Norris and his Southern Railway had their new freight cars rolling, and so did many another railroad which we had aided in buying equipment. After the war such cars cost twice what these men had paid in 1938 and 1939.

After we had kept the equipment certificates two or three or four years and payments were current, the market would take them from us. In addition to our own loans, we took over about $107,000,000 in equipment trust certificates from the Public Works Administration. All these were later sold or retired.

We encouraged railroads to put in streamlined trains and other up-to-date equipment when they could show there was a reasonable chance that such improvements would pay for themselves with the return of better conditions. Sometimes we suggested such purchases even before the borrowers broached the subject. We not only kept the Illinois Central out of the wringer; we helped its appearance.

Railroad managements were so accustomed to looking to their bankers to finance their properties that they were none too alert in thinking about it for themselves or in looking ahead. Under the RFC Act, we could authorize a loan and disburse it any time during the period of one year, but not longer. I kept a sort of record of railroad maturities and watched them. One day when I happened to meet W. Averell Harriman, chairman of the board of the Union Pacific, which controlled the Illinois Central, I suggested that the management of the Illinois Central had better get busy and make an application to the RFC for funds to meet a large debt which would mature in about fifteen months. I knew there was no likelihood the road would be able to get money from private sources to meet the maturing debt. I believed the Interstate Commerce Commission would at that particular time certify that the road was not in need of reorganization; and under that certification we could authorize a loan, whereas if the management waited the ICC might not be able to make the certification a year later and the road would go into receivership.

Accordingly, the application was made, we authorized the loan, and the road was saved from receivership. If the Illinois Central had waited a year to make the application, the ICC probably could not have given the proper certification. The road's gross revenues had dropped from $190,000,000 in 1929 to $89,000,000 in 1932 and its prospects were not too rosy.

In 1935, on one of the occasions when an Illinois Central official called on me, I asked why they had no Diesel engines or streamlined trains and whether they thought it would improve their road's situation if they had some. He seemed to like the idea, and we loaned the I.C. $2,500,000 to carry it out. Their first streamliner was christened the Green Diamond.

In 1937 the I.C.'s requirements exceeded their resources by $27,-000,000. We loaned them enough to keep them out of court. All the loans were fully repaid by 1943.

TILTING WITH THE VAN SWERINGENS

In the line of railroad operators who applied for help at the RFC nobody was ahead of the late Van Sweringen brothers—O. P. and M. J.—of Cleveland. Their two-billion-dollar "empire" had begun to crack almost as soon as they had patched it together in what the late historian, Dr. Charles A. Beard, aptly described as a crazy quilt of interrelated companies.

One of the railroads the Van Sweringens held in their vise was the Missouri Pacific. Their holding company, the Alleghany Corporation, had invested about one hundred million dollars to get control of the M.P. in May, 1930. On January 29, 1932, four full days before the RFC actually began operations, the Van Sweringens had an agent in Washington asking for a loan for the M.P. The road was heavily in debt to its bankers, and the bankers were pressing for payment.

When I was a young man the Missouri Pacific had been one of Jay Gould's sorely mistreated lines. Later it emerged from receivership, shortly before this country entered the First World War. When the war was over its run-down properties were unable to earn operating expenses and taxes. In 1923 an excellent rebuilding campaign was begun under L. W. Baldwin. He had been brought over to the M.P. as its president at $100,000 a year from the Illinois Central, where he had made an excellent record as vice president in charge of operations.

The late Mr. Baldwin was one of our ablest railroad executives. He practiced his preachment that "you can't run a railroad from a swivel chair." It took him only a few years to rebuild the badly deteriorated Missouri Pacific system. He had it out of the red by 1927. Reequipped to modern standards it was soon competing effectively with the better lines of the West and Southwest.

To modernize track, motive power, signals, and related facilities over thousands of miles of a large railway requires a great deal of money. Under Mr. Baldwin's guidance the M.P. made capital expenditures aggregating $200,000,000. Since the bond market was almost the only source of new railroad capital, he had recourse to it to the extent of $150,000,000 in eight years. Then the depression closed in and the rehabilitated lines found themselves unable to earn their fixed charges on the higher funded debt which improvements had created.

To make matters worse the road's cash resources were being exhausted by the complicated Van Sweringen interests, whose practical control had been obtained with the aid of money raised from the investing public by their bankers. At a time when the road could not wisely spare a dollar from its requirements, three millions were taken from its treasury to purchase its own securities. The road's treasurer, sitting in Cleveland at the Van Sweringens' elbows, simply called on the operating officials in St. Louis to send along the money. He used it to buy stock without informing either Mr. Baldwin or his lieutenants.

When our auditors went to Cleveland to check on the balance sheets which the Missouri Pacific had been asked to produce upon applying to us for help, they found its cash drawer empty. The money had been used to benefit other Van Sweringen properties.

The Missouri Pacific's original request of us was for loans of $23,500,000. The road's bankers had called for payment of a demand loan of $11,700,000. On February 1, 1932, the Missouri Pacific came to us for a loan of $14,700,000. One-half the amount was to be used to pay a loan to J. P. Morgan & Co., the road's banking house; one-half to meet other pressing needs.

Ogden Mills, Secretary of the Treasury and ex-officio member of our board, made a strong argument to our board in favor of the loan. I argued against it, that is, against that part of it which was to pay the bankers, because I didn't think the government should bail out private banking houses that for years had been profiting from railroad financing, especially when the bankers were amply able to take care of themselves, as was true in this case.

I felt that such a loan was not in the spirit of the law which had established the RFC, and that if we made a loan for the purposes stated—one-half to pay the private bankers—it would cause the RFC to be severely criticized in Congress, and would make it more difficult for the RFC to do the job it was created to do.

Finally General Dawes, then president of the RFC, proposed that the directors authorize the loan with me voting "No." I suggested to the General that we defer action until the following day, and that if I could not persuade other members of the board to my point of view I would not vote against it. I was unsuccessful in my efforts to bring the others to my way of thinking, so the loan was voted. Sure enough, when the loan became known several members of Congress sharply criticized it. The effect was exactly what I had felt it would be.

On Sunday, the day after our board voted the loan, I telephoned Mr. Baldwin in St. Louis. I told him the loan had been voted, and advised him not to take the part of it earmarked for payment to the bankers. The following Tuesday morning Herbert Fitzpatrick, general counsel for the Van Sweringens, came to see me. He explained that, while they appreciated my advice, they were not in a position to follow it.

I was not afflicted with any "anti-banker" complex, but felt in this particular situation and others of a similar nature that the bankers had no right to unload their bad or slow debts on the government. The bankers did not need the relief. I could see ahead of the RFC a long and ugly road along which we should need the confidence of the Congress if we were to revive the depressed state of our entire economy.

On February 1, 1932, one day before the RFC officially began operations, J. P. Morgan & Co. loaned the Missouri Pacific an additional $1,500,000 to meet a bond maturity, stipulating that the loan was made "only on the basis of the expectation that the RFC will lend you the sum necessary to repay such loan on February 15, 1932." Nearly five years later, at an inquiry into the affairs of the Missouri Pacific by the Senate Committee on Interstate Commerce, George Whitney, president of J. P. Morgan & Co., testified as follows under the questioning of Burton K. Wheeler, the Chairman:

THE CHAIRMAN. You would not have let the railroad bust at that time for $1,500,000?

MR. WHITNEY. We would have if we had not had assurances that the RFC was going to take care of them.

THE CHAIRMAN. Why?

MR. WHITNEY. Why not? It was a governmental body that the Congress had already passed a law to create for that very purpose.

THE CHAIRMAN. Not for the purpose, however, of—to use Commissioner Eastman's language—bailing out bankers' loans.

MR. WHITNEY. Maybe that was not the direct purpose. There were various other elements. For instance, the Texas & Pacific stock that we had as collateral, the RFC was very anxious to have a part of, for the basis of further loans if they made them. It was a very strong consideration in the paying off of a portion of our loan.

THE CHAIRMAN. Was there any assurance by anybody that the RFC would take the $1,500,000 over?

MR. WHITNEY. I do not think so; no. Certainly not, as far as I know, at least.

THE CHAIRMAN. There was this difference between the house of Morgan and the Government, and that is this, that you were already in for $11,700,000, when the Government was not—

MR. WHITNEY. Not in at all; no.

THE CHAIRMAN. I do not quite understand why you were afraid to make a $1,500,000 loan which was fully guaranteed at that time, the value collateralized at that time, unless the Government would come in and agree to take it over.

MR. WHITNEY. You do not understand it, or you—

THE CHAIRMAN. I do not understand your position. I do not understand why you would take that position. Well, we will pass it over.

* * *

Private banking houses render a useful service in distributing securities, but their charges should be commensurate with the service they render, and not measured by an assumed obligation of providing the borrower with funds whenever needed. They should be called note brokers instead of bankers, for they usually sell the securities before they buy or pay for them. They quit financing railroads in 1932 because they couldn't sell the securities.

Our total loans to the Missouri Pacific amounted to $23,134,000, and might as well not have been made, for on March 31, 1933, the road went into the courts to reorganize under Section 77B of the Corporate Bankruptcy Act.

In the autumn of 1930 soon after the Van Sweringens got control, the road had borrowed $10,000,000 from their bankers. Bank loans which the Van Sweringens had obtained for their Nickel Plate railroad had been secured by the Missouri Pacific stock bought on the rising market of the 1920's. As security prices slipped, more stock had to be put up. The M.P. used part of its stock purchases in 1930 to increase the Nickel Plate collateral. One block of this stock, for which it paid $1,000,000, was later sold for less than $200,000.

Previously, in October, 1929, just before the stock-market crash, the Van Sweringens through a wholly owned subsidiary of the Alleghany Corporation, which was called Terminal Shares, Inc., had paid better than $18,000,000 to buy real estate, warehouse, and belt-line developments in North Kansas City and St. Joseph. They bought these promotions from the Swift and Armour packing-house interests whose freight traffic they were eager to cultivate for the Nickel Plate and the Erie, which at that time they also controlled. Shortly after they got their grip on the Missouri Pacific the Van Sweringens unloaded onto that railroad the Terminal Shares promotions at a price above $20,000,000. In the purchase contract the M.P. agreed to make periodic payments of $400,000 quarterly. The M.P. had bought the property in bad times for more than the Van Sweringens had paid for it at the peak of the boom.

Though these were fixed obligations, the indebtedness was not shown on the railroad's balance sheet presented to the RFC and the ICC when the M.P. applied to us for loans. Had this disclosure then been made the Terminal Shares contracts would have been the subject of investigation.

Later we went to court to upset the Terminal Shares transaction. Subsequently Adolf A. Berle, Jr., and Cassius Clay, of our railroad division, successfully blocked the reorganization of the railroad as the Van Sweringens first proposed it. On November 15, 1935, in ruling on our suit in federal district court in Missouri, Judge C. B. Faris held the Terminal Shares contracts void on the grounds that they were improvident, unfair, unlawful, overreaching and had stuck the M.P. exorbitantly. The railroad sued to get back the several millions it had already forked over under the contract. After years of litigation a compromise settlement was reached in 1940.

In 1932, when the RFC was established, the Morgan bank and its associates or customers were creditors of Van Sweringen enterprises to the extent of more than $40,000,000, which included loans to the Vaness Corporation, the Cleveland Terminals Building Company, and sundry other promotions. Collateral securing these loans included for a time more than two million shares of Alleghany Corporation common. The Alleghany Corporation had been formed in

1929 to take over some of the Van Sweringen holdings. The banking
house of J. P. Morgan & Co. gave some of its customers the opportunity of buying the stock at $20 a share before it was offered to the
public at $24 a share. In 1930 the stock sold at $10, and during 1933
it dropped below $1. After the Chesapeake & Ohio, the Alleghany's
best source of income was supposed to be the Missouri Pacific.

In the reorganization of the bankrupt Missouri Pacific the Alleghany Corporation was allowed to remain in control of the property.
I seriously questioned the desirability of this. When the ICC was
holding its hearings on the reorganization plan in 1937 I wrote to
B. H. Meyer, chairman of Division 4 of the Interstate Commerce
Commission, who conducted them, suggesting that, as a matter of
public policy, an important railroad system should not be subject to
the convenience of its bankers and certainly not to that of a holding
company that controlled other large systems where the systems had
not been grouped together by the ICC.

The history of the Alleghany Corporation and the fact that it had
been abandoned by its sponsor bankers, J. P. Morgan & Co., and had
been put more or less on the auction block, seemed to me to dictate
exceeding care in determining its future participation in the affairs
of the Missouri Pacific—and I so informed Congress.

I also informed the ICC that in 1935, when O. P. Van Sweringen
discussed with me the reorganization of the Missouri Pacific, I had
taken the position, to which he finally agreed, that if the Alleghany
Corporation was to remain in charge of the property, after reorganization, it should in effect be permitted to do so on probation, by allowing it to name only one-third of the directors, the senior security
holders naming the other two-thirds, each class of senior securities
to have representation on the board. This would have left Alleghany
in charge of the property only so long as, in the opinion of
the majority of the board, its management was good. To this
Mr. Van Sweringen agreed. He had no choice if he was to have
our help.

A few months after our negotiations, he and his brother lost practical control of Alleghany to George A. Ball, the well known glass
bottle manufacturer of Muncie, Indiana. Mr. Ball and G. A. Tom-
linson of Cleveland took over the Van Sweringens' Alleghany securities to satisfy a loan. Two years later working control of Alleghany
was bought for a song by Robert R. Young, a Wall Street trader,

and his associates, just before the bottom was hit. Gradual recovery made him and his associates big railroad men and probably gave them big fortunes.

HOW THE FRISCO WAS TREATED

An ugly illustration of banker domination ruthlessly crippling a railroad was provided by the St. Louis-San Francisco, popularly known as the Frisco. Thoroughly stripped and wailing, that road was placed on our doorstep even before we opened for business. While declaring dividends through the years in excess of the road's real earnings, its banker-dominated board had drained eleven millions more out of its treasury to buy stock in other lines. Meanwhile the directors had compelled the president of the Frisco to pare expenditures to the point where some of its trackage and equipment was actually unsafe and many of its laid-off employees were going hungry.

When the Frisco came to us in February, 1932, asking for nearly $18,000,000, it was delinquent in its taxes. It had bank loans, bond maturities, and equipment trust obligations about to fall due. And it badly needed other money to use in capital expenditures—money which it had dissipated in misuse and improper dividends.

A week later we granted the Frisco $3,000,000—just enough to pay some taxes and meet a few equipment trust obligations. The system had been so involved by insiders there was no saving it from receivership in November, 1932, or from bankruptcy the following May.

To the Frisco the cycle of solvency, receivership, and reorganiza- was no novelty. In its ninety years it had been around that wheel several times. Characteristically each reorganization had given it a still larger structure and a heavier fixed debt.

Prior to the depression the Frisco's latest receivership had occurred in 1913. It was then reorganized under the joint auspices of two New York banking houses, Speyer & Co. and J. & W. Seligman & Company. Overnight the valuation of the assets carried on the company's books was jacked up $35,000,000—a sum which nicely fitted the amount of new security issues which had followed the banker-managed reorganization. In such circumstances it could scarcely be contended that all subsequent dividends were truly earned.

In 1925 James Speyer and E. N. Brown, then chairman of the

Frisco board, made a deal by which Speyer's banking house was to buy 275,000 shares of the common stock of the Rock Island, about 37½ per cent of the ownership of that line.

The Frisco put up more than ten million dollars to acquire two-thirds of these shares, the two men having agreed that the banking house would hold the other one-third. The bankers, in addition to charging the Frisco regular brokerage commissions for handling the transaction, also received under the Speyer-Brown arrangement $1.25 a share for each share bought for the railroad's account. That was a really nice gratuity—a little extra profit of several hundred thousand for the bankers.

Neither the Frisco's board nor its president was told of the deal until the whole job had been done. Then in January, 1926, the directors, some of whom had been put on the board by the bankers, ratified the purchase.

Such a vast acquisition constituted almost a "corner" in Rock Island stock and it rose from $60 to $130, whereupon the bankers began unloading part of their one-third at a profit exceeding $1,500,000. But the Frisco held onto its 183,333 shares for which it had paid $10,506,000. Mr. Brown and two other Frisco directors were placed on the Rock Island's board, Mr. Brown being made chairman of the executive committee at an added salary of $50,000. Upon Mr. Brown's advice the Rock Island then bought 25,000 shares of Frisco stock.

When the news got around that the Frisco had bought almost effective control of the Rock Island it alienated other railroads, such as the Burlington and the Milwaukee, which had had friendly relations with the Frisco and had habitually turned over to the Frisco a good deal of business at the Kansas City gateway and elsewhere. While willing to cooperate with the Frisco these lines looked upon the Rock Island as a direct competitor. They began to turn their friendly tonnage elsewhere. James M. Kurn, the Frisco's capable, forthright president, found his line was losing business at the rate of more than half a million dollars a month.

After taking that punishment for several months he sat down one day in July, 1927, in his office in St. Louis, and wrote a letter to Mr. Brown, who, of course, lived in New York. He told Mr. Brown how the purchase of Rock Island stock had lost friends and business for the Frisco. He suggested there should either be a consolidation of the properties or the financial interests of the two systems should be separated.

But the Frisco retained its Rock Island stock. When Mr. Kurn wrote that letter the Frisco might have begun selling its Rock Island portfolio at $130 a share, and made a profit of perhaps as much as ten millions. Later the stock was pounded down to little more than $1 a share.

A few months after Mr. Kurn made his appeal to Mr. Brown the bankers arranged another refinancing of the Frisco. They sold $100,-000,000 of a new bond issue and $50,000,000 of preferred stock to the public. Some of this money was used to retire at par an issue of bonds which still had forty years to run.

There was little Mr. Kurn could do about the way his road was being financed. As he later testified, he had been told when he got his job that he was to operate the railroad and the bankers would run its finances.

From 1923 to 1932 the road earned only $27,000,000; yet it paid out $38,000,000 in dividends, according to an accounting survey by Price, Waterhouse & Co.

In order to keep on paying dividends after the depression set in, the Frisco, in October, 1930, sold $10,000,000 of its holdings of its own bonds at 90. Then, in November, the Frisco's board declared dividends for the following year—1931—all four quarterly dividends on the preferred and a juicy January dividend on the common. Yet 1930 had been such a poor year for the road that, in carrying out orders from New York to cut expenditures, its shops had been closed 182 days out of the 365. Track maintenance had been slugged so severely that as many as twenty-five broken rails were reported in a single day, and, as Mr. Kurn put it, people who had worked for the road for years were starving.

After all this improvident saving the road showed a profit for the year of less than $900,000. Yet the directors, in their November meeting, ordered over $4,000,000 to be paid out in dividends during the next quarter alone. In letting the road deteriorate the responsible parties had destroyed much of its capital value. Maintenance had become what Mr. Kurn described as a "complete slaughter" of the property.

In April, 1932, shortly after we had doled out a part of the money the Frisco wanted from the RFC, a financial housecleaning of the system was ordered by the Interstate Commerce Commission before it would certify solvency of the road so that our agency might give the Frisco further assistance. In the following July the ICC approved an additional loan of $3,390,000.

Two-thirds of the money we handed to the Frisco was for interest payments, and the remainder for taxes. Once bankruptcy proceedings began the RFC had to wait a long time to get this money back, for the reorganization dragged on until 1947.

First as a co-trustee and later as chief executive officer of the bankrupt road, Mr. Kurn took advantage of this long respite from meeting interest payments and coupon dates to rebuild the system. Before his death in 1945 he had provided the road with one of the finest physical layouts among the lines serving the Southwest. He turned a deaf ear to the stockholders who clamored for some of the earnings when the war boom brought a big jump in the road's income.

In the reorganization the Frisco's fixed interest charges were reduced from twelve millions to a little above three millions.

While the Frisco was in bankruptcy Mr. Kurn and his co-trustee, John G. Lonsdale, brought suit against Mr. Brown and the Speyer and Seligman banking houses to recover $10,506,090 lost through the purchase of 183,333 shares of Rock Island stock. But on October 13, 1938, Justice Louis A. Valente of the New York State Supreme Court vindicated the defendants. He accepted their explanation that the purchase of Rock Island stock by the Frisco had been intended to precede a merger of the properties and held that the circumstances required a certain amount of secrecy in market trading to avoid paying higher prices. An error of judgment, his opinion said, was not a sufficient thing upon which to base liability.

"Wise or unwise," he wrote, "it was apparently for the good of the Frisco itself that the plan was set up in the way it was."

On that, of course, there could be differences of opinion.

REBUILDING THE ROCK ISLAND

The Rock Island system, with rails ranging along ten thousand miles of the wheat, corn, cattle, and cotton country between the Great Lakes and the Gulf, depends upon farm products for fully a third of its normal freight revenue. Consequently it suffered acutely from the slump in agricultural prosperity. Beginning in 1930, the road failed for eleven consecutive years to earn its fixed charges.

The Rock Island first sought aid from the RFC in the spring of 1932. For a time our help kept the system out of the courts; but it sank into bankruptcy in the summer of 1933 under the weight of a debt structure of nearly half a billion dollars.

Nine years later a rush of wartime traffic swiftly lifted the company's earnings. The RFC got its money back, as did the Rock Island's bankers, in 1945, a few days after the German surrender. The other creditors waited completion of a reorganization which had been bandied from plan to plan for more than a decade.

During most of that long stretch the collateral we held against our Rock Island loans wasn't worth the face value of the notes. In 1938, when nearly all railroad stocks and bonds went into terrific declines, the market value of all Rock Island securities, stock and bonds, was probably not more than 10 per cent of the face amount. The face value of the system's securities which we had accepted as collateral against loans of nearly $14,000,000 totaled nearly $42,000,000; but, at times, some of these securities would have brought very little.

Of our earlier loans over nine millions had gone to pay interest and meet maturities, and better than four millions was used to pay off notes due to banks, including the Chase National, the New York Trust Co., and the Continental Illinois National Bank & Trust Co. of Chicago. Probably no good purpose was served by our making the loans.

We finally decided, in 1936, that a change in management might help the situation and, through Ralph Budd, got John D. Farrington, a promising young operator, from the Burlington as the Rock Island's chief operating officer. The previous December Edward M. Durham, Jr., had left the senior vice presidency of the Missouri Pacific to become the Rock Island's chief executive officer. To that position Mr. Farrington succeeded when Mr. Durham retired in 1942. By then the road was again making ends meet. The Rock Island was restored to its owners January 1, 1948, with Mr. Farrington as president.

* * *

Among the roads we twice saved from bankruptcy is the Colorado & Southern, one of several lines that were being run by Mr. Budd. With him I had many dealings and conversations, both in regard to the systems under his management and on the railroad situation in general. We saw each other frequently during the two wartime years he devoted to service in Washington as adviser on transportation to the Council of National Defense.

As president of the Great Northern from 1919 to 1932 Mr. Budd had become one of the country's most highly regarded railway chieftains. The Great Northern and the Northern Pacific jointly control the Burlington, of which Mr. Budd later became president. The Burlington, in turn, controls the Colorado & Southern which, in its turn, controls, among other subsidiaries, the Fort Worth & Denver City. The Burlington shared with the Rock Island the ownership of the Burlington-Rock Island Railway Company in Texas. So Mr. Budd's influence as a railroader covered a lot of territory.

His Colorado & Southern, with lines running from Wyoming to the Texas coast, was barely able to keep its financial neck above water in the early years of the depression. Its properties—and traffic —took such a severe battering in the western floods of 1935 that the crippled road could no longer earn the interest on its obligations.

Mr. Budd came to see me. He had nearly $29,000,000 of 4½ per cent bonds falling due on May 1 of that year. The RFC purchased the bonds and extended their maturity for ten years. That was the first time we saved the C. & S. from bankruptcy.

The following year we advanced over $8,000,000 to the Fort Worth & Denver City to enable it to redeem an equal amount of 5½ per cent first-mortgage bonds due in 1961. We accepted as security a like amount of 4½ per cent first-mortgage bonds also due in 1961. This transaction enabled the road to reduce its fixed charges.

Late in 1941, in consequence of continued deficits and a worsening financial position, Mr. Budd foresaw that further changes in the debt structure of the C. & S. would be required to keep the road out of the courts. Its books had been in the red seven years out of the previous eight. Mr. Budd came to see us again. He brought along a cogent scheme of readjustment. He said he would try to get a voluntary agreement out of the security holders to accept it, which he did.

Under the readjustment plan he had worked out he proposed to reduce fixed charges from over $2,000,000 to less than $1,000,000 a year. He said he was determined to run his road as cheaply as was possible and to try to pay off its debts. He asked us to extend the maturity of the refunding bonds which we owned from 1945 to

1955 and reduce the interest from 4½ per cent to 4 per cent, of which 2½ per cent would be fixed and 1½ per cent contingent on earnings. The plan also provided for the extension of the Fort Worth & Denver City's note.

We accepted Mr. Budd's proposition, and the system again escaped bankruptcy.

All the road's general mortgage junior lien 4½ per cent bonds outstanding were modified to provide for fixed interest of 1½ per cent and contingent interest of 2½ per cent. In scouting for security holders to get them to agree to these readjustments Mr. Budd again demonstrated to what a great extent the railroads really belong to the public, to the small investor. They own them directly as well as sharing indirect ownership through their life-insurance policies and their savings-bank accounts. The C. & S. management discovered that three thousand individuals each held less than $5,000 of its bonds. Most of these people were small-town businessmen, lawyers, doctors, and widows. Some were guardians of local church funds.

Under the readjustment plan the RFC got the right to name two members of the railroad's board, but we did not exercise it. I considered Mr. Budd, who is a railroad man and not a promoter, and his fellow directors equal to the occasion, and left it to them. Mr. Budd retired from active railroading in 1949.

There were some other railroad boards about which our feelings were somewhat different. These, I shall discuss a little farther down the track. We sometimes exerted influence to bring about changes in both the board room and management.

LIGHTENING THE LOAD ON THE BOSTON & MAINE

Another readjustment plan which avoided a default, lightened the annual load of interest payments and convinced a great many private investors that a bird in the hand is worth two in the bush, was that of the Boston & Maine Railroad.

The Boston & Maine plan was largely worked out in a series of meetings between E. S. French, president of its system, and me in 1939 and 1940.

Notwithstanding that revenues were severely declining the B. & M., during the 1930's, had met over $32,000,000 of maturities. It had avoided resorting to the courts only by scraping the bottom of its barrel and simultaneously borrowing more than $20,000,000 from the RFC, the PWA and the bankers.

The road's bonds were selling in the market somewhere between 40 and 50 and had been down in the low 30's. About a year in advance of the maturity of its principal debt of a little over $100,-000,000, bearing 5 per cent interest, Mr. French came to see me for a loan to meet it. I explained to him that under the circumstances we could not make the loan, but suggested that if he would submit a plan to his bondholders, offering them two $500 bonds for each $1,000 bond—$500 in the form of a first mortgage, bearing 4 per cent interest and $500 in the form of an income bond, bearing 4½ per cent interest—the RFC would buy all or any part of the first mortgage 4 per cent bonds. He wasn't sure he could put it over, but thought the plan worth trying and certainly preferable to a receivership.

As I recall it he succeeded in getting 95 per cent of all bondholders to accept the plan. I regarded this as substantial compliance with our offer, and the plan was made effective. Most of the road's bonds were held in New England, and New Englanders are a frugal and practical people. Otherwise Mr. French probably could not have succeeded. The RFC was required to put up $26,000,000 for the purchase of bonds from bondholders who took part in cash and part in income bonds. The bonds the RFC took in exchange for the B. & M.'s notes which we held were later sold at a premium of $525,000. By reducing its fixed charges by more than $2,500,000 a year the railroad was kept out of the courts. Its security holders were able to cash coupons as each fell due and the RFC made a tidy profit out of its part in the transaction. The Boston & Maine's debt to the RFC has been entirely repaid.

One rather complicated railroad venture which we undertook was building through the heart of the Rockies the Dotsero Cut-off. Along with the famed Moffat Tunnel it shortened the rail distance between Denver and Salt Lake City by one hundred seventy-five miles and for the first time placed Denver on a main transcontinental route. The cut-off, which winds through thirty-eight mountainous miles, connects with the Denver & Salt Lake Railroad at Orestod, Colorado, and with Denver & Rio Grande Western at Dotsero, Colorado.

The proposal to construct the cut-off was authorized by the Interstate Commerce Commission on November 26, 1932, within ten months after the RFC began operations. The Commission authorized the Denver & Salt Lake Western to construct the cut-off upon condition that the Denver & Rio Grande Western be permitted to operate over it and over the Denver & Salt Lake into Utah Junction, three miles outside Denver, the agreement to run for fifty years with an option to renew for forty-nine additional years, the railroads splitting maintenance costs fifty-fifty.

On the previous September 15 we authorized at 5 per cent a $3,850,000 loan to the D. & R. G. W. to cover construction costs of the cut-off. Against this loan was pledged the entire capital stock of the Denver & Salt Lake Western. The RFC had loaned the D. & R. G. W. the money with which to buy control of the Denver & Salt Lake, and while this loan remained on the books the RFC took charge of voting that stock. It was necessary to maintain a proper segregation of the two operations, the two older railroads, and the cut-off which was under construction.

I decided the only way it could be properly handled would be to select a man of unquestioned integrity who would recognize the situation as between the old roads and the cut-off and the financial problems of all three, to reorganize the bankrupt Denver & Salt Lake. The cut-off had been opened to traffic on June 15, 1934. After consultation with all interested parties, I asked Wilson McCarthy of Salt Lake City, who had resigned a few months previously as one of the original directors of the RFC to resume law practice in Oakland, California, to give up that practice and go to Denver as president of the Denver & Salt Lake. He arrived there on December 22, 1934, and took charge as president.

In the autumn of 1935 when the Denver & Rio Grande went into trusteeship, Judge J. Foster Symes, of the United States District Court, asked Mr. McCarthy to become one of the trustees of that railroad, which he did.

Mr. McCarthy handled his dual job well. He had not been a railroad president many years before all the top railroad men accepted him as one of their best, a man of great integrity and good sense. Later when the two railroads were merged and brought out of the wringer through reorganization in April, 1947, he was elected president of the consolidated line—the Denver & Rio Grande Western. He has made a fine success of it.

HAROLD VANDERBILT AND HIS BANKERS

The New York Central was helped through the depression with $43,468,000 of government money, of which the RFC provided about 80 per cent and the Public Works Administration the remainder. The Central also borrowed heavily from the banks in its successful efforts to stay out of the courts. One of these bank loans was guaranteed by the RFC. Some of the others were made because we had agreed to lend the money if the bankers didn't. Here again we find an instance in which our agency was able to do a job without spending any money—simply by being willing and in a position to do it.

I did not always see eye to eye with the Central's bankers. In October, 1935, when the road had debts of $90,000,000 owing to its bankers and to the RFC, Harold S. Vanderbilt of its executive committee and F. E. Williamson, its president, asked us for a ten-year extension of a $15,600,000 note which was about to fall due. They were eager to take quick advantage of an amendment to the Emergency Railway Transportation Act which Congress, at our suggestion, had but recently enacted. This amendment permitted us to make long-term loans—up to ten years—but required that the loans be amortized over the period.

The New York Central directors, while asking for ten years on their obligation to us, were content to or were required by the banks to continue on a demand basis some $63,000,000 they owed the banks.

I wrote the ten banks concerned, suggesting that all the New York Central's notes, those that they held and those we held, be refunded into a convertible bond issue. I felt the Central's debt situation was unhealthy with so much short-time bank debt, and that such a refunding as I suggested would be beneficial.

The bankers admitted their lines of credit to the Central, though well secured, were frozen. I took the position, and told the bankers and Mr. Vanderbilt as well, that in the opinion of the RFC such a large demand debt by one of our major railroad systems constituted an unnecessary hazard, if not an actual menace, to railroad financing generally under the conditions then prevailing. But the bankers did not agree to my suggestion. They even accused me of asking them to do something illegal. As an alternative they recommended that all the Central's loans be put on a demand basis, each lender to agree to give six months' notice if he wanted his money.

Representatives of the ten banks sent a letter to Mr. Vanderbilt criticizing me for "agitating" publicly for a refunding of the loans. Mr. Vanderbilt then wrote me that my public references "to financial plans which cannot presently succeed is distinctly harmful to our company and might militate somewhat against the eventual culmination of some such issue."

In replying I gave Mr. Vanderbilt, whom I liked, as I also liked his bankers, some of my views on the American public's right to know about the financing of its railroads with government money. I told him that he and his bankers seemed to have forgotten that I was a government official lending government funds, and that the public was interested in the RFC and also in the New York Central's finances.

"You forget, too," my letter continued, "that these interviews to which you object are the result of pertinent inquiry by the press. But if you will search the newspaper files, you will find no statement by me that could be hurtful to the New York Central or to any other institution that has had occasion to borrow from the RFC.

"I appreciate that some bankers and corporate officials do not like publicity, but railroads are required by law to make public their entire activities, as is also the RFC. Yours is one of our prominent railroad systems, and the condition of its finances is of interest to the public. One very good way to avoid further publicity of this character would be to put your finances in order.

"I certainly have no desire to annoy you or your bankers, but I would be derelict in my duty if I did not do what I could to assist in correcting what I know to be an unhealthy situation. I am continuing these efforts in the belief that there will be no more opportune time than the present, and if your directors and bankers would enter into the matter with what I conceive to be the right spirit this could be accomplished."

In 1934, after we had loaned the New York Central more than $45,000,000 over a two-year period, the system found itself needing $60,000,000 more to meet maturities. We agreed to supply up to one-third of this sum, provided the road agreed to amortize all of it over a ten-year period. The Central raised the money by offering a 6 per cent, ten-year convertible note or bond issue. The banks took it all—which was another instance of our being able to do a job without spending any money. The bonds could have been marketed at 5 per cent. I advocated the lower rate, but it would have been less pleasing to the Central's bankers and their favored investor clients.

The road continued carrying its bank debts on a demand basis, but upon the RFC agreeing to charge the road only 4 per cent on its notes provided the banks charged it no more, the banks reduced their rate to that level. Finally, in 1936, the bank debts were refunded at favorable rates. Before the end of that year, the Central repaid its loans to the RFC at a premium to us of $118,000 and also retired nearly $7,000,000 of its notes which we had bought from the PWA. We purchased $9,000,000 of the Central's equipment trust certificates at par and later sold them to the public at 101.

During 1937 and 1938, in order to keep meeting fixed charges and avoid bankruptcy, the Central was compelled to institute various economies. In doing this the road laid off several thousand employees. Many of its bonds at that time were selling at sixty cents on the dollar. At our suggestion the Central agreed to use $5,000,000 in reemploying furloughed workers, according to our lending plan, to rehabilitate roadways and equipment. I suggested to the National City Bank of New York that, instead of our making this loan, they should make it and we would guarantee it. That is the way it was done.

BOLSTERING THE B. & O.

The Baltimore & Ohio got more help from the RFC than any other railroad. We were able to keep it out of receivership only by continued attention over a period of thirteen years, the length of my service with the Corporation.

The Baltimore & Ohio is the oldest and certainly one of the most important of our railroad systems. Its first application was made March 21, 1932, for loans aggregating $55,000,000.

By the middle of 1934 we had loaned the B. & O. $72,000,000, part of which helped it through a large refunding operation. In an effort to meet this situation we made an agreement with Kuhn, Loeb & Co., under which the RFC agreed to buy any part of a new $50,000,-000 five year 4½ per cent secured note issue which the bankers were unable to sell to the public. The issue was secured by $38,000,000 in B. & O. 6 per cent bonds and a large amount of the stock, both common and preferred, of the Reading Railroad, which the B. & O. controlled. Under that agreement we bought $13,490,000 which the bankers were unable to sell.

Subsequently the RFC continued lending additional funds to the road for various purposes, so that by August, 1938, the B. & O. owed RFC about $88,000,000. All of our loans had the prior approval of the Interstate Commerce Commission.

Including its debt to the RFC, the B. & O. would face maturities of approximately $185,000,000 in the next few years and Mr. Willard, then seventy-five years old, was anxious to avoid a receivership in the twilight of his long presidency of the system. Taking advantage of Chapter XV of the Bankruptcy Act, then known as the Chandler Act, which Congress had passed to meet just such situations as the B. & O.'s, Mr. Willard had his attorneys draw up a modification plan covering its principal debts. This plan involved extending the notes we held, as well as other principal creditors', and putting part of the interest on an if-earned basis. The plan lowered the road's fixed interest by $11,000,000 annually on about $542,000,000 of its outstanding securities.

Mr. Willard had risen from a locomotive engineer to the presidency of the B. & O. He had many friends in both houses of Congress. These friendships, I have no doubt, were effective in the passage of the Chandler Act, under which the rearrangement of his debts was made.

In the spring of 1944, nearly two years after Mr. Willard's death, the B. & O. officials came to us again. They requested further extension of the road's then indebtedness to RFC of $71,073,000, which would mature the following November. They had a great many other bond maturities coming along in the next two or three years. We told them that we would extend our loans if other creditors extended theirs, but not otherwise.

It seemed at the time that if enough effort were made the road could put its entire funded debt in a position to endure for a good many years and save a likely receivership.

Lending the road so much money and obviously being in the position of having to await better conditions before the government could get its money, I thought it advisable, as in some other situations, to strengthen its financial management. Accordingly, I suggested that Mr. Stewart McDonald, a sound business man, president of the Maryland Casualty Co. at Baltimore, headquarters of the B. & O., be put on the B. & O. Board of directors, and that he and Mr. Howard Bruce, a prominent banker and industrialist living in Baltimore, already a member of the road's Board, be put on the road's finance or executive committee.

When we explained to Roy B. White, the road's then president, that we would not extend our loans unless the other principal creditors did, he asked for a conference. The meeting, held in our office, was attended by Mr. White and three other directors, Stewart McDonald, President of Maryland Casualty Co., J. C. Traphagen, Chairman of the Board of the Bank of New York, and H. J. Cheston, a banker from Philadelphia. They were accompanied by Russell Snodgrass, financial vice president of the road, who had previously been an RFC attorney in our railroad division, and Cassius M. Clay, one of the B. & O.'s lawyers, who also was an RFC alumnus. Mr. Clay had gone to the B. & O. in 1942. He was the only man in the top bracket of our employees who ever accepted employment from a borrower of the RFC without first clearing it with me. If G. M. Shriver, the then financial vice president of the road, had asked me if it would be all right for the B. & O. to employ Mr. Clay, which he should have done, I would have told him that we would have no objection, but that such employment would not carry with it a key to our safe. And had Mr. Clay spoken to me about it I would have interposed no objection. Although a little ponderous in articulation, Mr. Clay was a good lawyer and had been with the RFC a number of years. While, as a rule, we did not secure positions for our employees, when we could spare those who had been faithful and were able to get better positions, we were glad to release them.

Many RFC alumni now occupy important positions in banking, industry and railroading, and in the practice of law. I know of none who have not made good. Most of these men had come to the RFC at small salaries during its early years when jobs were scarce. We could not expect them to remain with us always when they could get good positions that often paid several times their RFC salaries. RFC directors drew only $10,000 a year

When it was made clear to Mr. White and those of his directors who came to see us that we would not extend our 1944 maturity unless other principal holders of the road's securities would extend theirs, the road took steps to reorganize under the McLaughlin Act, passed by Congress in October, 1942. It was, in fact, an extension, with slight modifications, of the Chandler Act that had expired. The Act provided that 75 per cent of the holders of all the different issues of a road's indebtedness could speak for all of them. The plan, as I recall, was to extend to 1955 all bonds of the company which were to mature during the next several years. It put practically the entire debt structure on a long-term basis.

Due largely to the diligence and perseverance of the officials of the road, and of security holders' committees acting in their own interest, the plan was overwhelmingly approved. On some of the issues as many as 99 per cent voted favorably. Of the entire funded debt structure, more than 81 per cent approved. The plan, which was approved by the Interstate Commerce Commission, kept the road out of receivership. It saved many millions of dollars for the security holders, which included life insurance companies, savings banks, colleges, fiduciary institutions and private investors. It improved the road's debts to RFC.

For some unaccountable reason Mr. Clay, general solicitor for the road, opposed the plan even to the extent of resigning as a Baltimore & Ohio attorney and aligning himself with a Mr. Randolph Phillips to fight it. Mr. Phillips, as a bond holder, opposed the plan when it was heard by a special Federal court sitting in Baltimore. The court unanimously approved the plan. The court was composed of Judges Morris Soper and Armistead M. Dobie of the U. S. Court of Appeals, Fourth District, and Judge Calvin Chesnut of the U. S. District Court of the District of Maryland.

Later on, in 1947, long after I had left the Corporation, Senator Charles W. Tobey, chairman of the Senate Banking and Currency Committee, undertook to investigate the financial affairs of the B. & O. with respect to its RFC borrowings. He attacked the reorganization, but there was nothing done about it. Among those who testified for his committee were Mr. Clay, Mr. Phillips, and Robert R. Young. Mr. Young is the controlling factor of the Chesapeake & Ohio Railroad which is very rich and, in the opinion of many, would like to acquire the Western Maryland Railroad, which is controlled by the B. & O. The assumption was that if the B. & O. went into receivership Mr. Young might get the Western Maryland for the C. & O.

Notwithstanding Senator Tobey's investigation and his attack on the reorganization plan, the plan was consummated and the road's debt structure put on a sound basis.

At this writing (June, 1951) the RFC holds $76,300,000 B. & O. bonds, due in 1965. The bonds are secured by collateral having a present apparent quoted or market value of more than double the amount of the debt, and there has been no default. I am informed that the B. & O. has paid the RFC more than $57,000,000 interest on its borrowings which has yielded a profit to the Corporation of probably $15,000,000 over the cost of the money and the administration expenses incident to the loans. I regard the remaining B. & O. RFC loan as being as good as the average railroad security.

Railroads are regulated by the government and are dependent on their earnings to finance themselves, but it seems clear that the RFC will suffer no loss from its loans to the B. & O. However, with a little diligence on the part of the road's management, the entire balance due the RFC might easily have been placed with private investors during the era of cheap and plentiful money in 1948 and 1949. This would have been highly desirable from the government's standpoint, because the government should do no money lending where the borrower can get its money elsewhere, and even then only when an emergency exists.

The road has earned and paid all its charges since the last refunding, and has continually improved its position.

In Senator Tobey's investigation, he charged the Corporation with collusion, skulduggery and humbuggery. These charges were without foundation and undoubtedly were inspired by some selfish or vindictive motive.

LETTING THE ERIE SINK

Though we went to great pains to keep several roads from sliding into bankruptcy, there was one line—the Erie—about which we did not try any too hard. The Erie had for years been on the border line of solvency, earning little more than its fixed charges. However, it had a strong daddy or at least a big brother. The Erie was controlled by the rich and prosperous Chesapeake & Ohio. Yet when the C. & O. was asked to give a helping hand, either by guaranteeing payment of a further loan the Erie had requested from us, or by lending the Erie a mere $2,500,000 or $3,000,000 of securities to complete the collateralization of the loan, its directors refused. So we declined the loan.

A few days later—it was in January, 1938—the Erie, feeling itself unable to spare the cash to face a bond interest maturity of $1,-800,000, filed a petition in bankruptcy.

We had already loaned the Erie more than $16,000,000. And we had bought nearly $14,000,000 of its loans made by the PWA. When in the autumn of 1937 the road had come to us again, asking for a further advance of more than $6,000,000 to pay interest, sinking fund, and other obligations, the ICC specified, quite properly, in approving the loan that the C. & O. should either guarantee it or deposit collateral which, taken with the collateral the Erie itself could rake together, would provide acceptable security.

The strong C. & O. could easily have helped the Erie, in whose capital stock it had invested about $45,000,000; but it said no. Hence the receivership. Through the ten-year period 1928–1937, the C. & O. had been one of fewer than half a dozen railroads which were able continuously to pay dividends. In addition to paying all interest charges and pouring out an average of about $20,000,000 a year to its stockholders, during that decade when so many railroads were meeting with financial disaster, it had piled up earnings of more than $10,000,000 a year.

In 1937, the year it refused to lift a hand for the Erie, the C. & O. declared cash dividends of $29,000,000 and also a 4 per cent preferred stock dividend of $15,000,000. Probably if the directors had been less interested in fattening the Alleghany Corporation, the holding company which received a large part of the road's dividends, their course with the Erie might have been different, and the Erie could have avoided receivership.

When the Erie went bankrupt the RFC was given the right to name three directors on its board. I nominated Charles T. Fisher, Jr., of Detroit, who had been, but no longer was, one of our directors, James S. Knowlson, president and board chairman of the Stewart-Warner Corporation, who later became vice chairman of the War Production Board, and Frank C. Wright. Mr. Wright was our principal railroad official and a gracious gentleman. He had an extraordinary grasp on railroad affairs, and an exceptional capacity for understanding another man's position and problems. He was one of the reorganization

Fontaine Fox for Bell Syndicate.

managers of the Western Pacific and later a director. He also helped
reorganize the Denver & Rio Grande, and the Central of Georgia.
He came to us from the Public Works Administration, where he had
handled all that agency's railroad loans.

Another railroad on which we put three directors was the Chicago
& Eastern Illinois, to which we loaned six millions before it went
broke and five more millions when it had been reorganized. On its
board we put John W. Barriger III, who had headed our railroad
division, Frank O. Watts, chairman of the First National Bank of
St. Louis, and Roger C. Hyatt of the Continental Illinois National
Bank & Trust Co. of Chicago. Other creditors' interests in the first

year under reorganization proceedings had reappointed Will H. Hays on the C. & E. I. board, of which he had been a member since 1922. He had been Postmaster General in the Harding administration and chairman of the Republican National Committee before he went to Hollywood as overseer of the motion picture industry. But when the next election of directors fell due the interests which had placed him on the board did not renominate him. So I nominated Mr. Hays to take Mr. Barriger's place. Mr. Hays' law firm had been attorneys for the railroad and its predecessor road since 1883, and I saw no reason for leaving him off the board.

Mr. Barriger is now president of the Monon (the informal name of the Chicago, Indianapolis & Louisville Railway Co.,) and is doing a good job. He came to us as a bright young man in his early thirties. He well understood both the operating and the financing end of railroading and had an excellent comprehension of the whole nation-wide transportation problem. He stayed with us until 1941 when he became reorganization manager of the Chicago & Eastern Illinois.

Howard J. Klossner, who came up through RFC ranks to become one of its directors, holds, among other positions, a directorship of the Chicago & North Western, on which line I designated him voting trustee for the RFC in 1944, a year before he left the RFC.

My views as to the government's right to have a look-in on the management of railroads which came to it for aid were plainly stated in a letter I sent to Vice President Garner on November 6, 1934:

I am making it clear to the roads that need to come to the Government for help that we must have some look-in on the management. Probably a fair criticism of railroad executives would be that they are always reluctant to allow any sort of governmental interference. That is perfectly all right so long as they do not have to come to the Government for money, but if the Government must be the banker, it should exact intelligent and efficient management. Some are accepting it gracefully, others less so.

In all the railroad problems that came to us W. W. Sullivan, affectionately called Sully, was extraordinarily helpful. He seemed to know something about almost all the railroads, about the management, the character of the properties and the country through which they ran. We also had a very faithful lawyer, Meade Fletcher, who was devoted to the RFC and to his work in the railroad division.

8

✿

REVIVING THE REAL ESTATE MORTGAGE MARKET

WHAT is the largest single type of investment in which the American people put their money? It isn't railroads or highways or insurance policies or savings accounts or corporate stocks and bonds. It is the mortgage on real estate. From the ten-acre farm to the tallest skyscraper, almost every piece of property in the country has carried a mortgage at one time or another. Mortgages have financed the construction of nearly every home, factory, store, or office building in this country.

During the depression the almost measureless market for mortgages went into total eclipse. The RFC helped to bring it back into the light of day—and also into the light of reason.

That accomplishment required a good many years of hard work. Even after the banking structure had been made sound and agriculture was again moderately prospering, and most of the water had been wrung out of railroad finances, the real estate mortgage market remained immobile, congealed with fear. The part taken by the RFC in its recuperation was accomplished without cost to the taxpayer, although we used millions to put life into it. We got the money back and made a small profit for the government. Better still, we helped restore faith and confidence in the orderly financing of real estate.

When the RFC went directly into the mortgage business in 1934 countless mortgage loans were in default throughout the country. Thousands of costly, useful buildings, such as apartment houses, hotels, offices, stores, warehouses, and factories put up by corporations and covered by mortgage bonds, had gone into receivership.

At that time real estate mortgages on urban loans alone—all farm and rural properties being out of consideration—aggregated more than thirty-five billion dollars.

Of that sum about nine billion dollars in mortgages was held by commercial banks and trust companies and mutual savings banks, seven billions by building and loan associations, and six billions by life insurance companies. Five more billion dollars was in real estate mortgage bonds held by the public. The remainder was held by trustees, educational and charitable institutions, fire and casualty companies, and individuals.

Many of the properties then in default could have been safely reorganized both in the interest of the bondholders and equity owners and without loss to the new money. But there was no new money available in the real estate field—none for retirement of maturing mortgages, none for new construction except, in spots, from one of the more prosperous life insurance companies.

Between 1929 and 1934 the bonds of important, well-known buildings in almost every American city had sold at a fraction of their real value, simply because there was no fair market for them and no funds were available to reorganize the properties.

When the stock market crashed in 1929, properties in New York City alone had approximately two billion dollars of guaranteed mortgages and mortgage certificates in the hands of the public. Their experience with these investments became bitter and often tragic.

In Chicago, soon after the crash, about two and a half billions of real estate mortgages and bonds were in default. By the beginning of 1932 the aggregate amount of foreclosed Chicago properties approached one billion dollars. With the collapse of the boom unfinished buildings blurred the sky line of the city's suburbs. Weeds sprouted in the streets of many an outlying real estate development. Chicago's suburban banks, tied in closely with real estate promotion, went broke by the score. On a lesser scale, other cities and their surrounding areas were similarly smitten. Their pains were sometimes increased by collusion and graft in foreclosure proceedings.

In the booming 1920's many of our larger cities had been overbuilt, or at least expanded in advance of requirements by optimistic promoters.

The mortgage bond houses which financed these promotions not only charged excessive interest rates but, to make matters worse, required amortization payments much beyond the earning power of the properties even in prosperous times.

But this was not a valid reason for forever condemning real estate or real estate securities. Prior to the depression, billions and billions of dollars' worth of sound mortgages had been made, sold, and repaid. Unfortunately, the mortgage bond houses had in many instances sold more bonds against a business property than the cost of the property, and more than it could possibly earn and make amortization payments upon in addition to interest. Rates customarily charged by these mortgage bond houses were 6, 6½, and 7 per cent, and they would buy the bonds from the mortgager at 85 to 90 cents on the dollar. With heavy amortization and high interest rates, the building project could not possibly survive. The bond houses made a little temporary money, but most of them went bust trying to keep going.

Even so, the whole real estate market couldn't remain in collapse. With that thought in mind, we approached the problem, our idea being that if the country was sound—we felt it was—institutions of substantial capital and under capable management needed to be established to render again the essential service of making mortgage money available for new construction, extensions, renewals, and improvements.

In hundreds of banks closed in 1932 and 1933, our examiners had found perfectly good mortgages, current as to taxes and interest, which had matured or were maturing, and which we felt could safely be extended or taken over by a going concern. There also were many frozen mortgage loans in closed banks and elsewhere which could be revamped and made current on some basis. But nobody was willing to buy.

Having convinced ourselves that there was no mortgage money available to save the situation, we asked Congress in 1934 for authority to buy preferred stock in mortgage companies, somewhat as we had been doing in banks. When I was before the Senate Banking and Currency Committee asking for this authority, Senator Couzens, who was usually quite critical, was one of the first members of the Committee to speak; and he favored our being given the authority up to $100,000,000, which I think was the amount we had asked for. Congress gave us the requested authority up to that sum. But we were never able to get anyone to start a mortgage company. Times were so pessimistic that no one would put up money for common stock in such an enterprise.

In New York, where the greatest mortgage tragedies due to over-promoted and improvidently financed buildings had occurred, we tried to get a new mortgage company started. We offered to put $75,000,000 in preferred stock in a privately owned and managed mortgage company against $25,000,000 common stock to be owned by people interested in a rescue job, which could have been done on a sound and profitable basis. We wanted private investors to own the business, to do the work and make a fair profit. But we couldn't induce anyone to try it.

So, in the spring of 1935, we started the RFC Mortgage Company with a capital of $10,000,000 which later was raised to $25,000,000. The company did a lot of good, and it made some money for the government.

We bought and sold Federal Housing Administration mortgages to make a market and encourage the financial institutions to buy them. We wanted to prove that the mortgages were good and then withdraw from the field.

Before we entered the field, Congress during the Hoover administration had created the Federal Home Loan Bank, and early in the Roosevelt administration had authorized the Federal Land Banks to issue $2,000,000,000 in bonds to refinance farm mortgages. In June, 1934, the National Housing Act authorized the Federal Housing Administration to finance new construction, and to refund mortgages of homes, both single and multiple. Many homes were being built under that scheme.

When the farmer and the small home-owner had thus been taken under the government umbrella, there was still no provision for federal refinancing of such income-producing business properties as apartment houses, hotels, and office buildings. In that neglected field the RFC Mortgage Company began its financing of real estate.

It made loans on first mortgages on properties capable of producing enough income to pay operating expenses, taxes, interest, and reasonable amortization. It offered to make loans secured by first-mortgage bonds and certificates. In the debacle the mortgage and bond houses which had issued these bonds had ceased to exist.

We also financed first-mortgage loans to assist the construction of new buildings for which there seemed to be an economic need.

Our mortgage loan purchases were notably heavy in Detroit and Chicago, in Florida and, later, the Northwest. Conservative New England had not gone heavily into local real estate promotions. There was less need of the rescue program in that region. The call on us was comparatively light in California also, partly because out there the Bank of America remained active in mortgage financing.

Although many homes were being built with FHA government-guaranteed mortgages at an interest rate of 4½ per cent, financial institutions were slow to buy the mortgages. For the sole purpose of making a market for these insured mortgages, we created on February 10, 1938, the Federal National Mortgage Association. Owned and operated by the RFC, it started with a capital of $10,-000,000 and surplus of $1,000,000.

We immediately offered to buy any FHA-insured mortgage, wherever the property was located, at 99 per cent of the face value of the mortgage and to sell it at par. We soon had insurance companies and other big investors interested. Then we raised our price, paying par for the mortgages and selling them at a slight premium. They finally became a popular investment with fiduciaries and trust companies.

One of the first big investors in these securities was Morris S. Tremaine, Comptroller of the State of New York in the Smith, Roosevelt, and Lehman administrations. Mr. Tremaine was an astute man in financial affairs. He had large sums of public funds for investment. He began buying mortgages from us almost from the start and was soon paying us a premium of 1 per cent for them. After this had been going on for quite a time, he came to my office in Washington and asked me what price we would make him if he took all our FHA-insured mortgages on properties located in New York State. I told him the price would be 101½. He protested, asking why, if we would sell him one mortgage at 101, we wouldn't sell him all we had at the same price, or even for less. He bought them all—and paid 101½.

Mr. Tremaine also bought practically all the RFC's bridge and other public-works bonds that were secured by self-liquidating projects in New York State. For an issue of bonds for a bridge built across the Hudson River he paid us a premium of 19 per cent. He was glad to get the investment. Nowhere else could he get as good a rate of interest and as good an investment. He also bought from us $6,000,000 in bonds for the Jones Beach Recreation Centre on Long Island and another issue of about $4,000,000 for improvements in the spa at Saratoga Springs.

These RFC loans were to New York State corporations, but there was no recourse to the State of New York and no security except the property covered by the mortgage and its income. The loans turned out well. We were justified in making them. Mr. Tremaine made a good buy for the State of New York and the other public funds he had for investment.

In setting up the Federal National Mortgage Association to work exclusively in the handling of FHA-insured mortgages, we again entered the mortgage field only after our offers to become partners with private capital had fallen on deaf ears. The National Housing Act of 1934 had provided for the organization of National Mortgage Associations. To aid in starting some of them we offered, at the request of the Federal Housing Administrator, to match dollars with private capital by taking preferred stock. Nearly four years went by without our getting a single offer of cooperation.

We then formed the Federal National Mortgage Association. In the jargon of the government's alphabetical agencies, it quickly came to be called Fannie Mae. Before she was a year old, Fannie Mae had authorized and purchased 26,276 mortgages aggregating more than $100,000,000, and had found it necessary to start foreclosures on only twenty-five of them. While Fannie Mae bought insured mortgages on new homes, including large-scale housing projects, the RFC Mortgage Company continued to buy insured mortgages on old homes.

After the war the RFC Mortgage Company established a secondary market for the purchase of veterans' home loans. The Company bought these loans from banks and others at a price equal to the unpaid principal balance of the loan plus accrued and unpaid interest. No loan was to exceed $10,000. Bearing 4 per cent interest, they were to be amortized by monthly payments over a period of not more than twenty-five years. The banks or other institutions which made the loans in the first place continued to collect the monthly payments, receiving a service charge of ½ of 1 per cent a year.

Both the RFC Mortgage Company and the Federal National Mortgage Association became profitable enterprises for the government as well as a great help to the public. By Congressional dictate the

Mortgage Company was absorbed into the RFC on June 30, 1947, after more than twelve years of existence. It earned a net profit of $6,000,000 after interest and expenses of $16,000,000. It paid RFC $36,000,000 for money it used.

At the same date the accumulated net earnings of the Federal National Mortgage Association had risen above $23,000,000. In nine years Fannie Mae had purchased 66,966 FHA-insured mortgages totaling $271,716,894. She not only had helped restore a market for mortgages but had done a sizable share in filling the need for home properties for a growing population.

ALFRED E. SMITH AT THE DEDICATION IN 1934 OF KNICKERBOCKER VILLAGE

A New York City housing development financed by the RFC.

Acme Photos except top,
International News Photo

THREE BRIDGES FINANCED BY THE RFC

Top: The San Francisco–Oakland Bay Bridge. Center: Rip van Winkle Bridge over the Hudson. Bottom, left: The Huey P. Long Bridge over the Mississippi at New Orleans.

9

※

RESCUING SOME SURETY AND CASUALTY COMPANIES

Getting a Surety Company off the Rocks—Woes of the Maryland Casualty Company—The Prudence Loan—a Bad Situation—Unfreezing Chicago's Lake of Frozen Mortgages

ONE important rescue from the frozen mortgage field was that of the National Surety Company, which did business in every state in the Union. The immediate liquidation which threatened the company in 1933 would have caused wholesale cancellations of millions in bonds, which were widely distributed. It would have thrown onto sidewalks already swarming with discouraged job-hunters the company's several thousand employees. Such somber tragedies were averted by an arrangement which the RFC worked out with George S. Van Schaick, the New York State Superintendent of Insurance. After the bank holiday he had taken over the National Surety Company and a considerable number of other insurance concerns in New York State in order to rehabilitate or liquidate them.

Under an agreement with Mr. Van Schaick, the RFC released to him $5,000,000 in securities which we held to secure the National Surety Company debt to us. He used the $5,000,000 securities to organize a new corporation—the National Surety Corporation—which took over the business of the National Surety Company and assumed its contracts and liabilities. In lieu of the collateral which we released we accepted the capital stock of the new company as security to the National Surety Company debt.

The old company had admitted assets of nearly $50,000,000; but it had issued bonds and policies with a face value approaching $3,000,-000,000, and it had guaranteed to the extent of approximately $45,-

[153]

000,000 real estate mortgage bonds issued by more than a score of other corporations.

The public's rush to get these guaranteed securities redeemed cut deeply into the old company's treasury. The RFC began lending it money to give it liquidity. These borrowings, begun in the summer of 1932, had risen to nearly $15,000,000 by April, 1933, when the Superintendent of Insurance took the company over.

Both Superintendent Van Schaick and I felt its plant and good-will would be valueless in the event of liquidation, which also would entail cancellation of many bonds held by investors the country over. Arrangements to forestall such a catastrophe had to be made quickly if the business was to keep going. The process we employed placed ownership of all the new stock in the name of the rehabilitator of the old company subject to the lien of the RFC. The best assets of the old company were transferred to the new company. The insuring public accepted the change agreeably, and losses were light. Vincent Cullen, who had been a vice president of the old company, became president of the new, but most of the other top personnel was changed. The new company succeeded admirably. Our loans to the National Surety Company have long since been paid in full.

WOES OF THE MARYLAND CASUALTY COMPANY

One gloomy October day in 1933, there wound slowly into our offices a doleful delegation of gentlemen from New York, Newark, Baltimore, Hartford, and other cities to speak for the whole herd in the casualty insurance field. They asked us to save one of their bell cows, the Maryland Casualty Company of Baltimore. It, too, had bogged deeply in the mortgage guarantee mud. It had guaranteed payment of the principal on about $58,000,000 in mortgage bonds and certificates issued by various real estate companies.

The rush of investors to convert this paper into cash had so milked the company's treasury that it was hard pressed to find enough money to meet the day-to-day obligations of its regular casualty business.

The melancholy delegation predicted that if the Maryland Casualty Company sank there would be panicky repercussions throughout the whole realm of their business, and other companies would be battered into insolvency. They painted a black picture.

I was already somewhat acquainted with the situation. A short while previously, William H. Woodin, Secretary of the Treasury, had asked me to try to save the Maryland Casualty Company. He said that if it closed the Treasury would lose $3,000,000. Governor Albert C. Ritchie of Maryland also had spoken to us about the company. He was fearful that its collapse would do great harm throughout his state. Our board had been asked to consider advancing the company $7,500,000.

After several members of the visiting delegation had pleaded the Maryland's cause, almost in tears, I told them that their sad appeals recalled a picture in the second reader I had studied as a schoolboy.

The picture showed a farmer with his team of horses. One of the horses had dropped dead while hitched to the wagon. The other horse sagged wearily on all fours. A neighbor came up to the farmer, who was standing disconsolate beside his half dead, half alive team. The neighbor said: "Friend, I'm awfully sorry."

The farmer thanked him and asked, "How sorry are you?" As a measure of his sympathy the neighbor handed the farmer a $10 bill.

"The point to the story, gentlemen," I said, "is, how sorry are *you*?"

I then excused myself for half an hour or so to meet another delegation waiting in another office. When I returned to the casualty people, their spokesman said, "How sorry do you want us to be, Mr. Jones?"

"Gentlemen," I replied, "we will let you off light. You take the first $1,000,000 loss on the Maryland loan, and we will save the company."

They readily agreed to my suggestion. They went into a huddle and in a few moments subscribed a million-dollar pool. Later on, one of them told me they had been prepared to put up much more than that. As it turned out, there were so many of them to collect from that we did not trouble to pass the hat.

The casualty company officials were also disturbed about another Baltimore institution, the United States Fidelity & Guaranty Company, which was out on the mortgage limb, but not so perilously far. We were presently able to protect that company with loans and preferred-stock investments.

In tackling the Maryland Casualty's problem we began by lending

$7,500,000, the amount it was represented would save the company. Before we were done with that job, we had put in new management and loaned to and invested in the company and about a dozen of its affiliated debenture houses and other subsidiaries a total exceeding $50,000,000. Ultimately the RFC got back all that money, but it was one of our longest pulls. It took thirteen years.

The RFC acquired voting control of Maryland Casualty in April, 1934, when we first bought preferred stock in the Company. At that time we sent Silliman Evans to Baltimore to take the presidency of the company and Edward G. Lowry, Jr., of our legal department, to be its vice president and special counsel, each being elected a director. Mr. Evans later became chairman of the board. When he resigned that position in 1939 he was succeeded by Stewart McDonald, who was then the Federal Housing Administrator. That same year two RFC directors, Howard J. Klossner and Charles T. Fisher, Jr., were placed on the Maryland Casualty's board. When we got into the company, the situation was so much worse than had been represented that we felt it necessary to replace the management.

Mr. Evans is now publisher of the Nashville *Tennessean,* and Mr. Lowry is president and chairman of the board of the General Reinsurance Corporation and also chairman of the North Star Reinsurance Corporation.

Maryland's preferred-stock loans were paid off in full, with interest, on August 2, 1946, since which time the RFC has had no power of management or control in its affairs; but Mr. McDonald, an experienced businessman who was my deputy as Federal Loan Administrator for two years, has remained its chairman. He and his associates have made a notable success in the company's rehabilitation and operation.

The Maryland Casualty Company's $58,000,000 exposure under mortgage guarantees was but one sticky patch in a measureless slough of troubles. When it first besought our succor the company's assets and those of its affiliates ranged from small rugs and cuspidors to large office buildings. Many of these buildings were half empty. Their values had to be written down on the books to such an extent that, in at least one instance, the depreciation impaired a subsidiary's capital. Debentures which some of the affiliates had sold to the public totaled $3,630,200, of which $2,636,620 had no assets whatever behind them. We lent those allied corporations $22,600,000 in 1934 and 1935. Their borrowings were fully repaid by 1941.

Meanwhile—and on into 1943—Maryland Casualty itself continued to pay bitterly for its experience in mortgage guarantees, the losses on that score growing to $29,092,258. Nor does that large sum include the interest paid on the money borrowed from the RFC or the dividends paid on the preferred stock which had provided funds to meet the losses.

THE PRUDENCE LOAN—A BAD SITUATION

Just as one real estate promotion led to another in good times, so, when the deflation began, one default bred another. Many mortgagers could pay neither interest nor taxes. In order to meet interest payments or maturities some harassed companies borrowed from the banks, and others borrowed from the RFC. Our advances in the early 1930's to mortgage loan companies exceeded $250,000,000.

Only one of those loans—the $20,000,000 put into the Prudence Company, Inc., of New York—went sour. Eventually that company, with much added funds from the RFC and with patience and good management by the RFC, worked out. By 1950 the RFC had realized $14,000,000 in cash over and above the total of its loans and advances to the Prudence Company, and to a holding company which we established to preserve the Prudence assets. There were several more millions in sight as liquidation slowly proceeded.

This fine result was due to supplying ample capital and good management, and to the recovery of values in general that followed the great depression.

The splendid record of the Prudence account must be attributed in great measure to the persistence, patience, and perspicacity of Jerome Thralls, the RFC's special representative in New York City in charge of the Prudence Loan. Had the company and its conglomeration of forty affiliated and allied concerns been liquidated rapidly when a raft of them went on the rocks, tens of thousands of investors in their bonds, debentures, guaranteed mortgages, participation certificates, insurance policies and other side-lines would have suffered heavy losses—and so would the RFC. Even as it was, a great many investors lost heavily.

Hanging on to the bear's tail day after day for more than seventeen years, the pertinacious Mr. Thralls had all the while to fight off swarms of lawyers. Fees asked for in the course of the many Prudence liquidations and proceedings exceeded $12,000,000, there being 840 separate applications from lawyers. Mr. Thralls continually combated the more exorbitant of the attorneys' appraisals of their own worth. The courts awarded the lawyers $5,052,094, all of which came out of liquidating profits, not out of the RFC.

The Prudence set-up, its smash-up, and its reorganization under a plan proposed by the RFC were in many respects unique. Before the crash Prudence securities and those of its interrelated companies were held by eighty thousand investors. More than three thousand different real estate and other properties were covered by Prudence securities. The parcels varied from vacant lots, skating rinks, small shacks, and simple cottages to skyscrapers and, for a time, the Ringling Brothers Barnum & Bailey Circus. On the "biggest show on earth" Prudence possessed a lien through a $1,700,000 note held by one of its affiliates, the Allied Owners Corporation. This note was pledged to the RFC as part of the collateral against our loan. Luckily, we never actually had any of the elephants on our hands. When times got better the circus note was sold for nearly $2,000,000.

Another large property involved in the Prudence collapse was the Cleveland National Town and Country Club, a skyscraper promotion of the 1928–1929 boom, located on Euclid Avenue and dreamily intended to be the first link in a chain of pretentious town and country clubs in the wealthier cities. It cost over $2,500,000 to build, plus promotion fees. Among other attractions, it had a swimming pool on the twenty-sixth floor.

Mr. Thralls finally got $250,000 for the building, selling to Fenn College, a Y.M.C.A. school which now has 3,000 students. Though most of the Prudence properties were in the five boroughs of New York City, the company had under its crippled wing some real estate in Chicago, Toronto, and Birmingham, as well as Cleveland.

The Prudence people began dickering for a loan in January, 1932, a few days before we opened our offices. They wanted $25,-000,000. Although their accounts had once been sought by all the bigger New York banks, I did not particularly like their set-up, their rapidly freezing situation, or even some of their top personnel; but other mortgage loan people told us that a run on Prudence would bring pressure on all of them, and we decided that perhaps the shock would be softened if we helped Prudence. It was the opinion of Eugene Meyer, then chairman of our board, that the loan should be made.

One of the arrangements they agreed to before we gave them the money was to have Arthur H. Waterman retire as president of the company and elect to that office William H. Wheelock, a member of the real estate brokerage firm of Brown, Wheelock, Harris, Stevens. The $20,000,000 the RFC advanced was quickly distributed to people eager to cash in their guaranteed bonds and certificates. These wary investors were of all types, from charwomen to capitalists. Some of the Prudence participation certificates were in denominations as low as $50. Pressed hard for funds since it had promised to cash participation certificates at any time, at par, Prudence, in March, 1933, defaulted on a payment against the RFC loan. Soon thereafter its parent and guarantor, New York Investors, Inc., and a batch of its corporate cousins were blown into bankruptcy.

New York Investors, Inc., and the men who ran it, were also involved in numerous enterprises other than real estate. In 1929 the company had bought control of the St. Louis Southwestern Railway, known as the Cotton Belt, from the Kansas City Southern Railway and had installed its own chairman, Frank Bailey, a Brooklyn capitalist, as chairman of the railroad. William Marcus Greve, who was vice chairman of the Prudence Company and president of the parent concern, New York Investors, later became, for a time, a director of the Missouri-Kansas-Texas Railway. With these gentlemen, as we shall see, Mr. Thralls had his difficulties; but he finally collected from them every dollar they had personally promised as part of the guarantee of the RFC loan.

As security for the $20,000,000 loan Prudence put up collateral and guarantees with face values exceeding $30,000,000; but in the slumping market these soon appeared to us to be worth only a fraction of that sum. Most of the collateral consisted of mortgages, and more and more of these went into default.

When Prudence and its affiliates entered the bankruptcy proceedings, the endless tussles of Mr. Thralls and the lawyers began. But when the RFC proposed a reorganization plan for Prudence which was designed to provide machinery for the conservation, administration, and liquidation of its free assets, more than 16,500 creditors with claims totaling just under $100,000,000 accepted our plan. It was confirmed by the court in 1939 and became effective a few days later.

Two years previously the RFC had established a subsidiary, the Consolidated Realty Corporation, a holding company capitalized at $100, which took over the Prudence assets we had bought or were entitled to. These reorganized bond issues, other securities, and foreclosed buildings had belonged to about a dozen different allied corporations. To permit some of these to meet their bonds and other obligations and otherwise to assist orderly liquidation and the care and preservation of collateral, the RFC advanced to Consolidated during the early 1940's more than $7,000,000. Thus our loans on the Prudence account totaled $27,654,000. The fact that the RFC realized more than $14,000,000 over and above all its advances to the Prudence account, and after all expenses, is another proof that it pays to be patient and persistent, and to have sufficient capital to ride out a financial storm. It also proves the inherent value of real estate.

It took a great deal of persistence to collect most of the $1,000,000 in guarantees given by the officers and directors of Prudence partly to secure the original loan. The biggest individual guarantee was Mr. Bailey's $250,000—and every cent of it was paid. Mr. Greve was down for $140,000 and that, too, was collected; but it took many years of waiting and legal action to get the money. In the middle 1930's he disposed of many of his interests and moved away to Europe. He renounced his American citizenship and became a citizen of the tiny principality of Liechtenstein, which occupies part of an Alp between Switzerland and the Austrian Tirol.

One day Adolf Hitler cast his covetous eyes on the little principality, and Mr. Greve decided to return to his native side of the Atlantic. He came back quietly, through the Vermont frontier, paying the alien's $8 head tax to enter the United States as a visitor. The news of his return got around, and one night as he and a group of friends were leaving a swanky New York club he was handed a subpoena while a flashlight brightened the scene for a camera. The court awarded the RFC judgment for $149,589 against him, but Mr. Thralls settled for $140,000, the original amount Mr. Greve had guaranteed.

From Liechtenstein Mr. Greve moved to Bermuda. There he bought an estate which he adorned with a main house that was reported to be 214 feet in length. But the war also crept toward peaceful Bermuda. The property was taken over by the United States Navy for part of its Bermudan base, Mr. Greve being, of course, well paid for it. I do not know what country he now claims for his citizenship, but think he spends a good deal of time in New York.

While the Prudence stockholders and mortgage and debenture holders lost heavily on their investments, Mr. Greve was able to move about the world looking for other climes and he still seems to live in affluence.

The guarantees of other Prudence officers and directors ranged from Frank Fox's $11,000 to Mr. Waterman's $100,000. Except for one who became insolvent and two who died, full payments were eventually made by all of them and also $122,000 from Title Guaranty & Trust Company which had asked us to make the Prudence Loan as had its affiliate, Bond & Mortgage Guarantee Company. From the latter we also exacted a $122,000 guarantee; but the company went broke and couldn't pay it.

UNFREEZING CHICAGO'S LAKE OF FROZEN MORTGAGES

First of the large cities to have its frozen real estate mortgage market thawed out was Chicago. In that happy process the RFC cooperated with private business. The defrosting began when three of the largest Chicago financial institutions, the Continental Illinois National Bank & Trust Company, the First National Bank, and the Chicago Title & Trust Company, formed the Fort Dearborn Mortgage Company, which immediately began doing a heavy volume of business based upon a rediscount arrangement with the RFC.

At the time the company was formed, no one could get a dollar of mortgage money anywhere in Chicago. Any man who would have put up $100,000 could have bought the first mortgage on a Chicago hotel built at a cost of $2,500,000. Half of a loan which we made on one hotel, the Congress, immediately went to pay past due taxes.

Strewn all over the outlying residential and neighborhood shopping districts of Chicago was the wreckage of the "corner banks" which had become entangled in the financing of real estate promotions and had died of exposure to optimism. During the height of the boom 337 banks were in operation in Chicago. Of these, only 197 were left at the beginning of 1932. Of the survivors thirty more fell by the wayside in the first five months of that year. Twelve banks in one chain had to close because they had got deeply involved in real estate promotions. The large Foreman-State National Bank and its affiliate, the Foreman-State Trust and Savings Bank, were rescued only by absorption into the First National Bank and its trust and savings affiliate. Nearly $1,000,000,000 in mortgage bonds had been issued on Chicago real estate between 1925 and 1928, a large part of it after the building spurt had slowed down. The neighborhood banks peddled mortgages on local properties and occasionally guaranteed to buy them back if the customer wasn't pleased. Naturally those which they got back were the worst of the lot.

Twice stung and thrice shy, the Chicago investor in real estate securities became afraid even of an obvious bargain. To help thaw out the pipes between the money market and the Chicago property owner, the RFC approved loans of $30,000,000 to the above-mentioned Fort Dearborn Mortgage Company. Only $12,000,000 of this money was drawn because, once the defrosting set in, private funds began to flow again.

In 1933, when Congress ordered the separation of investment from commercial banking, the Chicago Corporation bought out the position of the three banks in the new mortgage company and installed other management. As one property after another was unfrozen, the Fort Dearborn Mortgage Company was able to sell the mortgages to insurance companies and pay off its debt to the RFC.

10

✦

SELF-LIQUIDATING LOANS

Al Smith Asks for a Check—Huey Long Hankers for a Bridge—San Francisco Quarterback Calls Time Out—Making Bridges and Other Improvements Pay Their Way

THE loans for self-liquidating projects which Congress authorized the RFC to provide to states, municipalities, and other political subdivisions and, for certain purposes, to private corporations were but one phase of our public-works program, begun in the last year of the Hoover administration. Today the nation is dotted, from coast to coast and from the Rio Grande to the Great Lakes, with useful monuments to the wisdom of that legislation—great bridges, electric power plants and lines, express highways, waterworks, sewer systems, college dormitories, modern low-rent housing, aqueducts, vehicular tunnels, and other facilities.

Some of these rank among the chief prides of the communities for which they were constructed and are familiar "sights" for tourists. The Bay Bridge linking San Francisco with Oakland, the super-highway from Pittsburgh through and around the Alleghenies to Harrisburg, the 244-mile aqueduct which carries water from the Colorado River to Los Angeles, San Diego, and twenty-six smaller communities in southern California, three bridges over the lower Mississippi, one over the Hudson, a tunnel beneath and a bridge above the East River, and, but recently opened, a tunnel bored under New York Bay from the lower tip of Manhattan to Brooklyn—these are but a few of the many improvements financed by the RFC on a self-liquidating basis.

For each grandiose enterprise which required millions, often many millions, to build, there were scores of small-town improvements arranged on a pay-for-itself basis that called for only a few thousand dollars; just enough, in some cases, to provide a village with a pump, a water tank and some pipe, or to replace its outdoor privies with indoor sanitation.

In size the loans ranged from the $208,500,000 required to funnel the Colorado's water to Los Angeles down to the $500 that was sufficient to put up a canning "factory" in a little independent school district near Yoakum, Texas. With few exceptions the small enterprises, like the large, have paid their way in the manner anticipated when the loans were made.

Occasionally the visitor who came to us with a self-liquidating project in mind was a gentleman of such distinction that our entire board of directors would assemble to listen to him. One of the memorable callers was Alfred E. Smith. He came campaigning for money as he had done for votes, with brown derby, cigar, and a group of smart advisers. When he asked us for an appointment he was no longer Governor of New York. His desk was then in the Empire State Building, which he had recently opened. But he still fondly regarded as his "baby" many a state institution which had been started under his regime in Albany for the health and enjoyment of the people of New York.

One of these was Jones Beach, a playground for New Yorkers to enjoy on Long Island, an easy ride from the city. He wanted a few millions to finance the building of bridges, causeways, and other approaches to that splendid seaside resort. To our meeting he brought the capable Robert Moses, his State Park Commissioner, and half a dozen alert advisers.

I have seldom met a group as well informed about every phase of a project they wanted to promote as those associates of the Happy Warrior. No matter what the question put to Mr. Smith—and most of our directors thought up something to ask him—he would turn to one or another of the men he had brought with him and provide an answer, quick, pat, and complete. Our discussions with him lasted a good part of an afternoon. The meeting decided that the Jones Beach loan was to be for $5,050,000.

"Now, gentlemen," said Al with an affable air, "each of you has been firing questions at me. Before we break up I'd like to know if I can have permission to put a question to your chairman." He was told he might ask as many questions as he liked of any or all of us.

"No," he said, "there's only one thing I want to learn from your chairman. Where do we go to get the check?"

He was told where to get the check, and the enterprise paid off.

HUEY LONG HANKERS FOR A BRIDGE

There was, about the same time, another former Governor who also wanted a bridge, and a big one: Huey P. Long of Louisiana, then a United States Senator. Unlike Governor Smith, the Louisiana Kingfish had many questions he wanted answered; so many that, day after day for several weeks, he would telephone our offices. He frequently asked for Harvey Couch, one of our directors. Couch's railroad and utility interests extended from his own state of Arkansas over into the Kingfish's kingdom. Long also made persistent telephone calls to Francis T. P. Plimpton, the RFC's general solicitor.

A bridge across the Mississippi at New Orleans was but one of many things he had in mind for us to finance in his neck of the woods. The subject of whether college dormitories could properly be considered as self-liquidating projects was then on our table. The Kingfish was hankering to get his hands on funds to enlarge the building program at Louisiana State University, of which institution he had come to think himself the chief panjandrum. He was so insistent in his daily telephoning that Mr. Couch finally called Mr. Plimpton and said: "I don't want you to do anything you shouldn't do, but please get the Kingfish off my neck."

Whether the Kingfish got off Mr. Couch's neck I don't know; but we did allocate $13,000,000 to build his pet bridge, $1,700,000 to construct dormitories at L.S.U. and A. & M., $1,500,000 for an airport at New Orleans, and smaller sums for other projects in Louisiana. All these loans turned out well.

Before the bridge was completed, the assassinated Kingfish had gone to his ornate grave; but the political and social conflicts he had started lived after him. On the day the bridge was opened an army of his admirers gathered on one side of the Mississippi, an anti-Long contingent on the other. There had to be two tape-cutting ceremonies. At one end of the bridge the late Senator's daughter held the scissors; at the other the snipping was accomplished by the daughter of the Mayor of New Orleans. That evening at the dinner to celebrate the occasion, the hostile groups occupied tables at opposite ends of the room. Morton Macartney, the chief engineer of the RFC, who had gone to New Orleans for the ceremony, had the delicate task of assuming a neutral position. Mr. Macartney supervised the building of the $208,000,000 water line from the Colorado River to Los Angeles, the San Francisco-Oakland Bay Bridge and many other projects, large and small.

During the war he had general supervision of the construction of plants for Defense Plant Corporation and measured up to the responsibilities of that very important job. He is still with the Corporation as its principal administrative officer, a most able, trustworthy gentleman.

On the Bay Bridge and the Los Angeles water line, we also employed Robert J. Cummins of Houston, Texas, one of the country's outstanding engineers, to make periodic inspections during construction of these two important projects in cooperation with Mr. Macartney and the engineers on the jobs.

Originally the self-liquidating loans were authorized by Congress in order to provide employment. It was a new field for all of us on the board of directors, and we were fortunate in obtaining at the outset, at President Hoover's suggestion, the services of five of the country's most distinguished engineers. They were Professor C. D. Marx of Leland Stanford University; Major General Lytle Brown, chief of engineers, United States Army; John Lyle Harrington of Kansas City; John Francis Coleman of New Orleans; and John Herbert Gregory of Johns Hopkins University, Baltimore.

When we employed outside engineers or other experts we could pay them only $30 a day; but none, regardless of his eminence, ever declined employment by us when requested.

To us, as well as to the people of Louisiana and their neighbors, the bridge across the Mississippi at New Orleans was a successful enterprise. We sold its bonds at a profit of about $900,000. The $1,700,000 loan for dormitories at L.S.U. and A. & M. College also seasoned well, as did similar loans to other state colleges and universities.

The two other bridges over the Mississippi, both vehicular, built under our loan program are at Natchez and Greenville, Mississippi. The New Orleans bridge was but one of many projects whose bonds we were able to sell to the public at a profit through investment houses, and with no recourse whatever on the Corporation. On the bonds of the San Francisco to Oakland Bay Bridge, for which we loaned $73,000,000, we made several millions. On the Metropolitan Water District of Southern California bonds of $208,000,000 we made about $12,000,000. These loans were authorized at 5 per cent interest; but, as the bond market improved and we were able to get a premium for securities we were selling, we reduced the interest rate, first to 4 per cent, then to 3½ per cent.

In all classes of RFC operations except disaster loans, we tried to make enough money on the bananas to offset our losses on the peanuts, and succeeded.

The 244-mile Colorado River Aqueduct, which is the lifeline for the people in the Los Angeles and San Diego areas of California and which cost more than $200,000,000, was, with the exception of $2,100,000, entirely financed by the RFC. It was started in 1933 and opened in August, 1941. Without this water, tapped from the Colorado River near Parker, Arizona, southern California could not support its present population. More than three and one-half million people now depend upon this supply, and it can meet the need of ten millions.

The Metropolitan Water District of Southern California, which operates the aqueduct, was created in 1928, five years after a far-sighted engineer, William Mulholland, had stuffed his pack and started out over the desert on a reconnaissance mission to the Colorado River. In July, 1929, F. E. Weymouth, who had had extensive engineering experience all over the United States and in Mexico, took charge. Three years later, when the RFC was authorized to make loans to self-liquidating projects, he made the first of his many calls on us in Washington. He died one week before the aqueduct went on an operating basis in 1941.

Interest payments on the aqueduct's bonds averaged about $7,-000,000 a year through the 1940's; but from 1952 until 1975 the load will be only a little over $5,000,000 a year. Thereafter, with maturities, it will gradually drop down yearly to the easy final payment of less than $35,000 in 1988.

SAN FRANCISCO QUARTERBACK CALLS TIME OUT

The San Francisco-Oakland Bay Bridge had been advocated by Herbert Hoover long before he became President. It had been recom-

mended by a commission of which he and C. C. Young, who was
Governor of California from 1927 to 1930, were the joint heads.
It was, of course, enthusiastically supported as a project by the
forward-looking businessmen of the San Francisco Bay area. Three
of these gentlemen, Leland W. Cutler, an insurance executive and
civic leader, Charles Purcell, an engineer, and Joseph Knowland,
publisher of the Oakland *Tribune* and father of United States Senator
William Fife Knowland, brought the bridge dream to Washington
and presented it to our board only a few weeks after we had begun
making loans on self-liquidating projects.

Though long on enthusiasm, they seemed a little short on data
we asked about, such as the annual revenue and daily traffic of the
ferries crossing San Francisco Bay. It was obvious they were somewhat embarrassed by an inability to answer some of the questions
fired by our directors. Director Harvey Couch, over whose desk
self-liquidating loans reached our board at that time, turned to Mr.
Cutler and asked him what position he'd played on the football team
when he was in school. Mr. Cutler said he'd played quarterback.

"And when the team got some signals mixed and seemed confused,
what would you do?" asked Mr. Couch.

"I'd ask for time out," Mr. Cutler replied.

It was then agreed he'd better ask for a week's time out, and we
set the bridge application on our order of business for seven days
later, at which time the requested information was on hand.

The Southern Pacific Railroad agreed to eliminate its automobile
ferry service when the bridge was completed. But there was no
accurate way of figuring how much traffic would develop for the
long, seven and one-half mile double-deck structure. Some San Francisco interests advocated using busses as public carriers across the
bridge; others favored electric trains. It was partly to get an outsider's independent judgment from a distinguished engineer who
had been in San Francisco only one day in his life that I asked Mr.
Cummins to go out there and make periodic reports, inspections,
and suggestions.

He recommended trains rather than busses. He was wise in doing
so. The engineers estimated that it would require a toll of 65 cents
for automobiles to meet the interest and principal payments on the
loan. A condition of our loan was that the toll for private automobiles
should be 65 cents, and that the bridge authority would not reduce

it without our permission as long as we held the bonds. It began earning so well that we soon allowed a toll reduction; first, I think, to 50 cents, then to 35. Today the toll is 25 cents, the bridge is making money, and the traffic is so thick that plans for a second bridge across the Bay are being evolved and its location debated.

MAKING BRIDGES AND OTHER IMPROVEMENTS PAY THEIR WAY

Our self-liquidating loans not only provided hundreds of thousands of jobs but acted as a nation-wide stimulant to business, since each contractor had to buy materials from many sources as well as hire labor on the task itself. When we started these loans in the summer of 1932, the market for nearly all securities had about dried up. Two or three years later, a fine bond market existed and continued for several years. This helped us dispose of many of our holdings at very satisfactory premiums.

Among the self-liquidating loans we authorized was $8,075,000 for Knickerbocker Village, a low-rent housing development in New York City; $6,090,600 to the Middle Rio Grande Conservancy District in New Mexico for the completion of an irrigation project; $3,400,000 for the Rip Van Winkle Bridge across the Hudson at Catskill, New York; $2,815,000 for the Niagara Frontier Bridges, near Buffalo; and $3,200,000 for the Spa at Saratoga Springs, New York. The bonds on the Saratoga Springs development were bought from us as an investment by the New York State Sinking Fund Commission.

To the State of Washington we loaned $3,520,000 to construct a vehicular bridge at Puget Sound. Two and one-half millions went into the building of a vehicular tunnel under the Mobile River on the Old Spanish Trail in Alabama. We loaned the City of Utica, New York, $7,900,000 to build a waterworks system and advanced $1,800,000 to Westchester County, New York, for a bridge.

Thousands of farmers benefited from our many loans on irrigation projects. One of these provided $5,000,000 for a series of dams and canals along the upper Rio Grande near Albuquerque, New Mexico. In carrying out another irrigation plan which we financed in Colorado, the engineers altered at one place the designs of Nature in creating the Great Divide. Through a tunnel built with RFC funds, water that had always flowed to the Gulf of Mexico was turned and headed down the slope which drains into the Pacific Ocean.

As the news got around that our purse strings were being loosened in Washington, city boosters in almost every section of the country began erupting with plans and dreams which, in many cases, looked quite pretty until one studied their potentialities for paying their way out of the debts they would need to contract. Before these well intentioned planners got the money, we often had to require them to tone down their visions. Our supervising engineers appreciated architectural beauty as well as the next fellow; but, like the rest of us in the RFC, they had been schooled to think black ink more attractive than red.

The heavy shifts of population which the war brought about more than justified one of our earlier loans—that of $10,500,000 to extend, improve, and refinance the Seattle municipal street railways. Had the lines not been lengthened and the equipment increased, Seattle would not have been able to handle the problem of moving daily from home to work and back again the vast civilian army of men and women who later flocked into that city to take jobs in the expanding defense industries.

On most self-liquidating loans we charged 4 per cent interest so long as the RFC held the security. We had started out, in 1932 and 1933, with higher rates—4½, 5, and 5½ per cent—but we came down to 4 per cent on April 1, 1934. If a loan had been made at one of the higher rates and had been reduced by us to 4 per cent, the higher rate was sometimes resumed when we sold the security. However, a reduction was frequently achieved by refunding.

On most of the self-liquidating projects our loans paid for the entire construction cost; but on many others begun under the New Deal we lent only part of the money needed to carry out a program. The remainder was provided as an outright grant by the Public Works Administration. This cooperation between the RFC and the PWA, the RFC lending 55 per cent of the cost and PWA making a grant of 4 per cent, proved helpful in promoting work through the construction of useful projects. As an example, to build the 160-mile toll highway from Pittsburgh to Harrisburg, RFC loaned the Pennsylvania Turnpike Commission $35,000,000, and PWA made a grant of the remainder.

*   *   *

We approved more than $145,000,000 in loans to drainage, levee and irrigation districts. We undertook to reduce and refinance the outstanding indebtedness of hundreds of drainage, levee, and irrigation districts which had overoptimistically sprouted in many of the agricultural states during the boom seasons of the 1920's. With the depression and tumbling prices for land and its products, many of these districts bogged down into their soggy debts. The farmers and other landowners had been unable to meet the water charges and other assessments on which the securities depended to be kept current.

The situation was particularly bad in rural Illinois, Missouri, Florida, Mississippi, Colorado, California, some areas in the Northwest, and the Rio Grande citrus belt in Texas. District after district, formed during the hopeful 1920's, had issued 6 per cent bonds on rosy assumptions of what the land could bear in assessments. When both land values and farm produce prices skidded to lower and lower levels, these reckonings went haywire.

Upon entering these melancholy pastures and farmlands, the RFC appraiser's job was to rejudge the ability of the land to produce and then establish a new price for the outstanding bonds. Our intention was to buy the slumped securities and refund the local district set-up, whatever it happened to be. This was a rather ticklish business. Often we thought it wise to buy the bonds at perhaps twice their depressed market value. These securities were held, for the most part, by individuals rather than by banks. Had word of our intention and the price we might pay got abroad, it would have opened up a luscious field for speculators in every neighborhood we entered. Thus it was essential that our appraisers keep their judgments secret. Before the job was done we had taken up in one manner or another some seven hundred projects scattered over twenty-six states. The holders of the old bonds received an average of 48 per cent of the face value of their securities.

In place of the 6 per cent bonds, we refinanced with 4 per cent issues. This interest reduction and a reduction in the face amount of the bonds cut the actual charges to the farmer to about one-third of what they had been. We estimated that this refunding program directly benefited 134,662 farms.

The obligations of these political subdivisions are nontaxable for federal income-tax purposes, whereas the federal government 2½ per cent bonds are taxable. So we found an excellent market. Usually, by holding the bonds awhile to let them season, we were able to sell them at a premium. With the improvement in agriculture and land prices, the entire list of seven hundred projects, with only one defaulting exception, was able to pay out or to keep current on its obligations.

It was June 14, 1933, before we got well into the reorganization of drainage and irrigation districts. To do the job, we looked about for a man who had had experience in that line. Henry T. Rainey of Illinois, Speaker of the House of Representatives, recommended Emil Schram, a farmer neighbor of his who was chairman of the board of directors of the National Drainage Association. We employed Mr. Schram, and he set about his task in a big way and did an excellent job.

11

AID TO STATES AND CITIES

*Bee Line by Governors and Mayors to the Dinner Table—
Gifford Pinchot Asks for the Moon—Paying Chicago's
Schoolteachers—Getting the "Little Flower" and the
Bankers Together—Moochers and Meddlers and FDR—
Mr. Ickes as a Doubting Thomas*

AT THE start it was not the intent of Congress that the RFC should
ever play Santa Claus with the public's money. As unemployment and other maladies of a depressed economy became epidemic,
many of the forty-eight states and hundreds of cities, towns and
counties sent politicians to Washington to plead for federal relief
funds. What they wanted was money they wouldn't have to pay back.

Partly in response to their entreaties, Congress passed the Emergency Relief and Construction Act of 1932. Among other new powers,
it gave the RFC, in that last summer of the fading Hoover administration, authority to distribute up to $300,000,000 for relief pur-
poses among the forty-eight states and three territories—Alaska,
Hawaii, and Puerto Rico.

That was the opening wedge for the siphon through which, later
on, the New Deal poured billions in grants, gifts, and doles. Between
1933 and 1937 more than $2,000,000,000, mostly earmarked for
relief, was funneled by Congressional direction through the RFC
to other government agencies. These agencies passed the funds along
to the ultimate recipients of the federal bounty. Some of the money
was used to feed, clothe, and shelter the destitute.

In handling those relief funds the RFC directors were given no
discretionary powers. We simply did what Congress told us to do.
We did it on such a scale that the allocations to other agencies, on

which we had no say, amounted to $2,785,867,007, including interest.

That money was not recoverable. So, in 1938, we asked Congress to direct the Secretary of the Treasury to cancel the RFC's notes to that extent, together with interest we had paid the Treasury on the money. Our request was granted. Our books once more were on a business basis. After all, those allocations had not been business transactions. The sum simply represented the cost of using the RFC as one of Santa Claus' many sleighs. It was divided as follows:

Allocations to other government agencies for relief and other purposes	$2,469,670,094
Advances for relief to States, Territories, and political subdivisions	282,825,767
Interest paid the Treasury on the foregoing funds	33,177,420

TOTAL $2,785,673,281

In 1932 the members of Congress intended that the States should reimburse the RFC for its relief funds. By 1933, harking to political ear poundings from back home, Congress changed its mind and authorized us to forgive those debts. The 1932 legislation had provided that the RFC would be repaid with 3 per cent interest, through deductions from future federal apportionments of highway funds to the States. Most of the $300,000,000 originally authorized had been distributed before the Hoover administration made way for the incoming Roosevelt regime.

Even before we rang the dinner bell there was quite a scramble among the governors to get a place near the head of our table. Under the law, 15 per cent of the $300,000,000 was all any single state or territory could get. If seven states first applying for aid had asked for and been granted $45,000,000 each, nothing would have been left for the other forty-four states and territories. That did not deter some of the applicants from asking for the moon.

GIFFORD PINCHOT ASKS FOR THE MOON

Three days before the Relief Act became law, the fiery Governor Gifford Pinchot of Pennsylvania, the second richest state, filed an application with us for what he called his state's "full share." He wanted $45,000,000, he said, and he asked that $10,000,000 of it be made available to him immediately.

Neither request was fully granted. Yet, before we were done with the program, Pennsylvania had received $34,929,875. Not, however, until at our insistence the Pennsylvania legislature had matched us dollar for dollar with appropriations for relief. At every step of the way Governor Pinchot kept repeating that his state was not able to do what the members of our board felt it could and should do— bear half the burden. But it did.

Illinois received the largest grants—$43,191,721—the distress among the unemployed in the Chicago area being extremely acute. Altogether we disbursed over $282,000,000 to the Governors of the various states.

After June 1, 1933, direct federal relief was taken over by Harry L. Hopkins and the new Federal Emergency Relief Administration. Soon the number of Americans on relief rolls increased to nearly 17,000,000.

What few millions the states had not drained out from our original $300,000,000 relief funds were loaned to cities and counties. We took their securities at 3 per cent. Those localized loans were almost fully repaid.

American municipalities, like the states, were far from bashful in begging Washington for help. Many of them had been prodigal and were using loans against next year's expected taxes to meet this year's bills. The Mayors of New York, Boston, Chicago, Milwaukee, and scores of smaller communities hustled to Washington, hats in hand.

After the breakdown of the banking structure in 1933, numerous municipalities had been unable to borrow further on tax anticipation warrants. In some cases the balances on such borrowings were frozen in closed banks. To make matters worse, many a taxpayer who owed such a stricken local government also had his funds tied up in the same closed banks, so that he could not get his money to pay his taxes. The delinquent's home became subject to sale for tax purposes. Often as not he had no job. In some cities teachers, policemen, firemen, civil servants, and the dogcatcher all were obliged to get along for various periods without their usual pay checks. In those dark days a city which seized a house or a business building to sell for taxes usually found there was no market for it. Early in 1934 New York City put up at a tax sale 600 parcels of real estate. There were bids on only two of the properties.

About that time a bill was introduced in Congress which would have empowered us to aid in financing boroughs, villages, towns, and cities by accepting their tax anticipation notes as security. I did not undertake to tell Congress whether it ought to enact such legislation. I did, however, give my views on the illimitable difficulties and political wire pullings the legislation would engender to the House Bank and Currency Committee during its consideration of the bill.

"I have never thought it desirable," I remarked to the Committee in February, 1934, "for the Government to start lending to States, counties and municipalities. It is a very dangerous procedure to embark upon. I do not know where it will lead. I think you will be subject to all the pressures in the world. They will get the loans first and repudiate them afterwards—or should we say they will find that they are not able to pay them?

"In the first place we have no way of knowing how much money it will take. If this is going to be done, certainly there should be a survey of the entire country to get some idea of what the problem is, and the size of it. I have thought also that if you should enact such a law as to permit this, that there ought to be a yardstick drawn, and that would be difficult.

"If a city is actually trying to live within its budget, and there are reasons for its being in debt, and having to borrow, I think I would be disposed to help; but, by and large, in these cities, politics do not permit trimming the budget.

". . . I think possibly there are cases where help is needed and would be justified. I am sure, however, you will want to give it very serious consideration. If you should take the bridle off and make it possible for anybody to come in, you gentlemen would pretty nearly have to abdicate; your constituents would all come to Washington and they would all be over here at the Capitol. It is pretty hard to continually say no."

PAYING CHICAGO'S SCHOOLTEACHERS

Congress did not take the bridle off. It did, however, further amend the RFC Act so as to permit us to make loans to cities to enable them to pay teachers' salaries due prior to June 1, 1934, when properly secured. The amendment was introduced by Representative

Adolph J. Sabath of Chicago. At that time—February, 1934—his city was two years behind in collecting taxes. Since the previous May there had been no salary checks for sixteen thousand schoolteachers and three thousand other employees of the Board of Education. The teachers had already taken cuts of 26 per cent in pay—and they were not receiving the reduced pay. Chicago's banks, eager to keep very liquid after the many failures of the previous years, wouldn't lend the city any more money, and the State made relief funds available only for current operations. Chicago's teachers were in a truly pitiable plight.

The following summer, after Representative Sabath's bill had become law, I went to Chicago and spent two days with the President of the Board of Education and its counsel and arranged to lend them $26,300,000 so they could pay the teachers' salaries long overdue. Many teachers had run out of funds to meet the rent or pay the grocer. On the morning of August 26, when the money was made available, more than five thousand teachers formed lines around the old bank building in North Wells Street where the checks were handed out. Some of them had been in line all night long.

Disbursal of the $26,300,000 greatly improved both economic conditions and general morale in Chicago and made it easier for the city to undertake subsequent financing in other quarters. Four months after making the loan we were able to sell it at a premium of $223,000. We purposely had held the securities until the city got its financing straightened out.

The Sabath amendment had authorized us to lend school districts up to $75,000,000 for the purpose of paying back salaries to teachers. It stipulated that we might accept security in the form of a first lien upon real property of such school districts provided the property was not used for school purposes. Of all the applicants only Chicago had such property, although back in 1818 when the State of Illinois was organized the Federal Government had ceded certain public lands to the State on the condition that one section—always Section 16—of such lands in each township should be kept in trust for educational purposes.

The Chicago Board of Education had held on to about 200 pieces of real estate other than its school buildings. Among them was an entire block in the heart of the downtown Loop district—the block bounded by State, Madison, Dearborn, and Monroe streets. Even in those days of depressed prices it was valued at $10,000,000. We took a lien on it and some other properties. Most of the communities which needed similar help for their unpaid teachers were unable to obtain it from us because they could offer as security only their school buildings.

Philadelphia was another city which let itself drop into a desperate financial condition. In 1939 its municipal employees were not being paid. John B. Kelly, the local Democratic leader, and Bernard Samuel, then chairman of the City Council's finance committee, appealed to us. The RFC arranged to cooperate with the leading banks of Philadelphia by buying half of a $41,000,000 issue of 3½ per cent revenue-trust certificates secured by assignment of $4,200,000 a year from the revenues of the Philadelphia Gas Works. This enabled the city to give its employees their back pay. In the early part of the depression, when Detroit was one of the blackest spots on the industrial map, we had been able to answer some of the appeals of Frank Murphy, then Mayor of that city, for financial help.

GETTING THE "LITTLE FLOWER" AND THE BANKERS TOGETHER

Sometimes we were able to help a city indirectly. I happened to be in New York in July, 1934, just after the City of New York had offered $75,000,000 of its bonds and had received only one bid, which came from a syndicate of seventy banks headed by the Chase National Bank. The bid was a stupid one in the manner in which it was submitted. For some unaccountable reason, the part of the bonds which matured in one year, as I recall, bore 6 per cent interest, but the average of the whole bid was 4.03 per cent. The latter was too high a rate for New York, our largest and richest city, to have to pay, and 6 per cent for one year was absurd. Mayor Fiorello H. La Guardia publicly accused the bankers of ganging up on him and appealed to me. On the evening of the day he opened the bid he came to my hotel accompanied by his City Chamberlain, Adolf A. Berle, Jr., who was an RFC alumnus, and City Comptroller Joseph D. McGoldrick. I told them we could not make the loan. The next morning at about eight o'clock, the Mayor came to my hotel room and told me that he intended to see Winthrop W. Aldrich, chairman of the Chase National Bank, and tell him he was going to borrow money from the RFC. I explained again to the Mayor that we could not make the loan. He said, "Please don't tell them so," and asked me to talk to Mr. Aldrich and see if we could not get the city a more favorable rate.

After my talk with Mr. Aldrich, he agreed to take the bonds at an average of about 3.75 per cent, or a saving to the City on that particular issue of about $3,500,000. The bonds were subscribed several times over when offered by the banks.

While I did not offer to buy any of the New York City bonds and the RFC had no authority to do so, the Corporation got credit for coming to the rescue of the city.

As a result of the reduced rate, all New York City bonds had an immediate advance on the market. Such deals had a wholesome effect on the whole bond-market situation.

In 1941 the State of Arkansas needed to refinance $136,000,000 of outstanding highway bonds. Some of these were the state's own bonds, others the issues of road districts. The bonds varied from 3 per cent to 5 per cent, and many of them were nearing maturity.

Governor Homer Adkins had been figuring with a banking syndicate, again headed by the Chase National in New York, to refund these bonds. He reported to me that the bankers thought they could handle only $90,000,000 of the issue, and he wanted the RFC to take the balance. That put us into contact with the Chase. They wanted 3½ per cent interest. I took the position with the bankers that the rate was too high for a state bond; that, if they would make it 3 per cent, the RFC would take half of the issue and allow them to sell their half first. This they declined. Then I suggested the same deal at 3¼ per cent. Again they declined. On the day before the bonds were to be sold, I told the bankers that we would bid for the entire issue. Accordingly, the RFC put in a bid at 3 per cent for $105,000,000 and 3¼ per cent for $31,000,000. I have forgotten what the Chase bid; but we bought the bonds and, the first day, sold $10,000,000 of the 3 per cent bonds to the Bank of America in California at a premium of 1 per cent, or $100,000.

Three weeks later we sold $15,000,000 of the 3's to Halsey, Stuart & Company, Chicago, and $35,000,000 to the Chase National syndicate at a premium of 1½ per cent—a profit of $750,000. Chase and

Halsey, Stuart found a ready market with the public at a substantial profit to them. The rest of the issue we sold to Halsey, Stuart at a still higher premium.

Over the life of the bonds the refunding operation will save the State of Arkansas $28,000,000 in interest. While the RFC made probably a million and a half dollars, the syndicates who sold the bonds to the public made their customary profits.

MOOCHERS AND MEDDLERS AND FDR

In our financial assistance to states, cities, and other public bodies, we occasionally had meddlers wanting to muscle in for a little private smoosh. These approaches were apt to come from any direction.

For example, the bond issue for power and flood-control developments on the lower Colorado River in Texas. Although this was a Public Works Administration project, the RFC bought the bonds, as in many PWA operations. When the payment of the securities we bought for public enterprises was dependent upon the income and earnings of the project, we usually held them until the enterprise had proven successful, because we felt that the government had no right to sell a doubtful security.

One day during a Cabinet meeting the President scribbled and handed to me a little note which read:

> "*Private*
>
> J. J.
>
> Don't sell the Lower Colorado River Auth.
>
> bonds without talking with Father.
>
> FDR"

What this meant was that some moocher had been to see the President, looking for an inside deal. I told the President we usually sold such securities to the highest bidder—and, later, we did in this case. The clients of the man who had seen the President were not the successful bidders.

Indirectly the RFC financed many PWA projects. In 1934 Secretary Ickes was eager for Congress to permit him to sell securities taken for Public Works projects in the market and reinvest the money. He wanted legislation comparable to that granted the RFC. The RFC was authorized to borrow money on the credit of the government, to lend it, and, when collected, to retain it for further use without having to go back to Congress for more money. That was what Mr. Ickes wanted for his PWA; but Congress did not give him the authority.

After consulting with me Congress did, however, authorize the RFC to buy his securities. I agreed with the Committee from Congress that, if Congress wished it, we would buy PWA securities that we thought were sound; but I told them we would want a limit of $250,000,000 on the amount we could have invested in such securities at any one time. This would permit us to sell and rebuy and thus serve as a clearinghouse for the PWA's securities. In that way Mr. Ickes got his money for much of his work by selling his bonds to the RFC instead of going to Congress. He did not especially like the arrangement, but it served his purpose.

MR. ICKES AS A DOUBTING THOMAS

When the law was passed authorizing us to buy PWA bonds, I realized that because of the peculiar nature of Mr. Ickes, who rightfully calls himself the old curmudgeon, he or his officers might possibly undertake to make the plan unworkable in order to go back to Congress for his funds. So I prepared a letter to him, agreeing to buy at par and accrued interest such of his securities as we thought were sound. In selling them, if we made a profit, we would pass the profit along to him; and if there were a loss it would be an RFC loss. Furthermore, I proposed that the RFC would bear the expense of buying and selling these securities. This was a one-sided contract, but my purpose was to avoid friction, and since it was all government money—a deal between two agencies—I thought it advisable.

I went to Secretary Ickes' office with my prepared proposal. All he had to do was accept it. He read it and, as I recall, exclaimed: "This won't even cost us a postage stamp!"

I said: "That's correct."

He asked: "Where's the catch?"

I replied that there was no catch, that it was simply cooperation between government departments in the interest of the government. He signed the agreement, and the matter was handled amicably between his department and ours.

By holding the securities taken over from the PWA and watching the market, we were often able to get premiums in selling them.

From June 19, 1934, to December 31, 1943, inclusive, we bought securities from the PWA having a par value of $694,739,787.58. There were more than four thousand blocks of these securities embracing in excess of three thousand different issues. Of these we sold during that nine-year period $557,628,031.54 at a premium of $14,472,618.75.

At the beginning we took the cream, buying at par the more easily salable securities in the PWA portfolio. Later we took the less desirable ones at a discount, usually 66⅔ cents on the dollar. The net premiums on the securities went to the credit of the PWA. Finally, when Mr. Ickes' work as PWA administrator was finished, his organization asked us to make an offer on their remaining portfolio, the bonds that were not up to par. We examined them carefully and paid, as I recall, 60 cents on the dollar for the balance. But under our agreement we had made profits enough for Mr. Ickes on the bonds we had sold at a premium to cover the discount on those that we bought at less than par, and to give him a profit.

In addition to the offerings of political subdivisions, the PWA sold to the RFC $199,000,000 in railway securities, practically all of which were disposed of in a few years' time. More than half of these were equipment trust certificates.

In the final wind-up, the RFC will make a substantial profit for PWA under our letter agreement. At the end of the fiscal year of 1949 the RFC still listed on its books $12,473,196 of securities taken over from the Ickes organization.

12

❊

LOANS TO BUSINESS AND INDUSTRY

*Saving a Department Store Chain—Pulling Passaic Out of
a Hole—The Postal Merger with Western Union—Zane
Grey's Characters Become Collateral—New Industries for
the South—Mice and Men and Money*

IN JUNE, 1934, Congress gave the RFC still another assignment.
We were authorized to make loans to business and industry. Such
loans were not allowed when the Corporation was created. Over
the next four years we made about nine thousand, aggregating almost
$500,000,000. Contrary to the impression some of our critics sought
to create, most of this money went to little-businessmen, rather than
to big corporations. More than a third of the loans were for $5,000
or less, well over half were for $10,000 or less. Loans of $50,000
and more amounted to only 17 per cent of the whole.

Our directors and executives gave a great deal of time to the
smaller business loans. We usually tried to get the applicant's home-
town banker to join us in such a loan. The law specified that we
should lend only where the borrower could not get the money from
others on reasonable terms.

At one time I sent a letter to every one of the 14,000 banks in
the United States asking their cooperation in making loans to business. Only 1 per cent acknowledged receipt of our letter. That seems
hardly credible, because more than half of the banks had been
directly assisted by the RFC and all had been indirectly assisted; but
it is human to forget.

Whenever possible we preferred that the bank share proportionately with us in the security and in repayments. Where the bank
wished us to do so we allowed it to carry the entire loan with a

definite commitment from the RFC to take over that part of the loan which we had underwritten without recourse on the bank. For the commitment the RFC charged a small part of the interest, but without additional charge to the borrower. This afforded the bank a profitable investment for its loanable funds which was convertible into cash at any time. Of our first nine thousand business loans banks shared in about twenty-five hundred.

Bankers had many reasons for reluctance to make business loans. From their recollections of the collapse in 1929–1930 emerged the realization that too much debt had been one of its principal causes. Even in good times banks do not like to make slow loans, or loans which the bank examiners class as slow. However, time loans are no longer criticized by the examining authorities. They afford the use of much of a bank's loanable funds.

Many of our business loans were made to keep people at work at a time when millions were walking the streets. Some were of a sort that no one would have expected a careful banker to make. They kept small enterprises from going under and dragging more men and women into the slough of the idle. Although we went further than banks should go, we did it with care and with due consideration of the surrounding circumstances.

In 1934, when Congress first authorized the RFC to make loans directly to industry, the law provided that they should be "adequately" secured. Previously the requirement on all loans had been "fully and adequately secured." The provision respecting loans to industry was later, at our request, changed to read that such loans be so secured as "reasonably to assure repayment." Partly because of this more liberal language and policy, the percentage of losses on our small business loans ran to about 10 per cent.

SAVING A DEPARTMENT STORE CHAIN

The ups and downs in the volume of sales by department stores register the changes in a community's economic condition about as well as any other gauge we possess. Whenever a store whose name for many years has been familiar to almost everyone within a city's trading area goes on the rocks, its liquidation hurts many people, especially the hapless men and women who were on its pay rolls.

The National Department Stores, Inc., with headquarters in New

Acme Photos

TWO SELF-LIQUIDATING PROJECTS FINANCED BY THE RFC

Top: Construction on Manhattan approach to the Brooklyn-Battery Tunnel.
Bottom: The World's deepest highway cut, on the Pennsylvania Turnpike.

ANOTHER JOB FOR DISASTER LOAN CORPORATION

Hurricane damage at New London, Connecticut, September, 1938.

York City, got into trouble. It had stores in Philadelphia, Pittsburgh, Cleveland, Detroit, Trenton, Atlanta, Memphis, Houston, San Antonio, Richmond, Minneapolis, St. Louis, and Portland, Oregon. Some of them were subsidiary corporations of the holding company, and were in good circumstances. But the parent company was reorganized in February, 1935, under section 77B of the Bankruptcy and Receivership Law.

Earl B. Schwulst, now President of the Bowery Savings Bank in New York, ran our Industrial Loan Department. He and Harry H. Schwartz, for the borrower, worked out a plan of rehabilitation. We made separate loans to eight of the stores, aggregating $2,250,000.

*   *   *

As a matter of policy we did not lend to pay existing debts, though thousands of borrowers and would-be borrowers would have liked us to. Before making our money available to Mr. Schwartz, we required him to get a general hold-off agreement from his bankers, landlords, venders, and others to whom his stores were indebted. His company agreed to pay its other creditors 25 per cent in cash and the remainder in 6 per cent preferred stock with the exception of the banks, which took notes instead. No dividends were allowed until the companies had paid off their debts to the RFC. By 1944 the last of these loans was paid in full.

Applicants would not always tell their true conditions, and frequently were overoptimistic as to when they could repay loans. Men in trouble are sometimes afraid to request enough money or sufficient time to repay for fear they will be turned down. I advised our executives and loan men, when authorizing a business or industrial loan, to use their judgment as to whether the applicant was asking for money enough or time enough in which to repay it. We adopted a policy in many cases of not making a business or industrial loan unless we were prepared to consider a second or third application.

PULLING PASSAIC OUT OF A HOLE

The case of the Botany Worsted Mills in Passaic, New Jersey, comes to mind. That concern is headed by Colonel Charles F. H. Johnson, a very able gentleman.

Colonel Johnson had been trying for some weeks to get an RFC loan. It was a doubtful situation, and our staff with my concurrence had about decided not to make the loan. The Colonel persisted. One of our directors asked that I see the Colonel, which I was glad to do. His application was for $1,000,000. When Colonel Johnson came in I asked him how much business he had done the previous year. He said $14,000,000. He said he had manufactured and sold that amount of merchandise. I then asked him how much money he had made, and he replied that he had made no money and had lost none. I remarked to him that our boys had told me he was a good salesman, but that I thought he was a poor salesman to manufacture and sell $14,000,000 worth of merchandise and not make any money. The trouble obviously was that he had been selling goods at sacrifice prices to meet pay rolls. I asked him how many people he employed. He said about five thousand. I then realized what it would mean if his company failed, and told the Colonel that we would lend him the million dollars he had applied for, and would probably have to lend him another million, if not more, but on the condition that we put a man on his Finance Committee to see that he did not sell merchandise except at a reasonable profit; that if he followed that course, and the million gave out, we would lend him another and maybe still another. We put A. B. Jones of New York City, an associate of mine in the real estate business, on his committee.

The Colonel worked out his problems, paid his debts, and kept the five thousand people employed. That saved the town of Passaic. Had the mill closed, practically everything else in Passaic would have withered. Colonel Johnson found A. B. Jones so useful as a constructive force in his organization that even after he had paid his debt to the RFC he continued Mr. Jones' employment as a consultant. For his mill to have closed, throwing five thousand people out of work, would have cost the government a great deal more than the loan, even if we had lost a part of it. As I thought might be the case, the million-dollar loan was not enough and was substantially increased from time to time; but it was fully repaid.

THE POSTAL MERGER WITH WESTERN UNION

A series of business loans made by the RFC led the way to the absorption of the Postal Telegraph Company by the Western Union after sixty years of unprofitable competition. Largely because of the development of wireless transmission and the growth of long-distance telephone service, the telegraph business had begun to decline even before the depression. With scientific advances competition sharpened yearly. By 1940, Postal Telegraph was about to go broke.

We nursed the company along for several years, making it loans up to $12,600,000. Finally, I suggested to Albert N. Williams, president of Western Union, and Edwin F. Chinlund, president of Postal, that they consolidate. The telegraph business seemed to me to be one of the few that could be accepted as a natural monopoly.

We used our influence on the Hill to have Congress enact the permissive legislation, which President Roosevelt signed on March 8, 1943. I then got the heads of the companies together again, and they worked out a plan by which Western Union acquired the Postal properties and agreed to take care of Postal's fifteen thousand employees. Postal's debt to the RFC was fully repaid the following January.

ZANE GREY'S CHARACTERS BECOME COLLATERAL

Another interesting loan—of $34,000—was made in 1934 to the Altadena National Bank in California, of which Mrs. Lina Elise Grey, wife of the novelist, Zane Grey, was president. The bank was suffering from dwindling deposits, and Mrs. Grey was eager to pay off all the depositors 100 per cent and close it. In analyzing its assets, we found that they were not sufficient to secure the necessary loan. Mr. and Mrs. Grey then pledged some of their properties on Catalina Island, as well as the royalties on Mr. Grey's novels and residuals derived from the sale of his stories to the motion picture producers, to secure our advances. The Security-First National Bank of Los Angeles, which had a branch in Altadena, consented to buy the deposits of the liquidated bank. Mr. and Mrs. Grey paid off the RFC loan in less than a year and a half. The excellence of the security may be judged from the fact that after Mr. Grey's death in 1939 his publishers continued to bring out new books from the mass of manuscripts he left behind—and the royalties, of course, kept rolling in.

America's first underground parking garage, which has 1,400 stalls on four levels under Union Square in San Francisco, was partially financed by an RFC loan. After the proposition had been studied for two years the City of San Francisco, which owns the square, leased the subsoil to a corporation formed by San Francisco businessmen, and construction of the garage began in 1941. Of the $1,500,000 it required, the RFC supplied $850,000. The remainder —in preferred stock—was raised in subscriptions by firms doing business within two blocks of Union Square. The enterprise has been profitable from the start and is probably the forerunner of similar parking facilities in many of the larger, traffic-congested cities of the country.

*   *   *

But for the many loans made by the RFC to the canning industry in California, particularly during the middle 1930's, the effects of the depression upon that business would have been disastrous. We also helped lumber companies in northern California, Washington, and Oregon, as well as in the South. In some of the lumber loans in the Northwest, to both pine and redwood industries, L. M. Giannini arranged for the Bank of America to participate.

In 1938 and 1939 we agreed to participate to the extent of 75 per cent in loans of $400,000, made by the Merchants National Bank of Mobile, to provide new plant construction for the W. T. Smith Lumber Company of Chapman, Alabama. Its cuttings and excellent replanting programs range over more than a quarter-million acres. The Company is operated by four alert and intelligent brothers— Earl, Floyd, Julian, and Nicholas McGowin.

The company paid the loans in full by November, 1941.

NEW INDUSTRIES FOR THE SOUTH

Some of our business loans created new enterprises for the South. A series of advances to the Southland Paper Mills at Lufkin, Texas, put into operation early in 1940 the process of making newsprint from pine. For several years previously Dr. Charles H. Herty had manufactured newsprint experimentally from southern pine wood in his laboratory at Savannah, Georgia. It is his process that has brought this new industry to the South.

Loans to the Crossett Lumber Company at Crossett, Arkansas, aggregating $4,500,000, established a kraft paper industry in the piney woods during the depression. Another such loan was approved for the Southeast, where there was a good deal of scrub pine, but the applicant did not avail himself of the loan.

Paper mills in the South require second-growth timber, which is a continuing crop in pine-timber sections and thus provides a market for farmers. The Crossett kraft-paper mill in Arkansas has turned out to be a valuable social as well as economic asset to its section of the country. Our loan to that company contemplated a plant with a capacity of 150 tons per day; but the mill is now producing twice that amount of kraft paper and employs seven hundred persons. In 1949 the company paid out approximately $2,000,000 to outsiders for pulp wood and furnished a use for wood produced by its sawmill logging operations, which would have been wasted had not the paper mill been close to its timber holdings.

A mark of the success of the newsprint plant at Lufkin is the fact that in the latter part of 1949 the founder and head of the mills, Ernest L. Kurth, was honored as that year's "Man of the South" at a testimonial attended by prominent businessmen from many areas. His Southland Paper Mills was an outgrowth of the Lufkin Land & Lumber Company, which had been sawmilling for more than a generation and had cut about all of its marketable "saw timber." It had in excess of 100,000 acres of land with much second-growth timber, and necessary sawmill facilities including thirty miles of railroad. The company put in its property and sold stock to many southern newspapers which would take their newsprint. RFC loans completed the project.

Mr. Kurth organized the Southland Paper Mills in 1938. Before definitely determining to start the newsprint mill, he brought Dr. Herty to see me. Being convinced by Dr. Herty of the feasibility of the project, and having complete confidence in Mr. Kurth, we authorized the loan.

Among the original stockholders in the enterprise were the leading newspapers of almost every large city in the South, except my paper, the Houston *Chronicle*. I did not buy any of the stock because I was on the lending end, and, unfortunately, have not benefited as other southern newspapers have from the products of this mill when newsprint has been scarce.

RFC's three loans and commitments to Mr. Kurth, made over a period of six years, aggregated $8,500,000, and helped his concern grow from the modest one-machine mill of 1940, which manufactured 32,000 tons of newsprint, to a 1949 production of 150,000 tons of kraft pulp, board, and newsprint. The loans have been paid.

MICE AND MEN AND MONEY

Our San Francisco office arranged a novel loan of $1,000 to enable a crippled student at the University of California, in Berkeley, to buy and house and experiment with 1,000 white mice. Getting about on crutches, the student, Robert B. Brown, had been working on an anti-influenza serum in which the Navy became interested. He needed money to enlarge his enterprise to the size the Navy desired. The loan we made him, in February, 1943, was repaid in a short time.

One of our smallest yet most beneficial business loans, was $500 to a wide-awake middle-aged Negro, Ed Sanders of Pasadena, California, who whipped the depression for himself and several dozen others with what he called a "Self-Help Plan." He took men off the relief rolls and put them to work cutting down trees no longer wanted on estates or in the yards of his neighbors. His staff also cleaned houses and did odd jobs.

Sanders started his little business in the summer of 1936 with a capital of $103. Within three months he had removed eleven men from the relief rolls of the Pasadena City Employment Office of which he had previously been in charge. Six months later he had accumulated enough wood to open a yard. Felled trees were split and sawed into cordwood. Boards gathered from wrecked buildings and back lots which Sanders' men had cleaned were cut into kindling. Each Saturday he employed young students to sack the kindling for sale.

By 1939 he had thirty-nine men on his pay roll, of whom twenty-three had come off relief. Five others were migrants from the Midwest "dust bowl." Of his gross take-in of $22,683 that year, Sanders paid out $19,401.55 in wages. It was to tide his helpful business over a lull and avoid laying off any regular workers that he approached the RFC for a $500 loan. He paid it off at the rate of $15 monthly, his truck and a power drag having been our security.

In 1938 we made a $30,000 loan to a real two-fisted borrower— Jack Dempsey. The former heavyweight champion used the money to refurbish his restaurant near Madison Square Garden, and the loan worked out all right.

During the thirteen years of my association with the RFC we

authorized, directly and in cooperation with banks, more than 22,000 business and industrial loans aggregating $2,650,000,000. Among these loans 10,300 were of $500 to $10,000, and 9,400 ranged from $10,000 to $100,000. Thus all but a small percentage of the loans went to little business, which in many ways is the backbone of our private enterprise system.

Prior to the war the RFC made just over 12,000 loans totaling $848,400,000 to business and industrial concerns. During the war the Corporation advanced almost $2,000,000,000 in business loans, mostly to small concerns, this figure being exclusive of the billions invested and lent by our subsidiaries directly for the war effort.

After Japan's surrender business loans became the principal occupation of the RFC, their number being greater than in the days of the depression. In 1946 alone the Corporation made more than 15,000 business loans, whereas in the twelve preceding years the grand total was just over 25,000. This should not have been necessary, and under proper management would not have been done.

It was always assumed the RFC was doing what private enterprise was not in a position to do, and that when the situation was met the Corporation would cease operations. Congress never had the thought of creating a government bank to compete with private enterprise or to socialize banking. The idea always was that the Corporation was there to do emergency jobs which could be accomplished in no other way.

Two circumstances I shall mention illustrate that if the directors of the RFC would try hard enough they could get cooperation from banks throughout the country so that the banks, instead of the Corporation, would carry the loans.

One day a man from Oklahoma City whom I had known slightly came to see about his troubles. He owned an office building which had a mortgage held by one of our largest life insurance companies. Rents had gone below the amount necessary to service the mortgage, and the insurance company had taken charge, leaving the owner nothing to live on—no income. I happened to know the building and knew it to be worth more than double the amount of the loan. The owner wanted to borrow from the RFC to pay the life insurance company, on terms and charges that would leave him a little something to eat on. I asked him who in the insurance company he did business with. He told me. I called the company's president and told him the RFC would, if necessary, make the loan, but that it was a poor come-off for his billion dollar company to force the government to make a loan to pay his company, or to take all the income from the building without leaving the owner a pittance to eat on. His reply was, "Mr. Jones, send him to me." The company reset his loan and reduced payments sufficiently to allow the man a livelihood.

The other case concerns an elderly gentleman who came to see me with a United States Senator from his state. He wanted to borrow several hundred thousand dollars to pay his bank. The bank had been rescued and recapitalized by the RFC and was in good circumstances. I looked over the borrower's financial statement and found his company was well entitled to credit in the amount he owed the bank. I called the banker by long-distance telephone while the Senator and the would-be borrower were at my desk. I told the banker of their presence and their purpose, that I had looked over the statement and saw no justification for the bank's attitude. The banker replied: "Mr. Jones, the loan is all right, but we don't like the way Mr. Blank runs his business." I replied, "Probably Mr. Blank doesn't like the way you part your hair." The banker then said, "Send him back, Mr. Jones, we will take care of him." We were able to help thousands of such cases with a little effort.

13

---------------- ☼ ----------------

DISASTER LOANS

FDR Talks Me Up Some Millions—When the Trees Fell in New England—Dollars Fell on Alabama

AMONG the good works of the RFC were 24,900 loans to sufferers from catastrophes variously attributed to Providence, Nature, and man's carelessness. Floods, droughts, freezes, hurricanes, explosions, and storms came in all sizes and in all manner of places.

So did the monetary responses of our Disaster Loan Corporation.

To one-mule farmers in the Deep South, male and female, white and black, who needed just a little money to tide them over a severe dry spell, we made individual loans as small as $15. To the Mande-ville Island Farms, Inc., of Stockton, California, we advanced $252,340.

During one of the overflows of the Ohio River, a small-town Kentucky barber, whose chair and combs, soap and shears, razors and strop had all been washed away, reckoned he could set himself up in business again if he could get hold of $20. We loaned it to him. A flooded-out Tennessee blacksmith was contented with $27 to buy a new anvil. Some flood, that washed away an anvil!

As part of the aftermath of the Ohio flood of 1937, we advanced $350,000 to the Gallatin County Housing Authority for the purpose of moving the entire community of Shawneetown, Illinois, out of the river valley onto safe, high ground. When the ruinous waters receded, Paducah, Kentucky, borrowed $300,000 to build a hospital. This was our second largest disaster loan, but there were others almost as big. Most of the loans, scattered through thirty-two states, were in sizes well in between the extremes just mentioned. Over the fourteen-year period 1933–1947, the average figured just above $2,000.

Under a special Act of Congress approved April 13, 1934, the RFC had authority to make what were known as disaster loans. Up to the end of 1936—the year of the Pittsburgh flood—it had made loans in that category of approximately $12,000,000.

Then came the great floods of January, 1937, which devastated large sections of the Ohio and Mississippi valleys, the waters covering vast areas in several states.

A committee from both houses of Congress, headed by Senator Alben Barkley of Kentucky, came to see me, asking that we set aside $50,000,000 to help the flood victims. Although there had been great damage over a rather wide area, I felt that when the water went down it would not turn out to be as bad as it looked. That is usually the case after high water. In an effort to reach a bargain with the committee, I suggested $5,000,000. Naturally the committee were not satisfied with my suggestion. They said they would go to the White House, to which I agreed.

I thought that it would require more than $5,000,000, but that nothing like $50,000,000 would be needed.

FDR TALKS ME UP SOME MILLIONS

When the gentlemen left my office I called Marvin McIntyre, the President's secretary, and told him that Senator Barkley with a committee was on the way to see the President about the flood situation, that they wanted $50,000,000, and that I suggested $5,000,000. I explained the matter fully to Mac and asked him to see Mr. Roosevelt immediately and suggest that he tell the Senator and the committee he would "try to talk Jess up to $20,000,000," which I was sure would be ample.

The President followed my suggestion, and we allocated $20,-000,000; but as it turned out only $7,000,000 was necessary for that flood.

In telephoning Mac I recalled to mind a neighbor whose ten-year-old son wanted a donkey and had located one that he could buy. The boy went to his father and told him he could buy the donkey for $14, and asked for the money. His father, thinking to teach the boy some trading tactics, gave him $7 and said: "Now, son, you take this $7, and if you try hard enough you can talk the man down to $7. When you see him, have the money in your hand so he can see it." The boy thanked his father, but before leaving the house he saw his mother. Later he came back home with the donkey. The father felt very proud, thinking he had taught the boy a good lesson in trading.

"Well, son," he said, "I see you got your donkey. You talked the man down to $7, did you?"

"Yes, father," the boy replied, "but he talked me back up to $14." The President talked me up to the $20,000,000.

Wishing to keep our disaster loans entirely separate from business loans, I asked Congress to create the Disaster Loan Corporation and authorize us to invest $20,000,000 in its capital. This was done on February 11, 1937. As the years went by and more catastrophes occurred, it was necessary to increase the capital stock to $40,000,000.

After a flood, a storm, an earthquake, or what not, it was our practice to have the citizens of each stricken community set up a committee whose members could appraise the real needs of their neighbors and recommend to us the size of each individual loan which seemed required. Such a local committee might consist of a banker, a farmer, a shopkeeper, a craftsman, a minister, perhaps a lawyer or a judge. They knew their neighbors, what their losses had been and each man's means, or lack of means, for making a comeback. Almost invariably we followed their recommendations.

Even before the magnitude of a disaster could be gauged, we would set up field offices and send examiners and attorneys into the afflicted areas to expedite the making of loans. As soon as the seriousness of the 1937 Ohio overflows became evident two of our directors, Emil Schram and C. B. Henderson, went to the flooded zone. They devoted several weeks to sizing up the distress and opening offices. How much money was needed from us, who was to get it, and the terms of repayment were questions which we left, in most cases, to the decision of the local citizens' committee. We usually let the borrower write his own ticket as to the way he thought he could pay back the loan. He might say he could pay $20 a month, or $100 a year, or $50, or whatever.

Very often these loans were made without any security. We tried to follow the spirit of the Act which had created the Disaster Loan Corporation, and expected to lose money. In that we were not disappointed. Yet we lost less than we had anticipated. When liquidated in 1945, the Disaster Loan Corporation was only a little more than

$5,000,000 in the red, out of a total loaned of nearly $55,000,000. Our practice of rushing field agents into afflicted areas was both arduous and expensive, but the needs were nearly always urgent. In some communities the distress was almost universal. In 1937, when the waters subsided in Shelbyville, across the Ohio River from Louisville, it seemed that almost every family deserved some outside help. The overflow had invaded almost every house and place of business in the community. We arranged that most of the small loans to people of Shelbyville should be repaid at a rate of $10 or $12 a month. The scrupulous manner in which those hard-hit citizens stinted to repay our loans—whose terms, by all local standards, were generous—testified touchingly to the fact that most "little" people, when treated fairly by a lender, will do their best to fulfill their obligations.

Some months after we had made the loans, the Mayor of Shelbyville came to Washington. He told us that, in order to keep their payments to the RFC on schedule, scores of his fellow townsmen had been falling behind in their local taxes and even on their grocery bills. We promptly sent out a representative. He arranged to extend the maturity date of the loans and reduce the payments. All but a few of these loans were ultimately repaid in full.

Another example of the honesty of most Americans, and of the RFC's effort to be a reasonable lender, was the situation in Paducah, Senator Barkley's home town, where the flood damage was sadly extensive. About seven hundred of the loans we made in Paducah were to men employed in the shops of the Illinois Central Railroad, family men whose homes and their contents had been soiled or ruined by the river's muck. A typical advance would be $500, half to be used for furniture, half for clothing, with a chattel mortgage on the furniture as the only security.

A few months after the loans were made, the railroad shops were shut down for a long period. Many of our borrowers were without work or pay checks. They simply couldn't meet the agreed payments. Yet, as soon as the shops reopened and pay days came regularly again, they began to whittle down their notes.

We charged no interest for the first four months, and only 3 per cent thereafter. All the expenses of making a loan, such as examination of titles and appraisal of properties, were paid by the Corporation.

After the 1937 flood the Disaster Loan Corporation set up thirty-six field offices from Wheeling, West Virginia, all along the Ohio and the Mississippi to New Orleans. We sent 375 examiners and 40 attorneys into the field. They authorized around 7,500 loans aggregating approximately $8,600,000, of which $7,027,300 was disbursed. Senator Barkley and his committee had thought it would take $50,000,000.

WHEN THE TREES FELL IN NEW ENGLAND

In September of 1938 we deployed forces into New England when that region was badly ruffled by a hurricane. There our agents quickly authorized 1,880 loans aggregating $4,062,000. Almost all our home repair loans, of which there were many in such battered communities as Providence, Hartford, New London, New Bedford and the surrounding countryside, were paid off in full and on time. The region stricken spread from New York City and Long Island almost to the Canadian border of New Hampshire. To handle the emergency expeditiously, we opened three offices in New York State, three in Connecticut, ten in Massachusetts, two in New Hampshire, and three in Rhode Island.

On the morning after the hurricane it seemed as though all New England were littered with fallen trees and broken branches. Cherished elms and strong oaks which had stood for centuries had crashed in the twisting winds. Helping farmers dispose of this timber provided us with an unaccustomed task. Many of the small farmers in the Northeast depend upon their wood lots for an annual cash crop, and these the storm had dolefully depleted. We were told that, unless the fallen timber could be cut up and got to the ponds before the winter of 1939, it was likely that bugs would ruin it. The problem involved salvaging as much as possible of some three billion feet of fallen timber, an enormous undertaking in an unfamiliar field. Ownership of the trees was spread among almost twenty-five thousand farmers and small landowners.

To facilitate our work, the Northeastern Timber Salvage Administration was formed. The Forest Service of the Department of Agriculture sent its agents into New England and the Federal Surplus Commodities Corporation was also called on for help. It established collecting stations and offered to buy, with RFC funds, all the fallen timber brought to designated assembling ponds.

We began by advancing the timber owners 90 per cent of the average market price of logs for the three previous years. Thus we bought and had cut into lumber about $15,000,000 worth of blown-down trees. We still had some of this lumber when the United States was blown into the war in 1941. We were gradually disposing of it at a good profit when the Office of Price Administration put on ceiling prices. On our sales from then on, we took a loss of about $1,500,000. The overhead costs of the entire operation were a little more than $3,000,000.

DOLLARS FELL ON ALABAMA

The timber-buying program had drawn so heavily on Disaster Loan Corporation funds that, early in 1939, we asked Congress to increase the Corporation's capital to $40,000,000. It wasn't long before new disasters brought more appeals. With the summer came a prolonged drought in the South. It blighted crops over a large section of Alabama and in parts of Georgia, Mississippi, and north-west Florida. The worst sufferers were the small-patch tenants or share croppers, poor folk who even in the best of times could scarcely hope for much credit at the bank, the grocer's or the feed store. The lingering drought dragged many of these folk not only down to their last dollar but well beyond it. Often there was no more hogback, cornmeal, or hominy in the kitchen, nothing to feed the mule, no more credit at the store or the bank for food or feedstuff or seeds to replant the burned-out acres.

In going to the aid of those people, the Disaster Loan Corporation really got down to the grass roots and the back-country roads. Within five months we made nine thousand loans, most of them between $200 and $500, to farmer folk eking an existence out of fifteen-, ten-, and even five-acre patches. They urgently required cash for such simple essentials as seed, sowbelly, and soap.

The majority of these loans were secured by a mule-and-crop mortgage. If the mortgaged mule died or the farmer died or moved away from the country, we knew we couldn't collect, and didn't bother much about it. Except when one or two of those three contingencies occurred, we usually got our money back, or most of it.

On top of the 1939 drought the summer of 1940 brought poor crops in most of the region, so it took the majority of the borrowers two years to reduce their loans. Yet in Alabama, where the situation was worst and the borrowing farmers poorest, 77 per cent of the

9,488 loans made were eventually collected by the field agents. Looking over the records, I note that on a $15 loan to one woman living near Dadeville we had a loss of 95 cents. On another $15 loan to a man with a rural delivery address out of Greensboro we collected all but $2.48. Evidently these poor people thought they had paid what they owed.

Altogether, out of nearly twenty-five thousand loans totaling $54,-000,000, those that had to be charged off amounted to $2,135,000. It was the general experience of the Disaster Loan Corporation that most of its uncollectable loans were to borrowers who died or lost their jobs.

The Disaster Loan Corporation was dissolved by Act of Congress on June 30, 1945. Thereafter its parent, the RFC, continued to make catastrophe loans as called upon.

14.

———————— ☼ ————————

THE BIRTH OF RURAL ELECTRIFICATION

SOME of the major achievements of the Roosevelt administration had their origin in casual conversations at the White House. Such was the case with the Rural Electrification Administration, which has been a great boon to a more comfortable life on the farm.

One day in 1935, while in conference with the President at the White House, I was preparing to leave when he told me that Senator George Norris of Nebraska was waiting to see him, and that the Senator had some grandiose idea about rural electrification. Would I see the Senator and find out what he had in mind? He then rang for the secretary, and the Senator was ushered in. The President said: "George, I want you and Jess to go in the Cabinet Room. You tell him what it is you want and see if you can work out a deal with him."

The Senator replied, "Mr. President, I don't think Jones and I can agree."

"Why?" the President asked.

"He wants too much interest and too much security."

"Well, go try and see how near you can come to an agreement, and then come back."

When we got in the Cabinet Room I asked the Senator what he had in mind. He said he wanted the farmers to have the benefit of electricity and explained his idea of groups of farmers organizing themselves and borrowing the money from the government to get electric service.

I asked the Senator how much money he thought it would take.

He replied, "A billion dollars."

"How fast can the money be spent?" I asked. "How much a year do you think will be needed?"

"Forty million dollars a year," he replied; "but we are not going to pay any 4 per cent interest."

"Well, what would you think, Senator, of our adopting your plan in principle by making a definite commitment for ten years? That is, we would make available $40,000,000 a year for the first ten years."

"That would be all right," the Senator replied, "but we are not going to pay your rate of interest."

"Do you think 4 per cent is too much?" I asked.

"Yes."

"What would you think about 3 per cent?"

"That would be the right figure," Senator Norris remarked.

"Then we are in agreement," I said. "The RFC will lend $40,-000,000 a year for the next ten years at 3 per cent interest, secured by notes of local rural electrification organizations such as cooperatives, with a 20 per cent margin to the RFC. That is, we will lend 80 per cent of the face value of the farmers' notes to the local agency."

Senator Norris was surprised that we were able to reach an agreement on such an important matter in less than ten minutes. We immediately sent word to the President that we were ready to report, and were soon ushered into his office.

"Mr. President," Senator Norris said, "Jones and I are in agreement." He proceeded to tell the President what we had decided to do.

"Fine," said the President, heartily congratulating us. That was the creation of the Rural Electrification Administration which has proven of immense value to rural sections throughout the nation.

On May 11, 1935, not long after my talk with Senator Norris, the President brought the Rural Electrification Administration into existence by an Executive Order authorizing a one-year program. A little later Congress enacted the Rural Electrification Act of 1936, authorizing a ten-year program.

Through the years the Rural Electrification Administration has lent more than a billion dollars at low interest to cooperatives, municipalities, and other public bodies and private utilities to finance the construction and operation of facilities to furnish electricity to persons in rural areas. More than 95 per cent of the loans have gone to cooperatives. Delinquencies have represented less than 1 per cent of the amounts due. Power lines financed by the Rural Electrification

Administration in forty-six states, Alaska, and the Virgin Islands serve upward of two million consumers. Thanks to electricity, these people now enjoy on the farm the modern refrigeration, lighting, power and labor-saving devices available but a few years ago only to those Americans who lived in urban areas.

15

---- ☼ ----

ELECTRIC HOME AND FARM AUTHORITY

I HAVE long felt that the best way to borrow money—or to lend it—is on the installment plan. Both the borrower and the lender are better off when the borrower is required to reduce the loan at conveniently spaced intervals, than when the interest alone is paid from time to time while the principal remains at the original figure until maturity.

If the principal remains undiminished until the note falls due, it is often necessary to renew the entire loan. This process may repeat itself several times, each time inducing a little more worry in the minds of both parties.

Of the efficacy of making installment loans to families of moderate means to facilitate the installation in their homes of modern heating, cooling, and labor-saving devices, the Electric Home and Farm Authority gave us daily examples over a period of several years. The Electric Home and Farm Authority had been orphaned by the passing of the National Industrial Recovery Administration, which gave it birth, and it had been adopted by the Tennessee Valley Authority before President Roosevelt handed it over to the RFC with our Mr. Emil Schram assigned to the role of foster father.

Under his guidance the Electric Home and Farm Authority spread its operations into thirty-seven states. It made loans, which averaged slightly above $150 each, to several hundred thousand tenants and home owners. It borrowed, in Wall Street and other money markets, as much as $15,000,000 at a time. Finally, upon liquidating its affairs, the Authority repaid the Treasury its capital stock investment of $850,000 and turned over to the government a tidy profit of $175,000.

After dealing with scores of thousands of people, the credit losses of the Authority came to less than ¼ of 1 per cent of its business. As Mr. Schram observed of this and other experiences he had in the RFC, if you lend money in small enough amounts to enough people, you'll get it back and some profits to boot. Most people are honest about paying their debts. Only a few of the borrowers with whom we dealt tried to trim us.

The main trouble with small loans is the proportionately heavy cost of making and collecting them. The Electric Home and Farm Authority went around that hurdle by arranging with the utility companies supplying electricity and gas to do the collecting. Along with the bill for their services they would send the consumer the monthly call for the installment due on the equipment whose purchase we had underwritten. For this service, regardless of the size of the contract, we paid the company $1 as an original booking charge on each account and thereafter 12½ cents per installment collected. The utility companies, both public and private, were pleased with the arrangement, for each piece of equipment a householder purchased either brought them a new customer or increased their business with an old one.

Our approach to the buyers of gas and electric appliances was through their local dealers. We made contracts with five thousand of these shops. The dealer would take the buyer's note, and endorse it to the Electric Home and Farm Authority, which purchased the paper from him. We thus had, as triple security, the obligation of the installment buyer, that of the dealer, and the value of the article itself.

To finance its operations the Authority was able to borrow money in the open market at 1 per cent. The banks were eager to take up this paper, which had the backing of the RFC. The installment buyers of the household appliances were charged at the rate of 5 per cent discount. For example, if a man bought a refrigerator for $100 and wanted a year in which to pay for it, his note was written for $105 and he paid it out with a down payment and twelve equal monthly installments. Figured in straight interest, a 5 per cent discount installment note works out a little more than 9 per cent yield. Our terms of payment ran up to four years on some heavy-duty units. The average paper was slightly above two years.

Mostly we carried on the business in sections where the larger installment finance companies chose not to go. They simply didn't want to bother with that type of financing in the smaller communities or in sparsely settled sections, finding it too expensive.

We did not, in general, enter the most densely populated sections, where private companies were finding such business quite profitable and seemed to meet the demand for installment loans. In New York State we did not have a single contract. In Connecticut the local banks became eager to take over our paper soon after we entered that field. We sold them our entire Connecticut portfolio. We had more contracts in California than in any other one state—above fifty thousand; Tennessee was second, Illinois and Georgia seesawing in third and fourth ranks, closely followed by Indiana, Minnesota, and Oregon. Among the New Englanders there seemed to be no demand for the program.

After wartime restrictions prohibited installment buying and stopped the manufacturing of many household appliances, an Executive Order of October 13, 1942, directed the RFC to liquidate the Electric Home and Farm Authority. Its assets then exceeded $8,-000,000. By having the dealers do all the selling and the utility companies the collecting, our administrative expenses for the program had been kept remarkably low. At the peak of its activity, with nearly three hundred thousand contracts outstanding, the Authority itself had fewer than one hundred fifty employees.

16

---- ☼ ----

SAVING SOME INSURANCE COMPANIES

NEVER in history were life insurance companies required to make so many policy loans, or cash in policies in such numbers, as they did during the early years of the great depression. People who had lost their savings in banks that failed or through real estate fore-closures or in mortgage bond defaults and then, perhaps, had also been dropped from their jobs, turned to their insurance policies as a last resort to raise cash to feed, clothe, and shelter themselves and their families and satisfy the tax collector. Until the depression pinched them, probably not many people ever thought of the fact that they could borrow on their insurance policies or cash them in while alive.

Swamped by this unexpected and unprecedented flood of demands, a number of weaker insurance companies had to be rehabilitated. Some others went into liquidation. To meet the pressure for cash, the companies were compelled to call their own loans and thereby bring hardship to their debtors, or to sell securities at a sacrifice price, or to borrow. Some were able to get help from the banks. One hundred and thirty-three insurance companies borrowed $90,-693,210 from the RFC.

Most of our insurance loans went to the smaller companies in New York, Detroit, Chicago, and Des Moines. There were also several in St. Louis, Indianapolis, and Dallas. A great majority of the companies were able, however, to meet their obligations without borrowing from the Government.

In addition to its loans the RFC bought preferred stock in six casualty and three fire insurance companies.

When the financial disintegration culminated in the closing of all banks, the New York Legislature gave dictatorial powers over some nine hundred insurance companies of every conceivable kind to the State Superintendent of Insurance, George S. Van Schaick. He was authorized to suspend any provisions of the insurance laws and amend any regulations. On March 9, 1933, while the banks were still blacked out, he forbade loans and cash surrenders under life insurance policies except in cases of extreme need or to meet pay rolls. Within a few months the liquidity of the companies had almost doubled and the new regulations were modified, then rescinded. During that doleful year Mr. Van Schaick was ordered by the courts to take over seventeen title and mortgage guarantee companies for rehabilitation and twenty-two insurance companies for liquidation and two others for reorganization. The next year, 1934, he took over thirty-nine insurance companies.

A few of these we helped him revive, among them the National Surety Company, which I have mentioned in Chapter 8, and the Globe & Rutgers Fire Insurance Company. The latter was the third largest fire insurance concern in the United States. It was annually writing about seven billions of insurance, doing business in forty-six of the states.

Had Globe & Rutgers, with its nation-wide chain of agencies, been liquidated, the unsettled state of the insurance community at that time would have been greatly worsened. The company's creditors and customers, whose claims numbered over 350,000, would have had to wait a long time to get paid. There were almost 500,000 policy holders.

Investment in corporate stocks was one of the gambles that got the company into trouble. In July, 1932, the company reduced the par value of its shares, cutting the outstanding capital stock from $7,000,000 to $2,000,000, thus releasing $5,000,000 in capital funds for transfer to the surplus account.

But this was quickly eaten into. A run began on the company's treasury with increased demands for return of unearned premiums. Concurrently came heavy cancellations of business. On March 24, 1933, the courts ordered Superintendent Van Schaick to take over Globe & Rutgers.

The RFC, which had loaned the company $10,000,000, was its principal creditor. On the following day we placed three men on its board: A. B. Jones, New York businessman and real estate consultant; Earl B. Schwulst of the RFC and Mortimer N. Buckner, chairman of the New York Trust Company.

The following August, negotiations were begun for purchase of control of the company from E. C. Jameson, who had been its president. The control was bought by two holding companies, the Tri-Continental Corporation and Selected Industries, the negotiations being arranged by two Wall Street investment houses, Hayden, Stone & Company and J. & W. Seligman & Company. After the change, the RFC joined with the new owners and Superintendent Van Schaick in plans to rehabilitate the concern and enable it to resume business.

Under this plan the RFC converted $3,500,000 of its $10,000,000 loan into first preferred stock in the reorganized company on condition that an equal amount of second preferred be bought by other creditors. The remainder of our loan was refunded and extended. A fund was set up to retire the preferred stock as rapidly as conservative management would permit. It was agreed no dividends were to be allowed on the common stock while any preferred stock was outstanding. It was further stipulated that while the preferred stock existed the RFC should have 51 per cent of all votes, and thereby control the concern.

The plan also provided that all claims of $500 or less were to be settled immediately in cash. On larger claims the settlement was 50 per cent in cash and 50 per cent in second preferred stock. With court approval the plan went into operation December 6, 1934. That is the first instance I know of in which a closed fire insurance company reopened its doors and resumed business.

It started out anew with capital funds of $6,000,000, directed by insurance executives of high standing. Olin L. Brooks, who had formerly been second vice president of the Firemen's Insurance Company of Newark, became the new president of Globe & Rutgers. So well did the company recuperate that in 1936 it was able to borrow enough from the banks at 2 per cent to pay off its loans from the RFC. The company gradually retired its first preferred stock. Its last tie to the RFC was severed in March, 1948.

THE PRESIDENT AND BASIL O'CONNOR'S FEE

In one of its amendments to the RFC Act, Congress had required the directors of the RFC to approve the size and appropriateness of the salaries, commissions, attorneys' fees, et cetera, of each borrower. In the Globe & Rutgers situation, when they were about ready for disbursements of the balance of the loan that we had granted, we asked for such an accounting in connection with the liquidation and reorganization. They were reluctant to give it to us until they had the money, claiming that they needed it to make the settlements; but we required it. Among other things, they submitted a list of attorneys' fees amounting to $619,500. The largest single fee was $200,000 to the firm of O'Connor & Farber, of which President Roosevelt had been a member.

We declined to allow these fat fees, and reduced them all we could. Since the President had been so much opposed to high salaries to railroad presidents—taking the position that $25,000 a year should be enough for such officials—and Mr. O'Connor was an intimate friend and former law partner of his, I brought these lawyers' fees and charges to his attention. I did it to tease the President. His comment was that he thought Basil might be charging a little too much and maybe I could get him to reduce it to $150,000. We had no notion of allowing him that amount.

I gave President Roosevelt a copy of a letter I had written about the fees to Earle Bailie of J. & W. Seligman & Company, which follows:

October 6, 1934

Dear Mr. Bailie:

Our board is unwilling to invest in or lend upon stock in an insurance company, if indeed we have the right to do so, that contemplates paying such lawyers' fees, reorganization or otherwise, as is proposed in the case of the Globe & Rutgers, which we understand from information to be:

Basil O'Connor	$200,000
Root, Clark, Buckner & Ballantine	165,000
Sullivan & Cromwell	95,000
Prentice & Townsend	50,000
Cravath, de Gersdorff, Swaine & Wood	37,500
Martin Conboy	35,000
Joseph V. McKee	25,000
Coudert Brothers	12,000

or a total of $619,500. Even the suggested reduction to a total of $426,000 would be very much more than what would appear to this Corporation to be proper fees to be paid by an insurance company that is being recapitalized with Government funds.

Yours very truly,

JESSE H. JONES

Under court orders Mr. O'Connor's firm was paid $100,000 in 1934 and $35,000 more the following year.

17

---- ☼ ----

REBUILDING THE BUILDING AND LOAN ASSOCIATIONS

WHEN the RFC opened its clinic for ailing financial institutions, there were about eleven thousand five hundred building and loan associations in the country, many of them in poor health. They had about twelve million members, nearly a tenth of the entire population of the country. If they had gone down, the losses would have been serious and widespread. They had about seven billion dollars invested in real estate mortgages on which they could not realize cash, and for which there was no market.

We helped more than eleven hundred of these associations, mostly in 1932 and 1933. Eventually we got back the $140,158,000 which we loaned to going building and loan associations and to the receivers of some others which had gone into liquidation. All together, in this particular field we authorized loans of $178,000,000; but $38,-831,000 of the authorizations were not taken.

The majority of building and loan associations in the United States were competently and carefully operated, their stock having long been a favorable form of investment for people of small means. However, a disappointing proportion of them seemed to have become merely promoters' schemes. Some of the others appeared to have been started because a butcher, a baker, and a candlestick maker wanted to be officers of a "financial institution." The situation was particularly bad in New Jersey. We made 382 loans to building and loan associations in New Jersey, 173 in Ohio, and 110 in Pennsylvania. Some lawyers in those areas chose to specialize as counsel for several building and loan associations, collecting a regular retainer from each. In New Jersey it was not unusual for one man to act as secretary for four or five building and loan associations, taking a salary from each for handling its routine day-to-day business.

The promoters of some of the Ohio concerns hawked their capital stock all over the country and pocketed 20 per cent of the money subscribed. When these outfits began to fail, many stockholders mistook their investments for deposits and clamored for their money. They lined up along with those who had "certificates of deposit" for the savings they had put into the broken concerns.

One of our early rescue missions in this field made an agreement to loan several million dollars to three building and loan associations in Dayton to enable them to pay at least 25 cents on the dollar on their "certificates of deposit." A group of stockholders sued to prevent this payment. The arguments were threshed out for several months in the Common Pleas Court. At the outset of the trial we dispatched George H. Hill, Jr., one of our young attorneys, to Dayton. He had to make his way through a swarm of several thousand people in and around the courthouse. In the corridors, cheer leaders were rallying the two groups as though they were attending a football game. The walls echoed cries of "Rah, rah, rah—depositors," and "Rah, rah, rah—stockholders," while in the downtown streets and hotel lobbies the certificates of deposit were sold as low as 10 cents on the dollar. Mr. Hill, a competent business lawyer, is now assistant to the president of the Cities Service Company, New York City.

The sorry plight of some of the building and loan associations helped to drag down a good many banks. During the banking crisis of 1933 there were several occasions on which we took over building and loan association paper which a bank held so that "the bank can open next Monday"—a familiar phrase in our offices in those days.

In Baltimore, as in Dayton, where a full dozen associations were in trouble, the difficulty was particularly widespread. There were several associations in Baltimore which had been organized among the Polish-Americans. They were brought together under the leadership of a Dr. Suwacki, who worked out a plan with our Mr. Tom Williams which saved the situation.

Generally in our deals with ailing building and loan associations we could lend only about 50 per cent of the face value of the collateral.

What finally cleaned up our loans to the associations was the refinancing of homes by the Home Owners' Loan Corporation, which had been created by Act of Congress in June, 1933. This Act provided for the establishment of federal savings and loan associations into which some of the old building and loan associations were reorganized. The situation was still further improved in June, 1934, by the creation of the Federal Housing Administration with its system for insuring first mortgages on residential properties.

18

---------- ☼ ----------

THE EXPORT-IMPORT BANK OF WASHINGTON

*Joe Stalin Breaks His Word—Business, Not Santa Claus,
in South America—Senator Borah and the New Deal*

AS ORIGINALLY established by Executive Order of the President
on February 2, 1934, the Export-Import Bank of Washington
was to devote itself exclusively to the promotion of trade with the
Soviet Union. Nothing came of that, for the reason that the Kremlin
refused to fulfill one of the promises made to the President by Maxim
Litvinov, People's Commissar for Foreign Affairs of the Union of
Soviet Socialist Republics, when he came to Washington in 1933 and
obtained American recognition of his government.

In those hopeful days William C. Bullitt, the first United States
Ambassador to the U.S.S.R., believed that a large trade with Russia
as well as good will could be built up if proper financing could be
arranged. The Soviet Union, which the Wilson, Harding, Coolidge, and
Hoover administrations had refused to recognize, needed many raw
materials and manufactured goods of which there were surpluses in
the United States. Previously, in July, 1933, before Washington recognized Moscow, the RFC, with the approval of President Roosevelt
and Secretary of the Treasury Woodin, had successfully financed a
one-year loan of $4,000,000 which enabled the Amtorg Trading
Corporation, an American concern owned by the Soviet Government,
to buy more than 60,000 bales of cotton from American exporters,
principally Anderson, Clayton & Company of Houston, and George
H. McFadden & Brother of Philadelphia.

Shortly after the President decided to create a government bank
to finance trade with Russia, Mr. Bullitt invited George N. Peek,
Administrator of the Agricultural Adjustment Administration, and
me to lunch. During the meal Mr. Bullitt, who apparently had discussed the matter with the President, urged Mr. Peek to accept the

presidency of the proposed bank. He later agreed to do so.

Voting control of the Export-Import Bank was vested, by the President's order, in the Secretary of State, Cordell Hull, and the Secretary of Commerce, Daniel C. Roper. I represented the RFC on the Bank's original board of trustees. To capitalize it, $1,000,000 was transferred by the President out of the $3,300,000,000 appropriation authorized by Sec. 220 of the National Industrial Recovery Act. The RFC subscribed for $10,000,000 of the Bank's preferred stock.

In this period our government was prohibited by the Johnson Act from lending money to any foreign country which was in debt to us for loans made during and following World War I. Russia was one of these countries.

The Kerensky Provisional Russian Government of 1917 borrowed more than $200,000,000 from Washington. These debts were repudiated by the Soviet regime which came into power in the autumn of 1917.

However, when Commissar Litvinov came to Washington to negotiate for American recognition of his government, he and President Roosevelt on November 15, 1933, initialed a "gentlemen's agreement" which stipulated that the Soviet Government would pay the United States on account of the Kerensky Provisional Government debt "a sum to be not less than $75,000,000 in the form of a percentage above the ordinary rate of interest on a loan to be granted to it by the Government of the United States or its nationals, all other claims of the Government of the United States or its nationals and of the Government of the Union of Soviet Socialist Republics or its nationals to be regarded as eliminated."

President Roosevelt was confident he could cajole Congress into accepting a sum of $150,000,000 in settlement of the Kerensky debt, but doubted if the Hill would favorably consider any smaller sum. Commissar Litvinov pretended to think a $150,000,000 settlement was excessive, but said he was inclined to advise Moscow to settle on $100,000,000.

To facilitate the gentlemen's agreement, the Export-Import Bank was created to finance Russian purchases in the United States and charge an excessive rate of interest, the excess above the going commercial rate to be applied to paying part of the Kerensky debt.

Commissar Litvinov did not remain in the United States to complete the arrangement. Negotiations were resumed when Alexander Antonovich Troyanovsky arrived in Washington as the first Soviet Ambassador. Meanwhile, Mr. Bullitt, who had reached Moscow, had conversations on the subject with the Commissariat of Foreign Affairs. The talks went on through the years, but no agreement satisfactory to both the Kremlin and the State Department was ever arrived at. The last serious discussion occurred in 1938, between Joseph V. Stalin and Joseph E. Davies, then American Ambassador to Moscow. Four days later, V. M. Molotov, who was President of the Council of People's Commissars of the Soviet Union, handed a memorandum to Ambassador Davies which said the Soviet Government was willing to agree to settle the Kerensky debt if it were reduced to $50,-000,000. Since the diplomatic negotiations of the Kerensky debt were never settled, the Export-Import Bank's directors granted no credits to the Soviet Government or its agents.

However, soon after the bank was created, there were other foreign requests for loans. Cuba, for example, wanted a loan to enable it to buy silver to be minted in the United States into Cuban coins. So, in March, 1934, the Second Export-Import Bank was set up to do business "with all countries except Russia." The reason the original Export-Import Bank did not take on the Cuban deal was the undated directive I had received from the President, which read:

THE WHITE HOUSE

WASHINGTON

My dear Mr. Jones:

In order that there should be no doubt in anyone's mind as to the purpose of the Export-Import Bank which was the subject of my Executive Order of February 2, 1934, I am writing you this letter to say that I wish this bank to concern itself solely with transactions with the Soviet Union and agencies thereof, and I do not wish it to be employed for any other financing whatsoever. If it shall seem desirable to use similar banks for other purposes, I wish such bank or banks to be set up as independent units, and not to be attached to the Export-Import Bank above referred to.

With all good wishes, I am,

Yours very sincerely,

FRANKLIN D. ROOSEVELT

The Second Export-Import Bank extended some credits to China as well as to Cuba. Later it was merged with the original Bank. The Second Export-Import Bank had a capital of only $2,750,000, of which all but $250,000 was preferred stock owned by the RFC.

In 1936 Mr. Peek resigned as President of the Export-Import Bank and as Special Adviser to the President on Foreign Trade. Secretaries Hull and Roper then requested me to take the presidency of the Bank and operate it. Lending money, they remarked, was not in their line. I agreed to accept responsibility for the Bank, to supervise it, finance it, and approve its loans; but I wanted it to have an active full-time president.

Looking over the Bank's organization I decided that Warren Lee Pierson, who was then the Bank's general counsel, would be best suited for the job. A California lawyer, he had joined the RFC in 1933 as special counsel to handle legal details of some large loans we had made in the West. Upon my recommendation the board of trustees elected Mr. Pierson president. Later on I became chairman of the board. At that time the Bank was a small-fry institution. It had outstanding loans of only $1,519,939.76 and undisbursed commitments of $4,538,404.77.

I encouraged Mr. Pierson to make a careful study of the various export credit agencies of other governments, particularly those of Great Britain, Sweden, France, and Japan. Accordingly, with the board's approval, he went to Europe in the summer of 1936 and passed several weeks conferring with officials of the British Export Credits Guarantee Department of the Board of Trade in London. Later he visited Sweden, Germany, and France and conferred with public officials and private businessmen regarding problems involved in the extension of export credits. In later years, because of the increased interest which the Bank had aroused both at home and abroad, we directed Mr. Pierson to make numerous trips to various parts of the world. He traveled extensively in Europe, throughout Latin America, and in the Far East.

His journeys brought to the Bank a first-hand knowledge of actual conditions existing in the trade centers of the world. Various members of the staff, notably Major Robert West, Hawthorne Arey, and John Fitch, likewise traveled widely and established close personal relations with foreign officials and businessmen. These were of great value. In 1938 I appointed as the Bank's solicitor Hampson Gary, a lawyer and diplomat with much experience overseas. He had been general counsel of the Federal Communications Commission.

Mr. Pierson left the Bank in 1944 to enter private business. He is now chairman of the board and chairman of the executive committee of Transcontinental & Western Air, Inc.

Under his presidency and my supervision the Bank was operated as an RFC institution that dealt entirely in foreign loans intended to be helpful to our national economy and to the borrowers. The Bank's expanded activities, as Mr. Pierson once remarked, ranged from "the importation of frozen Hungarian pheasants to the construction of mammoth hydroelectric plants in distant lands."

Before we got our teeth into Hungarian pheasants we had taken a bite of many dishes to which commercial bankers are generally allergic, such as medium- and long-term credits to encourage exports of durable goods or the construction or improvement of heavy industrial installations in distant climes. Short-term credits were granted to firms exporting agricultural products, especially cotton and tobacco.

One loan which was sharply criticized by a few impractical people, among them Secretary Morgenthau of the Treasury, was the $16,-000,000 advanced to the Franco government shortly after the conclusion of Spain's Civil War. The money was used to buy American cotton, of which there was an enormous surplus.

When the loan was first requested by the Spaniards in 1939 I asked President Roosevelt if he had any objection to our making it. I told him I thought we should make it for two reasons: one, to get rid of the cotton; the other, to stay on speaking terms with the Spaniards. He said to go ahead but to specify that none of the cotton either as raw bales or as manufactured goods was to be exported by Spain to other countries. On those conditions we agreed to finance 80 per cent of the credit for the 250,000 bales which the Franco government desired. The loan was paid off to the penny.

During the prewar years of '36 through most of '39 other cotton loans were made to Italy, Poland, and Czechoslovakia. All these were helpful to the distressed American cotton market.

Even after Stalin and Hitler struck Poland and divided that ill starred country between them, payments on our loan to Poland were kept up from funds held in this country to the credit of the Polish government in exile.

THE WHITE HOUSE
WASHINGTON

September 4, 1939.

MEMORANDUM FOR JESSE JONES:

This is to confirm our telephone conversation, in which I said regarding the Spanish cotton contract, that the President says, "Go ahead".

(E. M. W.)

The typewritten memorandum on the left was sent by General Edwin M. Watson, aide to President Roosevelt. The handwritten chit from F. D. R. on the right indicated some moocher was trying to pick up an acorn. He didn't get it.

BUSINESS, NOT SANTA CLAUS, IN SOUTH AMERICA

When Hitler set Europe afire the Bank's field of operations was somewhat restricted by the Neutrality Act. By then, however, its larger dollar funnels had been turned southward of the Rio Grande. The Bank assisted in financing highway construction in seven countries of Central America and the Caribbean area. These included loans to expedite construction of the Inter-American Highway in Mexico, Costa Rica, Colombia, Paraguay, and Bolivia. The Bank facilitated the placing of equipment orders in the United States for large electrical projects in Brazil, Chile, and Colombia. It financed the export of railway rolling stock and road-building machinery to Chile, Brazil, and Paraguay and the installation of packing plants in Venezuela.

Every one of the Bank's loans had the approval of the State Department, which was accorded more or less of a veto power. Only on two or three ocasions did the Department suggest our granting loans that seemed of a political nature; and these were not made.

Nowhere did we try to play Santa Claus. It was our practice to have specified in the papers covering a loan precisely for what the money was to be spent, and when and where and how. The Bank's first aid went to the American manufacturer and the American workman whose job often depended upon whether a plant's front office was successful in bidding for oversea orders. The foreign buyer of durable goods, such as locomotives, railway cars, and heavy machinery of all sorts, seldom pays spot cash. Heavy machinery must help pay for itself—and this takes time. What we did was to provide medium- or long-term loans to permit the exporting manufacturers to fill orders on long-term credit.

Sometimes an exporter would come to tell us of an order on which he wanted to bid, and we would agree to advance him money if his bid were successful. Usually we tried to cooperate with his banker in arranging the necessary financing.

An alternative method involved the appointment of the applicant's commercial bank as our agent to carry out all the details of a particular transaction. The bank was accorded the privilege of being reimbursed by us for its outlays, upon demand. Thus, while taking the risks unto itself, the Export-Import Bank encouraged commercial banks to supply the funds and the supervisory personnel to as great an extent as we could persuade them to go. By prompting commercial banks to service these loans we were able to handle all the Export-Import Bank's affairs with a staff of less than sixty.

On the other end of the line—in the countries to which the shipment of exports or the advances were made—we usually tried to get the purchaser's obligation guaranteed by substantial local banks in his country. Though in this way we dealt with several state-owned or state-controlled banks, we rarely did business with a foreign government itself. Banks cannot repudiate their obligations and continue in business. A state can. My feeling was that we should not lend money that we did not expect to get back. However, in some of the smaller and less prosperous countries we made a few small loans which I termed "soft"; but they worked out all right.

Examples of how foreign banks were brought into the picture were the credits of more than $12,000,000 arranged between 1937 and the war's beginning in 1939 for some one hundred different American cotton shippers who held orders from Italian spinners. We arranged to have the credits for the purchasers guaranteed, in varying amounts, by more than a dozen of the strongest banks in Italy.

Hardships—physical as well as financial—to which some of the foreign borrowers were put to meet their payments to us were particularly onerous in the case of the Chinese. Our first loan to China, made in 1937, was for $25,000,000. It was secured by the Chinese promise to deliver tung oil to the United States. This oil is an essential in the making of ink and certain varnishes. Although their railroads were in wretched condition and many of their ports were occupied by the Japanese, the Chinese somehow got that tung oil off to us, always on time and in sufficient quantity to meet the scheduled interest and capital payments on the loan.

The second of the Bank's loans to China was guaranteed by promises to deliver tin and tungsten. By then the internal situation in China was far worse than it had been when they had promised to to deliver the tung oil; but again they got the promised materials to such ports as were left to them and onto ships which crossed the Pacific bringing us valuable additions to the stockpile of critical materials being stacked against the day when we, too, should be hurled into hostilities. Without a whimper the Chinese paid off every dime of this second loan, like the first.

In our trades with the Chinese I had several meetings with T. V. Soong, the former finance minister of his country, who was then chairman of the Bank of China; with his successor as finance minister, Dr. H. H. Kung; with the Chinese Ambassador, Dr. C. T. Wang, and with Mr. K. C. Li, president of the Wah Chang Trading Corporation.

Mr. Li lives on Long Island and has his offices in New York City. He has a delightful family, and so has T. V. Soong. Mrs. Soong is a beautiful woman and they have three beautiful and talented daughters, all of whom speak perfect English as do Dr. and Mrs. Soong. All the Chinese with whom I dealt would impress anyone as being fine people in every respect. In my first few years in Washington, Sao-Ke Alfred Sze was the Chinese Ambassador. Socially, he was the most popular foreign diplomat in our capital at the time. The next most popular ambassador during that period was the Soviet representative, Alexander A. Troyanovsky. He was succeeded as Soviet plenipotentiary by Constantine Oumansky, who was probably the least popular ambassador in the whole diplomatic set. He was later transferred to Mexico and while there was killed in an airplane accident. On one occasion I asked Oumansky if it was true that Russia had a standing army of four million men. He replied: "Never less than twelve million."

*　　*　　*

During the early months of the European war in 1939–1940, we were able to extend a little help through the Export-Import Bank to our Scandinavian friends, whose normal trade practices had been stifled when their larger neighbors began to fight. To help meet their requirements the Export-Import Bank authorized commercial credits of $15,000,000 to Sweden, $10,000,000 each to Norway and Denmark, and $1,000,000 to Iceland.

During and after the Russo-Finnish war of 1939–1940 the Bank was able to render some nonmilitary assistance to America's friends the Finns. The Finnish Minister to Washington organized, under United States laws, the Finnish-American Trading Corporation with a paid-in capital stock of $1,000,000. To that Corporation the Bank extended a credit of $10,000,000 to finance up to 90 per cent purchases which received the prior approval of the Bank. This credit, later increased to $35,000,000, was employed in buying and shipping to Finland a variety of American goods, such as clothing, foodstuffs, machinery, and petroleum products. Purchases of arms and ammunition and other implements of war were prohibited.

From a strategic, as well as an economic standpoint, one of the most valuable of the Bank's actions was its cooperation in the development of the iron ore and steel industries of Brazil. The Mesaba Range in Minnesota, our principal domestic source of iron ore, will not last forever. Indeed there are some industrialists who question its capacity to meet the drain of a long Third World War. They foresee the day when we shall need to import large quantities of ore, from South America and Labrador.

The fabulous Itabira deposits in Brazil contain the purest iron ore known to exist. Because of transportation difficulties, only trickles of it—about 100,000 tons a year—used to come down from the Brazilian hills to the sea. First it had to be hauled twenty miles in trucks and old wagons to a railhead at Minas. From there it moved over a dilapidated railroad the 375 miles down to the port of Victoria, where hand labor slowly loaded it onto ships. Though possessing unlimited iron ore and some coal, Brazil habitually imported most of her steel, principally from Belgium and Germany. The war cut off these sources of supply. The Brazilians then worked out a plan to modernize their ore and steel industries.

They came to us for help. The British, too, were interested, the United Kingdom having been shut off by Hitler's conquests from its usual foreign sources of iron ore. In a tripartite agreement with the Export-Import Bank and the Brazilian Government, the British Government turned over, free of cost to the Brazilians, certain important Itabira iron-ore properties and the Bank advanced $14,-000,000 to put the Victoria Minas Railroad into shape to handle 1,500,000 tons of ore a year instead of 100,000. The most difficult sections of the railroad were relocated and rebuilt. Modern loading equipment was provided at the ore docks. The mine was newly equipped.

Other loans totaling $45,000,000 provided credits to pay for American goods and services required for the construction by Companhia Siderurgica Nacional of a modern steel mill at Volta Redonda, ninety miles inland on the main railway between Rio de Janeiro and São Paulo. These loans, repayable by semiannual installments running to 1965, were matched better than dollar for dollar by the Brazilian Government and private Brazilian capital, the Brazilians furnishing the equity capital and the Bank the loan.

In various other ways the Bank contributed to the improvement of Brazil's economy and the stimulation of trade between that country and the United States. The Brazilian Ambassador in Washington, Carlos Martins, was a very popular man in our Capital and was most helpful. Madame Martins, a gracious lady, is a well known sculptress and was prominent in the social life of Washington.

An over-all shortage of foreign exchange impelled the Brazilian Government during the 1930's to impose restrictions on the remittance of amounts due to American creditors on commercial transactions. The Export-Import Bank enabled Brazil to remove these restrictions by making $19,200,000 of dollar exchange available in that country. This was accomplished by authorizing a group of American commercial banks to accept three-month sight dollar drafts of the Banco do Brasil up to that amount. At each maturity part was to be repaid and new drafts accepted for the balance until the entire amount of each draft should be retired within two years, the interest rate being 3.6 per cent. The credit was fully utilized. During the loan negotiations I had several visits with Oswaldo Aranha, the Brazilian Minister of Foreign Affairs.

About the same time that this transaction took place Brazil was negotiating with German interests for the purchase of some steamships. The Moore-McCormack Lines came to us with a proposition which took the sale away from the Germans, provided Brazil with ships that later, under war conditions, played an important part in its commerce with the United States and, at the same time, strengthened the American merchant marine. The United States Maritime Commission was pushing a program to equip American steamship routes with modern high-speed ships. The Moore-McCormack Lines were eager to participate. The Bank made the company a loan of $2,275,000. The Company sold fourteen of its old ships to Lloyd Brasileiro, a steamship agency of the Brazilian Government, and then bought new-type C–3 vessels for its own use under the American flag. Meanwhile the Brazilians had broken off negotiations with the German shipping interests.

In Uruguay a hydroelectric plant which the Germans had begun in 1937 was completed, after Pearl Harbor, with American machinery financed through an Export-Import Bank credit of $12,000,000.

The Presidents of various Latin American countries personally sought assistance from the Export-Import Bank for their governmental projects. On May 22, 1939, the President of Nicaragua wrote to President Roosevelt that his country needed better roads and highways. He asked for American cooperation. The Export-Import Bank set up a $500,000 credit for the Banco Nacional de Nicaragua for exchange purposes and an additional $2,000,000 for public works. The credit was fully utilized. Ninety miles of modern highway were completed, and substantial purchases of road-building machinery were made in the United States on that loan.

As part of the plan of President Rafael L. Trujillo Molina to modernize the Dominican Republic his representatives requested a line of credit with which to make purchases in the United States and also certain Dominican materials and labor. The Bank gave them a $3,000,000 credit. Part of this was expended in constructing the handsome Hotel Jaragua at Ciudad Trujillo and into building an aqueduct, a modern slaughterhouse, and six schooners.

In the Republic of Haiti the drop in coffee prices and the forced repatriation of Haitian citizens from other countries had caused business stagnation and pathetic unemployment. There the financing of a three-year program of public works undertaken by the J. G. White Engineering Corporation was partly provided by an Export-Import Bank credit of $5,500,000, arranged in 1938.

After the economy as well as the terrain of Chile had been badly shaken by an earthquake in 1939 the Chilean Congress formed the Corporación de Fomento de la Producción to which, some months later, the Export-Import Bank provided a $20,000,000 credit.

SENATOR BORAH AND THE NEW DEAL

Shortly after war broke out in Europe in 1939 the President gave out a statement that he had in mind creating a $2,000,000,000 cartel of some sort to purchase the exportable commodities of South America. No sooner had the press carried the story than Senator William E. Borah, a strong Republican, began bristling with statements in vigorous opposition to any such procedure. The President did not pursue it because he knew, with Borah's opposition, Congress would not pass the necessary legislation.

A few weeks later, in conversation with the President, I asked him specifically what he had had in mind about this proposal. He explained to me that he would like to be prepared in case of war to show our friendship for South American countries. I then suggested to him that I might get Congress to give the Export-Import Bank $500,000,000 for additional loans and investments in South America, and that if it proved to be useful and was properly handled we could always get more from the Congress. "Go ahead," he said, "and see if you can get it." By this time Congress had become satisfied with the way we used the authority given us to lend money, and never denied our requests.

I had a bill prepared and presented to both houses which would give the Bank $500,000,000 to help stabilize the economy of nations of the Western Hemisphere. Senator Borah promptly blasted it in the press. I then called on Senator Borah. I gave him a complete statement of facts with respect to every loan the Bank had made and its current status, whether it had been paid, partly paid, or what not. I told the Senator that we operated the Bank as banks should be operated, and had no delinquencies.

Senator Borah said: "Well, if we give you this money, who will make the loans—you or the State Department?"

I explained to the Senator that I would make the loans, that I would always confer with the State Department, but that we would not make loans at the request of the State Department if, in my opinion, they should not be made. Senator Borah then said that upon that assurance he would favor granting us the authority. I had to testify many days to get the legislation. It was only after considerable and rather heated debate, particularly in the House, that we obtained it.

The bill would not have passed except for the strong support of three or four prominent Republican members of the Banking and Currency Committees. When I was testifying before the House committee, Robert Luce, a Massachusetts Republican, probably remembering a number of loans made by banks to some South American countries which had defaulted, asked me if we would have any assurance against revolutions, repudiations, or arbitrary defaults in some of those countries. I told him frankly we would not.

"Under those circumstances," he asked, "would you lend them money?" I replied that I would if I thought it to the best interest of our country.

That was the only question he asked me in my three or four days of testifying. He became a strong advocate of the bill, and made an excellent speech on the floor of the House in support of it. Without his help, we probably should not have got the legislation. There was much opposition to it.

Mr. Luce was a fine and able gentleman who had represented the 9th Massachusetts District in Congress for twenty years and was growing old when he sought reelection in 1940 and was defeated by a young Democrat. Soon after that he came to see me to tender his services without cost or expense to the government. He told me he would like to be helpful in connection with our South American activities and, if he could be of any assistance, would go to South America, paying his own expenses and without any compensation whatever. I thanked him, expressed appreciation for his help with the legislation and for the tender of his services, and told him we should be glad to have him and would fix him an office.

In Cabinet a few days later the President remarked, "If Jess would quit hiring lame-duck Republican Congressmen, more good Democrats could have jobs."

I made neither reply nor comment because what I would have said was better left unsaid. The President had been listening to some talebearer. Of these there were many with access to him.

Soon after his visit to my office Mr. Luce's health failed, and we were denied his services. I have pride in a tribute he paid the RFC, and me personally, in the course of the debate on increasing the lending authority of the Export-Import Bank, against which there was strong opposition.

As quoted in the *Congressional Record,* he said:

The R.F.C. is now under a man who, in my opinion, is the most intelligent, fairest, and honorable man in the Government. I refer to Jesse Jones. Under the R.F.C. we made good progress in lessening the hardships of the recession that took place. The R.F.C. has made money. As a whole it has not lost money. It has, of course, had some losses.

We shall not lend to South and Central America without loss. There will be losses. [Fortunately, there were none.] We grant you there will be losses, but, sir, if the lending agency to which I now refer, the Export-Import Bank, can continue to do what it has done in the last 6 years and more, then it will have made money for the Government. Perhaps it is an unfortunate thing to bring in here the profit factor, yet it is sometimes necessary to look at the advantages as well as the disadvantages of a transaction. If in this case we can make money by lending to South America without injury to ourselves, we shall have so much more money at our command to go through the hard years that are to come.

Why do you hesitate?. Why do you deplore? Why do you carp? Why do you criticize in minor details when the main thing is, are you willing to trust Jesse Jones, are you willing to trust the Secretary of the Treasury, are you willing to trust the Secretary of State, are you willing to trust the Secretary of Agriculture, are you willing to trust the Secretary of Commerce, and the President himself? We have no proof that any one of these men would deliberately do injury to any interest in this country or the interest of the country itself. They are honorable men, they are patriotic men, they love their country as much as you and I love our country. We can trust them, I believe, in this exigency to do that which is for the best interests of our country and the world itself.

The President was not willing to accept the services of the man that made this speech about him and his administrators, notwithstanding that we were by direction of Congress bipartisan politically. He chose rather to lend a willing ear to a malicious talebearer, and to do a mean little thing.

I felt the need of the services of a good man to go to South America for us. After Mr. Luce died I got Colonel James W. Flanagan, a native Texan who had been president of the Imperial Oil Company of Canada, to undertake the mission. He had lived a good many years in various South and Central American countries as a Standard Oil Company representative, and was well acquainted with the Spanish language. Colonel Flanagan, like Mr. Luce, volunteered to serve without compensation and to pay his own expenses. He died in 1950.

A major characteristic of our administration of the Bank was the cordial cooperation which existed between it and other agencies of our government. In addition to the RFC, which financed it, there were represented on the Bank's board of trustees the Departments of State, Treasury, Commerce, and Agriculture, and the Federal Reserve Bank. I served as chairman of the board of trustees until July 15, 1943, when, following my controversy with Vice President Henry A. Wallace, the President regrouped the agencies handling foreign economic matters and placed them under Leo T. Crowley as head of the Office of Economic Warfare, later the Foreign Economic Administration. Mr. Crowley, chairman of the Federal Deposit Insurance Corporation, became the chairman of the Bank's board, but at his invitation I continued as an active trustee until I left government service in 1945.

When I ended my connection with the Bank and the government I had a summary of its loans prepared, cumulative from its first transactions to January 23, 1945. The figures are given on page 230.

Later on in 1945 Congress established the Export-Import Bank as an independent agency, no longer connected with the RFC. It has since had an authorized capital of $1,000,000,000, with the law providing that it may not have loans outstanding of more than three and one-half times its paid-up capital.

In closing this chapter I want to emphasize that the success of the Bank was due in large measure to its president, Warren Lee Pierson. In most of his travels to a great many countries on the other side of both oceans in the interest of the Bank, he was accompanied by his charming wife traveling at her own expense. She was ever ready to go with him wherever the Bank's business called. They were both tactful, practical, and natural salesmen of good will.

EXPORT-IMPORT BANK OF WASHINGTON

January 23, 1945

Daily Summary of Loans
(Cumulative from February 12, 1934)

	Latin America	China	Other	Total
Authorizations	$808,922,140.61	$138,943,329.99	$248,852,771.12	$1,196,718,241.72
Cancellations and Expirations	266,937,040.37	4,526,800.00	124,784,442.56	396,248,282.93
Disbursements	262,280,515.84	117,809,672.43	104,363,937.14	484,454,125.41
Repayments	130,635,513.91	64,414,756.27	64,810,101.59	259,860,371.77
Outstanding Loans	131,645,001.93	53,394,916.16	39,553,835.55	224,593,753.64
Undisbursed Commitments	279,704,584.40	16,606,857.56	19,704,391.42	316,015,833.38
Total Undisbursed Commitments plus Outstanding Loans	411,349,586.33	70,001,773.72	59,258,226.97	540,609,587.02

19

❋

SOME LOANS WE DID NOT MAKE

Why We Would Not Lend to Newspapers—Thumbs Down on Oil and Motor Industries—No Soda for the Archbishop —Some Bright Ideas of James A. Moffett

ALTHOUGH the RFC, in one lending activity or another, directly or indirectly gave some degree of aid to every American citizen, there were certain entirely worthy types of institutions to which, as a matter of policy, we did not lend. Newspapers were on our "No" list. So were radio stations, churches, the drilling of oil wells, and the manufacturing of automobiles, all for reasons which I shall explain.

Before we had had any intimation that newspapers would want to borrow I read in a Washington paper that some organization or company was preparing to represent newspapers which might want to get funds from the RFC. We had had no applications from newspapers and had given the matter no consideration. A few days later, at my press conference, I was asked about loans to newspapers. I replied that we would not lend to newspapers. It was my thought that newspapers should not be under obligation to the government, that if we made them loans we would soon be accused of trying to dictate their editorial policies.

Soon thereafter one of the President's secretaries, Marvin McIntyre, called me about making a loan to the Philadelphia *Record.* The *Record* belonged to Dave Stern, who had been a strong supporter of Mr. Roosevelt. Mr. McIntyre told me that the President would like me to take care of Dave, and I told him to send him over. I knew Mr. Stern and liked him. I explained to him that we did not make loans to newspapers, but that I would try to get the money for him, mentioning that we were frequently able to get banks to make loans. He wanted to borrow $1,000,000. I regarded the loan as entirely good and was willing to recommend it to bankers.

I telephoned Harvey D. Gibson, president of the Manufacturers Trust Company in New York, and explained the situation to him. I told Harvey that I thought the loan perfectly good, but that I did not want the government to lend to newspapers. He promptly said, "Send Mr. Stern to me."

Mr. Stern went and was shunted to Henry C. Von Elm of Harvey's bank, but Mr. Von Elm was not interested. Mr. Stern reported to me that Mr. Von Elm was not even courteous, let alone interested in helping him. I had called Harvey Gibson because he and I had been friends for the better part of our adult lives and I had been helpful to him in obtaining business for each bank he was associated with since he started in the banking business in 1912 as assistant to Seward Prosser, president of Liberty National Bank. Furthermore, I had just gone to great pains to help him in saving the Manufacturers Trust Company, of which he was the president. Incidentally, he told me he was heavily in debt for the purchase of his stock in the Manufacturers Trust Company in 1931, only a short time before the depression.

At that period many bankers were timid about coming to the RFC for help, and Harvey was no exception. However, he and his attorney, Thomas L. Chadbourne, came to Washington with the facts and figures concerning his bank's situation. At his earnest request, I met them at their hotel in the evenings rather than at the RFC offices. They were afraid to be seen in the RFC offices for fear it would get noised around that they were seeking our help. We put $25,000,000 capital in Harvey's bank, the Manufacturers Trust Company, through the purchase of its capital notes. I had gone out of my way to help Harvey in his distress and had been glad to do so. Therefore, I felt free to ask his cooperation. I did not ask him to make the entire loan to Mr. Stern, but to set it up and take a part of it. I expected to place the balance with other banks, which I was in a position to do. But Mr. Gibson and Mr. Von Elm, having saved their own skins, were not interested.

I then queried another large bank in the West where for good reasons I felt free to do so, but got no cooperation from it. In the meantime Mr. Stern had become impatient and had gone back to the White House. Secretary McIntyre called me again and stated that the President was impatient. I told him to send Mr. Stern over. When Mr. Stern arrived I told him that if he expected to get the loan from the White House to quit bothering me about it. He was not necessarily to blame, because he was a strong supporter of the President, and felt he was entitled to call on him for assistance. I again told him that we would not make the loan, but that I would continue trying to get the money for him.

Having failed in my approach to two banks that could not have continued in existence except for our help in a big way, and from which we had every right to expect cooperation, I telephoned Joseph Wayne, Jr., president of the Philadelphia National Bank, and a Republican. I explained the situation to him. His reply was, in effect, to forget it—he would handle the loan. He had it set up by the Camden Trust Company, which took a participation of $100,000. Mr. Wayne, who was also a director of the Federal Reserve Bank at Philadelphia, put the Federal Reserve down for $350,000, his own bank for $250,000, the National City Bank of New York for $200,000, Bankers Securities Corporation for $100,000, and the Harrisburg National Bank for $50,000. Thus the matter was handled amicably, agreeably, and in every way satisfactorily. The loan was good. It was paid according to schedule.

Mr. Wayne ran a good bank. He had never asked the RFC for anything. To the contrary he had been most helpful to us in the Atlantic City situation and other troublesome problems in his territory. It would have been an easy matter to have the RFC make the Stern loan. But I went to all the trouble to place it elsewhere because I did not want to begin lending to newspapers. There was nothing in the law prohibiting loans to newspapers.

A little later I heard from the White House again. George Fort Milton of Tennessee, owner of the Chattanooga *News,* wanted a loan. This time the President mentioned the matter to me. I told him we did not make loans to newspapers.

"What the devil, Jess!" he said. "They are good friends of ours, and we ought to help them."

We did not make the loan. Once an exception was made, there would be no stopping. I had one other request. The publisher of a small county-seat newspaper in the South wanted to borrow $2,000. The suggestion came from a member of Congress for whom I had the highest possible regard. I explained that we did not make loans to newspapers and our reasons. His reply was that he did not think a $2,000 loan to a county newspaper with a circulation of a few thousand would be regarded as subsidizing the press. We did not make the loan, but I have been sorry ever since that it did not occur to me to send the little paper my own check for $2,000.

In our loan to the Canal Bank & Trust Company of New Orleans, which later failed, we got as collateral, among many other items, a $200,000 note secured by $250,000 of 6½ per cent bonds of the Tennessee Publishing Company, which owned the Nashville *Tennessean*. In our operations a borrower—and this was true of a bank receiver as well—could not sell or dispose of pledged collateral for less than its face value without our permission.

The liquidator of the Canal Bank, Harry G. Thompson, wrote us in the spring of 1935 that he had an offer of $200,000 for the $250,000 *Tennessean* bonds if he would sell them for a small down payment and the balance on credit. Knowing something about newspapers and wanting to recover as much as possible out of the collateral we held for the closed bank, I telephoned to Paul M. Davis, president of the American National Bank at Nashville, which also was a creditor of the *Tennessean*. I sold the bonds to Mr. Davis for $250,000 and took a note in payment with the bonds as collateral. Mr. Davis paid the note within a reasonable time and we saved $50,000 for the busted Canal Bank.

Silliman Evans, a former newspaperman, was at the time chairman of the Maryland Casualty Company, which the RFC had saved; he worked out a deal with Mr. Davis, and they reestablished the *Tennessean,* which was then in receivership, Mr. Evans becoming the publisher.

THUMBS DOWN ON OIL AND MOTOR INDUSTRIES

Our policy of not lending to the oil industry was based on two considerations: first, the oil business was profitable; it was able to command money when other kinds of business could not; secondly, if we loaned a man money to drill an oil well and another man owning the adjoining property sought a loan for the same purpose, we would be honor-bound to accommodate him. So, as a policy, we simply decided against lending to the oil industry, though we had ample opportunities, from Texas and probably from another state or two.

For many years we declined to make loans to the automobile industry, again for the reason that there was ample private capital available in that field, as well as enough automobiles. However, at the suggestion of William S. Knudsen, when war was approaching we made a few loans to some of the smaller automobile companies to keep them and their organizations intact. Later in the real war effort we used practically all the automobile companies; but they were serving at our request and not borrowing for their private purposes.

Early in the depression, from every part of the country, churches and religious schools and hospitals applied for loans. We had no direct authority to lend to them. We did not encourage Congress to grant us the authority, for it would have been an endless field.

The financial woes of the churches were particularly melancholy in Detroit and Buffalo, where banks, some of which were in liquidation in 1933 and 1934, held many millions of dollars in church notes and mortgages on church-owned property.

In November, 1934, representatives of three religious groups in Detroit—Protestant, Catholic, and Jewish—sent a memorial jointly to the President and to me. They wanted the RFC to take over their debts to the banks, cut them in half, and then lend the churches half for fifteen years at 2 per cent and rebate all the earlier interest payments which the churches had made.

Some members of the United States Senate seemed a bit astounded at that proposition. "Ask largely that your joy may be full" was quoted to them by a church representative from Ohio present when the Detroit memorial was read before the Senate Banking and Currency Committee, which had under consideration a bill introduced by Senator Arthur Capper of Kansas. The bill would have authorized the RFC to make loans to churches and church schools. It expired in the committee.

The directors of the RFC did not feel we should advise Congress in such legislative matters, but our board suggested that I express to the Senate committee our opinion that government lending to churches and private schools, once started, would require the appropriation by Congress of a great deal of money.

If we aided one denomination we should have to help them all.

We couldn't help the churches without being willing to help the schools and hospitals. It was my view that churches had always enjoyed good credit, and that they undoubtedly would again if they remained independent of the state, and I so told the Senate Committee.

It has always been difficult for hospitals to pay their way. They must be partially supported with either public or private funds; but to get the funds out of the federal purse in Washington rather than in the communities and states where they were needed would open a faucet which, I believed, had best be kept closed. As this is written, about all the faucets seem to be open, except perhaps the church faucet.

NO SODA FOR THE ARCHBISHOP

Catholic churches in Detroit owed the banks of that city about $21,000,000. They had excellent real estate security to offer and were rather insistent that we lend them money to pay their obliga-tions to the banks. We should have liked to help both the churches and the sorely tried Detroit banks, but we felt we could not aid one denomination without helping them all. Bishop Michael Gallagher of the Detroit diocese was much put out because we declined to lend him the money, particularly as he had ample security to offer. He expressed himself accordingly.

Bishop Gallagher died on January 20, 1937. By and by his successor, Archbishop Edward Mooney, came to see me. He gave me as good a sales talk to borrow money as I ever heard. He told me he was devoting more than half his time attending to the finances of the Archdiocese, and it was his business to look after the flock. He had plainly come to get the money and not to take No for an answer. When he had finished his story I told him frankly and definitely that we would not lend him the money, that if we loaned to his church we should have to lend to the Holy Rollers and all the others. I then said to the Archbishop, a delightful gentleman, that if he would listen I would tell him how to get the money. He listened attentively and I proceeded to say the following:

"You have two prominent Catholics at the head of two of the largest banks in your section of the country, Charles T. Fisher, Jr., president of the National Bank of Detroit, and Walter J. Cummings, chairman of the board of the Continental Illinois National Bank & Trust Co. of Chicago. Both of these institutions are in existence largely, if not solely, because of the RFC's assistance to them and to other banks. You get Fisher and Cummings together and make the same talk to them that you made to me. Tell them that henceforth you are going to devote your time to trying to save their souls, and watching after their morals, and that you have appointed them to look after the finances of the church. If you do that, I guarantee you will get the money."

The Archbishop followed my suggestion. Mr. Fisher got a number of bankers together and arranged a $21,000,000 loan by the Michigan banks. The Bankers Trust Company of New York agreed to take all of the loan that was not provided by Detroit interests.

After signing the note and agreeing to mortgage nothing, Archbishop Mooney arranged with the priests of the various churches under his jurisdiction to make annual contributions from their individual parishes. Evidently the Archbishop and his banker friends also went to work on some of the fat parishioners, for, in a few years, the bank debt was paid in full.

Shortly before the final payment the Archbishop came again one afternoon to tell me that within a few months his entire debt would be paid. I congratulated him and, it being about five o'clock, I asked if he would join me in a little Scotch and soda. He declined, telling me the following story:

An American was calling on a prominent English businessman at the latter's office in London about tea time. The Briton asked his caller if he would have a spot of tea. The American replied: "No tea, thank you."

"Perhaps you would have a cup of coffee?"

"No coffee, thank you."

"Well, how about a little Scotch and soda?"

"No *soda,* thank you."

SOME IDEAS OF JAMES A. MOFFETT

Of all the loans we did not make, that about which there was the most ado was the one we did not make to King ibn-Saud of Saudi Arabia. When the Middle East became one of the theaters of war in 1940, the King found his revenues shrinking, partly because there were no longer any great pilgrimages to Mecca, partly because some of the outlets for Arabian oil had been blocked.

Pinched for funds to support his court, his army, his sundry wives and families in the manner to which they had become accustomed through his oil royalties, the King—according to Mr. Moffett—borrowed from the Arabian American Oil Company to the extent of $7,001,653 in advances against future royalties. The company estimated its probable oil reserves in Arabia and Bahrein at fully 1,000,-000,000 barrels. The company was eager to stay always in the good graces of the King. Previously the name of the company had been California Arabian Standard Oil Company, Inc.

In 1941 the King requested more money from the oil company and also from the British Government, which looked upon Saudi Arabia as one of the countries in its sphere of influence, and a place it certainly didn't want Adolf Hitler to nose into. The King told the oil company he would be needing about $10,000,000 a year to cover his regal requirements. He hinted that the oil company would be smart to provide him with some of those millions against his future royalties. The British had promised him £400,000 sterling during 1941, and he was asking them to boost this to £900,000 sterling.

In April, 1941, James A. Moffett, chairman of the board of the California-Texas Oil Company and a friend of President Roosevelt's, went to the White House. To the President he is supposed to have quoted ibn-Saud as telling the American oilmen that unless the money he wanted were immediately forthcoming he had grave fears for the stability of his country. Mr. Moffett proposed to the President that the United States Government take up the burden of helping ibn-Saud. He suggested that the United States Government purchase petroleum products from the Saudi Arabian Government, the King to waive or defer royalties and the United States Navy to use the oil and gasoline.

Mr. Moffett then reportedly went to Secretary Cordell Hull and suggested that the State Department ask the British to increase the kitty for the Saudi Arabian monarch.

Then, on May 16, 1941, Mr. Moffett came to see me about a loan to the King. A few weeks later Harry L. Hopkins sent me the correspondence Mr. Moffett had had with the White House and a covering note which read:

THE WHITE HOUSE

WASHINGTON

June 14, 1941

PERSONAL AND CONFIDENTIAL

Dear Jesse:

The President is anxious to find a way to do something about this matter. I am enclosing confidential correspondence from the White House so you can see what goes on. Will you return it as soon as you have read it?

I am not sure what techniques there are to use. It occurred to me that some of it might be done in the shipment of food direct under the Lend-Lease Bill, although just how we could call that outfit a "democracy" I don't know. Perhaps instead of using his royalties on oil as collateral we could use his royalties on the tips he will get in the future on the pilgrims to Mecca.

The RFC has done some funny things since that man from Houston took charge of it.

Cordially yours,

HLH.

Meanwhile, I was told that Mr. Moffett had gone to Frank Knox, Secretary of the Navy, to try to sell him a bill of goods on the Navy using $6,000,000 worth of Saudi Arabian products each year. Secretary Knox wasn't interested.

Mr. Moffett continued bothering me about helping the King. We were not at war. We had no connection with the King of Saudi Arabia. As I saw it, there was no way we could, or any reason why we should do anything to help ibn-Saud. Not only was there no moral reason why we should do it, but the RFC had doubtful legal authority.

Having made up my mind that we were not going to do anything about ibn-Saud's demands, I told the President on July 18, shortly after a Cabinet meeting, that I was tired of being bothered about the King of Saudi Arabia. I told him I had no intention of making him a loan and I wanted to be able to tell the people who were trying to get us to help the King that it was not only my decision but the President's as well. I had scribbled a little note during Cabinet which I then handed to the President. I asked him to copy it in his own handwriting, so that I might show whoever was interested that it was not only my decision but the decision of the President that we were

THE WHITE HOUSE
WASHINGTON

7/18-41

Jms —

Will you Tell the British
I hope they can Take
care of the King of
Saudi-Arabia — This is
a little far afield for.
us !

FDR

not going to finance King ibn-Saud. The President immediately copied my exact wordage and handed it to me as a memo. It read:

7–18–41

Jess—Will you tell the British I hope they can take care of the King of Saudi Arabia—This is a little far afield for us!

FDR

At different times during the next few weeks I saw the British representatives: Lord Halifax, the Ambassador; Sir Edward Peacock, a director of the Bank of England; Sir Nevile M. Butler, the British Minister; Sir Frederick Phillips, of the British Purchasing Commission; and Carlyle Gifford, who was in charge of selling British-held American securities in order to obtain dollars. I told these gentlemen that Saudi Arabia was in the British sphere and added that if the British felt the King needed assistance it was up to them to furnish it. I showed the President's note to Sir Frederick Phillips. I told him the United States Government was not in a position either to finance ibn-Saud or to buy any oil in the ground in Saudi Arabia. After that meeting, I sent the following note to Harry Hopkins:

Dear Harry:

You wrote me on June 14 hoping I could find some way to assist King Ibn Saud. There appears no legal way that we can help the King, so, with the approval of the President, I suggested to Lord Halifax and Sir Frederick Phillips, also Mr. Neville Butler, that they arrange to continue taking care of the King.

Sincerely,

JESSE H. JONES, *Administrator*

Mr. Moffett persisted. So, on August 11, I sent him the following letter:

August 11, 1941

Dear Mr. Moffett:

Further and due consideration has been given to the matter of aid to the King of Saudi Arabia.

It is clearly the responsibility of the British to furnish the King with such aid as in their opinion he is entitled to and they feel would be helpful to their cause.

We would like to help the California Arabian Standard Oil

Company, but there is no way that we can do it unless they wish to borrow money on a properly secured note.

> Sincerely,
>
> JESSE H. JONES, *Administrator*

That might have stopped another man, but it didn't stop Mr. Moffett. I had told him, as I had told Secretary Hull, that the RFC had no authority to give money to the King of Saudi Arabia or to buy oil in the ground in Saudi Arabia in the expectation that it could ever be delivered to the Corporation.

Nothing daunted, Mr. Moffett came to see me again on September 10, this time suggesting that perhaps ibn-Saud could be cut in on Lend-Lease. In the hope of closing the subject once for all, I wrote Mr. Moffett another letter on October 9, which read:

Dear Mr. Moffett:

With further reference to your request that aid be provided by our Government for King Ibn Saud, through an advance of several million dollars, beg to advise I am informed that funds cannot be advanced to the King under the Lend-Lease Act, and no Government agency has the authority to provide the King with funds.

I discussed the matter with the President and the Secretary of State. They were both sympathetic with the King's needs and regretted that our Government was not in a position to make him a loan, or an advance on oil royalties that may accrue to him through leases held by your company at some future date.

At the instance of the President and Secretary, I suggested to the British Ambassador that Britain consider providing King Ibn Saud with such funds as in its opinion were necessary to meet his requirements.

The oil companies interested might, if they wanted to do so, work out some arrangement between the British Government and the King.

> Sincerely yours,
>
> JESSE H. JONES, *Administrator*

Subsequently, Mr. Moffett wanted me to give him a letter stating that I had stipulated that the British Government take care of King ibn-Saud out of the proceeds of the $425,000,000 collateral loan which we in the RFC had made to the British during the summer of 1941. I did not give Mr. Moffett such a letter because it would not have been true. I did not stipulate or instruct the British to do anything in regard to the King. I merely suggested that they follow their own judgment in the matter; but the talks were in no way in connection with the loan we were making the British on good collateral. My letters to Mr. Moffett of August 11 and October 9, 1941, were as far as I could truthfully go in response to his request.

Nearly six years later Mr. Moffett sued the Arabian American Oil Company for $6,000,000 as compensation for "influence" he pretended he had used in Washington in 1941 with President Roosevelt, Secretaries Hull and Knox and me, in his efforts to get money for King ibn-Saud.

He claimed in his suit that the oil company had promised to pay him a fair and reasonable value for these "services." The company denied making any such retainer or promise. In his complaint Mr. Moffett said that his services resulted "in the Government of the United States requiring the Government of the United Kingdom of Great Britain, as a part of certain financial negotiations then in progress between the U.S.A. and the U.K., to assume the budget requirements of the Kingdom of Saudi Arabia for the duration of the war."

Mr. Moffett was wrong again when he told the Senate Committee that this was one of the stipulations which the RFC made in granting the British loan.

I made the loan to the United Kingdom of Great Britain and Northern Ireland on perfectly good collateral and there was no such stipulation.

On February 15, 1949, the jury in New York which heard his case awarded Mr. Moffett $1,150,000 plus interest from 1941. Wisely and justly, the award was set aside on April 26, 1949, by Judge Edward A. Conger in the United States District Court in New York City, who held that the type of "services" which Mr. Moffett claimed he had rendered "were the kind that the law says may not be compensated for." The United States Court of Appeals affirmed the judgment. Mr. Moffett then appealed to the Supreme Court of the United States, but that court refused to hear the case, which ended Mr. Moffett's claim.

This was not my first acquaintance with Mr. Moffett. Jimmy claimed close friendship with President Roosevelt. In the early days of the New Deal he was appointed Federal Housing Administrator by the President and afterwards maintained fairly free access to the White House. During the depression, in an effort to create a market for mortgages insured by the Federal Housing Administration, we created the Federal National Mortgage Association, which quickly came to be known as "Fannie Mae." The purpose of Fannie Mae was to buy and sell insured home mortgages.

We invested in the capital stock of Fannie Mae $11,000,000 and it soon became a very profitable business, making about $10,000,000 in one year. After a few years I had one or more suggestions from the White House that maybe we would like to sell Fannie Mae and that Mr. Moffett was interested in buying it. With an invested capital of $11,000,000 and an annual profit in the millions, we were not interested in selling it to Mr. Moffett or to anyone else. It still belongs to the government.

20

---- ✵ ----

BUYING GOLD AND DEVALUING THE DOLLAR

Price Jiggling at FDR's Bedside—Morgenthau Gets on Acheson's Nerves

DURING a train journey from Atlanta to Washington early in his administration, President Roosevelt talked with me about devaluing the dollar. He asked who would get the profit on the gold in such an operation. I told the President that I did not know, but would look into it.

During the next few months the matter was discussed generally between the Treasury, the Department of Justice, and the RFC. It was finally decided by the lawyers that the RFC had authority to buy newly mined domestic gold or any foreign gold as a commodity, giving its notes in payment for the gold at whatever price might be determined by the RFC. The President's idea was that one way to lift the depressed prices of commodities would be to devalue the dollar by raising the price of gold.

A movement by the government to collect hoarded gold from the public had begun the previous March during the nation-wide bank holiday. Congress on March 9 had given the President dictatorial power over all forms of money. The total of gold coin and gold certificates in circulation on the day the President was inaugurated was $1,385,000,000. Two days later, on March 6, banks were prohibited by Presidential proclamation from any further paying out of gold coin and gold certificates. On March 8 the Federal Reserve Board requested the Federal Reserve banks to furnish a list of persons who had recently withdrawn gold and gold certificates, and who, by the approaching March 27, did not redeposit them. Between March 4 and March 31, $260,000,000 in gold coin and $370,000,000 in gold certificates were returned to the Federal Reserve banks and the Treasury. On

[245]

THE PRESIDENT

PRESENTS HIS RESPECTS

TO

THE SECRETARY OF THE TREASURY

AND TO

THE CHAIRMAN OF THE BOARD OF THE R. F. C.

Shiver me Timbers
    Over the Stones,
I, too, have a tale
    'Bout Jesse Jones.

One morning drear
    I had a cold,
And all I needed
    Was just more gold.

"O Jones, O, Jones,
    Give me some gold,"
And all I got
    Was just more cold.

Just then Bill Woodin
    Came along,
And joined to mine
    His beauteous song.

"O, Jones, O, Jones
    Give us some gold,
Or else we'll give you
    Back your cold."

As one we sneezed
    At Jesse Jones--
He handed out his gold
    With groans.

So now we hold
    This lovely gold,
We got with groans,
    From Jesse Jones.

Franklin D. Roosevelt

This jingle was composed by President Roosevelt in 1933.

March 31 the total of gold coin and gold certificates outside the Treasury and the Federal Reserve banks was $700,000,000, the lowest figure since 1923.

On April 5, my birthday, the President issued an Executive Order forbidding the hoarding of gold coin, gold bullion, and gold certificates. In mid-April he put a ban on exports of gold, and in June he signed an Act of Congress which outlawed the gold-payment clause in all moneys and other public and private contracts. By then some people in Wall Street were really getting the jitters and howling calamity.

On October 16, 1933, I sent to the President the following letter:

RECONSTRUCTION FINANCE CORPORATION

WASHINGTON

October 16, 1933

The President
The White House
My dear Mr. President:

In considering further the problem of the purchase of newly mined gold, I wish to make this suggestion.

Under Section 9 of the R.F.C. Act this Corporation is authorized, with the approval of the Secretary of the Treasury, to offer for sale "at such price or prices as the Corporation may determine with the approval of the Secretary of the Treasury," its obligations. We have authority to issue large amounts of notes, debentures or bonds. They could be offered by us for newly mined gold only or for gold coin, and we could agree with the holders of newly mined gold to accept bullion.

You and the Secretary could give us authority to sell this gold abroad. It need not be used but it would afford us a market should it be necessary, and thus would not result in a determined loss to this Corporation.

When Congress meets legislation could be passed which would authorize the purchase of this gold from us or we could pay our indebtedness to the Treasury with it, either on the dollar basis or on the gold basis as might be thought best.

You might desire to submit this suggestion to the Attorney General.

Very sincerely yours,
JESSE H. JONES, *Chairman*

Four days later, at the direction of the President and because of his action in outlawing the possession of monetary gold, the directors of the RFC adopted a resolution stating that there was no free market in the United States for newly mined domestic gold; that it would aid in the creation of such a market if such gold were purchased abroad; and that public problems arising from the absence of a free market for gold newly mined in the United States warranted action.

The board resolved that upon the President's request the RFC, subject to the Secretary of the Treasury's approval, would authorize an issue of $50,000,000 in short-term obligations to be offered for sale payable in newly mined domestic gold or gold imported from abroad.

A copy of this resolution was sent to the White House with the request that the President furnish us with a copy of the opinion of the Attorney General as to the legality of the proposed transaction. Two days later, on Sunday October 22, I prepared a letter setting forth the gold-buying plan as worked out by our general counsel and the Department of Justice and took it to a meeting which the President had called for two o'clock. I went a few minutes early to give the President an opportunity to read the letter before the others he had invited arrived. The President had hardly finished reading the letter when the others, who included several members of the Cabinet, came in. The meeting was in the Oval Room of the White House. No sooner had the men all assembled than the President proceeded to read aloud my letter. He then stated that he proposed to devalue the dollar by increasing the price of gold.

PRICE JIGGLING AT FDR'S BEDSIDE

The meeting was over in a few minutes. As we were leaving, the President turned to me and said:

"Jess, you and Henry [Morgenthau] drop by my bedroom in the morning, and we'll fix the price of gold."

That night, in one of his "fireside chats" on the radio, he gave the public an inkling of what was to come. He reiterated that "the definite policy of the Government has been to restore commodity price levels." He said that when these had been restored "we shall act to establish and maintain a dollar which will not change its purchasing and debt-paying power during the succeeding generation."

Then he said: "It becomes increasingly important to develop and apply the further measures which may be necessary from time to time to control the gold value of our own dollar at home." And he added that "the United States must take firmly in its own hands the control of the gold value of our dollar."

While the hair of many a conservative listener probably began to stand on end and his eyes to bulge, Mr. Roosevelt went on to announce the establishment of a government market for gold in the United States. He said he was authorizing the RFC to buy gold newly mined in the United States at prices to be determined from time to time after we had consulted with him and the Secretary of the Treasury.

"Whenever necessary to the end in view," he added, "we shall also buy or sell gold in the world market. . . . Government credit will be maintained and a sound currency will accompany a rise in the American commodity price level."

Thus he began to haul in the anchor to which the dollar had been tied for thirty-four years.

The next morning I went to the bedside of the President with Henry Morgenthau, Jr., who was then Farm Credit Administrator. It was the President's custom to have his breakfast in bed and to remain there a while reading the newspapers and some of his mail and memoranda of one sort or another before going to his office around ten o'clock. At that first meeting I suggested to the President that, to keep speculators from figuring what we were doing, we should not raise the price of gold on a formula, but should jump it around from day to day until the ultimate price was determined at which the dollar would be reestablished on a gold basis. We decided that morning the first day's price would be $31.36 an ounce instead of the then parity of $29.01. We agreed that gradually from time to time we would boost the price, but with no indications as to how much—or what the ultimate price would be.

On October 24 the President announced publicly that he had named Mr. Morgenthau, Dean Acheson, then Acting Secretary of the Treasury in the absence of Secretary Woodin, and me as a committee to fix the price at which the RFC would buy gold newly mined

C. K. Berryman in Washington Sunday Star.

in the United States. The next morning we announced that the price for that day would be $31.36—the figure hit upon earlier at the President's bedside.

That same day the President issued an Executive Order authorizing the RFC to acquire and to hold, earmark for foreign account, export, or otherwise dispose of gold newly mined in the United States and received by the mints and assay offices on consignment for such purposes.

The RFC thereupon announced that it would receive subscriptions for its ninety-day notes payable in gold so received. The circular for such notes was issued on October 26. At the same time, we jacked our paying offer from the previous day's starting price of $31.36 to $31.54.

We kept raising the price day after day, until we reached $34.01 on December 1. It remained at that figure through December 16, and then was moved up to $34.06, where we held it steady during the remainder of our gold-buying program, which was concluded January 17, 1934. By that time the RFC had bought 695,027.423 ounces

The initials on F. D. R.'s gold chit are those of R. F. C. Directors Jesse H. Jones, Carroll B. Merriam, John J. Blaine, Frederic H. Taber.

of domestic gold for $23,363,754.56, and 3,418,993.045 ounces of foreign gold in the London and Paris markets for $111,037,195.78, a total of $134,400,950.34.

The average cost to us for the foreign gold had been $32.48 per ounce, and for the newly mined domestic gold, $33.62 per ounce.

At the start the RFC had decided to issue $50,000,000 of notes with which to buy gold. This was increased by our board a few weeks later to $100,000,000 and then to $150,000,000.

MORGENTHAU GETS ON ACHESON'S NERVES

Habitually at our morning visits to his bedroom the President jotted down on a slip of paper the price of gold we had agreed upon for that day. He would then hand it to me, and, accompanied by Henry Morgenthau, I would go over to the Treasury and pass the slip to Mr. Acheson.

Although he had named Mr. Acheson a member of the committee of three, the President did not ask Dean to attend the morning bedside meetings in the White House. He had already determined to make Mr. Morgenthau head of the Treasury to succeed Mr. Woodin.

On October 20, the day the RFC directors adopted the resolution at the President's request to embark upon the gold buying program, one of Mr. Acheson's aides had prepared for him a memorandum setting forth the view that such transactions would be of doubtful legality and might "open wide the door for any and every kind of manipulation for ulterior purposes."

About the third or fourth morning that Henry Morgenthau and I went by Mr. Acheson's office to give him the price of gold for that day, I remained to talk with Mr. Acheson about another matter. When Henry was gone Dean remarked that, if the President wanted Henry Morgenthau to run the Treasury, he wished he would appoint him. The procedure was evidently getting on Dean's nerves.

Soon thereafter, on November 15, 1933, less than three weeks after we had begun buying gold, the President announced that he had accepted Mr. Acheson's resignation and had appointed Mr. Morgenthau Acting Secretary of the Treasury.

Mr. Acheson has been given credit by some and applauded for resigning from the Under Secretaryship of the Treasury because he disagreed with the President's determination to reduce the value of the dollar in terms of gold. As I understand the facts to be, Mr. Roosevelt announced Mr. Acheson's resignation without first telling him about it. I have not the slightest doubt that Mr. Acheson would have been glad to remain in the Treasury, either as Under Secretary to Mr. Woodin or as his successor in office and to cooperate in the dollar devaluing plan if wanted by the President. But I can understand that, feeling his superiority over Mr. Morgenthau, Dean would not serve under him.

Gradually, through the daily meetings of the President, Mr. Morgenthau, and me, the plan developed to fix the dollar at about 60 per cent of its old parity, which I am sure was the President's idea. This was finally done at the end of January. During that month Congress passed the Gold Reserve Act of 1934, which the President approved on his fifty-second birthday, January 30. This Act provided that all gold coin and gold bullion in every bank in the Federal Reserve System should pass to and be vested in the United States Treasury and be paid for in gold certificates. The Act authorized the Secretary of the Treasury to buy gold and to sell gold, "which is required to be maintained as a reserve or as security for currency issued by the United States, only to the extent necessary to maintain such currency at a parity with the gold dollar; and therefore, for the purpose of stabilizing the exchange value of the dollar . . . to deal in gold and foreign exchange." For that purpose a stabilizing fund of $2,000,000,000 was put aside.

At the President's request, the Act of May 12, 1933—the Thomas Amendment to the Farm Relief Act—was amended by Congress to provide that the weight of gold in the dollar be fixed at not more than 60 per cent of its then weight. Authorization was also given to the President to reduce in his discretion the weight of the silver dollar in the same percentage. At 3:10 P.M. on January 31, 1934, which was ten minutes after the New York Stock Exchange had closed for the day, President Roosevelt issued a proclamation fixing the weight of the gold dollar at $15\frac{5}{21}$ grains, $\frac{9}{10}$ fine, to become effective immediately. Thus the dollar was officially revalued at 59.06 per cent of the parity, which had been fixed for it in 1900.

The reduction of the gold weight of the dollar automatically gave the Treasury a book profit of $2,817,459,420.80. That was more than sufficient to take care of the following expenditures:

Exchange Stabilization Fund	$2,000,000,000.00
Melting losses, etc.	1,840,204.40
Paid to Federal Reserve Banks (Sec. 13b) Business loans	27,546,310.97
Retirement of national bank notes	645,387,965.45
	$2,674,774,480.82

Subtracting that total from the increment left a tidy balance of $142,684,939.98 for the Federal Treasury.

There are many Americans who stanchly believe that the Roosevelt Administration's tampering with the dollar and its repudiation of the gold clause were illegal and dishonest, a fraud upon every pocketbook in the land. It was only by a five-to-four vote that the United States Supreme Court, on February 18, 1934, decided Congress had the right to amend gold clauses in private contracts, but not in government contracts.

It is not for me to sit in judgment upon the morality of the course pursued. As I told a meeting of the East Texas Chamber of Commerce in Texarkana on April 23, 1934, we do not need to argue any longer about the advisability of devaluing the gold content of the dollar; or as to whether it was right or just to take gold out of actual circulation. These things had already been done, and our government bonds were selling higher than before the change. Enough promises to pay in gold had been made, both privately and governmentally, to make those promises impossible of fulfillment to any great extent—a situation that seemed little short of farcical. At best there is only enough gold in the world to act as a reserve, and a small one at that. Our gold, the basis for our circulating money, is now in the United States Treasury, much of it buried at Fort Knox.

With cotton selling at 5 cents a pound and corn at 15 cents a bushel—as happened in the dark days of the depression—one could not pay debts contracted when cotton was 15 cents and corn 45 cents. You cannot pay the debts of the world in gold when there is so small an amount of gold in the world.

What constitutes sound money? Is it a dollar that is so dear as to be oppressive? Is it a dollar that only a few can have? Or is it a dollar that the average person can get in sufficient quantities, in exchange for his labor and for the things he produces, to pay his taxes and interest and to provide his family with a comfortable life?

21

---- ☼ ----

RELATIONS WITH THE ROOSEVELTS,
THE CABINET AND TRUMAN

My Relations with FDR—FDR the Total Politician—Mrs. Roosevelt and Her Brother—The Unbalanced Budget— Mixing Politics with War—Anti-Fourth-Term Rumpus in Texas—Getting the Sack—I Was Not a New Dealer—Bailing Out Elliott Roosevelt—My Colleagues in the Cabinet— A New Face in the White House

MY RELATIONS with Franklin D. Roosevelt were cordial from the March day in 1933 when he inherited me from the Hoover Administration as a director of the RFC, until the January afternoon in 1945 when he asked me to step aside as Secretary of Commerce so that he could reward Henry A. Wallace whom he had not been able to get renominated for the Vice Presidency at the National Democratic Convention. However, there were occasional irritations from 1942 onward.

The President became vexed with me in 1942 because I did not have the RFC buy the 102-story Empire State Building in New York City at his request. Of that, more in Chapter 31. The following year he was miffed because of my controversy with Henry Wallace. That affair made it necessary for him to abolish Wallace's Board of Economic Warfare and with it, to Mr. Roosevelt's great disappointment, Wallace's succession to the Presidency—blessed be! But, whatever feelings the President may have harbored against me because of these irritants, they were not reflected in our current week-to-week dealings and were never referred to between us after the incidents had passed.

There was one other incident which the President didn't like, and which he held against me. I think he felt that I could have prevented the 1944 anti-fourth-term revolt against him by the Texas "Regulars" which I shall come to later in this chapter. However, I could not have prevented that revolt. The movement had jelled before I knew anything about it, and I was not a delegate to either the Texas state convention or the National Democratic Convention.

While the President remained cordial enough for all purposes, he was not quite the same after that. I knew he lent a willing ear to talebearers and mischief-makers, and there were plenty of them. One or two sat at the Cabinet table.

I never solicited any appointment or favor from the President directly or otherwise. After his election in 1932 he voluntarily told me that he wanted me to be chairman of the RFC. When his first Secretary of War, George H. Dern of Utah, died in August, 1936, Mr. Roosevelt asked if I would like to have that portfolio. I replied that I would not. The President then promoted Harry Woodring of Kansas, who had been Assistant Secretary under Mr. Dern. Soon thereafter the President again told me he wanted me in the Cabinet. I thanked him and told him that I was perfectly content in the work I was doing and was where I was probably needed most. Mr. Woodring headed the War Department until 1940, when the President relieved him and appointed the able and experienced Henry L. Stimson, a Republican, as his successor.

In 1939, when Secretary of the Navy Claude A. Swanson, who had been United States Senator from Virginia, became enfeebled with age, the President asked me to take the Navy portfolio and to find a trusteeship of some sort which would pay Mr. Swanson a living salary. I could easily have found something for Mr. Swanson, but I did not want to be Secretary of the Navy. I told the President I would be glad to look after Mr. Swanson for him, but that I scarcely knew the difference between a battleship and a canoe and preferred to stay where I was—in the business and financial branch of the government, even without a seat in the Cabinet, as that was the work I knew best how to do. Soon thereafter, on July 7, 1939, Secretary Swanson died, and the President named as Acting Secretary Charles Edison of New Jersey, son of Thomas A. Edison, the great inventor. He had been serving as Assistant Secretary of the Navy. A few days after Secretary Swanson's death the President created the Federal Loan Administration and appointed me its chief to be in charge not only of the RFC but of most of the other federal lending agencies. In 1940, at the President's request, Secretary Edison resigned from the Navy portfolio to run for Governor of New Jersey and was elected.

Naturally, any man in government service would like to be in the President's Cabinet. But I considered the proper operation of the RFC more important to the country than my having a Cabinet post. In 1940 the President told me quite casually that he was going to appoint me Secretary of Commerce to succeed Harry L. Hopkins, for whom he had other things in mind. I asked him if I would carry the loan agency with me. He replied that I would not. I then told him I preferred to stay where I was, that I was needed in the loan job and he should get someone else for Commerce. A few days later he sent me word that if Congress was willing for me to hold both jobs he was, and that the Attorney General was drafting a resolution to that effect. Under the law one man cannot occupy two government posts that carry salaries. Shortly thereafter, both Houses of Congress adopted a joint resolution permitting me to hold both positions but to draw only the Cabinet officer's salary.

The President was never genuinely friendly to business, and there was little the Secretary of Commerce could do for business and industry that the Federal Loan Administrator could not do; and I regarded the proper operation of the RFC as of paramount importance.

Later, on February 24, 1942, the President by Executive Order and without talking with me about it, transferred the powers and duties of the Federal Loan Agency and the Federal Loan Administrator, as they related to the RFC and its subsidiaries, to the Department of Commerce for supervision by the Secretary of Commerce. This accomplished nothing so long as I was both Federal Loan Administrator and Secretary of Commerce; but in effect it made the Loan Agency a part of Commerce.

* * *

I first met Franklin Roosevelt during World War I when he was Assistant Secretary of the Navy and I, Director General of Military Relief of the American Red Cross, but I saw very little of him during those two years. I was an alternate delegate to the exhausting Madison Square Garden convention in 1924 which nominated John W. Davis of West Virginia for President on the 103rd ballot, breaking a long deadlock between Governor Alfred E. Smith of New York and William Gibbs McAdoo of California. At that convention Mr. Roose-

Hal Coffman in Fort Worth Star-Telegram.

velt, making his first public appearance since 1921, when he had been stricken with infantile paralysis, put Governor Smith's name in nomination with his memorable "Happy Warrior" speech. Ballot after ballot, Alabama cast its twenty-four votes for its favorite son, Senator Oscar W. Underwood, a persistency which prevented either Smith or McAdoo from obtaining the necessary two-thirds vote. The convention had just about worn the delegates out before they compromised by nominating Mr. Davis for President. After the adjournment Mr. Davis asked me to take the position of Director of Finance for the Democratic National Committee and raise funds for the campaign. I tried to decline, since Mrs. Jones and I were on our way to Europe for a summer vacation, but Mr. Davis would not take no for an answer. Mr. Davis and I had been friends in the Woodrow Wilson Administration during World War I when he was Solicitor General in the Department of Justice.

During the drive for votes and dollars to finance the 1924 campaign Mr. Roosevelt occupied a desk part of the time at our headquarters in New York. I saw him again at the 1928 National Democratic Convention in Houston when he once more placed Al Smith in nomination for the Presidency. That time the Governor of New York received the nomination.

Four years later I was a member of the Texas delegation which swung the Presidential nomination to Governor Roosevelt in Chicago, when the plan of our delegation was to nominate John Nance Garner of Texas for Vice President. I talked with the Governor by long distance during the convention. During the ensuing campaign I called upon Governor Roosevelt at his office in Albany to discuss RFC matters. It had come to my attention that he contemplated attacking the RFC because of loans which it had been reported to him the RFC was making in the interest of President Hoover's campaign. I took with me a run-of-the-mine list of loans and explained to Governor Roosevelt the care that was being used in making most of our loans. I told him that instead of making reckless political loans the Corporation was being operated on a much too narrow basis. My purpose in going to see Governor Roosevelt was to prevent any blasts at the RFC during the campaign, and he made none.

I took no active part in the 1932 campaign except at the Chicago Convention which nominated the candidates. The tide of economic disaster was continually coming in, and we in the RFC were devoting ourselves relentlessly to trying to push it back; but it could not be stopped with the means at hand until it had engulfed the country. That happened after the election of Mr. Roosevelt, but before his inauguration. His first act as President, closing all the banks that were still open, was as wise as it was bold, and was followed by reopening all the sound banks—or those that appeared to be reasonably sound.

Five days after the President's inauguration Congress enacted and Mr. Roosevelt promptly signed an Act that enabled the RFC to put a new and solid foundation under the American banking structure by investing fresh capital, through the purchase of preferred stock in national banks and capital notes in state banks. These were not loans to the banks. These were investments in capital stock that the banks did not have to pay back except out of part of their earnings. We put more than $1,100,000,000 in preferred stock.

FDR THE TOTAL POLITICIAN

I do not understand exactly what Secretary of State Dean Acheson meant recently by "total diplomacy," but I understand perfectly what is meant by "total politician"—Franklin D. Roosevelt. He employed all the arts known to politics in getting and holding the confidence of a great majority of the American people and, along with it, the hatred of others—a hatred upon which he capitalized. He changed his tactics whenever politics seemed to dictate, and with no intention of leaving the White House until voted out—or carried out. In his twelve years in the Presidency he never looked back and never explained.

One serious problem with Mr. Roosevelt after the start of World War II in 1939 was that he was always fighting two wars at the same time, the political struggle for the Presidency, which he never lost sight of, and the military conflict. Regardless of his oft repeated statement "I hate war," he was eager to get into the fighting since that would insure a third term.

In his first campaign for the Presidency, he charged waste and extravagance in government, and promised economy; but immediately after his inauguration he started spending and spending, and never let up. In the beginning his purposes were undoubtedly high; but as the years went by and the mill seemed to require a new kind of grist to keep him in the driver's seat he never hesitated to provide it and, with his famous "You and I know" on the radio, to tell the people about it.

Usually the President's daily White House appointments were for fifteen minutes. If he knew or could divine what the caller was there to talk about, and was not particularly interested in discussing the matter, he was apt to grab the ball, as it were, the minute the visitor entered, talking about something other than what the caller was there for. Before the visitor knew it his fifteen minutes would be up and Marvin McIntyre, "Pa" Watson, or another of the President's secretaries would come in and remind the President that his next engagement was waiting. Mr. Roosevelt, of course, had plenty of time when it suited his purpose, regardless of a waiting caller.

He had a great habit of talking to one caller about the subject matter of his immediately preceding interview. This often happened; at least it did with me. I assumed it was to clarify his own thinking about a subject, and maybe get another opinion. He liked new ideas, even if they were radical, such as Wallace's plowing up every third row to reduce agricultural production, and killing little pigs to make meat scarcer, so as to raise prices. I have always thought the reason he liked Wallace so well was that Wallace was always popping up with some new idea—many of them screwball.

I tried to keep the President advised as to what we in the RFC were doing but did not bother him too much. Ours was largely a financial job. The law and circumstances dictated what we should do. Both as Chairman of the RFC and as Federal Loan Administrator I tried to take the responsibility for our board in making most of the decisions in doubtful situations, doing some things that appeared to be in the interest of the country even if a rather broad interpretation of the RFC Act was required. Whenever we did anything of importance that was on the border line of our authority, I would try at first opportunity to tell the President about it, but after the fact. He was always interested, and he never criticized.

He liked doing things rather than not doing them. I learned early that if I asked him how to do, or what to do, that he would tell me; and I also soon learned that it was my job to find the RFC answers, and not his. Furthermore, he was not experienced in business and finance and, after all, operating the Corporation was the responsibility of its board of directors, and it was a *bipartisan* agency.

Soon after I became chairman, Congress began looking to me for the RFC's operations; and I am glad to say that the President did also. In the twelve years I worked for and with him we never had an argument. We did not always see alike. If he asked me to do something which in my opinion we could not or should not do —and that happened only a few times—we just did not do it. For me that was the only way to operate without having a break with the President. He might or might not ask me about it later. Grace Tully in her book, "F. D. R., My Boss," said the President did not like this. I don't blame him, since he was President and I one of his appointees.

The President thought we in the RFC could do anything I wanted done, and, as time went on and Congress kept increasing our authority, we nearly could. Whenever we needed additional legislation to meet new situations I would take it up with Mr. Roosevelt, or he with me, and invariably he would tell me to get the bill enacted. I always did.

Except on "state" occasions, our relations were informal, which made for better cooperation. Once in a while I would be included in White House card games, but not often with the President.

He and I both suffered from sinus trouble. Almost invariably when he quit his desk in the evening, he would stop by Dr. Ross McIntire's office for a treatment. The doctor's office was in the basement of the White House. I had much the same habit in the winter seasons, though not as consistently. Frequently the President and I would be sitting in the doctor's office, our noses packed, chewing the fat. Mr. Roosevelt enjoyed a good story, and I was able to pick up quite a lot of them. The country never knew how much the President suffered from his sinuses in Washington. I understood it was not so bad elsewhere. The Washington climate is certainly not good except for a few months, in the spring and autumn.

Admiral McIntire was a delightful gentleman and a good doctor. He was loyal to the President to the last and subjected himself to criticism for not letting the public know how ill his patient was. The doctor, of course, had no choice except to quit his job, and that would have been unthinkable. He did call other doctors to see the President. That was fairly well known.

*   *   *

While the President knew I was on the conservative side, he frequently indicated to me that he thought my course a good antidote for the extreme liberals, a sort of balance, as it were. He allowed me to run my job my own way and soon learned that the Congress liked the way we operated. Over a period of twelve years Congress amended the RFC Act a great many times on my testimony, each time giving us more authority, and never declining any requests we made.

It will be remembered that in 1937 the President was very much provoked with the Supreme Court for not upholding some of his many New Deal laws and wanted Congress to increase the membership of the Court from nine to fifteen. The proposal met with strong opposition and was finally defeated in the Senate by a vote of 70 to 20.

When it began to appear that he would not get his way the President sent Thomas G. Corcoran—Tommy the Cork—to ask me if I would sound out some of my friends in the Senate as to whether it would be possible to increase the Court by two members. I had no sympathy with the plan to pack the Court, but went up the Hill and saw some of my friends. They made it clear to me that, had the President in the beginning asked for only two additional members for the Supreme Court, he probably could have got them, but as the score then stood, with everyone embittered, the Senate would not authorize any increase.

A few times over the years, when I felt that I should make suggestions to the President outside of my own work, I would put it on a strictly personal basis as Jess to Frank, reminding him the while that I was eight years his senior and had played most of the instruments in the business and financial orchestra, and was not unacquainted with politics.

My relationship with him was the same whether at his desk or away from the clamors of the Capital or in a friendly card game. In poker the President preferred wild cards and innovations to the kind of straight five-card draw poker most Texans were raised on.

I saw him occasionally outside Washington—at Hyde Park, New York City, Warm Springs. We fished in the Gulf, and at Houston inspected together the site for the San Jacinto Monument which marks the spot where Texas won its independence from Mexico. The monument cost approximately $2,000,000—mostly government money.

In 1926, ten years prior to its opening, I was chosen Director General of our Texas Centennial celebration. I determined to build a monument upon the historic battleground, comparable to the Washington Monument. With the help of Vice President Garner and Secretary of State Cordell Hull I got $400,000 from the Committee on Expenditures out of the government's $3,000,000 appropriation toward our Texas Centennial's cost. The State of Texas gave us $300,000. I was able to wangle another $250,000 out of Harold Ickes from his Public Works funds, which he gave up rather grudgingly. Harry Hopkins allocated about $1,000,000 from his Works Progress Administration funds. Harry gave us the money willingly, and I shall be ever grateful to him. Without his help we could not have finished the job.

The San Jacinto Monument, which attracts nearly half a million visitors each year, is about the same height as the Washington Monument. Some say it is a little higher. I say it depends on where you measure from. It is surmounted by a lone star—the symbol of Texas. Sam Houston's victory over General Santa Anna at San Jacinto opened another gateway for the westward sweep of the American people and brought closer the inevitable inclusion in the Union not only of Texas, but also of New Mexico, Arizona, California, Nevada, Utah, and portions of what are now Colorado, Wyoming, Kansas, and Oklahoma.

MRS. ROOSEVELT AND HER BROTHER

I did not see a great deal of Mrs. Roosevelt. Occasionally Mrs. Jones and I were at the White House at small, rather private dinners; and of course we attended Cabinet dinners and other formal White House functions. Once in a while Mrs. Roosevelt would ask me to a meeting to discuss some project, usually of a philanthropic nature. I was always glad to cooperate. Because of her many activities she might aptly have been termed Assistant President. She worked at the job.

Early in her husband's first Administration, she asked me to the White House to meet with her and a builder or architect from New York. The gentleman had a good idea, but that's about all he proposed to furnish. His plan was for the RFC to acquire property and construct a number of large apartment buildings on the lower East Side of New York City. The idea was good, but we did not have the authority.

Later, however, we made a loan to a builder for a large apartment development in that section, and it proved very successful. It was dedicated as Knickerbocker Village by Governor Smith with some ceremony. I attended and soon thereafter suggested to the Governor that he get a law passed at Albany that would permit the condemnation of property for a sort of glorified slum clearance operation. I had in mind condemning several hundred acres in that section, and building modern apartments, parking and spacing the property so as to make it attractive for residential purposes. The area was near to the business and financial section of Manhattan where many people work.

My idea was that the State of New York and the City of New York with RFC assistance could finance 100 per cent loans at government interest rates, and that the project would pay itself out in twenty or twenty-five years. It would have had the double purpose of creating an enormous amount of business and work, and of modernizing that section of our largest city. Governor Smith evidently did not think well of the idea, since I never heard from him about it. The Metropolitan Life Insurance Company in the last decade has acquired a substantial amount of property in that section and built modern improvements which rent readily at profitable rates.

The principle I had suggested to Governor Smith was adopted a few years later in the form of government-financed home building for people in the lower income brackets. There are now millions of homes throughout the country on which almost the entire cost was financed by government-guaranteed mortgages.

G. Hall Roosevelt, the President's cousin and Mrs. Roosevelt's brother, occasionally called us from the White House about loans. A call from the White House is always impressive. In those days it was intended to be so by some who went there to do their telephoning, particularly Hall Roosevelt and Tom Corcoran. I am sorry to say that this practice has been abused by some in more recent years.

Two or three loans were made in which it appeared Hall Roosevelt had some kind of interest. In one instance we had authorized a "work loan" of $1,250,000 to mine gold in Alaska. The operation was "pan-mining," where the gold is found in creek beds. A day or two after we had authorized the loan, Tommy the Cork came to see me. He said the President was very anxious for us to make this

Alaskan loan, that Hall Roosevelt could get a job with the company as chief engineer, and that the President wanted to get Hall as far from the White House as possible. I told Tom the loan had already been authorized. I suppose Hall Roosevelt got some kind of employment with the company as he soon flew up to Alaska; but he did not stay very long. Neither his efforts nor those of Tom Corcoran on behalf of the President had anything to do with the loan being granted. The borrower wanted a loan of $2,500,000. We loaned him half that amount.

THE UNBALANCED BUDGET

In the summer of 1937, the year following his second election, President Roosevelt got to thinking it might be a good idea politically to balance the budget. That was something he never achieved, either in 1937 or in any other year of his long Administration. There was a good deal of talk in Administration circles about cutting down on relief and other expenditures as one means of ending deficit spending.

So far as the budget was concerned, Secretary of the Treasury Morgenthau did not seem to know the difference between the RFC lending money and Harry Hopkins giving it away—the difference between disbursing funds which would be repaid, and dishing out doles and grants. When the economy proposals were being considered by the President and the matter of reducing public-works expenditures and relief payments came up for discussion, Mr. Morgenthau, who never liked the RFC, said to Wayne Chatfield Taylor, his Assistant Secretary:

"If we do it to Harold and Harry we will have to do it to Jesse." (Harold Ickes was running public works, and Harry Hopkins was ladling out hundreds of millions for "made" work.)

Mr. Taylor, without my knowledge, argued with the Secretary and asked if he had talked with the President about the difference between giving and lending. Mr. Morgenthau said he had not, but promised to do so.

Anyway, in early October of that year the President announced that no more Public Works Administration grants or loans would be made. A few days later, on October 18, on the advice of Secretary Morgenthau and without consulting me, he sent me a letter ordering us to stop all RFC lending. This was ill advised. First, RFC lending did not affect the budget. Of more importance, after four years of generally steady economic improvement, a definite recession in almost all lines had set in during the autumn weeks of 1937, with a marked slowing up in most business activities. Industrial production dropped. Car loadings were distinctly off. Operations in the great steel industry fell to a low level. Production in the heavy-goods and motor industries began to decline. Unemployment increased. There had been during the year a gradually falling market for securities. Bumper crops had caused commodity prices to slump. There were unusually large cotton and corn crops—five million more bales of cotton and a billion more bushels of corn than in 1936. It was obvious the Commodity Credit Corporation would have to make loans upon these crops to prevent ruinous prices, and the Commodity Credit Corporation was being operated and financed by the RFC.

Happily, the RFC at the time was returning money to the Treasury rather than drawing upon it, and we had already quit lending except in extraordinary circumstances, so that we were not contributing to the lack of balance in the Federal budget. But that made no difference with Secretary Morgenthau. He gave the evident impression that he would like the RFC discontinued.

A week after receiving the President's order to stop all lending I sent him a letter pointing out a number of cases in which our directors felt we were under moral obligation to make further loans and cited various commitments which I felt should be carried out. The President sent copies of my letter to Secretary Morgenthau and his Assistant Secretary, Wayne Chatfield Taylor, and Daniel W. Bell, Acting Director of the Budget, with a penciled message reading: "Will you talk this over with J.J.? It seems to me that we have to carry out moral obligations and legal directions. F. D. R."

My letter informed the President that we had a good many loans in the making, and that oftentimes in lending to industry it was necessary to make a second and sometimes a third loan to a borrower to prevent failure. Then there were the disaster loans and the fact that we had been buying FHA-insured mortgages on "new homes." Housing Administrator Stewart McDonald felt that if we discontinued buying these loans it would seriously interfere with home construction; and then there were commitments to pay depositors' money in closed banks and in fact many other situations which required our continuing, even if on a reduced basis.

C. K. Berryman in Washington Evening Star.

I finally convinced the President that economic recuperation would be speedier if we got back into the lending business which Congress had authorized. He made a timid start on November 11, 1937, by authorizing us to fulfill our undisbursed commitments of approximately $440,000,000.

Having figured the President could have a balanced budget without cramping our lending, I drafted a letter to me for his signature, pointing out that since our capital stock was unimpaired we should have ample borrowing capacity without ever calling upon the Treasury.

The President did nothing about it for three weeks, at the end of which he authorized me to resume lending in the following letter:

January 10, 1938

My dear Jesse:

With reference to our conversation of December 21, 1937, and the draft of a letter for my signature which you left with me for my consideration, I do not believe that it is desirable to give you general instructions at this time.

I agree with you that ample credit should be available for new construction, and while it is my intention to get the government out of the lending business as early as possible, credit must be available for all worthy purposes if people are to have work.

I understand that you have under consideration the submission to Congress of legislation which will in effect simplify the balance sheet of the Reconstruction Finance Corporation and eliminate those items which should not be considered extensions of credit, and in addition that you are considering the question of having the Reconstruction Finance Corporation finance its own requirements by the sale of its obligations in the market. The result of this second operation would be to eliminate Reconstruction Finance Corporation receipts and expenditures from the budget figures except that the proceeds from the sale of any Public Works Administration obligations held by Reconstruction Finance Corporation would come into the Treasury as a repayment on account of the Reconstruction Finance Corporation notes held by the Treasury and thereby be a credit against budget expenditures.

Pending the conclusion of these arrangements and within the limits of your Act, I desire that you give consideration to new construction loans which would tend to maintain or increase employment where there is an economic need for the construction. And in this connection that you discuss with me these requirements, the needs of the general situation and conditions prevailing in individual fields of credit.

Very truly yours,
FRANKLIN D. ROOSEVELT

Honorable Jesse H. Jones
Chairman,
Reconstruction Finance Corporation
Washington, D.C.

Accordingly, I discussed the entire situation with the President and resumed business across the board at my discretion.

MIXING POLITICS WITH WAR

One trouble with President Roosevelt, in both the preparedness program of 1940–1941 and the "home front" after Pearl Harbor, was that when it came to the mobilization of American industry for all-out war, he couldn't seem to make up his mind and stay put. This is best exemplified by the fact that one alphabetical agency followed another, most of them created by the President's Executive Orders, and none of them was given the power it needed.

The parade of successive agencies began on August 9, 1939, the second week of the European War, when, with the President's approval, the War and Navy Departments announced the formation of a Civil Advisory Committee to the Army-Navy Munitions Board. This group, which later came to be known as the War Resources Board, included E. R. Stettinius, Jr., chairman of the United States Steel Corporation; Dr. Karl T. Compton, president of the Massachusetts Institute of Technology; Walter S. Gifford, president of the American Telephone & Telegraph Co.; John L. Pratt, director of General Motors Corporation; General Robert E. Wood, chairman of Sears, Roebuck & Co.; Harold G. Moulton, president of Brookings Institution; and John M. Hancock, a partner of Lehman Brothers, New York bankers.

Simultaneously, the President created the Office of Emergency Management, composed of the Secretaries of War, Navy, Agriculture, Interior, Commerce, and Labor; but they did not get together until the following May, when France fell and everybody in Washington was scared.

During that melancholy month the President set up the National Defense Advisory Commission. It was composed of capable men, but it had no chairman. No man was told to head up the defense production effort or to settle the disputes and differences in approach and opinion which are bound to occur when strong men get together.

William S. Knudsen was called from the presidency of General Motors Corporation to oversee industrial production for the National Defense Advisory Commission. Mr. Stettinius was put in charge of industrial materials. Ralph Henderson was given price stabilization. Ralph Budd, president of the Burlington Railroad, was put in charge of the Commission's transportation studies, and Chester C. Davis of farm production. William H. McReynolds was appointed Secretary of the Commission. A little later Donald M. Nelson was called in from Sears, Roebuck to be the Commission's Coordinator of National Defense Purchases. The word "coordinator" was much in use and misuse in Washington at that time and continued to be for years thereafter.

The magnificent work done by Mr. Knudsen in the preparedness program and during the war is described in Chapter 22.

I have been told that it was Mr. Knudsen who first described his adopted country as the "Arsenal of Democracy"—a phrase given public dissemination by President Roosevelt. Whether he coined this happy locution seems uncertain, but surely Bill Knudsen, as much as any other man, made it ring true.

Born in Denmark, Bill Knudsen had come to this country penniless as a young man of twenty and had proved himself a genius in automobile production, first with Ford and then with General Motors.

In February, 1941, Mr. Knudsen organized the Production Planning Board and brought many of the country's leading industrialists to Washington.

In the summer of 1941 the President shifted civilian direction of the preparedness program to still another of his creations by Executive Order, the Office of Production Management. He asked Mr. Knudsen to take the job of Director General and told him he was appointing Sidney Hillman, the labor leader, Associate Director General. Mr. Knudsen asked the President who would be boss. The President replied, "I will be boss." Of course, the President would be the final boss, but what Knudsen meant was who would be boss as between him and Sidney Hillman. There and then Knudsen should have declined the appointment; but, being patriotic and willing to do anything the President wanted him to do, he accepted an impossible job. How impossible it was, the President made clear at his next press conference when in replying to a question as to the nature of the new organization he said it had "a single responsible head: his name is Knudsen and Hillman." As this two-headed condominium moved into action Mr. Knudsen represented business, industry, and production, with Mr. Hillman representing labor, New Dealism, and politics—an impossible, unworkable agreement.

On August 28, 1941, the President created still another organization to prepare for the exigencies of war and called it the Supply Priorities and Allocations Board, which was also supposed to do big things in winning the war. Its board, with Vice President Wallace as chairman, consisted of members of the Office of Production Management council, and included the Secretaries of War and Navy, and Harry Hopkins and Leon Henderson. Donald Nelson was executive director. A little later I was added to the board.

Shortly after Pearl Harbor the President decided to pull still another rabbit out of his fecund hat. This happened on January 13, 1942. I was attending a meeting that afternoon of the Supply Priorities and Allocations Board. At 4:30 or a little later, Henry Wallace and Donald Nelson excused themselves and left the meeting to go to the White House. I think none of us knew why—at least I did not. As our meeting adjourned about six o'clock and Mr. Knudsen walked into his office, his secretary told him she had just heard over the radio that Donald Nelson had been made chairman of a new Presidential creation, to be called War Production Board, which would take over direction of wartime industry.

When I reached my own office there was a White House call awaiting me. I answered, and Harry Hopkins told me what had been done. He said the manner in which it had been handled was brutal so far as Knudsen was concerned, and Bill was bound to feel badly hurt. Harry asked me to go see Mr. Knudsen as soon as I possibly could and urge him to accept a commission in the Army, a one-star or two-star generalship, and help Under Secretary of War Bob Patterson in his procurement problems.

I then telephoned Mrs. Jones that I would not be home for dinner and went straight away to Mr. Knudsen's Washington residence, in which he usually lived alone with only his servants about him. Occasionally Mrs. Knudsen and members of his family would come to Washington and spend some time with him. Arriving at his residence, I found a most unhappy man. I am sure that Bill Knudsen would rather have been shot than receive the treatment he got that day at the hands of the President, for whom he had the greatest possible reverence. I told him of Hopkins' request and that, while I agreed he had been badly mistreated, I believed he would be much happier in the end if he accepted a high-ranking appointment in the Army and continued in that capacity to push production. He was adamant. He said the President had kicked him out and he was going home to Detroit. Just the two of us were there. We talked all through dinner. I have never seen a more disconsolate man. After dinner this Great Dane, as he was admiringly called, sat at the piano and played and hummed sad tunes as though his heart would break. It was even tough for me. I finally got him to join me at cards a little, but when the discussion inevitably shifted back to my mission he was still firm in his intention to leave Washington. He was not critical; he was just plain hurt. Suddenly, about midnight, I picked up the telephone in his presence, called the White House, and asked for Mr. Hopkins. Taking a chance, I said to Harry: "Knudsen will accept a three-star generalship in the Army and report to Assistant Secretary of War Robert Patterson for service in promoting production for war." Knudsen said nothing; he was probably glad to have a friend decide for him.

Harry replied Bill could only be appointed a major general. I repeated, a lieutenant general. I had understood the latter was the highest rank to which a man not in the armed forces could be commissioned. I argued with Bill, of whom I was very fond, that I thought he would be much happier as a Lieutenant General in the Army, serving his country in time of war, than as chairman of any alphabetical agency of which there were great numbers. I also brought to his attention the fact that, to my knowledge, no other civilian had ever enjoyed such a distinction. I felt Bill Knudsen was entitled to the highest rank available to a nonmilitary man. It worked out that way the following day.

Knudsen proceeded to do a magnificent job, flying from plant to plant, seeing the men at work in the plants—as well as the bosses—and getting higher and higher production, *but he never got over the blow.* He was never happy again.

Meanwhile, the National Defense Advisory Commission had withered and passed away; but it was never given decent burial. Its members had their last meeting on October 23, 1941, but the organization itself was never officially terminated.

Knudsen was one of the most impressive public speakers that I ever heard. I attended a meeting of some fifteen hundred people on one occasion which he addressed. He talked for an hour and fifteen minutes without a note, and you could have heard a pin drop the entire time. No one thought the speech long, and everyone was inspired by the homespun eloquence of this foreign-born man who got his education in the workshop.

Telling of the creation of the War Production Board and the selection of its chairman by the President, Robert E. Sherwood in his history "Roosevelt and Hopkins" quotes from the memoranda of Harry Hopkins the following:

The amusing part of the whole business was that everybody was a candidate. Wallace, I am sure, hoped the President would ask him. Bernie Baruch was in a hotel room in Washington spreading propaganda for himself. A great many of my friends were pushing Bill Douglas. Morgenthau wanted it worse than anything in the world. So did Jesse Jones and, of course Knudsen.*

I cannot speak for the others, but I certainly was not angling for the job as chairman of the War Production Board and would not have accepted it had I been asked—for the same reason that prompted me in declining three proffered Cabinet portfolios, to remain with the RFC. I was already responsible for and doing the kind of war work I was best qualified to do, and knew it. I intended to stay with the RFC as long as I was in government.

ANTI-FOURTH-TERM RUMPUS IN TEXAS

Early in 1944 some of the old-line Democrats in Texas, fed up with the New Deal and the finaglings of the fourth-termers, organized themselves under the name of Texas "Regulars" to oppose the renomination of Roosevelt. When the Democratic party held its state convention in Austin in May of that year, the Regulars captured the convention from the pro-Roosevelt delegates, who then bolted to hold their own convention. Soon after these meetings certain troublemakers in Washington tried to make it appear to the President and others close to him that I had encouraged the action taken by the Regulars. This was due to the fact that George A. Butler, the husband of one of my several nieces, took a prominent part in the Regulars movement. In discussing this with the President, I told him that I had a good many in-laws, including several men who had married my nieces, and that I did not control them in their politics any more than he controlled his own family. I reminded him that his son Elliott, over my protest, had persisted in his purpose to second my nomination for the Vice Presidency at the 1940 Chicago Convention, after the President had chosen Henry Wallace, and of Elliott telling me that his father did not know what he was doing in wanting Wallace. Subsequent developments proved that Elliott was right about Wallace.

Being a member of the President's Cabinet, I was, of course, embarrassed by Mr. Butler's activities in the Regulars movement, but there was nothing I could do about it.

* Reprinted by permission of Harper & Brothers.

Jim Berryman in Washington Evening Star.

I would not, of course, remain in the President's Cabinet and be disloyal to him. During our conversation about the situation in Texas I told him I would try to find a way to correct the impression Mr. Butler's activities might have created, and assured him that he would, of course, carry Texas. In July, when the party held its national convention in Chicago, the credentials committee seated some of the pro-Roosevelt delegates from Texas and also some of the Regulars who favored Senator Harry F. Byrd of Virginia for the Presidential nomination. I was ill with pneumonia and did not attend the convention.

Following the nomination of the President for a fourth term, and in view of the party split in Texas, I wrote an editorial for the front page of my newspaper, the Houston *Chronicle,* advocating the President's reelection. The editorial was widely copied. In September, when the Texas Democrats held another state convention, this time in Dallas, the pro-Roosevelt faction was dominant.

During the fourth-term campaign Judge Sam Rosenman, the President's right-hand man and speech writer, came to my office to tell me Mr. Roosevelt wanted me to make a thirty-minute speech on a national radio hook-up, advocating his reelection. I told the Judge I would, but that my speech would have to be addressed to the business and financial world; that I would be glad to tell what had been accomplished by the Roosevelt administration for business and banking.

The Judge said that was exactly what the President wanted from me. I prepared the speech and submitted the manuscript to Judge Rosenman. He returned it with a few slight suggestions for changes, principally in language. After delivery of the speech I was told by Judge Rosenman that they all liked it. Later the President told me he liked it very much, and expressed his appreciation for my having made it. He knew I had not been well.

As a matter of fact, I took John D. Goodloe, general counsel for the RFC, with me to the broadcasting station so that if I were unable to complete delivery he could do it for me. I could not, of course, decline to make the speech when requested by the President, without its being misunderstood; and, as previously stated, according to my code I could not remain in his Cabinet and not support him.

Following the fourth-term nomination Postmaster General Frank C. Walker, a close personal friend of the President, told me the President thought each Cabinet member should help raise campaign funds. It had been my habit to contribute to the party fairly liberally since 1924, when I was director of finance for the Democratic National Committee and came to know how hard it is to get enough campaign money.

It was no particular chore for me to telephone a few friends and associates in Texas for contributions. Accordingly I raised something over $50,000, which included $5,000 each from Mrs. Jones and me, most of the balance being from my business associates. I have no way of knowing what, if anything, any other Cabinet member contributed or raised. Mr. Walker and Mr. Morgenthau could have, as also could Mr. Wallace; but Henry's contribution consisted largely of soapbox oratory.

GETTING THE SACK

When he was elected to his fourth term, I sent the President a letter of congratulations, as had been my custom. On November 21 he responded with this message:

Dear Jesse:

My warm thanks to you for your fine note of congratulations. Your good wishes are sincerely appreciated.

Affectionate regards,

FDR

Soon after the election there was gossip in Washington that the President would probably replace me in the Cabinet. Two or three of my close friends, including Harry Hopkins, told me as much. Harry said that Henry Wallace was insisting to the President on having my job, and Harry thought the President might give it to him. The President did.

Harry told me the President wanted Henry to accept the Commerce post without the Federal Loan Administrator job but Henry said he would not take the Commerce post unless he also got the Loan Agency. (The Congress, of course, saw to that, by separating the two agencies; so, after all, Henry did not get his hands on the RFC bank roll. He took what he could get.)

Before that happened I learned early in January, 1945, that a small borrower in Texas had written the President criticizing the manner in which the RFC had handled loans to his institution. He implied that I personally wanted to get hold of the Fuqua properties in the Panhandle of Texas through RFC loans. Because of this insinuation I wrote the President, January 11, 1945, that I had been furnished with a copy of the letter from the complaining customer in Texas. I took the occasion to inform Mr. Roosevelt in writing that I had never bought any property on which the RFC had made a loan, nor had anyone related to me or associated with me done so. And I added that I had not bought any property of any kind, anywhere, or a share of stock in any corporation since I had been in government service—thirteen years. I now might add that I have made no such purchases since leaving government. In fact, I have no investments other than those under my direct control and have not had for a great many years.

Because of the state of the President's health, I had not seen him very much for several weeks, as Cabinet had not been meeting. But Cabinet met Friday January 19th, the day before his fourth inauguration. During the session the President remarked that, although Henry Wallace would cease to be Vice President on the morrow, he would still be with us. He did not say in what capacity. After that Friday Cabinet, as was my custom, I discussed some RFC matters with the President with only the two of us present. He said nothing about replacing me. That particular meeting with the President was the first time I had noticed the deterioration of his mind. The matters I discussed were not new, but he had no recollection of them whatever.

On inaugural morning I attended as usual the ten o'clock service at the White House, then the swearing-in ceremonies on the South Portico of the White House, at noon. I stood within a few feet of the President when he took the oath and delivered his brief inaugural address. He could hardly go through with the short speech and had great difficulty in standing, even with the help of one of his sons, Colonel James Roosevelt, on one side, and Edwin Halsey, the Secretary of the Senate, on the other. I then realized how really enfeebled he had become.

About five o'clock that Saturday afternoon my office received a telephone call from the White House, the message being that I was asked to see the President at twelve o'clock noon, the next day. A few minutes later that Saturday afternoon I received by messenger the following letter:

THE WHITE HOUSE

January 20, 1945

Dear Jesse:

This is a very difficult letter to write—first, because of our long friendship and splendid relations during all these years and also because of your splendid services to the Government and the excellent way in which you have carried out the many difficult tasks during these years.

Henry Wallace deserves almost any service which he believes he can satisfactorily perform. I told him this at the end of the campaign, in which he displayed the utmost devotion to our cause, traveling almost incessantly and working for the success of the ticket in a great many parts of the country. Though not on the ticket himself, he gave of his utmost toward the victory which ensued.

He has told me that he thought he could do the greatest amount of good in the Department of Commerce, for which he is fully suited, and I feel, therefore, that the Vice President should have this post in the Administration.

It is for this reason only that I am asking you to relinquish this present post for Henry, and I want to tell you that it is in no way a lack of appreciation for all that you have done, and that I hope you will continue to be a part of the Government.

During the next few days I hope you will think about a new post—there are several Ambassadorships which are vacant—or about to be vacated. I make this suggestion among many other posts and I hope you will have a chance, if you think well of it to speak to Ed Stettinius, who will not leave to join me for several days.

Finally, let me tell you that you have my full confidence and that I am very proud of all that you have done during these past years.

With my warm regards,

Always sincerely,

FRANKLIN D. ROOSEVELT

The Honorable
The Secretary of Commerce

After reading the letter, I consulted with some of my associates, and on deliberate consideration, concluded that because of my long service and the responsible government portfolios I had held, and the fact that I was to be replaced by a man totally unfit for the great responsibilities I had been carrying, it was my duty to release the President's letter along with my acknowledgment, and comment.

I returned to the office on Sunday morning and, in view of having received the President's letter at so nearly the same hour the previous afternoon as the telephone call asking me to see the President at noon on Sunday, I had my secretary telephone the White House to ask if the President still wanted to see me. I was told he did.

I met him at twelve o'clock in the Oval Room where we had had many pleasant and constructive meetings over the twelve-year period I had served under him. He expressed great appreciation for the service I had rendered him and the country, and his deep regret at asking me to relinquish my post, but went on to say that he felt he owed Henry Wallace almost any post Henry might want. He told me Henry wanted to be Secretary of State, but if he could not have that post that he would take the Commerce job.

Continuing, the President told me he wanted me to stay in the government. He offered me the Ambassadorship to France, and elaborated on the possibility of a great reconstruction job in France as soon as the war was over—one for which he said I was especially qualified; or, if I would prefer, he would make me Ambassador to Rome, and probably later send me to the Court of St. James's.

I thanked the President, but told him that while I would like to be helpful until the war was over, I did not want an Ambassadorship and would not leave the country.

He then asked me to accept the chairmanship of the Board of Governors of the Federal Reserve System. He criticized the way the Board was being operated by Marriner Eccles, and enlarged upon the possibilities of a great job there. I again thanked him, but declined. Then he suggested that I set up any kind of organization, the headship of which I would accept, in connection with the finishing of the war and our readjustment thereafter. He said he would create such an organization and position by Executive Order and I could write my own ticket. Again I thanked him and declined once more. I did not want to undertake a new job at that stage and told him so. Furthermore, after twelve years of close association, to be dismissed in such a manner and for the reasons he gave, I could no longer have respected him or worked with him.

I asked when he wanted my desk vacated. He replied, when my successor was confirmed by the Senate. I arose, we shook hands, and I wished him success on his great undertaking at Yalta, and told him goodbye.

He said, "It's not goodbye; I'll see you when I get back."

I replied, "Mr. President, I think it is goodbye."

After this visit I shuddered at the thought of the President, weakened mentally and physically, as he obviously was, leaving that week for Yalta to meet Stalin and his horde.

Our last meeting was probably a mistake. Better he had let it go with the letter of dismissal, because it was not a happy occasion for either of us. My long association with him had been pleasant,

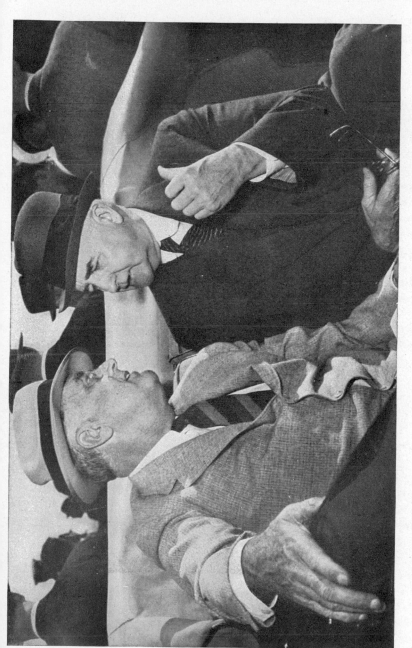

This photograph was sent to me by the President with the following inscription in his handwriting: "Franklin D. Roosevelt to the Hitch Hiker (see thumb)."

MEETING OF THE CABINET

The table with fifteen chairs was presented to the Cabinet by Secretary Jones in 1941 and is still used by President Truman's Cabinet.

and to have it end in the manner it did was a disappointment to me and not pleasant for him.

Because of the rumbling for some weeks prior to that date, I was not surprised at being relieved; but I was surprised at the manner in which it was done, though, knowing Mr. Roosevelt as I did, I should not have been. I had seen him operate for a dozen years and had in fact helped him replace men by getting them other jobs. He was at once one of the kindliest men I ever knew, and again he could be a near sadist. He did not like to meet unpleasant personal situations head on. When we were going to drop his friend Fred Taber from the RFC Board, he asked me not to let Taber come to him, saying Taber would make him cry. I knew perfectly what he meant because of my understanding of the President's peculiarly complex character.

It was a relief to be out of government service. First, I was tired and a little run-down, the result of two spells of pneumonia during the preceding two years, which came toward the end of thirteen years of incessant work. Next, which was important to me, I felt entirely satisfied with my record. I had rounded out fifteen years full time in two world wars and our country's most serious depression, with my salary checks going for philanthropic purposes.

In view of the President's decision, I sent to the White House on Sunday afternoon the following letter:

January 21, 1945

Dear Mr. President:

Inasmuch as you are sending Mr. Wallace's name to Congress tomorrow, I am releasing your letter to me and my reply.

I have eliminated from your letter any reference to your trip.

With all good wishes for a successful meeting.

Sincerely,

JESSE H. JONES

The President
The White House

When the above message had been delivered my secretary telephoned the White House to say it was my purpose to give out the letters at seven o'clock that night, which I did, not receiving any request from the White House not to do so.

My reply read:

THE SECRETARY OF COMMERCE

WASHINGTON

Dear Mr. President:

I have your letter of today, asking that I relinquish my post as Secretary of Commerce, which carries with it the vast financial and war production agencies within the Reconstruction Finance Corporation and its subsidiaries, so that you can give it to Henry Wallace as a reward for his support of you in the campaign.

You state that Henry Wallace thinks he could do the greatest amount of good in the Department of Commerce, and that you consider him fully suited to the post. With all due respect, Mr. President, while I must accede to your decision, I cannot agree with either of you.

You refer very kindly to our long friendship and our splendid relations during all the years, and state that you appreciate my splendid services to the government and the excellent way I have carried out the many difficult tasks during these years. You are also good enough to say that I have your full confidence, and that you are very proud of all I have done during these past years, and that you hope I will continue to be a part of the government, probably in a diplomatic post. It is difficult to reconcile these encomiums with your avowed purpose to replace me. While I want to be of any further service that I can, I would not want a diplomatic assignment.

I feel and have felt a great sense of responsibility to the Congress and to you for the proper administration of the laws with respect to the RFC, that have been passed in the expectation that they would be administered by me or someone experienced in business and finance.

I have had satisfaction in my government service because I have had the confidence of the Congress, as well as your own. I have had that confidence because I have been faithful to the responsibilities that have been entrusted to me. For you to turn over all these assets and responsibilities to a man inexperienced in business and finance will, I believe, be hard for the business and financial world to understand.

I appreciate the opportunity you have given me to serve my country through the depression and in time of war. My 13 years of government service are ample evidence of my desire to be of any assistance I can to the government. I can best be helpful in the line of my life's work—business and finance—but I seek no job.

With best wishes,

Faithfully yours,
JESSE H. JONES

The President
The White House

Talburt for Scripps-Howard newspapers.

Although the President had told me to continue until my successor was confirmed by the Senate, I wrote a note before leaving the office that Sunday evening to Chairman Charles B. Henderson of the RFC, asking him to accept as immediately effective my resignation as a director and chairman of the Corporation's five wartime subsidiaries: Defense Plant Corporation, Defense Supplies Corporation, Metals Reserve Company, Rubber Reserve Company, and War Damage Corporation.

I also sent a note to Leo T. Crowley, chairman of the Export-Import Bank of Washington, resigning as a member of its board of trustees, effective at Mr. Crowley's pleasure.

Then I wrote a letter to Wayne Chatfield Taylor, my Under Secretary in the Commerce Department, asking him to fulfill the functions of Secretary until my successor was confirmed. He ran the Department for six weeks.

It was not until March 1 that the Senate confirmed the Wallace appointment.

Meanwhile, I maintained my office as Federal Loan Administrator until, the two posts having been separated by Congressional passage of the George bill, the President appointed Fred M. Vinson (now Chief Justice of the United States) to succeed me. He took over on March 12.

In the interval the President sent a message to me from Yalta, "Keep your shirt on," that "We will work out something." He did not write me. He minded the maxim of old Senator Tom Platt of New York: "Don't write; send word." But I was through and never saw him again.

In the light of what the President did at Yalta and the promises he made, particularly to Stalin, the reader may be interested in a memorandum I dictated after attending the Cabinet meeting on the eve of his fourth inaugural.

MEMORANDUM:

At the Cabinet meeting Friday, January 19, the President stated that he was not going to make any trades on his contemplated meeting with Churchill and Stalin; that he was not going to make any commitments; that he was going to preserve his trading position, and if Stalin and Churchill pushed him for commitments, that he would tell them he wanted time to study their requests and to confer with Congress.

THE WHITE HOUSE
WASHINGTON

March 24, 1945

Dear Jesse:

Many thanks for those albums, with
the interesting pictures and history of the
Rogers Estate, together with that large aerial
photograph. I am glad to have them and much
appreciate your kindness in sending them to
me.

Always sincerely,

Franklin D Roosevelt

Honorable Jesse H. Jones,
Shoreham Hotel,
Washington, D. C.

Among other things, he referred to the fact that when President Wilson was taken seriously ill in late 1919, while on his speaking tour in the West, in the interest of the League of Nations, the Secretary of State (Robert Lansing), being the ranking member of the Cabinet, called a meeting of the Cabinet and that the President resented it very much, and soon thereafter appointed a new Secretary of State (Bainbridge Colby).

He stated that he would be away four or five weeks, and that he would have with him the Secretary of State, and that if the next ranking member of the Cabinet, Secretary Morgenthau, wished to do so, the President would have no objection to the Secretary of the Treasury calling a meeting of the Cabinet. In other words, that the next highest official of the Cabinet, Morgenthau, could carry on in his absence.

In cleaning out my desk before leaving I came across some albums with pictures and the history of the Rogers property adjoining the Roosevelt estate at Hyde Park, which I had arranged to purchase at the President's request. I sent the albums to him and on March 24 received a letter of thanks. Its signature, "Franklin D. Roosevelt," was that of a feeble hand. Twenty days later the President died.

* * *

I would like to have remained in charge of the RFC and its subsidiaries until the war ended, so as to have done something about recouping as much as possible from the vast investments we had made in plants and strategic materials. I could have saved the government many hundreds of millions of dollars in the preservation and disposition of these vast investments over what was realized by having them turned over to others who had no familiarity with them and, as often as not, no great amount of business experience. What I particularly had in mind was to bring to the attention of the President and the Congress the future of the RFC. Having completed its original purpose, to meet the depression, and its vast expansion for the war job, it had entirely too much authority and power, most of which had been given it on my testimony and in the expectation that I would direct its affairs. I wanted to put it away.

I was glad to have had the opportunity of serving my country during the depression and the war period in the capacities which I held, for I had been beyond the age of military service in both World War I and II. I had carried more problems and responsibilities than probably any man in government except the President and, at seventy-one, was feeling the strain.

*   *   *

In his climb to fame, Franklin Roosevelt was all things to all men —always a politician. He became President of the United States in a period of great depression and found he could break the depression with the people's own money, appropriated by Congress under his leadership. Of greater import he found that by the same method he could break the two-term Presidential tradition established by George Washington and respected by all previous Presidents.

When he had accomplished that, he was the exceptional man and began to see himself a great world figure of all time, a Caesar maybe, or an Alexander the Great. But he must bring Joseph Stalin under his influence. To do that it was necessary to get on a working basis with Joe. Overlooking the fact that Stalin had repudiated his agreement made with Roosevelt when, as President, he had the United States Government recognize the Soviet Union in 1933 after our Government had refused such recognition since the inception of the Soviet Union in 1917, at which time the Bolsheviks overthrew the Kerensky government, the President sent Harry Hopkins to the Kremlin in 1942 to tell Stalin that he would give him whatever war supplies and equipment he needed in his struggle with Hitler. This cost the American people more than $11,000,000,000 in money, materials, and equipment, and that was only a starter. Better he had let Hitler and Stalin destroy each other.

Next, the President must meet the Soviet dictator face to face; but Joe refused to travel far from Moscow. So, in 1943, the President took the long trip to Teheran, just across the Persian border from Russia, to meet Stalin. At Teheran the President made various promises and commitments to Joe. Still determined but in fast-failing health, weakened in mind and body, Roosevelt went to Russia in the dead of winter, 1945, to meet Stalin at Yalta. There he made still further commitments from which our country and the rest of the non-Communist world may never recover. A few weeks later he was dead—his ambition unattained.

I WAS NOT A NEW DEALER

In an obvious effort to justify Mr. Roosevelt for replacing me with Henry Wallace, Grace Tully wrote in her book, "F.D.R., My Boss" *:

Immediately after the 1944 election, the Boss had promised Wallace a new post in the Administration, and when the latter asked for the Commerce position, Roosevelt took steps to open it up for him. Jesse Jones was then doubling as Secretary of Commerce and Federal Loan Administrator. He had not favored Roosevelt's third and fourth term races. For that matter, he had never been a real New Dealer. Although he was in name a lifelong Texas Democrat, his private concepts of government and its role in our economy lay closer to the beliefs held in the Republican camp; he had in fact, been named a Director of the Reconstruction Finance Corporation by President Hoover in 1932.

While Jones had done a competent job in the vast Governmental empire he had brought under his control, Roosevelt knew of his early cooling toward New Deal policies, as well as his disapproval of the third and fourth terms.

On inauguration day, January 20, 1945, the President suddenly told me to take a note to Mr. Jones. He thereupon dictated a letter asking Jesse to relinquish the Cabinet post in order to permit the appointment of Mr. Wallace as Secretary of Commerce.

Though the President softened the tone of the letter by expressing his appreciation and admiration for Mr. Jones' long service—and though he suggested a possible diplomatic appointment—my personal feeling at the time was that it was neither a good letter nor the best way in which to handle a difficult situation.

Another instance of Mr. Roosevelt pleasing a friendly partisan writer is related by Jonathan Daniels in his biography of President Truman. He recounts that one day in June, 1944, while he and President Roosevelt were talking about "Jesus H. Jones"—the President often referred to me as Jesus Jones—Mr. Roosevelt drew his forefinger across his throat and made the statement that there would be a period between the election in November and the inauguration on January 20—meaning he would get rid of me before the fourth

* Reprinted by permission of Charles Scribner's Sons.

term began. From that statement one would think he would have asked for my resignation before the last hour of the last day, and that he would have done it in conference instead of by letter, since I saw him privately the day before he dictated the letter.

In this connection it is pertinent for me to relate that on the first day of June, 1944, which would have been but a little while before the unspecified date in that month when the President regaled Mr. Daniels with his "ear to ear" throat-slitting gesture in respect to me, there came to my office John J. Hardin of Oklahoma City and former Congressman Jack Nichols, also of Oklahoma. The fourth-term pot was boiling as the time for the Democratic National Convention approached. Mr. Nichols, then living in California, told me that he had had breakfast with the family at the White House, and that they were divided as to whether the President should stand for reelection. Mr. Nichols said some members of the President's family thought he was not physically able to make a campaign, let alone continue to bear the burdens of the Presidency, but other members wanted him to run again. Mr. Nichols then made the statement that if the President could be assured that his son James would be appointed Secretary of the Navy Mr. Roosevelt would not seek reelection. It will be remembered that F. D. R. had started his own national political career as Assistant Secretary of the Navy in the Woodrow Wilson Administration.

I had known Mr. Nichols only slightly when he was a member of Congress. When I asked him why he was telling me this story he said he was doing it at the instance of James Roosevelt. The inference was that I might do something about it. There was nothing I could or would do about such a scheme. It might have been that Jimmy assumed that if his father stepped aside he would, as a condition of not running again, name the party nominee to succeed him, and that the Democratic nominee would be elected. I never mentioned the matter to anyone. The visit from Messrs. Hardin and Nichols lasted only a few minutes, and I never heard anything further about it. I am now relating this story for the first time because Miss Tully said the President told her that I had tried to get a member of his own family to oppose his renomination. The President must have known better, or someone very close to him had done some tall lying.

Miss Tully's statement that I had not favored Roosevelt's third and fourth terms is not consistent with my actions. I was a member of his administration from the day he first took office and supported him without hesitation all four times he was a candidate. While I had much rather he had not broken the two-term tradition, in 1940 the war was on and he was a successful leader. In 1944 the war was at its height. I respected the President as he should be respected. I never asked him for anything except possibly a photograph for someone else. In no sense did I feel his superiority over other men except that he was President and the greatest politician our country has ever known, and ruthless when it suited his purpose.

I had been very much in favor of recovery during the President's first two terms and was heart and soul in the war effort. There were, however, many activities of some of the New Dealers, and certain phases of the New Deal, which I did not subscribe to, but said nothing about. I had enough to do "tendin' to my own knittin'," doing my own job. Most people who knew me knew that I was not a New Dealer, as did the President; but he also knew I was helpful to him and would not sell him down the river, regardless of the many talebearers who always had his willing ear. This brand of New Dealer did not know and did not care that the RFC was a bipartisan agency. They thought when Roosevelt was elected that everything was New Deal, and they would have had the RFC a grab-bag.

If Miss Tully had said my concepts of government were more Democratic than New Dealish, she would have been accurate. Although a Democrat, I could not keep up with all the New Deal procession any more than I could vote for William Jennings Bryan when the "Great Commoner" advocated free silver in 1896. I voted for William McKinley, his Republican opponent. At that time I did not have any silver or gold or property of any kind, but I didn't understand the "for free" silver business and voted accordingly. I had been brought up in the belief that the three most necessary things to a satisfactory life were family, religion, and money. Mr. Bryan wanted to monkey with the money, and I voted against him.

By the time the 1900 campaign came along Mr. Bryan had abandoned his advocacy of free silver, and I voted for him. I voted the Democratic ticket consistently thereafter until 1948. It was not because Mr. Truman was the candidate that I voted the Republican ticket in 1948 but in spite of the fact, for I liked him very much and regarded him as a personal friend. I did not know his opponent,

Governor Thomas E. Dewey. I voted the Republican ticket because I believe in the two-party system and thought the Democrats had been in power long enough and the country would be better off with a change. And I still think so. Otherwise we may some day be where Russia is, a "democratic" country with periodic elections but only one list of candidates on the ticket. You might scratch the ticket or even write in other names, but it probably would not be healthy.

I believe in a liberal government with proper social features, such as adequate provision for old people and those unable to work. But I do not believe in featherbedding everybody.

Of political aspirations I have never had the slightest. The Texas Democratic Convention held at Beaumont in 1928 instructed for me for President of the United States at the National Convention to be held in Houston in June of that year. Accordingly, former Representative Thomas H. Ball placed me in nomination at the national convention and the Texas delegation voted for me. I regarded it purely as a reward for my having secured the national convention for Houston to the complete surprise of the entire country, including Houston and myself. It was the first national political convention ever held in the South. While the vote of the Texas delegation was merely a "favorite son" gesture, it was a great compliment and one I appreciated. It was the first time a Texan had ever been placed in nomination for President of the United States at a national political convention of a major party.

When the Democratic National Committee had met in Washington in January, 1928, to choose a meeting place for the summer convention I had casually, as a matter of courtesy, invited it to hold the convention in Houston. We had before us invitations from several other cities—San Francisco, Detroit, St. Louis, and Kansas City. San Francisco offered the committee $250,000. To my invitation to come to Houston I attached my personal check for $200,000, thinking it a perfectly safe thing to do since it was $50,000 under the San Francisco offer. Each of the other cities, as I recall it, bid $125,000.

I had made no campaign to get the convention for Houston and, in fact, had spoken to no member of the committee about it. My invitation was a complete surprise to the committee, and their acceptance of it was certainly a complete surprise to me. I feel perfectly sure they gave my home town the convention simply because of my services during the previous four years as the committee's director of finances.

After Governor Smith was nominated for the Presidency at Houston, a member of the New York delegation came to me and asked if I would accept or like to have the nomination for Vice President. I replied that I would not. Senator Joseph T. Robinson of Arkansas was nominated for second place on the ticket.

I have never had any desire for government service and would not have been in government except for the great depression and the two world wars. I was offered the choice of two Ambassadorships by Woodrow Wilson when he was first elected President in 1912, and declined; and William G. McAdoo, Secretary of the Treasury in the first Wilson administration, offered me the Under Secretaryship. Colonel Edward M. House, who was Wilson's chief political emissary, asked me if I would consider accepting the portfolio of Secretary of Commerce or becoming a member of the Federal Trade Commission. All of these offers I declined.

In 1940 some friends wanted me to stand for the Vice Presidency, but I made no effort for it. I was a delegate to the National Convention that summer in Chicago. The morning before the convention met, I ran into James A. Farley and two or three other gentlemen gathered at a breakfast table in the dining room of the Blackstone Hotel. Mr. Farley turned to me and said, "I am going to place you in nomination for Vice President."

Since he had never before mentioned it, I naturally assumed he was joking; and, seeing that he and his friends were in conference, I moved on. A few hours later Elliott Roosevelt, son of the President, came to my apartment in the Blackstone. He told me that Mr. Farley was going to place me in nomination for Vice President, and that he, Elliott, was going to second my nomination. I told Elliott that under no circumstances would I permit it, that the President had already let it be known that he wanted Henry Wallace for Vice President.

That afternoon Elliott came back to my apartment and reiterated that they were going through with their plan, that Mr. Farley would put me in nomination and he would second it. It was then that Elliott remarked that his father did not know what he was doing in wanting Wallace. I again insisted that under no circumstances did I want my name proposed to the Convention, and immediately issued a statement to the press to that effect.

That night I went to the convention hall with Mrs. Jones and Mrs. Woodrow Wilson, Mrs. Wilson being our guest. I was sitting in the audience with them when I heard my friend Howard Bruce, of Maryland, placing someone in nomination for the Vice Presidency. I was astounded when he finally mentioned my name. I then went to the platform and addressed the convention. I thanked Mr. Bruce but requested that no one vote for me.

* * *

Frankly, after eight years' close association with the President and in various RFC legislative matters with Congress, where I had made many friends, if the President had chosen me as his running mate I would have been glad to accept. As Vice President, I could probably have been helpful to the President and continued to look after the RFC, since the Vice President has very little to do as such. However, as close friends as Harry Hopkins and I were, with apartments near each other in the Blackstone Hotel for the convention, and seeing him several times a day, I never mentioned to him anything about my possible nomination for the Vice Presidency. Harry was representing the President and had a private phone from his room to the White House.

The week end before the convention President Roosevelt had taken Mrs. Jones and me down the Potomac on his small yacht. No on else was aboard except the crew and "Missy" LeHand. Neither the President nor I mentioned the convention. We just fished and visited.

I would have liked to see William Bankhead of Alabama, then Speaker of the House of Representatives and a very fine man, nominated instead of Henry Wallace. We would all have been saved a lot of trouble.

BAILING OUT ELLIOTT ROOSEVELT

About nine o'clock on Sunday morning December 14, 1941—almost exactly one week after the Japanese attack on Pearl Harbor—President Roosevelt telephoned me at my office and stated that his son Elliott was in financial difficulties with his radio business in Texas. The President said Charlie Roeser and Sid Richardson, of

Fort Worth, were then with him at the White House. He asked me to see Sid and Charlie so that they could give me all the facts in the situation.

Messrs. Roeser and Richardson were wealthy oil men. They had stock in the Texas State Network, a radio chain of which Elliott held a controlling interest. Elliott had his home in Fort Worth, having eight years previously married Ruth Googins, an attractive Fort Worth girl, and she had borne him three fine children. The President said he would appreciate anything I could do to help Elliott, that he was in the Army Air Forces and would be until the war was over.

I told the President to send the boys over, that I would be glad to do what I could to help Elliott. A little later in the day Messrs. Roeser and Richardson came to my office and gave me a general outline of the situation. They told me that Elliott's radio company had lost its entire capital of $500,000, and that to buy his stock in the company Elliott had personally borrowed $200,000 from John A. Hartford, president of the Great Atlantic & Pacific Tea Company, $50,000 from David G. Baird, an insurance official of New York, and $25,000 from Judge Charles Harwood of New York, who subsequently, in the early part of 1941, had been appointed Governor of the Virgin Islands by the President.

As collateral to these loans, Mr. Hartford had received $200,000 par value of Elliott's radio stock and Mr. Baird, I think, $50,000 of the same. Judge Harwood thought he had Elliott's note, but apparently did not. He did, however, have $25,000 par value of the radio stock for the $25,000 he loaned Elliott.

Sometime later I was furnished with a financial statement of Elliott's radio company, the Texas State Network, Inc., as of December 31, 1941, which had been prepared by A. J. O'Brien & Company, certified public accountants of Fort Worth. The statement showed the company to be insolvent. Operating losses had exhausted all of its capital stock. It had book assets amounting to $395,555.31, and debts of $395,616.04—in other words, it was $60.73 worse off than nothing. These debts did not include what Elliott personally owed for the money he had borrowed to put into the stock of the company.

Messrs. Roeser and Richardson advised me in writing that they regarded their stock in the company as then of no value.

After I had got all the facts I could, I reported them to the President. He then said he would appreciate it very much if I would confer with Elliott's creditors and see what, if anything, they would be willing to do about his debts. He repeated that Elliott was in the Army and had no way of paying them.

Helping people in trouble was my business in Washington, and, while I did not particularly like this assignment, I could not very well refuse the request of the President.

Ruth, Elliott's wife, told me, and she also wrote Mr. Hartford and Judge Harwood, that aside from Elliott's Army pay and the small salary she was getting from the radio network, which she was trying to operate in his absence, they had no income. I was advised that their farm near Fort Worth, which I was told had been bought largely from a small inheritance of Ruth's, was mortgaged.

I did not know Mr. Hartford, Mr. Baird, or Judge Harwood but in the course of time got in touch with each of them. I first telephoned Mr. Hartford, since he was the largest creditor, and asked him if he would drop in to see me the next time he was in Washington. I told him the President had asked me to look into Elliott's affairs.

Mr. Hartford came to my office on December 30, 1941. I was interested in meeting him because of the great success he and his brother, George L. Hartford, had made with the Great Atlantic & Pacific Tea Company, a food chain whose stores are all over the country. We had a pleasant visit, and he told me a good deal about their business, its growth, etc., which was interesting.

When we reached the subject of Elliott's debt Mr. Hartford told me he was willing to do anything the President wanted him to do, that dollars meant very little to him, since from the standpoint of income they were worth about 11 cents as he was in or near the 90 per cent income bracket and at his death taxes would probably take 90 per cent of his estate. He also said that he did not want Elliott's notes in his estate while he was living or after he was dead.

It must be remembered that Mr. Hartford was a very rich man, to whom $200,000 was a small amount of money. Being asked by a son of the President of the United States for a loan to go into business for himself could easily have been regarded by him as an opportunity to make a friendly gesture that might bear fruit. Elliott had been introduced to him by the President's brother-in-law, Mrs. Roosevelt's brother, G. Hall Roosevelt—all fairly close to the purple.

Mr. Hartford had never met the President, yet when Elliott got his father on the telephone from Mr. Hartford's room, Mr. Roosevelt greeted him with his well known first-name come-on, "Hello, John." Then as reported, he went on to say, "While any business you have with my son must stand on its own merits, I will appreciate anything you do for him." And also, as reported, the President wound up the conversation by saying, "When you are in Washington come in to see me."

At the time Mr. Hartford loaned the money his company was being sued by the Federal Trade Commission under the antimonopoly laws. This was of course known to the President, but not to me.

Under that circumstance Mr. Hartford should not have loaned Elliott the money and the President should not have permitted Elliott to borrow it. Certainly, if I had known about the suit, I would not have had anything to do with Elliott's affairs with Mr. Hartford. I did not hear anything about the suit until long after the transaction.

Mr. Hartford came to see me a second time early in March, 1942. I told him I had learned the Texas Network stock had no present value, but offered him $4,000 to purchase the $200,000 par value of the stock which he held as collateral to Elliott's notes. And since he had said he did not want Elliott's notes in his files, I assumed he would destroy them or give them to Elliott, though he did not say so. I named the figure $4,000, because under the tax law $4,000 was the largest amount I could give to one person without paying a gift tax and, at the time, I had no expectation of getting the money back. I was simply doing a chore for the President, at his request; and it was not the first $4,000 I ever gave away. Mr. Hartford said he would accept my offer. In my letter to him, given to his lawyer on closing the transaction, I stated that I was buying the stock. This was on March 17, 1942, when Mr. Hartford's attorney, Caruthers Ewing, who was also counsel for the A. & P. store chain, came to my office with the stock and four notes for $50,000 each, signed by Elliott and his wife, Ruth. I sent my secretary to the bank for a cashier's check for $4,000, payable to Mr. Hartford out of my personal funds. I gave this check to Mr. Ewing, and he delivered the stock to me. He then took a pair of scissors from my desk and clipped out parts of each of the four $50,000 notes, threw pieces of them in the waste basket and put a piece of each note in his pocket. I noticed he tried to cut out Mr. Hartford's name.

If I had bought Elliott's $200,000 notes for $4,000 and had given the notes to Elliott, the claim might have been made that I was liable for a gift tax, just as Mr. Hartford might have been had he given Elliott his notes. He chose instead to destroy them.

Except for the fact that the Federal Trade Commission was suing the Great Atlantic & Pacific grocery chain, a circumstance that I did not know about, I would have seen nothing for which to criticize Mr. Hartford in lending Elliott money. Many rich people would give or spend that much for a friendship with the President of the United States and his family—especially with the Roosevelts.

On April 2, 1942, I gave the Hartford stock to the President with the following letter, which I had written in my own hand, making a carbon copy of it.

April 2, 1942

Dear Mr. President:

The enclosed 2000 shares of stock in The Texas State Network, Inc. were bought from Mr. John A. Hartford for $4,000.00 and are presented to Elliott and Ruth. Mr. Hartford held the stock as collateral for notes to him given by Elliott and Ruth in the sum of $200,000 which notes were destroyed in my presence. The stock has very little if any present value and Elliott advised Mr. Hartford that since the investment had failed he had no means of paying the notes particularly since he was now in the military service with no prospects as to when he would get out or how he would be able to make money enough to pay the notes and his other debts created for investment in the Radio business, all of which was lost.

Sincerely,

JESSE H. JONES

The President expressed his appreciation and told me Elliott would be able to pay the money back to me in about a year, explaining that Elliott would inherit perhaps as much as $10,000 from his grandmother, Mrs. Sara Delano Roosevelt, who had recently died.

Sometime later I concluded the purchase of a release of the stock held by Mr. Baird for $750.

I delivered the Texas Network stock I had obtained from Mr. Baird to the President on July 6, 1942, and he reiterated his appreciation.

New York City, N.Y. March 30 1939
the _____ after date we promise to pay
l'John A. Hartford _____
and _____ 00/100 Dollars
Guarant... interest of six (6)
ceived _____ annum from date
Due March 30th 1940
Elliott Roosevelt
Ruth J. Roosevelt

$50,000 00 New York City N.Y. Marc
twenty-four months _____ after date we prom
to the order of Joh.
fifty thousand dollars and 00/100
Payable at Guaranty Trust Co. N.Y.C. with interest of.
per annum
Value received
No two Due March 30th 1941
Elliott
Ruth J.

$50,000 00 New York City, N.Y. March
thirty-six months _____ after date we prom
to the order of Joh.
fifty thousand _____
Payable at Guaranty Trust Co. N.Y.C. with interest of
per annum
Value received
No three Due March 30th 1942
Elliott
Ruth J.

$50,000 00 New York City, N.Y. March
forty-eight months _____ after date we prom
to the order of Joh.
fifty-thousand _____
Payable at Guaranty Trust Co. N.Y.C with interest of
per annum
Value received
No four Due March 30th 1943
Elliott Ro...
Ruth J...

DEPARTMENT OF COMMERCE

OFFICE OF THE SECRETARY

WASHINGTON April 2ⁿᵈ 1942

Dear Mr President

The enclosed 2000 shares
of Stock in the Texas State Network Inc.
were bought from Mr John A Hartford
for $4000.⁰⁰ and are presented to Elliott
and Ruth. Mr Hartford held the stock
as collateral for notes to him given
by Elliott and Ruth in the sum of $200.000.⁰⁰
which notes were destroyed in
my presence. The stock has very little
if any present value and Elliott –
advised Mr Hartford that since the
investment had failed he had
no means of paying the notes particularly
since he was now in the military
service with no prospects as to
when he would get out or how
he would be able to make money
enough to pay the notes & his
other debts created for investment
in the Radio business all of which
was lost –

Sincerely
Jesse H Jones

[299]

I understand the stock was all given to Elliott's then wife, Ruth Googins, and their children in their divorce settlement.

No arrangement was ever concluded with Judge Harwood about his stock. According to my calendar, the Judge called at my office on eight different days in the month of March, 1942, and again in April, September, October and December of that year, and later in December, 1943, and September, 1944. He said he had been promised a federal judgeship when he loaned Elliott the money, and, if that was not available, he would take a commission as a general in the Army or in the high brass of the Navy, instead of Governor of the Virgin Islands; but his efforts in that direction were not successful.

At the time of my negotiations with Mr. Hartford and Mr. Baird for their stock I did not understand that either of them intended to take a tax loss. I understood the contrary.

Eventually, in 1945, after I had left government service the whole affair was aired in Congress. Many of the members sharply criticized the Treasury Department for allowing Mr. Hartford a $196,000 deduction from his income tax as a bad debt. He probably would not have been allowed the deduction except for the fact that the transaction concerned a Roosevelt, since he made little, if any, real effort to collect the money. Elliott was a young man and in time might have been able to pay the debt. He released the collateral for $4,000 but not the notes, and there was no agreement between Mr. Hartford and me or Mr. Hartford's attorney, Mr. Ewing, and me, that the purchase of the stock was a cancellation of the debt.

I have been informed that in testifying at the Treasury Department investigation Mr. Hartford said that on March 17, 1942, when the notes and stock were delivered to me, I had said I was going to present the mutilated notes and the stock to the "Boss." I made no such statement, and Mr. Hartford was not present. I told Mr. Hartford's attorney, Mr. Ewing, that I was going to deliver the stock to the President. Mr. Ewing had destroyed the notes, keeping a piece of each one and throwing the other pieces in the waste basket, which I later recovered and saved—just in case.

On Mr. Hartford's behalf Mr. Ewing, a careful lawyer, before delivering the stock to me, insisted on some evidence that I was representing the President or Elliott in acquiring the stock. He asked me to call the President at the White House in his presence while he was in my office. This I declined to do. I offered, however, to write

Jim Berryman in the Washington Evening Star.

Mr. Hartford a letter, and did so in my own hand. The letter follows:

Hon. John A. Hartford
New York City, NY

This is to advise you that Elliott Roosevelt and his wife Ruth Roosevelt are aware that I am arranging for the purchase of Two Thousand Shares of the capital stock of Texas State Network, Inc., held by you as collateral, and are very appreciative of your consideration of their financial problems and the fact that you are not embarrassing them by suit or otherwise because of their inability to pay their notes to you aggregating $200,000/00—Two Hundred Thousand Dollars—which you loaned them to invest in the Texas State Network, Inc. stock.

JESSE H. JONES

March 17, 1942

Five years later, somewhat to my surprise, I received from Elliott, who by then had become the husband of Faye Emerson, an actress, the following letter:

Hyde Park, New York

July 1, 1947

Honorable Jesse Jones
Houston, Texas
Dear Uncle Jesse:

It has come to my attention that in the settlement of my affairs in Texas, at the time of my divorce from Ruth, one item which I specifically required to be taken care of, namely the amount of money which you advanced in straightening out my affairs on the Texas State Network was never repaid to you.

I am extremely anxious that you should not be out of pocket for any sum advanced, and the purpose of this letter is to inquire the amount of indebtedness so that I may compute what the principal, plus interest, would be to date in order to settle the account with you.

I presume that a six per cent return on that investment would be agreeable.

Thanking you in advance for your kindness in looking up this matter, and with kindest personal regards, I remain,

Very sincerely yours,

ELLIOTT ROOSEVELT

I replied as follows:

July 5, 1947

Dear Elliott:

The stock bought from Mr. Hartford cost $4,000. The purchase was made March 3, 1942. The stock bought from Mr. Baird cost $750. The purchase was made May 2, 1942. Interest to this time at 4% per annum amounts to $991, or a total of $5,741.

With best wishes,

Sincerely,

JESSE H. JONES

Mr. Elliott Roosevelt
Hyde Park, New York

Two weeks later an envelope arrived in my office in Houston containing Elliott's check to me for $5,741. There was no covering letter or any other message in the envelope.

While the stock of the radio network had little or no value at the time of my negotiations, under different management, I understand, the company has since recovered its losses and is doing very well.

MY COLLEAGUES IN THE CABINET

My relations with my colleagues in the President's Cabinet were pleasantly varied. In his memoirs Harold Ickes has written that I used to sit silently in Cabinet with a "poker face," that he often wondered what I was thinking about. Several considerations might have motivated my reticence, one being the presence of Mr. Ickes. Through that gentleman much that went on in the Cabinet was passed to his buddy, Drew Pearson, and appeared in the Pearson column. Notwithstanding that Mr. Ickes probably felt he could do a better job in any Cabinet post, and even the Presidency, than was being done by the respective incumbents, he and I got along very well in our dealings, he as Public Works Administrator and I as Federal Loan Administrator, as well as Cabinet colleagues.

My principal reason for not having a great deal to say at Cabinet meetings was that there was no one at the table who could be of any particular help to me except the President, and when I needed to consult him I did not choose a Cabinet meeting to do it. I made no suggestions to other Cabinet members about their departments and asked none from them.

When I had anything to take up with the President which would require only a very few minutes, I would wait until Cabinet session ended and then speak to him privately. Most Cabinet members at one time or another waited until after Cabinet for a few private words with the President. This custom I dubbed "prayer meeting." Those waiting had their private talks in the order of their rank—the Secretary of State being first, then Treasury, War, Attorney General, Postmaster General, Navy, Agriculture, Commerce, and Labor.

Matters of high governmental policy were seldom discussed at Cabinet meetings. In opening the meeting, the President ordinarily would have something to say, but not always. He usually asked the

Secretary of State if he had anything to report and went on down the line. There was not a great deal of discussion.

After we began preparations for war in the summer of 1940, I almost invariably saw the President after Cabinet because all RFC war and defense purchases and work were done at my direction, with the approval of the President. This was clearly set out in the Act that gave RFC the authority. The RFC could not do anything in the defense and war efforts except at my request with the President's "O.K." In day-to-day operations we could not wait to get the President's approval before proceeding with each war undertaking. So in practice, to save his time and mine and not delay starting work on war projects, I would instruct the RFC to proceed. Then, when I went to Cabinet, I would take with me a batch of my directives. When Cabinet was over the President would put "O.K. FDR" on each project. Oftener than not he did not look to see what he was initialing. From June, 1940, to January, 1945, there were hundreds of such directives, and he never questioned one.

My Cabinet colleagues varied widely in their personalities. Cordell Hull, the Secretary of State, is able and a man of high purpose. He has a good knowledge of foreign affairs and was faithful to the President, though the President was not always considerate of him. By nature Mr. Hull was above the activities and meddlesomeness of some in his department, and one or two other departments. In character, understanding, ability, and dignity, he was a great Secretary; but he needed an Under Secretary or Assistant Secretary for administration— a general manager, as it were—a "tough hombre" to run the Department and ride herd over a large bureau composed in substantial part of career people filled with their own opinions as to how the Department should be run, some of whom wore lace. Mr. Hull had neither the disposition, the time, nor the will to do that. He choose to ignore the irritations or put up with them rather than thrash it out with Mr. Roosevelt and demand help of his own choosing—help that would look to him. The President encouraged some in secondary places to come direct to him. Whatever his motive, it was not a good practice, particularly with a man like Mr. Hull. My relations with Mr. Hull were very close, and our concepts of government much alike.

Henry Morgenthau, Jr., the Secretary of the Treasury, had had no previous business or financial experience. His appointment was purely personal, but he maintained dignity and character in the office.

Happily Mr. Morgenthau usually had a good Under Secretary who acted as a sort of general manager in running the Treasury. Among the capable men who successively served in that capacity were T. Jefferson Coolidge, John W. Hanes, and Daniel W. Bell, any one of whom would have made a good Secretary of the Treasury. Mr. Morgenthau leaned heavily upon his general counsel, Herman Oliphant, who was extraordinarily prolific and proficient in New Deal ideas. The Secretary also received considerable assistance from Harry D. White, an economist who had joined the Treasury Department in 1934 and became its director of monetary research. In 1943 Mr. White formulated the White Plan for international monetary agreements, many of his proposals being adopted at the Bretton Woods Conference the following year. It was reported that he drew up the "Morgenthau Plan" for postwar Germany which would have changed the economy of that country from industrial to agrarian. In 1946 he left the Treasury to take a tax-free $17,500 salary as United States executive director of the International Monetary Fund.

Two years later it was charged before a Congressional Committee that he had given documentary information to Communist spies. It seems the FBI had been on Mr. White's trail for some time, that when the "pumpkin papers" which figured conspicuously in the conviction of Alger Hiss were turned up by Whitaker Chambers they included letters in White's handwriting. I understand that while Mr. White, for the Treasury, was in charge of the introduction of "occupation currency" for West Germany there appeared almost simultaneously identical currency which it was said was printed in Russia or occupied East Germany, and from plates which experts believed were made from the same set of dies—and those dies of course were made in the United States Bureau of Printing and Engraving in Washington. That trick, it will be recalled, caused a great deal of confusion and at one time was reported as costing the United States Government $1,000,000 a day to block distribution of the Russian counterfeit.

"Who's Who in America" appears to give no birthplace or background of Harry D. White. It simply starts him off as an economist with a Ph.D. from Harvard in 1930. After leaving government service he went to Fitzwilliam, New Hampshire. There he was found dead on August 16, 1948, with an empty bottle beside him, that had contained strong tablets.

I saw a good deal of Mr. White since he frequently attended meetings at my office representing the Treasury. I knew he was shrewd, but I had no reason to suspect him and can well understand that Mr. Morgenthau would not.

My relations with Secretary Morgenthau were cordial, though I think few in government were close to Henry or liked him. He was always serious and punctual in his appointments, but when the business of the meeting was over there was never any time for chewing the fat. He trusted few people outside of some of his own organization.

Because of his intimate relations with the President, Mr. Morgenthau, like Mr. Ickes, was inclined to interfere with departments other than his own. At one Cabinet meeting a question arose that required cooperative action between the State and Treasury Departments concerning China and Russia. Knowing that the feeling between Messrs. Hull and Morgenthau was none too cordial, the President immediately grabbed the ball and turning to me said:

"Jess, you see Henry and Oumansky tomorrow and straighten this matter out." Constantine Oumansky was the Soviet Ambassador.

The next morning I suggested to Mr. Morgenthau that he invite Oumansky to meet us at the Secretary's office in the Treasury. The three of us met and, as usual, Morgenthau had his stenographer taking notes of the conversation on a stenotype machine.

Morgenthau started making a statement which was being taken down by the stenographer. He had not gotten far when Oumansky interrupted. Looking first at the stenographer to be certain his words were being recorded, but addressing Secretary Morgenthau, he said, "Mr. Secretary, the relationship between your country and mine is getting to be very strained, and I do not know how long I will be here . . ." He proceeded in this strain, and Henry became obviously disturbed, fearing, I suppose, that he had said the wrong thing. Soon I rather rudely interrupted.

"Mr. Ambassador," I said, "I am not concerned about the relationship between your country and mine, but I am concerned about your relationship and mine personally.

"I enjoyed cordial relations with your predecessor, Ambassador Alexander Troyanovsky. We played bridge together and he often sent me vodka and caviar. Since you've been here, I haven't had a blankety-blank thing from the Russian Embassy."

That clarified the atmosphere, and the purpose of the meeting was accomplished. Next day I received from the Russian Ambassador a large carton of caviar and two bottles of vodka. I ate the caviar but didn't drink the vodka.

I am inclined to think the Kremlin replaced Troyanovsky because he was socially too friendly in Washington. Oumansky indulged in no social activities other than the formal functions where protocol required his appearance.

Secretary of War Henry L. Stimson came to the Cabinet with such wide and varied experience, both in and out of government, that he was eminently—indeed, ideally—suited for his position. He exhibited delicate skill in being able to disagree with the President without rubbing his fur the wrong way or "getting his Dutch up." It was said that on several occasions Mr. Stimson told the President privately that if certain things were done he would have to resign— and they were never done. I held Mr. Stimson in high esteem.

During my time in the Cabinet we had two Attorneys General: Robert H. Jackson, now Associate Justice of the Supreme Court— probably promoted to make a place for a more amenable Attorney General—his successor, Francis Biddle. Mr. Jackson was the abler of the two, and the stronger in his opinions. When he was not in full agreement with the President it was interesting to observe the finesse and polished courtesy in his discussions. He was usually able to avoid doing what he thought should not be done. I liked him very much.

Mr. Biddle, on the other hand, always agreed with the President and did to the best of his ability what he thought Mr. Roosevelt wanted done—not a bad policy ordinarily; but the President of the United States has so much coming to his desk that he needs men about him who will not rubber-stamp everything he proposes, but who will be helpful in presenting their views, which may sometimes disagree with his own. Biddle is a fine gentleman, with ability enough, but I thought he was too ready to please the President.

Frank Knox, Secretary of the Navy, was a delightful personality, but was handicapped by the fact that he had to recognize that the President could not help wanting to run the Navy. Though unnecessary, this was natural because of Mr. Roosevelt's love of the sea and his personal fondness for the Navy, of which he had been Assistant Secretary during the First World War. Mr. Knox was a fine character, a great gentleman. He and Secretary Stimson, both Republicans, were appointed to their posts in order to have a bipartisan Cabinet during the war. It would have been difficult not to like Knox.

Frances Perkins, the Secretary of Labor, was quite competent. Whether a woman should have been Secretary of Labor is not for me to say; but Miss Perkins certainly did her work to the best of her ability, and a very good job at that. She never shirked her responsibilities. Frequently, when she had meetings with groups of labor people, she would ask me to join her; and I was always glad to give her any assistance that I could. I liked her very much. To me, one of the most interesting jobs in the Cabinet is that of Secretary of Labor, because it involves dealing strictly with human problems. In all my rather busy life, which has included extensive building operations, extending over a period of almost fifty years in Texas and New York City, I have never had a strike except on one occasion, when there was a general strike. I was always able to reason with labor and avoid strikes. I number many labor leaders among my friends and believe a different approach to our labor problems than we have had would get better results; but of course you are at a disadvantage in negotiating wage agreements, working conditions, et cetera, if you are negotiating for votes at the same time.

Only a short time ago, when it was necessary to arbitrate under the labor contract in one of my institutions, the manager of my business asked the labor leader to name his representative for the arbitration. He promptly replied, "We'll take Mr. Jones."

Two of the ablest Secretaries, who started as Under Secretaries, were Robert P. Patterson, the War Secretary, and James Forrestal, the Navy Secretary. Bob and Jim were two of America's strongest men in fighting the war. They gave all their great energies and extraordinary abilities to their respective jobs in cooperation, and were superbly effective. To know Bob Patterson is to admire him and love him. To know Forrestal was to admire and respect him. Few men got close to Jim. He was a much abler man than Knox, but, unfortunately, he carried his problems to bed with him and was up late and early with never any relaxation. He took no time out for social functions even in the evenings. He would occasionally appear at one as a matter of protocolar courtesy but would remain no longer than absolutely necessary. The fact that he was unable to find relaxation finally destroyed him. Secretary Patterson was of a different temperament. He could fight it out with all comers, but when the day's work was done could relax and rest.

Claude R. Wickard of Indiana, appointed Secretary of Agriculture in 1940, after Henry Wallace had resigned to run for Vice President of the United States, was an earnest and sincere public servant. He succeeded to a greatly expanded Department of Agriculture, which, under Henry Wallace, had just about spread over the lot. Claude Wickard did not have a great deal to say in Cabinet. He was a hard worker, a high-class gentleman and attended to his own business. I liked him—as a farmer likes a good mule that jumps fences.

Frank C. Walker, who followed Jim Farley as Postmaster General, was a fine agreeable gentleman and a confidant of the President. He had little to say in Cabinet except occasionally to report progress in his Department. The Post Office Department largely runs itself, through 1st, 2nd, 3rd, and 4th Assistant Postmasters General, with the Cabinet officer looking after the politics of the Administration. Although Frank Walker could not do that as well as Jim Farley, he did it competently, and was most likable.

As for Ickes, who trusts no one and likes few, I can only say that, while we never had a cross word, there may have been times when I felt like swatting him in the jaw. However, I will borrow Will Rogers' famous saying, "I never saw a man I did not like" (except probably just a few), and in spite of the old curmudgeon's sardonic disposition, I liked him.

A NEW FACE IN THE WHITE HOUSE

When Harry S. Truman succeeded to the Presidency on the death of Mr. Roosevelt, I sent him my good wishes and offered to be of any assistance I could. I recommended that he appoint John W. Snyder Federal Loan Administrator. A short time thereafter the President telephoned me and said, "I am sending John Synder's name to the Senate as Federal Loan Administrator, and wanted you to be the first to know it." Mr. Snyder, for the previous five years, had been assistant to the directors of the RFC in important war work and before that, manager of its St. Louis agency. He is now Secretary of the Treasury, doing a good job, in keeping with the policies of the President, and is probably the President's closest friend. They were in World War I together and have been fast friends ever since.

In the Senate Mr. Truman was ranking member of the Interstate Commerce Committee, through which all railroad legislation originated. I found him always cooperative in giving us authority to help keep as many of the railroads out of receivership as possible, and in our "make work" loans to them. Later on, when he became chairman of the Senate Committee to Investigate Defense Expenditures, my contacts with him continued to be frequent. Among these expenditures I directed the disbursement of about thirty-two billion dollars. In his investigations I found Senator Truman to be a man of understanding and fairness.

I saw him frequently at lunch with groups of Senators at the office of Colonel Edwin Halsey, Secretary of the Senate, and later his successor, Leslie Biffle. Mr. Biffle is a close friend of Mr. Truman's. One day in February, 1944, after lunching with Senator Truman and several others at Leslie Biffle's office, I told the Senator that he would be President Roosevelt's running mate in the coming fall election. The Senator pooh-poohed the idea. I felt sure that when the convention met in July it would not accept Henry Wallace, and that the Senator from Missouri, because of the favorable reputation he had made in the Senate, and coming from the Midwest, would appeal to the delegates looking about for a logical candidate. I am sure the date of my prediction was February, 1944, because Arthur Krock, of New York *Times* fame, recently reminded me that I had related the story to him at that time. It was obvious that President Roosevelt would succeed himself again if he could, and I did not believe he could carry Mr. Wallace.

In 1948, two days before the convention that nominated Mr. Truman for the Presidency was to meet in Philadelphia, President Truman telephoned me at my office in Houston. He told me that three of my friends were in consultation—he, Secretary Snyder, and Senator J. Howard McGrath, who was chairman of the Democratic National Finance Committee. The President said they wanted me to accept the chairmanship of the Finance Committee to raise funds for the campaign. I thanked the President, but told him I could not accept the appointment. I hated to decline because I liked Mr. Truman very much, but had about reached the conclusion that the Democrats had been in power long enough, and that a change would be helpful to the country.

I asked President Truman if he had determined who would be his running mate. He said that he had not, though it was generally understood he wanted Justice W. O. Douglas. I told the President that in my opinion he had but one choice, that Senator Barkley was the man, that Barkley knew the political score from A to Z, that he did not have to ask anybody anything about how to run for office, that he made a good speech and held his audiences. Evidently the Convention thought as I did and made Senator Barkley the Vice Presidential nominee. Soon he became the nation's "Veep," then, a little later, our number one bridegroom.

Although as a publisher I opposed President Truman's election in 1948, my personal relations with him have remained on a cordial basis.

HEARING OF SENATE BANKING AND CURRENCY COMMITTEE

Left to right: Senator Carter Glass, Secretary of the Interior Harold L. Ickes; Jesse H. Jones, Senator William G. McAdoo.

WITH SENATOR HARRY S TRUMAN, OCTOBER, 1944

A few days later Mr. Truman was elected Vice President of the United States

PART II

Preparedness and War

22

---- ☼ ----

DEFENSE PLANT CORPORATION

We Build 2,300 War Plants for $9,200,000,000—Cooperation in Big Business—Trading with Alcoa's Arthur V. Davis —Wartime Aluminum Expansions—Henry Kaiser Tries His Hand in Magnesium—Financing the Biggest Airplane in the World—Some Spectacular Wartime Projects—The Men Who Did the Job

THE accelerated expansion of American industrial capacity during the Second World War was of a magnitude without precedent in all the world's economic evolution. Much of this great accomplishment was financed by the RFC through its subsidiary, Defense Plant Corporation, acting at the requests of the War and Navy Departments, the Office of Production Management, the War Production Board, the Maritime Commission, and occasionally other government agencies. They told us what they wanted built—and, usually, where and by whom. We saw to it that the plants were constructed, equipped, and, in most instances, competently operated.

Between its creation on August 22, 1940, and the military victories of 1945, Defense Plant Corporation disbursed approximately $9,200,-000,000 on twenty-three hundred projects in forty-six states and a few foreign lands. Most of this money built new factories and mills and equipped them with tools and machinery.

With few exceptions the plants were leased to private companies to operate. These companies proceeded to turn out all manner of materials and supplies, from tiny jewel bearings to giant guns, tanks, ships, and airplanes.

The leases varied. Some companies merely rented the plants for a nominal $1 a year. Others were based on volume of production, or percentage of sales, or percentage of profits. Occasionally we shared in the profits but agreed to take the losses, should the projects run into the red. That stipulation was made in a number of the contracts for the operation of aluminum plants.

In spending billions without stint to speed the victory, the government acquired a dominant position in several industries—aircraft manufacture, nonferrous metals, machine tools, synthetic rubber, and shipping. It became a large investor in an infinite variety of other industries, light, medium, and heavy.

It is interesting to compare the expansions of the 1940's with those of 1917–1918. During the First World War the government's investment in new industrial plants amounted to only about $600,000,000, mostly in shipping facilities and powder and chemical plants. Nine-tenths of the six billions expended in the United States on plant expansions for World War I was supplied by private funds.

At the close of World War II, Defense Plant Corporation's investments alone embraced 96 per cent of the nation's synthetic rubber capacity, 90 per cent in magnesium metal, 71 per cent in the manufacture of aircraft and their engines, 58 per cent in aluminum metal, and nearly 50 per cent of the facilities for fabricating aluminum.

About half of Defense Plant Corporation's huge outlays flowed directly or indirectly into aviation. To build aircraft, their engines and parts—from bolts to bomb sights, gas tanks to shimmy dampeners —the Corporation directly invested $2,600,000,000 in land, buildings, machines, and other equipment in several hundred new plants. Of the fifteen largest airplane engine plants put up during the war, fourteen were wholly or partly financed by the Corporation. Another quarter of a billion dollars constructed and equipped forty-five plants which produced high-octane aviation gasoline exclusively. And aviation got the lion's share of aluminum and magnesium. Into the expansion of those two industries we put about $1,500,000,000. To assist the War Department's pilot-training program, the Corporation bought and enlarged sixty-two flying schools and provided planes and housing for the cadets, all at a cost of $41,000,000. We leased the schools to private operators, who billed the War Department for their work.

Enlarging steel and pig-iron capacity took almost another billion out of the Corporation's purse. It was necessary to produce unexpectedly large amounts of pig iron to replace the sorely needed shiploads of scrap which had been sold to foreign customers—including our future enemies—in the years just before the war. When we first approached the steel companies with our propositions, months before Pearl Harbor, they were reluctant to undertake extensive enlargements. Most steel executives felt the country did not need any more capacity in their line. They had a natural fear that abnormal expansion would plague them once the emergency ended. But a survey which a distinguished engineer, Gano Dunn, had made in the spring of 1941 for the Office of Production Management indicated the country might face a steel deficiency of six million tons in 1942. He estimated that to increase capacity by ten million tons would require $1,250,000,000 and two years' time. I thought and convinced the President that ten million tons of new capacity was the least amount we should undertake.

On such a program we set out in the summer of 1941. Before the job was done, Defense Plant Corporation had made trades with all the larger steel companies and put almost $1,000,000,000 into plants to manufacture steel and pig iron and into scores of foundries and other small auxiliaries of the industry. The RFC meanwhile made business loans of more than $100,000,000 to steel companies to help finance their privately undertaken expansions. The Navy and War Departments and the Maritime Commission directly financed another $250,000,000 of steel-making facilities.

When I was discussing the necessity for increased capacity with President Roosevelt he drew a small, crude map of the United States and marked on it where he thought we should build steel plants. One was in New England, a big mill in Utah, one in the extreme Northwest, another in southern California and one in Texas, and there was an ore installation in northern New York.

The project in New England was not practicable, but we did something about the ore in New York State and built the big plant at Geneva, Utah. Nothing was done about the project in the Northwest. We planned to build in southern California, but Henry J. Kaiser borrowed the money from the RFC and did that job. A small plant was built in east Texas, which is now being enlarged with government funds.

The Corporation allotted many millions for plants and machinery which made tanks, guns, bombs, shells, and a thousand other implements of war. It also financed the building of ships and dry dock facilities. Tens of millions went to enlarge production of chemicals and synthetics, from old-fashioned bleaching powder to ultramodern Plexiglas.

To stimulate production of machine tools we made advances to manufacturers against purchase orders up to 30 per cent of the delivery price. These agreements, instituted the day after Pearl Harbor, were in effect underwritings. The machine-tool commitments ultimately aggregated almost $2,000,000,000. They provided tool manufacturers with supplementary working capital.

For machinery to equip one hundred and nineteen new plants assigned to make lenses for optical instruments Defense Plant spent $217,000,000. Transportation projects took $335,000,000. Notable in that category were the Big Inch and Little Big Inch pipe lines through which petroleum and its products were pumped from Texas to the New Jersey seaboard, thus freeing tankers from the coastal runs to vital overseas services for the armed forces. The Corporation also financed tugboats and barges for river transportation to take some of the War Department's load off the overburdened railroads. We ordered twelve hundred sleeping cars and four hundred kitchen cars for troop trains and bought tank cars to haul butadiene for the synthetic rubber program.

Early in 1941 I had suggested to the President that the RFC build five thousand railway passenger cars especially designed for mass capacity, so that they would be available for the transportation of troops should the occasion require. My thought was that the cars could later be used for reduced-fare service.

The President said: "No, the troops could be moved in box cars."

I also suggested we build a stockpile of freight cars, to which he again said "No." Better that he had said "Yes."

A little later the Act of June 10, 1941, specifically authorized us to acquire or purchase railroad equipment, and we did. We also bought new busses and streetcars and even feeder railroads to carry war materials and workers to and from plants rapidly built in areas which had been sparsely inhabited. In thirty such communities Defense Plant Corporation financed housing developments. These, by the war's end, showed earnings of about $3,000,000.

The variety of projects seemed endless. We financed development of milkweed to relieve the shortage of kapok for stuffing life preservers. We financed production of desalting kits for installation in life rafts. To breed rodents at New City, New York, for use in medical laboratories we assigned $138,000. At a cost of $7,000,000, the Corporation contracted for five laboratories which produced penicillin. Nearly $2,000,000 was required to convert an underground limestone quarry in Atchison, Kansas, into refrigerated storage space for perishables.

One could go on and on with the list. Other millions provided facilities for dehydrating, curing, and concentrating fruits and vegetables which were distributed to American troops and our allies and liberated peoples the world over.

*   *   *

In carrying out its program the officials of Defense Plant Corporation negotiated and worked with most of the outstanding men in the wartime government and in American industry. Of them all, none played a finer role in the war than William S. Knudsen.

Months before the establishment in 1941 of the Office of Production Management, of which he was to become director general, Mr. Knudsen had been called to Washington from the presidency of General Motors Corporation to advise the Council of National Defense. He hurled himself, heart and soul, into the intense work of helping get his adopted country ready to defend itself against whatever blows might fall. Better than anyone else he knew how to engage a particular industry to manufacture certain war materials, to build plants to furnish arms to the British, to meet the ever increasing demands of the preparedness programs of our own fighting services.

Mr. Knudsen's first office in Washington was a small one in the Federal Reserve Building, with only one secretary to help him. I went there frequently to see him. His office expanded rapidly. It soon became necessary for us to have a direct telephone line from his desk to mine. Several times a day he would want to talk about contracting with some one to build an airplant plant or an engine plant or some other kind of plant. He would simply lift the receiver and ask me if we had $5,000,000 or $10,000,000 or even $100,000,000, as the case might be, and I always said "Yes."

"O.K.," he'd say. "I'll send a man over to see you."

After negotiating with the man or men, and becoming favorably impressed myself, I would call Knudsen back to confirm that he felt confident the fellow or his firm was qualified to do the proposed job. If he said "Yes" without qualification, in nine cases out of ten the man would leave my office after an hour, or maybe three hours, or perhaps only a few minutes, with a Letter of Intent from the RFC, authorizing him to acquire the necessary property and build the plant.

In the beginning most of our industrialists were rather cautious about having their companies undertake war work. They didn't want to invest a lot of their own funds in equipment to manufacture things they believed would not be in demand after the shooting ceased.

I recall one of the first such contracts that we made. Mr. Knudsen had asked me to come to his office to talk with the head of Colt's Manufacturing Company about taking an order that would require installation of a substantial amount of new equipment. This rather oldish gentleman had come to Washington at Mr. Knudsen's request. He finally agreed to make the guns which Mr. Knudsen wanted to order, but said that we would have to put the necessary equipment into his plant to manufacture the guns, and remove it at our expense when it was no longer required. We made the contract on exactly his terms, and many similar ones thereafter with other industrialists.

On Mr. Knudsen's orders we had committed, prior to Pearl Harbor, more than $2,500,000,000 for war-plant construction. By the early spring of 1942 this amount increased to approximately $7,000,000,-000. Later it grew to more than $11,000,000,000 for Defense Plant Corporation alone; but of these authorizations only about $9,200,-000,000 was spent.

For this great wartime job Mr. Knudsen was the ideal man. He knew the manufacturing industry, the manufacturing technique, and the manufacturing men of this country better than anyone else. He knew what firm, man, or corporation could best be engaged to do any specific job. The soul of honor, he was an inspiration to all of us and especially to the men working in the plants. When he was commissioned lieutenant general and appointed director of production for the War Department by Robert P. Patterson, Under Secretary of War, he traveled many thousands of miles by plane to inspect plants and encourage workers. Secretary Patterson once told me that, without exception, each time he visited a plant, even if only to walk through it saying "How are you getting on, boys?" production immediately jumped.

In my view, Bill Knudsen had as much to do with winning the war as any other man, in or out of uniform. He was the right man on the right job at the right time.

COOPERATION IN BIG BUSINESS

While there are always a few chiselers to be found wherever opportunities abound, the industry of this country performed its wartime mission with patriotism and high excellence. When the chips were down and the facts were laid before any corporation and the directors were told the government wanted them to build a certain plant or make a specified article, or both, they were entirely responsive, ninety-nine times out of a hundred, and reasonable in their own demands. Even in the early lend-lease days, months before our country was blasted into the war, the heads of many of our large industries, in taking on government contracts, made it plain that they would be content just to break even financially on the jobs we asked them to do.

Several cases come to mind. We had been directed to employ the United States Steel Corporation to build several plants, including large ones at Homestead and Duquesne, Pennsylvania, these two to cost nearly $100,000,000. U.S. Steel agreed to acquire the sites and build the plants at out-of-pocket cost to their subsidiary, the Carnegie-Illinois Steel Corporation. No part of the company's general overhead was to be included in the cost of the new mills, which Defense Plant Corporation would own and rent to U.S. Steel on a percentage scale based on proportion-of-capacity production.

Later we were directed by the War Production Board to have a huge steel plant built in the West near Provo, Utah, which cost about $200,000,000. We were told by the War Production Board to employ the U.S. Steel Corporation to build it. They agreed to construct the plant for out-of-pocket cost and without a fee, if they were employed to operate it. If we employed some one else to operate it, U.S. Steel would expect a reasonable fee for building it. That was our proposal, and they accepted it.

When it came time to get an operator for the plant we were again told by the War Production Board to employ U.S. Steel. Their executives and ours worked out an operating contract under which they were to be paid about 1 per cent of the value of the material manufactured. This seemed a very reasonable fee; but when applied to the vast volume of which the plant was capable it would amount to about $1,000,000 a year. I told our boys we couldn't agree to a fee of that size, although I recognized that, relatively, it was quite modest. After further negotiations the Steel Corporation agreed to accept a fee of approximately one-half that amount. This I thought entirely reasonable, and authorized the contract on those terms.

The next day, Sunday, I got to thinking it over and put in a telephone call for Benjamin F. Fairless, president of U.S. Steel. When the operator located him he was at an Army billet in Atlantic City visiting his son, who was in the service.

"Mr. President," I said to him, "I would like to tell you how to run your business."

"Go ahead," he said. "What do you have in mind?"

I remarked that we had agreed upon the operating contract for the plant in Utah which was in every way reasonable and satisfactory to the RFC.

"But," I said, "I would like to suggest for your consideration that you operate the plant without any fee or other consideration as long as our country is at war."

He thanked me and replied that he would call me back Tuesday, after seeing his associates. He telephoned Tuesday before noon and said the company would be glad to operate the plant during the war without any fee.

That was big business doing business in a big way, and patriotically. We rarely had much trouble with either the big fellows or "little business."

Another circumstance: In our synthetic rubber program we were directed by the War Production Board to buy the Neoprene plant of the Du Pont Company at Louisville, Kentucky. Neoprene is a highly developed synthetic rubber. Du Pont was willing to sell the government the plant but wished to be allowed to repurchase it when the war was over—a perfectly reasonable position to take, since Neoprene was Du Pont's own product. After negotiating some days with the Du Pont representatives our boys reported that the option was the only thing in the way of closing the trade. Our policy was not to give options on plants. I asked to see a top official of the company. Walter S. Carpenter, Jr., president of Du Pont, came to Washington. In an effort substantially to meet his views I proposed that when the government was ready to sell the plant we would advertise it for sale for all cash. Since his company would know more than any other about the plant, would own the patents and have the cash, in all probability it would get the plant.

Mr. Carpenter said, "Mr. Jones, that will be satisfactory."

It had taken us less than twenty minutes to dispose of the matter.

Two tough but fair traders with whom we dealt were Eugene G. Grace, head of Bethlehem Steel Corporation, and Tom M. Girdler, chairman of both the Republic Steel Corporation and Consolidated Vultee Aircraft Corporation. Though both men were exceptionally exacting in negotiations, they performed well once the trades were made; and that was what we wanted.

In contracts for steel plants, our business with Mr. Girdler and his associate, Charles M. White, Republic's vice president in charge of operations, ran up to about $175,000,000, the biggest item being a $90,000,000 plant which we financed for them to operate in South Chicago.

For the plants, expansions, and facilities for Mr. Girdler's aircraft company in San Diego, New Orleans, Nashville, and Allentown, more than $40,000,000 was allocated, the planes going to both the Navy and the Army Air Forces.

All the "scrambled" facilities and machinery which we put into plants carried options of purchase by the plant owner at rates quite fair to the government. Generally the options ran for ninety days after the cancellation of the operating contract; in a few instances, six months. The option price was cost to Defense Plant Corporation less depreciation at 5 per cent per annum on buildings, 12 per cent on machinery, and 25 per cent on tools. The first steel company to exercise its option to purchase was Bethlehem. We had put scrambled facilities in four of their plants. One day in December, 1943, Bethlehem's treasurer telephoned our office to ask how much money we had spent putting scrambled facilities in their plants. The figure was $20,500,000. In the mail a few days later, we received Bethlehem's check for that amount. They had decided to pay for their own scrambled facilities—which, under the wartime law, they could depreciate in five years.

They may have been influenced by another circumstance. It will be remembered by some that after World War I there was much litigation between the government and corporations which had done war work or built plants for it. One such suit was that of the Bethlehem

Steel Corporation. It was not until the Monday following Pearl Harbor Sunday in 1941 that the Supreme Court finally decided the Bethlehem case, after twenty-three years in court. The decision was in favor of Bethlehem. I suppose Mr. Grace and his associates did not feel like risking another twenty-three years' litigation with the government after World War II.

In cases where plant owners did not want to buy the equipment we had installed, we agreed to remove it and restore their property to the condition in which we had found it—a reasonable arrangement.

Another example of the attitude of big business is that of the Dow Chemical Company. We were directed to employ them to build a magnesium plant on the Texas coast at an estimated cost of about $60,000,000. Our executives figured with their executives, but didn't make much progress toward hammering out an agreement. After the negotiations had stuck in an impasse for several days, I telephoned Dr. Willard H. Dow, president of the company, and asked if he would come to Washington to discuss the matter with me. He arrived the next day. We had not met before. After customary greetings, he said:

"Mr. Jones, I know you are a busy man. On just what basis do you want us to build and operate the plant?"

I told him what we thought would be a proper basis. His only reply was: "That will be perfectly satisfactory. Have the contract drawn, and we will proceed."

We did just that. They built and operated the plant, and it was a great success. Like many another plant financed by the government just before or just after Pearl Harbor, the Dow magnesium plant in Texas is a great national asset for, as these lines are written, the war clouds are thickening again, and the plant is being expanded.

TRADING WITH ALCOA'S ARTHUR V. DAVIS

Magnesium and aluminum were two of our most urgent wartime requirements. In each case only a few people knew anything about the business. The Dow people were the only ones who were making magnesium commercially, and the Aluminum Company of America was almost alone in its field. The War Production Board directed us to employ the Aluminum Company—"Alcoa," as it is commonly called—to build six or seven new plants and operate them for the government.

I knew absolutely nothing about aluminum or how it was made. I did not even know that for years the United States Government had been prosecuting Alcoa as a monopoly. My first problem was to find out something about aluminum. The best man to find that out from was the man we had to employ to do the job. He was Arthur V. Davis, chairman of the Aluminum Company. He was then about seventy-five years of age. He had started with the business at its birth, having poured the first commercial ingot of aluminum when he was a young man of twenty-one working for Alcoa's predecessor, in Pittsburgh.

Now when you are told to trade with a man, and the man knows you must trade with him, you are in a bad trading position. That was the situation we were in, in substantially all our plant construction and plant operations. After finding out as much as we could about the business and about Mr. Davis, we started our negotiations. It took a good many days to thresh out such a large and involved deal. We finally worked out a trade whereby Alcoa was to design and build the plants, operate them, and sell the material, retaining 15 per cent of the net profits of the operation and no other fee. Mr. Davis had asked for 20 per cent, and I had countered with an offer of 10 per cent. We compromised on 15 per cent, both trading. The fact that I have always been a trader came in handy in all our war work.

The selling price of aluminum had but recently been reduced from 19 cents a pound to 17 cents. After we had agreed on everything in connection with building and operating the plants, I suggested to Mr. Davis that he reduce the price from 17 cents to 15 cents a pound.

"I thought we had already traded," he said.

I replied that we had and that we would sign the contract exactly as agreed, but that I thought in his own interest the price should be 15 cents. I had become convinced from the things he had told me that the over-all cost of producing aluminum was about 12 cents a pound, and thought 15 cents would be a fair price and would afford the company profit enough. Again he reminded me that we had already traded, and once more I responded that we had and that we would sign the contract accordingly. But I repeated that, everything considered, I thought in his own interest as well as that of the government he should reduce the price to 15 cents.

"O.K.," he finally said, "if you insist." The 15-cent price yielded Alcoa a substantial profit.

As a matter of fact, because of excess profits taxes and renegotiations later authorized by Congress it did not make too much difference what price Mr. Davis and I agreed upon.

I learned not only to have great respect for Mr. Davis but to hold him in high esteem. At seventy-five, he was still hitting the ball. While our government had for years been prosecuting his company as a monopoly, it had never been able to prove its cause, and has not to this day.

Later on—in the spring of 1941—we were directed by the War Department to buy a large amount of aluminum from Alcoa's Canadian subsidiary, the Aluminum Company of Canada, of which Edward Davis, brother of Arthur, was the head. To enable the company to provide the necessary facilities to manufacture the aluminum, we first advanced them $25,000,000, then another $25,000,000 as our demands increased. Still later, as our needs grew by hundreds of millions of pounds, we made additional advances to the Canadian company.

A substantial amount of the money we advanced them—which was to be returned to us at the rate of 5 cents per pound on the aluminum delivered—was used to build the Shipshaw dam in Canada. We were criticized by several members of Congress for lending money to build that dam, since it would compete with power in our own country. We had no choice. We had done what the War Production Board directed. But when the criticism in Congress got hot President Roosevelt became concerned. He had an ear to the ground for the political angle in every situation, war or no war. On April 19, 1943, he sent me a memorandum which read:

> "Please let me have a copy of the Shipsaw Dam Contract with the Aluminum Company. Honestly I do not remember specifically approving the contract—but I may be wrong.
>
> F. D. R."

It was a rare occasion when Mr. Roosevelt admitted he might be wrong. In this case he was, but it was not to his discredit. With the multitude of things he had to do and remember, it was remarkable how well he kept up with what was going on.

When Congress in June, 1940 gave the RFC authority to do almost anything in the interest of our national defense, the one restriction was that it so act only at the request of the Federal Loan Administrator and with the approval of the President. That was inserted in the bill at my request to concentrate the responsibility, which was so very broad. I never hesitated to take the authority to proceed without the President's O.K. unless it was an unusual situation such as constructing the dam in Canada, or something that might have a political angle. The Shipshaw dam could easily have been forgotten by him, since he more often than not signed my directives to the RFC without reading them. Knowing the political aspects of the Shipshaw dam project, I called it to his attention.

The Canadian company fulfilled its contracts with us promptly and efficiently. The proposed plants were all built, and we got the material when it was needed. Without it the war would have lasted longer than it did, for aluminum is an essential material in aircraft construction.

Later, in December, 1944, when it was possible to see the end of hostilities, I called Edward Davis at his office in Boston and suggested that he pay in cash the balance of the money that we had advanced to the Canadian company instead of our taking it out of future shipments of aluminum. It amounted to several million dollars. He promptly complied with my request. He could have insisted on repaying it in aluminum.

As busy as he was with other matters, the President never forgot the government's case against Alcoa for being a monopoly. He wanted competition in aluminum. This was achieved in a small way before the war started and continued during the war as we built and financed aluminum facilities for others than Alcoa. On March 23, 1942, I got a memorandum from the White House initialed "F. D. R." which asked, "What about this story about twelve new aluminum plants—all to be operated by Alcoa?"

I sent back the following reply:

> We were requested by War Production Board or its predecessors to contract with Alcoa to build and operate the plants.
> In checking the progress of the plants, we find that they are all well organized and progressing on schedule.   J. H. J.

In the summer of 1940 we had made a loan of about $16,000,000 to the Reynolds Metals Company of Richmond, Virginia, to build an aluminum plant. The Reynolds people were in several other lines, and we were not so sure they would make a success in this new field; but they gave us what we regarded as satisfactory security other than the aluminum plants to be built, and we were glad to accommodate them, because war clouds were already threatening and if the enterprise were successful it meant more aluminum. I recall very well finally approving the Reynolds loan. The RFC Board had approved it in principle, and the executives had worked out the details with the Reynolds people. Then they came to my office with Richard S. Reynolds, head of the company. As I remember it, Mr. Reynolds told me he had signed more papers and given more security for his RFC loan than he had ever had to give when dealing with banks. Yet he had done only what he had offered to do in requesting the loan. Then he said, jokingly, "Now, Mr. Jones, is there anything else you want me to sign?"

"Yes, Mr. Reynolds," I said. "Since you ask, we want one more thing. We want an Oklahoma guarantee."

"What is an Oklahoma guarantee?"

I told him that when a farmer goes into a country bank in Oklahoma for a loan, and has mortgaged his prospective crop and a mule or two, and whatever else he may have, he is asked, just before putting his signature to the note, to insert one more line which reads: "And if I don't pay this note I'm an S.O.B."

WARTIME ALUMINUM EXPANSIONS

A gauge of the tremendous increase in production of magnesium and aluminum which the war necessitated may be had from a note I sent to the President on August 16, 1943:

MEMORANDUM FOR THE PRESIDENT:

Government owned plants produced 31,410,000 pounds of magnesium in July, and Dow Chemical Company, the only private producer, 3,500,000 pounds. Prior to the war, total production in this country was 500,000 pounds monthly.

Aluminum produced in Government owned plants for the month of July was 73,292,000 pounds; production by Alcoa and Reynolds Metals, 77,600,000 pounds—a total of something over 150,000,000 pounds, compared to a pre-war monthly output of about 25,000,000 pounds.

We appear to be well out in front on the production of both of these metals.

JESSE H. JONES
Secretary of Commerce

As the war wore on, President Roosevelt continued expressing his desire to see more competition in the aluminum field. Whenever I heard from him in this vein I knew that some meddler had been talking to him. In answer to one of his inquiries I sent on November 25, 1944, the following letter:

Dear Mr. President:

Reynolds Metals Company has had exceptional treatment from the RFC in all of its operations. It now owes the Corporation $36,681,333, secured by its various plants.

The principal debt is due in 1955, with easy amortization payments in the meantime.

The Company owns an aluminum plant at Listerhill, Alabama, costing $16,529,244, with an annual capacity of 100,000,000 pounds of aluminum. This investment includes an alumina plant sufficient to supply the mill.

It owns an aluminum plant at Longview, Washington, costing $8,106,997, with an annual capacity of 60,000,000 pounds.

It owns a sheet, rod and extrusion plant at Louisville, which cost $5,050,001, and miscellaneous facilities at various plants that cost an additional $3,144,803.

We loaned Reynolds the money for all these plants, and in addition, about $10,000,000 for working capital, and to pay bank notes.

In addition to the foregoing, Defense Plant Corporation owns a sheet, rod and bar mill plant at Listerhill, Alabama, with an annual capacity of 72,000,000 pounds of sheet and 60,000,000 pounds of bar and rod. This will cost Defense Plant Corporation $1,276,943, and is under lease to Reynolds.

Defense Plant Corporation owns a complete aluminum extrusion plant at Louisville with an annual capacity of 48,000,000 pounds, which is under lease to Reynolds. This plant cost $5,001,855.

Defense Plant Corporation owns another plant at Louisville for the manufacture of aircraft parts. The plant cost $2,467,658, and is under lease to Reynolds.

Defense Plant Corporation owns a plant at Springfield, Massachusetts, formerly leased to Springfield Bronze and Aluminum Company. This lease terminated May 30, 1944. The plant is to be used by Reynolds as a foundry to produce permanent mold aluminum castings for aircraft. The plant cost $2,893,153.

The Company is in a good financial condition, and has certainly had excellent treatment at the hands of the RFC, although they are seldom satisfied.

Sincerely,
JESSE H. JONES

I might have added in this letter to the President that we had put Reynolds in the aluminum business in a big way.

The Reynolds loans for aluminum plants at Listerhill and Longview were arranged in the summer of 1940. Both plants were in operation before Pearl Harbor. After that we quickly made additional loans so that the prewar capacity of those two plants was soon more than doubled. Contrary to some of the criticism provoked by the aluminum program, the requirements of our nation and our allies for that metal were fully met. Production rose from 300,000,000 pounds per year to 2,500,000,000 pounds, or more than eight for one. There was never a shortage of aluminum.

Whatever one's opinion concerning competition *vs.* monopoly or near monopoly, it was unwise, especially in wartime, to request a manufacturing concern, however well managed, to undertake something in which it lacked experience, as some of our largest, most efficient corporations were the first to admit. For example, we were asked by the Office of Production Management to engage Alcoa to build aluminum reduction plants at Los Angeles and Spokane but upon completion to have them operated by others—the Los Angeles plant by Bohn Aluminum & Brass Company and the Spokane plant by Union Carbide & Carbon Corporation. When both these plants were well on the way to completion, the two chosen companies asked to be excused. They told us they had all the war work they could well say grace over, and said further that they had no experience in making aluminum. They told us they felt the best interests of the war program would be served by employing Alcoa to do the job. So, with the concurrence of Donald M. Nelson, chairman of the War Production Board, we had Alcoa operate the plants. Among the concerns which were put into aluminum fabrication were the Big Three of the automobile industry, General Motors, Chrysler, and Ford.

Some members of Congress also continually clamored for more competition in aluminum. The preparedness program intensified that desire, and the contracts made by Defense Plant Corporation brought about its fulfillment. The subject recurred when I was testifying before the Truman Committee on September 15, 1941. Senator Joseph H. Ball of Minnesota said the Committee was concerned that we were using Alcoa so much in increasing our aluminum production and feared that company would come out of the emergency with its monopoly position strengthened.

I told the Committee I did not think so, that with our loans to Reynolds Metals Company and others to construct aluminum plants there would be, as then planned, an American capacity of approximately 1,500,000,000 pounds of aluminum production annually, Alcoa accounting for about half of it. Thus in aluminum the situation would be somewhat comparable to steel where the United States Steel Corporation competes with Bethlehem, Republic, Inland, and other smaller companies. I predicted we would have plenty of competition in aluminum to insure reasonable prices. That's the way it has worked out.

Magnesium, another metal essential in aircraft production, is also required in the manufacture of incendiaries, flares, and certain munitions. In 1939, when the European war began, Dow Chemical Company, the one concern manufacturing magnesium in the United States, was producing only about 7,000,000 pounds a year. During 1940 Dow expanded its capacity to 18,000,000 pounds.

In magnesium as in aluminum, private enterprise was reluctant to make large expansions because of a probable lack of postwar uses for the increased capacity.

HENRY KAISER TRIES HIS HAND IN MAGNESIUM

There was one industrialist, Henry J. Kaiser, who was ready to try anything if the government would put up the money. We helped him get into both magnesium and steel, but when he later wanted to go into synthetic rubber and building airplanes as well I told him "No." I thought he had enough to do.

He was busy building ships by the hundreds on the Pacific coast for the Maritime Commission. When the War Production Board ordered us to build a magnesium plant at Los Altos, south of San Francisco, Mr. Kaiser heard about it and came to Washington to see us. The private capital he proposed to put up to go into magnesium manufacturing was only $100,000—the stock of the Permanente Metals

Corporation which he had organized. He wanted to borrow a good many millions. He employed Thomas G. Corcoran, a White House favorite of the Roosevelt days and a former attorney in the legal division of the RFC, to help him wangle a loan. Mr. Kaiser knew nothing about manufacturing magnesium, so I was a little skeptical.

There seemed to be various processes for extracting magnesium. One was the Hansgirg process. Mr. Hansgirg, a Hungarian, claimed to have built plants, as I remember, in Japan and Hungary. Mr. Kaiser said he had contracted to buy the Hansgirg process or patent and to pay $750,000 for it. He was also going to employ Mr. Hansgirg to build and operate the plant, and did. The whole set-up looked a little screwy to me, one that would be of doubtful outcome.

I understood Mr. Kaiser was building ships on a fee basis which netted him a profit on each ship of from $60,000 to $110,000. So I told him we would lend him the money to build the magnesium plant but not to buy the patent. I told him that, in addition to a mortgage on the plant, we would require an assignment of his shipbuilding profits. He demurred at this; but it was the only way he could get the money, and he finally agreed. Lucky it was that we required the ship profits as collateral, because the enterprise was not a success. Furthermore, after Pearl Harbor, Hansgirg was thrown in the hoosegow as an enemy alien.

Mr. Kaiser's Permanente plant was built in units, with us advancing the money as required, starting with a loan of $3,500,000. We ultimately loaned $28,000,000 on that project, always secured by the assignment of shipbuilding fees. Through these fees we collected our money in full; but the project was not a success.

Later on, when Mr. Kaiser heard the government wanted a steel plant built near the Pacific coast, he went to see Sam Husbands, President of Defense Plant Corporation, and proposed to build and own the plant himself if RFC would lend him the money, taking a mortgage on the plant and an assignment of shipbuilding fees from three of his shipyards. Sam agreed and Kaiser built the steel mill. He capitalized his Fontana steel company for $100,000 and borrowed the balance of the money, for construction and operating capital, something more than $111,000,000, from the RFC. His shipbuilding fees applied to payment on the steel mill during the war amounted to nearly $18,000,000. Since ship plates and structurals were Fontana's only products the RFC, toward the end of the war, loaned Kaiser $11,000,000 additional to put in a pipe mill for postwar use.

Mr. Kaiser was smart to invest his ship fees in plants because, if he had not done so, probably 90 per cent of them would have been taken from him in excess profit taxes.

By comparison with others, Mr. Kaiser was no great shakes of a success in magnesium. Take the plant of Basic Magnesium, Inc., RFC's own plant near Las Vegas, Nevada. After a poor start under the management of a Cleveland industrialist, we employed Anaconda Copper Company to operate the Basic Magnesium plant, which we built in the desert in heat that sometimes soared to 120°. The plant was in production in September, 1942, within a year of breaking ground, and was fully completed in April, 1943. Before it was shut down in December, 1944, because of a surplus stockpile—and a need for its labor in shipbuilding yards—it had produced one-fourth of all the magnesium made by all the various processes during the war. In one year—1943—this one plant provided 39 per cent of the nation's magnesium production. The plant cost $130,000,000.

Under Anaconda Copper's management, the Las Vegas plant got its production cost of magnesium down to 18 cents a pound, whereas the Kaiser operation at Los Altos never got its production costs under 30 cents a pound, and Metals Reserve Company, another RFC subsidiary, had to subsidize Mr. Kaiser to the tune of $2,500,000 by buying his product at higher than market price.

* * *

When the Senate Committee on Defense Expenditures, headed by Senator Harry S. Truman, went out West to investigate the aluminum and magnesium situation, which had become a subject of Congressional controversy, the Committee's counsel, Hugh Fulton, wrote a report which reflected on the RFC. He praised the Kaiser magnesium plant, which had been almost a complete flop, and condemned the Nevada plant, which was a success. While I was in the process of writing a reply to the report I telephoned Senator Truman that I wanted it put in the record. He said: "Pay no attention to the report. Fulton wrote it. Forget it."

I was before the Truman Committee a number of times. Its counsel, Mr. Fulton, was typical of a small-town district attorney. His main job seemed to be to build up Mr. Truman and criticize everybody else.

I was informed he expected to be made Attorney General when Vice President Truman succeeded to the Presidency. I was told that he was at Mr. Truman's residence the morning after Mr. Truman became President, probably to tell him how to run the Presidency, as he had done in running the Truman Committee.

Altogether, the RFC put more than $150,000,000 into Mr. Kaiser's wartime enterprises including his Permanente magnesium plant, his Fontana steel mill in California, and working capital. His plant for making ship plates and structurals like the Permanente was a heavy loser.

Mr. Kaiser came to me one day with the story that his profits in building ships for the Maritime Commission the previous year had been about $29,000,000, and that Admiral Emory Scott Land, chairman of the Maritime Commission, wanted to cut him to about $17,000,000. Mr. Kaiser proposed to me that if I would persuade the Admiral to allow his $29,000,000 fees to stand he would apply $12,000,000 on his Permanente magnesium plant debt. I did not take the bait, and I suppose the Admiral cut his fees.

The RFC sold the Geneva plant in Utah to U.S. Steel for $40,-000,000, having advertised for bids and received no others. That was much too low a price, and it was no way to sell the plant. It should have been a negotiated sale. When Mr. Kaiser heard of the sale he asked for a reduction in his debt to the RFC for Fontana; but Mr. Husbands and his board very properly declined.

In 1947 Kaiser asked the RFC, with which I was no longer connected, to write off $74,000,000 of his debt as "excessive wartime cost" of the Fontana plant; but the directors quite rightly refused his request. Mr. Kaiser chose to borrow the money to build the plant rather than have Defense Plant Corporation build and own it. And if the war had lasted six months longer Kaiser would have paid for the plant out of his profits from building ships, rather than paying 90 per cent of his profits as income and excess profits taxes. He fared very well at government hands. His Fontana loan was paid in full in November, 1950, with a check for $91,476,989.92. This money was from a $125,000,000 financing arranged through the First Boston Corporation, Goldman, Sachs & Co., and other underwriting bankers. But the Kaiser-Frazer Corporation still owed the RFC $44,500,000 and a few weeks later received a further loan of $25,000,000 to be used in manufacturing and carrying automobiles—a sorry business for the RFC.

FINANCING THE BIGGEST AIRPLANE IN THE WORLD

One of Mr. Kaiser's wartime ambitions was to build a large fleet of long-range cargo aircraft which, as he visualized them, would be bigger than any planes the skies had yet known, each one capable of carrying a whole company of soldiers with their equipment. Apparently there was much difference of opinion as to the practicability of such a plane in the Cargo Plane Committee, which was composed of representatives of several government agencies. It had been set up by Chairman Nelson of the War Production Board. Mr. Kaiser, who did not seem to be making progress with his idea, was smart enough to get Howard Hughes to join him.

That, of course, put a different face on the situation because Howard Hughes was a recognized authority in building and flying airplanes. After getting Mr. Hughes interested Mr. Kaiser evidently sold his idea to the President. At all events Mr. Nelson came to ask me if we would finance the construction of three such planes, one prototype and two for use. I told him that of course we would if he directed us to. Kaiser-Hughes were given the contract to build three planes at an estimated cost of $18,000,000 but were required to build them without the use of much critical metal material, which was a ridiculous restriction. The planes were to be built of wood.

When Mr. Hughes undertook to construct the plane he did not want Mr. Kaiser around, and I have been advised that Mr. Kaiser never got inside the plant where it was built and assembled.

After a good many months the question of the practicability of the plane arose again; and the experts evidently condemned it, because I had a letter from Mr. Nelson directing us to cancel the contract. About $13,000,000 had already been spent on the prototype alone, and it was not yet near to being finished. We notified Mr. Hughes to stop work on the plane. He immediately came to Washington. He wanted to complete the plane. At the first Cabinet meeting after we had been ordered to cancel the contract I remained, as I frequently did, to discuss our work with the President. I mentioned to the President that Mr. Nelson had ordered us to cancel the contract for the Kaiser-Hughes plane. The President said, instantly:

"You can't do that."

"Well," I said, "we have already notified Mr. Hughes to stop work."

A few days after this I had a letter from Mr. Nelson directing us to reinstate the work. In the meantime Mr. Hughes had been in Washington. We finally agreed with him that we would complete our commitment of $18,000,000 on the condition that he pay any additional cost himself. So work was started again. I understand Mr. Hughes has put $8,000,000 or $10,000,000 of his own money in addition to the RFC's $18,000,000 to complete the plane. He was determined to prove its feasibility.

In the meantime Mr. Kaiser eliminated himself and had no further part in it; but, since it was his promotion in the beginning, he cost the government and Mr. Hughes probably $25,000,000 or $30,000,000 in money and the war effort a great deal of labor and materials.

After I had left government service and after the war was over, Defense Plant Corporation agreed to provide an additional $500,000 to move the big plane from Culver City to Long Beach, California, and to reimburse Mr. Hughes up to $1,000,000 for flight-testing expenses. Although he once flew the plane a short distance I do not believe it has ever had a real test flight. And he is still spending millions of his own funds to prove its feasibility.

SOME SPECTACULAR WARTIME PROJECTS

There were, of course, many cases of excessive costs in wartime, but most of these were necessary if victory was to be hastened. No such case was more striking than the use of half a billion dollars' worth of silver coins and bullion which we borrowed from the Treasury to convert into bus bars and transformer windings as a substitute for critically needed copper. These electrical installations made of silver were used in aluminum plants. In the tremendous industrial expansions of wartime copper had become a very precious metal indeed.

We began the silver substitute scheme by borrowing 35,329 pieces of that metal valued at $63,000,000 to ship on specially guarded trains to an aluminum plant at Riverbank in the San Joaquin valley of California.

Before releasing the metal, Secretary Morgenthau took the precaution of obtaining an opinion from the Attorney General, which the

President approved, saying he had authority to permit such use to be made of the Treasury's silver provided we returned a like amount of it after the war in the form and fineness of the quantities received.

Later we installed silver electrical apparatus in lieu of copper in aluminum metal and fabricating plants in New York, Louisiana, North Carolina, and elsewhere, borrowing some 474,194,633 fine troy ounces which the Treasury valued at $551,795,879. To convert it into bus bars, etc., cost over $5,000,000. After the war it was remelted into bullion.

Next to the Geneva steel mill in Utah, the costliest single project of Defense Plant Corporation was the $176,000,000 Dodge-Chicago plant in which aircraft engines were manufactured to power the B-29 Superfortresses and the B-32 Dominators. Among the engines built in Chicago were those which powered the planes that dropped atomic bombs on Hiroshima and Nagasaki.

At first it was estimated the plant would cost about $100,000,000, but the demands of General H. H. Arnold, commanding the Army Air Corps, kept climbing until, in the end, there had been brought into operation the largest single industrial plant in the country. With its own steel forge and aluminum foundry, Dodge-Chicago was the only factory which took in pigs of magnesium and aluminum and bars of steel at one end and turned out finished engines at the other.

The plant's nineteen one-story buildings sprawled over 6,300,000 square feet—about 145 acres—of floor space near the southwest outskirts of Chicago where, before the war, corn had grown. So deep was the mud at intervals during the day-and-night construction period that the contractor mounted some of his foremen and timekeepers on horses.

Lester L. Colbert, whom the Chrysler Corporation chose from its executives to be general manager of the giant enterprise, used to say that he could put Ford's aircraft assembly plant at Willow Run—another Defense Plant Corporation offspring—in one of his larger buildings in Chicago and have space left over for several baseball fields. The army of men and women under his command built 18,413 engines and was never once behind schedule. The engines were shipped for installation to airplane factories in Wichita, Omaha, Seattle, Marietta, Fort Worth, and San Diego. When the plant was about to be handed back to the government after the war, "Tex" Colbert, just turned forty, was elected president of Dodge division, the largest unit in the Chrysler Corporation. In November, 1950, he succeeded K. T. Keller as president of Chrysler. The Chicago plant is now being used by the Ford Motor Company to build matériel for World War III.

Defense Plant Corporation had large-scale dealings with practically every automobile maker in the country and with scores of firms that supplied them. Our disbursements to construct and equip plants in which General Motors built airplane engines exceeded $300,000,000. We put nearly $170,000,000 more into other plants which that corporation operated to turn out various war materials. One of our earliest defense disbursements in 1940 was $50,000,000 to the Studebaker Corporation for a plant to make airplane engines and parts. I became well acquainted with Studebaker's president, Paul G. Hoffman. In 1942, when a group of the country's outstanding businessmen met in my office in the Department of Commerce and formed the Committee on Economic Development to make plans for an orderly postwar reconversion of industry, I selected Mr. Hoffman to head it, and William Benton, now a United States Senator, to assist him. They did a good job. In 1948 President Truman appointed Mr. Hoffman to direct the European Recovery Program, to carry out the Marshall Plan. After three years of executing the Marshall Plan, Mr. Hoffman is now president of the $300,000,000 Ford Foundation.

Big business may have its faults, but it also has its virtues and a gleaming record of good deeds. The vast capabilities of our largest industrial corporations were necessary to win the recent war and will be necessary to win the next one. They are necessary to our modern peacetime economy. Orders and demands from the fighting services and the requests of our allies were so enormous that, in thousands of instances, only a gigantic organization could fill the bill efficiently and quickly. Of the $9,200,000,000 with which this chapter is concerned, nearly $4,000,000,000 went into projects carried out by only twenty-five of the nation's biggest concerns.

The list of twenty-five top-liners appears on the facing page.

It was not Defense Plant Corporation or the RFC that selected a certain big company to undertake a specified big job. Each project was requested or recommended by some other government agency, such as the War Production Board, Army, Navy or Maritime Commission. Generally the agency specified the concern with which it wished us to deal.

Company	Defense Plant Corporation Investment
Aluminum Company of America	$508,800,000
General Motors Corp.	470,500,000
United States Steel Corp.	372,000,000
Curtiss-Wright Corp.	358,100,000
Republic Steel Corp.	187,900,000
Chrysler Corp.	180,600,000
Ford Motor Co.	172,500,000
Anaconda Copper Mining Co.	170,200,000
Dow Chemical Co.	150,700,000
United Aircraft Corp.	143,200,000
General Electric Co.	137,100,000
Union Carbide & Carbon Corp.	134,500,000
Standard Oil Co. of New Jersey	103,600,000
Bendix Aviation Corp.	94,200,000
Goodyear Tire & Rubber Co.	79,500,000
Koppers Co., Inc.	74,000,000
Studebaker Corp.	73,700,000
American Rolling Mill Co.	66,500,000
Continental Motors Corp.	65,900,000
Mathieson Alkali Works, Inc.	60,400,000
Packard Motor Co.	59,900,000
B. F. Goodrich Co.	53,200,000
Nash-Kelvinator Corp.	53,100,000
E. I. du Pont de Nemours & Co.	50,700,000
The Sperry Corp.	50,600,000
Total	$3,871,400,000

Small business enterprises came into the orbit of Defense Plant Corporation not only indirectly as subcontractors by the tens of thousands, but directly in hundreds and hundreds of contracts. Defense Plant Corporation's parent, the RFC, made 4,100 defense loans totaling nearly $4,000,000,000, mostly to comparatively small concerns working on government orders. The RFC also took participations with banks in 3,362 other loans amounting to nearly $400,-000,000 under a defense loan program which I announced on May

20, 1940, just as Hitler was making his rapid conquest of France. The announcement said:

> In order to be of assistance to those industries that may need credit to meet increased demands upon them as a result of the program of National Defense, the RFC will cooperate with banks in making loans either for production or plant expansion, by taking 75% of any such secured loan that a bank may make, the bank carrying 25% of the loan.
>
> Where a bank wishes to carry the entire loan, the RFC will give the bank a definite take-out agreement for 75% of the loan under the schedule of rates now in force, or that may be agreed upon.

Congress had authorized us to make defense loans "on such terms and conditions and with such maturities" as we might determine.

After Pearl Harbor, we increased our participation to 90 per cent of a bank's defense loan at any time during the life of the loan at the option of the bank to meet the needs of any manufacturer having a government contract or, similarly, the needs of a subcontractor. Our interest charge in these cases was 4 per cent.

Our participation charges on a bank's defense loans ranged from 1 per cent down to ½ of 1 per cent. The larger the portion of a note not covered by the agreement, the less our participation charge. This arrangement had the effect of providing the banks with the equivalent of a short-term government security yield from 3 to 3½ per cent, less their servicing costs, on that portion of the loan in which the RFC participated.

Although it was not organized until the summer of 1940 the genesis of Defense Plant Corporation really goes back to the previous winter, when a strange quiet prevailed on the narrow western front while Hitler prepared his spring offensive. At that time I asked Hans A. Klagsbrunn of our legal staff and another lawyer to join with certain Treasury officials in a study of the problem of how we could assist the British in financing an increased use of American industrial facilities in their effort to arm themselves adequately.

In April, 1940, a few weeks before the German onslaught, these gentlemen drew up a memorandum suggesting various methods by which our manufacturing potentials might be increased. They mentioned special tax incentives, such as allowances for rapid depreciation, and also government ownership of facilities to be operated by private contractors under a management-fee agreement. Alternatively, they suggested government ownership and lease of facilities, a method that would give wider freedom to contractors, since a lease could be for a nominal $1 a year.

On May 16, 1940, less than a week after the Wehrmacht and Luftwaffe stormed into Holland, Belgium, Luxemburg, and France, President Roosevelt addressed Congress on preparedness. Among other measures, he advocated gearing up the country's ability so that it could produce 50,000 airplanes a year. To most of his listeners that figure seemed incredible and impossible. The American aircraft industry then had its sights on a maximum output of 12,000 planes a year, which would be more than double the industry's pre-1939 capacity.

Ten days later, in a radio broadcast, the President told the country the government stood ready to advance whatever money would be necessary to enlarge factories and build new plants to strengthen the nation's defenses.

At his suggestion the RFC then requested Congress for powers to make defense loans for plant construction and expansion, and to buy equipment. We asked authority to create subsidiary corporations which could engage in all manner of preparations for meeting the threat of war. We also requested Congress to extend the RFC's life five more years and to increase its lending power another $1,500,-000,000.

Some of the Senators seemed appalled. My friend Arthur Krock, chief Washington correspondent of the New York *Times,* wrote in his column that I was asking for the dictionary. Congress gave it to us. Before the war was won we had thumbed almost every page of it.

The Act of June 25, 1940—which gave us the dictionary—authorized us to purchase plants, lease plants, build plants, whatever we wished, and in any way we might find feasible. It empowered the RFC to manufacture arms, to train aviators, to do almost anything else that would strengthen the nation's armed might. We could buy or build anything the President defined as strategic or critical.

The fact that seventeen months before Pearl Harbor the RFC had —and freely used—the authority and the available funds to buy critical materials and equipment and to build plants probably shortened the war's duration by a good many months.

Once the American preparedness program got under way, no

request of the War or Navy Department was ever questioned by the RFC. We began construction of plants in September, 1940. By the following April—nine months before Pearl Harbor—Congress had authorized defense expenditures aggregating $40,000,000,000. A large proportion of this spending was through the RFC and its subsidiaries. Even then our preparedness spending was running at the rate of about ten billions a year. We had already made more than 14,000 separate prime contracts and promoted probably above 100,000 subcontracts for the manufacture of everything from a corporal's chevrons to bombers. At that time 784 new defense plants, costing more than $2,000,000,000, had been built or were under construction for the War and Navy Departments. In addition, the RFC was financing scores of other projects for making war materials.

I questioned the judgment of those Americans who were out of step with our defense program. I doubted if they understood the real meaning of the conflict which already involved almost the whole of the Eastern Hemisphere.

"These people," I said in a public address, "think this war is just another struggle for power and territory—just another European war. If I thought that, I, too, would favor going about our own business and letting them shoot it out.

"To me this war is a life and death struggle between two powerful world forces with totally different concepts of life and government. One force seeks savagely to restore the State to a position of absolute power represented by the dictum 'The State can do no wrong.' The other fights desperately against great odds to preserve the hard-won freedom and dignity of man. I am on that side, heart and soul, hook, line and sinker."

Defense Plant Corporation's original capital was only $5,000,000, subscribed for in cash by the RFC. All of Defense Plant Corporation's additional funds were obtained by borrowing from the RFC at the rate of 1 per cent per annum—the rate at which RFC was borrowing from the Treasury. On June 30, 1945, when Congress, by joint resolution, dissolved Defense Plant Corporation and merged its powers, assets, and liabilities with those of its parent, it owed the RFC for capital and loans the sum of $4,740,155,251, on which accrued interest of $120,997,124 was also due. Administrative expenses had amounted to only $18,751,019.

Though many of the wartime projects inevitably failed to pay for themselves, quite a number turned in spectacular profits. Two of these were the Big Inch and Little Big Inch pipe lines which brought oil and gasoline from Texas to the eastern seaboard. But for the services those pipe lines rendered, the war, in the opinion of many people, would have lasted much longer. Together they were able to deliver daily more than 550,000 barrels of petroleum and its products, which was about one-third the average delivery to the east coast by all methods in the year 1941.

Big Inch, with a diameter of two feet, was authorized in June, 1942, when German submarines were taking a heavy toll of tanker shipping off the Atlantic and Gulf coasts. It had become obvious that the nation's tanker fleets could not supply the internal needs of the country and simultaneously carry out the overseas traffic which fighting a two-ocean war would require. Soon after our entry into the war, fifty American tankers had been transferred into British service. With one thing and another, the eastern states soon began to feel the pinch of an oil shortage.

Starting at Longview in the east Texas field, Big Inch was in operation as far as Illinois in December, 1942, and was completed to its New Jersey terminus in August, 1943. It cost $79,000,000. Construction of Little Big Inch was authorized in February, 1943, and the job was completed in March, 1944, at a cost of $69,000,000. Little Big Inch started on the Texas coast and was used to transport gasoline and light petroleum products, while Big Inch brought crude oil to the eastern refineries.

The construction of those two pipe lines was by men who knew how to do it well. At the inception of the projects, eleven oil companies had put up $1,000 each to capitalize the War Emergency Pipe Line, Inc. As its president, they selected W. Alton Jones, the hard-driving chief of Cities Service Company.

I had told Secretary Ickes, the Petroleum Administrator for War, that the RFC would finance the pipe-line project through Defense Plant Corporation. Fnally it was decided to rest ownership of the lines in Defense Plant Corporation.

We promptly drafted the services of Captain W. R. Finney of the Standard Oil Company of New Jersey, who had been chairman of the engineers committee which had surveyed the route and planned Big Inch when it was first proposed to have it privately owned. All the best "pipe liners" in the country were eager to join his staff on the biggest job ever undertaken by men of their calling. As field generals in driving the line through in surprisingly fast time, he had Burt E. Hull of the Texas Company and A. N. Horne, who had been drafted from the Texas-Empire Pipe Line Company, subsidiary of the Texas Company. Technicians and laborers, many of them veterans of pipe-line construction in the deserts of the Middle East and in the swamps and hills of Colombia and Venezuela, all toiled with great energy to push Big Inch through forest and field, under rivers and over mountains.

Once built, the lines were turned over to another RFC subsidiary, Defense Supplies Corporation, to operate. Defense Supplies arbitrarily set the transportation price a little higher than the cost of carrying oil from Texas to New York by tanker. In three years the two lines yielded a net profit of $109,000,000. Then the RFC sold them to private operators for $143,000,000, which was slightly more than they had cost to construct ($6,000,000 of the original outlay had been returned to us by a pipe manufacturing company because of the failure of a substantial amount of the pipe it had furnished).

Four smaller oil pipe lines were constructed during the war by direction of Defense Plant Corporation. Two cut across Florida; a third funneled from Greensboro, North Carolina, to Richmond, Virginia; and a fourth served industrial areas in Ohio. Their operations brought a $9,000,000 profit into Defense Plant Corporation. Further to ease the oil transport situation, the Corporation spent $96,000,000 to build tugs, towboats, and barges.

We expected, in the rush of wartime, that mistakes would be made; and they were, plenty of them. Among the failures were the attempts to offset the loss of our principal source of hemp—the Philippines—by establishing hemp fiber plantations in the Middle West. At the request of Commodity Credit Corporation, which was then in the Department of Agriculture, we invested more than $12,000,000 in land, buildings, machinery, and tools for hemp production in Illinois, Wisconsin, Iowa, Indiana, and Minnesota. The rope we got from them would scarcely have sufficed to string up all the war criminals. In January, 1942, before the Philippines had fallen, we arranged to finance the planting and processing of hemp fiber on six plantations in Costa Rica, Guatemala, Honduras, Panama, and Haiti. In these projects about $13,000,000 was invested under agreements which

Courtesy Chrysler Corp.

THE END OF A LONG LINE

Assembling airplane engines at the Dodge-Chicago plant, financed by Defense Plant Corporation.

STEEL PLANT AT GENEVA, UTAH

A $200,000,000 enterprise financed by the Defense Plant Corporation.

continued until 1948. The sale of more than seventy million pounds of hemp fiber grown on those plantations brought only about half what it had cost to produce; but it was necessary.

On January 15, 1945, just a few days before my services with the government were concluded, I sent a report to the President and the Congress summarizing the war activities of the RFC and its subsidiaries. At that time Defense Plant Corporation had financed 2,098 plants and other projects in forty-six states for which our commitments totaled $7,939,465,000. Some 920 of the plants were complete, integrated establishments wholly owned by Defense Plant Corporation in the amount of $6,055,000,000. We had committed another $750,000,000 to expansions owned by Defense Plant Corporation on land which it either bought or held on long-term leases.

The way the plants and projects were distributed by states is shown by the following list:

State	Plants and Projects	Commitment	State	Plants and Projects	Commitment
Alabama	16	$73,733,000	Nevada	5	150,259,000
Arizona	16	98,402,000	New Hampshire	3	2,521,000
Arkansas	12	88,853,000	New Jersey	132	298,337,000
California	120	323,206,000	New Mexico	4	5,268,000
Colorado	5	6,235,000	New York	166	577,542,000
Connecticut	63	152,866,000	North Carolina	9	13,420,000
Delaware	7	3,383,000	Ohio	232	778,515,000
District of			Oklahoma	20	46,985,000
Columbia	3	4,850,000	Oregon	26	43,019,000
Florida	14	16,008,000	Pennsylvania	172	581,663,000
Georgia	11	4,279,000	Rhode Island	13	6,937,000
Idaho	1	225,000	South Carolina	11	8,050,000
Illinois	132	695,679,000	Tennessee	23	47,545,000
Indiana	84	507,485,000	Texas	92	647,000,000
Iowa	20	14,999,000	Utah	18	248,601,000
Kansas	10	44,544,000	Vermont	6	4,126,000
Kentucky	56	161,432,000	Virginia	10	16,553,000
Louisiana	27	232,816,000	Washington	30	149,068,000
Maine	2	352,000	West Virginia	12	93,093,000
Maryland	42	72,598,000	Wisconsin	56	171,463,000
Massachusetts	71	94,901,000	Wyoming	4	12,899,000
Michigan	209	808,000,000	Facilities in		
Minnesota	27	29,376,000	more than		
Mississippi	55	1,620,000	1 state: pipe		
Missouri	32	161,808,000	lines, etc.	60	398,268,000
Montana	3	12,478,000			
Nebraska	6	28,125,000	Total	2,148	$7,939,385,000

Defense Plant Corporation also made commitments for facilities in foreign countries to produce critical and strategic materials, the sum aggregating nearly $43,000,000. These included the production of copper in Chile, nickel in Cuba, vanadium concentrates in Peru, peat in Canada, fluorspar in Newfoundland, and balsa wood in Ecuador.

THE MEN WHO DID THE JOB

During all but the last few months of its corporate existence, the operations of Defense Plant Corporation were conducted under my general supervision. By law, my authority as Federal Loan Administrator transcended that of the boards of directors of the RFC and its subsidiaries. Of Defense Plant Corporation, as of most of the other subsidiaries, I took the board chairmanship, with Emil Schram, then chairman of the RFC, as president of this new corporation. When Mr. Schram left us in July, 1941, to accept the presidency of the New York Stock Exchange, Sam H. Husbands, another RFC director who had been running Defense Supplies Corporation under the supervision of Mr. Clayton, took on the presidency of Defense Plant Corporation. He remained its president throughout the war. All of its other directors and officers were likewise selected from the board and the staff of the RFC.

I cannot speak too highly of Sam Husbands. As the operating head of Defense Plant Corporation, his dealings generally were with topflight industrialists in every field. He was an excellent judge of human nature, and not afraid to take responsibility. When the going got rough the boys who headed all our subsidiary corporations and RFC departments would sometimes ask me to hold their hands, as it were. Time was of the essence, and we acted. The question was to get the job done. Sam Husbands always did.

Four divisions were set up within Defense Plant Corporation. The chief of each reported directly to Mr. Husbands. Frank T. Ronan headed the administrative division which investigated the financial responsibility of lessees and plant operators and guided the machine tools program. Walter L. Drager, as head of the engineering division, supervised plant construction. Once a plant went into operation, our plant servicing division, of which Herbert R. Rutland was the chief, kept an eye on operations—and rentals. The acquisition of real estate was in charge of Louis H. Bean.

During the war John Francis Coleman, a brilliant engineer and very personable gentleman of New Orleans who at President Hoover's suggestion had assisted us in the early days of the RFC in supervising some of the self-liquidating public-works projects, returned to us to give particular attention to some of the constructions undertaken by the Defense Plant Corporation. I knew something of Mr. Coleman's ability for, as chairman of the Houston Harbor Board in 1912, when we first got deep water at Houston, I had employed Mr. Coleman to plan our port facilities. Another distinguished engineer upon whose services we were able to call during the war was F. E. Lamphere of Philadelphia.

In directing Defense Plant Corporation, we adopted a by-law constituting any two members of the executive committee as a quorum and gave this committee all the authority and power of the board of directors when the board was not in session. Thus, in practice, any two directors could handle the day's top decisions, leaving the others free to get on with other work. An inkling of the immensity of detail which had to be handled may be had from the fact that the minutes reporting the meetings of the board over a period of slightly less than five years take up approximately seventy thousand pages.

We received much help and cooperation from businessmen and industrialists, some of whom gave us their full time for weeks or months at a stretch. Fifteen days after Pearl Harbor I telephoned Clarence Francis, president of General Foods Corporation, and asked him to come to Washington from New York and help us speed the building of war plants. He did. He flew down during Christmas week, went back to New York the same evening to get a leave from his board, and, just after New Year's, returned to work full time for us. He got out a map, divided the country into zones and asked himself who would be the most capable executive to take charge and act as a liaison man or red-tape cutter in each area.

Among the executives he persuaded to cooperate in this task were Edward S. French, president of the Boston & Maine Railroad, in New England; W. Gibson Carey, Jr., president of Yale & Towne Manufacturing Co., in New York; Lee H. Bristol of the Bristol-Myers Co., who took over the troubleshooting in the northern New Jersey area; and Richard P. Brown, chairman of the board of Brown Instrument Co., Philadelphia, who was assigned eastern Pennsylvania and Maryland. Among Mr. Brown's contributions to the war effort was the share-a-car idea which came to him when he noticed that most of his own employees drove to work alone so long as the tires lasted and the gasoline ration held out.

Other businessmen and industrialists who pitched into our war-plant program under Mr. Francis' direction were:

Buffalo-Rochester area: Edward P. Lupfer, president, Edward P. Lupfer Corporation, Buffalo; and Henry P. Werner, chairman of the board, Best Foods, Inc., Buffalo.

West Virginia, eastern Ohio, and western Pennsylvania area: George H. Willock, Pittsburgh.

Cleveland area: Harvey H. Brown, vice president, Stewart Furnace Corporation.

Detroit area: Jean T. Sheafor, secretary and treasurer, Michigan Bell Telephone Co.

Indianapolis area: E. S. Pearce, president, Railway Service & Supply Corporation.

Chicago area: R. Douglas Stuart, vice president, Quaker Oats Co.

Minnesota area: Harry W. Zinsmaster, president, Zinsmaster Bread Company, Duluth.

St. Louis area: William McClellan, chairman of the board, Union Electric Company of Missouri.

Omaha and Kansas City area: W. Dale Clark, president, Omaha National Bank.

Seattle area: H. B. Friele, general manager, The Nakat Packing Corporation.

Arizona, California, Nevada, and Utah area: Arthur C. Stewart, Union Oil Company of California, Los Angeles; and Clifford W. Lord, sales manager Pacific coast district, Oil Well Supply Company, Los Angeles.

Texas area: M. Tilford Jones, engineer and ranchman, Houston; and Thomas W. Griffiths, Dallas.

Southeast area: Crawford Johnson, Sr., Crawford Johnson & Co., Birmingham.

Cincinnati area: Harry R. Drackett, president, The Drackett Co.

Much of the road and field work between the zones was ably and tirelessly done by Al Schindler of St. Louis, who later became Under Secretary of Commerce.

At every plant during the period of construction, Defense Plant

Corporation had a Johnnie-on-the-spot. We didn't pinch pennies, or millions either, but, even in a war, those of us trained in the RFC didn't want to see any of the taxpayers' money unnecessarily wasted. It was all done in the most businesslike way possible in the circumstances.

23

---- ❊ ----

DEFENSE SUPPLIES CORPORATION

Getting Started on Aviation Gasoline—Stockpiling Wool and Silk—Some Rougher Fabrics—Controversy over Quinine—Driving Nazi Airplanes Out of South America—Taking French Leave from Madagascar—Subsidizing the Butcher and Baker—A $50,000,000 Deal with the Soviets—Cooperation from the Customs

BY FAR the most versatile member of RFC's sturdy brood of wartime offspring was Defense Supplies Corporation. It was a catch-all, go-anywhere, do-anything organization. In buying, lending, and subsidizing it disbursed $9,226,000,000 in the United States and forty-five foreign lands as a part of the government's preparedness and war-making activities. It has wound up about $2,600,000,000 in the red, a result Congress foresaw and specifically authorized.

At the continuous requests of the armed services and other government agencies Defense Supplies Corporation ran all manner of essential errands and performed critical chores on every continent. For one thing it bought, stockpiled, and distributed more than $5,000,000,000 worth of commodities of two hundred-odd different kinds, ranging through the alphabet from abaca to xylidines. The products it bought and distributed were deemed essential to winning the war.

For another thing Defense Supplies Corporation disbursed more than $2,700,000,000 in subsidies and grants. These were poured out on directives issued by me as Federal Loan Administrator with the President's approval. The requests upon which the directives were based came from the War Production Board, the Office of Price Administration, the Board of Economic Warfare, the Maritime Commission, the armed services and, occasionally, other qualified agencies.

Some of the subsidies were granted to stabilize consumer prices, some to reimburse a primary producer, processor, or shipper for abnormal expenditures attributable to the dislocations of wartime. Occasionally a subsidy was arranged to do a diplomatic favor for the State Department in cultivating friends and annoying enemies in neutral lands. Others were granted to encourage marginal producers of such things as minerals to dig up more materials for America's arsenal. The biggest of all the subsidies had the simple purpose of holding down the price the public paid for its bread, meat, and butter.

Defense Supplies did not itself initiate policies or particular procurement programs. It merely carried out, in as businesslike a manner as the circumstances permitted, the legally authorized directives, suggestions, and recommendations of others, with all of whom, except Vice President Wallace's Board of Economic Warfare, its relations were, from beginning to end, amicable, cooperative, and mutually helpful.

The gigantic growth of Defense Supplies Corporation may be measured with the fact that the total amount the Corporation authorized its agents and representatives to spend approached $13,500,000,-000. About $2,500,000,000 of those authorizations were canceled, some of them because private industry or another government body undertook the assignments.

The cumulated net cost of Defense Supplies' operations—about $2,600,000,000—was slightly less than the total amount the Corporation gave away in the form of subsidies, grants, and contributions. In its trading in commodities the Corporation showed an overall profit. Goods that cost it $5,534,000,000 were sold, mostly on War Production Board allocations, for $5,922,000,000.

For the magnitude of its almost world-wide operations, the administrative expenses of Defense Supplies—some $12,500,000—were, I think, remarkably small. As far as possible we relied on established commercial enterprises whose personnel were experienced in one or another of the many fields that were strange to us.

Defense Supplies' highly useful existence had many facets. It financed the manufacture of industrial alcohol needed by the newborn synthetic rubber industry, and it bought every available raw material for the making of the alcohol, from dehydrated potatoes to strap molasses. It helped the State Department purge the air lines of South and Central America of German and Italian capital, direction, and operating personnel and paid for the training in the United States of Latin American pilots, mechanics, and engineers to replace them. By a series of exclusive purchasing agreements with South American republics it closed those markets to buyers for the Axis countries months before Pearl Harbor.

Defense Supplies bought and sold to the air services more than $2,200,000,000 worth of 100-octane gasoline. It helped the oil industry make plant conversions and expansions which that immense undertaking required.

As a feeder to the alcohol and synthetic rubber programs, the Corporation bought all of Cuba's sugar and molasses crops for three years. It transported and stored, partly for the United States, partly for Great Britain, the bulk of the Australian and New Zealand wool clips, which ran into hundreds of millions of pounds. With loans of more than $71,000,000 it financed the Army's Post Exchanges in every military camp at home and in every alien land to which American forces carried the flag.

Defense Supplies sponsored industries new to America, such as the making of jewel bearings, for which this country had previously been almost completely dependent upon the craftsmanship of the Swiss. The Corporation put up the money to develop the growing of sisal in Haiti, of cinchona and abaca in Central America, of other needed products in various parts of the United States, Brazil, Mexico, and elsewhere. It backed geological explorations both at home and abroad. When Newfoundland became a jumping-off place for the military air ferry across the Atlantic, Defense Supplies loaned more than $1,500,000 to improve the railway facilities in that colony so that they could adequately serve the air fields.

The Corporation bought and stored quinine, typhus fever serum, opium, and other medicines required by the Army and Navy. It bought and stored the nation's entire frozen stocks of raw silk, primarily needed for parachutes and gunpowder bags. It handled the idle tire and scrap rubber collections, relieved manufacturers and dealers of frozen inventories of automobiles, refrigerators, stoves, and other severely rationed articles. It built up stockpiles of radio parts and equipment, aluminum rivets, fibers and fabrics, leather and hides, goatskins, hog bristles, sheep linings, horsehair manes, even shark livers and Mexican prairie bones, all of which had a part to play in waging war.

When it served their country's interests as a belligerent, Defense Supplies' operatives were not above a bit of duplicity or even sabotage. In their dealings with diamond dies, a strictly legalistic mind might have accused them of smuggling. Dies made from industrial diamonds are employed in drawing ultrafine wires used in manufacturing certain airplane instruments, the timing apparatus on bombs and other delicate mechanisms. The holes are sometimes so small as to be invisible to the naked eye. Excellent vision is required even to see the thinnest of the wires. Some are so light it requires about 135 miles of length to weigh one pound. Laid across a sheet of plain white paper the thin strand is hardly visible.

The making of such dies is a specialty of craftsmen in a few communities in France. An industrial diamond that originally might have been worth no more than $1 will sometimes fetch, when it leaves their superbly skilled hands, $50 and up. To get a stock of these dies out of a France occupied by the Germans required devious and surreptitious methods. Defense Supplies had been asked to get out a stock, and it did—tens of thousands of dies. Our British friends, who had cultivated good clandestine contacts behind Hitler's barriers, were very helpful in that enterprise.

To the Soviet Union's Amtorg Trading Corporation, Defense Supplies loaned $50,000,000 which was used to purchase war materials in the United States. We collected that debt by importing from Russia finished platinum, manganese, chrome ores, and other materials which increased the armed might of the United States.

In our dealings with other foreign countries the procurement of metals and ores was assigned to another RFC subsidiary, Metals Reserve Company. Almost everything else the national defense and war programs required from abroad, except rubber, fell into the ever expanding province of Defense Supplies.

William L. Clayton, one of the sagest Americans both in foreign trade and in diplomacy, a gentleman who before beginning his distinguished government service career had built up the world's largest firm of cotton merchants, was my assistant as Secretary of Commerce and one of my Deputy Federal Loan Administrators. He was in general charge of the overseas procurement activities of Defense Supplies and our other wartime subsidiaries, Rubber Development Corporation, Metals Reserve Company and, later on, the United States Commercial Company.

When Defense Supplies began operations in August, 1940, it had but a single immediate objective—to procure and store a supply of high-octane gasoline for the Army and Navy air services. At that time American industry's capacity for producing 100-octane gasoline was only about 30,000 barrels a year. Before the war ended Defense Supplies had handled more than thirteen billion gallons of it.

With the potent part high-octane fuel played in winning the war it seems strange that when its increased production program was first proposed to the procurement branches of both Army and Navy air services they showed no particular interest. In those unprepared days of the summer of 1940, just after the fall of France, only a few American pursuit planes were fed with 100-octane gasoline. The commercial air lines and the majority of our military aircraft burned ordinary aviation fuel.

It was a former professor of chemical engineering at Massachusetts Institute of Technology, the foresighted Dr. R. E. Wilson, that first convinced us we ought to get going on a high-octane gasoline expansion program. Dr. Wilson, who has since become chairman of the Standard Oil Company of Indiana, was then president of the Pan American Petroleum & Transport Company. He was brought to my office by Edward R. Stettinius, Jr., of the Council of National Defense (who later became Secretary of State). After he had outlined what he believed increased requirements would be if President Roosevelt's proposed expansion of Army and Navy aviation were carried out, I told him that if the Army and Navy would take the gasoline off our hands later on we would finance the necessary plant expansions in the oil industry and establish a stockpile.

George Hill of our legal department went with Dr. Wilson to visit the services' procurement offices. To their surprise, they received what they considered somewhat of a brush-off. Later on, however, both services were continually clamoring for higher and higher production, so much so that we were never able to establish a stockpile. As fast as the gasoline flowed from the refineries it was sent on its way to air bases and carriers.

Taking full advantage of the *carte blanche* powers Congress had accorded the RFC in the Act of June 25, 1940, to aid the national defense program, Defense Supplies' charter authorized the Corporation to take any action toward that end which the President and the Federal Loan Administration might deem necessary. In addition to this all-embracing clause the charter specifically empowered Defense Supplies to produce, buy, sell, and store critical and strategic materials; to buy or lease land; buy, build, or lease plants; engage in the manufacture of arms, ammunition, and implements of war; produce or buy railroad equipment, airplanes, aviation training fields and camps; buy and control transportation facilities in and between other American countries in the Western Hemisphere and the United States.

At the start Sam H. Husbands, one of the RFC directors, was elected president of Defense Supplies Corporation, and I took the chairmanship. John D. Goodloe was chosen executive vice president. In July, 1941, when Mr. Goodloe was appointed general counsel of the RFC, George H. Hill, Jr., succeeded him as executive vice president of Defense Supplies. Stuart Barnes, who had been with the RFC in its early years, returned to us from the Securities and Exchange Commission to join Defense Supplies. Upon Mr. Hill's retirement, Mr. Barnes became executive vice president. Stuart Barnes is now an officer of the Guaranty Trust Company of New York and George Hill is assistant to the president of Cities Service Company. For a short time Mr. Husbands was president of both Defense Plant and Defense Supplies. Defense Plant alone was a man's size job; so, in 1943, we relieved Sam of the Defense Supplies presidency, which was taken over by Harry Mulligan who had been with the RFC since its inception.

Almost from the start Defense Supplies had scores of materials to concern itself with, other than engine fuel for Army and Navy airplanes. Eventually, however, the original program for high-octane gasoline became the Corporation's largest single procurement undertaking. To reimburse us for expenses in administering that program we charged the Army and Navy a fee of $1/200$ of a cent per gallon of fuel delivered.

Before the program hit its peak a large part of the nation's petroleum industry had been diverted to the refining of aviation gasoline. To help finance the additional facilities this change-over required, we loaned the participating oil companies more than $65,000,000, charging them 2 per cent interest. We also agreed to reimburse refiners for unusual expenses incurred to increase production. On that score we paid out approximately $100,000,000. These costs were added to the price charged the services for the gasoline. The refiners paid off their loans, including more than $5,000,000 in interest, with fuel deliveries of equivalent value. For tax purposes they were allowed five-year amortization on the new plants. The $\frac{1}{200}$ of a cent a gallon which Defense Supplies charged the services for overhead and administration expenses brought in more than $600,000.

Linked to high-octane gasoline was a procurement program for benzol, an essential ingredient. Benzol was also required in producing styrene and butadiene which went into the manufacture of synthetic rubber, an enterprise in which Defense Plant Corporation was investing more than $700,000,000. Thus the RFC had two direct interests in boosting the output of benzol.

Benzol is obtained as a by-product of coal coking. Steel plants are the principal sources of the domestic supply. During the war Defense Supplies bought and distributed more than two hundred million gallons. Almost exactly half of it came from domestic sources, the other half being imported from the United Kingdom under reverse Lend-Lease arrangements.

STOCKPILING WOOL AND SILK

During its early months while waiting for the armed services to indicate their likely requirements in high-octane gasoline Defense Supplies Corporation was directed into scores of other procurement activities. Its first large-scale undertaking was the buying and storing of a considerable part of the Australian and New Zealand wool crops, and, later, a portion of the clips from the sheep of South Africa and Uruguay.

Immediately after the outbreak of the war in 1939, the British government had contracted to purchase the entire Australian wool clip each year until twelve months after hostilities were concluded. As merchant marine dislocations and losses at sea accumulated during the early months of the war the British found they could not spare sufficient shipping for all the long voyages that would be required to transport their wool stocks from the Antipodes to United Kingdom ports. Meanwhile—even before the creation of Defense Supplies— farsighted plans were broached in Washington for establishing a stockpile of Australian wool in the United States. Our country is not self-sufficient in wool. The administration felt a shortage might result in a major emergency.

We knew, of course, that the British wanted dollars. They also desired, for their own stockpile, to have some of their wool closer to home than Australia, though not necessarily in England where wool warehouses along the Thames were among the first sufferers from the German blitz on London. The long haul from Australia had been stretched even farther when the Mediterranean became so perilous that "the life line of Empire" had to be moved down around the southern tip of Africa. So, as we sat down to trade with the British, it was a case of each fellow having something the other wanted.

We had called John Goodloc back from Commodity Credit Corporation which, less than a year before, had been moved from the RFC to the Department of Agriculture. He joined Mr. Clayton on our side of the Anglo-American table. A tentative agreement was soon reached for the storage in this country of a substantial amount of Australian wool. President Roosevelt approved it. He wrote on October 3, 1940, asking me to submit to him as quickly as possible my recommendation for financing the transport and warehouse charges involved in the proposed arrangement.

"The matter is urgent," his letter said.

I promptly suggested that he dip into his "Emergency Funds for the President." The next day he transferred $12,000,000 from that account to me, as Federal Loan Administrator, and authorized me to use the money in acquiring an "adequate supply" of wool. I credited the money to Defense Supplies, and we resumed conversations with the British.

The British Ministry of Supply contracted to establish in bond in the United States a strategic reserve of Australian wool, we to pay the freight and storage charges. We also made warehouse space available in this country for wool in transit to the United Kingdom.

Deliveries began early in 1941. By the summer of that fateful year the administration had raised its sights as to our possible needs in an emergency. The Office of Production Management recommended a billion-pound wool stockpile and outright purchase of such Australian wool as was already in storage in the United States. Messrs. Clayton and Goodloe then opened new negotiations with Sir Frederick Phillips and his British colleagues. After various proposals and counter proposals they hit off a trade on October 10, 1941. We contracted to purchase all the Australian wool already received or afloat, plus further shipments up to 250,000 pounds. The British agreed to sell this wool at 10 per cent under the then f.o.b. price Australian ports—about 8 per cent above what they had paid for the clip. The transaction gave the United Kingdom some needed dollar exchange, and the United States the wool.

In March, 1942, it was further agreed Defense Supplies would store 400,000 bales of African wool owned by Great Britain, all of which we could purchase if we wished. In March, 1943, all these previous agreements were superseded by an arrangement whereby Defense Supplies Corporation and the Ministry of Supply shared fifty-fifty the freight, storage, and other charges on wool and we took a fee of ten cents a bale in lieu of 3 per cent interest.

During the course of the war and the months immediately afterwards Defense Supplies purchased and sold 337,000,000 pounds of foreign wool. Over the same period the United Kingdom stored in transit in this country 577,000,000 pounds, on the handling of which our 50 per cent share of the expense came to $7,500,000. We looked upon that cost as an insurance premium for the protection of having the wool here during the emergency.

By the end of 1943 private importations and domestic production were meeting American requirements to such an extent that the War Production Board recommended gradual liquidation of Defense Supplies' stockpile. We decided on periodic sales at public auctions primarily conducted by the National Wool Market Corporation acting as our agent on a commission basis. Our net gain from trading in wool amounted to almost $70,000,000. A substantial portion of the inventory which remained on hand at the conclusion of hostilities in Europe was shipped to France, Belgium, and Holland under Lend-Lease arrangements.

The Corporation's purchase of 34,600,000 pounds of Uruguayan wool for $12,685,000 was made partly to aid in the stabilization of Uruguay's economic situation. The Uruguayan portion of the stockpile was sold at auction for $18,912,992, a profit of more than $6,000,-000.

Silk has been an essential war material ever since armies began using gunpowder. Silk is the material of which powder bags are made. Even before the development of the airplane added a new element to warfare, silk was used for parachutes by balloonists. Substitutes for silk have been found adequate in making parachutes and women's stockings—but no synthetic has yet appeared that can satisfactorily take the place of silk in fabricating powder bags for large-caliber guns.

The Corporation began stockpiling silk several months before our country was attacked by Japan, which had long been our principal source of that material. Small quantities had been imported from China, Italy and France. The United States has never produced silk in commercial quantities.

In July, 1941, an Office of Price Administration order restricted sales of raw silk to the Defense Supplies Corporation and to manufacturers requiring it to fill military contracts. Simultaneously the OPA clamped on ceiling prices. With the intention of building a 50,000 bale stockpile, Defense Supplies began buying raw silk from domestic importers and from manufacturers' inventories. Within a month the War Production Board upped the stockpile target to 100,000 bales. After Pearl Harbor all raw silk held by American importers and processors was requisitioned for purchase by Defense Supplies.

We bought and requisitioned nearly nine million pounds at a cost exceeding $26,000,000. Since our selling tag was the same as the purchase price, the Corporation lost the cost of handling and storing —about half a million dollars. Some dealers contended the price we paid for requisitioned stocks resulted in losses to them and they sued to recover. Their claims ran to another half a million dollars.

SOME ROUGHER FABRICS

Of the rougher fabrics and fibers, Defense Supplies and its sister corporation, United States Commercial Company, were potent purchasers in most parts of the world still open to American buyers. Burlap, customarily made from jute, goes into the manufacture of bags for industrial, chemical, agricultural, and sundry military purposes. After the President had defined it as a strategic and critical material on September 5, 1941, Defense Supplies purchased about a billion and a half yards in India and Brazil and also requisitioned 118,000,000 yards from domestic sources when the War Production Board froze the American stocks.

Defense Supplies made about $12,000,000 trading in burlap, which it sold at Office of Price Administration prices on War Production Board allocations. Subsequently the United States Commercial Company imported $60,000,000 worth of burlap which it sold at a profit exceeding $5,600,000.

We also bought millions of dollars' worth of cotton and cotton linters in Peru, Egypt, Brazil, and Mexico, cotton towels in Spain, jute in India and the Belgian Congo, kapok and sisal all over the world, rope and twine in Mexico, Cuba, and elsewhere.

The only satisfactory substitute for burlap in making certain bags was Osnaburg, a medium-heavy cotton fabric. On Office of Production Management's recommendation Defense Supplies bought up all available Osnaburg at normal sources and then contracted for its manufacture by domestic mills which had not previously produced it. Much of it was shipped to Africa as garments for natives whose friendship was valuable to our armed forces.

In trading in agave fibers, principally sisal and henequen, which are used for wrappings, twine and stuffing for cushions, we lost nearly $5,000,000, about $2,000,000 of which represented freight allowances. These in reality were subsidies granted to reimburse purchasers for the difference between freight rates from ports customarily used and those through which wartime cargoes were diverted.

From April 2, 1942, onward, all fibers were considered strategic and critical. With Philippine sources cut off, price ceased to be a deciding consideration. But in selling what we had bought we bumped our heads against the price ceiling and were hurt financially.

Some of the purchases we were directed to execute in South and Central America were motivated more by political than by economic or military considerations. When France and the Low Countries fell to the Germans, the republics of Latin America lost their principal European markets. President Roosevelt and some of his advisers feared that economic chaos might creep into the southern half of our hemisphere, and that this could beget political storms of which the Nazis would take full advantage. Both within the administration and in Congress there were influential men who advocated creation of a one- or two-billion-dollar government consortium to buy the products of South American countries and store them until normal markets had been restored.

On February 16, 1942, in summarizing our operations in the acquisition of critical and strategic materials and the activities of the

Export-Import Bank, I had concluded a long memorandum to President Roosevelt with the following observations:

We are buying and will continue to buy every exportable commodity produced in Latin America which may be requested by WPB, the Department of State and the BEW. Also we are buying and will continue to buy, wherever available, such critical and strategic materials as may be recommended by these departments.

No application to the Export-Import Bank for a loan from any Latin-American country has been declined. To the contrary, every application has been worked out and authorized to the satisfaction of the applicant, though sometimes at lesser amounts than applied for.

The integrity of the Bank has been preserved, and must continue to be if it is to render a real service in both war and post-war problems.

In the five years between the launching of the preparedness program in 1940 and the conclusion of hostilities, the United States, largely through RFC subsidiaries, bought more than $5,000,000,000 worth of goods from other American republics. Long before Pearl Harbor we were buying from most of them—and denying to the Axis—everything they had for export that the British did not require.

Led by Brazil, one country after another sent commissions to Washington to trade with us. The Brazilian commission was headed by Senhor Valentin Boucas. From the outset his cooperation and statesmanship and that of the Brazilian Ambassador, Carlos Martins, were unfailing. When both our countries had become belligerents their devotion to the war objectives of the United Nations made an outstanding personal contribution to the success of every program that came within their ken, as many of ours did. In general, the trading patterns which Senhor Boucas, Mr. Clayton, and their associates established were fair and equitable; and, on the whole, the contracts were carried out with complete integrity.

While the South and Central American countries were, for the most part, exerting every effort to expand production to meet our needs, the administration in Washington did all it could to keep their various national economies on an even keel. Sometimes this meant the purchasing of their raw materials and manufactures beyond our foreseeable requirements.

Our principal purchases in Latin America were minerals and metals. These are reviewed in Chapter 29. Brazil, Mexico, and some of the other countries made agreements with us limiting their exportation of specified strategic materials exclusively to the United States.

Outside of metals, our chief interest in Latin American production in the early days of the defense program lay in hides, wool, linseed, and quebracho. When Manila hemp could no longer be brought out of the Philippines we arranged with the United Fruit Company, on a cost-plus-fee basis, for a large-scale effort to grow abaca in Panama. We dealt with United Fruit because they were the only available people experienced in growing abaca, and they had the seed. Furthermore, the State Department objected to our taking a lease on the land in Panama and growing the abaca ourselves.

The abaca development program, in which our investments and loans exceeded $26,000,000, provided for planting about 30,000 acres in Costa Rica and other Central American countries. The program barely got beyond the development stage.

Mr. Wallace's BEW roped us into financing a sisal development in Haiti. We put nearly a million dollars into that project. Before it reached the production stage the war was over.

CONTROVERSY OVER QUININE

The scale and pace of our activities in the procurement of quinine and the growing of cinchona bark, from which that antimalaria drug is manufactured, was one of the many things misrepresented by Mr. Wallace in his public outburst against me in June, 1943. Our subsequent exchange of amenities is dealt with in detail elsewhere in these pages. Overlooked or omitted by Mr. Wallace in his blasts against our work was the fact that the United States Army had on hand before we entered the war several years' supply of quinine sulphate. When Atabrine was developed as a quinine substitute the Army had no use for its quinine sulphate stockpile.

Nevertheless, Defense Supplies had bought and stored two million ounces of quinine, as recommended by the Office of Production Management as early as August, 1941. Although the War Production Board informed us a few weeks after Pearl Harbor that a four years' supply was on hand, and that further stockpiling was unnecessary, we went ahead at the request of Mr. Wallace, and contracted for the delivery of several million more ounces from the Netherlands East Indies. Our purchases and efforts to purchase were summarized in a letter sent me by Mr. Clayton on April 24, 1942, fourteen months before Mr. Wallace let loose his tirade.

Mr. Clayton's letter follows:

Dear Mr. Jones:

Here is our record on quinine:

August 1941, we bought 2,000,000 ounces on recommendation of OPM. The next recommendation to buy quinine came in a letter from Morris Rosenthal, Assistant Director of BEW, which was received by us January 21, 1942, confirming his verbal recommendation, January 15th.

Notwithstanding the fact that all stockpile recommendations were, by Executive Order of the President, to come from WPB and not from BEW, we started negotiations, January 15th and were advised, January 22nd, by the Netherlands East Indies Trade Commissioner, that there was no quinine available in Java for prompt delivery, but we were offered 2,000,000 ounces monthly, March through June 1942. We immediately took the matter up with WPB, and were advised that our quinine supply was comfortable, approximately 14,000,000 ounces, or four years' requirements, and that further stockpiling was unnecessary.

February 16th, we received another letter from Morris Rosenthal, recommending the purchase of 3,000,000 ounces from the Netherlands East Indies. You immediately conferred with Mr. Donald Nelson, and on his verbal approval we ordered the 3,000,-000 ounces for March and April shipment, having been previously advised that there was no quinine available for immediate shipment.

February 26th, we were advised by Mr. Finletter, of the State Department, that 2,500,000 ounces of quinine in the bark could be bought for prompt shipment from Batavia. We made the purchase within the hour, and later the same day bought an additional 665,000 ounces from another source.

Batavia was occupied by the Japanese ten days later, and, as far as we know, none of this quinine was shipped.

Sincerely yours,

W. L. CLAYTON

Special Assistant to the Secretary of Commerce.

For quinine developments in Costa Rica and Guatemala, Defense Supplies disbursed more than $4,000,000, bringing the Corporation's total expenditures in the quinine and cinchona bark programs to nearly $30,000,000. The Corporation also financed the purchase of machinery and equipment for processing antimalarials while the parent RFC financed the assembling by the American Pharmaceutical Association of the principal domestic supply of quinine made available to the armed forces after the fall of Java. This supply was collected from thousands of domestic stocks, large and small, held by druggists and others throughout the nation. Much of it was donated.

Quinine was but one of several medicines and medicaments we were asked to acquire and stock against the accidents and casualties of war. While Defense Plant Corporation was financing the penicillin manufacturing program and the expansion of facilities for making certain other drugs, Defense Supplies spent $665,000 for half a million pounds of iodine, $190,000 for typhus fever vaccine, $500,000 for sponges, and small sums on a miscellany of medicinal barks. On one occasion we were asked to allocate $1,350,000 for a stock of ipecac, and we did; but the directive was later rescinded. In the meantime, without expending any funds, our staff acquired quite a stockpile of ipecac jokes.

*   *   *

One of the procurement programs into which Defense Supplies was pushed by a directive from Mr. Wallace's BEW was that of contracting with inexperienced operators to deliver Mexican mahogany. I shall leave it to Lindsay C. Warren, Comptroller General of the United States at the war's conclusion, to tell that story. Here are the words he submitted to Congress in the General Accounting Office's report of its audit of Defense Supplies from that Corporation's inception through the fiscal year ended June 30, 1945:

> In November 1942 at the direction of BEW, the Corporation [i.e., Defense Supplies Corporation] entered into a contract with the Export-Import Lumber Company of Buffalo, N.Y., for the production and delivery of 2,500,000 board feet of Mexican Mahogany. The performance of the contract was to be accomplished by the Tehuantepec Lumber Company, under stumpage leases on certain tracts of land in Mexico understood to be con-

trolled by Resources Corporation International of Chicago, Ill. The principals of Resources Corporation were under indictment at the time, charged with fraud in connection with stock transactions of that company. The Export-Import Lumber Company was a partnership composed of a father and son, neither of whom had had any previous experience in the lumber business.

The Corporation's [DSC's] representatives objected strongly to contracting with inexperienced operators, but were directed to do so nevertheless. Mexican Government officials were also reluctant, and final arrangements with the Mexican Government were completed only upon the personal intervention of the United States Ambassador.

That the preliminary doubts as to the success of the venture were well founded is evidenced by the troubles encountered in the operations.

The Tehuantepec Lumber Company became involved with the Mexican Government as the result of cutting logs on Mexican public lands. At one time that Government ordered all operations stopped and troops were stationed on the property to enforce the order. Only at the intervention of the United States Ambassador were the difficulties settled.

The Corporation made advances of more than $500,000 to the Export-Import Lumber Company and was never able to get an adequate accounting for the expenditure of the funds. An audit of the Mexican operations was requested, but the auditors found the records in such confusion that a satisfactory audit could not be made.

The lumber company was unable to deliver the 2,500,000 board feet of logs required by the contract; the cost of the lumber which was delivered exceeded the original estimated cost by more than $100 per thousand board feet.

On April 10, 1944, this operation was transferred to U.S. Commercial Company in accordance with Executive Order 9361. USCC reimbursed DSC for all advances, losses, equipment and other transactions appearing in its accounts and assumed the burden of completing the contract.

The results of this operation proved the irresponsibility and inexperience of the operators and justified the reluctance with which the Corporation had undertaken the project. It is an interesting sidelight that, for a 6-month period during the course of this operation, the senior forestry specialist of BEW was an ex-official of Resources Corporation International, and at the time of his employment in BEW, was under indictment for fraud.

BEW was also instrumental in involving the Corporation in the leasing of a plantation in Guatemala for the production of cinchona bark. The officials of the Corporation were not consulted during the preliminary negotiations for this lease, and, when they were drawn into them, they expressed reluctance to proceed under the terms agreed upon by BEW.

However, BEW insisted and the Corporation paid $1,700,000 for a 30-year lease on a 1,200 acre plantation, planted primarily in coffee, for the purpose of growing cinchona trees and harvesting the bark. The lease was effected April 28, 1943, and was transferred to USCC on March 31, 1944.

The plantation was owned by a foreign corporation the majority of the stock of which had been seized by the Alien Property Custodian. Before its principal asset was leased to Defense Supplies Corporation, the stock of the plantation owner was quoted at from $1 to $2.50 per share. After $1,700,000 had been paid to this company by the Corporation, the stock had a liquidating value of approximately $58 per share. Presumably, the foreign shareholders were among the beneficiaries of this bonanza.

Original estimates of bark harvest from this plantation were from 5,000 to 10,000 tons of bark during the first year. Later estimates contemplated that the harvest would be 750 tons. A qualified expert stated that the value of the land, for which $1,700,000 was paid for a 30-year lease, was $60,000.

So much for a couple of deals into which we were directed by Mr. Wallace, whom the President had given the power to tell us what to do, and where, and how much to pay and to whom.

It is significant that of the seven contracts for a total of 47,000,000 board feet of mahogany into which Defense Supplies reluctantly entered at the direction of Mr. Wallace's organization, not a foot of mahogany had been delivered up to the date on which the Vice President launched his attack on me.

DRIVING NAZI AIRPLANES OUT OF SOUTH AMERICA

Between the two world wars German enterprise pushed into a dominant position in commercial aviation in large areas of South and Central America and gave the State Department a shock by requesting landing rights in Florida. German airway expansions through the South American continent were greatly accelerated after Hitler hopped into the saddle in 1933, just a few weeks before President Roosevelt's first inauguration.

Such a situation, within short striking distance of the Panama Canal, gave grave concern to the War, Navy, and State Departments. In 1940 the administration began designs to denazify South America's airways and replace their commercial services with new companies owned by South American or North American interests or by the two jointly. It was an enterprise of extirpation that called for diplomacy, dollars, and doggedness, a silk glove in one spot, a lot of tough talk in another.

In June, 1940, German personnel were ousted from Scadta (Sociedad Colombo Alemana de Transporte Aéreo)—the German-Colombian Air Transport Company, which had pioneered commercial aviation in Latin America as early as 1920 with a line from Bogotá to Barranquilla.

Our cleansing campaign was fully under way by the spring of 1941. At the request of both State and War Departments an American Republics Aviation Division was created within Defense Supplies Corporation to direct and finance the purge. American airplanes and other equipment had to be supplied to replace German facilities. Prospective pilots and student mechanics from various Latin American countries had to be brought to the United States and trained. The Germans, in most of their Latin American air-line operations, had run their own shows with their own people. Consequently there were not many trained nationals of those countries ready to replace them.

A variety of pressures, delicate or blunt, had to be applied to squeeze Scaff out of Colombia, chase Condor and the Lufthansa from Peru and its neighboring lands, rid Brazilian aviation of Italians as well as Germans, and so on.

The Peruvian government was persuaded to expropriate Lufthansa Peru in April, 1941, on the ground that it had conducted flights over forbidden territory. This method turned out to be a helpful device in many places. A few weeks later the government of Bolivia, with which Allen W. Dulles, the brother of John Foster Dulles, had conferred on our behalf, removed German influence from Lloyd Aéreo Boliviano by nationalizing that system. The Bolivians signed a contract with us to eliminate all non-Hemisphere stock ownership and personnel from air lines operating in their country.

We had already begun negotiations with Brazil toward the same end. By the following September, Ecuador requisitioned the Sedta air lines (Sociedad Ecuatoriana de Transportes Aéreos) which, since its inception, had been owned and operated by Lufthansa. Lati, the Italian air service in South America, having been cut off from its fuel supplies, ceased operations on Christmas Eve, 1941.

When other methods failed we were in a position of denying aviation gasoline, and spare parts, to South American countries. Though Defense Supplies Corporation never did succeed in eliminating Condor from the Argentine, we bled that line white of gasoline. The United States allowed the delivery of just enough aviation fuel to Argentina to meet the requirements of that country's military services. Chile was treated to a similar freeze-out.

The American oil companies were scarcely enthusiastic when we first asked them to assist in applying these squeezes. They were understandably anxious to cultivate customers for the years ahead when the war would be a thing of the past. In bringing them around to our program Nelson Rockefeller and his associates in the Office of the Coordinator of Inter-American Affairs were influential. The name Rockefeller swings a lot of weight in oil circles and in many another circle as well.

Mr. Rockefeller's organization drove the denazification campaign forward in various ways. Their showcase was "culture." But ballet dancers, singers, lecturers, movie stars, and other entertaining or enlightening elements of the North American population were not the only persons they sent around South America. Behind the publicized window dressing of the culture carriers various unreported activities helpful to the anti-Axis cause were quietly accomplished by men who couldn't carry a tune, or make a speech in public without becoming flabbergasted. Sundry American business interests also cooperated.

After Pearl Harbor and the entry of several of the South American republics into the war, we found the going much easier. Uniform policies were agreed upon at the Pan-American Conference in Rio de Janeiro late in January, 1942.

Mr. Clayton had general supervision of the financial and operational phases of the denazification program. Adolf A. Berle directed the diplomatic negotiations for the State Department. From National Aviation, an investment trust, W. A. M. Burden came to us in March 1941, as vice president of the American Republics Aviation Division; and William Harding was loaned to the RFC by Mr. Rockefeller's organization. In those busy days Mr. Rockefeller and I had an arrangement to visit together once a week in my office.

Messrs. Burden and Harding alternated between Washington and South American points, swapping posts at six-month intervals. In 1943 I had Mr. Burden appointed Assistant Secretary of Commerce. The War Department's part in the program was directed by Robert A. Lovett, then Assistant Secretary of War for Air. Reed Chambers, of U. S. Aviation Underwriters, Inc., a World War I pilot with flying experience—and useful acquaintances—in many parts of the world, aided the program both in this country and in South America. During the dural shortage Mr. Clayton and Under Secretary Lovett arranged with General H. H. Arnold, head of the Army Air Forces, to have a Philadelphia concern build planes out of nonstrategic materials, but only seventeen of these were completed.

Major General Davenport Johnson, who was in charge of training Army pilots, agreed to enroll Latin American student fliers, mostly at Randolph and Kelly fields. Defense Supplies paid for their traveling expenses, subsistence, and tuition. Pilots were brought here on a quota basis from almost all of the Latin American Republics. To save time only candidates who could speak and read English were accepted. Many of these men now hold prominent positions in both the military and civil aviation of their countries.

Each of the 260 pilots and 121 service mechanics brought up from Latin America received seven months' instruction before returning to his homeland, while more than 100 imported instructor mechanics and administrative engineers were given two-year courses. The training program cost Defense Supplies $1,833,183.

With the object of improving weather forecasting in the South American republics, some of which lay on the air forces' ocean-hopping route to Africa and the European Theater of Operations, Defense Supplies and Mr. Rockefeller's office jointly provided funds to the United States Weather Bureau to permit it to operate the Inter-American Meteorological Institute at Medellín, Colombia. The Institute trained South Americans as weather observers. Defense Supplies' part of that bill came to $155,350. If it resulted in saving even one airplane crash it was well worth the price.

TAKING FRENCH LEAVE FROM MADAGASCAR

Early in 1941 the War Production Board appealed to us to buy and import mica, quartz crystals, and graphite for use in manufacturing radio equipment and batteries. That assignment brought us anxious days and provoked some tense experiences for several ships of the American merchant marine. Mr. Clayton's agents had located available stocks of the desired materials on the island of Madagascar, off the southeast coast of Africa. Madagascar's colonial government was under rigid domination of the Vichy French regime. British naval forces were blockading the island. Nor was much love lost between Washington and Vichy.

On six or seven occasions Mr. Clayton went to New York to confer with American importers who, he learned, had made contracts for Madagascar graphite prior to the Hitler-Pétain armistice. They had not been able to get the stuff loaded onto a ship. They agreed to turn their graphite over to Defense Supplies if we could get at it.

Mr. Clayton appealed to the British authorities to permit us to send a ship to Madagascar unmolested; but he was never able to get an answer out of them as to what they would try to do if we attempted to run a freighter through their blockade. After much palaver the Vichy government informed us that they would have no objection to the exportation of the graphite, quartz crystals, and mica. Mr. Clayton thereupon contracted with the States Marine Corporation to dispatch their freighter *Lone Star* for the cargo. He then said to the British: "We're going to send the *Lone Star* to Madagascar. She will be flying the American flag. Don't bother her."

The ship went in through the blockade without incident, but while she was loading, in May, relations between Washington and Marshal Pétain's government deteriorated considerably. The owners feared for her in the event of a break in diplomatic relations between Vichy and Washington. They consulted Secretary of State Cordell Hull. He advised them—and us—to order the ship away from Madagascar without delay. The Navy's wireless moved the message in code. Without even asking for clearance papers or waiting the return aboard of three men in the crew who had gone ashore, the *Lone Star*, with only half her intended cargo loaded, slipped out to sea late that night. Several weeks later she reached New York.

The following September, Vichy's feathers having been smoothed somewhat by Washington, we succeeded in getting a nine-knot freighter of World War I vintage to go to Madagascar and pick up the 5,000 tons of cargo the *Lone Star* had left behind—and also her three abandoned sailors along with a stranded American writer. The poky old ship crept into Capetown in November with her engines needing repairs. A few days later Germany declared war upon the United States, and the waters of the South Atlantic became happy hunting for the enemy's submarine commanders. We were keenly concerned as to what might happen to such a slow ship, whose cargo was now doubly valuable to us, if she attempted the homeward voyage alone. Mr. Clayton appealed to the Navy to lend us two destroyers to bring the cargo to the United States, but the Navy, still benumbed from the blow at Pearl Harbor, did not feel fighting ships could be spared for such a purpose. Finally we dispatched three sixteen-knot cargo vessels to Capetown, where the cargo was distributed equally among them in order to spread the risk. All three got home in good order.

In August, anticipating possible hostilities with Japan, we had begun to hold weekly meetings in which the State Department, the RFC, the Maritime Commission, and two or three other agencies took part. The object was to speed up shipping from the Orient.

Instead of bringing the Far Eastern tin and rubber and abaca to the Atlantic coast in the normal way, we decided to have it unloaded at our Pacific ports so the ships could make a quicker turn-around.

At that time the transcontinental railways did not appear to have enough cars to handle promptly all freight that would be coming in at Pacific instead of Atlantic ports. We would have to hire storage space. Railroad rates from the west coast would make the cost of delivery to eastern industrial centers much higher than usual. Far Eastern rubber shipments customarily came through the Panama Canal and up to east-coast ports convenient to Akron, the principal consuming center. So did most of the tin, the bulk of which is processed in the eastern states. Our staffs estimated the excess transportation and storage charges might amount to as much as $3,000,000. I immediately approved the spending of it.

Beginning in 1940, and continuing as long as possible after the Japanese struck us, Admiral Emory Scott Land, Chairman of the United States Maritime Commission, and his chief of traffic, F. M. Darr, had actively sped along our program to obtain shipping space and even divert vessels from the regular runs in order to fetch all possible rubber and tin out of British Malaya and the Dutch East Indies, chromite and manganese ore from India and China, and Manila fiber and other strategic materials from the Philippines.

In January, 1941, the American President Lines allocated space for our cargoes on every ship they had scheduled in their transpacific and round-the-world services for the full year ahead. The Waterman Steamship Lines canceled some of their sugar sailings from the Philippines and postponed others in order to divert shipping to more vital imports into the United States before the expected storm should break in the Pacific. Other American steamship interests were similarly helpful.

SUBSIDIZING THE BUTCHER AND BAKER

Subsidies of one sort or another stacked up until they became the largest single class of expenditures by Defense Supplies Corporation. We paid subsidies to producers, processors, or venders of certain commodities which had been defined by the President as strategic and critical. Some were granted to stimulate production; others, to stabilize prices. Industrial alcohol is an example of the first type. Into the second category fell the subsidies on meats, flour, and butter. These were begun in 1943 as a part of the President's program to "roll back" the rising cost of living to the levels of September, 1942, and to "hold the price line" generally against the inflationary influences of a trillion-dollar war.

Defense Supplies' books recorded the total of direct subsidies allowed up to the time of the Corporation's dissolution on June 30, 1945, at $1,694,518,025. But that was only part of the story of giveaways. There were so many indirect and obscured transactions which were subsidies in effect if not in name that the total amount of federal funds disbursed in that category as part of the general war effort can never be definitely determined. At the close of the fiscal year 1949 Defense Supplies' balance sheets on the RFC books listed its direct subsidies, grants, and contributions since its inception in 1940 at $2,741,000,000, or about $140,000,000 in excess of the Corporation's cumulative net losses over all those years. Subsidies granted by other RFC subsidiaries, particularly those paid by Metals Reserve Company to stimulate the mining of copper, zinc, and lead, brought the total well above $3,000,000,000.

Meat subsidies made up the biggest item on the list, $937,000,000 up to June 30, 1945, and a good many more millions after that. Meat subsidies were continued until the autumn of 1946, nearly fourteen months beyond the duration of hostilities. Subsidies on metals continued until June 30, 1947.

The policy of employing handouts to stimulate production was established in the Emergency Price Control Act of 1942. Congress vested in me, as Federal Loan Administrator, the authority to make the payments, subject to the President's approval.

If the subsidy program was to achieve its purposes, the disbursements had to be made promptly upon the presentation of claims by everyone entitled to them. This necessary haste increased the hazards of overpayment and probably encouraged a little fudging here, a little rooking there, on the part of the small minority whose patriotism was warmer in their mouths and hearts than in the neighborhood of the pocketbook. Some producers who were not entitled to subsidies got our checks and cashed them. Full responsibility for discovering and reporting violations of the subsidy regulations had been assumed by the Office of Price Administration and the War Foods Administration. Defense Supplies Corporation had no police functions. It was merely a disbursing agent. We tried, however, to make our regulations as cheat-proof as possible. In most cases we were successful.

Subsidies on meats originated May 7, 1943, when I received a directive from James F. Byrnes, then Director of Economic Stabilization. He left it to me and to Prentiss M. Brown, the Price Administrator, to decide on the amounts to be paid and the manner of making the payments.

On the previous day the President had designated beef, veal, pork, lamb, mutton, coffee, and butter as strategic and critical materials. Mr. Brown and I decided the meat subsidies should be paid to the packer at the time of slaughtering. The Office of Price Administration then decreed a 10 per cent reduction in the wholesale and retail prices of meats. But it did not lower the price the stockman or farmer was to receive for his animal on the hoof. Consequently we set the size of the packer's subsidy at a sum sufficient to reimburse him for the reduction in the ceiling price at which he had to sell his product. Varying with the cuts, the meat subsidies ranged from just under 1 cent a pound to 3½ cents. All together some 270,000 separate claims for livestock slaughter subsidies were paid during the war, and a good many other thousands after it was over.

The butter subsidy—5 cents a pound—was paid to the creameries. Since the ration was only one pound a month, this saved the individual consumer no more than 60 cents a year. On the face of it such a subsidy seemed silly. But it was the administration's theory that if the price line were dented anywhere, the whole thing might be badly bent. Later the Office of Price Administration raised the ceiling on butter, and our subsidies to the creameries ceased. By then they had cost us about $160,000,000.

Millers, like packers, were being squeezed between the farmer on their buying end and price ceilings on the selling side. To hold down bread prices, total subsidies of $175,000,000 were paid on flour. A person with an agile pencil probably could prove in a jiffy that what we lost in subsidies was saved by the Army and Navy in buying their mountains of meat and flour in a held-down market.

Soon after Pearl Harbor the President put alcohol on the growing list of materials we were to buy. The making of domestic whiskies ceased. Every American distillery that could do so was turned to the production of high-proof alcohol for industrial purposes. Defense Supplies was authorized to buy the nation's entire output of alcohol and to distribute it to the armed services, commercial users, and government agencies. Finding sufficient storage facilities was a tough task. At one time we leased an entire tank farm at Morgantown, West Virginia, and filled it with alcohol.

We also set out to buy every available raw material from which alcohol could be produced. Here again we dangled subsidies as bait and took some losses. Up to the week of my departure from government service the Corporation's commitments for alcohol purchases had totaled nearly $900,000,000, and for sugar and molasses about $306,000,000.

Molasses had been defined as strategic in September, 1941. The

Office of Production Management promptly recommended that the RFC serve as sole purchasing agent for the 1942 Cuban sugar crop in order to provide distillers with sufficient raw materials to insure capacity production during that year. We contracted with the Cuban Sugar Stabilization Institute not only for the 1942 crop in the form of raw sugar, invert molasses, and blackstrap molasses, but also for a large proportion of the 1943, 1944, and 1945 crops.

To purchase, ship, and sell those products, the Corporation appointed as its agents the four commercial companies which had normally dealt with more than 90 per cent of Cuba's exported molasses. They had their own transport and storage facilities and seemed well placed to do the job. But a few months after they had undertaken it we were at war, and German submarines began severely disrupting shipping between Cuba and the United States. Sugar could no longer be exported from Cuba on the planned schedules. Storage facilities on that island became overburdened. Planters, humanly enough, insisted upon being paid promptly even if we hadn't received delivery.

In April, 1942, we made an agreement with the Cuban Sugar Stabilization Institute to advance cash to producers against sugar in Cuban warehouses and to consider these as non-interest-bearing loans. Here again we employed experienced agents to relieve us of details. We arranged with three banks, the Chase National and the National City of New York and the First National Bank of Boston, to make the advances for us. We agreed to reimburse the banks upon demand and to pay them ½ of 1 per cent per annum on outstanding balances.

Our molasses procurements were directed by Samuel H. Sabin, who left a vice presidency in Commodity Credit Corporation to become executive vice president of Defense Supplies.

We lost $32,000,000 in our transactions in sugar and molasses, but earned $40,000,000 in buying and selling alcohol. Since both programs were parts of a single enterprise, the Corporation came out ahead on it. The taxpayer didn't. Our losses on molasses were due to the fact that the sales price was set at a sum which would permit distilleries, without loss to themselves, to sell the alcohol distilled from molasses at the ceiling price of 48 cents a gallon. The profit on alcohol resulted from a selling policy which provided that losses sustained on commercial sales at ceiling prices would be offset—and then some— by increasing the price charged government agencies.

The average cost of producing the alcohol handled by Defense

Supplies was just under 75 cents a gallon. Although 19 per cent of the production was sold to commercial users at the 48-cent ceiling, the government agencies were charged an average of 85 cents for the 76 per cent of the production which they bought. We also acquired some alcohol in Canada, Mexico, and Cuba.

Our subsidies saved the eastern states from what threatened to be a paralyzing shortage of oil and gasoline. Losses of torpedoed tankers and the transfer of other tankers from the usual coastal runs to meet the overseas requirements of the Army, Navy, and Maritime Commission, caused the tank-car and pipe-line facilities of the country to be overtaxed. The costs of transporting petroleum and its products from the mid-continent and southwestern production areas to consuming centers on the east and west coasts were jacked up to a point that made it impossible for the refiners to sell at ceiling prices without losing large sums of money. We were called upon to plug that gap with more gifts.

In peacetime 95 per cent of the eastern seaboard's normal requirements of 1,500,000 barrels of oil and gasoline daily had been shipped northward in tankers. By June, 1942, less than 200,000 barrels was delivered in that manner and 700,000 barrels a day was all that railroad tank cars could supply. Even that was a manifold increase of their prewar deliveries. At first the oil companies formed a pooling arrangement for the equitable sharing of these higher transportation expenses; but the price increases they asked the Office of Price Administration to grant would, that agency thought, imperil the Administration's "hold the line" policy. The Office of Price Administration requested me, as an emergency war measure, to make funds available through the RFC to compensate the oil companies for their higher transportation costs.

The War and Navy Departments requested the RFC to arrange to absorb the increased costs of delivering oil and gasoline to them and to contractors manufacturing facilities on their orders. Both of these government departments promised to pay us back later. Neither did, but that doesn't matter. It would merely have been taking money out of one of the government's pockets to put it in another. Eventually the oil transportation subsidies cost us nearly $300,000,000.

After Germany surrendered, the concentration of military operations in the Pacific created a demand for petroleum and gasoline on the west coast which far exceeded the supply of crude oil available

Lieutenant General William S. Knudsen receives a decoration for his services in directing the country's wartime industrial production. Left to right: Robert P. Patterson, Secretary of War; Jesse H. Jones, Federal Loan Administrator; General Knudsen; James V. Forrestal, Secretary of the Navy.

THE BIG INCH PIPE LINE

Workmen pushing the line over the Alleghenies.

from the wells in that area. West-coast refiners could not obtain the oil from Texas and sell it under the existing price regulations because of the extremely high cost of transportation. At the request of the Army and Navy Petroleum Board, Defense Supplies Corporation agreed to subsidize the sale of west Texas crude oil in California at less than cost in west Texas plus the overland transportation.

To encourage production from stripper wells—submarginal units pumping only a few barrels a day—the Office of Price Administration granted them price increases ranging from 20 to 75 cents a barrel, based on location and output. Defense Supplies then paid a subsidy to buyers of their oil to reimburse them for the excess price. Transportation subsidies on coal, sugar, and nitrate of soda diverted over expensive emergency routes totaled nearly $80,000,000.

The Corporation was asked to do all manner of odd chores. Farmers howled that they couldn't buy barbed wire at a time when meat was a "strategic and critical" material. Yet the Army had more wire than it knew what to do with. But the War Department was bound by red-tape regulations from selling it to the men whose cattle, sheep, and hog fences needed repairs or replacement. Nothing had been put on paper to prevent the Army from selling the wire to another government agency, so Defense Supplies bought a lot of the surplus and, on War Production Board allocations, resold it to the farmers—at a loss of about $100,000.

Stirrup pumps gave us another headache. Defense Supplies at the request of the Office of Civilian Defense underwrote the manufacture of several hundred thousand stirrup pumps designed to be employed when, as, and if any of our communities were bombed by enemy incendiaries. The stirrup pumps could not be readily sold to civilian defense organizations or to the public in general. We tried to get people to buy them from us to water their gardens since rubber hoses were scarce or unobtainable. But the idea didn't catch on, perhaps because a stirrup pump, unlike a hose or sprinkler, takes elbow grease to operate. Thus we had another loss—about $2,500,000.

Still another loss, amounting to $17,500,000, resulted from the Office of Price Administration's request for us to deal in automobile tires and tubes. The government had frozen all new tires in the hands of manufacturers and dealers. The dealer wanted to be thawed out and relieved of the cost of carrying his inventory. So did some of the manufacturers. We bought nineteen million of their tires, nearly eight million tubes. Whenever he was permitted to make a sale, under ration and price regulations, the manufacturer or distributor would buy some of the stock back from Defense Supplies. The purpose of this program was to conserve supplies and facilitate redistributions among consumers whose cars or trucks were classified as essential—a word much overworked through the war.

When the Office of Price Administration ordered the civilian motoring public to surrender all tires, new or used, above the number of five per car, Defense Supplies was once again designated as a repository with the American Railway Express Company acting as its collection agent.

William J. Hobbs was then vice president of Defense Supplies. He took charge of the "Idle Tire Program," as it was called. To store the mountains of turned-in tubes and tires he had to rent warehouses all over the country so that the surrendered materials could be examined for defects, their values appraised, and the owners properly paid.

As a reaction to that program we received nearly four thousand letters, most of them from irate automobile owners. They accused us of having robbed them. Actually the appraisals were made by representatives of the Rubber Manufacturers Association of America, acting as our agents, on a fee basis. In a land of more than thirty million automobiles, perhaps four thousand such squawks isn't many. Anyway, there was a sweeter side to the public's reaction. It was the donation by automobile owners of $1,500,000 worth of tires and tubes for which they could have demanded compensation had they so desired.

Sponsoring new sources of supply was one of the Corporation's manifold functions. The principal program of this type was the manufacture of jewel bearings. Before we entered that strange pasture Switzerland was the only source of such bearings, which were necessary in the manufacture of many instruments employed by the Army and Navy as well as in their familiar role inside the watches everyone carried. With democratic Switzerland entirely surrounded by dictatorships, it was occasionally necessary to smuggle out bearings to fill our urgent needs.

In 1942, at the request of the Office of Production Management, we called upon all the principal watchmaking concerns in the United States to send representatives to Washington to confer with us. At that meeting we arranged with them to sponsor and finance an experi-

LOTS OF BOUNCE TO IT, ANYWAY.

C. K. Berryman in the Washington Evening Star.

mental and training program at a cost of approximately $1,100,000. A year after that our watchmakers had, so to speak, got their bearings in an endeavor which was new to them.

We then made contracts with them for production. During the following years American watch companies delivered 13,160,000 jewel bearings to Defense Supplies at an average price of 62½ cents each. This compared with 79,000,000 bearings the Corporation had bought from Swiss sources at an average price of 4¾ cents each. There are still a good many things in this world which some foreign people do better than Americans!

* * *

Defense Supplies' largest loan was one with which I think the whole American people may well be pleased. We were glad to arrange it, and I like to think it helped bring some joy and comfort to every soldier who served in the army at home and overseas. It was a series of advances totaling $71,153,521 to the Army Post Exchange Service to finance the establishment and operation of Post Exchange stores. And it was fully repaid before the end of the war.

Wherever our troops were sent they usually found convenient to their stations a PX (Post Exchange) in which they could buy some of the everyday articles and amenities which had been familiar to them as civilians at peace with all the world. In many a far corner of the globe a PX blossomed with American ice cream, American soft drinks and beer, watches, cigarettes, tobacco, and candies, as well as native souvenirs the G.I. could buy to send back home without leaving a counter with the feeling he had been taken for a sucker by some local tradesman whose language he didn't understand.

I summarized the story of the PX loans in the following letter to President Roosevelt:

December 26, 1944

Dear Mr. President:

You will recall having, at my request, approved loans to the Army Post Exchange Service between September 18, 1941 and December 24, 1943.

A total of $91,000,000 of loans was authorized, $71,000,000 of this amount was disbursed, and the balance cancelled. The entire loans have been paid.

Major General Joseph W. Byron was in to see me about his new prospective assignment, and expressed appreciation for our assistance to him in the Army Post Exchange. He reported that starting with no capital and operating entirely on borrowed money, he had not only repaid the $71,000,000 borrowed from the RFC, but has on hand merchandise and other assets to the probable cost of $60,000,000.

In discussing "merchandising" on a big scale and at widely diversified areas, he reminded me that the Army Post Exchange Service was doing business at the rate of $1,000,000,000 a year in sales. Approximately two-thirds of this is in this country and one-third at various points overseas. He stated that the entire operation was working smoothly and rendering a great service to our armed forces.

The Army Exchange loans were not the first experience we have had with Major General Byron. We have always found him especially competent, and confident.

Sincerely,

JESSE H. JONES

A $50,000,000 DEAL WITH THE SOVIETS

During the summer of 1941, and prior to the extension of Lend-Lease to the Russians, the President asked me if we could lend Russia a little money which the Soviets needed to buy military supplies in this country.

I immediately sent for the Soviet Ambassador, Constantine A. Oumansky, and we loaned the Amtorg Trading Corporation, a Russian purchasing agency in New York City, $50,000,000 against a purchase contract with the Russians for materials that we ordinarily imported from them. Soon after our agreement to make a loan to Russia and to buy critical materials, Ambassador Oumansky was transferred to Mexico and the purchase contracts were worked out with Andrei Gromyko who had succeeded him in Washington. Gromyko was not the most pleasant mannered man with whom we ever dealt, but he knew what he wanted. And, of course, so did we. There was no real difficulty in our trading with him, because we were in a position to write the ticket. Other Americans who have since dealt with him in post war international conferences have been in a less happy situation.

After the Russians were granted Lend-Lease, in October, 1941, they wanted us to cancel their debt to the RFC; but we declined, and the loan was paid.

To expedite Russian deliveries to our ports we thought it would be a good idea to hire someone experienced in dealing with Soviet citizens in general and Amtorg in particular. We engaged Leonard J. Buck, Inc., of New York, to act as our agent in handling the details of buying, receiving, and disposing of the Russian materials.

Mr. Buck, an importer of world-wide experience, had been dealing with the Soviet export trust and with Amtorg for many years. Several months before the deal with Ambassador Oumansky we had engaged him to fly down to Rio with a party of ten or twelve men, mostly of his own selection, to arrange for the buying of about $20,000,000 worth of Brazilian quartz crystals, industrial diamonds, and mica. His small efficient group got the job done well and speedily on a businessman's basis. They did it at a time when Vice President Wallace's Board of Economic Warfare had several hundred agents swarming around Brazil on buying errands without purchasing as much material as Mr. Buck and his dozen able assistants acquired and got delivered to the ports. The job Mr. Buck and his associates did should have been done by Mr. Wallace's wandering agents.

Mr. Buck's tradings with the Brazilians, and later, at our request, with Mexico, were on a strictly commercial basis. Unlike the boys in the Wallace gang, he didn't try to reform the native laborer's eating habits, improve his hygiene, or convert him either to vitamins or to "social conciousness." When he later dealt on our behalf with Moscow, an alien "ideology" was not among the items he arranged to import from the Soviet Union.

I suppose it was an ingrained habit of secrecy that caused the Soviet's disinclination to let us have any definite information as to when we could expect one of their shipments. Then suddenly, after our inquiries had received a run-around, the telephone would ring and Amtorg would notify us that a ship loaded with, say, X tons of manganese or Y tons of chromite would be at such and such a pier in Brooklyn the next morning, or that a ship with so many pounds of pig bristles and maybe a hundred thousand goatskins, some horse-mane hair and goose down, had just tied up in Philadelphia.

Horse-mane hair, of which the Russians sent us more than a million pounds valued at $922,000, was mixed with pig bristles in making brushes for the Navy and Army. Deliveries of pig bristles also totaled more than a million pounds from Russia and about 2,500,000 more pounds from other foreign countries for the account of Defense Supplies Corporation. These bristles mostly went into paintbrushes for the services.

A city-bred American might think Iowa or Missouri or Texas could fill that bill. But it seems that, whatever other virtues the American hog may have, whatever may be his many other contributions to our well-being, he is not a good provider of commercial bristles. Some people say this is because, with us, the pig is turned into ham sandwiches or pork chops before it is old enough to have bristles that are really tough. Others tell me that the coldness of the climate makes the porcine overcoat heavier in Russia and northern China, the sources of most of the bristles tough enough to satisfy our Navy and the mills which use the bristles for combing wool. Some of the longer and tougher bristles are worth more than any other part of the pig—up to $15 and even $20 a pound.

Our pig-bristle stockpile turned out profitable. During the war, Defense Supplies Corporation made nearly $3,000,000 trading in bristles; and it had 1,500,000 pounds of them in its inventory when Japan surrendered. The average price had been $6.22 a pound.

One million five hundred thousand goatskins which Amtorg delivered to us were used in making jackets for aviators. Russian goose down, nearly half a million dollars' worth, insulated the jackets our fliers wore into the high sub-freezing altitudes and also went into the Navy's lighter mattresses.

Strategically our most important imports through Amtorg were the metals. Chrome ore, nearly 300,000 tons, tagged at more than $17,000,000, led all the rest in value. The 175,000 ounces of platinum the Russians sent us were not risked in ships sailing the seas where the U-boats roamed. The platinum was turned over to our agents in Iran. From there, the base of the United States Army's Persian Gulf Command, the bars were flown by the Air Transport Command across the Middle East, Africa, and the Atlantic to New York. Until needed they were stored in the Federal Reserve Bank's vaults. We paid Amtorg $35 an ounce for the platinum. Later its wartime price got as high as $100. So we didn't do so badly on that deal.

Manganese ranked third among our metal imports in the Russian trade with 52,000 long tons valued at $1,836,000. Iridium was fourth, its mere 2,090 ounces being valued at $349,991. An ounce of iridium cost as much as five tons of manganese.

We also got about $3,500,000 worth of Russian lumber. Most of it was carried in Soviet freighters through the Japan Sea prior to the Kremlin's last-minute lunge into the fight against a beaten Japan. It was unloaded at Adak and other Aleutian outposts of our Army and Navy.

Though slow, the Russian deliveries turned out to be sure. We got our money back with interest, a not too common occurrence in government-with-government deals, particularly when Uncle Sam happens to be the lender.

On the day Defense Supplies Corporation was created President Roosevelt proclaimed certain chemicals to be strategic and critical.

From time to time others were added to the list. To us was delegated the task of rounding up, storing, and distributing them on War Production Board allocations.

One of the largest of these programs involved the purchase of nearly 800,000,000 pounds of calcium carbide. To increase its production we set the Tennessee Valley Authority up in that branch of activity, and also a Canadian government-owned corporation, War Supplies, Ltd. To put the Tennessee Valley Authority into calcium carbide manufacture two RFC subsidiaries, Defense Supplies Corporation and the Rubber Reserve Company, paid a $2,650,000 bill for plant construction and reconditioning. It was stipulated that these facilities would remain TVA's property.

The Tennessee Valley Authority produced nearly half the calcium carbide Defense Supplies acquired. The other half came mostly from other domestic sources.

Defense Supplies Corporation and United States Commercial Company lost nearly $15,000,000 trading in nitrate of soda. That program began in November, 1940, and was continued throughout the war. Much of the loss can be put down to subsidies, overt and otherwise. We subsidized the American farmer by selling him imported fertilizer at or under the OPA ceiling price of $30 a ton, although it had cost us more. The theory in Washington was that a rise in agricultural prices would thereby be avoided. As recompense for excess distribution costs we subsidized the Chilean nitrate sales trust and, indirectly, the Chilean government, which got a 25 per cent cut of the monopoly's profits. We subsidized transportation costs when wartime conditions caused the nitrate cargoes to be detoured to unusual ports of entry on the Pacific coast.

On cork we took a loss of several millions, partly through deterioration of surplus stocks—but we kept the cork out of the enemy's reach. We bought about sixty million pounds of shellac, mainly in India through arrangements with the British Ministry of Supply, and took over the frozen domestic stocks. The shellac program showed a profit of about $1,500,000.

We stocked more than ten million ounces of opium, a lot of it bought in Turkey where the Germans were in the market for it. Later we sold the opium, under stringent allocations, at a profit of about $900,000.

COOPERATION FROM THE CUSTOMS

Critical appraisals of the RFC have contended that the balance sheets of its wartime subsidiaries do not give a true picture of the costs to the taxpayer of the materials dealt in because of the fact that billions of dollars' worth of imports purchased abroad were admitted duty-free through the customs. Up to the end of the war, according to estimates by the Comptroller General of the United States, three of our subsidiaries had saved—and the Internal Revenue had lost—about $410,000,000 through import duty exemptions granted our imports of strategic and critical materials. Of this sum about half was attributable to imports by Metals Reserve Company, $75,000,000 to imports by Defense Supplies Corporation, and the remainder to the overseas procurements of the United States Commercial Company.

From the Treasury's standpoint—or the taxpayer's—what difference did it make? What the government lost from one pocket it gained in another. Our position with respect to the exemption from import duties was expressed in a letter I wrote the Comptroller General on March 11, 1944, in response to a letter which he had written challenging the propriety of Defense Supplies Corporation's omission to pay duties on imported wool which was later sold to industrial consumers at public auction.

"Payment of customs duties by an agency of the United States," I wrote, "results only in the transfer of funds upon the books of the Treasury and does not improve the financial condition of the Government. Payment of customs would impose upon the government an incalculable cost in man hours and money. It would require the examination and valuation of large quantities of goods for customs purposes on docks and warehouses now overburdened with vital exports and imports. It would require the maintenance of a vast and intricate system for the tracing and control of each item imported by government agencies to its ultimate end use."

The privilege of duty-free importation by a government agency originated with the Navy through the Act of June 30, 1914 (38 Stat. 399). This law enabled the Secretary of the Navy to avoid payment of customs duties on repair parts purchased by Navy personnel while in foreign waters, or on materials bought abroad and imported for testing or research purposes.

As the nation moved toward the vortex of the Second World War the Comptroller General of the United States held that this 1914 legislation was still in effect, and that, under the First War Powers Act (1941) its privileges could be transferred by the Navy Department to other government agencies. Accordingly, early in 1941, at my request the President, the Secretary of the Navy, the Secretary of the Treasury, and I arranged to have Secretary Frank Knox write me a letter asking Metals Reserve Company to act as the Navy Department's agent in acquiring and disposing of stocks of minerals and other articles as emergency purchases of war materials, and requesting that these be admitted duty-free.

24

☼

UNITED STATES COMMERCIAL COMPANY

Cordell Hull Asks Us to Begin Preclusive Buying in Neutral Countries—Sabotage and Black Marketing to Forestall the Axis—We Lose Eighty Millions to Starve the German War Machine of Wolfram—Blankets for the Red Army—Cornering the Sardine Market

SHORTLY after the United States entered the Second World War, the Secretary of State, Cordell Hull, asked the RFC to undertake preclusive buying such as the Ministry of Economic Warfare and the United Kingdom Commercial Corporation had long been performing for our British allies. This meant going into neutral countries and collaring, regardless of price, raw materials and manufactured goods which the enemy wanted.

For that purpose, with the President's approval, we created the United States Commercial Company on March 26, 1942. It was entirely owned and financed by the RFC.

To achieve the Corporation's singular, punitive aims meant purchasing, often at previously unheard-of prices, some materials of which we already had a sufficiency, but which we knew the enemy vitally required. It meant trying to bankrupt the German in his foreign exchange holdings in Spain, a goal we ultimately all but attained.

Preclusive buying involved dealing with questionable characters as well as with men of integrity. It led to private fees, sabotage, black markets, hidden deals under the table, secret funds, and, at times, slick stunts which smacked of cloak-and-dagger drama.

Such unbusinesslike goings-on made losses inevitable, but these were less than might have been anticipated. United States Commercial disbursed nearly $2,000,000,000. Its balance sheet, brought up to the middle of 1949, when substantially all its inventories had been liquidated, showed a cumulative net loss of only $172,000,000.

Once United States Commercial was established, we promptly put the company into a fifty-fifty partnership with our more experienced British allies. United States Commercial made an agreement to work in double harness with the United Kingdom Commercial Corporation in Spain, Portugal, and Turkey, each sharing equally the expenses of certain specified buying programs.

The No. 1 objective was to starve the German war machine of wolfram, the extraheavy ore which is the source of tungsten and is used to harden steel. Modern warfare cannot be waged without wolfram. It is essential in making armor plate and providing tungsten carbide cores and fire heads in armor-piercing projectiles. Once the Germans had been shut off from South America, almost all of their tungsten supplies had to be bought in the Iberian Peninsula. Their competitive bidding against the British had driven the price of Spanish wolfram from a few hundred dollars a ton to several thousand dollars.

One of our first agreements with the British was to boot the bidding up to $22,000 a ton. Ultimately it went as high as $35,000. Obtaining wolfram at that price drained Germany's peseta account. To replenish it, the Berlin government shipped to Spain wheat, barley, and even oil, all of which the Axis badly needed for its own uses. The more the Germans were forced to spend for wolfram, the fewer pesetas they could spare for other essential purchases.

Intelligence reports quickly reflected the effectiveness of our preemptive buying campaign. Before the end of 1943, the Germans discontinued the use of tungsten carbide cores in their armor-piercing projectiles. A little later they had to forbid the use of tungsten carbide for cutting tools in other than armament production. They were forced to reduce the amount of tungsten used in carbide tool tips, which meant lowering their machining speeds.

A few members of Congress were at first startled at the prices we were offering for certain foreign materials, particularly wolfram. My view of our operations in that respect was expressed to the Senate Banking and Currency Committee on December 2, 1942.

"In the cases of these materials we know," I said, "that we are paying very high prices, sometimes ten or twenty times the normal market price.

"But if it is a critical material that would be of value to the enemy, there is no way to measure in dollars and cents its value to us. The real measure of the value of such material is the lives of our boys. Our job is to keep such material from going to the Axis if dollars will do it. It may be true that such things on a trial balance would look bad, but the circumstances must be taken into consideration. For instance, you may build a ship knowing it is likely to be sunk, and yet you must build the ship."

As a result of Allied economic pressure—largely our control of her oil supply—Spain placed an embargo on wolfram in February, 1944. Portugal followed suit four months later, on the day the armies under General Dwight D. Eisenhower made their first landings on Normandy's coast. The liberation of France severed Germany from Spanish markets, except for an occasional airplane shipment. With the retreat of German forces away from the Pyrenees, we were able to call quits to the preclusive buying in Spain and Portugal.

So dire became the enemy's shortage of tungsten that toward the end of the war submarine cargo space was allocated for the heavy wolfram ores on the long U-boat runs through the Allied blockade across the Indian Ocean, around the continent of Africa, and up the Atlantic to the ports remaining in Hitler's grasp.

Getting hold of enough Portuguese escudos and Spanish pesetas to pay for some of United States Commercial's activities sometimes took us into devious paths. Spain and Portugal both had currency problems. Their governments would provide local money in large sums to foreigners only when they were shown how it was to be spent. In economic warfare there are many occasions when one doesn't want to show the cards in his hand. And there are times in clandestine dickering when the only money that will take is hard money. We had the Navy take a stock of gold coins to Gibraltar where they were conveniently available for our operatives across the Spanish border to use in ticklish situations.

Sosthenes Behn, head of the International Telephone & Telegraph Corporation, had sold that company's extensive holdings in Spain but had not been able to convert all of the resulting pesetas into dollars. We offered him 5 cents per peseta, but he held out for the official rate, around 9 cents. So United States Commercial turned to the American motion picture concerns and to other exporters and made deals with them. All the Hollywood films shipped into Spain during the remainder of the war were handled by United States Commercial. We paid the movie people dollars in this country and picked up the pesetas owing to them in Spain. Our men were not amateurs in foreign trade. On exchange differentials the Corporation's books recorded a gain of about $6,000,000.

In the joint United Kingdom and U.S.A. preclusive operations in the Iberian Peninsula, more than 10,500 metric tons of wolfram and tungsten concentrates were obtained at a price of nearly $175,000,-000. There were additional expenditures of nearly $20,000,000 in that program for which no commodity was received. Not all of those expenditures were legal or aboveboard or could be explained in public ledgers. The polite phrase was "disruptive outlays." These were made to disrupt Axis attempts to obtain tungsten. Sometimes sabotage was employed; at other times black market operations. I was told of a contract the Germans negotiated with one mine owner to buy his entire year's supply of wolfram, about 120 tons a month. To clinch the deal they deposited nearly 100,000,000 pesetas in the mine owner's bank account. But they didn't get his wolfram. Since the Allies had broken the German's commercial code, our agents were often tipped off beforehand as to persons and places to be approached by German buyers eager to make a deal in Spain or Portugal. To paraphrase the formula of the Confederate General Nathan Bedford Forrest, it was then our job to get there fustest with the mostest money.

The Spanish Government made no effort to control the production or sale of wolfram. Anyone who paid a fee could obtain a "production permit" from the government. In Spain large quantities of ores and concentrates occur in superficial deposits cropping out of the earth's surface. The fabulous prices—often twenty times or more what was being paid for wolfram elsewhere in the world—attracted thousands of Spanish farmers and city workers alike to tackle these deposits with pick and shovel. Naturally they exploited the unusual situation for all it was worth. Wolfram ore is so heavy that a fistful will weigh a kilogram (2.2 pounds) and the average price we and the British paid for Spanish wolfram over the whole preclusive buying period was $21.03 a kilogram. We sold it at an average of $1.22 a kilo. United States Commercial's share of the losses in trading in wolfram exceeded $80,000,000.

We got wolfram much cheaper in Portugal than in Spain, the average price being $7.52 a kilo compared to the above-mentioned $21.03. This wide variation was due to the fact that the Portuguese

Government required all wolfram mined in that country to be sold only to the Portuguese Metals Commission, a government agency. The Commission placed its purchases in three pools. Into one went production from mines owned or controlled by British or American interests; and these stocks were then sold to the Allies. Into another pool went production from mines owned or controlled by Axis nationals and this was then resold to Germany or her satellites at the same price the Allies had been charged. All other production was put in a third or "neutral" pool whence it was resold either to the Allies or to the Axis, depending on allocations made from time to time by the Portuguese Government.

Such a situation begat a robust black market. In the bitter, constant struggle between Anglo-American agents and the Germans to prevent the other side from tapping these illegal sources, the United Kingdom Commercial Corporation and the United States Commercial Company together paid out a total of nearly $18,000,000 to purchase mining properties, options, and equipment and for sabotage, smuggling, and other disruptive activities.

In general the Portuguese Government regulated the sale of most critical and strategic materials on a fifty-fifty basis as between the Axis and the Allies. But the Spanish customarily sold to the highest bidder. We bought large quantities of rabbit furs, fleece-lined gloves, wool, and blankets in Spain, not because the Allies needed them, but to keep them from the Germans. Hitler's troops painfully wanted warm covering for their winter campaigns across the frozen plains and forests of Russia.

Some of the blankets we bought in Spain were offered as a gift to the Lord Mayor of London for the bombed-out people of his courageous city. His Worship's envoy felt the quality of Spanish wool was not up to that to which the British were accustomed, and the offer was declined. Later, under Lend-Lease, the blankets were shipped to the Soviet Union. I wonder whether Stalin, who has spoken so harshly of General Franco's regime, ever learned that part of the Red Army was being warmed by blankets from Spain, where Russian fliers had fought against Franco's forces during the Spanish Civil War.

The help General Franco received from Germany during Spain's Civil War was, oddly enough, one of the reasons we had to bid the price of wolfram skyward in order to deplete Germany's reserves of pesetas. Hitler had billed Franco 380,000,000 reichsmarks for the services of the German Army's Condor division. Against this was Franco's later bill to Hitler for 130,000,000 reichsmarks for the use of Spain's Azul (Blue) division on the Russian front during the Second World War. Thus on that one balance alone the Germans had a call on 1,000,000,000 pesetas—that being the exchange value of the difference of 250,000,000 reichsmarks between the two bills.

To make the going rougher for Germany's purchasing agents, our representatives in Madrid suggested to the Spanish Government that they slap an export tax of about $10 a kilogram (nearly $5 a pound) on wolfram. They did so. Governments like to have someone suggest new sources of revenue. As a quid-pro-quo the British and American authorities, who were in a better position than the Germans to supply Spain with the goods she wanted most, imposed heavy surcharges, usually 100 per cent, on certain exports to that country, and to Portugal as well. These surcharges, while they lasted, mitigated somewhat our trading losses on the Peninsula.

United States Commercial Company purchased ammonium sulphate and nitrate, petroleum products, and cellulose in the Western Hemisphere and sold these to the Spanish and Portuguese at approximately twice their cost. The British imposed similar surcharges on the sugar, rubber, potatoes, and copper sulphate which they delivered. United States Commercial Company's profits from the surcharges exceeded $16,000,000.

Another quid-pro-quo deal brought about abolition of the surcharges. By the latter part of 1944, United States Commercial owed the Spanish Government about 175,000,000 pesetas, roughly $17,-000,000, in taxes. Alfred W. Barth (now a vice president of the Chase National Bank) negotiated a simple settlement as our exchange expert in Spain: Spain agreed to cancel the tax debt; we agreed to cease surcharging.

Since armies move on their bellies, food is an instrument of war. Everybody knows the German fondness for sausage. United States Commercial made a point of purchasing all the sausage casings the Turks would sell. The company still had nearly 3,000,000 of them in its inventories when the war ended. During two successive years we contracted to buy Portugal's entire output of sardines. The Portuguese needed tin and the Germans hungered for sardines—and olive oil— as, indeed, did the British. To get the entire crop of Portuguese sardines United States Commercial agreed to ship to Portugal and sell at cost sufficient tin to can the sardines and, in addition, to sell quantities of other tin—at a profitable price—ample to meet Portugal's further requirements. Since the Allied fleets had the power to control what went into and came out of Spain and Portugal by sea, the British and American authorities refused to permit those countries to import edible oils in sufficient quantities to allow reexporting to Germany or Italy.

As Federal Loan Administrator I had general supervision of U.S. Commercial only during its first fifteen months. Then the President, on July 15, 1943, directed the transfer of all foreign activities of RFC subsidiaries to a new Office of Economic Warfare headed by my friend Leo T. Crowley. He made no changes in the personnel which the RFC and the State Department had placed overseas as agents for United States Commercial Company. One of these men was William Walton Butterworth, Jr., a State Department career man. Secretary Hull had loaned him to us at the time he asked us to begin preclusive buying. Mr. Butterworth was named director general of United States Commercial's operations in the Iberian Peninsula, the most important preemptive buying region of them all. At home Mr. Clayton had general charge of the foreign activities of all RFC subsidiaries. As executive vice president of USCC he was able to obtain the services of Robert Ducas, an American businessman who had lived in England and was familiar with some of the experiences of the United Kingdom Commercial Corporation. In Spain and Portugal, by sharing offices and activities with the United Kingdom Commercial Corporation and the State Department as well, we were able to keep our American personnel to a limited number.

Alvin House (now an executive of the Goodyear Tire & Rubber Company in Akron, Ohio) was directly in charge of the company's activities in Portugal. Another of Mr. Butterworth's assistants was Robert P. Furey (now vice president of the Central Hanover Bank & Trust Company in New York). Before asking me to undertake preclusive buying, Secretary Hull had sent Henry R. Labouisse, Jr., of the State Department to scout the strategic materials situation in Spain and Portugal.

From start to finish, with a few exceptions, United States Commercial Company's preemptive purchases were carried out in cooperation with the United Kingdom Commercial Corporation. The first agreement entered into by the two corporations provided that either party would furnish to the other its organization, methods, services, and facilities in the various countries in which operations were being or would be conducted. The United Kingdom Commercial Corporation agreed to make available to us the information, knowledge, and experience it had acquired during the period prior to America's entry into the war. Each party was to reimburse the other for the costs of goods procured and for services rendered, but without profit to either party.

It was then intended that all operations would be conducted jointly, with purchases on a half-and-half basis. Experience quickly proved this to be impractical. A later agreement provided for a division of purchasing responsibility in the field.

In Turkey the financing of preemptive purchases was left to the joint discretion of the American and British ambassadors. They formed an Anglo-American Purchasing Committee which decided which agents and what means were to be employed on any particular occasion.

In Washington United States Commercial had no domestic personnel of its own. RFC employees and, later on, Foreign Economic Administration employees as well were assigned to it on a full-time or part-time basis, depending on the type of work they were doing. After Mr. Crowley's organization took over our foreign procurement programs, United States Commercial established overseas offices in more than thirty countries around the world and opened branches in New York and San Francisco, mostly to handle warehouse problems.

As far as feasible, the company continued to pursue the RFC's policy of helping maintain private trade channels of American importers and exporters to the fullest possible extent and of withdrawing from an activity whenever private enterprise could be relied upon to do the desired job expeditiously and on reasonable terms.

United States Commercial's foreign offices were located in the following countries and cities:

Algeria, Algiers	Guatemala, Guatemala City
Angola, Luanda	Haiti, Port-au-Prince
Argentina, Buenos Aires	India, New Delhi
Australia, Sydney	Kenya, Mombasa
Belgian Congo, Léopoldville	Liberia, Monrovia
Bolivia, La Paz	Madagascar, Antananarivo

Brazil, Rio de Janeiro
Chile, Santiago
China, Chungking
Colombia, Bogotá
Costa Rica, San José
Cuba, Havana and Santiago
Dominican Republic, Ciudad
    Trujillo
Ecuador, Quito and Guayaquil
Egypt, Cairo
French West Africa, Dakar
Gold Coast, Accra

Mexico, Mexico, D.F.
Mozambique, Lourenço
    Marques
New Caledonia, Nouméa
Peru, Lima
Portugal, Lisbon
Spain, Madrid
Switzerland, Bern
Turkey, Ankara
Union of South Africa,
    Johannesburg
Venezuela, Caracas

Amid the dangers of wartime there is many a slip between the buying of materials abroad and getting them safely home. United States Commercial reported cargo losses in the amount of nearly $5,000,000 resulting from the sinking by enemy action of ocean vessels whose freight was not covered by war-risk insurance. More than half these losses were in tungsten concentrates and copper. An additional $2,300,000 was lost in contract cancellations in various countries, mostly in South America.

As with its other wartime subsidiaries, RFC capitalized United States Commercial at $5,000,000. United States Commercial got its additional funds by borrowing from the RFC at 1 per cent.

At the close of the government's fiscal year 1945, United States Commercial owed to the RFC, for capital and loans, $322,654,000 plus accrued interest of $4,619,750. At that time, in its trading in strategic and critical materials—which is not to be confused with its necessarily costly preemptive purchases—it had just about broken even. In trading in some commodities it had made about fifty millions and in dealing in others had lost almost the same sum. In its cleaning-up work and a few postwar activities it continued to break almost even. The cumulative balance sheet from its inception in 1942 up to June, 1949, showed sales of commodities totaling approximately $1,690,-000,000 against cost of commodities sold at $1,709,000,000.

In the postwar unscrambling of wartime agencies the United States Commercial Company on October 10, 1945, was returned to the RFC, which rapidly closed all but a few of its foreign offices.

25

❖

STOCKPILING OF RUBBER

A Trade with the Big Five—Lord Beaverbrook Lends a Hand—Transport Difficulties Across the Pacific—Japan Finds the Cupboard Bare in Malaya and the Dutch East Indies

M Y INTRODUCTION to our rubber situation came late in May, 1940, as France was falling. Harry Hopkins casually mentioned that the President wanted me to buy some crude rubber and some tin for stockpile purposes. When I next saw the President I told him of this message from Hopkins, and he said, "Yes, I think you'd better." He made no further comments or explanations.

I told him that we would have to have legislation giving us the authority. He said, "Go ahead and get it." I then had our attorneys prepare the necessary bill for submission to the Congress.

After I had testified at great length before the Banking and Currency Committees of Congress, which handled all our RFC legislation, the Act giving the RFC the authority to buy rubber and tin was passed. President Roosevelt signed it June 25, 1940, the day of the Franco-German armistice.

As was my custom when entering a field that was strange to me, of which there were many, I sought information from the men best qualified by familiarity in that field. I called A. L. Viles, president of the Rubber Manufacturers Association. In a few days he brought to my office the heads of the five biggest rubber manufacturing corporations in the country. These gentlemen were: Paul W. Litchfield, chairman of the Goodyear Tire & Rubber Company; Harvey Firestone, Jr., vice president of the Firestone Tire & Rubber Company; John L. Collyer, president of B. F. Goodrich Company; William F.

O'Neil, president of the General Tire & Rubber Company; and F. B. Davis, Jr., chairman of the United States Rubber Company.

I explained to those gentlemen and to Mr. Viles the problem President Roosevelt had presented to me, and asked for their cooperation and assistance. After a general discussion I suggested that the RFC and the rubber industry go partners. But the rubber company executives, recalling the heavy losses they had suffered from inventories in the past due to fluctuating markets, were not inclined to dip into their working capital to make the investments that would be necessary to carry a large surplus of raw rubber. Furthermore, out of their experience they cautioned me that if we began bidding for raw rubber even a few cents a pound above current market prices the Far Eastern rubber growers, instead of moving more rubber into the ships, would begin to hold their stocks in the expectation of still higher prices.

We had no intention of competing with the rubber industry in buying crude rubber, but felt it was necessary to have a working agreement with them. We then concluded an arrangement whereby the RFC would furnish the money to buy and carry the rubber and the industry would go fifty-fifty on the cost of carrying and storing the rubber.

It soon became apparent that a more practical way to handle the situation would be for the RFC to buy all the rubber that was to come to this country during the emergency and sell it to the industry at cost plus carrying charges, which was more satisfactory. The President had not indicated any particular amount of materials he wanted us to buy or the reasons, but this later was obvious. I proceeded on the theory that if we were to need any rubber at all, due to a war danger, we should have all that could be obtained.

At my suggestion Mr. Viles telephoned to London and asked the International Rubber Regulation Committee, on whose advisory panel he was the American delegate, to send a representative to Washington to negotiate an agreement with us.

The International Committee, set up by the British and Dutch governments, had for years controlled the flow of raw rubber into the world markets. From quarter to quarter the Committee fixed the proportion of the potential crop which would be exported from the growing areas.

In response to our request, Sir John Hay arrived in the United

States from London on June 13 and we immediately began negotiations with him and signed a contract with the cartel three days after the President signed the bill giving us the authority.

Under this authority the first two corporations we created were the Rubber Reserve Company and the Metals Reserve Company. We created them on June 28.

Even while Congress and its committees were considering our legislation we were negotiating with the British and the Dutch for tin as well as rubber. Howard J. Klossner, one of the five RFC directors at that time, became president of Rubber Reserve; Stanley T. Crossland, who had been for some years with the RFC, executive vice president; and I, chairman of the board.

We lost no time in starting the stockpiling. At first the British and Dutch, who controlled probably 90 per cent of the world's raw rubber, were none too anxious for us to accumulate large quantities. They feared we might hurt the industry by dumping our stocks on the market after the war. To satisfy them on this point, we gave them an agreement to market our rubber in cooperation with theirs after the war.

Even so, they were very slow about shipping rubber. After much prodding by us, I was finally told that the rubber growers did not want to crowd their producing trees, particularly since the British profits taxes took from the plantation owners substantially all the profit they might make.

Lord Beaverbrook, the British Minister of Supply, came to see me about war supplies in general. I told him that we were not getting rubber, and recounted what I had heard were the probable reasons. After that we began receiving rubber shipments in greater quantity. Without the intervention of "the Beaver," we would not have gotten as much rubber as we did.

Lord Beaverbrook, who was born William Maxwell Aitken in Canada, was reared in rural New Brunswick, where his father was a Presbyterian minister. Having made a fortune by the time he was thirty, he moved to England, was soon elected to Parliament and given a government post in the First World War. He multiplied his fortune on the London Stock Exchange and became one of Britain's biggest newspaper publishers. After being knighted and then made a baronet, he was elevated to the peerage. When that happened. he took as the title of his barony the name of the creek in which, as a boy, he had paddled and fished.

Between the twenty-eighth day of June in 1940 and Pearl Harbor Day, we piled up in the United States, or had afloat, the largest stock of rubber that had ever been accumulated at any time in any country, but nothing like enough to feel comfortable. What we had brought in, however, was accomplished despite a shipping shortage and the slowness of the rubber people to ship rubber. Making the situation more uncomfortable were the increasing demands for rubber by American civilians for non-defense purposes—mostly for automobile tires—reaching an all-time high rate in 1941 of more than 900,000 tons a year.

In amassing this stockpile we received full and generous cooperation from the American rubber industry. Without their help we could not have succeeded. Except for our first early bids for about 10,000 tons of rubber from Indo-China, all Rubber Reserve Company purchases were made through a buying committee headed by Mr. Viles and composed of five experienced buyers loaned to us without compensation by the five leading rubber manufacturers. Their services were freely given to the government during the entire crude rubber program. From time to time as we kept raising our sights we successfully drummed away at the International Committee in London, persuading them to authorize larger and larger export schedules. Instead of the originally contracted 150,000 tons, the most Sir John Hay would then agree to sell, we had, before Pearl Harbor, arranged to buy 800,000 tons.

Rubber Reserve Company became the sole importer of crude rubber for the entire country, and likewise was made the sole distributor of these imports to the manufacturing industries.

Buying the rubber was one thing. Getting it across the Pacific was another. The commitments of shipping to the war in Africa, and to supplying the United Kingdom and its armies, caused such a very heavy withdrawal of British and Dutch freighters from the Far Eastern routes that it became necessary for us to look around for American bottoms to bring the rubber to this country. Starting in March, 1941, Rubber Reserve Company made arrangements with the Maritime Commission, the War Department, and various steamship interests to provide adequate American shipping space for all its purchases in the

Far East and elsewhere. Army transports which took troops and equipment to the Philippines went on before returning home to pick up rubber at Singapore or in Dutch East Indian ports.

As a result of these measures, enough shipping space was provided to transport all the rubber available out of most of the Far East up to the fall of Singapore. When the Japanese armies took Malaya and Java they found the rubber cupboard bare. During the eight weeks between Pearl Harbor and the surrender of Singapore, 114,000 tons of rubber were shipped across the Pacific and safely stored in the United States. That was only a few tons less than the entire stock of natural rubber which had been on hand in this country in 1939 when the European war began.

A week after the attack on Pearl Harbor, we were able to make a new agreement with the International Committee calling for American rubber purchases throughout 1942 at the unprecedented rate of 100,-000 tons a month. If they had shipped rubber that fast in the beginning, we would never have been short of it. The rapid conquests by the Japanese in the producing areas quickly relegated that contract to the realm of dreams that couldn't come true. In seven weeks Singapore fell; in five more weeks Java had to give in. In exactly three months after the strike at Pearl Harbor, 90 per cent of the world's natural rubber production facilities had fallen into the enemy's grasp. The only considerable production area remaining available to our allies and ourselves was Ceylon.

Luckily, almost all the rubber we bought overseas reached our shores. Out of nearly a million long tons purchased by the Rubber Reserve Company in every available part of the world, only 24,753 tons were lost as a result of enemy action.

A few weeks after Pearl Harbor, our stockpile reached its maximum—630,356 tons. We had by then made agreements with private interests in Liberia and with the governments of seventeen South and Central American countries to encourage the production and export both of plantation and of wild rubber and had arranged with the British to take over from them a large portion of the distant Ceylon output. We bought all the scrap rubber in the country. We never got as much natural rubber as we wanted or tried to acquire, but we did get all that was available.

Yet, with America engaged in global war, and on a motorized basis, all this would not be enough. Fully a year before Pearl Harbor we had begun, at first on a modest scale, the great gamble on synthetic rubber. Before we finished that vast program we invested $700,000,-000 and built a new industry which produced more than three billion pounds of synthetic rubber for the war effort.

26

---------------------------------- ☼ ----------------------------------

BUILDING THE SYNTHETIC RUBBER INDUSTRY

Getting the Big Five Together—FDR Isn't Interested—
Patriotic Pooling of Secrets—We Raise Our Sights—The
Baruch Committee Report—William Jeffers Drives Our
Program Through—Synthetic Production Hits Its Stride

IN 1945, when the war was brought to an end, 87 per cent of the
rubber being consumed in the United States was synthetic—and
nearly all of it was coming from government-owned plants built with
RFC money under RFC direction. The production of these plants
exceeded 700,000 tons in 1944 and rose above 800,000 tons in 1945.
It adequately met all military requirements and every really essential
civilian need as well. The capacity of the plants exceeded 1,000,000
tons a year.

The military requirements were staggering. For example, the national output of airplane tires, which had been 33,000 in 1939, rose
almost to 1,500,000 in 1944. Between Pearl Harbor and the day the
Japanese surrendered aboard the U.S.S. *Missouri,* more than 40,-
000,000 heavy-duty truck tires were turned out in American plants
and sent rolling along the roads to victory on every continent of the
earth.

The synthetic rubber baby was put on my lap in the late summer
of 1940. I had discussed its possibilities in May with John L. Collyer,
president of the B. F. Goodrich Company, which had successfully
pioneered in the development of a synthetic rubber suitable for tires.

Mr. Collyer was familiar with the German synthetic rubber industry
and felt that the successful manufacture of synthetic rubber in the
United States would show the world that America could quickly put
itself in a position to replace natural rubber with synthetics, a neces-

sity he then foresaw should the Far Eastern plantations fall into unfriendly hands.

For some time the National Defense Advisory Committee had been discussing the pros and cons of developing a synthetic rubber industry. They threshed over its complexities, both technical and financial, without reaching a decision. At the end of a long exchange of ideas around a table presided over by Clarence Francis, president of General Foods Corporation, A. L. Viles, I am told, finally suggested that they "wrap this whole thing up in one package and take it over to Jesse Jones." It was Mr. Viles' argument that our office was the one place in Washington that had the money and the authority to undertake the job.

The question of getting the money was the least of our worries. The whole idea of setting up what amounted to an untried industry was greatly speculative, involving processes still in the experimental stage. Four of the major rubber companies and the Standard Oil Development Company were already engaged in development work in the synthetic rubber field, but on a small scale not fully emerged from the test-tube stage. Other large chemical and petroleum companies, including Du Pont, Dow, Monsanto, Koppers, and the Carbide & Carbon Chemicals Corporation, were experimenting with the production either of synthetic rubber or of ingredient materials such as butadiene and styrene. Each company had its own carefully guarded processes. No three people seemed to have the same formula. We were not yet at war. To persuade these concerns to pool their patents and exchange technical information would not, I knew, be easy.

FDR ISN'T INTERESTED

Edward R. Stettinius, Jr., and William L. Batt, vice chairman of the War Production Board, both members of the Advisory Defense Committee, came to see me about synthetic rubber. They told me they had just come from talking with the President about it but could not interest him. They wanted me to talk to him. They thought we should allocate $100,000,000 to build plants. The following day I reported to the President what Stettinius and Batt had said.

The President was not concerned. He told me that we could always build the necessary plants in a year's time and that we would always have ample notice if it should become necessary. Either the President thought there would be no necessity for building a synthetic rubber industry, or he was woefully ignorant of the problem. I advised Messrs. Stettinius and Batt of the President's attitude. They were greatly disappointed and concerned. Mr. Batt pounded my office table with his fist and said he would have to do it (meaning the President would have to O.K. it). To that I replied that I had been working for and with President Roosevelt for a good many years and had not yet seen anyone make him do anything that he did not want to do.

However, I felt as they did, that inasmuch as we in this country had not perfected the making of synthetic rubber we should at least learn the know-how. Accordingly I prepared a letter to the President, leaving the number of dollars blank until I could see him. I felt sure I could convince him that we should get started. I had adopted the principle of putting my recommendations to the President in letter or memorandum form. The letter follows:

FEDERAL LOAN AGENCY

WASHINGTON

September 16, 1940

Dear Mr. President:

With further reference to synthetic rubber and Mr. Stettinius' Memorandum to you of September 12th, beg to advise that, based upon the studies I have made of this subject with Mr. Schram and other RFC officials in cooperation with Mr. Stettinius, Mr. Batt and others of the Defense Council, and Assistant Secretary of War Robert Patterson, and Under Secretary of the Navy James Forrestal, I am prepared to recommend that the RFC finance the construction of synthetic rubber manufacturing plant or plants preferably to be built and operated by one or more of the companies that have been experimenting with synthetic rubber.

The following companies have made some progress in developing synthetic rubber, all by somewhat different methods: The duPont Company, Standard Oil of New Jersey, B. F. Goodrich Company, Firestone, and Goodyear. It appears that none of the methods has been sufficiently proven to warrant the construction of expensive plants *except in an extraordinary emergency*.

The Rubber Reserve Company has obligated itself to buy 330,-000 tons of raw rubber, and unless interrupted this should be in hand by the middle of 1941. 53,560 tons have already been bought under this arrangement for shipment over the next two or three months. In addition, the barter rubber will increase our stockpile to 415,000 tons. If the raw rubber supply is not cut off or seriously interrupted, we can increase our stockpile beyond the amount already arranged for. Sir John Hay thought we would get the first 150,000 tons by the first of next year and the 180,000 tons by July of 1941. He may, of course, be a little optimistic, but they are extremely anxious to sell the rubber and are not enthusiastic about our building synthetic plants.

If under the circumstances you think the situation warrants it and that we should do so under existing law, we will pursue the matter with a view to building one, two or three small plants at a total cost of not more than $_____.

Sincerely yours,

JESSE H. JONES, Administrator

The President
The White House

The President read my letter very carefully and asked how much money I would suggest. I told him about the $100,000,000 figure which Stettinius and Batt had asked for but added that I thought we might start with $50,000,000. He said, "Definitely no." He told me he thought the whole thing unnecessary but that we might spend up to $25,000,000. That amount, he remarked, would do as much good as $100,000,000.

"These wealthy rubber companies," he said, "ought to build their own plants."

PATRIOTIC POOLING OF SECRETS

With the President approving my recommendations, but only up to $25,000,000, we sent letters on December 5, 1940, a year and two days before Pearl Harbor, asking the rubber companies to submit plans for pilot plants. On March 28, 1941, after we had received their replies and held many conferences with them, we requested four of them—Goodrich, Goodyear, Firestone, and United States Rubber Company—to submit proposals for four pilot plants, each to have a 10,000-ton capacity. The estimated cost was $10,000,000 each, a total of $40,000,000. Although the President had authorized only $25,000,000, I took the responsibility of going ahead without bothering him further, as he had enough problems.

As the political skies over the Pacific continued to darken we went ahead without further discussion with the President, developing plans in cooperation with private industry for an expanded program. Into these conferences we brought the heads of some of the largest industrial concerns in the country, among them William S. Farish, president of the Standard Oil Company of New Jersey; F. B. Davis, Jr., of United States Rubber; James A. Rafferty, chairman of Carbide & Carbon Chemicals Corporation; J. P. Williams, Jr., president of Koppers Company; W. Alton Jones, president of Cities Service Company; Harry C. Wiess and Hines H. Baker of the Humble Oil Company; W. S. S. Rodgers, president of the Texas Company; Colonel J. Frank Drake, president of the Gulf Oil Corporation; Robert H. Colley, president of the Atlantic Refining Company; Frank Phillips, chairman, and K. S. Adams, president, of Phillips Petroleum; Jan Oostermeyer, president of Shell Chemical Corporation of San Francisco; Harry L. Masser, executive vice president of Southern California Gas Company; Willard H. Dow, head of Dow Chemical Company; Charles Belknap, president of Monsanto Chemical Company; and Ernest Bridgewater and E. G. Robinson of the Du Pont enterprises.

Finding a convenient day to get these busy men together was difficult enough. Inducing them to pool patents and share their secrets with competitors and with us was not fully possible—until Pearl Harbor and the attack on Malaya. Then, in February, 1942, they met at ten o'clock one morning in our offices, continued their session straight through until three o'clock the next morning, resumed after a few hours of sleep, and by early afternoon had arranged an agreement to work together and with the Rubber Reserve Company in complete cooperation on a program which called for pooling patents and secrets and for plants that would produce 400,000 tons of synthetic rubber a year.

One night early in 1942 there was a meeting at the White House which included the President, Prime Minister Winston Churchill, Lord Beaverbrook, one or two others, and myself. Many problems were discussed. Finally, Lord Beaverbrook asked me how much synthetic rubber we were planning to manufacture; that is, what ton capacity per year. I replied that our plans were set for 400,000 tons a year. He commented that that would be "the greatest of plenty." I had not yet cleared this with the President. That was all that was said that night about rubber.

The next morning I prepared a press release announcing that we were contracting for synthetic rubber plants to produce 400,000 tons a year at an approximate cost of $400,000,000. As a matter of fact, we had purposely rated the plants at about 75 per cent of what the experts thought they would produce. I went to the White House and showed the President my release because I did not yet have his approval. I told the President that the experts thought the program would turn out not less than 500,000 tons instead of 400,000. He replied that 400,000 tons was enough, but we continued as we had planned.

Later events rapidly proved that we should increase—which we did.

On January 13, 1942, Lord Beaverbrook sent to Prime Minister Churchill a memorandum of which only recently he forwarded a copy to me from his files. It read:

PRIME MINISTER
Rubber

On Sunday morning I came to an understanding with Jesse Jones about production of rubber.

His statement in the newspapers is entirely satisfactory except for synthetic rubber.

We must persuade him to increase production of synthetic rubber from 400,000 tons to 600,000 tons per annum.

He has an understanding with me to give us 50,000 tons of synthetic rubber per annum, on the basis of 350,000 tons of production. If production falls short, then Great Britain's share is reduced proportionately.

We have an understanding with OPM to supply us with 25,000 tons of reclaimed rubber in 1942.

I am not sending you any reports on Raw Materials.

Do you want tin?

It is a Jesse Jones business.

BEAVERBROOK

WE RAISE OUR SIGHTS

Soon after Singapore's surrender to the Japanese, on February 15, 1942, which cut us off not only from Malayan rubber but also from the largest tin smelter then in existence, we increased our synthetic rubber goal to a rated capacity of 805,000 tons a year, continuing to underrate the capacity of the plants. The War Production Board advised against more than 600,000 tons. The plants could in fact produce more than 1,000,000 tons a year. In taking the responsibility for increasing the plants and underrating their capacity, it was my judgment that none of us knew how well they could work, whether they would all work, or how many of them might be destroyed by accident, sabotage, or other causes.

Of this 805,000-ton rated capacity which we announced, 705,000 tons would be GR-S (butadiene-styrene, sometimes called Buna-S, or general purpose rubber) and the remainder Butyl and Neoprene. Butyl was a product developed by Standard Oil and was regarded as the most suitable rubber substitute for the manufacture of tubes and barrage balloons. Neoprene, a Du Pont synthetic, had already been in commercial production on a small scale for several years. We bought Du Pont's Neoprene plant at Louisville and expanded it.

Although the War Production Board approved my recommendation that all priority and allocation assistance needed to carry out our program would be given us, we continually ran into unexpected difficulties and delays. The heavy toll taken by submarines off the Gulf and Atlantic coasts spurred a sharp increase in the building of escort vessels while upward changes in the airplane production program required ever larger allocations of materials for the aviation gasoline program. Both of these industries needed many of the same things the rubber program required—pumps, compressors, motors, pipes, and other types of machinery. The Army and Navy had vastly underestimated what their needs would be; and, as the war progressed, these were continually changing, always upward.

An ever growing number of government agencies, as well as the armed services, were directly interested in obtaining or allocating rubber. To get the tugging and pulling into one arena, Stanley Crossland and I, beginning early in May, 1942, held meetings every Monday morning with a committee drawn from all the interested depart-

A LOAF OF SYNTHETIC RUBBER

Defense Plant Corporation spent nearly $700,000,000 developing this new industry. The photograph was taken in June, 1943, at the Institute (West Virginia) plant. Left to right: William M. Jeffers, Rubber Director of the United States; James A. Rafferty, president of Carbide & Carbon Chemicals Corporation, which produced the raw materials; F. B. Davis, Jr., chairman of the United States Rubber Co., which made the loaf, and Jesse H. Jones.

Photo Office Production Management

THE WAR PRODUCTION BOARD, 1942

Left to right (seated), Leon Henderson, James V. Forrestal, Jesse H. Jones, Frank Knox, Donald Nelson (chairman); Vice President Henry A. Wallace, Robert P. Patterson, William S. Knudsen.

ments, boards, and agencies. Ferdinand Eberstadt sat in for the Army-Navy Munitions Board, of which he was chairman. General Lucius D. Clay represented the Army as assistant chief of staff for material service of supply. Rear Admiral Ernest G. Small came over from the Navy Department. Among the other Monday morning regulars were Clarence Francis from the Council of National Defense, Edward R. Weidlein, director of the Mellon Institute of Industrial Research, who then was in the chemical division of the War Production Board, and others sent by the Department of Agriculture, the Office of Price Administration, and the Office of Petroleum Coordinator.

Robert P. Patterson, the Secretary of War, told me he would like to review our weekly decisions. I suggested he assign a man to attend our sessions. He selected one of his special assistants, Michael J. Madigan, a New York engineer. From then on Mr. Madigan joined us as long as the meetings continued.

We had to consider all phases of the program, including selection of processes, availability of raw materials, plant locations, scheduling of completions, and, of course, the obtaining of allocations of sufficient construction materials and such ingredients as industrial alcohol and petroleum.

The Monday meetings continued until September, 1942, by which time our program was set and construction under way. In the early stages of the enterprise, the only major raw material which appeared to be adequately available was petroleum. It was not until May, 1942, that the alcohol production situation improved sufficiently for the War Production Board to allocate any grain alcohol for synthetic rubber.

New processes and formulae were advanced almost daily by people anxious to help—or to make money out of government contracts— but we would never have gotten any considerable amount of synthetic rubber if we had jumped from one process to another each time an oil company or alcohol company or an inventor, however patriotic, wanted the government to adopt a particular process. We sought what we believed to be the best available technical advice and followed it.

Early in our consideration of synthetic or substitute rubber I asked the distinguished scientist and industrial inventor Dr. Charles F. Kettering to organize a committee to make recommendations as to procedure. A diligent and very helpful gentleman, Dr. Kettering brought together a group of technical experts from the rubber, oil, and chemical industries and gave a great deal of his own time to our problems. He made recommendations for the manufacture of a material called thiacol which could be produced rather quickly. We built a plant and manufactured some of the material, but it did not prove very satisfactory, though it made tires that carried light loads when handled carefully. It was only intended as a stopgap while the synthetic program was getting under way.

Another great contributor to our success with rubber was John W. Livingston. In 1942 he gave up a $60,000-a-year vice presidency of the Monsanto Chemical Company to serve the government at $10,000. His experience in chemistry and engineering and his untiring efforts throughout the war made him invaluable to our program.

Though we had the largest-ever stockpile of natural rubber on hand when the Pacific War began, it was not sufficient, with further supplies largely cut off, to care for the customary civilian requirements of a people owning three-fourths of all the automobiles in the world and at the same time to meet the country's military program, requiring tens of thousands of airplanes and hundreds of thousands of motorized vehicles and weapons carriers.

Giving up, or curtailing, the habit of riding in automobiles would seem to be the last thing millions of Americans would ever want to do. It was so during the great depression when many people drove cars to the relief stations to collect governmental doles. It remained so in considerable degree during the war. When it became almost impossible for a civilian to buy a new tire, there was criticism and much uninformed complaining that our rubber program was a failure. The fact is that 45 per cent of the more than three billion pounds of synthetic rubber sold by Rubber Reserve Company during the war was designated for use directly on war contracts, and 54 per cent was sold, substantially at the OPA ceiling prices, for other uses.

THE BARUCH COMMITTEE REPORT

With the continued curtailment of rubber tires for business and private use and the inconvenience to everyone caused by this shortage, it was but natural that nearly everyone should offer suggestions as to how to get tires. Washington was filled with smart people who thought they could do the job better than it was being done. The President was finally persuaded by Harold Ickes (according to that gentleman's memoirs) to create an investigating committee headed by Bernard M. Baruch. Harold frequently tried to interfere with or criticize some other fellow's department. He probably thought he could do a better job. Maybe he could. He did a very good job as Public Works Administrator.

I knew that some meddler or meddlers—there were plenty of them —had persuaded the President that an investigation was necessary. I was glad to have it because we were working on a new problem, the success of which might determine the outcome of the war. The other two members of the investigating committee were Dr. James Bryant Conant, president of Harvard University, and Dr. Karl Taylor Compton, president of the Massachusetts Institute of Technology. They were told to investigate the rubber situation and make recommendations to the President.

They drafted other prominent men to assist them. These included Edward Eagle Brown, president of the First National Bank of Chicago; Clarence Dillon, head of Dillon, Read & Company, Wall Street bankers; and John M. Hancock, a partner in Lehman Brothers, also Wall Street bankers. They were probably two months at their task before giving the President their report on September 10, 1942.

They recommended the appointment of a Rubber Director to have charge of the entire rubber program. The committee suggested "a man of unusual capacities and power, a thoroughly competent operating and manufacturing executive, preferably with experience in the rubber industry." The War Production Board already had a Rubber Coordinator, Arthur B. Newhall, with whom I kept in closest possible contact, and who concurred in everything we were doing.

The Baruch Committee report made a number of criticisms of our program which were not justified, but wound up by saying the program *would produce rubber* and that we were trying to do in two years what ordinarily would take twelve years to accomplish. Incidentally President Roosevelt had told me, when he was reluctant to approve even the original pilot plants, that we could always build a synthetic rubber industry, if needed, in one year. At the end of two years we had a capacity of close to a million tons of synthetic rubber a year.

In making his report my friend Baruch was willing to give me a little dig—for reasons of his own, maybe. Probably Mr. Baruch and his committee colleagues, Messrs. Dillon and Hancock, like some other Wall Streeters, were none too pleased that the RFC, the biggest banking and industrial corporation in history, could be run without calling on some of them.

After the Baruch Rubber Committee report was made public, I wrote a memorandum to the President and took it to the White House and handed it to him. It read:

> I think it a great mistake to allow the country to get the impression from the Baruch report that a great deal has not been accomplished in the rubber situation, both crude and synthetic. About all has already been done toward synthetic rubber that the Baruch report recommends, and the balance can be contracted within a few days, if the critical materials can be spared.
>
> Construction would have been further along with better priorities. A 15% factor of safety will give us a million tons.
>
> JESSE H. JONES

The President read the memorandum, laid it aside, and said he would handle it. It was his press conference day, and I thought the proper time for him to comment on the report was while it was fresh in the public's mind. I stayed for the press conference and sat just back of him, which I occasionally did if I happened to be at the White House on press conference days, but he made no reference to the Baruch report.

WILLIAM JEFFERS DRIVES OUR PROGRAM THROUGH

As Rubber Director, the President appointed William M. Jeffers, president of the Union Pacific Railroad. It was a wise selection, although Mr. Jeffers had no rubber or other manufacturing experience. He had risen from trackwalker on the railroad to its presidency. He is both competent and effective in whatever he is willing to undertake. Under his direction we continued our rubber program and carried it out and completed it 97 per cent as we had planned it and had it well under way before the Baruch Committee report or the appointment of a rubber director.

Mr. Jeffers directed us to do a few things which the Baruch committee had recommended in their report, but soon rescinded most of those orders. As for natural rubber, he made no suggestion to us.

The really great service Mr. Jeffers rendered, which was paramount, was in hammering away at getting materials for the construction of the synthetic rubber plants. He was continually at cross purposes with the War Department in fighting for materials. And we got them.

He drove the program through as he found it. For this great contribution, I shall ever be grateful. When he resigned to return to his railroad, he sent me the following letter:

UNION PACIFIC RAILROAD COMPANY

OMAHA, NEBRASKA

WM. JEFFERS
President

Washington, D.C.
September 7, 1943

PERSONAL

Dear Jesse:

Before leaving Washington, I would be remiss if I did not tell you how genuinely appreciative I am of the understanding and consistent support you have given me in ironing out some of the synthetic rubber problems.

The synthetic rubber program, after all, was your program, and we have succeeded in driving it through. I feel well repaid for the effort.

It has been a great pleasure and a great comfort to have known you better, and I hope in the years to come that our paths will cross often. You are a great fellow!

Remember me affectionately to Mrs. Jones.

Sincerely,

WM. JEFFERS

Colonel Bradley Dewey, the distinguished chemist who had served as Mr. Jeffers' deputy, succeeded him as Rubber Director and continued his technical advice to us. There was never any friction between those two gentlemen and the RFC agencies.

One unpardonable error in the Baruch Committee's report, and one undoubtedly prompted by a disposition to be critical (a disposition which Dr. Conant and Dr. Compton did not share), was the statement that we had the service of only one part-time rubber expert-scientist-chemist, in doing this big job. As a matter of fact, we had the help and services of most of the experts, chemists, and scientists of the rubber industry, the oil industry, and the chemical industries. True, they were not on our pay roll; but the leaders of these industries had put their experts at our disposal in a patriotic way, and without cost to the RFC. Several other observations in the Committee report could be attributed to a propensity to find fault.

The Baruch Committee also criticized us for "failure to obtain information concerning the Russian process for making synthetic rubber." I felt that we would get nothing from the Russians in time to be of any value to us, if ever, and in this I was not mistaken. Upon the recommendation of the Rubber Survey Committee, Mr. Jeffers dispatched a mission of technical experts to Russia in the early part of December, 1942. The mission returned home in March, 1943, having obtained no information that could make any contribution to the American synthetic rubber program. *The commission never got inside any Russian plants.*

SYNTHETIC PRODUCTION HITS ITS STRIDE

The American rubber program, which produced more than 700,000 tons in 1944, was operating at a rate in excess of 1,000,000 tons a year when the war ended. Compare those figures with the accomplishments of the Germans. Prior to the war the Germans were generally conceded to possess greater knowledge of synthetic rubber production than any other people. During the war their supplies of natural rubber were so extremely limited that they had to rely almost entirely upon their synthetic production. When their records became available after the surrender, we learned that their annual production never rose above 109,173 tons, that peak having been reached in 1943.

We handled the rubber situation, both natural and synthetic, in a businesslike way and got results. As a contribution to winning the war, our accomplishments in less than two years in the rubber field will stand comparison with those of any other industry. At the start we did not have the knowledge, but we went out to get it, and did, just as we did in many other fields.

A friend asked me how we did so many things we did not know

how to do, which brought to mind a story about General Charles G. Dawes. When Mr. Dawes was taking his examinations for a commission in the Corps of Engineers of the War Department in World War I, the opening question put to him was: "What is the first thing you would do if you were told to survey a field?" Mr. Dawes replied, "I would employ an engineer." He got his commission.

Altogether, fifty-one government-owned plants were designed, constructed, and put in operation. In carrying out the program, forty-nine rubber, chemical, petroleum, and other industrial companies participated under the supervision of Rubber Reserve Company. (A list of the plants, giving their locations, costs, and the nature of their products, will be found in the appendix.)

Our investment in these plants approximated $700,000,000. When the program really got going, expenditures for materials, utilities, services, etc. ran around $2,000,000 per day. All these plants were constructed under the auspices of another RFC subsidiary, Defense Plant Corporation, which leased them to the various operating companies at a nominal rental of one dollar per year. Nearly all of them were operated on a cost-plus-management-charge basis.

Since alcohol and petroleum were the principal feeder bases, the plants were built convenient to the sources of those raw materials. Twenty-one plants were in the east central States, twenty-three in the Southwest, principally in Texas and Louisiana. The remaining seven were in southern California. Fifteen of the plants produced Butadiene, five produced Styrene, nine produced other chemicals, and nineteen turned out the finished product—synthetic rubber. Of the cost of production, 86 per cent went for materials. For alcohol more than $500,000,000 was spent, and for petroleum more than $100,000,000. It was the predominant importance of petroleum in synthetic rubber production that motivated placing nearly half the nation's capacity in the Gulf Coast area of Texas and Louisiana.

Although four grades of rubber were manufactured, the principal production was the GR-S type, known commercially as Buna S. (The symbol GR-S stands for Government Rubber-Styrene.) Of Buna S more than three billion pounds were sold by Rubber Reserve during the war. By the war's end the accumulated average cost of production of GR-S had dropped to 31.41 cents a pound. Sales to the Army, Navy, and other government procurement agencies or to manufacturers for use directly on government orders were, in effect, made at average cost. About half the sales were war orders. The other half brought only the OPA ceiling prices—and we had to take a loss.

However, the whole net operating deficit of the plants up to December, 1948, had amounted to only $33,481,000, according to G. B. Hadlock, director of the RFC's Office of Rubber Reserve. The big loss—nearly $250,000,000—was for depreciation of the plants. Yet that was a very small price to pay for synthetic rubber's contribution to the victory and its guarantee that our country shall never again be wholly dependent on distant sources for its supply of such an essential article.

During the war the whole huge enterprise was administered by Rubber Reserve Company with a personnel of fewer than 300 directly assigned employees. On V-J Day there were about 24,000 employees engaged in operating the plants. Although they were working with new processes and sometimes with strange materials and machinery, they were credited by the Department of Labor in the last year of the war with the third best accident prevention record in the nation.

Long before the end of the war we had enough rubber on hand, in sight, and in plant capacity, to keep going for another two years. Because of all the criticism and hullabaloo over rubber and to keep the record straight, I summarized the situation in the following memorandum to President Roosevelt:

December 16, 1944

Dear Mr. President:

Through November our 1944 imports of natural rubber have been about 102,000 tons, and we expect probably 10,000 tons in December. Consumption of natural rubber for the year will be about 142,000 tons, or approximately 30,000 tons more than our imports.

December 1, Rubber Reserve Company's stockpile of crude rubber was approximately 75,000 tons, and industry had about 22,000 tons.

Rubber Reserve Company had a stockpile of 61,000 tons of synthetic rubber, and industry about 71,000 tons.

Production of synthetic rubber for 1944 will run about 760,000 tons. This includes 23,000 from private industry. Our own facilities are presently adequate to produce 1,000,000 tons a year, if necessary.

From 1935 to 1939, inclusive, rubber imports averaged 460,000 tons annually. In 1940–41–42, when accumulating our stockpile, we imported 2,107,000 tons.

Indications now are that consumption of natural rubber will be somewhat greater in 1945 than in 1944, but if we continue to get the greater part of the rubber produced in Ceylon, we should be able to get enough natural rubber to carry us through at least another two years.

Sincerely yours,

JESSE H. JONES

Earlier—on August 28, 1944—I had written a long letter to the President, telling him that the synthetic rubber program was substantially completed, and functioning successfully. I pointed out that it was virtually the identical program of Rubber Reserve Company in effect prior to the appointment of the Rubber Survey Committee in August, 1942. My letter reviewed the accomplishments in all three phases of the rubber program—stockpiling, the creation of an immense synthetic rubber industry, and the collection of wild rubber in South America. It evoked this response:

THE WHITE HOUSE
Washington   August 31, 1944
Dear Jesse:

I have your letter of the 28th and agree with you that the success of the rubber program is indeed noteworthy.

Those who have contributed to the development of this industry are entitled to great credit and I am sure that credit will be given them by the people when the story is told.

Sincerely yours,

FRANKLIN D. ROOSEVELT

This, then, is the story.

*   *   *

As this is written the world situation seems to grow tenser each day. President Truman has ordered the reopening of several of the synthetic rubber plants which had been put on a stand-by basis. With the war clouds gathering again, an American synthetic rubber industry with a capacity of one million tons a year is a mighty good thing for the nation to possess.

27

---------------------- ☼ ----------------------

THE WILD RUBBER PROGRAM

Henry Wallace Butts in with an Idea for Feeding Every-
body Along the Amazon for Free—Jeffers Gives Wallace
the Boot—Nelson Rockefeller Extends His Assistance

WHEN Malaya and Java had fallen to the enemy early in 1942,
cutting off nine-tenths of the world's sources of raw rubber, the
chief plantations left open to the United Nations—those of Ceylon,
India, and Liberia—had a combined production of only about
115,000 tons a year. The requirements of the United States and our
allies were then estimated at 1,200,000 tons a year. The great gap
between supply and demand could not be bridged merely by drastic
rubber conservation, maximum utilization of reclaimed rubber, and
the immediate development of a vast synthetic rubber industry. It
would be necessary to procure wild rubber from the tropical jungle
lands of Central and South America. We promptly set about that
delicate and difficult task.

For twenty-five years the once prosperous trade in wild rubber
from the upper reaches of the Amazon and its tributaries had been
moribund. Four days before the fall of Java an agreement to revive
it was made between our Rubber Reserve Company and the Government of Brazil. In succeeding months similar agreements were
entered into with sixteen other rubber producing countries south of
the Rio Grande and in the Caribbean. There then began one of the
most intimate, extensive, and long-continued collaborations between
an agency of the United States Government and the Governments of
Latin America ever undertaken. These collaborations were smooth
and fruitful despite the interventions, interruptions, and irritations

during a nine-month period by Vice President Henry Wallace and his reformers in the Board of Economic Warfare.

From April, 1942, until January, 1943, President Roosevelt accorded those gentlemen full policy control over all overseas economic activities of the United States, including the procurement and production programs administered by the RFC. They were given power without responsibility, and we, for a time, had imposed upon us responsibility without power.

Jurisdiction was divided, personnel duplicated, red tape tripled, and debate and discussion quadrupled when speed was important. In 1942, it should be remembered, the tides of war were not running in our favor.

Despite frictions and the meddling of the BEW the revival of the trade in wild rubber was well under way before that year was out.

Production of wild rubber is an isolated individualistic type of operation not susceptible of such organization and control as is customary in growing plantation rubber, where trees are concentrated 100 to 150 to the acre and labor can be conveniently assembled. In the jungles of Latin America wild rubber trees occur on an average of about one per acre. The collection of their rubber has been compared to the activity of a fur trapper in the Far North, or a mining prospector in remote regions. Because the sources are so scattered and difficult of access, wild rubber costs substantially more than plantation rubber.

We had to hurry. Haste, of course, added to the cost. We had such extra expenses as maintaining a regular air service between the coast of Peru and the upper Amazon. We were obliged to set up wireless stations, establish steamship transportation along the Amazon and some of its tributaries and arrange with the Brazilian Government to move more than thirty thousand laborers from the southern parts of that vast republic into the steaming upper Amazon country, where the population was sparse. Though the Amazon Basin is larger than the continental United States, its estimated population is only 1,500,000.

Despite all these expensive and difficult undertakings Rubber Reserve Company and its successor, Rubber Development Corporation, brought more rubber out of Latin America than had been anticipated and at a cheaper price than anyone had estimated. During the years the inter-American agreements were in operation, the program brought to the United States 153,545 long tons of wild rubber at an over-all cost of $203,636,178.65. That was an average-unit cost of just under 60 cents per pound, delivered to United States ports.

Preliminary estimates of alleged experts had run from $1 to $5 a pound. Vice President Wallace testified before a Senate Committee that in his opinion the cost would "push $2 per pound." And so it probably would, had he been able to have his way. One plantation his bright young disciples originated in Haiti (against the advice of the qualified rubber authorities recruited by our organization) succeeded in spending nearly $7,000,000 to produce about enough rubber to fill a large truck. Its production cost $546 a pound. (That's right, a *pound,* not a ton.)

Senator Hugh A. Butler of Nebraska, after a trip to South America, reported to the Senate his opinion that to bring wild rubber out of that Continent would cost at least $5 a pound. On the other hand Douglas H. Allen, the experienced foreign trader who took charge of our procurement program in the Amazon basin and later became president of our Rubber Development Corporation, had given a Senate committee in early 1943 his estimate that the average cost, after all expenses and losses were met, would be less than 75 cents a pound. His figure was received at the time with considerable skepticism. The actual average cost finally came to 59⅕ cents a pound.

It should not be forgotten that there had been, during many months of the war, the possibility that the Japanese might capture Ceylon and the Germans overrun Africa. Had that happened, the United Nations would have been left almost entirely dependent upon Latin America for their supplies of natural rubber. Until the surrender of Japan, every pound of natural rubber we obtained was of critical importance and desperately needed.

Out of Liberia, almost entirely from plantations of the Firestone Tire & Rubber Company, there was brought during the period of the international rubber agreements nearly 65,000 long tons of crude rubber at a cost of $44,000,000, or about 30 cents a pound, and also more than 20,000 tons of latex.

Rubber from Africa other than Liberia, and from Ceylon and India, was left to the administrative responsibility of the British Government and was subject to reverse lend-lease, while all the rubber produced in the Americas was made our responsibility.

The agreements reached with the seventeen Latin American countries established a single cooperative system for the equitable control of rubber consumption and for the encouragement of maximum production. The Department of State, in conjunction with Rubber Reserve Company, negotiated the agreements. These provided for the sale for a term of years, at a fixed price, to the United States of their exportable surpluses and for limiting consumption in the producing countries. In turn the United States gave assurance to our good neighbors to the south that their essential requirements for rubber and manufactured rubber goods would be supplied in so far as the war needs of the United Nations permitted. The price was adjusted from time to time.

The seventeen countries with which substantially identical agreements were made were Brazil, Bolivia, Peru, Venezuela, Colombia, Ecuador, Nicaragua, Honduras, British Honduras, Costa Rica, Guatemala, Panama, Mexico, El Salvador, British Guiana, Dutch Guiana, and Trinidad.

To the greatest possible extent the financing of the program was done through private banks or through credit instrumentalities of the local governments, so that an agency of the United States Government would not be put in the position of directly lending money to producers of rubber. For example, in Brazil a specialized credit concern, called the Banco de Crédito da Borracha, was set up. The Brazilian Government subscribed $4,500,000 to the capital of this bank, and the Rubber Development Corporation subscribed $3,000,000. The bank handled all the financing of rubber production in Brazil. In Peru the Peruvian Amazon Corporation was established for a similar purpose.

Everywhere the foreign governments cooperated splendidly with the program. In the Amazon Basin, through arrangements with the three countries concerned—Brazil, Peru, and Bolivia—effective steps were taken to discourage the production of non-essential commodities so that almost the only activity that could be engaged in was the production of rubber. This was an extraordinarily generous thing for the three governments to do and their peoples to accept.

Field technicians were sent to the principal producing areas to teach improved methods to the tappers and investigate new developments. These men, not a few of whom were loaned to us by American rubber companies, led a hard and dangerous life. Some of them died in line of duty. Others incurred disabling tropical diseases.

On the Amazon additional river steamers were supplied between Belém at the mouth of the river, and Manaus a thousand miles upstream, to offset the withdrawal of the ocean freighters which in normal times served Manaus. During the period of the rubber program, which continued until 1947, freight moving through the port of Belém more than doubled. On smaller rivers tugs, barges, and motor boats were assembled to handle the revived traffic. Most of the rubber trees in the Amazon Basin are two thousand to twenty-five hundred miles from the Atlantic Ocean.

My friend Cordell Hull was Secretary of State from March 4, 1933, to November 27, 1944. Though our Rubber Development Corporation was continually involved in complex and delicate negotiations with foreign governments, we received his full cooperation and that of his staff, in Washington and abroad, especially Under Secretary Sumner Welles and Herbert Feis, the Department's adviser on economics. Since a representative of the State Department served always as a director of Rubber Development Corporation, there was a continual and informed liaison between our two establishments.

HENRY WALLACE BUTTS IN WITH AN IDEA

The friction and the interagency troubles over rubber in 1942 and 1943 were directly attributable to the executive order issued by President Roosevelt on April 13, 1942, giving Vice President Henry Wallace's Board of Economic Warfare final policy control over natural rubber procurement abroad, with power to issue directives to the Rubber Reserve Company. This was within six weeks of the signing of the first agreement—with Brazil—and Douglas Allen had already gone to that country on behalf of Rubber Reserve Company to implement the agreement and get production started.

Mr. Wallace and his chief aide in the BEW, Milo Perkins, promptly began to deploy platoons of their ideological pals into South America. They set up an almost complete parallel operating organization to Rubber Reserve's—and damn the expense!

Some of his social-reformer colleagues persuaded Mr. Wallace that living conditions would be improved and production increased if he would give food away free to everyone in the Amazon Basin. He had the power to try to do this, or to direct us to do it.

When Douglas Allen returned to Washington from Brazil in the summer of 1942, I thought in view of his intimate knowledge of the Amazon he might be able to dissuade the Vice President from such a grandiose gesture. I arranged a luncheon to bring the two men together. Mr. Perkins was also invited, as were Messrs. Clayton and Klossner of our organization and Dean Acheson of the State Department, and perhaps a few others.

Let Mr. Allen tell the story of that luncheon.

"I was placed next to the Vice President at the table," Mr. Allen recalls. "He inquired how many people there were in the Amazon, and I replied that I didn't know and no one else knew, but the best estimates were in the neighborhood of 1,500,000. He then asked me whether it was not a fact that the people of the Amazon Basin suffered from an inadequate and unbalanced diet. I replied that that was entirely true. The Vice President then made a rough mental calculation and said that in his opinion 350,000 tons of staple foodstuffs, particularly including flour fortified with vitamins, would enable the people of the Amazon to have a more adequate and balanced diet. This, in turn, he argued, would make them more productive and thereby aid the rubber program. He, therefore, proposed that food be given away free to everyone in the Amazon.

"In commenting on this proposal, I mentioned that there was an acute shortage of shipping and that if the 350,000 tons of foodstuffs were to be taken out of the allocation of cargo space to Brazil, which was already inadequate to meet that country's essential import needs, I felt sure the Government of Brazil could not and would not agree. On the other hand, if an additional allocation of space were to be asked of the War Shipping Administration, I doubted they would be able or willing to provide it.

"The Vice President replied that that was no problem at all.

"I then remarked that, assuming shipping space and the 350,000 tons of foodstuffs were available, it was my opinion that if food were given away free to everyone in the Amazon Basin we would, instead of getting more rubber, get no rubber at all, since the people down there, like most people all over the world, work only because they want to eat. If they were fed free, many of them would do no work at all and, therefore, there would be little or no rubber.

"A long discussion followed in which everyone present participated with the Vice President still insisting the free food should be sent. Finally, Milo Perkins leaned across the table and said, 'Henry, I guess we just can't give away food in the Amazon and still get any rubber; maybe we had better forget about it,' whereupon he and the Vice President departed. That was the end of the proposal for the time being.

"On another occasion I was talking with Mr. Clayton and Vice President Wallace about a recommendation I had made that certain airplane facilities be made available in the Amazon. The Vice President asked what was being done about it. Mr. Clayton replied that he had sent my recommendation to the Aviation Division of Defense Supplies Corporation for study of the technical details and to prepare an estimate of the capital investment and operating cost of the proposed facilities.

"At that Vice President Wallace turned purple in the face and said to Mr. Clayton: 'Will, you don't mean to say that you are thinking of cost!!'

"Mr. Clayton replied that in order to obtain the funds required that it would be necessary to have an estimate made of the original capital investment and how much would be needed to operate the airplane service. It was apparent that, to the Vice President, the idea that anyone under any circumstances would think about the cost of any government project was either inconceivable or altogether reprehensible."

Mr. Wallace did not long delay in returning to his pet free-food project. Soon after Mr. Allen got back to Brazil, he received a cablegram from the BEW once more pressing the question. The message authorized and directed him to begin immediately the purchase of 350,000 tons of foodstuffs for prompt shipment to the Amazon. The cable advised him the BEW was arranging to send an 11,000-ton ship loaded with foodstuffs, including a large quantity of rice.

In reply Mr. Allen cabled the Wallace organization that, for three years prior to 1942, the entire imports of the Amazon Basin, including bottled beverages, had averaged only about 110,000 tons annually, and that since the people down there were still alive and apparently in as good condition as they had ever been it was reasonable to assume they did not need 350,000 extra tons of food. As for the rice which the BEW was shipping, he pointed out that the state of Pará, at the mouth of the Amazon, was a large exporter of that commodity and even then was shipping rice to the Guianas and the West Indies.

Another cable from the BEW advised Mr. Allen the Wallace organization had arranged with a Latin American oil pool for oil companies to purchase rubber at "their gasoline filling stations along the Amazon." Apparently some of Mr. Wallace's "progressive-minded" disciples had picked up an idea from the arrangements made by our Rubber Reserve Company in buying scrap rubber in the United States through the ubiquitous gasoline stations. It was necessary for Mr. Allen to remind them that there are no gasoline filling stations along the Amazon. The large oil companies merely had some storage tanks at Belém. They sold gasoline and other petroleum products to merchants, who, in turn, distributed them in tins or drums throughout the Basin. Up the river at Manaus the oil companies did not have even storage tanks, let alone filling stations.

Mr. Allen's message also observed that the United States had no right to buy rubber in Brazil from producers, since, under the terms of our intergovernmental agreement, all rubber within the country was to be purchased by the chosen instrumentality of the Brazilian Government (at that time the Banco da Borracha) which, in turn, sold it to the United States f.o.b. shipside.

On another occasion in 1942, Mr. Allen received a BEW cablegram stating that, according to a report from one of their field "technicians," social conditions along one of the remote tributaries of the Amazon were deplorable. The BEW demanded to know what he proposed to do to remedy the situation. Mr. Allen replied that our job was the production of rubber. He pointed out that social conditions in some parts of the United States were still deplorable despite the efforts of federal and state governmental agencies extending over many years, so it seemed hardly surprising that conditions in a remote area of the Amazon Basin were not altogether ideal.

The Vice President's disciples proposed sending a large American personnel to the Amazon to engage in many kinds of activities which, under the terms of the rubber agreement between the United States and Brazil, we were not to engage in without specific consent of the Brazilian Government. Large sums were to be spent on various developments, some of which were so "social" as to be practically eleemosynary. Finally, the BEW drew up an organizational chart of the way they thought the rubber program and the more abundant life should be integrated. The planners contemplated, as I recall it, an expenditure of some $400,000,000 on an "Amazon Project."

Mr. Allen informed Mr. Clayton that, in his opinion, no matter what was done in the Amazon, it would be impossible to obtain enough rubber to justify spending $400,000,000. He rightly predicted that, if the natural rubber program continued under the direction of the BEW, there would be a national scandal. He asked to be relieved of responsibility for the Amazon part of the program unless the BEW was removed from the picture.

JEFFERS GIVES WALLACE THE BOOT

A few months previously, Mr. Jeffers had been appointed Rubber Director. Mr. Allen asked if Mr. Clayton and I would have any objection if he placed the whole situation before Director Jeffers. We had no objection, so Mr. Allen went to Mr. Jeffers and told him, if nothing was done to end the interagency interferences, he planned to resign and publish his reasons for doing so. He added that, if Mr. Jeffers would remove the BEW, he would be glad to continue his endeavors to keep the program on a proper, realistic basis.

Mr. Jeffers remarked that Mr. Allen was asking him to remove the Vice President of the United States from a responsibility which had been assigned to him by the President. Politically, he said, that was not an easy thing to do. But he promised to think it over. A little later he sent for Mr. Allen and told him he had decided to remove the BEW from all connection with the natural rubber program. Shortly thereafter, in January, 1943, he issued a directive to that effect. As a result, the whole rubber procurement program once more came back to the RFC.

We then formed a new subsidiary, Rubber Development Corporation, and, with Director Jeffers' concurrence, vested in it sole jurisdiction over the procurement and development of natural rubber outside the United States, subject to such policy directives as he might issue. Rubber Reserve Company continued its functions within the United States.

The State Department and other government agencies with a vital interest in the rubber program were represented on the new corporation's board. The RFC named only two of the directors, Mr. Clayton, who was elected chairman, and Mr. Allen, who was asked to be president.

As rapidly as possible, Rubber Development Corporation liquidated the unsound elements of the BEW's Amazon projects, and others.

From then on, complete harmony and cooperation prevailed both within the Corporation and in its relations to other agencies and all the foreign governments concerned.

A few months later, President Roosevelt removed Mr. Wallace from the Board of Economic Warfare and reconstituted that organization into the Office of Economic Warfare, at whose head he placed Leo T. Crowley, who had previously been Alien Property Custodian and, prior to that, chairman of the Federal Deposit Insurance Corporation. Mr. Crowley got along well with Mr. Clayton and me. He agreed to exercise his new authority, so far as rubber was concerned, only by taking over the chairmanship of the board of our new Rubber Development Corporation and leave our operation intact.

There was, he and I agreed, to be no other link between his Office of Economic Warfare and our Rubber Development Corporation, which would continue to function on its own in Latin America. At Mr. Crowley's suggestion Mr. Clayton, after handing over the chairmanship, continued to serve as adviser to the Corporation.

One of the inheritances from the BEW's meddlings in rubber which we proceeded to liquidate was the project in Haiti for growing cryptostegia, a vinelike rubber-yielding plant. This project, as I mentioned earlier, had been initiated and carried out in pursuance of one of Mr. Wallace's directives against the advice of our people. The BEW originally proposed the planting of 100,000 acres in cryptostegia and of spending $30,000,000 on the development. Later the acreage was reduced to 40,000. On it they produced exactly five and one-half tons of rubber at a cost of $6,725,615.64. That works out at $546 per pound of rubber.

As opposed to Mr. Wallace's philosophies, our own school of thought had, throughout the program, been to maintain a profitable and stable price for rubber, but not a boom price. We tried to work in close cooperation and partnership with the governments of the producing countries, having scrupulous regard for their sovereignty and national pride. We never concerned ourselves with reforming the habits and customs of foreign peoples.

We sought to limit American personnel in those countries to the minimum and to depend to the greatest feasible extent upon local agencies and regular trade channels, avoiding, so far as possible, competition with established private enterprise. The peak number of American personnel engaged in the Latin American rubber program, in Washington and in the field, was 725 in June, 1943. This number was gradually reduced by a policy of replacing Americans in the field with local personnel whenever warrantable.

NELSON ROCKEFELLER EXTENDS HIS ASSISTANCE

I do not, of course, pretend that we did not make mistakes or were innocent of inefficiencies; but we did try to administer the affairs of the Corporation in as businesslike a manner as wartime conditions and objectives permitted, and we sought the services of the ablest and most experienced personnel available. "It is obvious, however," as Messrs. Allen and Francis Adams Truslow wrote in a report to me on the wild rubber procurement program, "that operations as complex as those of the Rubber Development Corporation, conducted in the most primitive areas of some seventeen foreign countries through a hastily improvised wartime organization and in conjunction with the governments of those countries, could not be carried out without some instances of waste and extravagance."

In carrying out the rubber development program we had the able help of many men long experienced in the areas concerned. Mr. Allen had been engaged nearly all his business career in foreign trade. At the suggestion of Thomas K. Finletter, then special assistant to the Secretary of State, Mr. Clayton and I asked Mr. Allen at the very inception of the program in March, 1942, to take charge of procurement in the Amazon Basin countries, Brazil, Peru, and Bolivia. Serving without compensation, he remained with us until he resigned as president of the Rubber Development Corporation, October 1, 1944.

He was succeeded in that office by Mr. Truslow, who had been our special representative in Peru from the start of the program until February, 1944, when he was brought to Washington as vice president of the Corporation. Mr. Truslow resigned November 19, 1945. He is now president of the New York Curb Exchange.

J. W. Bicknell, who was executive vice president of Rubber Development Corporation, had, for many years, been in charge of the Far Eastern operations of the United States Rubber Company.

Henry Linam, the Corporation's vice president in charge of field operations, had spent seventeen years in Latin America, twelve of them as president of the Standard Oil Company of Venezuela.

Maurice McAshan of Anderson, Clayton & Company was Rubber Development's resident vice president in Brazil, of which country he had intimate knowledge. He had previously been chairman of the United States Purchasing Commission in Brazil.

R. B. Bogardus of the Goodyear Tire & Rubber Company was also a vice president of Rubber Development Corporation.

James Roberts of the Firestone Tire & Rubber Company was associated with the program from its inception.

E. E. Kaiser, the manager of our Amazon division, had spent many years in South America, a number of them as acting managing director of General Motors Corporation in Brazil.

Carl Sylvester, who directed the Rio de Janeiro division, had lived for thirty years in Brazil, where he managed public utility properties.

James Russell, manager of the Rio division, had spent most of his business career in the cotton business in Brazil and Mexico.

The Corporation was fortunate in securing the services, as officers or in other responsible positions, for the length of time their private affairs would permit, of a number of other men with much experience in Latin America or other foreign fields.

Among these gentlemen were William E. Mitchell, head of the Georgia Power Company; Paul B. McKee, president of the Portland Gas & Coke Company and formerly in charge of public utility properties in Brazil; C. B. Manifold of the Department of Agriculture, who organized and directed the staff of field technicians; Charles Atwell, who had previously supervised construction of the pipe line for the South American Gulf Oil Company in Colombia; Frederick Utz, formerly in charge of public utility properties in Chile, and Donald Knapp, formerly general manager of the rubber plantations of the United States Rubber Company in the Far East.

The American rubber trade in general made its facilities and personnel freely available to the Corporation. So did many other private companies experienced in South American business. The William Wrigley, Jr., Company initiated and carried on for some time a particularly successful operation in Nicaragua. The Chicle Development Company likewise acted for the Corporation in certain field areas. Several oil companies were also most cooperative.

William Beck and Nathaniel Royall of the RFC served as financial officers of Rubber Development Corporation, and H. Clay Johnson of the RFC's legal department was its general counsel. All of these gentlemen had the unselfish devotion and wise guidance of Mr. Clayton.

Nelson Rockefeller, as Coordinator of Inter-American Affairs, extended the full assistance of his organization throughout Latin America. He rendered us much aid, through the Inter-American Institute, in the serious public-health problems involved in getting wild rubber out of barely accessible areas in the tropic jungle.

28

✲

COLLECTING SCRAP RUBBER

A FEW weeks after Pearl Harbor I suggested to Donald M. Nelson, who had just been made chairman of the War Production Board, that an agency be set up to see that no one should waste a pound of rubber, and that a campaign to collect scrap rubber be started. My memo to Mr. Nelson read:

THE SECRETARY OF COMMERCE
WASHINGTON

February 27, 1942

Dear Donald:

As you know, we have a very substantial stockpile of raw rubber. Including some still afloat and stocks with the manufacturers, we have approximately 700,000 tons. There is more than 1,000,000 tons of scrap or used rubber in the country, that should yield from 40 to 50% of usable rubber, providing at least another 500,000 tons.

With the proper conservation and use of this rubber, it will last until we can bring in the synthetic production, but we will not have any to spare; and unless very strict regulations and enforcement of those regulations are put into effect throughout the country, we will find ourselves short of rubber vital to our war effort.

It seems to me that you should create a department, under extra-competent direction, to see that no one wastes a single pound of rubber. Probably the first and greatest offender will be found in the Government agencies, particularly the War Department (including the Quartermaster Corps, Air Corps, Ordnance Department, Corps of Engineers, Signal Corps, Chemical Warfare, and Medical Department, listed in order of rubber volume consumption), the Navy Department (including the Bureau of Ships, Yards & Docks, U.S. Marine Corps, Aeronautics, Supplies & Accounts, Coast Guard, Medicine & Surgery, and Ordnance, listed in order of rubber volume consumption).

Several months were permitted to elapse before the campaign was launched. President Roosevelt announced the first scrap-rubber collection drive on June 12, 1942. Rubber Reserve Company then offered to buy scrap tires and miscellaneous scrap rubber at $25 per short ton in carload lots at any shipping point in the country. A few days later the Office of Price Administration amended the maximum sales prices at consuming centers to range from $10.50 to $34 per short ton for tires, from $5 to $37.50 for miscellaneous scrap rubber and from 4 to 18 cents per pound for tubes and mechanical and unvulcanized scrap rubber. It was our joint intention to relieve collectors of shipping expenses, which in some cases were prohibiting sales.

To carry out the program Rubber Reserve entered into agreements with four of the larger scrap-rubber dealers, promising to reimburse them for their actual expenses. Oil companies under the direction of the Petroleum Industry War Council conducted the first drive, which lasted about four weeks and resulted in the collection of 454,000 tons of scrap rubber.

The oil companies paid 1 cent a pound, or $20 a ton, for the rubber and sold it to our Rubber Reserve Company for $25 a ton. The amounts resulting from the differential of $5 a ton, plus returns from the sale of donated rubber aggregating approximately $2,500,000, were distributed among four organizations; namely, United Service Organizations, Inc., Army Emergency Relief, Navy Relief Society, and the American Red Cross. All expenses of conducting the campaign, estimated to have cost several million dollars in out-of-pocket expenditures alone, were willingly paid by the oil companies.

After the first drive the country's four largest scrap-rubber dealers carried on the program. These nominees were Nat E. Berzen, Inc., Lowenthal Company, H. Muehlstein & Co., and A. Schulman. Rubber Reserve became the sole distributor of scrap rubber, acquiring altogether some 1,150,127 short tons at a purchase cost of $29,857,645, an average of $25.96 per short ton. Wartime sales at OPA ceiling prices, which averaged $25.87 a ton, consisted of 987,764 short tons, from which the proceeds were $25,460,930. This was expensive—but we got the rubber!

It cost us almost as much to handle, store, ship, and distribute the scrap as to buy it. This fact ran the Corporation's wartime losses nearly $23,000,000 deeper into the red, or more than $22 a ton.

At the end of the war Rubber Reserve Company, which had been methodically liquidating its stockpile, had on hand about 150,000 short tons of miscellaneous scrap, which rapidly diminished in value almost to zero—another loss of nearly $5,000,000.

29

---- ☼ ----

METALS RESERVE COMPANY

Building the World's Biggest Tin Smelter from Scratch—
Copper Becomes Precious Metal—Donald Nelson Makes
Us Junk Dealers—Flying the Oceans with Quartz Crystals
and Platinum—Arsenic and Poison Gas

METALS Reserve Company, created by the RFC on June 28, 1940, spent nearly $2,750,000,000 before the war's conclusion in acquiring half a hundred different minerals and metals in fifty-one foreign countries, thirty-eight states of the Union, and Alaska and the Philippines. It disbursed nearly a billion dollars more, partly on freight, storage, and operating expenses, but mostly in subsidies and premium price payments granted to stimulate the development of new sources and the marginal production of the last possible pound of those metals and ores which were not in sufficient supply to forge all the needed implements of war.

Long before Pearl Harbor, in cooperation with the State Department, Metals Reserve made exclusive agreements with South American countries which denied vital supplies of almost the whole Western Hemisphere to Japanese buyers as well as to the Rome-Berlin Axis. I asked Secretary Hull to let me deal with the North American copper interests who had engaged to sell some of their Latin-American production to Japan, and he agreed. I asked the copper people to say to Japan that they would have to *delay* shipment a few months. At that stage we were not at war with Japan, and I could not ask that contracts be canceled. But the delays were arranged—and we got that copper.

As one of its side lines Metals Reserve Company financed scrap-collection campaigns throughout the United States. As another it financed development projects for the purpose of getting more ores and metals out of South America and Mexico.

The Company did not initiate procurement programs or set its selling prices. In scanning the globe for materials it acted merely as a purchasing agent for the armed services, the War Production Board, and other government institutions. They told us what was wanted, and to whom to sell it. In most cases the Office of Price Administration fixed the selling price. Sometimes this was high enough to give a profit, but often we were obliged to sell at a loss. There was, of course, no way to recover the hundreds of millions shoveled out in subsidies. These went mostly to producers of zinc, copper, and lead, less to those of iron and a few other metals.

Congress specifically authorized our so-called defense subsidiaries to deal in commodities and materials at a loss. Considering its purposes and functions and the wartime circumstances, Metals Reserve Company has come out of its world-wide experiences with a balance sheet for which, I think, no apologies are required. At the end of the war it owed the RFC about $800,000,000. Postwar liquidation of its inventories and other holdings has run up the cumulative net cost of the Corporation to $876,000,000.

The balance sheet at the end of the fiscal year 1949 showed Metals Reserve through the years had spent $2,750,000,000 buying materials and had sold them for $2,800,000,000. It was the other expenses, principally subsidies, which ran the books into the red. But there are compensations not to be measured in dollars and cents. Today our country's defense establishment, which was so ill prepared in 1940, has large stockpiles of strategic materials for future emergencies.

Each metal in which we dealt had its own story, at home or abroad, or both. Without these metals the immense expansion of America's industrial might, a major contribution to the victory, could not have been brought about to the amazement—and envy—of the whole world.

I shall begin with the story of tin.

BUILDING THE WORLD'S BIGGEST TIN SMELTER

In their swift conquest of Holland the Germans captured, among other valuable properties, the principal tin-smelting plant of the western world. One of the many worries in Washington at that moment was the fact that there were utterly no facilities in the United States for smelting tin. And this country was the world's largest consumer of tin.

Today the Government of the United States owns the largest tin smelter on earth, thanks in large part to the push provided by two RFC subsidiaries, Metals Reserve Company and Defense Plant Corporation. The plant, known as the Longhorn smelter, is located at Texas City, on Galveston Bay. In the latter years of the war it was capable of smelting all the ores then available to the Allies. Since the war it has produced a precious stockpile against future emergencies in addition to meeting much of the nation's peacetime needs.

When the President asked me to begin accumulating stocks of tin, I discovered scarcely anyone in this country had ever mined or smelted that metal. Our continent is almost barren of tin-bearing ores. Nor had we any facilities for refining imported ores. We were completely dependent on foreigners for every pig of tin our processors turned into cans, solder, bearings, etc.

Our first move was to communicate with the International Tin Committee in London, controlled by the Dutch and British, who had both political and commercial dominance over most of the Far Eastern and African lands which yield tin-bearing ores. The committee rushed a representative, Victor A. Lowinger, to Washington, in June, 1940. We told him we would readily purchase all the tin produced which could be exported to this country, and which was not bought by private American interests.

As a starter the Dutch and British agreed to raise their controlled production quotas and to sell us, between June, 1940, when we hit off the bargain, and the end of 1941 some 112,500 tons of refined tin produced in the Far East. Before this source of supply was cut off by the invading Japanese early in 1942, we had received from the Dutch and British about 41,000 tons of fine tin and 12,728 tons of fine-tin ore. However, we had also imported for our stockpile about 12,000 tons from China and the Belgian Congo and had brought crude ores up from Bolivia sufficient to manufacture 35,000 tons of tin. At the time the Malayan and Dutch East Indies sources were cut off, a few weeks after Pearl Harbor, our cache of tin and tin ore contained about 100,000 tons.

The ores, of course, had to be smelted. In 1940 the Council of National Defense had appointed a technical committee to study various proposals for the construction and operation of a tin smelter in the United States. During the First World War there had been but two small smelters operating in this country, one in New Jersey, the other in Rhode Island; but they had long since been shut down and dismantled.

After the committee made its report, the Council of National Defense recommended to the RFC early in 1941 that Phelps Dodge Corporation, which produces copper, be given a contract to build and operate a tin smelter, or, if we were unable to make a deal with them, that the American Metal Company should next be considered. Although the Dutch and British both had plenty of experience in tin smelting, few Americans even had a smattering. Notwithstanding that fact, the Office of Production Management told us they wanted an American concern to undertake the task.

When I talked with the officials of Phelps Dodge and American Metal they both confessed there was a good deal about tin smelting they didn't know and couldn't learn overnight. Both companies advised us to employ the Dutch to do the job.

The previous June, when we were negotiating with the International Tin Committee for our stockpile purchases, I had had several meetings with Dr. Johannes van den Broek, a fine Dutch gentleman. He and Mr. Lowinger signed the stockpiling agreement with us on behalf of the International Tin Committee. Of all the men I consulted about tin, Dr. van den Broek struck me as being the ablest. He was managing director of the N. V. Billiton Maatschappij, the principal Dutch tin company. It owned the large smelter at Arnhem, Holland, which the Germans had captured. The Billiton company had taken its name from one of the three tin-ore producing islands which lie between Borneo and Sumatra, the other two being Singkep and Bangka. Dr. van den Broek had come to the United States as head of the Netherlands Purchasing Mission. He later became his government's finance minister. He died in 1946.

In my conversations with him, after the recommended American concerns advised me to let the Dutch build and operate the projected smelter, we soon reached an agreement under which we employed his firm to design and build the plant, paying them a fee. We also employed them to operate it. They set up an American subsidiary, Tin Processing Company, to carry out these tasks.

The question arose as to where the plant should be built. The

American concerns we had originally approached had insisted upon Baltimore, which was convenient to their headquarters. They cited the fact that most of the tin consumed in America is processed into its final forms within the highly industrialized triangle of which Baltimore, Chicago, and Boston are the angles. President Roosevelt suggested we might locate the smelter just outside Quantico, Virginia, about thirty miles south of Washington. I asked Charles B. Henderson, then President of Metals Reserve and a director of the RFC, to have an investigation made of all the ports from Baltimore to Brownsville and to choose the most suitable. Then the Joint Chiefs of Staff for strategic reasons insisted the plant be located between the Alleghenies and the Rockies. To make good sense economically the smelter would have to be built on or very near the seaboard, so the Army's decision almost reduced the possible sites to ports west of Mobile—to the Louisiana and Texas coasts.

Mr. Henderson had drafted G. Temple Bridgman of San Francisco, one of the country's outstanding mining engineers, to be executive vice president of Metals Reserve. It fell to him to seek a location for the smelter. He visited every port from Baltimore to Brownsville and then recommended that the plant be built either at Texas City or at near-by Deer Park, which is on the Houston Ship Channel.

Aside from conforming to the suggestions of the Joint Chiefs of Staff, three factors motivated his choice. Both places were deep-water ports where ores would be unloaded near the smelter; there was an abundance of cheap fuel—natural gas—and, because of the proximity of many oil refineries, a plenitude of hydrochloric acid, a by-product of petroleum and an essential chemical in the smelting of tin ores. The cost of this acid transported to either the Texas City or the Deer Park location was figured at $7.50 a ton, compared with about $20 to Baltimore.

I telephoned Colonel Hugh B. Moore, who was operating the belt railroad serving the port and industries in Texas City, and suggested to him that he give the government a site for the plant. Colonel Moore gave us the site, which was ideal, and the affair was closed.

The first two Dutch technicians who started for Texas City to meet Mr. Bridgman and investigate the site were killed in the airplane crash near Atlanta in which the famous "indestructible" Captain Eddie Rickenbacker, president of Eastern Air Lines, was so seriously injured.

Other Dutch technicians were sent to Texas City, and ground for the smelter was broken in March, 1941. Thirteen months later the first furnace went into production. By then we had sufficient ores on hand to meet the plant's capacity for a full year. I sent a souvenir of the occasion over to the White House with the following note:

Dear Mr. President:

I enclose the "Roosevelt tin dollar" made from the first run of fine tin smelted at the government's wholly-owned tin smelter at Texas City, the first run being on May 5th.

We have an excellent tin smelter that will have an annual capacity of 50,000 tons of fine tin.

As it turned out the capacity was somewhat greater.

During the last three years of the war the Longhorn smelter produced 40 per cent of all the new tin consumed during that period; 90 per cent of its production was in the form of "Three Star" metal, the highest commercial grade. It didn't make money during the war. It wasn't meant to. The Office of Price Administration had set a ceiling of 52 cents on finished tin, while the purchase price of ore bought in Bolivia—our principal source of supply after the Far East fell to the Japanese—was sometimes as high as 60 cents and never lower than 48 cents. The smelting cost, exclusive of amortization of investment in plant and equipment, came to more than 5 cents a pound.

Refined tin produced in the Belgian Congo and in China during the war was purchased by United States Commercial Company, another RFC sudsidiary, at prices, f.o.b. shipping point, which ranged up to 55 cents a pound.

In January, 1941, we contracted with the National Resources Commission of China to buy $39,500,000 worth of tin. After Japan grabbed nearly the whole China coast much of this tin was flown "over the Hump" by the Army's Air Transport Command and brought by air to the United States, an expensive process.

Since the war and up to the time of this writing the Dutch firm has continued to manage the smelter on behalf of the tin division of RFC and has done so very successfully. Until the summer of 1949 the RFC continued to be the sole United States importer of tin and the only source of supply to private American firms. The market has since been reopened to private traders.

COPPER BECOMES A PRECIOUS METAL

Most of us associate copper with the cheapest coin in our pockets, or telephone wires gleaming in the sunshine, or a battery of pans shining in an old-fashioned kitchen. In war copper becomes a truly precious metal. Demand for it started soaring the moment France fell. Consumption swiftly reached unprecedented proportions.

Normally the United States had been self-sufficient in copper and occasionally had exported a surplus to Europe. But as our preparedness program swung heavy industry into vast expansions Metals Reserve was asked to go into foreign lands and buy all the copper it could find. Meanwhile, spurred by our loans and subsidies, domestic output was multiplied several times.

From South and Central American countries we imported copper by the millions of tons. Yet there was never enough at hand to satisfy the insatiable appetite of the war machine. Almost every back lot, barnyard, and junk pile in the country was scouted for scrap from which electrolytic copper could be recovered. The federal mints began using substitutes to coin the Lincoln penny.

Thanks to the subsidy and premium-price policies the base ceiling price of copper was maintained throughout the war at 12 cents a pound. Copper subsidies by Metals Reserve exceeded $75,000,000. On its sales of more than $800,000,000 in copper which it had acquired at home and overseas the Company lost nearly $17,000,000 more.

Since we were dealing in millions of tons, the over-all cost of the copper program to the national economy was comparatively small. It worked out around 1 cent a pound. Compare the 12-cent price level held throughout the Second World War with the fact that at the end of the First World War copper was selling at 32 cents a pound.

Our foreign procurement program began modestly but grew rapidly. President Roosevelt had recommended in December, 1940, that I arrange to buy 100,000 tons of foreign copper, principally in Chile. The following January, after discussions with the Army and Navy Munitions Board, I suggested the importation be increased to 200,000 tons and, in February, to 300,000 tons. In April we boosted the goal again—to 500,000 tons.

Our encouragement of new copper developments in foreign lands

WORLD'S LARGEST TIN SMELTER

The Longhorn Tin Smelter at Texas City, Texas, built by Defense Plant Corporation. Top: Roasting kilns. Bottom: Poling kettles and hand casting line.

WITH THE PRESIDENT AT THE SAN JACINTO BATTLEFIELD

Behind Mr. Jones is Senator Morris Sheppard, of Texas.

was largely undertaken on War Production Board recommendations. After many conferences with James R. Hobbins, president of Anaconda Copper Mining Company, and his principal associates, we advanced about $23,000,000 to one of their subsidiaries, Greene Cananea Copper Company, for the development of a body of low-grade ore and construction of concentrating facilities at Cananea, in the state of Sonora, Mexico, a few miles southwest of Douglas, Arizona. Since the location was within 100 kilometers of the border, and therefore forbidden territory for foreign investment, it was necessary to negotiate with the Mexican government for special permission.

Construction began in October, 1942. The properties started producing in November, 1944. At first the copper from these low-grade ores cost about 20 cents a pound to produce, but we had anticipated it would be more. Anaconda agreed to pay Metals Reserve a royalty up to 1954 of one-tenth of a cent a pound on all the tonnage sold from the Sonora mines at more than 16 cents. In recent years those royalties have been yielding the RFC about $500,000 a year, and I am advised there is a prospect that the agency will eventually break even on what looked to be a losing proportion.

During his negotiations with Anaconda officials my deputy, Will L. Clayton, on January 21, 1942, made an extraordinarily accurate prediction as to how long the war would last. In a memorandum which he sent me that day, reporting on a conference the previous night with Mr. Hobbins and estimating what the project would cost and would yield over given periods, he began one paragraph with the phrase, "If we should assume that the war will be over by mid-summer of 1945." Which is when it did end.

Metals Reserve Company advanced funds to Phelps Dodge Corporation to defray the cost of rehabilitating a Mexican copper mine owned by one of its subsidiaries in Sonora and then bought its production at cost plus 1½ cents a pound, the wartime average being about 17 cents. It allocated $20,000,000 for new facilities in Chile, and nearly $30,000,000 to provide sixty thousand tons a year of additional production from the Morenci mine in Arizona. We also assisted some Canadian producers to meet capital costs necessary to increase their output.

Since every ounce was urgently in demand as fast as delivered, it was not until a few months before the end of hostilities that the Company was able to begin stockpiling a reserve. There were times during

1942 and 1943 when the supply was so far behind the expanding consumption program that General Electric, Western Electric, and various other large concerns busy with war orders were threatened with temporary shutdowns of some of their operations. During one phase of the shortage Metals Reserve called the leaders of the copper industry together for help in searching out every bit of unused copper the country possessed. They organized the Copper Recovery Corporation to act as our agent in buying scrap and idle inventories, on the sale of which we lost more than $10,000,000. Among the items acquired were forty million square feet of insect-screening which the Army and Navy found useful in the tropics.

DONALD NELSON MAKES US JUNK DEALERS

In addition to copper Metals Reserve collected many types of scrap—iron and steel, brass, nickel, tin, anything that could be remelted and fed into the voracious jaws of the war industries. It was in February, 1942, that Donald M. Nelson, chairman of the War Production Board, made junk dealers of us all. He thought we might require $750,000,000 for that end of our business, and would probably lose about half of it. I asked Senator Charles B. Henderson, president of Metals Reserve, to set the sum aside. Actually, when the war ended, our losses as scrap dealers had come to less than $30,-000,000.

The collection campaign included the demolition of buildings, bridges, railroad and streetcar tracks and other installations which had fallen into disuse or were not needed. Streetcar lines were uprooted in about two hundred New Jersey communities. The abandoned New York, Westchester & Boston Railroad was torn up. Using $2,500,000 which Metals Reserve Company had advanced, the Work Projects Administration dispatched workmen from farm to farm and to many a remote spot to pick up scrap metal and rubber. Some of it was donated by the owners. The remainder we bought.

Subsidies were offered to stimulate the recovery of metal from tin cans. We bought the entire inventories of surplus parts and materials owned by five aircraft manufacturers.

Steel mills needed scrap in such quantities that the amount available in the United States, however far and wide we searched, was not enough. The Company ordered its agents to ferret out scrap in Alaska, Cuba, and the cities of Central and South America.

We even resorted to requisitioning. About 140,000 tons of iron and steel were acquired in that way, mostly from railroads. A few branch lines were taken over in their entirety.

We engaged C. Walter Nichols, chairman of the board of Nichols Engineering & Research Corporation, of New York, to head up the scrap procurement program. As chief rustler he obtained the gratuitous services of Philip W. Frieder of Cleveland, who had formerly been president of the Institute of Scrap Iron & Steel. Mr. Frieder seemed to know all the principal wreckers and scrap dealers the country over. From a telephone in Washington he got in touch with one after another of them. His persuasiveness often induced a man, as an act of patriotism, to demolish a plant or tear up a car line without profit to his firm, or even at a loss.

In order to increase the iron supply Metals Reserve subsidized marginal producers in certain areas, buying their ore and pig iron at prices above the OPA ceilings at which we distributed it. On that venture, the loss was about $500,000.

NICKEL

For nickel, one of the metals essential to the steel industry, the United States must go abroad for almost its entire supply, mostly to near-by Canada and far-away New Caledonia. During the war, Canadian production was increased. Metals Reserve purchased the New Caledonian output, which in peacetime had largely gone to France. Those two sources accounted for about three-fourths of the wartime imports of nickel.

The remainder came from Cuba, where Metals Reserve collaborated with its sister subsidiary, Defense Plant Corporation, in developing a large deposit. It was mined by the Nicaro Nickel Company, which leased the properties at a dollar a year. Nicaro Nickel Company is owned by the Freeport Sulphur Company. In the construction and equipment of Nicaro's nickel-producing facilities in Cuba and in Wilmington, Delaware, Defense Plant Corporation invested about $33,000,000. Trading in nickel and nickel products during the war cost Metals Reserve nearly $7,000,000.

TUNGSTEN

How we dropped $80,000,000 in preemptive purchasing of Spanish and Portuguese tungsten ores (wolfram) in cooperation with the British, I have reviewed in Chapter 24 on the United States Commercial Company, which was especially created for the purpose of acquiring materials on a noncommercial basis. Our other experiences with tungsten were happier from the standpoint of the balance sheet.

Long before the United States Commercial Company moved into the neutral European markets, Metals Reserve Company had been taking every ton of tungsten that was for sale in Latin America and China. At the outset of our stockpiling campaign North American companies which owned or operated tungsten mines in South America agreed to the request of the State Department to incorporate in their contracts of sale to foreign countries a cancellation clause to be exercised if the materials should be required for the defense program of the United States.

We lost no time making that agreement effective. The companies readily canceled all contracts which gave promise of eventually delivering materials into the hands of the Rome-Berlin Axis. Early in 1941 Metals Reserve set out to sever Japan from Latin American sources of any metal that could be used in waging war. By then the scramble for tungsten had pushed up its price in South American markets to about double the peacetime quotation of $8 per unit. (There are sixty-seven units of tungsten to a metric ton.) In May, 1941, we engaged to buy Bolivia's entire output for the next three years. Originally they agreed to sell at $17 a unit; but because of the activities of other buyers, particularly the Japanese, they asked us to increase the offer to $21 per unit, or above $1,300 a ton. We did. It was no time for haggling.

A little later we contracted similarly with Peru, Argentina, and Mexico and opened negotiations to the same end with other Latin American countries. The resulting contracts closed that continent to Axis buyers.

Of the 62,000 tons of tungsten ore and concentrates imported by Metals Reserve during the war, more than 14,000 came from China. Like Chinese tin, much of the Chinese tungsten was flown "over the Hump" and brought to the United States in Army planes. The War

Department did not charge us for that expensive emergency service. Based on commercial air-line rates it was estimated that this free transportation saved the Company about $6,000,000. More than half a million dollars' worth of our tungsten purchases was lost in storage in China or en route. We contracted for $30,000,000 worth of Chinese tungsten ores and concentrates as early as October, 1940, and arranged in January, 1941, to buy an additional $16,000,000 worth from the National Resources Commission of China.

At home Metals Reserve motivated a phenomenal expansion of tungsten production by offering both temptingly high prices and substantial subsidies. Most of the domestic output came from three operators in Idaho, California, and Nevada.

ZINC

The metal most heavily subsidized by Metals Reserve was zinc. Premium prices and grants paid to stimulate its production exceeded $100,000,000. The war brought such extraordinary demands for zinc, particularly as an ingredient of cartridge brass, that it became necessary not only to encourage expansion of the domestic supply, which had been adequate in peacetime, but to buy more than two million tons of ores and concentrates in Canada, Mexico, Australia, Argentina, Peru, and Bolivia.

While Defense Supplies Corporation was subsidizing the producers, Defense Plant Corporation was financing construction and rehabilitation of smelters needed to refine the constantly increasing deliveries of ore. To guarantee a future stockpile, Metals Reserve Company entered into long-term contracts with various concerns both for ore supplies and for the refined products. These contracts enabled the companies to enlarge their facilities. As a further stimulus we made cash advances against future production and in that manner brought about the reopening of old mines and the refitting of abandoned smelters.

What made the zinc subsidies necessary, if we were to avoid any impairment of the military schedule, was the government's decision to hold to a ceiling price of 8½ cents. By the summer of 1941 it had become obvious that the desired zinc production wouldn't be forthcoming at that price, particularly from the important tristate area, Missouri, Oklahoma, and Kansas, where ore reserves of profitable grade were speedily approaching exhaustion. We had to make the mining of marginal ores a paying proposition.

In 1942 the subsidies were supplemented by the premium price plan. Under that scheme, operators of copper, lead, and zinc mines sold their output at OPA ceiling prices and received premium payments from Metals Reserve on all production in excess of quotas established by a joint committee of War Production Board and Office of Price Administration representatives on the basis of the previous year's production.

Up to June 30, 1945, the Company had made premium payments of about $211,000,000, distributed among thirty-one hundred mines. In its actual trading in zinc Metals Reserve's books recorded a wartime gain in excess of $2,000,000; but that figure does not take into account the vast sums poured out in subsidies to zinc-mine operators.

CHROME ORES

For the manufacture of armor plate and projectiles chrome ores were essential. The steel industry also required them for other purposes, as did refractories and certain chemical plants. Normally only a small amount of these ores is obtained in the United States. From 1940 onward Metals Reserve bought chrome ores in practically every available foreign area—South Africa, Russia, Turkey, Cuba, the Philippines, Rhodesia, India, Canada, and elsewhere.

To get at ore deposits in the Custer National Forest in Montana, Metals Reserve spent $700,000 building hard-surface roads while Defense Plant Corporation was investing $12,300,000 in three Montana plants which we engaged Anaconda Copper Mining Company to operate. We also obtained chrome ore from deposits of black sand in Oregon.

The Company bought antimony in Mexico, Bolivia, and China, mercury in Mexico, Chile, Canada, and Peru, manganese in Asia, Africa, and South America, crude platinum in Colombia, and refined platinum in Russia.

MICA

Constant developments in radio equipment and electronics made mica one of the most sought-after minerals in wartime. The structure of micas permits them to be divided easily into extremely thin sheets, often less than a thousandth of an inch in thickness. Before the war Brazil had supplied only 2 per cent of the world's output; the United States, only 10 per cent. Three-fourths of the production came from India.

Metals Reserve set out to expand Brazilian and American sources to the fullest possible extent. In Brazil our agents advanced funds against future production, bought and loaned machinery to mine operators, and offered tempting prices to obtain exclusive sales to the United States and Great Britain. At home several hundred thousands of dollars were advanced to hundreds of mica producers to cover development costs and provide working capital. Much of the money was unrecoverable.

The responsibility for acquiring and allocating India's entire production to the Allied nations was assigned, early in 1942, to the British-supervised Joint Mica Mission. They promptly eliminated private buyers from the inflated markets. Metals Reserve agreed to share the costs of the Indian program. At the same time we formed Colonial Mica Corporation, a nonprofit organization with paid-in capital of only $10, to act as our agent in buying, processing, and distributing foreign and domestic mica, all its outlays to be paid by Metals Reserve. By the end of the war we had bought nearly five million pounds of mica, of which 11 per cent, rather than the prewar 2 per cent, came from Brazil, while the United States provided close to 15 per cent rather than its customary 10 per cent.

Many of the procurement programs were of such magnitude no one industrial concern could handle them. In such cases we would persuade an entire industry to form a nonprofit corporation with nominal capital to act as agent for Metals Reserve Company. This was done by the copper industry in forming Copper Recovery Corporation to handle the scrap collections, by the steel industry in creating Steel Recovery Corporation, and by the tin industry in forming Tin Salvage Institute to collect old cans.

Whenever possible outsiders with skill and experience were hired to act as Metals Reserve's agents. We employed specialists to arrange foreign purchases and importations. Altogether Metals Reserve Company entered into 419 agent contracts. For the most part the agents operated without profit. The industrial specialists whom we hired individually to obtain quick results were generally paid a commission or fee based upon the volume of business handled.

German submarines took a comparatively small toll from sea-borne metals. To a great extent quartz crystals, like platinum, were spared the perils of the wartime oceans. They were so urgently needed in the making of radio transmitting and receiving sets, detection devices, and certain precision instruments that a large proportion of the seven million pounds which Metals Reserve imported were delivered by airplane, mostly from Brazil.

The Navy Airplane Shuttle Service carried the crystals from the interior to Natal whence Army planes ferried them to Miami, Florida. Metals Reserve did not replace the industry's private buyers. They supplied more than half the country's wartime requirements. For the air transportation from Brazil the private importers of quartz crystals were charged only $1.50 a pound. So extensive were these importations that the cargo charge ultimately aggregated more than $900,000. Until the end of the conflict allocations restricted the use of quartz crystals to manufacturers of war materials. In its trading in the crystals Metals Reserve recorded a profit of nearly $4,000,000.

SILVER AND GOLD

Though silver was not among the metals designated either strategic or critical, we were directed by the War Production Board in 1942 to buy 10,000,000 ounces of foreign silver at 45 cents an ounce— 10 cents an ounce above the Treasury Department's price. Subsequent directives increased our purchases to 25,000,000 ounces. The differential, which I recommended and President Roosevelt approved, was necessary to maintain production at satisfactory levels, to keep the Mexican Government satisfied, and to support the economy of that country.

Metals Reserve also acquired gold—nearly 375,000 ounces of it— as a by-product from the refining of copper, zinc, and other metallic ores. We usually sold the gold at prevailing market prices to the smelters and refiners of the ores from which it had come. The gold cost Metals Reserve, exclusive of interest and administrative expenses, $13,022,749. Receipts from its sale totaled $13,022,866. Thus it gave us a net gain of $117—one of the smallest sums to be found in our books.

While Defense Plant Corporation was investing hundreds of millions in aluminum facilities for the aircraft program, Metals Reserve made heavy purchases abroad of both primary aluminum and bauxite, which is used in making the metal. Buying, storing, and distributing Canadian primary aluminum was one of Metals Reserve's largest single enterprises. We purchased it to the extent of nearly $250,000,000 and lost more than $35,000,000 selling it at or below ceiling prices to American manufacturers and fabricators. About 7 per cent of our Canadian aluminum purchases went to the British, and about 3 per cent to the Russians, under lend-lease agreements.

To help finance Aluminum Company of Canada's plant expansions Metals Reserve loaned that concern $68,500,000 at 3 per cent. The loan was repaid before the close of the war with interest amounting to nearly $4,000,000.

In Greenland, where very few people ever go shopping, Metals Reserve purchased 40,000 tons of ore containing cryolite, a substance used in preparing alumina for the electrolytic recovery of metallic aluminum.

ARSENIC AND POISON GAS

Poison gas was not employed in the Second World War. Had the enemy used it the Allies were prepared to retaliate. The War Production Board told us in June, 1942, to encourage the production of arsenic, which is needed in the manufacture of lewisite, a poison gas. In peacetime most of the arsenic consumed in the United States is used in agricultural insecticides and weed exterminators. The Chemical Warfare Service could not legally pay a price higher than the established OPA ceiling of 3½ cents a pound, and quickly expanded production could not be achieved at that figure. So Metals Reserve contracted with Jardine Mining Company to purchase 5,000 tons of refined arsenic at a subsidy price of 6 cents a pound. To finance expansions the Jardine Company borrowed $365,000 from the Smaller War Plants Corporation.

Before the end of the war, Metals Reserve acquired nearly 37,000 tons of arsenic—28,000 tons from domestic sources, the remainder from abroad—and, of course, lost money on every ton of it.

The Company leased the Gold Hill mines in Utah from the United States Smelting, Refining & Mining Company and operated them on a royalty basis. Not all of the wartime production of arsenic went into the poison-gas stockpile. Some was assigned to the customary killing of bugs and weeds.

The delegation to outside agents of as many of its undertakings as seemed feasible enabled Metals Reserve to keep its pay roll and other administrative expenses remarkably low. There was never a time when it employed more than 450 men and women. Yet frequently between 8,000 and 10,000 persons in the employ of firms with which the Company had agreements would be devoting full time to our business. From its creation in 1940 to its dissolution in 1945 Metals Reserve's pay roll and its out-of-pocket expenditures for personal and professional services totaled only a little above $5,000,000, a modest sum for an organization that dealt with nearly $3,000,000,000 worth of materials bought all over the globe.

We were fortunate in the types of men who pitched in to help with the job. One of the executives who came to us on a voluntary basis was G. Temple Bridgman, who was consulting engineer with Guggenheim Brothers. He had been a leading figure in the metals trade both in this country and abroad for many years. Henry DeWitt Smith, vice president of the Newmont Mining Company, was loaned to us to take charge of domestic operations. We borrowed David D. Irwin (now a vice president of the Pure Oil Company) to manage the procurement of foreign metals. Harry Hamilton (now a vice president of the New York Trust Company) was another of the well known mining authorities loaned to us. From within the RFC family Metals Reserve drew Harvey J. Gunderson, later an RFC director, who had much procurement experience with the Army as well as with our organization. When Mr. Bridgman returned to his own affairs in 1944, Mr. Gunderson succeeded him as Metals Reserve's executive vice president.

Like the RFC's other wartime subsidiaries Metals Reserve obtained all of its operating funds by borrowing money from the RFC at 1 per cent—the rate we were paying the Treasury. When dissolved on June 30, 1945, Metals Reserve owed the RFC for capital, loans, and interest nearly $700,000,000. Its net losses attributable to subsidies, premium payments, and trading activities up to that date exceeded $300,000,000, and its inventories represented an investment of nearly $540,000,000.

30

---------------------------------- ☼ ----------------------------------

THE WAR DAMAGE CORPORATION

IMMEDIATELY following the attack on Pearl Harbor, the American people, particularly those living on the Pacific coast, became frightened about the possibility of being bombed. To our knowledge, insurance companies were not prepared to write this character of coverage, so I suggested to the President that RFC create a war damage insurance company with a capital of $100,000,000. He approved the plan, and I immediately announced it through a press release which was carried by newspapers throughout the country:

FEDERAL LOAN AGENCY

WASHINGTON

December 13, 1941

Jesse Jones, Federal Loan Administrator, announced today that, with the approval of the President, the Reconstruction Finance Corporation has created the War Insurance Corporation, with a capital of $100,000,000 to provide reasonable protection against losses resulting from enemy attacks which may be sustained by owners of property in Continental United States through damage to or destruction of buildings, structures and personal property, including goods, growing crops and orchards.

Pending completion of details, any such losses will be protected from December 31, 1941, up to a total of $100,000,000.

Accounts, bills, currency, debts, evidences of debt, money, notes, securities, paintings and other objects of art will not be covered.

For the time being, no premium will be charged for this protection, and no declaration or reports required, unless there is a loss.

Other terms and conditions for such protection will be announced as established. No protection will be available to owners of property who, in the opinion of the President, are unfriendly to the United States.

We immediately set about organizing on a business basis and, as was our custom in operating in any new field, summoned a group of insurance executives to meet with us in Washington. We were able to work out a plan with them whereby the industry would write the insurance and take a 10 per cent participation in the enterprise; that is, sharing in the profits or losses to the extent of 10 per cent. The companies and their organizations were to be paid as near as could be determined their out-of-pocket expenses in handling the business, including modest commissions to the agents who wrote the insurance.

Obviously, people should pay a reasonable premium for such insurance, just as they pay for any other insurance. Charges for the insurance were arrived at by consultation with the industry, and these were not too expensive, since we knew the spread would naturally be very wide and most people would want protection.

A few large bombs dropped on Los Angeles or San Francisco, or any other big city, would have been calamitous both in their effect and in the cost. Happily, the accident of geography and the circumstances of the conflict spared our country the destructive ordeals suffered by the principal cities of our principal allies and all of our enemies. The existence of our War Damage Corporation, which was in fact the Government of the United States operating under that name, gave millions throughout the country a sense of financial security.

On March 27, 1942, Congress ratified our informal creation of the War Damage Corporation and directed the RFC to provide it with funds up to $1,000,000,000 when requested to do so by the Secretary of Commerce with the approval of the President, The borrowing authority of the RFC was also increased by that amount in the same Act.

The operation eventually included the services of 546 fire insurance companies and 83 casualty insurance companies.

Some of our largest industries took out policies of enormous amounts. The properties of the United States Steel Corporation were covered by one policy for $1,297,000,000. The American Telephone

& Telegraph Company, which left it to its various subsidiaries to decide whether they would take insurance and to what extent, was covered by several policies totaling $1,419,000,000.

Our insurance policies provided for payment to policy holders on losses resulting from enemy attack or from actions or accidents which might occur in resisting enemy attack. The latter provision we stretched generously. For example, we indemnified policy holders in Brooklyn for damages caused to their property by an explosion on a Navy cruiser which was approaching its berth after a tour of sea duty. We paid for damages done to property in the Los Angeles region by falling anti-aircraft missiles. We also paid for the damage done to the Equitable Building in the Wall Street district on March 13, 1942, when one of eight shells accidentally fired from an anti-aircraft gun on the East River waterfront exploded against a cornice of the skyscraper just beneath the floor in which the Bankers Club has its premises. No one was injured, and we never learned where the other seven shells landed.

In the San Francisco Bay area a claim of $10 was paid for damage caused by the impact of a Navy blimp against the insured's dwelling. The blimp had been on actual patrol against the enemy, and its pilot had reported it was investigating a suspicious looking oil slick. About three hours later the blimp drifted in from sea, unmanned, partially deflated, with engine stopped and door open—another of the war's mysteries.

A claim exceeding $12,500 was paid for the destruction of a building which resulted from the falling of an American plane shot down by U.S. forces because of mistaken identity due to lack of signals from the aircraft. In connection with this claim, the Corporation took the position that when, through an honest but mistaken belief, U.S. forces took action to oppose a supposed enemy, the action constituted "resistance to enemy attack" within the meaning of the statute authorizing us to provide compensation.

From the Philippines came six hundred claims, aggregating $172,-806,361. So far as War Damage Corporation was concerned, these were canceled after June 30, 1945, when Congress established the Philippine War Damage Commission.

Although the War Damage Corporation was created informally by the RFC seven days after Pearl Harbor, Congress passed a law March 27, 1942, approving it and providing that the benefits of the program might be extended without cost or contract to persons who sustained losses after December 6, 1941, and before the date on which the Corporation's premium insurance might become effective. After organizing and giving people ample time in which to take out insurance with us, if they wanted it, free insurance no longer prevailed. The legislation gave me as Secretary of Commerce the authority to determine the date for the ending of this "free" coverage, and I fixed July 1, 1942. We were authorized to adjust claims for damage done before that day "as if a policy covering such property was in force at the time of such loss or damage." On that score we subsequently paid out $372,000. Conforming to my decision, the Corporation made its rates effective as of July 1, 1942.

The charter of the War Damage Corporation provided for a total authorized capital stock of $100,000,000, all to be subscribed by the RFC, but the only funds we made available to the War Damage Corporation were the initial subscription of $1,000,000 for capital stock. The premium revenues were nearly $246,000,000, more than enough to meet all expenses and pay all approved claims.

* * *

With the tides of war definitely turned in America's favor, and taking into consideration the few losses which had been paid or then seemed likely, the War Damage Corporation on April 1, 1944, extended all insurance then in force for an additional period of twelve months without premium or other charge. And when that year was up another twelve months of "free" insurance was provided to policy holders. All new or additional insurance was, of course, subject to the usual full payment.

Almost half the insurance written under the general program covered business properties. There was also a substantial coverage on residential properties, hotels, apartment houses, churches, hospitals, schools, museums, libraries, and publicly or privately owned utilities.

As with our other wartime subsidiaries, I took the chairmanship of the board of War Damage Corporation. W. L. Clayton became its president. The other directors, in addition to the five directors of the RFC, were Frederic A. Delano—who was Uncle Fred to President Roosevelt—and George E. Allen. Stanley T. Crossland, as vice president, was our chief liaison man with the insurance industry. We worked in close cooperation with Frank Christensen, vice president of the Continental Insurance Company. As chairman of the Advisory Committee of Insurance Men, he worked without salary—and worked very hard. Later, he, too, became a vice president of War Damage Corporation.

In its final liquidation of War Damage Corporation, the RFC paid into the federal Treasury $209,827,810, representing profits realized from its operations, exclusive of the 10 per cent participating interest of the insurance companies which did most of the work and earned their 10 per cent for the risk they had taken. Their over-all expenses and agents' commissions in writing billions in insurance amounted to about $21,000,000 and their 10 per cent interest in the profits or losses yielded them a profit of $20,000,000.

31

---- ☆ ----

FDR ASKS US TO BUY THE EMPIRE STATE BUILDING

An Obligation to Al Smith and John Raskob—Offer of a Swap for Equity in the Tallest Skyscraper—Al Smith Declines—A Nice Million His Agents Didn't Get—Al Smith's Real Feeling Toward FDR

I READ in a Washington newspaper one day in 1942 that former Governor Alfred E. Smith of New York had called on President Roosevelt at the White House. Knowing that the feeling between the two had not been cordial since Governor Smith took a walk at the Chicago convention which first nominated Mr. Roosevelt for the Presidency, I wondered why the call.

It was explained a day or two later when I saw the President about a routine matter. He handed me an envelope containing a lot of facts and figures about the Empire State Building and asked me to study them and see if we could justify its purchase.

I took the file with me. On top of everything else was a penciled note which read:

J. Jones—

> To put together and justify if possible.
>
> F. D. R.

There was also a typewritten memorandum from the President to me which read:

> I have long felt that it would pay the Federal Government to put all of the Federal offices in and around New York City into one central building.
>
> We all know that the Empire State Building is a losing proposi-

THE WHITE HOUSE

WASHINGTON

Noted JHJ SEP 22 41

July 25, 1941.

CONFIDENTIAL

MEMORANDUM FOR JESSE JONES:

I have long felt that it would pay the Federal Government to put all of the Federal offices in and around New York City into one central building.

We all know that the Empire State Building is a losing proposition, but on the other side, it is ideally located for a central Federal Office Building.

I wish you would look into this whole subject, without passing it over to anyone else or speaking to anyone else about it. We can talk it over next week.

F.D.R.

To put together - notify if possible.

tion, but on the other side, it is ideally located for a central Federal Office Building.

I wish you would look into this whole subject, without passing it over to anyone else or speaking to anyone else about it. We can talk it over next week.

F. D. R.

If the President wanted the government to buy the world's tallest skyscraper for government use, he should have asked the Public Buildings Administration to buy it; but he probably knew that the Congress would not authorize the money, so he turned to me.

I already knew a good deal about the Empire State Building. I had built a number of office buildings in the Grand Central area and at one time had considered buying the old Waldorf-Astoria Hotel (the site of the Empire State Building) and putting up an office building in its place. But I decided the location was none too good for that purpose. Besides, the asking price for the land was much too high.

In addition to going direct to the President, Governor Smith, who was managing the Empire State Building, employed John R. Todd, a real estate man, and Lester S. Abberley, a lawyer, both of New York, to negotiate the sale of the property to the government.

The building was owned by a corporation in which, I was advised, John J. Raskob, former chairman of the Democratic National Committee and a very rich man, owned 82 per cent, Pierre S. du Pont of Delaware 8 per cent, and Governor Smith 10 per cent. The Governor had probably been given his stock by Mr. Raskob when, being out of politics, he became president of the building company and assumed its management, at a salary of, I think, $50,000 a year.

There was a first mortgage on the property for $27,000,000 to the Metropolitan Life Insurance Company and, according to the record, a second mortgage of $13,500,000 which, I understood, was held by Mr. Raskob or his interests.

According to the building company's report to the Internal Revenue Bureau, the cost of the building was $28,189,000 and of the land, $17,494,000—a total of $45,683,000, though in offering the property to the government for $45,000,000 it was represented to have been more than $50,000,000. This probably included carrying charges and losses in operation. It is my recollection that the building company had bought the old Waldorf-Astoria Hotel for $14,000,000, and had started constructing the skyscraper at the very height of the boom which started busting in 1929 and brought on a general real estate debacle along with every other kind of financial disaster.

Opened early in the depression, the building had not rented well and had not earned its charges. The Metropolitan Life had reduced their interest on the mortgage to 2 or 2½ per cent. I understood that even a part of that had to be contributed by the owners.

In trying to determine what, if anything, could or should be done by the government toward acquiring the property, I talked with Frederick H. Ecker, chairman of the Metropolitan Life, about the mortgage. Mr. Ecker told me that if the government bought the building, his company would continue to carry the loan at an interest rate comparable to long-time government bonds, that is, 2 or 2½ per cent, and without the government assuming the debt. With the government owning, occupying and operating the property, the mortgage would have been perfectly good. After a thorough examination of the building, and considering the President's obvious desire to own it, I finally decided that if we could get the equity cheap enough, and pay for it in foreclosed real estate that we had taken for debt, we might afford to recommend a trade, as government rent would pay the mortgage. Accordingly, I suggested to Messrs. Todd and Abberley that I would recommend trading the Essex House for the equity over the $27,000,000 mortgage.

The Essex House was a new hotel on Central Park South that had cost its builders $5,000,000 or $6,000,000. The RFC had inherited it through foreclosure on a loan to the Prudence Company, a defunct real estate mortgage house. The hotel was operating in the red. The RFC sold it some ten years later for, as I recall, $5,400,000.

Before suggesting to Messrs. Todd and Abberley that I might consider recommending such a trade, I talked with the President about it. I explained to him that, because of the extreme height of the Empire State Building, it was not well adapted to government occupancy and, furthermore, that its operation—a continuing charge— would be very much greater than that of buildings of normal height. I also told him that the government could not use more than half of the building, and the balance of the space would have to be rented in competition with private business. Moreover, we could provide the same amount of space in a moderate-size building suitable for government occupancy for less than half the asking price of the Empire State, and in doing so would be helping recovery through furnishing employment and buying materials.

"Yes, Jess," the President replied, "all that is probably true, but I would like to do something for Al Smith. He is broke and has an expensive family."

Governor Smith died a few years later. His estate was reported to be several hundred thousand dollars.

If the government had bought the building at the owners' last offer of $38,000,000 it would have given Mr. Raskob, holder of the second mortgage and the principal stockholder, $11,000,000 in cash over and above the Metropolitan's mortgage. What Governor Smith would have got out of the deal would have been the sum Mr. Raskob might allot to him, as the total amount would not have paid the second mortgage in full. While taking a substantial loss on the building, Mr. Raskob would have recovered a good part of his equity investment at a time when the outlook for the building was not good.

It will be remembered that Governor Smith and Mr. Raskob had persuaded Mr. Roosevelt to run for the Governorship of New York in 1928, when Mr. Smith was a candidate for the Presidency and Mr. Raskob was chairman of the Democratic National Committee. Mr. Roosevelt was elected Governor, and four years later, President, but Governor Smith had not carried his own state for the Presidency. When Messrs. Smith and Raskob were trying to get Mr. Roosevelt to run for the Governorship, he demurred, giving as his reasons not only the state of his health, but the fact that he was heavily in debt on his Warm Springs property. Mr. Raskob offered to bail him out on that debt and, I understand, did. So, in buying the Empire State Building from Mr. Raskob and Governor Smith, the President would be doing something for the two men who had done the most to make him President.

Messrs. Abberley and Todd came to see me a number of times about the building. Finally I asked Mr. Abberley why they were so persistent. He told me quite frankly that Governor Smith was paying them $50,000 for compiling the necessary information and trying to sell the building to us, and that if the sale were made they would be paid a commission of $1,000,000.

I then wrote the following letter to the President:

THE SECRETARY OF COMMERCE
WASHINGTON

July 29, 1942

Dear Mr. President:

As stated by Governor Smith in the memorandum he left with you July 9, I have seen him and his representatives a number of times since you first asked me to investigate the Empire State Building with a view to determining whether or not the Federal Government would acquire it and concentrate all the Federal Government offices and employees in the vicinity of New York City in one building.

Where practical, it would appear desirable to have the various government agencies in one building if it can be accomplished on the right basis, but the price they are asking for the Empire State Building cannot, in my opinion, be justified.

From figures furnished me by Mr. John R. Todd and Mr. Lester S. Abberley, who have been employed by Governor Smith to negotiate with us for the sale of the building, the property cost $48,400,000; $17,000,000 odd of which was the capitalized cost of the land, but this was a very high price. Deducting the land would leave $31,400,000 for the building, which is approximately $15.00 per square foot for the rentable space and 85¢ per cubic foot. Either of these figures is a very high price for a first class office building. Approximately $10.00 per square foot of rentable space and 60¢ per cubic foot are good prices for first class office buildings.

According to the company's report to the Internal Revenue Department, the cost of the building was $28,189,000, and the land $17,494,000, a total of $45,683,000. The building was completed in 1931, and the company has computed its depreciation in its reports to the Internal Revenue Department at slightly more than 3% per annum. This depreciation for 11 years would amount to $9,302,370 and reduce the depreciated value of the building to $18,886,630. I doubt if the land could now be properly valued at more than $6,000,000 although it is assessed at $10,250,000. But valuing it at $7,000,000 would give a total of present value of the property of $25,886,630. If we figured the depreciation at 2% instead of 3%, the present value would be $28,987,420 ($21,987,420 for the building and $7,000,000 for the land).

In these figures I have deducted nothing for the extraordinary cost of operating the Empire State Building due to its abnormal height, as compared to buildings of normal height, say 20 to 30 stories. This extra operating cost would probably average 18¢ per square foot or $400,000 a year, which is 2½% on $16,000,000. The increased operating cost could be offset by increased rates if the building was rented commercially, but this would not apply to government occupancy.

It is well-known that, until recently and due largely to a substantial amount of space being rented to government war agencies, the Empire State has never earned interest on the $27,000,000 mortgage, let alone any return on the equity investment. I am advised that the Metropolitan Life reduced the interest some years ago to 2½%, and that a substantial part of this had to be contributed by the owners, as the building did not earn it. The interest was later reduced by Metropolitan Life to 2%.

As a private investment, I would not regard the equity in the Empire State Building above the $27,000,000 mortgage as of any real value, but if the government used the entire building, it could afford to pay something for the equity, but not a great deal.

Mr. Abberley advised me that he and Mr. Todd were being paid $50,000 to negotiate the sale, whether or not a sale is effected, and that the Governor had given them a letter agreeing to pay them $1,000,000 if they were able to sell the building at $45,000,000 and that, while nothing was said about it, he assumed this fee would be proportionately reduced if the building was sold at a lesser figure.

I am giving you this information because Mr. Abberley advised me that Governor Smith has decided that, because of my views with regard to the value of the property, he would prefer to negotiate with someone else representing the government.

Sincerely yours,

JESSE H. JONES
Secretary of Commerce

The President
The White House

On the following day, or at least soon thereafter, the President asked me to return the papers to him, which I did.

Several months later Harold D. Smith, Director of the Budget, came to my office and told me that at the request of the President he had taken up the purchase of the Empire State Building with the Public Buildings Administration, but that they were not interested in buying the property. He told me that he thought the problem would be back in my lap in a few days.

It was. The President returned the papers to me, and requested that I continue negotiations to buy the building. With this request, he enclosed the following message from Budget Director Smith:

November 4, 1943

MEMORANDUM FOR THE PRESIDENT

We have carefully studied the adaptability of the Empire State Building to meet space requirements of Federal agencies in New York City, including probable extent of use, cost of maintenance, taxes, amortization and similar factors. In this survey we were aided by the Public Buildings Administration.

Our conclusions are:

(1) Probably little more than one-half of the total available space would be required in this location by Government agencies after the war; the balance would be leased to business firms, thus competing with private business.

(2) At the suggested price of $38,000,000 an appropriation for its purchase would not be economically justified, due to the high percentage of land value in the cost, the type of space, its vertical distribution and similar drawbacks.

(3) Without having available complete or independent appraisals, I would think that an offer of approximately 80% of the suggested figure might be worth consideration, and that the cost of space for Federal activities at such a price might be economically justified.

In view of these conclusions, I suggest that the Reconstruction Finance Corporation be asked to continue discussion with the owners of the Empire State Building to determine if more advantageous terms than those now proposed can be arranged.

Attached is an analysis of Federal space requirements in New York City and the suitability of the Empire State Building to meet them.

HAROLD A. SMITH, *Director*

Attachment.

I did nothing further about it, and the President never again mentioned the matter to me, nor I to him. But I am sure he was displeased that I had not carried out his wish to buy the property, and that he never forgave me for not doing it. We had no direct authority to buy the building, but he thought I could do it if I wanted to. I probably could have, but did not think I should.

According to my calendar, Messrs. Todd and Abberley first saw me February 5, 1942, and one or both of them called subsequently on March 7, April 15, May 27, June 23, July 23 and 24, August 18, and December 3 and 16 of that year and on January 6 and 28, 1943. It will be noted I had no calls from them between August 18, 1942, and December 3, 1942. During that period they were trying to negotiate sale of the building to the Public Buildings Administration through the Director of the Bureau of the Budget.

Governor Smith came to see me two or three times during the negotiations and indicated clearly his real feeling toward the President —which was that of utter contempt. He made it plain he had gone to the White House to see the President only to help his friend Mr. Raskob get some of his money out of a losing venture.

32

---- ☼ ----

BUYING THE ROGERS ESTATE AT HYDE PARK

*Father Divine and a Heaven Near Hyde Park—Squabble
of Country Squires—We Come Out Ahead on the Deal*

THERE was a property—the Rogers estate adjoining the Roosevelt
home on the Hudson—that the President wanted the government
to acquire. The estate was Crumwold Farms, a property of 742 acres
which had been owned by the late Archibald Rogers.

One day in 1942, after a Cabinet meeting, the President talked
with Claude R. Wickard, Secretary of Agriculture, about buying the
property. The President thought the Department of Agriculture should
acquire the place and use it for reforestation and other experimental
purposes, as Mr. Rogers had planted thousands of trees on the property.

I was in the room, and the President asked me to talk with Claude
and see if a way could be found.

Father Divine, the noted Negro preacher-leader, had bought a
large estate just across the Hudson from the President's home, and
it was rumored that he considered buying Crumwold Farms and
becoming a neighbor of the President. This was not mentioned by Mr.
Roosevelt, though he might have heard the rumor.

It developed that Secretary Wickard had no funds with which to
buy the farm. The President then asked me to try to arrange for its
purchase. Joseph P. Day, one of New York's most prominent real
estate brokers, had talked to him about the property and told him it
could be had by the government for $150,000 and was worth much
more. I had seen the estate on some of my trips to Hyde Park.

In foreclosing on a $20,000,000 loan to the Prudence Company, a
mortgage bond and real estate company in New York, we had ac-

quired all of the assets of the company, which included a number of subsidiary corporations dealing in and related to real estate that were not in bankruptcy. I discussed the matter with our people in New York and asked if any of the affiliates of the bankrupt company, which the RFC was operating, had the money available to buy the farm. They had, and they concluded the purchase.

Crumwold Farms adjoined the northern end of the Roosevelts' Hyde Park estate, and the two were linked together by private roads. Sloping high above the Hudson, with broad lawns and a profusion of fine trees, it was one of the most attractive private estates in the East. It had provided Franklin D. Roosevelt in his boyhood with a spacious playground and the companionship of Archibald Rogers' children.

Mr. Rogers died in 1928, a few months before his now famous neighbor was elected Governor of New York; but Mr. Roosevelt, both as Governor and as President, continued to enjoy some of the amenities of Crumwold Farms. During his visits to Hyde Park he frequently drove through his neighbor's grounds.

The Rogers manor house, Crumwold Hall, is a massive, almost fortresslike structure of granite. The stone had been brought by ship from Maine, down the Atlantic and up the Hudson to the Rogers' own river-bank landing. Divided by the Albany Post Road, the estate was dotted with some thirty buildings, including a large stone garage, barns in which the owner had stabled his blooded horses and his prized dairy herd, a conservatory, a formidable concrete bull pen and the residences of household and farm employees. A swimming pool, a fishing pond, and a boathouse on the river, reached by a private bridge over the New York Central Railroad tracks, were but a few of the recreational pleasures Crumwold Farms provided.

Up the river a few miles had been the country home of Frederick W. Vanderbilt, which is now a park operated by the State of New York. Across the river from the Roosevelt and Rogers properties was Cragston, which had been the country domain of the senior J. P. Morgan.

Near Morgan's Cragston was Krum Elbow, the estate of Howland Spencer. He and President Roosevelt had got into a public disagreement over the President's contention that the old Dutch name, Krum Elbow, really belonged to the Roosevelt property on the east bank. Mr. Spencer insisted the name had been given to his headland on the west bank in the year 1609 by no less distinguished a name-giver than the explorer, Henry Hudson.

It was while this dispute of country squires was being aired that the public was regaled, in 1938, with the announcement that Mr. Spencer had sold Krum Elbow to Father Divine, who promptly created upon it another "heaven" for the followers who look upon him as a deity.

Six years later Mr. Day called at the White House and told the President the Rogers place could be had by the government at a bargain price.

Instead of Secretary Wickard's using the property for the Department of Agriculture, the Army occupied it ostensibly as a training camp for military police. First a company, then a whole battalion, was quartered there, largely to protect the President's Hyde Park home, I suppose. The Army paid a rental to the bankrupt Prudence Company for the property, sufficient to pay the real estate taxes and 4 per cent interest on this investment.

After the war, the President having died, the Army moved the M.P.'s out, and the property was sold in 1947 for $210,000—a tidy profit for the government.

33

☼

BUILDING DEFENSE HOMES

Dormitories for War Workers—The Evalyn Walsh Mc-Lean Estate—Building a Hotel for Women Employees in Washington

WHEN the United States embarked upon industrial expansion for defense purposes in the summer of 1940, great shiftings of populations set in which created sudden demands for shelter for people who had left their old homes to take employment in helping build or operate new plants or to find places on the expanding federal pay rolls in Washington and elsewhere.

The National Capital and many "defense areas" became exceedingly congested. On October 23, 1940, to assist in meeting the swelling needs for housing, the RFC created another subsidiary, Defense Homes Corporation. For its capital stock President Roosevelt assigned to me, as Federal Loan Administrator, $10,000,000 from his Emergency Funds. Defense Homes then borrowed $65,700,000 from the RFC.

With this money it built and operated 10,964 housing units, ranging from small individual homes to dormitories, apartment houses, and a hotel. These were scattered across the country in thirteen states and the District of Columbia.

After the war they were sold to individuals and corporations at a net profit to the government of about $2,100,000. There were losses on only three of the projects. Two others—dormitory residences which had been built for Negroes in Washington—were transferred by Congressional authority to Howard University.

Construction began several months before Pearl Harbor. By the summer of 1942 we had 3,800 housing units completed in seventeen localities and 7,000 more units in seven locations were under way. We built whatever and wherever the Federal Housing Administrator designated; but we built for permanence—and it paid to do so. All the projects were completed by June, 1944, including nearly 3,000 individual homes, dormitories with nearly 2,500 rooms, and a number of large apartment houses, particularly in Washington.

President Roosevelt took a keen personal interest in some of these projects. While I sat at his desk he drew on a sheet of paper the first rough draft of the dormitories to be built in Washington. Only a few of the general ideas in his offhand sketch were adopted by the architects in designing some of the buildings which were put up in McLean Gardens after our corporation had bought the eighty-odd-acre McLean Estate in the heart of fashionable Washington from Mrs. Evalyn Walsh McLean for a consideration of $1,000,000. The price was cheap.

I had spoken to the President of buying the McLean property after the Cabinet meeting of December 19, 1941. He gave his approval and immediately reached for a pencil and began sketching his ideas of how the dormitories should be designed. He suggested two-story wooden structures with corrugated iron partitions and even jotted down the details of the furniture each cubbyhole might contain: "bed, bureau, chair and desk."

But we decided to build for permanence because of the excellent location of the property. Though some advocates of make-haste-whatever-the-waste criticized us, it was a wise decision. Some of the "temporary" or "emergency" housing pitched in Washington by other agencies during the war was so rickety it could not be used for human habitation.

Kenneth Franzheim, a New York and Houston architect, planned the dormitories and apartment buildings in McLean Gardens, and also the neighboring Fairlington development which provided 3,439 apartments. Those two projects cost more than $46,000,000 to develop. They were later sold at a gross profit exceeding $4,500,000. In the Southeast section of the Capital, we built Naylor Gardens, containing 757 apartments. On that development, which cost $6,607,000, Defense Homes took one of its few losses.

There was a great shortage in living quarters for government workingwomen in Washington, and one day in April, 1941, at a Cabinet meeting, I addressed a note to the President suggesting that we build a

At Cabinet meeting 4/4/41

THE WHITE HOUSE
WASHINGTON

Mr President — You
allocated from your
special Emergency fund $10,000,000.
to the Federal Loan Ad-
ministration to purchase
the Stock of a corporation
to provide financing for
housing necessary for
national defense. I.e.
to let the company form
the Defense Homes Corp.
which it building definite
housing in 15 different
localities. There is
a need for girls dorms
a need too for where
young women in government
service can get board all
rooms at prices they can
afford, and accommodation
cannot be had from
private renters over

THE WHITE HOUSE
WASHINGTON

If you approve I will
have Defense Homes Corp.
build such a hotel and
have it operated probably
by the YWCA — or at
all events on a non
profitable basis — and basis
probably no rent basis
for the property — living
the emergency — to build
it may cost or much as
and equip — or equip enough
$1,000,000. to do enough
to do much good.
Sincerely
Jesse Jones

We will make it pay ut
FDR

april 2 1941

FEDERAL LOAN AGENCY
OFFICE OF THE ADMINISTRATOR

DATE December 19th

Noted JHJ
DEC 21 #1

Memorandum to

Speak to the President about buying
Friendship, approximately 80 acres at
$12,000 an acre. Use to construct
small apartments.

residential hotel for women, and passed it across the table to him. The President returned the note with the inscription: "O.K., but make it pay out. . . . F. D. R."

We built the Meridian Hill Hotel, which made homes for 715 women government employees at very reasonable rates. It is located on Euclid Street facing Meridian Park between Fifteenth and Sixteenth streets, an excellent home for workingwomen. Mrs. Roosevelt took a great interest in the project and spoke at its opening ceremonies.

The hotel cost $1,824,970. Earnings from its operation were more than enough to pay its carrying charges, and the corporation sold the property after the war to private investors for $2,775,000, a handsome profit.

Total cost to the government of the Defense Homes Corporation projects was about $75,625,455. Profits from operations reduced the government's total investment to approximately $61,520,627. Net sales realized from its properties, including the book value credited to its account by RFC, as authorized by Congress, on the transfer of the two dormitories to Howard University, totaled about $69,202,470, leaving a net profit to the government of $2,100,000 after deducting expense of operation and interest on the investment.

The list of properties and their balance sheets will be found in the Appendix.

34

✦

THE BRITISH LOAN

EARLY in 1941 the dollar position of Great Britain began to get very low. The United Kingdom had been ordering vast quantities of war materials in the United States and needed dollars to pay for them. The British Government had already sold nearly $1,500,000,000 of American securities which British subjects had been obliged to surrender to it. The sale of so many of these securities was forcing the market down, and the return to the British represented much less than true values. Among the British-owned investments in the United States was the American Viscose Corporation, the largest producer of rayon in this country and a very profitable institution. It was owned at the time by Courtaulds, Limited, of London. Thrown on the market through Wall Street banking houses in March, 1941, it brought less than half its worth even in bad times.

British selling under pressure was hurtful to the market generally, and to our entire economy. If the British continued to throw on the market their American investments, market conditions would continue to get worse. Furthermore, we wanted the British to get the maximum dollar value for what they sold, to give them more dollars for war supplies. So, four days after Sir Edward Peacock, a director of Baring Brothers & Co., bankers, and of the Bank of England, who was in the United States representing the British Treasury, announced that he had made arrangements for the sale of Viscose to an investment banking syndicate in Wall Street, I wrote the following letter to President Roosevelt:

[472]

March 20, 1941

Dear Mr. President:

If the British are required to sell their United States investments on a forced sale basis, they will probably not be able to realize their fair value, and the fact that these investments are hanging over the market will have a depressing effect on the entire market, and in that way adversely affect investments of our own citizens.

Furthermore, the British have made a point of the fact that many of their investments in this country are an important factor in their economic affairs. The income from them is being used to buy our products, and otherwise to provide them with dollar exchange.

I think we all feel that the British should pay as long as they can, and should use their foreign investments to fight the war and buy war supplies. But it may not leave a very good feeling with them if they are forced to sell investments that are vital to their existence.

I suggest that we arrange to lend on these investments at approximately the cost of money to us, and for a period—not too long—that will enable them to sell in an orderly way, and probably save some of these investments by applying the earnings toward interest and in liquidation of the debt.

In the case of the Viscose, as I understand the deal, it was hurried and forced, the bankers advancing $40,000,000, and agreeing to account to the British for 90% of the sale price over the $40,-000,000 advance, and their fees of $2,700,000, and expenses estimated at $150,000.

In other words, from the total sale price, after paying the advance and the bankers' fees and expenses, aggregating approximately $43,000,000, the bankers take 10% of any excess.

The Company is in excellent shape with almost $40,000,000 cash on hand and a substantial amount of other liquid assets. Its earnings for the past two years have been approximately $9,700,000 a year. This may have been before income taxes, but even allowing for taxes, the net earnings would be more than $7,000,000 a year.

If the bankers should sell the property at, say, $75,000,000, which would not be a big price, the bankers' total fees will be in the neighborhood of $6,000,000, or a net to the British of approximately $68,000,000. The British will be justified in feeling that this is a very big price to pay the bankers, particularly since they are selling their choicest United States investments.

If we had loaned $68,000,000 against the property at 3%, the earnings would have paid the interest on the loan, and amortized the entire debt in approximately ten years, based upon the last two years' earnings.

Sincerely yours,

JESSE H. JONES, Administrator

The President
The White House

Prior to the sale of Viscose I suggested to Sir Edward Peacock that the RFC would be glad to lend the Viscose Corporation up to $75,000,000, which was many millions more than they finally got for the company by selling it. If they had borrowed $75,000,000 from the RFC, they could have loaned or given the money to their government and kept their property and the earnings from it would have completely liquidated the debt with interest in approximately ten years. And they would have still owned their property. Sir Edward, however, seemed to be afraid Secretary Morgenthau would not like it if he borrowed this money from the RFC. I told Secretary Morgenthau of my proposal to make the company the loan, but he said definitely that he did not want us to make it, that he wanted the property sold. I never knew why, unless he wanted to favor his Wall Street friends. It meant that Dillon, Read & Co., would make a few millions in fees and would sell the company to friends who made many more millions out of the deal.

A few weeks later, as a part of the national defense program, Senator Prentiss M. Brown of Michigan, at my suggestion, introduced a bill to amend the RFC Act so as to permit the RFC at my request, with the President's approval, to make loans to foreign governments or their central banks or agents "for the purpose of achieving the maximum dollar exchange value in the United States" for their securities or other property in this country. The amendment provided these loans were to be permitted "notwithstanding the provisions of any other law"—meaning the Johnson Act. This Act prohibited loans to foreign countries that had repudiated or defaulted on loans they had gotten from the United States Treasury during and after World War I. The new bill provided that such loans as we might make should be secured by United States Government, state, or municipal bonds, or the securities of privately owned American corporations.

Senator Brown's bill became law on June 10, 1941. During hearings on it a month earlier before the Senate Banking and Currency Committee I testified that its purpose was to aid the best possible realization on British securities sold in this country so they could pay for orders placed for war supplies.

I illustrated my point by telling the Senators of a loan we had made to the British-owned Brown & Williamson Tobacco Co. of Louisville, a Delaware corporation. It was arranged under our authority to lend to business. The company was strictly an American business but was British-owned. The British Government was threatening to commandeer the capital stock and sell it to get dollars. Colonel Joseph M. Hartfield, counsel for the owners, came to see me about a loan to the company. We loaned it $40,000,000, taking its very profitable business as security. The Brown & Williamson Tobacco Co. in turn gave or loaned the $40,000,000 cash to its owners, the British American Tobacco Co., Ltd., of London. The British American Tobacco Co. then loaned the $40,000,000 to the British Government, and they still owned their profitable American business. The loan was perfectly good from our standpoint, and it enabled the owners to help their government and still keep their business. The company was doing business in five or six of our tobacco-growing states. It owned several factories and fifteen or more drying barns, and employed a large number of people. The loan was paid in full on April 26, 1946. We could have handled the Viscose situation in the same way.

Pursuant to the legislation of June, 1941, the RFC authorized a loan of $425,000,000 to the United Kingdom of Great Britain and Northern Ireland. The loan matured serially over a period of fifteen years with interest at 3 per cent. In considering the collateral which the British offered, Harry Mulligan, one of our directors and for a number of years our treasurer, estimated the income from the securities would amount to approximately $36,000,000 a year. It is interesting to note that the income from this collateral averaged approximately $37,000,000 annually for eight years and then increased very substantially.

If the current rate is maintained the loan should be retired well before its maturity in 1956. The British will then regain possession of these American investments having a value of probably more than

$1,000,000,000. The securities include listed and unlisted stocks and bonds of many of the most highly regarded American corporations, the capital stock of forty British-owned American insurance companies, and the assets in this country deposited to secure the liabilities of forty other British insurance companies doing business in the United States.

If, in order to raise $425,000,000, the British had been required to sell these American investments, it would have been a hardship on them. First, they would have been deprived of their properties and the income from them. Next, if forced on the market, the securities would not have brought anything like their value.

In 1941, when I broached the idea of making an RFC loan to the British Government, I was attacked in some quarters of London as "an enemy of England," as one who was trying to take advantage of that country's difficulties. They see it differently now, as the London *Evening Standard* remarked in an article published in December, 1949.

"It is thanks to Jesse Jones," the article said, "that we still have in the United States a huge dollar asset—the largest single dollar asset left—instead of nothing at all. . . . When the last dollar is paid off, Britain will regain possession of a huge portfolio of some of the most valuable securities in the world.

"And much more important, from the dollar-gap point of view, we shall once again benefit from the income of these investments, which lately has been running somewhere between $45 million and $50 million a year.

"The security handed over to the Americans was hundreds of thousands of shares in American enterprises, taken from their British owners by force under the wartime regulations, and which it had originally been Whitehall's intention to sell.

"A very high proportion of the sequestered shares were preferred and common stocks in some of the finest companies in America, recognized 'blue chips' of steadily increasing value. The market quotation on almost all of the certificates has climbed continuously since 1941, when the RFC handed them over to the Federal Reserve Bank in New York for safe keeping. From the start the British taxpayer has never had to pay a single penny to square our account with the RFC. . . .

"What will happen to these valuable securities when they return to full British control? Do the original owners get them back?

"As a matter of equity, it would appear at first sight that they should. But it was purely accidental that these investments were not sold, as millions of others were before and after the RFC arrangement. THEN there were 4.03 dollars to the pound; NOW there are 2.80."

35

---------- ☼ ----------

WE SEIZE MONTGOMERY WARD & COMPANY

ABOUT the most awkward thing the White House asked me to do
was to seize the headquarters and main Chicago plant of Montgomery Ward & Company in April, 1944. It seemed that Sewell Avery,
head of Montgomery Ward, had ignored a White House directive
telling him to extend a contract with a labor union. Mr. Avery had
refused on the ground that Montgomery Ward & Company was not
engaged in war work, and had violated no law nor denied any
privileges to the union.

The President was in Warm Springs at the time. He left it to James
F. Byrnes (now Governor of South Carolina), who had resigned
from the Supreme Court and, as Director of War Mobilization, was
acting for him. Mr. Byrnes directed me to take over the plant and
operate it. I was not in sympathy with the move and did not want
the responsibility. However, I had no choice. I tried to persuade Mr.
Byrnes to give the job to Donald Nelson, who had had experience in
this line of business as executive vice president of Sears, Roebuck &
Company prior to coming to the government as head of the War Production Board, or to Harold Ickes, also from Chicago. I thought
Harold would enjoy a tussle with Sewell Avery and that the enjoyment
would be mutual. But Byrnes insisted that I do it, saying that I was
the only man in Washington who could handle Sewell Avery. I appreciated the compliment, but he was 100 per cent wrong. No one can
handle Sewell Avery. When Sewell thinks he is in the right all the
king's horses can't move him. He is able and a square-shooter—two
good characteristics.

The War Labor Board, which was piqued at Mr. Avery for ignoring its "orders," had consulted both the Justice and the War Department, as well as my Department of Commerce. Benjamin V. Cohen and some other bright young fellows in White House favor had drawn up a batch of directives, applications for injunctions, and other legalistic scribble-scrabble. The shooting license they wrote out for us wasn't any good. But we did the best we could to comply with the White House order.

I selected Wayne Taylor, my Under Secretary of Commerce, to go to Chicago. Mr. Taylor was accompanied by Ugo Carusi, then executive assistant to Attorney General Francis Biddle. I also sent along John D. Goodloe, then general counsel of the RFC. My orders were to take over and operate the Montgomery Ward plant unless Mr. Avery gave the President an affirmative answer that he would extend his contract with the union.

Mr. Taylor, having formerly lived in Chicago, knew Mr. Avery, and went to his office accompanied by Mr. Carusi, representing the Attorney General. He read his directives to Mr. Avery and explained that he was acting on the advice of Attorney General Biddle.

"Well," remarked Mr. Avery, "all I've got to say is that you are getting some damn bad advice."

Mr. Avery refused to turn over his business to the government. He said that he would offer no physical resistance to his ejection, but that, to establish the government in possession of his business, at least certain moves indicating force would be necessary. He added, according to Mr. Taylor, that he wouldn't leave unless carried out bodily. The next day, while Mr. Taylor was on the telephone talking to me in Washington, a detachment of military police dispatched by the Army arrived at the plant. Fortunately for me—and a great relief it was—Attorney General Biddle had also arrived on the scene about that time. He instructed the major in charge of the military detachment to remove Mr. Avery from the building. Two of the soldiers were then ordered to carry Mr. Avery out of the building, and they did. He was told he could return only for the stockholders' meeting, scheduled the following day, April 28.

Meanwhile my instructions to Messrs. Taylor and Goodloe were to let Attorney General Biddle carry the ball and to do only those things the Attorney General told them to do. It was deemed advisable to get the soldiers out of the plant as quickly as possible so that an

C. K. Berryman in the Washington Evening Star.

election could be held to determine whether the employees wished the union to be their collective bargaining agent. The election was set for May 9. On May 8 I went to the White House with Mr. Taylor, who had returned from Chicago, and we conferred with Mr. Byrnes, Benjamin Cohen, Attorney General Biddle, and probably some others. They drew up an order which I was to release the following night terminating the government's possession, control, and operation of the plants and facilities and returning them to Montgomery Ward & Company. The President had by then taken the position that, if the election showed the union lacked a majority of the employees, that would end the case, whereas, if the election gave the union a majority, the management had declared its willingness to continue its contract, and that, too, would end the case. In the election the CIO won the collective bargaining privilege by a vote of 2,440 to 1,565.

Both the White House and the War Labor Board continued to be displeased with the manner in which Mr. Avery operated his business. Late in 1944 they again contended that the company's labor troubles were threatening to spread and impede the war effort. On December 26 Major General Joseph W. Byron, through whom, as chief of the Army Exchange Service, the RFC had loaned more than $70,000,000 to finance the Army post exchanges, came to my office and told me he was leaving Washington on a new assignment—to command troops which the President would order to take over sixteen Montgomery Ward properties in half a dozen cities. I sympathized with the General. The Executive Order was issued the following day, and on December 28 the properties were seized. Both Mr. Avery and the company's president, Clement D. Ryan, were barred from their administration building. When the Secretary of War, Henry L. Stimson, took possession of the plants, President Roosevelt allocated to him $5,000,000 from the President's emergency funds to operate the Montgomery Ward facilities and indicated his willingness to allocate up to $5,000,000 more. Secretary Stimson estimated that he would probably need additional funds for financing the operation and asked me to make them available. I thereupon requested Defense Supplies Corporation to make funds available to the Secretary of War for the purpose of carrying out the Executive Order in an amount not to exceed $50,000,000.

It was not until October 19, 1945, that a new President, Harry S Truman, restored to Mr. Avery the control of the properties.

36

PETROLEUM RESERVES CORPORATION

THE Petroleum Reserves Corporation, which was created by the RFC on June 30, 1943, at President Roosevelt's request, remained under our aegis only fifteen days and then was transferred by the President to the newly established Office of Economic Warfare headed by Leo T. Crowley, with Harold L. Ickes, Secretary of the Interior, acting as its president. Though it remained in existence until November 9, 1945, it never achieved its primary purpose, which was to acquire ownership for the government of the oil concession held by a privately owned American oil company in Saudi Arabia. The Corporation undertook only one venture, the building of a refinery in Saudi Arabia, and that turned out to be a fizzle, abandoned in its early stages after it had cost $111,853.

Secretary Ickes had written to the California Arabian Standard Oil Company on September 4, 1943, that the completion of the refinery at the earliest possible date was of vital importance to the war program. It had been designed for an initial output of 100,000 barrels per day of aviation and motor gasoline, Diesel oil and special fuels for the Navy. Exactly one month later, Mr. Ickes sent another letter to the oil company calling the entire thing off on the ground that "no reasonable basis for an agreement between our respective corporations has been presented or intended."

The concept of Petroleum Reserves Corporation grew out of the worries of the Joint Chiefs of Staff. They were gravely concerned over the rapid dwindling of domestic reserves of petroleum caused by wartime demands. During June, 1943, a number of meetings were held in the War Department to consider the situation. These were attended by Herbert Feis of the Department of State; Robert P. Patterson, then Under Secretary of War; General Boykin C. Wright and Colonel W. E. R. Covell of the War Department; William C. Bullitt and Captain W. J. Carter of the Navy Department and Abe Fortas of the Interior Department. They recommended, among other things, that the government make secret contracts with the presidents of the Texas Company and the Standard Oil Company of California which jointly owned the California Arabian Standard Oil Company, and negotiate for the purchase of 100 per cent of the latter's capital stock. They also recommended that a government official be dispatched to the Middle East to sound out Alexander C. Kirk, the American Minister to Egypt and Saudi Arabia, as to what, if anything, ought to be done to arrange appointments and conferences with King ibn-Saud. All these plans and proposals were then submitted to Cordell Hull, Secretary of State; Henry L. Stimson, Secretary of War; James Forrestal, Acting Secretary of the Navy, and Secretary Ickes of the Interior Department. These four gentlemen then went into a huddle with James F. Byrnes, who at that time was the Director of War Mobilization. They concurred in the recommendations which their subordinates had made, and sent a letter to President Roosevelt on June 26, 1943, suggesting the creation of the Petroleum Reserves Corporation before July 1. On June 29, the President bundled up the secret recommendations and sent them to me with a memorandum which read:

> I approve this and ask that it be carried out today. This instruction applies merely to the act of incorporation. No further action of any kind is to be taken pending further instructions from me.
>
> —FDR

The reason the President sent the matter to me was to take advantage of the authority Congress had given the RFC to create corporations for any wartime purpose. I had Petroleum Reserves Corporation set up the following morning, the intention being that as soon as we received instructions from the President the RFC would provide it with capital stock of $1,000,000. Fifteen days later, the President transferred Petroleum Reserves Corporation to Mr. Crowley to supervise, and Mr. Ickes to operate.

Secretary Ickes was elected President of the Corporation. Other members of its board were Secretary of State Hull, Secretary of War Stimson, and Secretary of the Navy Knox. Since they were using RFC money, I suggested to Mr. Byrnes that I should be on the board of directors; but Secretary Ickes would not have it. The President let Harold have his way.

On August 17, 1943, Mr. Crowley, to whom the President had assigned over-all supervision of the new Corporation, requested that the RFC lend it a million dollars, the money to be advanced from time to time in $100,000 installments. We gave him the first $100,000 the next day, and, as I explained above, it went down the sink a few weeks later.

As Petroleum Administrator for War, Secretary Ickes began borrowing the personnel of the Petroleum Reserves Corporation and kept it up until, from December 6, 1944, onward, the Corporation had only one salaried employee who had not been loaned to the Petroleum Administration for War.

Although it had accomplished nothing and was doing nothing, Petroleum Reserves Corporation continued in existence as such until November 9, 1945, when, by charter amendment, its name was changed to War Assets Corporation and it became a disposal agency for surplus property left over from the wartime expansions.

On January 8, 1946, its full authorized capital of $1,000,000 was, at last, paid in by the RFC.

On March 25, 1946, by the provisions of Executive Order 9689, the Corporation's functions as a disposal agency were transferred to War Assets Administration. On June 30, 1946, the Corporation, unwept and little sung, was dissolved by the RFC. Happily enough, its dissolution by this merciful method had been authorized in its charter.

37

---　✲　---

HOW HENRY WALLACE MISSED THE PRESIDENCY

*A School of "Social" Reformers—Congress Refuses
Them a Checkbook—Henry Gets on a High Horse—
Greasing the Skids for Wallace—The Ax Falls in Chicago*

MY CONTROVERSY with Henry Wallace, which flared up publicly in the summer of 1943, burned the bridge over which that
gentleman expected to cross to the Presidency. That he should succeed
Mr. Roosevelt in the White House was obviously the President's intention from the day he chose Wallace as his running mate in the
1940 election. To the President, Mr. Wallace had become the crown
prince.

My difficulties with Mr. Wallace, whom I rarely saw except at
Cabinet, or Commodity Credit Corporation meetings, arose principally from the impractical directives which he and his appointees
on the Board of Economic Warfare gave to the RFC.

The Board of Economic Warfare was created, coddled, and finally
killed by President Roosevelt himself. He created it on July 30, 1941,
to provide Vice President Wallace with important war work so that
he would remain the logical successor to the Presidency. Twenty-nine
days later the President also made Mr. Wallace chairman of the
Supply, Priorities, and Allocations Board to spearhead our war
effort; but that alphabetical agency soon flopped and was succeeded
by the War Production Board, of which Donald Nelson was made
chairman. Mr. Wallace was one of a dozen members of this new
board and sat alongside Chairman Nelson. The meetings started at
two in the afternoon and ran until five or six o'clock. Mr. Wallace
usually dozed in his chair at these meetings, often sleeping fifteen or
twenty minutes at a stretch. I envied him his ability to sleep so easily.

In creating the Board of Economic Warfare with a wave of the Executive Order wand, the President gave Mr. Wallace, and anyone Wallace saw fit to appoint, authority to duplicate the purchase and stockpiling of critical and strategic materials from all parts of the world which various RFC subsidiaries had been performing since June 28, 1940, when Congress gave the RFC the authority. The Order creating the BEW provided that its purchases should be financed by the RFC. It gave the new Wallace organization power to direct the RFC to pay for anything purchased by it outside the United States, anywhere, at any price that Mr. Wallace and his appointees might contract for. The President was overriding Congress, as the funds and authority had been given to the RFC.

Before bringing the BEW into being, the President spoke to me on two occasions, some weeks apart, about Wallace wanting him to create such an organization. I explained both times that there was no need for the agency, that it would simply be duplicating work already being done efficiently by the RFC and its subsidiaries, and that we were buying everything available in the way of critical and strategic materials throughout the world, and without fanfare. The President agreed with me on both occasions but later gave in to Wallace's wishes. Ironically enough, his creation of the BEW thwarted his own purpose to make Wallace his successor. Wallace, already Vice President, would have been automatically renominated with the President in June, 1944, except for the BEW fiasco.

By the President's selection, the Board of Economic Warfare had an impressive list of directors. Headed by the Vice President as chairman, members of the Board included Secretary of State Hull, Secretary of the Treasury Morgenthau, Secretary of War Stimson, Secretary of Agriculture Wickard, the Attorney General, and myself; also later on, the chairman of the War Production Board, the Coordinator of Inter-American Affairs, and the Lend Lease Administrator. Thus the Vice President had a cabinet of his own—like the President—and composed mostly of the same officials. Henry could sit in the big chair once a week and "play like" he was already Mister President, grooming himself to occupy the White House. Wallace wanted to be President so badly that, with the cooperation of his friend, Mr. Roosevelt, he dug his own political grave.

MILO PERKINS AND OTHER REFORMERS

While Wallace had an impressive cabinet, not many of its members attended the meetings. I attended two or three but saw none of the White House Cabinet members present except the Attorney General. Without consulting his board of directors, Mr. Wallace appointed his man Friday, Milo Perkins, a former bag salesman and self-ordained cultist "priest" from Texas, as Executive Director of the BEW. Milo had made a name for himself by playing second fiddle to Mr. Wallace when the latter was Secretary of Agriculture in the early years of the New Deal. It was in that capacity that Mr. Perkins hatched a scheme for getting rid of surplus products by handing a buyer two bushels each time he bought one and for the price of one.

Long before Henry Wallace's concern with curious cults became known, Mr. Perkins had ordained himself or otherwise become "priest-in-charge" of what he called a parish in the "Liberal Catholic Church of the United States of America." As such it was supposed to be his habit in Houston over a period of some years to don his "religious" robes Sunday mornings and climb up to the windowless attic of his home at 2412 Southmore Boulevard and conduct services for his "parishioners." He named his home the "Church of Saint Raphael the Ark [sic] Angel" and then proceeded to persuade the tax authorities of Houston that his homestead belonged to Saint Raphael's Church and that it was used for church purposes. Thus, through the years 1929 to 1934, inclusive, he spared his purse the trouble of paying city taxes on his home. After 1934—by which time Mr. Perkins had become a priest-in-charge of many mundane affairs in the Department of Agriculture—his home in Houston was put back on the municipal tax rolls.

I was informed that one of the tenets of Milo's "Liberal Catholic Church of the United States of America" was supposed to be the transmigration of the soul. Also that Milo became a vegetarian for a time—probably in the thought that it would be unseemly of him to lunch off a deceased uncle or grandparent who might have returned to earth in the form of an animal.

In addition to Mr. Perkins, Vice President Wallace appointed as Assistant Directors of the BEW one Hector Lazo and a Mister Morris Rosenthal, both extrasmart—of the Wallace type. As General Counsel

Parrish in the Chicago Tribune.

he selected Monroe Oppenheimer, also plenty smart. These gentlemen were all chosen by Wallace without consultation with his board. At least, I was never consulted.

During its brief but bustling life, the organization puffed its personnel up to nearly three thousand men and women, scores of whom traveled all over the world at the government's expense having the time of their lives, trying to duplicate work already being efficiently done by RFC's wartime subsidiaries, in purchasing and stockpiling all manner of strategic and critical materials.

What burned Wallace, Perkins, Rosenthal, Lazo, and Oppenheimer were the RFC's refusals to execute their orders without considering the advisability or appropriateness of doing so. For a full year before Mr. Wallace came on the preparedness scene the RFC and its subsidiaries had been doing the work that the BEW was set up to duplicate, and we knew the score. Our overseas work was under the direction of W. L. Clayton, my Deputy Loan Administrator and Assistant Secretary of Commerce, a world trader in cotton and later Under Secretary of State. He had cosmopolitan contacts and knew his way around in world business, and what conditions were in practically every country on earth.

* * *

While the President had directed the RFC to follow the orders of the BEW and to pay out money on its orders, we nevertheless felt a responsibility to Congress for the money appropriated to us. We didn't have the same confidence in Henry that the President had. When we were told to do something by the BEW we wanted to know what it was all about. In taking time to make such inquiries, no war effort was delayed, because we were already buying all over the world and had been for a year. But our attitude was resented by Mr. Wallace and his supersmart gang. They accused us of obstructing their outfit (which we did) and of hampering the war effort by failing to buy materials, et cetera, et cetera (which we did not). What we actually obstructed were their efforts to throw money away to no good purpose. We thereby prevented them from hampering the war effort, but they did succeed in squandering a lot of money.

Mr. Wallace's desire to take charge of the spending was made perfectly plain in a long statement containing his charges that we hampered the war effort. He sent his statement to the Senate Committee on Appropriations on June 29, 1943, and released it to the press.

"It seems to me," he wrote to the Committee, "that we could end this wrangling and improve the administrative efficiency so essential to winning this war if program money were appropriated directly to the BEW for its purchase and development of *all* imported strategic materials."

I have included the complete text of Mr. Wallace's outburst in the appendix of this volume. My point-by-point reply to his outburst is also in the appendix.

After the first two or three meetings of the BEW, having seen how farcical its discussions were, I attended no more. Mr. Clayton represented me. He not only knew the score, world-wide; he knew Milo, Henry, Hector, and Morris.

CONGRESS REFUSES THEM A CHECKBOOK

There was no need whatever for the creation of the BEW; but, had it been put in charge of practical men and in its proper place, it would have been a relief to me and to the RFC because we had so very much war work. The burning wish of Henry Wallace, Milo Perkins, Morris Rosenthal, and Monroe Oppenheimer was for a direct appropriation from Congress to carry out their ambitious plans, which they never got. However, they did get $12,000,000 in 1942 for salaries and expenses which they spent and wasted lavishly. They were never trusted by Congress with a checkbook of their own with which to make purchases of materials, and should not have been given the $12,000,000 for expenses. What they hankered for was a large appropriation to finance their ideologies. Mr. Wallace's purpose seemed to be to make a big splurge to help him win the Presidency.

Our worst difficulties with the Wallace crowd had their genesis in Executive Order No. 9128, issued by the President on April 13, 1942. This order was intended to give Mr. Wallace control of all overseas economic activities of governmental agencies engaged in the importation of the materials of war. In addition to permitting them authority to direct us what to buy and where and when, and to pay no attention to the price tag, the Executive Order authorized the Wallace gang to advise the State Department with respect to the terms and conditions to be included in the Master Agreement with each nation receiving lend-lease aid. They were also to represent the United States in dealing with the economic warfare agencies of the nations allied against the Axis powers. And, what was dear to the ambitions of Mr. Wallace and his reformers, the Executive Order ordained that they should send abroad such technical and economic representatives as they might deem necessary.

When we thought their orders were proper, we complied promptly. When we thought the orders were not what they should be, we tried with great patience to reason with them. By them, I mean Messrs. Wallace, Perkins, Rosenthal, Oppenheimer and their more uppity underlings.

In disbursing many billions of dollars on preparedness and wartime directives under authority from Congress, we in the RFC never had the slightest difficulty with any agency except the BEW. If we had a request from some other agency, such as the War or Navy Department, the War Production Board, or the Maritime Commission, and wanted more information before complying, we took it up with that agency. All were invariably reasonable—all but the BEW.

At the outset, the socialist-minded uplifters with whom Mr. Wallace had surrounded himself began demanding that we insert "work clauses" in the procurement and production contracts which various RFC subsidiaries had made with Latin American countries and their nationals. What Mr. Wallace really demanded was that we interfere not only with the sovereignty of those republics, but also with the eating, housing, hygienic and working habits of their peoples. Previous to the creation of the BEW, all our contracts had been made on a commercial basis with responsible private and governmental agencies from the Rio Grande almost to the Straits of Magellan. I have told in Chapter 27 of Mr. Wallace's desire to provide free food for everybody in the Amazon Basin and of his dream of strengthening them with vitamin pills and vitaminized flour.

The work clause they kept harping upon would have compelled Latin American producers to pay their employees wages with sufficient purchasing power to equal the North American scale and also to supply sundry allegedly "social" benefits.

Mr. Wallace had a notion it would make for a happier world to teach the Indians in the jungles of the Amazon to grow vegetables in the North American manner. He dispatched an "expert" from the Department of Agriculture down to the Amazon to instruct the inhabitants how to grow spinach, string beans, lettuce, cauliflower, and other greens to which they, in their innocent content with a corn-meal and frijole diet, were totally unaccustomed. Upon his return to Washington the inspired agriculturist regaled the board of directors of the BEW for about forty-five minutes with the story of his accomplishments along the Amazon and of many other wonders yet to come. At the conclusion of his dissertation one of the directors inquired: "Who is going to teach them to eat it?" That broke up the meeting.

Another example: We were getting tin ores from Bolivia high up in the mountains where labor is more or less indifferent and hard to hire. Mr. Wallace and his gang thought that in addition to paying the contract price for tin ore we should agree to give the workers in the mines one good hot meal a day, free of any charge. The reader should understand that we had nothing whatever to do with mining the ore. Offering the mine employees a free meal would not have gotten any more tin ore but less, since the miners worked only because they had to work to eat. This plan was not made effective.

HENRY GETS ON A HIGH HORSE

President Roosevelt's Executive Order No. 9128 of April 13, 1942, giving the BEW final policy control over natural rubber procurement abroad, with power to issue directives to RFC's Rubber Reserve Company, was bad enough in provoking irritations, but there was worse to come. The following January, while the President was in Casablanca, Vice President Wallace issued his arrogant "Order No. 5," in which he sought to usurp for the BEW all of the powers to buy, stockpile, and sell foreign critical materials which the Congress had conferred upon the RFC. He unburdened himself of this ukase without notifying us or suggesting any preliminary discussions. We did not obey the order to the letter.

In a final exasperated effort to try to please Mr. Wallace and get his long-haired, incompetent, meddlesome disciples out of our hair, I went with Mr. Clayton to the Vice President's office on May 29, 1943. We arrived at an oral agreement that, if the President approved, we would turn over the RFC's United States Commercial Company, which was engaged in preemptive buying in many parts of the world, to the Wallace organization and, with certain precautionary exceptions, let it handle the development and procurement of strategic and critical materials in foreign markets. When Mr. Wallace's aides got around to reducing our oral agreement to a written draft I detected that the boys of the BEW were trying to grab much more than we had agreed to. That helped to brew the storm which broke a few weeks later when Mr. Wallace publicly assailed me and the RFC. Meanwhile, on June 1, 1943, the Vice President had sent the following letter to the President, who promptly forwarded a copy to me:

June 1, 1943

The President
The White House

Dear Mr. President:

Mr. Jones and I have agreed that, if you approve, the U.S. Commercial Company be turned over to the Board of Economic Warfare for the purpose of handling, with certain exceptions, the development and procurement of all strategic and critical materials abroad as well as for the preclusive buying in which it is now engaged.

However, the actual mechanics of the transfer have not yet been agreed upon or cleared with the Bureau of the Budget. Obviously, the mechanics are very important. In view of the fact that the transfer of the Corporation from RFC to the Board of Economic Warfare should be submitted for your signature, I am suggesting that when the presentation is finally made to you that Jesse and I come in together. Jesse and I are both hopeful that this will result in greater peace in the family.

Respectfully yours,

H. A. WALLACE

The next day I wrote the two following letters—one to the President, the other to the Vice President:

June 2, 1943

Dear Mr. President:

I am in receipt of a copy of Henry Wallace's letter to you of June 1st, and enclose copy of letter I am writing him today in regard to it.

I hope you will allow the matter to be handled the way I suggest and that you will let me talk with you a few minutes about it before it is made definite.

Sincerely yours,

JESSE H. JONES
Secretary of Commerce

The President
The White House

June 2, 1943

Dear Henry:

I have before me a copy of your letter of June 1st to the President.

I would appreciate it very much if our respective staffs, with you and I approving, could reduce our understanding of Saturday, May 29th, to writing and not have someone else undertake it.

As you know, Executive Order 9128 was issued at your instance, without either the State Department or ourselves having seen it, and yet we were expected to work under the Order.

At the request of the State Department, the Order was later modified in so far as State was concerned.

We have asked for no modification, but have tried to work under it without bothering the President.

Your Order No. 5, issued while the President was in Casablanca, went beyond any reasonable interpretation of Executive Order 9128 and has proved unworkable. This Order also was issued without our having an opportunity to discuss it, or even to see it until it was published in the Federal Register, notwithstanding we were expected to operate under it.

We have authorized the expenditure of more than $20,000,-000,000 in the war effort, at the request of, or by direction of, war policy-making agencies, including OPM, WPB, War and Navy Departments, Maritime Commission, and the Director of Economic Stabilization. Our relationship with all of them except BEW has been both satisfactory and cordial.

We are prepared to proceed in all of the matters, but our respective staffs should get together and reduce the agreements we reached Saturday, May 29th, to writing, and not have someone else attempt to do so.

When this is done and we get the approval of the President, I will ask Congress to instruct us to make funds available to the U.S. Commercial Company under BEW management.

Sincerely,

JESSE H. JONES
Secretary of Commerce

The Honorable
The Vice President

Unknown to us, Messrs. Wallace and no doubt some of his smarties were at work the while on the statement to Congress and the public attacking me and my associates—principally me.

As soon as I had read the Vice President's vituperations I demanded a full Congressional investigation of our controversy. Mr. Wallace's smearing statement had been addressed to the Senate Committee on Appropriations, from which he was eager to obtain a checkbook for the BEW. He released his statement "for consideration by this Committee, by the entire Congress and by the public at large." Specifically he attacked our conduct of the stockpiling programs, activities in which Metals Reserve Company, Defense Supplies Corporation, Rubber Development Corporation, and the United States Commercial Company were vigorously engaged. As all of these corporations were subsidiaries of the RFC, the charges of "impeding the war effort" by not throwing billions out of the window were really aimed at me. I was the stumbling block in Wallace's way. Until the time he released his attack on me and the RFC, we had had no public controversy.

President Roosevelt was apparently surprised by Mr. Wallace's attack. If he knew about it in advance, which I doubt, he was equally guilty with Wallace. At all events, he quickly got in touch with his "assistant President" and Director of War Mobilization, James F. Byrnes, whose offices were in the White House. He requested Mr. Byrnes to get Wallace and me together and "demobilize" us. Mr. Byrnes set the hour of the meeting for the afternoon of the following day, June 30.

I purposely arrived at the White House fifteen minutes late. I wanted to give Henry time to state his case to Mr. Byrnes. Entering the White House grounds, I passed through a crowd of several hundred gathered outside the gates. When I stepped inside the door leading to Mr. Byrnes' office, Mr. Wallace said, "Hello, Jesse." I did not return his greeting.

Mr. Byrnes wanted us to compose our differences. Henry and Jimmy did most of the talking. Finally I told Wallace that he had lied about me and I wanted him to prove his lies, to which he made no reply. Mr. Byrnes talked quite a lot about the damage the quarrel was doing to the Administration. He said he thought we owed it to the President to settle our squabble. I had done no quarreling either privately or publicly. In the course of the meeting I said to Mr.

Gregg in the Denver Post

An Old Story Up-to-Date.

"Herod . . . said, Ask of me whatsoever thou wilt, and I will give it to thee. And he sware, Whatsoever thou shalt ask of me, I will give it thee, unto the half of my kingdom."

Wallace that I understood he was a praying man and suggested that when he said his prayers that night he should ask God to stop him from lying. In a few minutes I absented myself from the office purportedly to make a telephone call. I really wanted to get out of the room to give Mr. Wallace a little more time to talk with Mr. Byrnes. I returned in a few minutes and, as soon as convenient, excused myself and left the meeting. Nothing was accomplished, and I was

Alley in the Nashville Banner

determined nothing should be until I had answered the malicious diatribe which Wallace had released to the press.

Later in the day Mr. Wallace issued the following statement:

> We have talked with Mr. Jesse Jones. He and I have agreed for the time being to continue the present arrangement under which the Board of Economic Warfare is functioning. Preparatory to the Congress reconvening, the Board of Economic Warfare will initiate steps through the Budget Bureau which will result in a proposal to the Congress that there be made available to BEW the necessary program funds for the procurement and development of all imported strategic war materials under public purchase so that BEW may be completely independent of RFC. Mr. Jones did not object to this policy decision.
>
> I advised Mr. Jones that in my statement to the press I had no intention to reflect upon his patriotism or his interest in the war effort. I did not state or intend to create the impression that his personal motive was deliberately or intentionally to delay the war effort.
>
> Our difficulties have had to do with strong differences of opinion with regard to the quantities of various products to be obtained at a given time and place. That there should be these differences of opinion may reflect upon the judgment of the individuals involved but such differences do not reflect upon the desire of the individuals to serve their country.

I promptly issued this brief comment for publication:

> Mr. Wallace, in his statement tonight, repeats that delays of the Reconstruction Finance Corporation have retarded the war effort. This dastardly charge is as untrue as when he first made it.
>
> As for the rest of his statement, Mr. Wallace was not authorized to speak for me. I will continue to speak for myself and, as previously stated, I shall insist upon a Congressional investigation.

In cooperation with my associates in that branch of our work, I devoted a considerable portion of the next day or two to preparing a full reply to Mr. Wallace's charges. I sent it in the form of a statement to Senator Carter Glass, chairman of the Senate Committee on Appropriations, with the following covering letter:

July 5, 1943

Dear Mr. Chairman:

June 29, Vice President Wallace, in his capacity as Chairman of the Board of Economic Warfare, released to the press a statement prepared for the Senate Committee on Appropriations containing grave charges against me and my associates in the RFC.

In my eleven years as a government official, I have consistently refrained from any public criticism of other government departments, and reluctant as I am to burden the Congress and the public with a detailed reply to Mr. Wallace, his tirade is so filled with malice, innuendo, half-truths, and no truths at all, that considerations of self-respect and of common justice to my associates force me to expose his unscrupulous tactics.

Mr. Wallace offers as an excuse for his charges that in my testimony before the Byrd Committee I gave it certain misinformation about the Board of Economic Warfare. This is a falsehood out of whole cloth. The truth is that in answer to questions as to the connection between BEW and RFC I merely testified that, by Executive Order 9128, issued April 13, 1942, BEW was given authority to issue directives to RFC agencies with respect to the purchase of critical and strategic materials from abroad.

Mr. Wallace implied that I testified before the Byrd Committee that RFC had received a directive to pay employees of the BEW. There is no truth in this. Both Mr. Wallace and Milo Perkins, who undoubtedly assisted him in the preparation of his amazing statement, must know this, because Mr. Perkins asked me by letter, June 7, if I had so testified. June 8, I replied by letter that I had not, and gave Mr. Perkins a copy of what I had said about BEW in my appearance before the Byrd Committee.

Mr. Wallace's statement that I have harassed administrative employees of BEW in "their single-minded effort to help shorten this war by securing adequate stocks of strategic materials" is as silly and ridiculous as it is false. It is completely refuted by the record, which reveals that of RFC foreign purchases and commitments totaling $3,500,000,000 made since the middle of 1940, not more than 10% has been acquired under programs initiated since BEW entered the field, April 13, 1942, and that of $1,600,000,000 in foreign materials already paid for by the RFC, less than 5% has come from such programs; and this after 15 months during which time BEW has frantically sent at great expense many "missions" composed mostly of inexperienced men to all parts of the world. Furthermore, the 10% initiated since BEW entered the field would have been undertaken anyway by RFC under recommendations of the War Production Board, which is the planning and policy-making agency of the Government for war production, and the procurement of strategic materials, and from which agency BEW gets recommendations for which it gives RFC directives.

In the war effort, RFC functions as a service agency, and not as a war policy-making agency. RFC acts on recommendations of the President, War Production Board and its predecessor agencies, the State, War and Navy Departments, the Rubber Director, the Maritime Commission, the Petroleum Coordinator for War, and the Board of Economic Warfare.

A very significant thing in this controversy is the fact that not one of these agencies has had reason to complain, nor has any except BEW ever complained, of RFC's performance in the war effort, which has involved the authorization of expenditures of more than $20,000,000,000.

RFC began foreign purchases in the summer of 1940, and has complied efficiently and speedily with every request made of it by the President or any war policy-making agency.

Because of the nature of some of the directives from BEW, some of the trades they make and contracts they prepare for execution by RFC agencies without consulting RFC, it has been necessary to call their attention to errors and poor practices in some of the contracts. Their reluctance to admit anything but in-fallibility has sometimes required a few days to make the necessary corrections, and sometimes they refuse, but no delay in any important material has been occasioned by RFC agencies.

RFC has always believed, and after years of experience now believes more strongly than ever, that the maximum production and procurement of materials can be obtained, in a minimum of time and at a minimum of expense, without resorting to methods bordering on the hysterical.

The foreign purchase program of the RFC has been conducted under the personal direction of W. L. Clayton, who has had wide experience in the field of foreign trade for many years. He has been assisted by a number of competent men, among them G. Temple Bridgman, Executive Vice President of Metals Reserve Company, who has been a leading figure for many years in the metals trade, both in this country and abroad.

RFC has felt, and it has learned, that production is best brought out and handled through established and experienced agencies, and not by sending great groups of inexperienced men to overrun foreign countries. A few well-selected men, under proper leadership, can accomplish much more in foreign countries, utilizing the citizens of such countries as much as possible, than scores of our own people hastily brought together and sent abroad with little knowledge of what they are to do or of the country to which they are sent.

While generous prices are desirable and often necessary in the war effort, lavish prices do not always increase production. Our immediate efforts in the foreign field should be concentrated on war procurement needs, and not on post-war ideologies. Furthermore, it is the unspectacular rather than the spectacular methods, and the quiet rather than the noisy approach, which accomplish the most.

Mr. Wallace speaks of sending a hundred men to Brazil alone, on a single program. It is our belief that those hundred men, hastily recruited as they were, and with little or no familiarity with the work they were to do, have done little more than get in each other's way, and substitute confusion for order. That program would be in better shape today if most of those hundred men had stayed at home.

If the policy of the RFC in dealing with private business at home and abroad, when possible, subjects me to Mr. Wallace's criticism, that cannot be helped. It is my belief that Government should seek to preserve private business, use it wherever possible in the war effort, and operate directly only when necessary.

The statements made by Mr. Wallace and Mr. Perkins before the Senate Banking and Currency Committee in December, 1942, and to which the former again refers, were at that time shown to be unjustified and some of them untrue. My answer is contained in the hearings of that Committee. My detailed reply to his present accusations is attached.

The President's Executive Order 9128 gave BEW authority to issue directives to the RFC with respect to foreign purchases. That Mr. Wallace's own Order No. 5, issued while the President was in Casablanca, has equal force, is open to serious question.

Under Mr. Wallace's Order No. 5, officials of the RFC are allegedly given no choice but to sign, without question or inquiry, any contract or make any commitment which BEW negotiates and prepares and gives a directive for, regardless of the terms and conditions of the contract or the extent of the Government obligation assumed.

The RFC and its operations are well known to Congress. It is bi-partisan by law and in its administration. Its Directors are men of character, experience and ability. They are appointed by the President, and confirmed by the Senate. Their duties and responsibilities cannot be properly discharged by signing blank checks or executing without careful examination contracts that commit the Government for hundreds of millions of dollars.

The directives RFC receives from BEW are signed by Milo Perkins, Morris Rosenthal, or Arthur Paul. At the pleasure of Mr. Wallace they may be signed by any employee of BEW whom Mr. Wallace designates.

These directives are not considered or approved by the members of the Board of Economic Warfare. The members know very little of BEW operations. To my knowledge, and I am a member of the Board, few, if any, purchase or development contracts have been considered at Board meetings, much less formally approved by the Board.

As for the charge which Mr. Wallace appears to regard as a major crime, that I have attempted to safeguard the taxpayers' money, I must plead guilty. Squandering the people's money even in wartime is no proof of patriotism. The RFC does not pay $2.00 for something it can buy for $1.00. Maybe no one does, but the point is that some men know when you can buy it for $1.00, some don't know, and some don't care as long as they are spending other people's money.

It takes a long time and a lot of hard work to build an organization of men who are competent to trade and to handle vast sums of money properly—particularly public money. The RFC has such an organization, and I am proud of it.

I will appreciate your placing this letter and my accompanying statement in the official record.

Sincerely yours,

JESSE H. JONES
Secretary of Commerce

Honorable Carter Glass,
Chairman, Senate Committee on Appropriations,
Washington, D.C.

GREASING THE SKIDS FOR WALLACE

Having publicly answered Mr. Wallace, I gave little further thought to the matter and made no effort to see the President. The controversy raised reams of newspaper and magazine comment. From coast to coast columnists and cartoonists had a field day, much to the President's discomfort. After reading about the rumpus for two weeks, the President on July 15, without any advance notice to me, issued an Executive Order which purported to relieve me of all responsibilities in foreign economic matters and at the same time abolished Wallace's Board of Economic Warfare and all its works and pomps. The foreign economic responsibilities which had fallen under my jurisdiction as Federal Loan Administrator, such as the preemptive purchases of the United States Commercial Company, the stockpiling procurements of several other RFC subsidiaries, and the foreign-trade loans of the Export-Import Bank, were ordered to be transferred to a new Office of Economic Warfare, at the head of which the President appointed my friend Leo T. Crowley. Mr. Crowley and I went on working together in harmony. He made no changes in what we were doing abroad. Mr. Wallace was out of a war job. He was once more just the Vice President with little to do but wait for the President to die, which fortunately did not occur while Henry was Vice President.

Simultaneously with his issuance of the Executive Order of July 15, the President made public a letter which he had addressed jointly to Mr. Wallace and me. It follows:

Gentlemen:

I have come to the conclusion that the unfortunate controversy and acrimonious public debate which has been carried on between you in the public press concerning the administration of foreign economic matters make it necessary, in the public interest, to transfer these matters into other hands.

In the midst of waging a war so critical to our national security and to the future of all civilization, there is not sufficient time to investigate and determine where the truth lies in your conflicting versions as to transactions which took place over a year and a half ago.

My action today is not intended to decide that question. The important thing is to clear the decks and to get on with the war at once. To do this requires a fresh start with new men, unencumbered by inter-agency dissension and bitterness.

I am persuaded that the present controversy indicates that future cooperative action between your two agencies is impossible, and that without full cooperation between you the program of economic warfare cannot be carried out.

I am sure that the American people understand that both of you have attempted to do your duty as you have seen it; but we must go forward without any further public debate as to matters which are now academic as far as winning the war is presently concerned.

I have therefore issued today an executive order of which I am attaching a copy for your information and guidance.

Very sincerely yours,
FRANKLIN D. ROOSEVELT

The President knew where the fault lay; but because of his great friendship for Wallace he would not directly put the blame where it belonged—on Mr. Wallace—except to abolish his agency and his war job. But the country got the point.

Along with his letter to Mr. Wallace and me, the President on the same day addressed identical letters to the heads of all government departments and agencies telling them that if they got into an inter-departmental row and released a statement about it without first submitting it to him, he would expect to receive a letter of resignation from the author of the statement.

The press release which the President issued to convey his referee's decision in the dispute between Mr. Wallace and me, said:

MY TWO SPONSORS

Senator Carter Glass and Speaker John N. Garner at a baseball game in Washington.

OUR TWO HOMES

During the depression the Corporation's headquarters were in the building at the left. In 1941 the agency moved into the newly built Lafayette Building. (Both photos Underwood & Underwood, Washington, D.C.)

The President today issued an Executive Order to unify the policy of the various administrative agencies engaged in different phases of foreign economic matters. The order also relieves both the Vice President and the Secretary of Commerce of any responsibilities or duties in this field and transfers such responsibilities and duties to other hands.

1. The present Board of Economic Warfare, of which the Vice President is chairman, is abolished.

2. All of its powers, functions and duties are transferred to a new Office of Economic Warfare, headed by a director. Mr. Leo T. Crowley has been appointed such director.

3. The United States Commercial Corporation, the Rubber Development Corporation, the Petroleum Reserves Corporation, the Export-Import Bank of Washington, and all the other subsidiaries of the Reconstruction Finance Corporation which are now engaged in financing foreign purchases and imports, are transferred from the Department of Commerce and from the Reconstruction Finance Corporation to the new Office of Economic Warfare to be administered by the new director.

4. Until such time as the Congress provides other means of financing the Office of Economic Warfare, the Reconstruction Finance Corporation is directed to turn over to the Office of Economic Warfare all funds necessary to carry on its operations.

5. The director of the Office of War Mobilization is given the responsibility of unifying and coordinating the policies and programs of the agencies engaged in foreign economic matters in conformity with foreign policy of the United States as determined by the State Department.

The letter which the President sent to the heads of departments and agencies follows:

Dear Sir:

On August 21, 1942, I sent to the head of each department and agency of the Federal Government a letter, copy of which is attached.

I call your attention to the statement contained in that letter that "disagreements either as to fact or policy should not be publicly aired, but are to be submitted to me by the appropriate heads of the conflicting agencies." Notwithstanding these positive instructions, disagreements between agencies have been publicly aired on several occasions.

I realize the nervous strain under which Government officials are working in war time, but I cannot overlook any further violations of my instructions.

By this letter I do not place any restriction upon your furnishing statements in response to Congressional inquiries.

But if when you have a disagreement with another agency as to fact or policy, instead of submitting it to me or submitting it to the Director of War Mobilization for settlement under the terms of the order creating that office, you feel you should submit it to the press, I ask that when you release the statement for publication, you send me a letter of resignation.

If any subordinate of yours violates my instructions in this regard, I shall expect you to ask for his immediate resignation.

Sincerely yours,

FRANKLIN D. ROOSEVELT

After reading the new Executive Order and the President's letter to me and that to the heads of departments, I issued the following statement:

I concur most heartily in the President's determination to have harmony and cooperation between government officials and agencies in the war effort. The Department of Commerce and the Reconstruction Finance Corporation and its subsidiary corporations engaged in foreign purchases will render every possible assistance to the new Director of Economic Warfare.

The director will find the affairs of all RFC agencies engaged in foreign purchases, as well as the Export-Import Bank, in excellent condition. He will find the organizations functioning with a maximum of efficiency and at a minimum of expense.

The President could not have selected a better qualified man for the important assignment of Director of the Office of Economic Warfare than Leo T. Crowley. Mr. Crowley is well and favorably known to the business and financial world because of his able administration of the Federal Deposit Insurance Corporation and as Alien Property Custodian.

THE AX FALLS IN CHICAGO

The controversy wrecked the political career which the President was carving out for Mr. Wallace; but he continued to groom Wallace to be his running mate again in 1944, so that the Chief Executive's mantle would ultimately fall to Wallace. The President remained hopeful of having Mr. Wallace as his fourth-term running mate until a few hours before the Democratic Convention opened in Chicago in mid-July of 1944. He had written a letter to Senator Samuel Jackson, temporary chairman of the convention, to be read to the delegates, saying he had been associated with Henry Wallace during the past four years as Vice President and for eight years earlier while he was Secretary of Agriculture, and even before that.

"I like him and I respect him," the letter continued. "For these reasons, I personally would vote for his nomination if I were a delegate to the Convention."

However, before the convention opened the President's best informed political advisers, particularly Robert E. Hannegan, the Democratic National Chairman, Ed Flynn, boss of the Bronx, Ed Kelly, Kingpin of Chicago, and Frank Hague, nabob of New Jersey, made it clear to him that he wouldn't be able to cram Wallace down the throats of a majority of the delegates. When convinced of that, the President wrote another letter, this one addressed to Bob Hannegan, saying that he would be happy to have either Senator Harry S. Truman or Associate Justice William O. Douglas as the Vice Presidential candidate. As the President originally drafted it, the letter said William O. Douglas or Harry S. Truman. Mr. Hannegan, who hailed from Senator Truman's Missouri, persuaded the President to transpose the names, putting Senator Truman's ahead of Mr. Justice Douglas'—a master political stroke which explains Mr. Truman's presence in the White House. In view of the foregoing, it is interesting to record that according to James F. Byrnes the President had assured him in 1944 that he was to be his running mate.

It was current gossip that Tom Corcoran, Secretary Ickes, and Attorney General Biddle busied themselves at the Chicago convention trying to manuever Truman out and Douglas in. Bob Hannegan told me there were five Cabinet members at the convention, and, so far as he could figure out, they controlled a total of one delegate vote. I was not at the convention, being ill at the time with pneumonia.

During the campaign Mr. Wallace, being out in the cold politically, made soapbox speeches for the Roosevelt-Truman ticket.

The suggestion sent to Congress by President Roosevelt on the day after his fourth inaugural that Mr. Wallace, who possessed odd and mystic notions about business and finance, should be placed in charge of the government's lending agencies, which were then dealing in billions of dollars, startled the country and shocked the Congress into immediately taking steps to see to it that, whatever else Mr. Wallace got hold of, he wouldn't get his hands on Uncle Sam's checkbook. This sound sentiment was shared by a large portion of the Democratic Representatives and Senators, along with the Republicans.

When the President nominated Mr. Wallace to replace me as Secretary of Commerce, Senator Walter F. George of Georgia introduced a bill to separate the Federal Loan Administration, which included the RFC and its subsidiaries, from the Department of Commerce. The Senate Commerce Committee voted 15 to 4 in favor of the bill, 6 of those opposing Mr. Wallace being members of what was then his own political party. Then, by a vote of 15 to 5, the committee rejected a motion to report favorably on Wallace's nomination to be Secretary of Commerce—one of the few such instances in the history of the Republic. Mr. Wallace, it should be kept in mind, had just concluded a four-year term as Vice President of the United States and presiding officer over the deliberations of these Senators.

The George bill passed the House on February 16, 1945, by a thumping vote of 400 to 2. The only two Representatives who apparently wanted Mr. Wallace as Federal Loan Administrator were William Lemke of North Dakota and Earl Wilson of Indiana.

The Senate, after passing the George bill, 74 to 12, confirmed Mr. Wallace as Secretary of Commerce by the far from flattering vote of 56 to 32. The Senate made a mistake, which I am sure it soon recognized. The President had sent Wallace's name up to the Hill in January. So abiding was the objection to him that it was not until March 1 that he was confirmed, under what to many another man would have been embarrassing circumstances.

The Vice President is not a member of the Cabinet; but it became the custom during the first Roosevelt administration to invite the Vice President to all meetings of the Cabinet, and this practice had

Goldberg in New York Sun

been continued after Mr. Wallace succeeded Mr. Garner. At the Cabinet sessions Mr. Wallace was free to discuss problems and report his impression of conditions on the Hill; but, as a matter of fact, he was less acquainted with what went on in the Senate and the House than almost anyone else at the Capitol. He seemed to have no contacts in the Senate nor any social relations with its members and was seldom in the chair. While almost every Senator was a personal friend of Vice President Garner, scarcely any of them seemed to know Henry Wallace, probably because he didn't live in their world.

Wallace seemed always to be critical of the State Department. It was his ambition, as another step toward the White House, to be Secretary of State. He and Secretary Ickes of the Interior became self-appointed Secretaries of the Exterior, it being the custom of both those gentlemen to deluge the President with letters of advice and counsel on all manner of subjects external to the responsibilities of their own offices.

When I saw the President in the Oval Room at the White House on the Sunday noon following his fourth inaugural and my receipt of his letter telling me he was going to appoint Wallace to replace me as Secretary of Commerce, he explained to me that he had promised Henry almost any post in the government that he wanted and that Henry wanted to be Secretary of State. But, the President continued, he had told Henry he did not feel he could give him that. Henry then chose to become Secretary of Commerce, which included the Federal Loan job. Congress, of course, by passing the George bill saw to it that Wallace did not get hold of the loan agencies and Henry took what he could get—Secretary of Commerce. Vice President Truman, at the request of President Roosevelt, lobbied among the Senators for Wallace's confirmation. Otherwise he would not have been confirmed. Six weeks later, as President, Mr. Truman inherited Wallace as a member of the Cabinet. The new President was not long in giving Henry the boot.

Jim Berryman in Washington Evening Star

38

———————— ☼ ————————

THE MEN WHO RAN THE RFC

*How the RFC Was Organized—I Become a Director—
President Hoover Looks for a Democrat—President
Roosevelt Looks for Republicans—I Become Federal
Loan Administrator—Joining the Cabinet—Our Alumni
Make Good*

LATE in 1931, when the bill which brought the RFC into being
was under consideration by Congress, I was asked by some friends
in the Senate what I thought of the idea. I told them I thought something of the kind was desirable.

Early in January of 1932 I went to Washington to attend a meeting
of the Democratic National Committee. While I was there a number
of Senators asked me for suggestions for the Democratic members
of the Board of Directors of the RFC. I told them the directors should
be men of business experience who realized that most of our country
lies west of the Hudson River, and none of it east of the Atlantic
Ocean. I had in mind the many foreign loans that had gone sour,
loans made both by our government and by investment bankers. I
gave them two or three names, but none was appointed. I expressed
the view that the directors should be men who were willing to go all
out and take a chance on the country.

When asked by two or three Senators if I would consider going on
the Board, I replied that I could not, that my own rather extensive
affairs required all of my attention.

The bill, when passed, provided for seven directors, not more than
four of whom could be of one political faith, thereby making it a
bipartisan agency. It provided that the Secretary of the Treasury, the

Farm Loan Commissioner, and the Governor of the Federal Reserve Board should be ex-officio directors of the RFC. Since all three of these men were Republicans that left only one Republican appointive position. It went to former Vice President Charles G. Dawes. Andrew W. Mellon was Secretary of the Treasury; Paul Bestor, Farm Loan Commissioner; and Eugene Meyer, Governor of the Federal Reserve Board.

Prior to the passage of the original RFC bill on January 22, 1932, the House of Representatives had become Democratic by one vote, through the death of a Republican member who was succeeded by a Democrat. The House had then elected John N. Garner of Texas as its Speaker. President Hoover advised with him and other Democratic leaders as to the selection of the three Democratic members of the RFC Board.

Senator Joseph T. Robinson of Arkansas, minority leader in the Senate, suggested his fellow Arkansan, Harvey C. Couch, a public utility and railroad executive with whom Mr. Hoover had become friendly during flood-control work in 1927. Later I was told that our Texas Senators gave Mr. Hoover a list of five Texans from whom to choose, if a Texan were to be included. My name was on the list. Other names, I assume, were suggested to the President by Senators from different sections of the country. I understood later that Mr. Garner, although he had never spoken to me about it, insisted on my appointment, and that Senator Carter Glass of Virginia, ranking minority member of the Banking and Currency Committee, which handled the RFC legislation, concurred with him.

While Mr. Garner was a fellow Texan, my acquaintance with him was slight, since we lived in different sections of our rather large state. I had known Carter Glass in Washington during World War I, when he was a Representative in Congress. I had also seen a good deal of him in Houston during the Democratic National Convention in 1928.

Senator William H. King of Utah recommended Wilson McCarthy of Salt Lake City. That completed the three Democrats. General Dawes became president of the Corporation, and Eugene Meyer, chairman.

Earlier, talking with me about Democrats to be appointed to the Board, Senator Glass said quite frankly that if the President asked his advice he would recommend my appointment. I told Senator Glass, as I had two or three of his colleagues, that I could not accept the appointment if it should be tendered me.

From the National Committee meeting in Washington on January 8, I had gone to New York. Two weeks later my secretary, William C. Costello, reminded me that Bascom N. Timmons, Washington correspondent for my paper, the Houston *Chronicle,* was to be inaugurated president of the National Press Club that evening. Mr. Costello thought I should attend, and I did. The next morning— a Sunday—I had a telephone call from President Hoover asking if he could send my name to the Senate as a director of the new RFC. I replied to the President that I would be glad to be of any assistance that I could. I had had a glimpse of him the evening before at the National Press Club meeting honoring Timmons. I had known Mr. Hoover slightly during World War I when he was Food Administrator.

While in New York during those two weeks in January, 1932, I had learned that conditions throughout the country were much more serious than I had thought. I felt it my duty to do anything I could in the general interest, regardless of my personal affairs. I had the impression, however, that the RFC directors would employ executives to operate the Corporation, and that the principal job of the Board would be to outline policies and supervise the operation, and that it would not be a full-time job. I had not read the law.

Had I known it would be a full-time job, I doubt if I would have thought it possible to accept the appointment, although each of my business enterprises was under competent management: the bank, the newspaper and radio stations, the building operations, and the mortgage company. As it turned out, I went to work two days later with General Dawes, the only other appointive director on the job, and even before our nominations were confirmed by the Senate. We used the offices of the Comptroller of the Currency, who was temporarily in California because of the critical situation in the Bank of America, with a strong proxy fight being waged for control of its vast empire of banks.

In a few days we were occupying two floors of an office building on H Street, with an organization which Chairman Meyer had hurriedly set up. It was composed largely of former employees of the old War Finance Corporation, of which Mr. Meyer had been the head during and following World War I. Within a year we were occupying the entire building. Later—in 1939 and 1940—we erected a new and much larger home, the Lafayette Building. We made a loan to construct this building with an option to buy it, and soon exercised our option.

HOW THE RFC WAS ORGANIZED

When we set up shop in 1932 I soon found that being a member of the board of directors of the RFC required fifteen to eighteen hours a day, Sundays not excepted. I telephoned my wife to join me, and, much against her wish, she did. We spent the next fourteen years in Washington hotels.

I had had some experience with troubled banks in Houston during and following the panic of 1907, and again in October, 1931, when we cleaned up our home town's banking troubles. So I was not an entirely green hand at bank and business rescue work. I had been a money borrower all of my business life, and a money lender most of it, and had a fair understanding of the problems and points of view of both sides of the desk. But, in the beginning, none of us had any conception of the extent of the gathering troubles.

When President Hoover signed the RFC Act on January 22, 1932, the directors, who took office ten days later, were confronted with the gigantic task of quickly organizing a general office in Washington, with branch offices wherever there were Federal Reserve Banks. Under the law, the "Federals" were fiscal agents for the RFC. This was done almost entirely by Eugene Meyer, our chairman, and he did a good job. Being Governor of the Federal Reserve Board gave him contacts with the banks in cities throughout the country where there was a Federal Reserve bank or branch bank. These banks were helpful to him in suggesting men he might employ for both our Washington office and our thirty-three agencies.

The agencies, each in charge of a manager with a staff selected or approved by the Board, were located in the following cities:

Atlanta	Houston	Oklahoma City
Birmingham	Jacksonville	Omaha
Boston	Kansas City	Philadelphia
Charlotte	Little Rock	Portland, Ore.
Chicago	Los Angeles	Richmond
Cleveland	Louisville	St. Louis
Dallas	Memphis	Salt Lake City

Denver	Minneapolis	San Antonio
Detroit	Nashville	San Francisco
El Paso	New Orleans	Seattle
Helena	New York	Spokane

The agencies received applications for loans and transmitted them to Washington with their recommendations. Competent local advisory committees, the members of which served without compensation, were appointed by the Board to assist the managers in passing on loans. On these advisory committees, with 363 members at the start, were some of the leading bankers, farmers, industrialists, and businessmen of their respective sections of the country. Their names had been suggested largely by the Federal Reserve banks and branch banks.

Recruiting competent personnel was in itself a big undertaking. Mr. Meyer quickly put together a skeleton staff from the old War Finance Corporation and the Federal Reserve banks.

There was another aid to our rapid mobilization of a working force—a little black address book carried by Leopold H. Paulger, a former Iowa banker. Leo Paulger had been assistant to the directors of the War Finance Corporation for five years and then for four more years was chief of the Division of Examiners of the Federal Farm Loan Board. He had been all over the country. He brought in scores of his acquaintances from all directions. During the early months he was made chief of our examining division.

Finding available men who knew something about banking was not too difficult. So many banks had failed that unemployed bankers were numerous. With forms to prepare and legal procedures to establish, we also needed attorneys. In those depressed times the woods—and city skyscrapers—were full of bright young lawyers who weren't sure whether there would be enough fees to pay next month's rent. So that part of early mobilization of help was comparatively easy, except for the fact that we were pressed for time, as the economic situation was rapidly, desperately deteriorating.

Secretary Mellon attended only one or two of the daily meetings of our Board. On February 5, three days after the RFC was launched, he was confirmed as American Ambassador to Great Britain. He relinquished the Treasury post and Ogden L. Mills, his Under Secretary, was appointed Secretary and thereupon became an ex-officio member of the Board. During the early months Secretary Mills, a forceful and capable man, and Chairman Meyer largely determined the policies of the Corporation. They, of course, consulted with President Hoover, as did General Dawes and occasionally Mr. Couch.

It took some time for the seven directors to get really acquainted. They had come from different climes, economically and socially as well as geographically. Mr. Couch was from Arkansas, Mr. McCarthy from Utah, Messrs. Mills and Meyer from New York, Mr. Bestor from New Jersey, General Dawes from Illinois, and I from Texas. Several months passed before Chairman Meyer and Secretary Mills seemed to think it necessary to regard the Democratic directors as their equals on the Board, a fact that brought on clashes with Mr. Meyer and sometimes differences with Secretary Mills. When Mr. Mills could not attend our meetings, Under Secretary Arthur A. Ballantine represented the Treasury. He was most helpful. He treated us Democratic members as if we had a share in the responsibility.

I have given Mr. Meyer credit for having set up a good organization. But his attitude toward his fellow directors left much to be desired. I shall cite two or three instances. G. A. Marr, our first general counsel, worked himself to a frazzle and lost his health after a few months. In his absence the work was carried on very satisfactorily by Walston Chubb, a dynamic young man from St. Louis who was an assistant general counsel. Then, one day Mr. Meyer announced to the Board that he had employed Morton Bogue of New York as general counsel to succeed Mr. Marr. Mr. Bogue had been handling our railroad loans. I promptly objected. Mr. Meyer wanted to know what I had against Mr. Bogue. I told him nothing, but that he should have consulted his Board before engaging Mr. Bogue or anyone else in so important a position; that Mr. Chubb as acting general counsel was doing a good job, and I saw no reason why he should not be given the position. Third, I did not think it was necessary for us to go to New York for everything.

I had nothing against Morton Bogue as a man and a lawyer, and I had never seen Mr. Chubb except in the RFC; nor did he know about the discussion. The matter was deferred. On hearing about it, Mr. Chubb asked me not to urge his appointment.

A few days later General Dawes told me that President Hoover agreed with my position in the matter and wanted to know if a certain attorney in another section of the country, whose name it is unnecessary to mention here, would be acceptable to me. I looked up the gentleman's record and decided he was none too well suited for the job.

Some ten days or two weeks later Mr. Meyer, assuming that we were going to employ the gentleman President Hoover had suggested, asked if the Board was prepared to consider the appointment of a General Counsel. Much to his surprise and that of my codirectors, I immediately placed Mr. Bogue in nomination for the position, and he was chosen.

I thought Mr. Bogue better suited for the job than the other man who had been suggested and, furthermore, believed I had succeeded in putting over the point that Mr. Meyer should consult the Board before appointing executive officers in the Corporation, and that, whoever these officers might be, they should understand that they were working for the Board and not alone for the Chairman. But sometime later Mr. Meyer announced at a Board meeting that he had employed Lynn P. Talley as special assistant to the Board at a higher salary than the directors were drawing.

Again I objected, and for the same reasons that I had originally objected to the engagement of Mr. Bogue. Mr. Talley was a Texan who had held good positions in banks in both Houston and Dallas, and who, more recently, had been chairman of the board of the Bank of America in San Francisco, the big Giannini bank, at a time when that bank was under the control of Elisha Walker of New York. When A. P. Giannini regained control of it in February, 1932, Mr. Talley lost his position.

I liked Mr. Talley and knew he was qualified. After letting Mr. Meyer understand again that the other directors should be consulted in important matters, we approved Mr. Talley's employment. He rendered exceptional service to the Corporation for a number of years, especially as President of Commodity Credit Corporation, until his health gave way. These clashes and probably a few others were necessary to establish a proper relationship among the directors.

Our business had started with a bang and never let up. Our first bank loan, conditionally authorized on February 2, was $15,000,000 to the Giannini bank. It had, I suppose, been under consideration by the Secretary of the Treasury and Mr. Meyer before we opened the RFC. The Bank of America loan was negotiated by them. Two days after our opening we authorized a $200,000 loan to the Commercial National Bank of Lafayette & Trust Company of Lafayette, Louisiana, and the first installment of $6,000,000 eventually loaned to the East Tennessee National Bank of Knoxville. The troubled Tennessee bankers had applied to General Dawes and me while we were still in the Comptroller's offices.

A number of loans to other banks were made during our first two weeks, and several to railroads, including the Pennsylvania, the Missouri Pacific and the Frisco. In the division of work among our directors after I was elected chairman in 1933, the railroads became one of my particular assignments, and remained so as long as I was a director of the Corporation or Federal Loan Administrator.

At the start the RFC had a capital of $500,000,000 and the authority to borrow $1,500,000,000 from the Treasury. This seemed a lot of money at the time, but it was only the beginning of a flow that ultimately totaled $50,000,000,000 authorized by us to fight, first the depression, then the Second World War.

In our first month of operation we authorized almost exactly 1,000 loans, including $158,000,000 to 858 banks and trust companies, nearly $61,000,000 to sixteen railroads, and about $10,-000,000 to mortgage loan companies and building and loan associations.

Even at the start some of our directors favored freer lending; but the majority of the Board was cautious. Mr. Couch thought the Corporation should help everybody. Mr. McCarthy proved an excellent director and was particularly interested in helping the cattle and sheep people. He had courage and good judgment. He had one or two rather blunt and bitter clashes with Mr. Meyer over some sheep and cattle loans, which he handled. He understood stockmen's problems better than the rest of us, and did the job well.

Mr. Bestor was excellent, but a fairly conservative mortgage lender. He was accustomed to government service, which Couch, McCarthy, and I were not. Mr. Meyer and Mr. Mills wanted to help the railroads and seemed more interested in the larger situations. I do not mean by that that they were not sympathetic with the smaller problems, but, living in New York and dealing with expansive affairs, they seemed to feel that we should first take care of the big situations. We country boys were thinking also of the little fellow and the country at large.

During the first year of the Corporation's life, Congress was quite skeptical of it. This was not necessarily to its discredit, since the government had embarked on a new type of operation, putting government money behind the whole national economy.

The first change in the Board of Directors came in June, 1932, when General Dawes resigned and returned to Chicago to try to save his own bank.

It soon became apparent that the Act which created the RFC was much too restrictive, that the task of economic reconstruction and restoration of confidence required a broader approach than our financial and political leaders had foreseen. The original Act did not permit loans for public works, for direct relief or loans to business, or for putting capital into banks and insurance companies. Nor was it effective in immediately reviving business, or even to any great extent in halting the downward trend, which did not reach bottom until March, 1933. The Act provided that we could lend only on full and adequate security, and it was not easy to determine what constituted full and adequate security.

In early June of 1932, Representative Henry T. Rainey of Illinois, the Democratic leader of the House, introduced a bill to broaden our powers. The bill passed both houses, but President Hoover vetoed it. It would have provided, among other things, for relief funds to states and territories, self-liquidating loans, and a public-works program. It would also have authorized the RFC to lend to individuals and to states and municipalities and their political subdivisions.

Of loans to individuals President Hoover, in his veto message, wrote: "This proposal violates every sound principle of public finance and of government. Never before has so much power for evil been placed at the unlimited discretion of seven individuals." The seven individuals were the directors of the RFC. The President was right in regard to lending to individuals.

In vetoing the bill Mr. Hoover recommended that a compromise be reached on terms suggested by certain members of both houses and both parties. He asked Congress not to adjourn until this could be accomplished. Congress immediately reconsidered and passed the Emergency Relief and Construction Act of 1932, which the President approved on July 21. It enlarged our powers, increased our borrowing authority and provided for replacing two of the three ex-officio Board members—the Governor of the Federal Reserve, and the Farm Loan Commissioner—with appointive members. Thus Mr. Meyer and Mr. Bestor departed from our directorate.

PRESIDENT HOOVER LOOKS FOR A DEMOCRAT

In July, President Hoover appointed Gardner Cowles, Sr., a Republican publisher of Des Moines, to take General Dawes' place on the Board, but he did not give him the title of president. So now there were both the presidency and the chairmanship to fill.

About this time, Ogden Mills told me in his office when I was there on RFC business that the President was going to appoint the biggest Democrat in the country as chairman. I replied to Secretary Mills that I thought by then they should know whom to make chairman, but he didn't take the hint.

Later, I was told, but without confirmation, that President Hoover offered the chairmanship to Owen D. Young, head of the General Electric Company, and for the presidency of the Corporation had sounded out both Melvin A. Traylor, president of the First National Bank of Chicago, and Newton D. Baker of Cleveland, who had been Woodrow Wilson's Secretary of War, but all three of these distinguished Democrats had declined the invitation. Owen Young would undoubtedly have made a good chairman and Mr. Traylor a good president. Both had had broad executive and administrative experience in business and finance. Newton Baker was an excellent man, but had not had the kind of experience needed to operate the RFC.

In seeking a Democrat for chairman, Mr. Hoover, who had just been nominated by the Republican party for a second term in the White House, told some of his associates that, with the Presidential campaign approaching, he wished the majority of the RFC Board to be Democrats so that he would not be accused of "playing politics with the miseries of the people."

The Democrat he appointed as our chairman was Atlee Pomerene, a lawyer and formerly United States Senator from Ohio. Simultaneously the President named Charles A. Miller, a lawyer and savings-bank official of Utica, New York, and a Republican, to fill the other vacancy and assume the title of president of the Corporation. Mr. Miller, on the recommendation of Owen D. Young, had previously been appointed the first manager of the RFC's agency in New York.

Thus, on August 1, 1932, we again had a full board of seven members, but now four were Democrats and three were Republicans.

Because Congress was not in session, neither Mr. Pomerene nor

Mr. Miller was confirmed by the Senate; so when the new administration came in on March 4, 1933, they were automatically retired. Mr. Pomerene and Franklin D. Roosevelt were not mutually congenial, and Mr. Miller, whose health had become impaired under the strain of work, didn't like the new President either; so neither of these directors would have remained on our Board after March 4, even if his nomination had been confirmed.

The law firm of which Senator Pomerene was a senior member, was counsel for the RFC's Cleveland agency. It had been selected by Chairman Meyer in the beginning and was retained when I became chairman. The Cleveland agency was one of our biggest, both in dollar volume and in number of loans. The firm's services were exceptionally satisfactory, and the cost to the RFC per dollar volume was much smaller than in any of our other agencies. Not many months after Mr. Roosevelt became President another law firm or two in Cleveland, with Democratic political ties more of the New Deal type than Pomerene's, began angling for the RFC's legal business, and I would hear from the President about it. In each such instance I would give the President a written memorandum showing the cost to the Corporation of the Pomerene firm's services compared to that of all our other agencies. After a few years the President thought we could afford to give at least one other firm in Cleveland a part of the business, and we did. Incidentally, the most expensive law services we received in any agency were from a firm in Florida of which Senator Claude D. Pepper had been a partner. He had secured the business.

A month after Mr. Roosevelt took office, Mr. Cowles resigned. He was an excellent man but was very conservative, and, I think, did not wish to stay on under a Democratic administration. With his departure there were three vacancies on the Board. All four of the remaining directors were Democrats, the original three appointed by President Hoover and President Roosevelt's newly named Secretary of the Treasury, William H. Woodin, who had replaced the outgoing Secretary Mills in our deliberations. Mr. Woodin attended only one or two meetings, so McCarthy, Couch, and I had the full responsibility.

Once again our Corporation had neither chairman nor president. Mr. Roosevelt had told me he wanted me to be chairman. Under the law, as amended, the Board of Directors of the RFC select their own chairman; but as a matter of policy he should be acceptable to the President, and that practice has always been followed.

After President Roosevelt's inauguration, thinking he might perhaps have changed his mind and would prefer someone else, I called the White House to remind him that we were without a chairman. Raymond Moley, who was working closely with the President, answered my call and delivered the message. He came back to the phone and told me the President said for me to go ahead as acting chairman. I said nothing, but did not follow the suggestion. I thought we should have a permanent chairman. For several weeks we had no chairman.

All of the board members expected me to be chairman, but I suggested that we rotate, each director being chairman for a day. This plan was adopted. After about two months of rotating, I ran into Postmaster General James A. Farley one morning at breakfast in the Mayflower Hotel, where we were both living. I explained our situation and told him that if he cared to take the message, I would be glad to have him tell the President, if he wanted me to be chairman of the Board, to say so. I explained that it was not good for the organization to be without a head. About an hour later Secretary of the Treasury Woodin telephoned me and explained that the President thought I was already chairman. He said that, of course, the President meant me to be chairman. I told Mr. Woodin that, since he was a member of our Board and had attended only one or two meetings, he should attend at least one more and put me in nomination. He did so that same morning, apologizing for his neglect.

It soon developed that Secretary Woodin was not in good health. He told me he was going to resign as soon as the President would let him, and he wanted me to succeed him as Secretary of the Treasury. Mr. Woodin was a good man and a gentle character.

Arthur Ballantine, a Republican, who had been Under Secretary of the Treasury in the Hoover administration, graciously offered to remain with Mr. Woodin until the bank emergency was straightened out. Mr. Ballantine was entirely capable of administering the office of Secretary and was very helpful during the first few months after Roosevelt took office. The President appointed Dean Acheson Under Secretary May 19, 1933.

The new banking laws provided for conservators of banks to be appointed by the Comptroller of the Currency, who was under the Secretary of the Treasury. Immediately following the bank holiday, the banking situation in Detroit was one of the worst. Secretary Woodin asked me to work out a plan of conservatorship so that the

Detroit depositors could get some of their money pending reopening or reorganization. It was a new situation for all of us, but I worked out a plan which was soon put into effect and which enabled some eight hundred thousand distressed depositors in Detroit to get a part of their deposits. During the first few months of the Secretary's term of office I saw him almost daily, not only about RFC matters, but about his own job. He was new in government and not too strong. He was not suited to the rough-and-tumble going with respect to bank repair work and conservatorships, and leaned on me heavily.

Because of the state of his health, Secretary Woodin tendered his resignation in October, 1933. The President wouldn't accept it. Instead, he gave Mr. Woodin an indefinite leave of absence and appointed Henry Morgenthau, Jr., Acting Secretary of the Treasury. Mr. Woodin went to Tucson, Arizona. From there he kept in touch with me by mail and telephone about our bank-rescue work. We had become close friends though I had not known him until his appointment as Secretary of the Treasury. His health did not improve, and at the end of the year he persuaded the President to let him resign. He returned to New York and died a few months later.

PRESIDENT ROOSEVELT LOOKS FOR REPUBLICANS

As I have said, the three vacancies on our Board which President Roosevelt was called upon to fill in the early days of his administration had to go to Republicans. The President waited until June to fill the vacancies. He asked me for recommendations. I gave him only one suggestion: Carroll B. Merriam, a banker of Topeka, Kansas, with whom I had been associated in the American Red Cross during World War I. He was appointed. The other two appointees were Frederic H. Taber of Massachusetts, who had been a classmate of Mr. Roosevelt at Harvard, and John J. Blaine, a lame-duck Senator from Wisconsin. He had been defeated in the election that sent Mr. Roosevelt to the White House and gave him a Democratic Congress.

I was told by a Democratic Senator who had served with Mr. Blaine that we would have trouble with him. I had never met Mr. Baine, but I knew that in the Senate he had been critical of the RFC. Rather than trouble, I got from him the most constructive cooperation. He was a diligent worker. No one ever served the Corporation with greater zeal to be helpful to anyone in trouble or anyone who, under the law, had a right to come to us for assistance. He was quick to detect a phony, but always fair. He had a critical mind, particularly of people trying to get something they were not entitled to—and there were plenty of them about in those days. There still are, and I am ashamed to say they are meeting with magnificent success.

Mr. Blaine gave his life in the cause of the country's economic reconstruction. As a courtesy to him I had suggested that he take our chief examiner John McKee and go back to his home state, Wisconsin, and help his neighbors work out their banking problems, and formulate plans for payment of deposits tied up in closed banks. He greatly appreciated the assignment but took pneumonia and died while on his arduous mission. He had the respect of all his associates in the Corporation and the genuine affection of many of us, certainly my own.

The directors of the RFC were appointed for two years, and all appointments expired simultaneously. Invariably I would have to remind the President when it came time for him to name a new Board or reappoint the old one. Just as invariably he would ask if I wanted the same Board reappointed. I would reply in the affirmative, and it would be done. In 1938, when I gave him the biennial reminder, he said: "Well, you want the same Board, don't you?" I then said, "I do if you do, but your classmate from Massachusetts [Taber] has been causing us considerable criticism." To which he replied: "He has, hasn't he? Why not reduce the Board and leave him off and tell the Congress you will drop a Democrat next year?"

I replied that I would work it out. I went to see Henry Morgenthau, Jr., Secretary of the Treasury, and said:

"Henry, you don't attend meetings of the RFC Board. Would you mind not to be on the Board?"

He replied that he would prefer not to be on. I then told the President of my conversation with Henry—that I would ask Congress to reduce our Board from seven to five members, dropping the ex-officio Secretary of the Treasury and Mr. Taber.

Mr. Taber owned a cotton milling business in Massachusetts which I think he had inherited from his father. His mill got into financial difficulties, and the RFC made him a loan of $100,000, and by and by another loan and still another, until our advances to the Taber mill aggregated about $400,000. The property securing the loan was worth the money. Under the law all our loans were made public once a month. Each time a loan to the Taber mill was publicized, we would get criticism from other mills in the same line of business. For every protesting letter I got, the President probably received several. So it was a relief to him to get rid of Mr. Taber, who was an excellent gentleman, but none too experienced. He was very cooperative as an RFC director, and we all liked him. The Taber loans were strictly legal and proper and were finally paid.

When I was testifying before the House Banking and Currency Committee which was considering the bill whose provisions included the reduction of our Board by two members, Representative Charles L. Gifford, an able Republican Congressman from Massachusetts, noting that Mr. Taber would be left off, facetiously asked me: "Who will represent New England?" I replied that I would. Mr. Gifford remarked that that would be perfectly satisfactory. By that time, the Republican members of Congress had learned that we were operating the Corporation as the law provided—on a nonpolitical, businesslike basis.

In September, 1933, Mr. McCarthy had resigned from the Board, moved to Oakland, California, and resumed the practice of law. This vacancy was filled a few months later by the President's appointment of former Senator Charles B. Henderson of Nevada. Mr. Henderson was then living in San Francisco, and his name had been given the President by western Senators. The President asked me to investigate Mr. Henderson and see if I thought he would be a satisfactory director, which I did, and recommended his appointment. We had no director from the Far West, and the President thought we should have one. I thought so too.

The next chair to become vacant after Senator Henderson joined the Board was that of Mr. Couch. He resigned in August, 1934, to return to his business. It was not until the following April, after the death of Senator Blaine had created still another vacancy, that we again had a full Board.

Several times I had suggested to the President that we fill the vacancy caused by the resignation of Mr. Couch. But he would invariably put me off and say, "Come over some day, and we will go through a list of names that have been recommended to me." After Senator Blaine's death I insisted that the President fill the two vacancies, one Democrat and one Republican, telling him the work was heavy and we needed the two directors. As a matter of fact, the Presi-

dent had come to feel that we needed no directors except for patron-
age purposes.

For the Couch vacancy the southern Senators thought the successor
should be from the Atlanta Federal Reserve District. Senator Pat
Harrison of Mississippi, who stood high in the political councils, had
had a name in the hat ever since Mr. Couch resigned. In the meantime
Hubert Stephens, the junior Senator from Mississippi, had been defeated for reelection by Theodore Bilbo. After that, Senator Harrison
came to see me. He wanted me to talk to the President about appointing Stephens instead of the man he had first recommended. I saw the
President and reported Senator Harrison's talk.

The President said to me, "How would you like to have Hubert?"

I replied that if he would like to appoint the Senator it would be all
right with me. I knew the Senator well, and while he was not a
financial or a business man he was a fine gentleman and, I was sure,
would cooperate. And he did.

The President then said, "Go up to the Hill and clear Hubert with
the Senators from the four or five southern states that have candidates.
The first man for you to see is Bilbo."

Several months previously I had recommended to the President the
appointment of Charles T. Fisher, Jr., of Detroit, to the Republican
vacancy. Mr. Fisher was manager of the RFC Agency at Detroit,
and I knew his excellent capabilities.

As I was leaving the White House after discussing Hubert Stephens
with the President I encountered Senator Walter F. George of
Georgia. The Senator got in my car to ride with me to the Capitol.
En route I told him of my purpose to see some of the southern
Senators, including him, and he remarked:

"I don't think the President is going to appoint your man Fisher;
FDR is afraid of Labor." I had said nothing further to the President
about Fisher and had been looking about for another Republican to
suggest to him.

Charles Fisher was of the Fisher Body and General Motors family.
Evidently Senator George had been talking with the President about
Hubert Stephens for our Democratic vacancy, and the President had
undoubtedly told him about my wanting Fisher to fill the Republican
vacancy. Arriving on the Hill, I saw Senator Bilbo and told him the
object of my visit. He said:

"It is all right by me. In our campaign in which I defeated Senator

Stephens, I told the people of Mississippi that when I got to Washington one of the first things I would do would be to get Hubert a job."

I then cleared Hubert with the other southern Senators.

After returning to my office from the Capitol that afternoon, I telephoned William Green, President of the American Federation of Labor, whom I had known for a good many years. I asked Mr. Green if he would be good enough to come to my office. When he got there I told him my problem, explaining that I wanted Mr. Fisher appointed to our Board and that the President was hesitant because of Labor. Mr. Green promptly said:

"I will be glad to recommend him if it will help."

At my request, he sent me a letter within the hour recommending the appointment of Mr. Fisher.

The next morning I saw the President and reported to him that while each of the southern Senators wanted his own man appointed, Senator Stephens would be acceptable to them all. I then handed the President William Green's letter about Mr. Fisher. He read it and said:

"Go tell Rudolph to send both their names to the Senate this morning."

Rudolph Forster was a faithful White House executive clerk of long standing, a friend whom I had known since the Woodrow Wilson days. He sent the names of Messrs. Stephens and Fisher up to the Senate, where both were immediately confirmed.

When Senator Blaine died leaving a Republican vacancy on the Board I asked the directors and our executive staff to see if we had a Republican in one of our thirty-two agencies that we could recommend for a directorship. My thought was that it would be helpful to the Board to have on it a member that had agency experience. They reported almost at once that Charles T. Fisher, Jr., our manager in Detroit, was the man; that he had been with the agency since its inception and manager of it for some months. That was the basis of my recommending "Chick" Fisher for a directorship.

In December, 1936, Frank Murphy, Governor of Michigan and a Democrat, asked me to release Mr. Fisher, a Republican, so that he could appoint him banking commissioner of his home state. Three years later the President appointed Governor Murphy Attorney General of the United States, and a few months afterwards elevated him to the Supreme Court bench. Meanwhile, in January, 1938, Mr. Fisher was elected president of the National Bank of Detroit.

On my recommendation, Mr. Fisher was succeeded on our Board in 1936 by Howard J. Klossner, Republican, of Minnesota. Mr. Klossner had been in the examining division of the Corporation since July, 1932. Prior to coming to us, he had served as an examiner in the banking department of the State of Minnesota for six years.

In 1942, when another Republican vacancy occurred, I induced Mr. Fisher to take a leave of absence from his bank and come back to us. The President promptly appointed him. I wanted him with the organization because our war work had become exceedingly heavy and he understood industry and was extraordinarily competent. He worked hard with our wartime subsidiaries. During his absence from Detroit he received no salary from the bank. Early in 1946, the war work completed, he again resigned from the RFC and returned to the National Bank of Detroit. In cooperation with the General Motors Corporation, the RFC had established that bank following the debacle in 1933. In my long experience in business and banking, few men have come to my notice who are better equipped by native ability, natural poise, trustworthiness, and all-around good sense than "Chick" Fisher, who is still a young man.

In 1936 Emil Schram of Illinois succeeded former Senator Hubert Stephens, who had not been reappointed. When the vacancy occurred, I had suggested Sam H. Husbands of South Carolina, since he had been with the Corporation longer than Mr. Schram. The President indicated he would rather have a man from farther West, inasmuch as the South was already well represented. It was election year, and the South was, of course, in the bag for FDR. I thereupon suggested Mr. Schram, who had come to us in 1933 on the recommendation of the Speaker of the House of Representatives, Henry T. Rainey, and was a constituent of his.

Shortly after I became chairman, I suggested to our Board that we amend our by-laws so as to give any three directors, regardless of their politics, authority to make loans. Within the Board we had an executive committee composed of three directors, again regardless of political affiliations. In practice the committee was interchangeable from day to day, and without formality. Any three members of the Board could constitute themselves an executive committee and make commitments. Then when the Board was in session, which usually was daily, what an executive committee had done would be reported and confirmed, or become board action. This procedure enabled us to act faster. While a little unorthodox, it worked. I can truthfully say that politics never influenced any action of our Board from the time I became chairman. And I never saw any sign of such influence, even before that.

In my time with the Corporation, we went on the principle that, if any director could give a valid reason why a loan should not be made, generally it was not authorized. Once in a while a director might be recorded as not voting, or even as dissenting, but always because of the apparent insufficiency of the security offered. Usually we acted unanimously. As I have mentioned, there were, during the first six months of the Corporation's work, some clashes and differences of opinion at Board meetings; but when Mr. Meyer was no longer with us we had complete harmony. Mr. Cowles, an ultraconservative and sound man, probably dissented more than any other director, but not to his discredit. He had no patience with the New Deal and very little with incompetence and failure.

After being reduced to five members, our Board went from February, 1938, to July, 1939, without any change, the members being Messrs. Merriam, Henderson, Klossner, Schram, and myself.

I BECOME FEDERAL LOAN ADMINISTRATOR

In July, 1939, President Roosevelt created the Federal Loan Administration by Executive Order and appointed me Federal Loan Administrator to retain general supervision of the RFC while assuming over-all direction of other government lending agencies, including the Federal Housing Administration, Home Owners' Loan Corporation and the Export-Import Bank. I had no previous knowledge that he was going to do this. The first I knew about it was when it was publicly announced from the White House. There was gossip to the effect that I had been kicked upstairs in order to get more liberal administration of the RFC; but this talk did not reach me at the time, and I continued to direct the affairs of the Corporation as long as I was in government service, as I had always done since becoming chairman.

The President never discussed with me his purpose in adding the

Home Owners' Loan Corporation and the Federal Housing Administration to my responsibilities. I supposed it was simply to group the various lending agencies under one head and to relieve him of direct contact with those two agencies. Both were in good hands. I advised with Stewart McDonald, Federal Housing Administrator, and appointed him a Deputy Federal Loan Administrator. I also advised with John H. Fahey, head of the Home Owners' Loan Corporation, with respect to their agencies, and we all got along fine.

On preparing to assume the Federal Loan Administration job, I recommended to the President that Mr. Schram be made chairman of the RFC, which was done. When the question arose of filling the vacancy on the Board caused by my resignation as a director, I suggested Sam H. Husbands, and Mr. Schram recommended him to the President. The President told Mr. Schram that he preferred a man from the West, and that he wanted the RFC to have an "Emil Schram Board, not a Jesse Jones Board." Fortunately, I did not hear of this until recently. Whatever the President's real feelings may have been, he nevertheless sent Mr. Husbands' name to the Senate and he was confirmed as a director.

Upon appointing me Federal Loan Administrator, the President wrote the following letter:

THE WHITE HOUSE

WASHINGTON

July 18, 1939

Dear Jesse:

I have received and accepted your resignation as a member of the Board of the Reconstruction Finance Corporation—but I do so only because of your undertaking the work of Federal Loan Administrator.

The Reconstruction Finance Corporation under your Chairmanship has made an amazing record of financial efficiency while at the same time assisting many banks, corporations and individuals to continue solvent and to do their part in giving employment and keeping the wheels of industry turning.

Your statement that the Reconstruction Finance Corporation "has sound assets sufficient to pay all of its debts and return to the Treasury the entire capital stock invested in it, with something in addition," reminds me that in 1933, 1934, 1935, and 1936 a few

Mr President

I should like to operate the Federal Loan Agency with borrowed help – (as far as possible) from the different agencies in this group —

Adjusting the expense between them + reimbursing, with approval of the Budget Director

Jesse H Jones

7/15/39

people in the Executive Branch of the Government, more people in the Congress of the United States, and many individuals and newspapers in civil life were announcing to the Nation that the Reconstruction Finance Corporation was broke and that the Government would not get back more than fifty cents on the dollar.

These people were in some cases honest in their belief, but in many cases were making these ghoulish statements with the hope that their own types of partisanship would thereby be served. In either case their action did little to encourage the "confidence" they were so loudly talking about. In either case their gloomy predictions proved false.

I call this matter of history to your attention because it is illustrative of the difficulties which public servants find in carrying out their duties.

You, the fellow members of your Board, and all of us who have some confidence in the good sense of the American people, and confidence in the ability of honest Government to cope with difficult situations, which have not been solved by wholly private efforts, have a right to some measure of pride in the Reconstruction Finance Corporation.

Very sincerely yours,

FRANKLIN D. ROOSEVELT

Some months after Mr. Schram became the Corporation's chairman, there was a vacancy in the office of Governor of the Federal Reserve Bank of Chicago. Walter J. Cummings, chairman of the Continental Illinois National Bank & Trust Company, suggested to the Federal Reserve Board that Mr. Schram be appointed, but this did not materialize. The suggestion got into the press, however, and soon thereafter a committee from the New York Stock Exchange was sent to see me.

The committee was composed of Robert P. Boylan, Curtis Calder, John A. Coleman, Russell E. Gardner, Jr., Charles B. Harding, William McChesney Martin, Jr., Paul V. Shields, and Robert L. Stott. Mr. Martin, having been drafted into the Army, was retiring as the Exchange's president. Two of the committeemen came to my office

---

Note: On becoming Federal Loan Administrator, I wrote the President the note on page 532. The Federal Loan Administration had only a small force and very little expense.

as spokesmen for the group. They asked me what I thought of Mr. Schram for president of the Exchange.

The Stock Exchange, along with every other part of our economy, had had its troubles. One of its former presidents had been sent to Sing Sing. I told the committee I thought Mr. Schram would be an excellent selection—that he had extraordinary ability, that he was a positive character, that he had proven his ability by handling many difficult problems. Soon thereafter Mr. Schram was elected president of the Stock Exchange.

While he had a farm in Illinois, he was not a man of means. Our RFC directors' salaries were only $10,000 a year, so, while as patriotic as anyone could be, the salary the Stock Exchange paid its president and the public service he could render as president of our country's greatest market place entirely justified Mr. Schram in accepting the employment. That he made a success was evidenced by the fact that when his contract of employment with the Exchange expired it was renewed, carrying with it extraordinary benefits for retirement at his pleasure, as well as a substantial increase in salary. As president of the Stock Exchange, he has rendered the country a fine service. A strong man, he was always so intent on doing a good job of whatever he undertook that he overtaxed himself and paid the penalty by a severe illness in 1949 and 1950. Happily, he is now back with the Exchange but tells me he is soon to retire.

Mr. Husbands was one of the young men we had recruited, in 1932, out of Leo Paulger's little black address book. He had been the cashier of a country bank that went to the wall in South Carolina. He began with us as an examiner at $200 a month, became head of the Examining Division in 1936 and was made president of our Federal National Mortgage Association two years later along with his many other duties.

Subsequently he and the other RFC directors were put on the boards of most of our wartime subsidiaries. Sam's outstanding achievement in that period was his work as president of Defense Plant Corporation. Alert, amiable, and able, he was one of my most versatile colleagues. He left the Corporation in January, 1946, to go to San Francisco as vice president of the great Transamerica Corporation, of which A. P. Giannini was the head. In 1949, on the death of Mr. Giannini, Sam was elected president.

When Mr. Schram left us in 1941 there was a vacancy on the Board as well as the office of chairman. On my recommendation, Henry A. Mulligan, of New York, succeeded to the vacant directorship and Charles B. Henderson, then the senior member of the Board, became chairman. Harry Mulligan, as he was known to all, was the RFC's treasurer. He had been with the Corporation from the outset and in government work almost all his adult life. He came to us from the Federal Farm Loan Bureau, where he had headed the division of examinations. During the war he was for a time president of Defense Supplies Corporation and was a director of each of our other defense subsidiaries.

While he had little experience in business, I regard Harry Mulligan as one of the ablest administrators with whom I have ever been associated. He knew more about the RFC than any of us. This was in part because the books and accounts were in his charge, and also because he felt great responsibility for the Corporation and its every operation. He was meticulous to the penny and to the letter.

Whenever I went before Congress for amendments to the law under which we operated, Harry Mulligan was always at my side. When any question was asked for which I did not have a ready answer, he gave me the necessary information.

I felt much gratitude to each director of the Corporation after I became chairman, but I probably had greater affection for Harry than for anyone in the Corporation. Because of failing health, he resigned from the Board in the spring of 1950. His leaving was a great loss to the Corporation.

JOINING THE CABINET

In the summer of 1940 when President Roosevelt asked me to join his Cabinet as Secretary of Commerce I asked him if I would carry with me the job of Federal Loan Administrator; he replied that I would not. I therefore told him that I thought it best to stay where I was, that I was needed in the Federal Loan job. Some days later, he sent me word that, if Congress was willing for me to hold two jobs, he was. Shortly thereafter a joint resolution, which had been favorably reported by the Banking and Currency Committees, unanimously passed both Houses in the following words:

To authorize Jesse H. Jones, Federal Loan Administrator, to be appointed to, and to perform the duties of, the Office of Secretary of Commerce.

Resolved by the Senate and House of Representatives of the United States of America in Congress assembled, That notwithstanding any provision of law to the contrary, Jesse H. Jones, Federal Loan Administrator, may continue in such office and be appointed to, in the manner now provided by law, and may exercise the duties of the Office of Secretary of Commerce: Provided that the total compensation to be paid him as Secretary of Commerce and as Federal Loan Administrator shall be that provided by law for the Secretary of Commerce.

Meanwhile, I had been out of Washington for a few days, and wrote the following letter to Vice President Garner:

Friday, just before leaving Washington, the President asked me to become Secretary of Commerce, and to continue to act as Federal Loan Administrator. This will require a joint resolution which the Congress may or may not be willing to adopt. I could probably carry the new work with very little additional effort, as it is all in the line of business.

I feel that I should continue the supervision particularly of the RFC, since much of its authority has been given to it by Congress upon my advice and testimony, and in the belief that I would administer it. I feel this responsibility keenly, and would not like to be taken away from it—for any cause.

The war situation will probably have an influence on the election. That the world situation is about as bad as it could be is apparent. Just how and when Hitler, if victorious, will undertake to give us trouble is a question. He might not, but I am convinced that we should arm to the teeth. If we are well prepared there will be no real danger. Even a bully seldom takes on a superior.

Fortunately, he is finding it difficult to cross the English Channel, and, of course, would find it much more difficult to cross the Atlantic, although a foothold in South America, sufficient to put the Panama Canal out of commission, would make it possible for him to give serious trouble from that approach.

Through all my years in Washington, Mr. Garner remained my confidant and friend. In the years he was Speaker of the House and

THE ORIGINAL BOARD OF THE RFC

Swearing in the directors, February 2, 1932. Left to right: James L. Dougherty, RFC counsel (reading oath), Ogden L. Mills, Paul Bestor, Harvey Couch, General Charles G. Dawes, Jesse H. Jones, Eugene Meyer. Messrs. Mills, Bestor, and Meyer were already government officials and were not required to renew their oaths.

RFC DIRECTORS AND DEPARTMENT HEADS IN 1936

then Vice President, it was my custom to keep in touch with him. He was wise and, from long experience, knew all the ropes in Washington.

Soon after I had qualified as a director of the RFC in 1932, Mr. Garner advised me to keep a record of my actions. I decided that the records of the Corporation would be my record, or at least record enough for me. I had no time to keep a diary.

Whenever I was made the target of criticism, I would receive encouraging words from him. During the war, after I had been accused by New Dealers and some other trouble-makers of possessing a "banker mentality" and even of sometimes seeming to be "more interested in saving a few pennies than in saving the nation," I received a letter from Uvalde which said:

> Don't let Drew Pearson and some scandal mongers discourage you in any way. Stick to your guns because we need men of your type to serve the country, especially at this time. I can tell you that the people of the United States admire and have the greatest confidence in your ability and patriotism. As long as your health holds out, stick to your jobs.

I promptly telegraphed Mr. Garner that I had no worries about Drew Pearson or others of his ilk.

The following summer, when my controversy with Vice President Wallace was crackling in the press, I received another letter from Uvalde, which read:

> July 9, 1943
>
> Dear Jesse:
>
> I know you are not running away. That much I do know. Politically speaking, it is more honorable and the better policy to stand up and be shot than to surrender. My suggestion is to stay with the ship. Stand your ground even if your head comes off by force.
>
> I have had no desire to go back to Washington since I left, but I surely would like to be there for three or four days to have a little conversation with some of my "amigos" on the Hill and get them to sustain you in your position. I am hoping and praying that you will win out.

Mrs. Garner is about as usual. I am fine as can be and don't permit anything to worry me.

We join in love to you and the good woman.

Sincerely, your friend,

JNO. N. GARNER

I did not feel the need of these encouraging letters, but they were, of course, good to have. The way to be able to serve the government best is to be ready to go home at any time, and fortunately I always had something to go home to.

My predecessor as Secretary of Commerce was Harry L. Hopkins. When the President sent his nomination to the Hill and a Senate committee opened hearings on his qualifications, Mr. Hopkins felt that many members of the Senate did not trust him. He asked me to accompany him to the hearings on the day he was interrogated. I was glad to go with him, for, as a matter of fact, I liked him and knew him to be a faithful and loyal helper to the President. We walked into the committee room arm in arm. He took the witness chair, and I got back of the table with the Senate committee members who were to question him. I remained there until the hearing was over. Harry Hopkins' appointment was confirmed, but only after a rather severe and critical quizzing by members of the committee. He was taunted about the famous statement credited to him in defending the New Deal—that we will "spend and spend, tax and tax, and elect and elect." At one time in the examination he was rather put to it for a proper answer to a question, and I have always thought that his response was the principal contributing factor in his confirmation. After some hesitation he replied to the difficult question, "I am on the team, and when the captain calls the plays, I play." This answer was so true that I felt sure it impressed the members of the committee. Certainly it did me, and I knew it to be true.

After I had become Secretary of Commerce I continued to spend most of my time at RFC headquarters. I found that I could better detail many of the operations of the Department of Commerce to Under Secretary Wayne C. Taylor than I could pass on to others the manifold problems and vast operations of the RFC and its subsidiaries in war work. And I felt responsible to Congress for the RFC.

When in 1940 the defense program made it necessary for us to create several subsidiaries, it was my policy to have one of the RFC

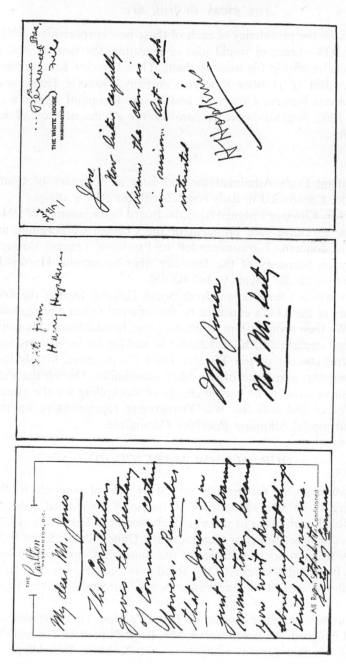

At left: a tip from Harry L. Hopkins that I would be named to succeed him as Secretary of Commerce. At right, a note from Hopkins written at a Cabinet meeting.

directors take the presidency of each of these new corporations, while
the other RFC directors would join or constitute the new boards. I
held the chairmanship for most of them. Thus Director Klossner became President of Rubber Reserve Company, Director Henderson
headed Metals Reserve Company, and so on. The point to this was
that the RFC directors were responsible for all the acts of all its
subsidiaries.

*　　*　　*

As Federal Loan Administrator and later as Secretary of Commerce, too, I continued in daily contact with the RFC's affairs.

When Mr. Klossner resigned from the Board in the summer of 1945
to become executive vice president of the Chicago Corporation, an
investment concern, I recommended to President Truman through
John Snyder, Secretary of the Treasury, that he appoint Harvey J.
Gunderson to fill the vacancy, and he did.

Harvey was a young lawyer from South Dakota. During the first
three years of the RFC's existence he was counsel to our Minneapolis
agency. We then brought him to Washington. In addition to his work
in our legal department, he was active in making business loans and
was general counsel of our Disaster Loan Corporation, Metals Reserve Company, and some of our other subsidiaries. During the war,
as a major of cavalry, he was in charge of stockpiling for the armed
service forces and was the War Department representative on the
Interdepartmental Shipping Priorities Committee.

OUR ALUMNI MAKE GOOD

The lawyers who successively served as general counsels to the
RFC have made fine reputations in the legal or judicial spheres.
Stanley Reed, who came to us as general counsel in December, 1932,
later was appointed Solicitor General of the United States. Since 1938
he has been an Associate Justice of the Supreme Court by appointment of President Roosevelt. Mr. Reed was brought into the RFC
principally because of his experience as general counsel of the Farm
Board.

With us he succeeded Morton G. Bogue, a New York Republican,
who had resigned. As noted above, Mr. Bogue's predecessor and the
Corporation's first general counsel was G. A. Marr, Republican of

Utah, who had held a similar position with the War Finance Corporation.

In 1935, when Mr. Reed left us to become Solicitor General, James B. Alley of New York, who had well earned the promotion in our legal division, was chosen as our next general counsel. He had for three years been occupied with the legal end of reorganizing and recapitalizing banks which required government help. Mr. Alley left us in 1937 to practice his profession in New York and has done well. He was succeeded by Claude E. Hamilton, Jr., a young lawyer who had come to us in 1933, from Greenville, Alabama. Mr. Hamilton remained general counsel until 1943; then, like Mr. Alley, he went to New York. There he joined the well-known law firm of White & Case in the Wall Street district. John D. Goodloe, another young lawyer who had been my executive assistant, succeeded him. Mr. Goodloe later became a director and then chairman of the Board. In 1949 he joined the Coca-Cola Company, of which he is now Vice President.

The Corporation's general counsel as these lines are written is James L. Dougherty, who has been with the organization from its very first day. It was before Jim Dougherty as a notary public, that I and the other original directors took our oaths of office in February, 1932.

Of all the RFC personnel, none has been more faithful or rendered more consistent service than Jim Dougherty. He came to the Corporation before it was really organized. He had had experience in government work as counsel with the old War Finance Corporation and the Federal Farm Loan Board. He has a thorough understanding of government service and, besides, is an excellent lawyer and a good administrator. I never suggested his appointment as general counsel during my administration for the reason that I thought he was too old to carry the work. I knew that he was one of the best counselors we had and handled all work in his charge perfectly; but twelve to fifteen hours a day six and a half days a week, I thought, would be too much for him. In this I was probably wrong because he doesn't appear any grayer, older, or less vital today than he did in February, 1932. So, Jim, this is my apology!

* * *

In the busy thirteen days between the signing of the RFC Act and the start of operations, George Cooksey, the Corporation's first secretary, and David B. Griffin (now assistant treasurer) came over to us from the Farm Board. George Cooksey regarded himself as the guardian of the RFC directors, responsible for seeing that everything was done according to law. His records were perfectly kept. George did not mind calling any of us to task. Unfortunately, he did not live to see the job through. He died in July, 1941.

Mr. Cooksey was succeeded as secretary of the RFC by Ronald Allen. When Mr. Allen was appointed naval attaché in the American Embassy at Moscow, A. T. Hobson of Missoula, Montana, who had been secretary of our Defense Plant Corporation, succeeded him. Mr. Hobson proved a good man and very useful.

Hugh Leach, our first treasurer, had been managing director of the Baltimore branch of the Federal Reserve Bank. He is now president of the Federal Reserve Bank in his native Richmond.

Among the men Mr. Leach recruited in our early days were Harry L. Sullivan, who had been in the Memphis branch of the Federal Reserve Bank of St. Louis, and David B. Griffin, who came from the Federal Land Bank in Louisville. Griffin and Charles Boysen went to work on January 27, 1932, before the Corporation was officially organized. Mr. Griffin is now its acting treasurer. Another pioneer in the Corporation's work was Walter Joyce. During the war, Sam Husbands made him vice president of Defense Plant Corporation in charge of engineering, and he did a very capable job. So did Francis J. O'Hara, Jr., who came to Washington in the autumn of 1940 to help in the over-all policy forming for Defense Plant. Schuyler W. Livingston, who had been with the RFC as an attorney since 1934, became Defense Plant's assistant chief counsel. Just before Pearl Harbor, when we were getting well into our stride in war work, we had George C. Summers, who had been counsel of our New York agency since 1934, come to Washington to help Mr. O'Hara and Hans Klagsbrunn in Defense Plant. He left us to go into the Navy, but returned to the RFC when the war ended and became chief counsel of the Office of Surplus Property.

The important work of establishing the loan agencies across the country was initiated by Roy A. Brownell. Roy is still with the Corporation, an efficient and loyal administrator, in charge of the 32 agencies.

Upon Postmaster General James A. Farley's recommendation, Norman W. Baxter joined the RFC in its early days as personnel and press relations officer and remained with us until 1937. He came back three years later and stayed on as my very capable, level-headed assistant, both in the RFC and in the Department of Commerce. Having been a newspaper correspondent for many years at home and in Europe, Mr. Baxter had a sound knowledge of the economic and political climates not only of Washington but of the Western world. When I left the government Norman joined me on the editorial staff of the Houston *Chronicle,* stationed in Washington.

My secretary, W. C. Costello, as I noted earlier in this chapter, was with me when I went to Washington in 1932 to meet with the Democratic National Committee a few days before President Hoover asked me to become a director of the RFC. From then on Bill Costello was with me constantly, first as my secretary and then as assistant to the chairman. He remained at my side from the beginning to the very end of my long stay in Washington. He was most faithful and extraordinarily helpful. I could hardly have got along without him. Bill Costello had authority to sign my name to anything but a contract or commitment, and he penned my signature so perfectly that I couldn't deny it. I frequently had to eat my words when denying I had written a certain letter. He is now with the J. A. Zurn Manufacturing Company as its vice president.

With Mr. Costello on my personal staff were four loyal and tireless helpers: John H. Tanner, who had come to me on the recommendation of Senator Reed Smoot of Utah; Dennis Joe Toomey, who until recently was on the personal staff of the Secretary of the Treasury, John W. Snyder; Dorothy Robbins, of Washington; and Mrs. Gladys D. Mikell, who had been my P.B.X. operator at Houston and later was assistant to Bill Costello. Mrs. Mikell came to Washington in August, 1932, to reorganize our telephone room and improve its service. She arrived under the impression that her stay would be temporary; but she soon became head of our secretarial department, and it was not until after the Second World War that she got back to Houston.

There are many other capable men and women who served in the Corporation who are entitled to favorable mention, but there is just not room to name each one. I do, however, want to cite Mrs. Edna Collins, the capable chief of the telephone department.

The RFC had the reputation of having the best telephone service of any government agency. We had to have it to do the job during the busy years—and most of them were busy. At the peak of our operations we had sixty telephone operators, and the switchboard worked day and night.

At the start, the Corporation had but a few score employees. The unemployment situation being severe, there were scores of applicants for every opening we created. Tons of forms, including job application papers, had been printed. When it became known in Washington that a new government agency was being established, applicants for jobs filled an entire corridor of the Treasury building. Their outstretched arms at the time a clerk opened the door to pass out the blank forms reminded Jim Dougherty of baby robins opening their mouths to be fed.

In 1938 the personnel of the RFC numbered slightly above 3,000. With the launching of the defense program and the creation of subsidiaries to help the war programs, the rolls grew. Personnel reached a peak above 12,000 in 1934, and I don't believe that any comparable number of men and women ever accomplished more work. After the war, one-third of this staff was lopped off in a year's time, and substantial reductions were made in subsequent years. The number of employees at the end of June, 1949, had dropped to 4,599, of whom 1,499 comprised the Washington staff, the remainder being assigned to the loan agencies or to other duties in the field.

The RFC's rapid recruitment of good personnel was facilitated by the fact that it was not under civil service regulations on hiring and pay scales. The Corporation did not come under the Civil Service Act until January 1, 1942.

During the depression it was possible, of course, to hire competent men and women for modest salaries. At the end of our first month of operations only forty-seven persons on the RFC pay roll, including directors, were receiving more than $400 a month. A director's salary was $833.33 a month. We paid some of the lawyers as much as $1,250 a month.

There has never been a school of business experience comparable to the RFC. In the period from 1932 to 1945, every imaginable type of transaction came to the Corporation for analysis and handling. With only twenty-four hours to the day, it was physically impossible for the directors personally to make every decision. We had to allocate different situations and varying problems to the man or men we thought best suited to handle them and then ratify their decisions. There was no friction and no politics.

One of our most appreciated tributes came from Herbert Hoover on December 10, 1947, when he graciously left a sick bed to appear at a dinner given for me by the "Alumni" of the RFC at the Waldorf-Astoria Hotel. Mr. Hoover said: "Under the leadership of Jesse Jones the RFC has been a fabulous success for the American people." He said the organization, operated according to the creating Act, had prevented many efforts to abuse it. Of me he said: "I take great pride in these fifteen years of friendship with a man of the opposite political party. Jesse Jones never lets politics or personal friendship interfere with his concept of public service."

* * *

In my sixty years in business I have never seen an organization that worked more cooperatively and unselfishly than the men and women who composed the RFC. When I became chairman I let them know that politics was to have no consideration in the operation of the Corporation, that there was to be no toadying or catering, that efficiency and speed were expected, that the integrity of the Corporation was paramount, that the staff should bring to the directors their best judgment in each application or situation, that when that was done their responsibilities ceased. The directors would make the determinations. This principle was adhered to invariably and literally.

The organization was composed of as fine a group of men as I have ever seen in one enterprise. This is especially striking in the light of the fact that we had been drawn together from all sections of the country and in a particularly great hurry. If any one of our people had an ax to grind other than to help in a difficult situation, it never developed. There was no angling for position or authority. They were proud of their association with the Corporation and glad to have a chairman who would back them up and was not afraid to make decisions.

Because of those busy years of experience in dealing with all manner of business problems, our men developed independence of judgment and the courage to back that judgment. Just as doctors get extraordinary experience in time of war, so in the RFC our men got unusual experience in business, industry, finance, and law. As a result, there are among the alumni of the RFC probably more than 100 executives of big business, in industry, finance, and the railroads. Among them are men who are now directing some of the most important institutions in the United States. They did not get those jobs because of RFC influence. What happened was that as the top men in various lines came in contact with the RFC, they soon observed men in our organization who had developed under the emergency and were drawing $10,000 a year and less, who in private industry would be paid five to ten times that much.

One of our troubles was to avoid having our best men taken away from us before we could spare them. In addition to operating the Corporation properly the directors had at heart the welfare of each employee. When we could spare one for a permanent position in business or industry, we did. But we never sought jobs for them. Without exception they have done well in the important positions they have occupied since leaving the Corporation.*

* A list of some of the RFC alumni who have "made good" in private enterprise is in the appendix.

COLLABORATOR'S ACKNOWLEDGMENTS

——————————— ☼ ———————————

THE word "collaborator" was one of the casualties of the Second World War. All that remained of it in common use was its sinister definition—to assist an enemy. For the past three years I have collaborated with Mr. Jesse H. Jones in the first and finest sense of the term—that of aiding a friend in assembling material and in writing.

Largely this book has been a work of picking men's brains and cudgeling their memories rather than lifting a fact here or filching a line there from what others have written. Perhaps some pedantic authority on unapplied economics will detect the absence from this volume of a bibliography. Though tens of thousands of pages have been perused, they were almost exclusively government reports, the minutes of board meetings, correspondence, sundry memoranda, and the terms on which hundreds of loans and investments were negotiated and made by the Reconstruction Finance Corporation.

At the suggestion of Mr. Jones, whose name has been for me an open sesame to almost any door, I journeyed the country over to interview scores of men about their bygone dealings, trades, and relations with him and the RFC. First among them my thanks go to a former President and two former Vice Presidents of the United States, Herbert Hoover, John Nance Garner and Charles Gates Dawes. Some may imagine it might have been worth while to have sought out still another former Vice President of the United States; but that gentleman, I hope the reader has found, has been adequately disposed of in the outpouring of Mr. Jones's rich store of recollections.

When this work was begun John D. Goodloe was chairman of the Board of the RFC. He and two of his fellow directors—Henry A. Mulligan and Harvey J. Gunderson, each keenly sympathetic with the labor in hand—gave generously of their time, information, and guidance over long periods, as did other officials of the Corporation,

[547]

including James L. Dougherty, general counsel, A. T. Hobson, secretary, and Morton Macartney, chief engineer. A goodly number of members of the staff were also graciously helpful. Among all the persons interviewed, but a single man failed to be kindled with a cooperative spirit. This could be a record of some sort; it is certainly a tribute to Mr. Jones.

Among those I saw, interviewed and found helpful are:

Douglas H. Allen, New York, formerly President, Rubber Development Corporation; James B. Alley, New York, formerly General Counsel of RFC; Leland Anderson, of Anderson, Clayton & Co., Houston, Texas.

Arthur A. Ballantine, New York, formerly Under Secretary of the Treasury; H. D. Barnes, Comptroller, Chicago & North-Western Railway; Russell Barnes, Detroit *News,* Detroit; Stuart K. Barnes, Guaranty Trust Co., New York, formerly with Defense Supplies Corporation; John W. Barriger III, President, Chicago, Indianapolis & Louisville Railroad Co.; Alfred W. Barth, Vice President, Chase National Bank, New York, formerly with United States Commercial Co.; Norman W. Baxter, Houston *Chronicle* bureau, Washington, D.C.; Robert Beach, Department of Agriculture, Washington, D.C.; Malcolm W. Bingay, Editor, Detroit *Free Press;* Morton Bodfish, Chairman of the Board, U.S. Savings and Loan League, Chicago; Morton G. Bogue, New York, formerly General Counsel of RFC; Milton S. Briggs, Washington, D.C.; Olin L. Brooks, President, Globe & Rutgers Fire Insurance Co., New York; Edward Eagle Brown, Chairman of the Board, First National Bank of Chicago; Prentiss Brown, Chairman of the Board, Detroit Edison Co.; Leonard J. Buck, importer, New York; Ralph Budd, formerly President, Chicago, Burlington & Quincy Railroad; William A. M. Burden, New York, formerly Assistant Secretary of Commerce; William Walton Butterworth, Jr., Department of State, Washington, D.C.

Reed M. Chambers, U.S. Aviation Underwriters, Inc., New York, formerly with Defense Supplies Corporation; Dale W. Clark, President, Omaha National Bank, Omaha, Nebraska; William L. Clayton, Houston, Texas, formerly Assistant Secretary of Commerce, formerly Deputy Loan Administrator, and later Under Secretary of State; B. A. Clements, formerly Vice Chairman, American Arch Co., New York; E. G. Cleverdon, Vice President and Cashier, Merchants National Bank of Mobile, Alabama; Lester L. Colbert, President,

Chrysler Corporation, Detroit; Sidney B. Congdon, President, National City Bank of Cleveland; William C. Costello, Washington, D.C., Vice President, J. A. Zurn Manufacturing Co., formerly special assistant to the Board of Directors of the RFC; Stanley T. Crossland, Vice President and Treasurer, Ethyl Corporation, New York, formerly Executive Vice President, Rubber Reserve Co.; Leo T. Crowley, Chairman of the Board, Chicago, Milwaukee, St. Paul & Pacific Railroad Co.; Thomas Cuffe, President, Pacific Far East Line, San Francisco; Walter J. Cummings, Chairman of the Board, Continental Illinois National Bank and Trust Co., Chicago; Robert J. Cummins, Consulting Engineer, Houston; Leland W. Cutler, Vice President, Fidelity & Deposit Co. of Maryland, San Francisco.

Don M. Dailey, Director of Financial Research, U.S. Savings & Loan League, Chicago; Arthur V. Davis, Chairman of the Board, Aluminum Company of America, New York; J. H. Dean, Department of Agriculture, Washington, D.C.; Robert P. Doherty, President, National Bank of Commerce, Houston, Texas; J. Paschal Dreibelbis, Vice President, Bankers Trust Co., New York.

Frederick H. Ecker, Chairman of the Board, Metropolitan Life Insurance Co., New York; David Elliott, Economist, Cleveland Trust Co.; R. P. A. Everard, Assistant to the President, Bank of America, San Francisco.

Benjamin F. Fairless, President, United States Steel Corporation; William J. Farthing, formerly Manager, New York Agency of RFC; Charles T. Fisher, Jr., President, National Bank of Detroit, formerly Director of RFC; Vernon W. Foster, Vice President and General Counsel, Illinois Central Railroad Co.; Clarence Francis, Chairman General Foods Corporation, New York; Kenneth Franzheim, Architect, Houston; Jesse Fraser, RFC Agency Manager, Cleveland; Robert P. Furey, Assistant Vice President, Central Hanover Bank & Trust Co., New York, formerly with United States Commercial Co.

Loring L. Gelbach, President, Central National Bank of Cleveland, formerly Manager, Cleveland Agency of RFC; A. P. Giannini, Founder and late Chairman of the Board of the Bank of America, San Francisco; L. M. Giannini, President, Bank of America, San Francisco; Robert E. Lee Grayson, Chief Librarian, New York *Herald Tribune.*

Hector C. Haight, Manager, San Francisco Agency of RFC; Claude E. Hamilton, Jr., New York, formerly General Counsel of RFC;

William B. Harding, Attorney, New York, formerly President of American Republics Aviation Division, Defense Supplies Corporation; George Leslie Harrison, President, New York Life Insurance Co.; Colonel Joseph M. Hartfield, Attorney, New York; William D. Hassett, formerly Secretary to President Franklin D. Roosevelt, now Secretary to President Truman; George W. Healey, Special Representative of RFC in New York; Charles B. Henderson, San Francisco, formerly Chairman of RFC; Charles H. Hewitt, Vice Pres., The Detroit Bank; George H. Hill, Jr., Assistant to the President, Cities Service Co., New York, formerly Executive Vice President of Defense Supplies Corporation; Julian Hinds, General Manager, Metropolitan Water Board of Southern California, Los Angeles; Sam H. Husbands, President, Transamerica Corporation, San Francisco, formerly Director of RFC and President of Defense Plant Corporation.

Alfred Jaretzki, Director, Globe & Rutgers Fire Insurance Co., New York; William M. Jeffers, Pasadena, Calif., formerly President, Union Pacific Railroad, formerly Rubber Director; A. B. Jones, Real Estate Consultant, New York; Col. Charles F. H. Johnson, President, Botany Mills, Inc., Passaic, N. J.

Herman Kahn, Director, Franklin D. Roosevelt Library, Hyde Park, N.Y.; Miss Kathryne Marie Killeen, Washington Bureau of Houston *Chronicle;* Howard J. Klossner, Vice President, Chicago Corporation, Chicago, formerly Director of RFC.

Henry R. Labouisse, Jr., Department of State, Washington, D.C.; Clifford B. Longley, Attorney, Detroit.

Paul Meyer Mazur, partner in Lehman Bros., New York; Wilson McCarthy, President, Denver & Rio Grande Western Railroad, formerly Director of RFC; John S. McCullough, Jr., Manager, San Francisco Agency of RFC; Stewart McDonald, Chairman of the Board, Maryland Casualty Co., Baltimore, formerly Deputy Federal Loan Administrator; Earl M. and Floyd N. McGowin, W. T. Smith Lumber Co., Chapman, Ala.; John Keown McKee, New York, formerly Chief of Examining Division, RFC; A. W. McKinley, Comptroller, Metropolitan Water District of Southern California, Los Angeles; Walter Scott McLucas, Chairman of the Board, National Bank of Detroit; Mrs. Gladys Mikell, Houston, Secretary to Mr. Jones; Wilson W. Mills, Attorney, Detroit; Herbert G. Moulton, Engineer, New York.

Sterling Newell, Attorney, Cleveland; William J. Nichols, and Edgar B. Nixon, Franklin D. Roosevelt Library, Hyde Park, N.Y.;

Ernest E. Norris, President, Southern Railway, Washington, D.C.; Miss Mae Nyquist, Assistant Librarian, New York *Herald Tribune.* Irving S. Olds, Chairman of the Board, United States Steel Corporation.

Robert P. Patterson, former Secretary of War; Warren Lee Pierson, Chairman of the Board, Transcontinental & Western Air, Inc., New York, formerly President, Export-Import Bank; Francis T. P. Plimpton, New York, formerly General Solicitor of the RFC; Reed Pond, Department of Agriculture, Washington, D.C.

Silas B. Ragsdale, Editor, *Petroleum Review,* Houston, Texas; Stanley Reed, Associate Justice of the Supreme Court, formerly General Counsel, RFC; Miss Dorothy Robbins, Washington, D.C., formerly Secretary to Mr. Jones; Horace Russell, U.S. Savings and Loan League, Chicago.

Samuel H. Sabin, formerly Executive Vice President, Defense Supplies Corporation; Emil Schram, President of the New York Stock Exchange, formerly Chairman of the RFC; Harry H. Schwartz, President, National Department Stores Corporation, New York; Earl B. Schwulst, President, Bowery Savings Bank, New York, formerly Special Assistant to RFC Board of Directors; W. F. Sheehan, Chief Examiner, Federal Reserve Bank of New York; John W. Slacks, New York, formerly President, RFC Mortgage Co.; Edward D. Stair, financier, Detroit.

Wayne Chatfield Taylor, formerly Under Secretary of Commerce; Jerome Thralls, Special Representative of RFC in New York; Bascom N. Timmons, Washington Correspondent of Houston *Chronicle;* John Tripp, Department of Agriculture, Washington, D.C.; Francis Adams Truslow, President, New York Curb Exchange, formerly President, Rubber Development Corporation.

John R. Van Horne, Secretary, Globe & Rutgers Fire Insurance Co., New York; George S. Van Schaick, formerly New York State Insurance Commissioner; A. L. Viles, Manager, National Rubber Manufacturers Association, New York.

Richard Wagner, President, Chicago Corporation; Brigadier General Paul L. Wakefield, Austin, Texas; Ethelbert Warfield, Attorney, New York; Rowland L. Williams, President, Chicago & North Western Railway; James C. Wilson, President, First Bank & Trust Co., Perth Amboy, N.J., formerly Assistant Chief Examiner, RFC.

* * *

Among the many members of the headquarters staff of the RFC in Washington who provided information and material and patiently sought answers to innumerable questions—many of which sent them burrowing into the archives—are:

George F. Buskie, Special Assistant to the Board of Directors; Mrs. Edna Collins, Chief of the Telephone Department; Facius W. Davis and Henry W. Davis of the Comptroller's Office; Edward Edelman, Public Works Division; Robert C. Goodale; Charles Griffin, Examing Division; Matthias W. Knarr, Assistant Secretary; W. F. McKinnon, Chief, Tin Division, Office of Production; William Roselle; Herbert Rutland; Edward Stansfield; George Stoner, Deputy Director, Office of Defense Supplies; W. W. Sullivan, Chief of Railroad Division; W. E. Unzicker, Assistant Controller; J. Frank Williams; Thomas Williams; Thomas Wilson and Walter H. Young.

I wish also to express appreciation of occasional help and constant tolerance from my three office companions in New York, Messrs. Daniel L. Ross, Francis B. Henry, and Harry S. Vecchio, and my gratitude to the ladies who at various times assisted in research and in the incessant dictation, typing, retyping, and revisions of the manuscript. They are:

Mrs. Geneva Fulgham, Miss Jennette Tomlin, and Mrs. Madeline Withoff of Houston; and Miss Anne D. Hamilton, Miss Elizabeth McDowell, Miss Jane McQueen, and Miss Patricia Schoeck of New York.

My debt to the above ladies is exceeded by that which I owe to Mrs. Billie Brauner and Miss Paula Frantz of Houston, and Miss Louise H. Turner of Danville, Va. All three stayed with the job to the finish, ignoring the clock.

Through the many months Mrs. Jeanne Allen, Mrs. Thelma Monroe, and Mrs. Rosine McKinnon of Houston and Mrs. Marjorie Palmer, Miss Joan Rice, and Miss Bernice Rynne of New York efficiently handled hundreds of long-distance telephone calls.

Alvin Thigpen of Houston, toiled late and cheerfully into many a night running off final copies of the manuscript.

My thanks also go to the New York *Herald Tribune* for permission to use its excellent files and reference library.

*   *   *

Working with Mr. Jones has been interesting, informative, and inspiring—and an antidote to indolence. Our collaboration has been so close and constant, and the rewritings so often repeated, that there remains scarcely a paragraph of this story which is entirely his or entirely mine. The eggs were scrambled in almost every dish, with Mr. Jones putting in the salt and pepper.

Arrived at an autumnal seventy-seven, Uncle Jesse, as so many of his countrymen refer to him, is still on the job at least six full days a week, hankers for home work almost every night, ignores most national, state, and local holidays, and sometimes devotes part of his Sundays to the workaday grindstone.

After striving for three years to keep pace with such a regimen, I feel, in coming to the end of this task, not unlike the odd character who beat a tattoo on the wall with his head because it felt so good when he stopped.

EDWARD ANGLY

New York, June 14, 1951

APPENDIX I

THE JONES-WALLACE CONTROVERSY

STATEMENT BY VICE PRESIDENT WALLACE
CHAIRMAN, BOARD OF ECONOMIC WARFARE
JUNE 29, 1943

Vice President Wallace today made public a statement originally prepared for the Senate Committee on Appropriations. In releasing this statement he said:

"On June 4 my good friend, Senator McKellar from Tennessee, said certain things about the Board of Economic Warfare on the floor of the Senate which moved me to prepare a statement. After sleeping over the matter for several nights I decided not to make it.

"Milo Perkins, Executive Director of the Board of Economic Warfare, recently appeared before the Senate Committee on Appropriations to discuss the work of the Board. During his testimony he indicated that, in the interest of unity, he was reluctant to discuss the failure of the Reconstruction Finance Corporation to build adequate government stockpiles of strategic materials as authorized and directed by the Congress nearly 18 months before Pearl Harbor.

"Since his appearance before the Senate Committee on Appropriations, the effort to misrepresent the facts concerning the work of the Board of Economic Warfare has continued. Some of these misrepresentations which have been called to my attention during the past week have been of such a nature that I have decided to release the statement as originally prepared. I am asking Senator McKellar to make it part of our hearings.

"It seems to me that on a matter such as this, I, and only I, as Chairman of the Board of Economic Warfare, can make the kind of presentation that will set the record straight.

"There are times when the sense of public duty outweighs the natural, personal reluctance to present facts of this nature. This is such a time."

[555]

STATEMENT BY VICE PRESIDENT WALLACE
CHAIRMAN OF THE BOARD OF ECONOMIC WARFARE
AS ORIGINALLY PREPARED FOR
THE SENATE COMMITTEE ON APPROPRIATIONS

On June 4, 1943, the Chairman of this Committee discussed the work of the Board on the floor of the Senate. His statement contained certain inaccuracies for which the Senator was not responsible. He was basing his comments on testimony which he said Mr. Jesse Jones had given before the Joint Committee on the Reduction of Non-Essential Federal Expenditures.

I realize that when the distinguished Senator from Tennessee made his remarks on the floor of the Senate he felt he had been correctly informed by the Secretary of Commerce. The actual facts are at variance with the information given the Senator, however, and I feel compelled to state the correct information for the record.

Senator McKellar said on June 4th: "No Congressional appropriation has ever been made for the payment of a single person employed in the Board of Economic Warfare. The Senate Appropriations Committee, of which I happen to be temporarily the head, has never appropriated any money for the Board of Economic Warfare."

On May 30, 1942, the President transmitted for the consideration of Congress an estimate of an appropriation for the salaries and expenses of the Board of Economic Warfare for the fiscal year 1943 (Document No. 760, 77th Congress, 2nd Sess.). After hearings before the House Appropriations Committee, during which we gave detailed testimony, that Committee favorably reported HR 7319, which contained an item for salaries and expenses of the Board of Economic Warfare (Report No. 2295, 77th Congress, 2nd Sess.). The bill passed the House on June 30, 1942, and was reported by Senator McKellar, for the Senate Committee on Appropriations, on July 10, 1942. The report suggested changes in some other items in the bill but left unchanged the item for salaries and expenses of the Board of Economic Warfare (Senate Report No. 1542). The bill as passed by the Senate on July 16, 1942, and approved by the President on July 25, 1942, contained an item in the amount of $12,-000,000 for salaries and expenses of the Board of Economic Warfare (Public Law No. 678, 77th Congress). Mr. Perkins was not called upon to testify with regard to the item when it was considered by the Senate Committee on Appropriations. However, on October 12, 1942, Mr. Perkins appeared before the sub-committee of the Senate Committee on Appropriations, with Senator McKellar presiding, to explain the need for certain amendments in the appropriation language, primarily to take care of the payment of living and quarters allowances to employees stationed abroad. These amendments were included in an item entitled "Board of Economic Warfare" in Public No. 763, 77th Congress, approved October 26, 1942.

In the same statement on the floor of the Senate on June 4th, 1943, Senator McKellar said: "Mr. Jesse Jones testified a day or two ago before the so-called Economy Committee, that Mr. Milo Perkins absolutely ran the entire establishment of 2,620 employees; that his word was law, even over him, Mr. Jesse Jones, and that he had received a directive from Mr. Perkins to furnish the money to pay all these employees."

The Board has never obtained money for administrative purposes from the Reconstruction Finance Corporation, nor has the Board ever directed Mr. Jesse Jones or any Reconstruction Finance Corporation subsidiary to furnish money to pay the salaries of any of the Board's employees or any of its administrative expenses. All such salaries and expenses are paid from funds appropriated by the Congress to the Board of Economic Warfare.

There have been a few occasions where, in connection with the joint operations of the Board of Economic Warfare and the Reconstruction Finance Corporation field staffs in foreign countries, arrangements have been worked out jointly for the payment of certain joint staff expenses by either the Board or the Corporation. In these cases reimbursement by the one agency or the other has been made in accordance with established government procedures.

On June 4, Senator McKellar also said: "The Board of Economic Warfare was not created by the Congress."

The Board of Economic Warfare was established by the President on July 30, 1941, by executive order, as were other war agencies. From time to time additional functions have been transferred to the Board of Economic Warfare by the President pursuant to authority vested in the President by the Congress, particularly by the First War Powers Act of December 18, 1942 (Public Law No. 354, 77th Congress). Congress has appropriated the monies which the Board is using to discharge these responsibilities. Furthermore, Congress has specifically directed in Public Law No. 638, 77th Congress, approved June 30, 1942, that unless the President shall determine otherwise, the Board of Economic Warfare shall administer the Export Control Law.

It is not enough to make these corrections. The false impression which Mr. Jones created before the Byrd Committee is similar to the impression he created in early December before the Senate Banking and Currency Committee. It is time to prevent further harmful misrepresentations of this nature.

On April 13, 1942, the President vested in the Board of Economic Warfare complete control of all public purchase import operations. Mr. Jones has never been willing to accept that fact. He has instead done much to harass the administrative employees of the Board in their single-minded effort to help shorten this war by securing adequate stocks of strategic materials.

The report of the Truman Committee, dated May 6, 1943, has set the proper pattern for dealing with situations of this kind. Two brief paragraphs from that report are of particular relevance:

"Energetic, aggressive men, striving to meet war needs, will tend to clash when their duties bring them into conflict. But destructive, wasteful feuding must be suppressed.

"The task of control and guidance is of utmost importance. Clear leadership in strong hands is required. The influence from above must be always towards unity. Where necessary, heads must be knocked together."

The President's Order of April 13, 1942, provided for "clear leadership" in programming the import of strategic materials. As a consequence of Mr. Jones' reluctance to accept that leadership there has been too much "destructive, wasteful feuding." The Board of Economic Warfare has tried for over a year now to do its job in spite of the obstructionist tactics Mr. Jones has employed from time to time.

The Congress showed great foresight, very early, in authorizing government stockpiling of strategic materials by passing legislation and by making funds available for this purpose way back in 1939 and 1940. In June of 1939, the Secretary of the Treasury was empowered to purchase and stockpile strategic materials as directed by the Secretary of War and the Secretary of the Navy. This program was comparatively small. Then in the summer of 1940, the Congress made substantial funds available to the Reconstruction Finance Corporation for carrying out a program for purchasing and stockpiling all critical and strategic materials.

From the summer of 1940 until well past December 7, 1941, the Reconstruction Finance Corporation failed dismally, so far as the import field was concerned, to build the government stockpiles authorized and directed by the Congress nearly eighteen months before Pearl Harbor.

During this period, of course, private purchasing of imports continued on a somewhat increased scale due to better business, and the Reconstruction Finance Corporation entered into various under-writing agreements with some countries under which we agreed to take surpluses if they were not bought privately. This seems to us to have been a timid, business-as-usual procedure; at least it was a "far cry" from the aggressive government stockpiling which the Congress directed and authorized so that this Nation might have a margin of security in its imported raw materials inventories.

On December 8, 1942, Mr. Perkins and I testified before the Senate Banking and Currency Committee and gave partial evidence of the delays to our work for which we felt Mr. Jones responsible. We gave testimony on his failure to meet the Office of Production Management's directives to stockpile industrial diamonds and black mica. We gave evidence on the extent to which he had delayed the foreign rubber program and cited specifically his stalling in the gathering of wild rubber in South America and the planting of rubber plantations in Africa and in the planting of cryptostegia for natural rubber in the Caribbean. We also presented evidence on the months of delay in starting a preclusive buying program in European neutral countries to prevent strategic materials from going to the Axis. These delays took place before Pearl Harbor and extended beyond Pearl Harbor right up to the 13th of April, 1942, at which time the President transferred import powers from the Reconstruction Finance Corporation and its subsidiaries to the Board of Economic Warfare.

The evidence which we presented on December 8, 1942, to the Senate Banking and Currency Committee was only partial evidence. It is a matter of public record in Hearings on S. 2900.

I now desire to present additional evidence on government stockpiling—commodity by commodity—for consideration by this Committee, by the entire Congress, and by the public at large.

PERFORMANCE RECORD ON CERTAIN PUBLIC PURCHASE RECOMMENDATIONS ISSUED IN 1941

1 Commodity	2 WPB (or OPM) Recommendation	3 Import Contracts Executed before April 13, 1942	4 Import Contracts Executed as of December 31, 1942	5 Chief Countries of Origin	6 Chief Uses
Beryl Ore	December 1, 1941: 3,000 m. t.	300 m. t.	4,118 m. t.	Argentina, Brazil, India, South Africa	In production of master beryllium-copper alloy
Castor Seeds	November 19, 1941: 178,571 l. t.	None	73,799 l. t. (spot purchases) 220,000 l. t. 9 (future delivery)	Brazil, Central America	Castor oil used as hydraulic brake fluid
Cobalt	November 17, 1941: 2,500 s. t. of contained cobalt metal November 18, 1941: 6,000 l. t. (subsequently increased)	159 s. t.	876 s. t.	Canada, Brazil, Belgian Congo	High speed cutting steels
Corundum		None	12,000 l. t.	South Africa	Abrasive for grinding optical glass telescope lenses
Fats and Oils (General)	October, November (1941); January, February (1942): 317,499 l. t. (subsequently increased)	2,200 l. t. (approximate)	276,622 l. t. (spot purchases) 500,000 l. t. (future delivery)	Africa, Brazil, Canada, Central America, South America, South Pacific	Edible oils; glycerine (for explosives); manufacture of synthetic rubber; lubricants; paints; tin plate manufacture
Palm Oil	October 20, 1941: 30,000 l. t.	None	23,928 l. t.	Belgian Congo, Nigeria	Manufacture of tin plate
Flax Fiber	October 27, 1941: 6,500 s. t.	None	8,000 s. t. annually for duration	Canada, Egypt, Peru	Parachute webbing; industrial sewing thread
Jute	September 5, 1941: 80,000 l. t.	1,210 l. t.	88,000 l. t.	India	Marine cordage; twines and ropes
Sisal	September 5, 1941: 100,000 s. t. (subsequently increased)	33,600 s. t.	310,000 s. t.	Caribbean Area, Africa, Mexico	Binder twine
Tantalite	December, 1941; March 13, 1942: 1,000,000 lbs.	None	322,000 lbs.	Africa, Argentina, Brazil, Nigeria	Contact points in radio tubes
Zirconium	September 5, 1941: "reasonable amounts"	None	21,575 s. t.	Australia, Brazil	Tracer ammunition; flares; signal; blasting caps

I want to point out first that all of our administrative work on imports is done under the broad direction of the War Production Board and in some cases under the broad direction of the War Food Administration. I now feel it my duty to get down to specific cases. For reasons of military security, I shall not include figures which might be of value to the enemy. The figures I am able to use, however, have not been previously presented to the Congress. They appear in the following table which I desire to discuss, commodity by commodity:

BERYL ORE

Beryl ore has very important military uses, the outstanding one being its use as an alloy with copper.

On December 1, 1941, the Office of Production Management, the forerunner of the War Production Board, recommended the purchase by Reconstruction Finance Corporation of 3,000 metric tons of beryl ore.

As of April 13, 1942, the day the President transferred import powers from the Reconstruction Finance Corporation to the Board of Economic Warfare, one 300 ton contract had been made, and no deliveries effected.

As of December 31, 1942, eleven contracts calling for the delivery of 4,118 metric tons of ore from four different countries (Argentina, Brazil, India, South Africa) had been made; 640 tons had been delivered. This was done under Board of Economic Warfare directives.

CASTOR SEEDS

The oil extracted from castor seeds is vitally important for war purposes. Among other things, it is used as a hydraulic fluid for jacks and brakes in war machines, as a solvent in paint, and (dehydrated) as a special protective coating for testing airplane motors. No adequate substitute is known.

On November 19, 1941, the Office of Production Management recommended to Reconstruction Finance Corporation the purchase of 178,571 long tons of castor seeds.

As of April 13, 1942, over four months after Pearl Harbor, none had been purchased.

As of December 31, 1942, at the direction of the Board of Economic Warfare, spot purchases totaling 73,799 long tons had been made and long term contracts had been executed for another 220,000 long tons.

COBALT

Cobalt is vitally important to our military effort, its chief use being in high speed cutting steels.

On November 17, 1941, Office of Production Management recommended to the Reconstruction Finance Corporation the purchase of ores containing 2,500 short tons of cobalt metal.

As of April 13, 1942, contracts had been made by the Metals Reserve Company for the purchase of ores containing only about 159 tons of cobalt metal. As of December 31, 1942, government contracts for ore purchases from foreign sources totaled about 876 short tons of cobalt metal. Increased private purchases have now put us in a comfortable supply position.

CORUNDUM

Corundum, vitally important for its use as an abrasive for grinding optical glass and telescope lenses, is obtained almost exclusively from South Africa. There is practically none in the United States, although there are some interesting experiments being carried on now, in the Southeastern section of the country.

On November 18, 1941, the Office of Production Management recommended to the Reconstruction Finance Corporation the purchase of 6,000 long tons of South African corundum. The recommendation was subsequently increased.

As of April 13, 1942, over four months after Pearl Harbor, no purchases had been made.

As of December 31, 1942, there were under contract (one contract; made by Metals Reserve Company in June, 1942) 12,000 long tons of South African corundum for delivery during 1943 and 1944. This was done under the Board of Economic Warfare directives.

FATS AND OILS

The fats and oils group includes approximately 25 different products, ranging all the way from sunflower seeds to curicury nuts and whale oil. These products are critically needed in the war effort for a variety of industrial uses as well as for human consumption.

There is one large group of edible oils, needed for Army, Navy, Lend-Lease and civilian uses.

Another group, which includes babassu nuts, coconuts, palm kernels, muru muru nuts, tucum nuts, and ouricury nuts, contains a high percentage of lauric acid, from which glycerine—used in the manufacture of explosives—is derived. These products are also used for plasticizers (to reduce brittleness) and in the manufacture of soap and synthetic rubber.

Oiticica oil and linseed oil are used as solvents in paints.

There is no adequate substitute for cashew nut oil, which is used to impregnate and toughen brake linings and for magneto harness coverings.

Neatsfoot oil is used in impregnating leather.

Tallow, seal oil and whale oil are used in soap making processes, in the course of which glycerine is produced.

Palm oil is essential in the manufacture of tin-plate.

Certain marine engines require rapeseed oil as a lubricant.

Sperm oil is used as a special lubricant for airplane engines (allowing the "cold" breaking in of motors), in the rifling of gun barrels, and as a high pressure smokeless lubricant in Diesel engines.

One would think, in view of the critical military urgency of going out to get these imported raw materials, that Mr. Jones would have moved aggressively to build government stockpiles of these fats and oils, and yet here are the facts:

In October, 1941, the Office of Production Management recommended to the Reconstruction Finance Corporation the purchase of approximately 30,000 long tons of various types of fats and oils from foreign sources. In November this total was increased to 208,571 long tons; in January, 1942, to 308,571 tons; in February to 317,499 tons. (The total has, since April 13, 1942, been increased much beyond this last figure.)

As of April 13, 1942, the Reconstruction Finance Corporation had purchased (according to the best information we have) only 2,200 long tons (rapeseed oil); none had arrived in this country. The purchases were all spot: no development program had been even devised. There may be a minor error in this particular figure due to the inadequate commodity accounting records of the Reconstruction Finance Corporation, but we believe the figure to be substantially accurate. For all practical purposes, however, virtually nothing was done by Mr. Jones to build a government stockpile of fats and oils even after Pearl Harbor, when the Japs were conquering the Far East from which we had been getting tremendous supplies.

The Board of Economic Warfare, shortly after it was given its responsibility in the import field, on April 13, 1942, shifted the financing of the fats and oils program to the Commodity Credit Corporation, but retained general administration of it.

As of December 31, 1942:

(1) 276,622 tons of foreign fats and oils had been bought on a spot purchase basis.

(2) The Board of Economic Warfare had negotiated and the Commodity Credit Corporation had entered into development and long term purchase contracts calling for the delivery of 500,000 tons. Several additional development contracts beyond this total were subsequently negotiated.

(3) The private import trade, dealing in fats and oils, which was threatened with extinction because of distortions in the world price structure, was organized into the Emergency Group for Foreign Vegetable Oils, Fats and Oil-Bearing Materials, and its services made use of as an integrated part of the program.

(4) Agreements for joint purchasing were made with the British and Canadians, eliminating competitive buying and resulting in a substantial reduction in the prices paid for a number of fats, oils and oil-bearing materials.

PALM OIL

Since there is no adequate substitute for palm oil, which is used in the manufacture of tin plate, I desire to call special attention to it.

On October 20, 1941, the Office of Production Management recommended to the Reconstruction Finance Corporation the purchase of 30,000 long tons of palm oil.

As of April 13, 1942, none had been purchased.

As of December 31, 1942, purchases (spot) totaled 23,928 long tons. This took place under Board of Economic Warfare directives.

FLAX FIBER

I now want to discuss flax fiber which is used for parachute webbing and which is also used as industrial sewing thread for high tension purposes.

On October 27, 1941, the Office of Production Management recommended the purchase by the Reconstruction Finance Corporation of 6,500 tons of flax.

As of April 13, 1942, the day the President transferred import powers from the Reconstruction Finance Corporation to the Board of Economic Warfare, no purchases had been made.

As of December 31, 1942, contacts had been made for approximately 8,000 tons annually from Canada, Peru and Egypt under Board of Economic Warfare directives.

JUTE

Jute is another commodity which must be imported from abroad. On September 5, 1941, the Office of Production Management had directed the purchase of 80,000 long tons of jute, nearly all of which comes from India.

As of April 13, 1942, over four months after Pearl Harbor, the Reconstruction Finance Corporation had done practically nothing to fulfill this important directive, having bought only 1,210 long tons, although the situation in India during this period was highly uncertain.

As of December 31, 1942, the Board of Economic Warfare had arranged for the purchase of the full 80,000 long tons, plus another 8,000 long tons to cover a supplementary directive. Moreover, most of this jute was shipped from Indian ports by the end of 1942.

The Board of Economic Warfare's insistence on maintaining in Calcutta, India, a special agent with a full business background in this industry, has been an important factor in the establishment of this performance record.

SISAL

Sisal is a hard fiber needed particularly in the manufacture of binder twine for the harvesting of our grain crops.

As of September 5, 1941, the Office of Production Management had recommended the purchase of 100,000 short tons of sisal (increased to 250,000 tons on March 18, 1942).

As of April 13, 1942, the Reconstruction Finance Corporation had purchased only an approximate 33,600 short tons against this urgent directive.

As of December 31, 1942, the Board of Economic Warfare had negotiated contracts for approximately 310,000 short tons, all to be produced by June 1945, and of which 150,000 tons is expected to be produced by the middle of 1943. By December 31, 1942, some 38,000 tons had been delivered.

We lost many of our fibers sources in the Far East to the Japanese. By

December 31, 1942, the Board of Economic Warfare had entered into contracts for the development and purchase of a number of hard fibers in Mexico and Caribbean areas as well as in Africa as part of a tremendous development program. We are planning to put 70,000 acres in these crops. 40,000 acres have already been planted. During a war we have to fight as vigorously to buy goods as we have to fight in peacetime to sell them.

TANTALITE

Tantalite is another strategic material carrying the very highest military priorities. It is used, among other things, for contact points in radio tubes.

In December, 1941, there was an exchange of correspondence between the Office of Production Management, the State Department and the Reconstruction Finance Corporation which made clear the necessity of increasing substantially United States tantalite imports by public purchase. On March 13, 1942, the War Production Board formally recommended the purchase by the Reconstruction Finance Corporation of 1,000,000 pounds.

As of April 13, 1942, over four months after Pearl Harbor, no tantalite had been purchased by the Reconstruction Finance Corporation.

As of December 31, 1942, some 322,000 pounds had been purchased.

This increase has been due in large measure to an aggressive Board of Economic Warfare program of tracing down every possible source of an ore which occurs only in very small and scattered deposits. Most purchases have been in exceedingly small lots.

In order to open up new sources of supply which will permit fulfilling the purchase recommendations we have received from the War Production Board, the Rare Metals Section of the Board of Economic Warfare's Metals and Minerals Division has contacted private producers or government representatives in Australia, Brazil, South Rhodesia, Argentina, French Equatorial Africa, Nigeria, Portuguese East Africa, India and Uganda.

It is estimated that, very largely as the result of Board of Economic Warfare efforts, 1943 imports into the United States may be 60 per cent above 1942 imports and ten times the total world production in 1939. This program is typical of the way in which the Board of Economic Warfare fights for every pound of strategic materials as though a soldier's life depended upon it— which, of course, it does.

ZIRCONIUM

I now desire to discuss zirconium which is so important in the manufacture of flares, signals, tracer ammunition, and blasting caps.

On September 5, 1941, Office of Production Management recommended to the Reconstruction Finance Corporation the purchase of "reasonable amounts" of zirconium from Brazil.

As of April 13, 1942, the day on which the President transferred import powers from the Reconstruction Finance Corporation to the Board of Economic

Warfare, no purchase contracts had been made under the Office of Production Management directive.

As of December 31, 1942, contracts had been made for the purchase from foreign sources of 21,575 short tons of zirconium ores, of which 16,500 short tons were from Brazil. This was done under Board of Economic Warfare directives.

As previously indicated, I have deliberately given figures of the Board of Economic Warfare accomplishments through December 31, 1942, only, for the purposes of military security. The progress in the foreign field for the first six months of 1943 is even more encouraging, considering the difficulties we have faced, than it was during the last six months of 1942. As an over-all figure for this Committee to bear in mind, I should like to point out that total purchases of imported raw materials subject to Board of Economic Warfare directives will run roughly a billion and one-half dollars for the 1943 fiscal year and slightly over two billion dollars for the fiscal year of 1944. Over two hundred critically needed strategic materials will be included in these public purchase programs. Contracts will be made in over thirty foreign countries.

Mr. Perkins is in position to give this Committee detailed and current information on any imported strategic material in a completely secret and off-the-record discussion if this Committee desires to have such facts placed before it in this manner. He can indicate the figures for the full fiscal year 1943 as well as contemplated figures for the 1944 fiscal year. Under no conditions would we make such current information a matter of public record. We are, however, very anxious to inform this Committee as to how such vast sums are being spent. I used the word "spent," but imported strategic materials are, of course sold by subsidiaries of the Reconstruction Finance Corporation to our war industries. Public purchase is used to assure adequate supplies. Detailed information has already been given the House Committee on Appropriations. We want to give the fullest possible information to the Senate Committee.

Since the 13th of April, 1942, when full import powers were transferred from the Reconstruction Finance Corporation to the Board of Economic Warfare, tremendous progress has been made in stepping up the procurement of certain strategic materials, shortages of which could not adequately have been foreseen by the Office of Production Management prior to Pearl Harbor. Outstanding among these is the increased production of balso wood and mahogany, largely in this Hemisphere. When the full story can be told, it will be one of the most dramatic successes of the war effort. Our country can be proud of having achieved what seemed to be almost impossible on this front.

Although the President, on April 13, 1942, transferred full control over the programming of imported strategic materials from the Reconstruction Finance Corporation to the Board of Economic Warfare, which operates under broad directives received from the War Production Board, Mr. Jones has never fully accepted that authority. He and his personnel down the line have thrown a great many obstacles in the way of our exercise of the powers given us to carry out our war-time assignments. Some of these obstructionist tactics have been minor and annoying and some have been of major consequence in this gigantic job of waging total war. I now desire to inform this Committee and the Congress and the public at large about some of these delays, which have not yet seen the light of day.

First of all I desire to discuss quinine. Brig. Gen. H. C. Minton has informed us that: "Antimalarial preparations derived from cinchona are, of course, essential to adequate control and treatment of malaria, in conjunction with the accepted synthetic anti-malarials."

Far East cinchona bark contains 7 to 10 per cent quinine sulfate; Latin America bark about 2 per cent.

On April 14, 1942, General MacArthur wired Washington that two million seeds of a high grade strain had been brought out of the Philippines (on one of the last planes leaving for Australia); adding that they "must be planted *without delay.*"

I am sorry to have to inform this Committee that Jesse Jones and Will Clayton stalled for months on this program. As I indicated to the Senate Banking and Currency Committee last December, there are times when what we need is more fights and fewer shortages.

Lt. Col. Arthur F. Fischer, who brought those seeds from the Philippines to the United States, came to the Board of Economic Warfare with his proposal—to plant the seeds in Costa Rica—on August 24, 1942. Within three weeks, the Board of Economic Warfare had worked out a detailed plan and submitted it to the other interested agencies. Reconstruction Finance Corporation representatives at first acquiesced in the proposal when it was discussed with them on September 11 and 29. Under Secretary of War Patterson approved it formally on October 7, 1942.

Then, on October 10, the Reconstruction Finance Corporation notified the Board of Economic Warfare that "the matter requires further consideration." Those "considerations" continued for four months. Mr. Jones said that our proposal was post-war planning because of the time it takes for cinchona trees to come to full maturity for profitable stripping. The Fischer trees couldn't be harvested for 2½ years at the earliest; normally, seven years pass before stripping of the bark begins.

During 1941 Mr. Jones may have felt that this would be a short war in which we wouldn't become involved; in any event he did not buy quinine during that period in adequate amounts for government stockpiles; during 1942 he acted as though the war might be over by 1944 if we can take his attitude toward this quinine project as a criterion. A United Press story in the New York Journal of Commerce of February 3, 1942, quotes Jesse Jones as follows: "Secretary of Commerce Jesse H. Jones told the House Banking Committee today that he believed the United States will be getting 'all the rubber we need from the Dutch East Indies' by the end of 1943 despite the present Japanese threat to that area." Mr. Jones may be right, but we dare not take chances and base our imports work on any such optimistic estimate.

As a matter of fact, Mr. Jones may have been considering something else. He takes great pride in the profits of the Reconstruction Finance Corporation and some of its subsidiaries, as evidenced by his recent testimony before the Byrd Committee. If the cinchona trees which we have been discussing have to be stripped after 2½ years because of desperate military needs for quinine, they will yield about 10,000 ounces of quinine—and a $125,000 loss to the Reconstruction Finance Corporation. That will mean red ink on the books of the Reconstruction Finance Corporation. I do not like to assign motives, but it is difficult to escape the conclusion that a possible dollar loss held up this production project. Like many things in total war this project may, of course, prove to be an expensive undertaking in terms of dollars. It seems to us to be a wise investment in terms of saving lives, however.

Whatever his reasons may have been, the facts are that Mr. Jones disregarded the constant proddings by the Board of Economic Warfare, and for a while he ignored the fact that I, as Chairman of the Board of Economic Warfare, had personally investigated the matter and recommended immediate action. His "considerations" continued right on through the battle—with malaria and with the Japs—at Guadalcanal.

It was not until late January, 1943, that the Reconstruction Finance Corporation finally announced that it would spend some money for this quinine project. For all the full power the President has given the Board of Economic Warfare over imports, we are helpless when Jesse Jones, as our banker, refuses to sign checks in accordance with our directives. Finally, we have won out in all such cases, but the time lost has been precious time which there was no excuse for losing. There have been many other times, of course, when personnel down the line in both the Reconstruction Finance Corporation and the Board of Economic Warfare have found themselves in complete agreement and have moved forward together with speed. The situation is better than it was a while back, and Mr. Perkins emphasized this fact in his recent testimony before the House Appropriations Committee.

Colonel Fischer is now in Costa Rica and the quinine project is underway. Some of his seeds have been germinating in the Department of Agriculture's experimental station in Beltsville and are about to be sent to Costa Rica. The rest will be planted there. It will be 1946 before quinine from the seeds brought out of the Philippines by Colonel Fischer can be put to work fighting malaria in the tropics. Even so, our Armed Forces may need it desperately by that time if they are still fighting in the malarial regions of the Southwest Pacific.

We and the Army would be quite willing to strip a greater part of the young trees at the end of 2½ years if we have to do so to get quinine for our soldiers, even though the Reconstruction Finance Corporation may lose a little money through not waiting seven years to let the trees mature for the most profitable period of stripping.

In fairness to the Reconstruction Finance Corporation I want to report that on a recent development project in Guatemala, where three hundred million cinchona trees for quinine are being planted under Board of Economic Warfare directives, we have thus far had no opposition from the RFC. We had previously won our fight in terms of principle on the Fischer project just described and Mr. Jones has not yet opposed us on the much larger project we have worked out in Guatemala.

The other quinine programs of the Board, such as gathering wild cinchona bark in Latin America, have been pushed aggressively by the Board of Economic Warfare, and Army officers are now surveying this work in the foreign field with members of our staff. Even this work, I am sorry to report, was held up by Mr. Jones in the late summer of 1942, some nine months after Pearl Harbor. I want to submit the following facts:

In February, 1943, the Board of Economic Warfare took over the actual import purchase negotiations under Order No. 5 which I signed as Chairman of the Board of Economic Warfare. Order No. 5 is part of our formal budget presentation. These negotiations had previously been handled by the Reconstruction Finance Corporation subsidiaries. The 1942 record of Reconstruction Finance Corporation's purchases of cinchona bark, under Board of Economic Warfare directives, illustrates why the procedures were changed in the interest of shortening this war.

(1) On June 19, 1942, the Board of Economic Warfare gave Defense Supplies Corporation a detailed outline of a program for purchasing Latin American cinchona bark from United States importers, and directed that it be put into immediate effect. A checkup five days later revealed that nothing had been done; the Federal Loan Administrator had "objected to the tone of finality" about the letter of June 19. Another week was lost because Mr. Clayton "has apparently mislaid the directive and requests another copy." That's the way the Reconstruction Finance Corporation was handling the cinchona program for quinine three months after we had lost Bataan.

(2) The Reconstruction Finance Corporation waited one month to accept an offer of 25 tons; by that time the particular bark had been sold to Brazil. Another offer for 20 tons was withdrawn—five weeks after it had been made. Those delays meant the loss of 1,800 ounces of anti-malarial alkaloids for United States soldiers fighting in the tropics. In three months the Reconstruction Finance Corporation bought just 75 tons of bark. In the following seven weeks a single Board of Economic Warfare agent got firm commitments for 750 tons for immediate shipment, 1,500 more for future delivery. By this time, our Imports Office was better organized than in the Spring of 1942, and swinging vigorously into action.

(3) The Board of Economic Warfare learned that the Reconstruction Finance Corporation was getting firm offers on cinchona bark but referring them to processors—with whom the importers were then haggling about price—while the bark stayed in Colombia and Ecuador. When the Board of Economic Warfare directed the Reconstruction Finance Corporation to accept all firm offers, the Reconstruction Finance Corporation responded by calling two meetings, each after another ten day delay. Then the Reconstruction Finance Corporation explained its reluctance; it didn't want to take the risk of financial loss involved in dealing with unknown and possibly "irresponsible" suppliers.

The Reconstruction Finance Corporation thus held up the vital quinine program while it objected to the "tone" of our letters, mislaid papers, forgot about offers, and handpicked its suppliers from the "right kinds of people," instead of making a desperate fight to buy every pound of cinchona bark it could locate from any source whatsoever, regardless of the financial risks involved.

QUARTZ CRYSTALS

I now desire to discuss quartz crystals, the use of which is so utterly important to some of our war industries.

For two years now Brazilian quartz crystal, essential element in airplane, tank and submarine radio sets, has been in critically short supply.

During 1941 and early 1942, the Reconstruction Finance Corporation agent in Brazil bought 2,000 tons of crystals. He was paid a commission of 1½ per cent on his gross purchases, and he bought those crystals without checking to see whether they were of the quality needed and paid for. Over 85 per cent of them weren't. The government lost between two and six million dollars, and we have heard that United States quartz fabricators began raiding museums to get usable crystals.

Shortly after April 13, 1942, the Reconstruction Finance Corporation replaced this agent although it gave him equally lucrative work in New York. But the situation in Brazil wasn't improved. The Reconstruction Finance Corporation had been burnt where it hurt most, by having to take a loss on a hazardous undertaking. The new Reconstruction Finance Corporation agent began eliminating dollar losses the easy way. Not a pound of quartz crystal was purchased by the Metals Reserve Company for six months. The Board of Economic Warfare finally had to send a top official to Rio to get the public purchasing resumed. I feel that Board of Economic Warfare personnel should have fought the delaying tactics of the Reconstruction Finance Corporation more vigorously in this instance.

The Board of Economic Warfare finally insisted upon inspection facilities in Rio so that crystals could be tested before payment and shipment. The Army Signal Corps has been of great assistance to us on this project by supplying 20 trained inspectors and the necessary arc-lights, inspection baths, polaroid screens, etc. The Army, of course, had a critical military stake in this phase of our work and has cooperated readily and effectively.

Reconstruction Finance Corporation policy had been to keep a staff in Rio— and to wait for the business to come in. When the Board of Economic Warfare sent 100 engineers and qualified purchasing agents into the up-country areas where the crystals are mined, Reconstruction Finance Corporation representatives in Brazil at first cooperated in supplying purchase money and contracting authority; then they refused to cooperate—on "instructions from Washington." The Board of Economic Warfare set up a purchasing station at outlying Campo Formoso; then we had to move it back to Bahia—so that Reconstruction Finance Corporation funds could be spent through the Bank there.

In April, 1943, Board of Economic Warfare representatives in Rio advised that restrictions put upon Metals Reserve Company agents' purchasing authority by Reconstruction Finance Corporation was preventing our meeting market prices in our buying there and that purchases were coming to a halt. The Board of Economic Warfare, therefore, directed the Reconstruction Finance Corporation to relax its restrictions. Reconstruction Finance Corporation refused, stating that we didn't need quartz enough to pay any more for it. Three weeks later, after advice from their own Brazilian representatives, they reconsidered—and changed their instructions. But not in time to head off the Special Representative of the Board of Economic Warfare in Brazil. Fed up with Reconstruction Finance Corporation obstruction to his Brazilian program, he arrived in Washington to report. It took his report, plus a morning which I spent with Jesse Jones and Will Clayton, to break this particular log-jam. Throughout the period of these bureaucratic, obstructionist tactics on the part of the Reconstruction Finance Corporation, the need for quartz crystals was critically urgent.

As I previously indicated, the reason Mr. Jones could hold up our quartz crystal and quinine programs is because he signs the checks to pay for the procurement and development of these commodities. To put it differently, he has been able to delay this part of the war effort because of his position as banker for us, notwithstanding the complete delegation of powers over imports which the President gave the Board of Economic Warfare on the 13th of April, 1942, following the failure of the Reconstruction Finance Corporation to build the government stockpiles of strategic materials which Congress authorized and directed in the summer of 1940.

The delays on the two programs just mentioned were major matters. More annoying, because there are more of them, have been the minor delays which have taken place from time to time throughout this past year. I now desire to discuss some of these, more by way of illustration than by way of presenting any completely documented case:

Since February, 1943, the Board of Economic Warfare has been negotiating and drafting all imported materials contracts, getting them executed by the sellers, then sending them to the Reconstruction Finance Corporation subsidiaries for execution. This has been done under Order No. 5 to which I referred earlier. The purpose in establishing these new procedures was to eliminate delay and duplication.

Those purposes have been in large measure accomplished—but only in the face of an exasperating rear guard action by Reconstruction Finance Corporation officials who are still fighting the war with peacetime red tape, corporate technicalities, and with what seems to us to be an unnecessary caution. None of the following obstructionist efforts of the Reconstruction Finance Corporation is major in itself, but the cumulative effect has been maddening to the businessmen with foreign trade background who have left lucrative positions in private industry to work for the Board of Economic Warfare at government salaries for the duration in a patriotic effort to help shorten this war.

The tactics are better illustrated than described. During the past four months, for example, one of the Reconstruction Finance Corporation subsidiaries, Metals Reserve Company:

(1) Took four weeks to execute a group of three metal contracts drafted by the Board of Economic Warfare which the sellers had executed and returned within ten days.

(2) Held a copper contract for five weeks because one letter had been left out of one unimportant word and because two minor clauses "could have been

more clearly stated." (The seller had supplied the missing letter and had found no difficulty in understanding the two clauses.)

(3) Wrote three letters to the Board of Economic Warfare complaining because a form recital clause (without legal effect) referred to the Board of Economic Warfare's "direction" that the contract be entered into. (A similar reference to the War Production Board had always been included by the Reconstruction Finance Corporation draftsmen.)

(4) Demanded that a simple five-ton wash sale contract for tantalite be broken up into two contracts—so that Reconstruction Finance Corporation attorneys might draft one of the two. The wash sale technique was used on this small lot in order to provide Government ownership while in transit, as it was necessary to ship the goods by air and the Air Transport Command carries only Government owned materials.

(5) Refused to sign a contract with a Nigerian tantalite producer before the producer signed it—even though the alternative meant a three-week delay in getting a new mine into production.

(6) Refused, on a legal technicality, to honor a directive authorizing the "loan *or* rental" of equipment to the Brazilian Government—because of information from Government representatives in Rio, received subsequent to our directive, that the equipment would be *rented,* and not *loaned.*

(7) Held a Brazilian tantalite contract for four weeks because it had been entered into without a formal approval required by the Secretary of Commerce.

All this, and I want to emphasize it, is bureaucracy at its worst; it is utterly inexcusable in a nation at war.

We are quite willing to rest our case with the Congress and stand on our record. While I realize that the suggestion which I am about to make is not a matter directly before this Committee, I should like to express a personal judgment.

It seems to me that we could end this wrangling and improve the administrative efficiency so essential to winning this war, if program money were appropriated directly to the Board of Economic Warfare for its purchase and development of *all* imported strategic materials, just as money is now appropriated directly to us for administrative expenses in connection with our imports work. These difficult war time jobs cannot be tackled effectively, as pointed out so truly in the report of the Truman Committee from which I read in the early part of this statement, without the full power to carry out specific assignments.

The Board of Economic Warfare is a war agency; it is not a part of the permanent machinery of Government. We have recruited what we feel to be an extremely competent group of businessmen and technical engineers with foreign trade background to carry out our job of importing strategic materials. Shortly after the war is over most of these men will be wanting to get back to their peacetime responsibilities.

For the duration, however, I feel that they should be given adequate latitude for a job which is extremely difficult even under the best of conditions. They should be free from this hamstringing bureaucracy and backdoor complaining of Mr. Jones and his employees. It is my hope that this statement has cleared up any misunderstandings which may have been caused by Mr. Jones' appearance before the Byrd Committee.

REPLY OF JESSE H. JONES, SECRETARY OF COMMERCE TO VICE PRESIDENT WALLACE
JULY 5, 1943

(In the procurement and development of critical and strategic materials, both at home and abroad, the RFC operates through subsidiary corporations such as Metals Reserve Company, Defense Supplies Corporation, Defense Plant Corporation, the U. S. Commercial Company, Rubber Reserve Company and Rubber Development Corporation.

The Directors of the Reconstruction Finance Corporation and the Secretary of Commerce largely constitute the Boards of Directors and management of the subsidiary corporations.

Therefore, for convenience in this statement RFC is used throughout instead of the particular subsidiary involved.)

Mr. Wallace's statement of June 29, 1943, says: "I now desire to present additional evidence on government stockpiling—commodity by commodity— for consideration by this Committee, by the entire Congress, and by the public at large."

That statement indicates an intention to review the entire foreign program. Actually only a few items are mentioned.

The metals will be discussed first.

RFC is purchasing 37 different metals. Mr. Wallace confines his discussion to six, with a reference to two others.

The 29 metals which are not mentioned account for 97% of RFC's dollar commitments and 99% by weight, and include such major items as aluminum, copper, lead, manganese, tin and zinc.

Mr. Wallace's detailed discussion covers beryllium, cobalt, corundum, tantalum, zirconium and quartz crystal. He also makes reference to testimony previously given before the Senate Banking and Currency Committee, with regard to mica and industrial diamonds; but that testimony was refuted by me at the time.

Mr. Wallace's charges with respect to the six items which he discusses in detail are answered below.

Many of the statements made are false; others are purposely misleading. The net effect of these statements is to create the impression that failure to obtain these materials in larger quantities, or more promptly, has impeded the war effort. This implication is maliciously false. While the situation on tantalum and corundum has been tight, there has been no shortage; and in so far as beryl, cobalt, quartz crystal and zirconium are concerned, our stockpiles are large and are increasing.

BERYLLIUM: **Mr.** Wallace states that although OPM recommended RFC purchase 3,000 metric tons of beryl ore in December, 1941, only one purchase had been made prior to April 13, 1942. The facts are:

The OPM recommendation requested that RFC "consult Mr. Masters [then chief of the OPM beryllium branch] as to the details of purchase, ore specifications, etc." On consultation with Mr. Masters he asked that existing private contracts for importation of beryl ore be completed before RFC undertook purchase. The principal supply was under contract to come to this country until June, 1942. At that time RFC immediately began buying this material, literally as requested by WPB.

While imports of beryl ore during 1942 by RFC were relatively small, this was due to two causes beyond our control—a government embargo on Argentine exports (lifted only in October) and to heavy shipping losses by submarines. Furthermore, as consumers' stocks in this country were fully adequate to cover requirements, RFC continued to purchase and hold beryl abroad, for shipment when the risks of sinkings were less, all in accordance with the views of WPB. Improvement in shipping has changed this situation. Our present stockpile of beryl ore in government hands is large and is still increasing.

RFC staffs in Washington and in the field handled negotiations for beryllium until February 25, 1943, and there has been no shortage.

COBALT: Mr. Wallace refers to the OPM recommendation of November 17, 1941, for the purchase of materials containing cobalt. He points out that contracts made by RFC prior to April 13, 1942, covered only 159 tons of cobalt metal. The OPM recommendation included both domestic and foreign materials. Therefore, the comparison with foreign purchases only, as made by Mr. Wallace, is deliberately misleading. The facts are:

When the recommendation was made by OPM only two foreign sources of cobalt materials were available to RFC—Canada and Burma. The principal foreign producer, Belgian Congo, would not sell to the U. S. Government for stockpile but agreed to produce at a maximum rate and import into U. S. for its own account. To this date, 15 months after the responsibility has been with BEW, no purchase of Belgian Congo cobalt has been made.

Cobalt from Burma had been purchased by RFC and received prior to April 13, 1942, after which time the supply from Burma was cut off. Canadian cobalt had not been bought because facilities for treatment in the United States were limited (the ore presents serious metallurgical problems) and WPB did not advise purchase. In the spring of 1942, at the request of WPB, RFC began construction of a plant to treat arsenical cobalt ores and negotiations for cobalt ores were promptly concluded with the Canadian Government.

Because of continued heavy imports from Belgian Congo, stocks of cobalt have been growing steadily. Recently substantial quantities have been obtained from French North Africa, thanks to the armies of the United Nations, and not as the result of anything BEW has done.

Both WPB and the Combined Raw Materials Board have recently indicated that RFC purchase of additional quantities of cobalt is not warranted.

CORUNDUM: Mr. Wallace refers to the OPM recommendation for the purchase of 6,000 long tons of South African corundum, made in November, 1941. He points out that no contract was made until June, 1942. Again this is misleading. The facts are:

Usable corundum for abrasive purposes is largely controlled by a single producer in South Africa. This producer, at the time of the OPM recommendation, had a contract with the only large consumer in the United States extending to June 30, 1942. With the full approval of OPM, therefore, RFC contracted for the purchase of this material available after June 30, 1942. Terms had been agreed upon prior to BEW's entry into this field.

The entire output of the producer in question has come to the United States since November, 1941, (except for a small quantity shipped to the United Kingdom). Whether this material came consigned to a private consumer or to the Government cannot have affected the war effort.

TANTALUM: Mr. Wallace refers to WPB recommendations in December, 1941, and March 13, 1942, to purchase tantalum. He points out that on April 13, 1942, four months after Pearl Harbor, no tantalum ore had been purchased by RFC. The facts are:

OPM, under the direction of SPAB, of which Mr. Wallace was Chairman, State Department and RFC had correspondence relating to purchase of tantalite in December, 1941. RFC was asked to buy material "not purchased by private industry." On February 25, 1942, WPB wrote us: "As for the purchase of these ores, it is doubtful whether any large quantity would be offered to our Government for purchase, as industry is buying every pound available."

These quotations made clear that SPAB, OPM, and WPB were in full agreement as to the policy pursued. On March 13, 1942, WPB, which determines policy, asked that RFC proceed forthwith to buy tantalum ore, including a large stock already in the United States. This was promptly done, and on April 16, 1942, RFC approved a contract for 537,000 pounds of tantalum ore already in the United States, though of foreign origin. Mr. Wallace makes no mention of that purchase when he speaks of 322,000 pounds purchased as of December 31, 1942.

To date about 85% of our supply continues to come from Brazil and Belgian Congo, the two major sources which were well developed by RFC prior to the activities of BEW. Mr. Wallace's statement that as a result of BEW activities, U. S. imports of tantalum in 1943 will be "ten times the total world production in 1939" is of very doubtful accuracy. I am advised that world production in 1939 was at least 50% of the present level.

ZIRCONIUM: Mr. Wallace indicates a desire to "discuss zirconium, which is so important in the manufacture of flares, signals, tracer ammunition, and blasting caps."

We are informed by WPB that zirconium is not now being used in the manufacture of flares, signals or tracer ammunition. About 300 to 400 pounds of zirconium metal goes into blasting caps annually. If these were the real uses for zirconium, the RFC stockpile would cover requirements for 100,000 years.

OPM recommended on September 5, 1941, the purchase of "reasonable amounts" of zirconium from Brazil. In May, 1941, RFC had arranged with the Brazilian Government to embargo shipment of strategic materials to Axis countries, zirconium being one of these materials. RFC agreed to buy all zirconium ore not bought by U. S. consumers. Because private trade was importing sufficient quantities, RFC made no purchases, with WPB knowledge and approval.

On March 13, 1942, WPB recommended that RFC purchase 5,000 tons of Australian zircon already in the U. S. as an incentive to import additional quantities of combined rutile-zircon ores. This was done promptly, the contract being approved on April 11, 1942.

On May 18, 1942, WPB recommended to BEW that 15,000 short tons of Brazilian zirconium ore be purchased. This contract was promptly negotiated by RFC and BEW.

It is significant of the war demand for zirconium that none of the RFC stockpile has been used; that zirconium has been denied shipping priorities (except in the case of combined rutile-zirconium ore, valuable for the rutile contained); and that consumption for metallurgical purposes, the principal expected war use, has dropped to virtually nil.

QUARTZ CRYSTAL: Mr. Wallace states: "For two years now Brazilian quartz crystal, essential element in airplane, tank and submarine radio sets, has been in critically short supply."

This statement is misleading. There has been no actual shortage. All consuming demands have been met. There is now a large stockpile in Government hands, which is increasing. RFC's sales of quartz crystal to manufacturers during the last three months have been the smallest in more than a year, in part because the demand for this material is leveling off, and in part because consumers hold ample stocks.

Morris Rosenthal, head of the BEW Imports Office, cabled to the BEW representative in Brazil on May 27th saying "stock position here is such that it is not necessary to reach for quartz in Brazil at present"; and on June 26th BEW wired its representative in Argentina that the quartz crystal situation was easier and that therefore the examination of an Argentine deposit was not warranted.

Mr. Wallace states that during 1941 and early 1942 the RFC agent in Brazil "bought 2,000 tons of crystals . . . without checking to see whether they were of the quality needed and paid for" and that over 85% of them were not. Mr. Wallace says the Government lost between two and six million dollars. Those statements are largely incorrect and deliberately misleading.

RFC purchases to April 13, 1942, amounted to approximately 1,600 tons. The cost of this material was $7,750,000.

During the period in question, RFC purchased all of the quartz crystal available in Brazil, whether of good grades or poor, under an arrangement with the Brazilian Government to prevent any crystals from reaching Axis sources. Instead of more than 85% being of no value, however, between 35 and 40% of the 1,600 tons are suitable for radio use (which is the normal recovery based on the experience of private importers). It is estimated and our opinion that no loss will be sustained by the Government on the material in question. This result has been brought about by the technical discovery that much material previously considered unusable can be fully utilized. It is, therefore, fortunate that RFC bought the entire output, good and poor.

Mr. Wallace refers to a commission of 1½% having been paid the RFC agent on his gross purchases. The following are the facts:

In May, 1941, the RFC, with the cooperation of the State Department, entered into an over-all purchase agreement with the Brazilian Government covering twelve strategic and critical materials of Brazilian production. Under this agreement the Brazilian Government issued a decree confining the exportation of these materials to the United States, and the RFC agreed to purchase all of such materials at prices agreed upon. Due to the fact that considerable quantities of these materials were at that time being exported to Germany, Italy and Japan, quick action had to be taken in order to stop this traffic. Rather than attempt quickly to set up a buying organization in Brazil, we decided that both time and money could be saved by employing a capable American firm, experienced in the business of importing metals, to handle this business for us. This we did, paying a commission of 1½% which was less than we could have done the work for ourselves and is far less than it is costing the BEW at the present time.

Mr. Wallace also states that RFC refused to "relax its restrictions" on the purchase of quartz crystal, because "we didn't need quartz enough to pay more for it."

This statement is not true. RFC did not refuse to relax its restrictions. It merely asked BEW for certain information before it acted.

Starting in October, 1942, RFC has purchased in the United States, under BEW directive, $2,500,000 in scarce equipment for shipment to Brazil to be used in mining quartz, mica and tantalum, but predominantly for quartz. These minerals have usually been produced by hand labor, but BEW thought production could be increased by mechanizing operations with bulldozers, tractors, compressors, rock drills, etc. In addition to the aforesaid equipment bought in this country and shipped to Brazil, substantial amounts of such machinery have been bought in Brazil by RFC, under directive of BEW.

We are advised that much of this machinery has not been put to work, but is lying idle and rusting. Considering that this equipment is vital to our war effort, the loss cannot be measured in terms of wasted money alone. Notwithstanding this and the fact that much of the machinery already on hand is not being used, BEW continues to direct RFC to buy additional machinery and equipment.

May 12, 1943, BEW's Brazilian representatives estimated that exports of quartz crystal during the second half of 1943 would average 113 short tons a month. This compares with an average of over 160 tons a month during the first year RFC bought quartz in Brazil, and before BEW had sent 100 or more engineers and purchasing agents to Brazil and had directed RFC to buy so much machinery.

CONTRACT DELAYS: Mr. Wallace refers to the "obstructionist efforts" of the RFC, and gives seven examples of the "tactics" employed.

The desire and efforts of RFC agencies to comply with their statutory and administrative responsibilities cannot properly be described as "tactics."

Since February 25, 1943, all negotiations are handled by BEW. More's the pity. In some cases RFC is informed on the negotiations as they progress; in other cases RFC's first knowledge of the contracts is obtained when they are sent by the BEW to the seller for execution, with a copy to RFC; in still other cases, RFC knows nothing of the contracts until after they have been executed by the seller, and are sent to RFC with a directive for execution.

When a contract comes to RFC from BEW, it is examined by our legal and administrative staffs. The Directors of RFC have not felt free to execute contracts, as received from BEW, with directives, without examination as to the legal effect of the contracts and the obligations assumed by the Government under them. Consequently, where any contract contains provisions which might not give proper protection to the Government, we have given BEW our views and have awaited their replies before proceeding. In many cases such contracts have contained errors which had to be corrected.

Mr. Wallace gives seven examples. Two of these examples (1 and 2) we have been unable to identify from the statements as given.

In example No. 3, reference is made to certain correspondence regarding a form recital clause. Regardless of the merits of the question (which was of corporate importance to RFC) this correspondence caused no delay in signing the contract.

In example No. 4, it is implied that RFC wished a contract divided into two parts in order to make work for RFC's attorneys. This statement is ridiculous. BEW lawyers no doubt have time to waste. Not so with RFC. RFC sought to provide for the required allocation by the War Production Board, which had been omitted; and also to avoid confusion by separating the foreign purchase, which is under control of BEW, from the domestic sale with which BEW has nothing to do.

In example No. 5, Mr. Wallace speaks of a "three week delay in getting a new mine into production," because RFC "refused to sign" the contract until prior signing by the producer. RFC actually expedited this transaction by authorizing the BEW representative in London to sign the contract immediately upon its execution by the producer. There was no delay.

In example No. 6, Mr. Wallace suggests that RFC refused to honor a directive authorizing the "loan *or* rental" of equipment to the Brazilian Government because of information that the equipment would be *rented* and not *loaned.* This statement is both untrue and misleading. The facts are that a cable from the BEW's representative in Brazil indicated that this equipment might be given away. RFC pointed out to BEW that it lacks authority to give away government property and therefore asked for assurance that the equipment would either be sold or rented. This assurance being given, the directive was approved.

In example No. 7, reference is made to a Brazilian contract being delayed for four weeks pending "formal approval" required by the Secretary of Commerce. This contract involved a substantial advance payment. Under the law, advance payments can only be made with the approval of the President. The contract had been signed in Brazil, and was approved by the Secretary of Commerce for the President as soon as it was received here.

*   *   *   *   *   *

Reply to Mr. Wallace's charges relating to materials other than metals follows:

Most of these materials that Mr. Wallace mentions were, on May 20, 1942, more than 13 months ago, transferred by BEW to the Department of Agriculture, so that RFC has had no responsibility concerning them since that time.

Mr. Wallace's charges concern only ten of these materials, although RFC has dealt in 64 such commodities.

QUININE, CINCHONA BARK, AND THE FISCHER PROJECT: Mr. Wallace's statement about quinine and cinchona bark from which quinine is produced, and about the so-called Fischer Project, is full of distortions, omissions, and inaccuracies.

Here are the facts:

QUININE

August, 1941, we bought 2,000,000 ounces of quinine as recommended by OPM. The next recommendation to buy quinine came in a letter from Morris Rosenthal, Assistant Director of BEW, which was received by us January 21, 1942, confirming his verbal recommendation of January 15th.

Notwithstanding the fact that all RFC stockpile recommendations were, by Executive Order of the President, to come from WPB and not from BEW, we started negotiations January 15th, and were advised January 22nd, by the Netherlands East Indies Trade Commissioner, that there was no quinine available in Java for prompt delivery, but we were offered 2,000,000 ounces, for shipment 500,000 ounces monthly, March through June, 1942. We immediately took the matter up with WPB, and were advised that our quinine supply was comfortable, approximately 14,000,000 ounces, or four years' requirements, and that further stockpiling was unnecessary.

However, February 16, we received another letter from Morris Rosenthal, recommending the purchase of 3,000,000 ounces from the Netherlands East Indies. I immediately conferred with Mr. Donald Nelson, and on his verbal approval we ordered the 3,000,000 ounces for March and April shipments, having been previously advised that there was no quinine available for immediate shipment.

February 26, we were advised by the State Department that 2,500,000 ounces of quinine in the bark could be bought for prompt shipment from Batavia. We made the purchase within the hour, and later the same day bought an additional 665,000 ounces from another source.

Batavia was occupied by the Japanese ten days later, and none of the quinine covered by this latter purchase was delivered.

THE FISCHER PROJECT

The project for the planting of cinchona trees in Costa Rica was initiated by the Army through Colonel A. F. Fischer. Mr. Wallace states that the project was proposed to BEW on August 24, 1942. The proposal was known to the BEW at least a full month before that date. On April 9, 1943, 9 months later, the BEW, after it had finally worked out its plan of operations, first asked RFC to establish credit for the initiation of the Col. Fischer project, and such credit was promptly established. This credit would have been established many months earlier if the BEW had acted promptly. The fact is that BEW did not submit to RFC even a tentative proposal until October 7, 1942. Our reply of October 10 did not, as Mr. Wallace asserts, state "the matter requires further consideration" but advised that the "plan will receive prompt consideration." The proposal submitted to RFC at that time involved the organization, under the auspices of BEW, of a cooperative non-profit association. All financing and responsibility would rest upon RFC. BEW finally abandoned this plan after the State Department had indicated that it could not approve an arrangement under which the operation of the United States Government in a Latin American country would be concealed in an association purporting to be a cooperative organization. Mr. Wallace's statement that the BEW's proposal was objected to because it would not be profitable is, therefore, false.

CINCHONA BARK

The BEW's handling of the procurement of cinchona bark has been vacillating as to policy and disorderly in administration. Despite prior promptings by the WPB, RFC, and others interested, the BEW failed to formulate any plans or issue a directive under which RFC could act until June 19, 1942.

Mr. Wallace implies that BEW was not responsible for cinchona bark procurement until February 25, 1943, when his Order No. 5 became effective. BEW reiterated to us again and again after April 13, 1942, that it was responsible for the procurement of cinchona bark down to smallest detail.

The policy finally established by the BEW directive of June 19, 1942, was abandoned by it in approximately 90 days and a second policy was established by BEW. During the next 90-day period a third policy was established by BEW. The three policies overlapped and much confusion resulted. None of the plans recognized that the procurement of cinchona bark, particularly in Latin America where it was not well understood, requires skilled and experienced handling. Those business firms whose background best qualified them to meet the problem were largely ignored by BEW, and firms with little experience which were called on by BEW were not given competent guidance by it. The third policy established by BEW ignores entirely the possibility of aid through private business and substitutes direct purchases in foreign countries by BEW employees who are, in the main, inexperienced in this field.

In shifting from policy to policy, BEW has caused confusion and uncertainty among the suppliers of bark in Latin America, several Latin American

Governments, and the American importers. A very small quantity of cinchona bark has been produced as a result of BEW's activities, notwithstanding the time which has elapsed and the money which has been spent.

The principal additional supply of quinine made available to our armed forces since the fall of Java was procured through the splendid services of the American Pharmaceutical Association financed by RFC acting under directive from the WPB. A substantial quantity of quinine in its various forms has been assembled from thousands of domestic stocks, large and small, held by druggists and others throughout the nation, much of it donated to the Government.

CORDAGE FIBERS: Mr. Wallace states that September 5, 1941, OPM recommended the purchase of 100,000 short tons of sisal and as of April 13, 1942, only 33,600 tons had been purchased. The facts are:

Mr. Wallace's statements about sisal and other cordage fibers are false in detail and give a distorted picture of the situation. He gives the impression that present supplies result solely from BEW enterprise, ignoring the fact that all of our present substantial sources of supply were opened by private enterprise and RFC prior to any participation by BEW.

Mr. Wallace states that only 33,600 short tons of sisal had been contracted for prior to April 13, 1942. BEW knows that on December 26, 1941, RFC contracted for the importation of 23,000 long tons of sisal from British East Africa, 13,000 long tons on April 7, 1942, and 14,500 long tons on April 10, 1942, a total of 55,500 short tons. In addition, RFC contracted for approximately 22,500 tons of Philippine fiber, of which over one-half was brought from the Philippines before Pearl Harbor. An additional 20,000 tons of cordage fiber were procured for stockpile from private importers and holders. In addition, RFC negotiated in Mexico the purchase of 210,000 tons of Mexican henequen sisal. These negotiations were commenced in February, 1942, and continued to a successful conclusion by representatives of RFC sent to Mexico for that purpose, without any direction by BEW.

Thus, RFC, without participation by BEW, contracted for a total of 308,000 short tons of cordage fibers, of which a substantial portion was actually delivered during 1941 and 1942. The BEW's participation in the fiber program subsequent to April 13, 1942, has not resulted in the opening of substantial new sources of fiber, nor has it expedited or increased the quantities of deliveries in any appreciable way. On the contrary, under BEW handling, it took from April 13, 1942, to November, 1942, before another contract for British East African fiber was ready for execution. During this delay the shippers of African sisal, impatient of the delay in negotiations, shipped large quantities of sisal to RFC without a contract.

Mr. Wallace states: "We are planning to put 70,000 acres in these crops [fibers]. Forty thousand acres have already been planted."

The clear implication here is that BEW is responsible for the planting of these 40,000 acres. This is not true. Late in 1941, RFC and United Fruit Company entered into negotiations for the planting of fiber in Costa Rica and Panama. These negotiations culminated in the signing of two contracts on January 30 and February 9, 1942, for the planting of 20,000 acres of abaca fiber in these countries and the construction of the necessary processing plants. Discussions regarding the planting of an additional 20,000 acres were taking place at the time BEW entered the field, April 13, 1942. Their intervention in the matter caused the negotiations to be so prolonged that it was not until the end of September, 1942, that a contract for the planting of these additional 20,000 acres was made.

CASTOR SEEDS: Mr. Wallace states that on November 19, 1941, OPM recommended to RFC the purchase of 178,571 long tons of castor seeds and that as of April 13, 1942, none had been purchased. The facts are:

November 19, 1941, OPM recommended that the RFC *underwrite* the purchase of 400,000,000 pounds (178,571 long tons) of castor seeds during the year 1942. OPM recommended further that the agreement provide for Government purchase on the following conditions:

"1. Government will purchase for stockpile that proportion of the total not taken up by private industry through regular channels of direct purchase, except when a specific purchase will prevent slip [shipment] to Axis countries.

"2. That such purchase will be made under conditions agreeable to OPM with respect to price and quality."

It was agreed that Brazil's production was adequate to meet the requirements and that castor seeds would be included in our over-all purchase agreement with Brazil, made in May, 1941.

On December 4, 1941, the State Department cabled the Embassy in Brazil asking the Embassy to ascertain whether the Brazilian authorities would accept in principle an offer to purchase that part of the Brazilian exportable surplus of castor oil and castor seeds for 1942 which was not acquired by private purchasers in the United States, United Kingdom, or other American Republics. At the same time an outline of the proposed underwriting agreement with Brazil, covering 400,000,000 pounds of castor seeds, which had been prepared in cooperation with the State Department and OPM, was submitted to our Embassy in Brazil.

In the meantime investigations disclosed that private interests in this country were buying substantially all of the castor seeds available for export from Brazil.

Following Pearl Harbor, however, American buyers began competing with each other in the Brazilian castor seed market to such an extent that the price rose rapidly and finally reached a point so high that the American importers could not buy without sustaining loss. We were advised of this trend in February, 1942, and immediately took up with the WPB a proposal that the United States Government, acting through RFC, be designated as the sole importer of castor seeds.

On March 28, 1942, RFC advised the Embassy in Brazil through the State Department that it was willing to purchase the exportable surplus of Brazilian castor seeds up to 200,000 metric tons to be shipped during the next 12 months at a price of $75 per metric ton. Ten days later castor seed was put under General Imports Order M-63 by WPB.

Between April 28, 1942, and May 4, 1942, RFC authorized American importers to purchase approximately 28,000 tons of Brazilian castor seeds. These negotiations were conducted without the assistance of BEW, although to comply with Executive Order 9128 confirming directives were requested by RFC and received from BEW. Almost immediately thereafter the castor seed program, along with certain other agricultural commodities, was transferred to Commodity Credit Corporation, which is operated by the Department of Agriculture, and since that time has not been a responsibility of the RFC.

PALM OIL: Mr. Wallace states that on October 20, 1941, OPM recommended the purchase by RFC of 30,000 long tons of palm oil, and that as of April 13, 1942, none had been purchased. The facts are:

October 20, 1941, OPM recommended the purchase of 30,000 tons of plantation palm oil, for the purpose of establishing a "stockpile specifically earmarked for the tin-plate industry, to be released only upon recommendation of OPM."

It was found that the amount of palm oil used by the tin-plate industry constituted only a small percentage of the oil normally imported by this country. It was further ascertained that the tin-plate industry had a year's supply of palm oil on hand (28,000 tons). To assure two years' supply for the tin-plate industry, OPM proposed to restrict the domestic use, and on December 15, 1941, RFC confirmed to OPM its understanding that the RFC was to do nothing concerning palm oil until further advised.

There were no further stockpile recommendations to RFC with respect to this commodity. Appreciable quantities of palm oil were being imported by the trade, a monthly average of 12,500 long tons having been imported during the last six months of the year 1941 and 8,000 long tons monthly during the first quarter of 1942. In February, 1942, WPB placed palm kernels and palm kernel oil under General Imports Order M-63, but rather than request RFC to purchase, WPB granted exemptions to importers which made it unnecessary for RFC to purchase palm oil.

JUTE: Mr. Wallace states that on September 5, 1941, OPM had directed the purchase of 80,000 long tons of jute, and that as of April 13, 1942, RFC had only bought 1,210 long tons. The facts are:

September 5, 1941, OPM submitted to RFC a general request setting forth the commodities to be acquired under public purchase programs. The list includes jute to the extent of 80,000 long tons.

Conferences were held with the industry and OPM in August and September, 1941, in regard to the desirability of RFC purchasing a stockpile of jute. The Schlichter Jute Cordage Company was experiencing difficulty at that time in obtaining shipping priorities for jute purchases. They were particularly interested in fulfilling orders of jute for electrical insulation, and it was considered essential by OPM that an effort be made to obtain shipping space. Consequently, RFC entered into agreements with the Company under which RFC purchased the jute at cost and resold the same to the Company upon arrival in the United

States. This procedure enabled the jute to obtain a higher shipping priority. The transactions covered 1,210 long tons.

With the exception of the foregoing transactions, it appeared to OPM that there was no need for further government purchases of jute at that time. RFC maintained close contact with the Textile Branch of OPM and was prepared to make purchases whenever it appeared necessary to OPM to take such action. Heavy purchases of jute were being made by the trade during this period and with the exception of the Schlichter supply, shipments were coming forward in a satisfactory manner. This condition continued until late July, 1942. At that time WPB decided to amend the jute order for the purpose of further restricting uses of jute in the United States. It was further recommended that RFC make public purchases of jute in order to assure a more orderly shipment of the jute and, particularly, to stabilize prices in India. On August 3, 1942, BEW directed RFC to negotiate for the purchase of approximately 80,000 long tons of jute. RFC immediately negotiated and executed the contracts.

It is significant that BEW did not direct the purchase of jute until 4½ months after it acquired control over foreign purchases. If the situation were as critical as appears in Mr. Wallace's statement, such direction should have been made immediately after April 13, 1942.

FLAX FIBER: Mr. Wallace states that OPM recommended on October 27, 1941, that RFC purchase 6,500 tons of flax and that as of April 13, 1942, no purchase had been made. The facts are:

October 27, 1941, OPM recommended the purchase by RFC of a stockpile of flax fiber of 5,000 tons of line and 1,500 tons of tow. In this recommendation it was suggested that we not buy tow except as part of a general trade, and not more than 1,500 tons because plenty of tow was available.

In connection with this recommendation, OPM also outlined a tentative plan which had been discussed informally with the British. This plan provided for the purchase by RFC of 25 to 50% of the Egyptian crop and that portion of the Canadian crop which was not needed by the British; also, that we buy in South America.

The British offered us 25% of the Egyptian crop, but a maximum of 1,500 tons, as a result of discussions with them, the State Department and OPM. Because of the necessity that drafts of the proposed agreement on the Egyptian flax be submitted to and approved by London, substantial time was necessarily consumed in working out the agreement. However, with the exception of final clearance by London, the agreement was approved by all interested parties prior to BEW participation.

During the period of negotiations for Egyptian flax RFC was also working in cooperation with the State Department and WPB in an effort to acquire a portion of the Canadian flax production. A contract covering 4,000 long tons of Peruvian flax per year was concluded early in May, 1942, as a result of RFC negotiations. The negotiations referred to involved a quantity of flax substantially in excess of the amount recommended for stockpile.

RAPE-SEED OIL: Mr. Wallace states that as of April 13, 1942, the RFC had purchased only 2,200 long tons of rape-seed oil. The facts are:

February 26, 1942, the WPB recommended that we purchase and hold for stockpile 5,000 short tons (10,000,000 lbs.) of Argentine refined rape-seed oil. RFC immediately proceeded to meet this requirement and before April 13, 1942, had contracted to purchase 2,782 short tons, and by May 5, without the assistance of BEW, RFC had contracted to purchase a total of 3,900 short tons. No further purchases were made by RFC due to the fact that the fats and oils program was transferred to the Commodity Credit Corporation.

FATS AND OILS: Mr. Wallace says that in October, 1941, OPM recommended to RFC the purchase of approximately 30,000 long tons of various types of fats and oils from foreign sources; that by February, 1942, this total had been increased to 317,499 tons and that "for all practical purposes virtually nothing was done by Mr. Jones to build a Government stockpile of fats and oils," etc.

Reply is made elsewhere in this statement as to palm oil and rape-seed oil.

COPRA AND COCONUT OIL: January 13, 1942, OPM recommended that the RFC purchase 100,000 long tons of coconut oil, or the equivalent in copra. This recommendation implemented General Imports Order M-63 which made RFC the sole importer of copra and coconut oil.

At the time the recommendation was received, the Philippine Islands, which produced about 85% of the copra imported into the United States in 1941, had already been cut off as a source of supply. The Netherlands East Indies, which had provided 10% of the imports in 1941, were also in the war theatre.

Some stocks were believed to exist in East Africa, but the largest remaining potential source was found to be the South Pacific Islands, including Fiji, Samoa, New Caledonia, New Hebrides, and Papeete.

It was estimated that forty to fifty thousand long tons of copra could be lifted in that area in a reasonably short time providing shipping space could be made available, and steps were immediately taken to provide a plan for purchases. Various copra crushing companies on the Pacific Coast were immediately contacted, and on February 9 a plan was formulated whereby RFC would sell to those companies all copra it was able to purchase in the South Seas. This agreement was signed as of March 2, 1942, and submitted to WPB for consideration and clearance through the Department of Justice on March 9, 1942. Department of Justice reviewed the agreement and approved it in principle on April 10, and WPB returned the agreement on April 15. The agreement was executed by RFC the following day.

Chaotic conditions had prevailed in the islands, shipping space was problematical and communications were poor. Local governments in both the British and French islands were reported to have taken control of all the available supply. On February 18, the State Department informed us that the entire Fiji and Tonga production had been sold to the British Ministry of Food for an indefinite period and on February 19, RFC suggested to the State Department that they "discuss with the British authorities the possibility of releasing this copra" to the United States.

Conditions were such in the islands controlled by the Free French that no firm offerings could be obtained, and it was found that even in areas under British control, suppliers having commitments with American firms were using excuses of every nature to cancel contracts which involved over 15,000 long tons in order to obtain higher prices. This last situation was brought directly to the attention of the British Food Mission in Washington on April 2 with the earnest request that they "make every possible effort to have the authorities in London impress upon the suppliers . . . the advisability of fulfilling their original contractual obligations."

On March 10, it was reported from Ceylon that there were "no significant stocks . . . on hand which (were) not under contract." Investigation developed that there were no available surpluses in India, and further that there were "no current or prospective exportable supplies" in Brazil.

Although exhaustive efforts were made by RFC's agent under the agreement with the Pacific Coast crushers to obtain firm offers of copra, because of the reasons stated no copra was immediately available.

During the same period, in order to utilize all possible facilities for acquiring copra, WPB with the approval of RFC granted exemptions from General Imports Order M-63 to private importers. Under these exemptions a number of contracts for purchase of South Seas copra were arranged by importers who had private buying organizations in the field. The African production available to the United States was accounted for by this means. For example, on February 26, 1942, an authorization was given by WPB to a private firm to lift approximately 3,000 long tons of copra from Portuguese East Africa, and shortly thereafter an authorization was granted covering 2,000 long tons from British East Africa, and later another covering 4,000 tons of "East African copra from other than British territory."

Although our reports show that only about 4,000 tons of copra were purchased by us under the Pacific Coast copra purchasing agreement prior to the time the fats and oils program was transferred to the Department of Agriculture, there is little doubt that our actions and conversations with British authorities directly and through the State Department resulted in the acquisition of substantial quantities of copra by private buyers in this country during the first eight months of 1942.

BABASSU OIL: Of all the fats and oils needed for the war effort, perhaps the most troublesome from the procurement standpoint is babassu oil and kernels. Although it was not until April 23, 1942, that the WPB recommended that RFC purchase 75,000 metric tons of babassu kernels for storage and resale in this country, our experience with the babassu problem dates back to December of 1941. At that time OPM discussed with us the need for increasing the production of babassu kernels in Brazil, resulting from the fact that with the supply of copra from the Philippines being cut off, a serious shortage of glycerine was imminent, and babassu oil has a high glycerine content. Moreover, the babassu nut grows wild in great quantity in Brazil so that a substantial amount of glycerine was available there if a satisfactory means could be devised for collecting the nuts and separating the kernels from the shells. This problem was extremely difficult of solution because no satisfactory or efficient method had theretofore been developed by which the nuts could be cracked and the kernels removed in the jungle. On the other hand, since the shell of the babassu nut weighs approximately eight times as much as the kernel, and since there are no roads between ports and the area of production, it was almost impossible to transport the nuts themselves out of the jungle in any large quantity. The situation was further complicated by the fact that labor was very short in that part of Brazil and was badly needed in rubber development.

It became apparent immediately that large sums of money and material would be used in an effort to increase the quantity of glycerine derived from this source, with small chance of any compensating results. Conferences were held between representatives of RFC and WPB and other interested agencies. An expert was sent to Brazil to investigate the possibilities of increasing the production of babassu kernels. In addition, the problem was discussed at length with representatives of Brazilian interests who suggested plans for its solution, and General Mills made an exhaustive study of the babassu situation in Brazil as a result of which they made certain general proposals. None of the plans presented was approved by the various federal agencies concerned, including BEW. Finally, on May 4, 1942, a meeting was held at which representatives of the BEW, State, the Department of Commerce, WPB, the Department of Agriculture, and RFC were present. There was considerable difference of opinion expressed concerning the steps that could and should be taken to increase production of babassu kernels and oil in Brazil. However, it was agreed at the meeting that an attempt should be made immediately to negotiate with the Brazilian Government an agreement whereby exports would be permitted only to an agency of the United States Government in consideration of a definite agreement to buy the entire available supply of kernels and oil for a two-year period at prices as high as permitted under the United States ceiling. At about that time all fats and oils programs were transferred by BEW to Commodity Credit Corporation.

* * * * * *

Mr. Wallace seeks to give the impression that BEW has somehow accomplished the impossible.

In view of the vicious attacks made on me by Mr. Wallace, charging delay, inaction and even obstruction in the war effort, I give below a few of the many examples afforded by our experience with BEW of their incompetence in the work they are attempting to do.

MAHOGANY: The Mahogany Program has been handled almost exclusively by BEW.

Discussions concerning the program were started by BEW in June, 1942, but it was not until November 7, 1942, that RFC was directed to make the first of seven contracts for the production of mahogany. The contracting concerns, selected by BEW, were largely inexperienced in this field.

It is significant that out of seven contracts for a total of 47,000,000 board feet of mahogany, no mahogany has been delivered even at this late date.

An additional contract for a spot purchase of mahogany was entered into with one of these contractors, but only 100,000 board feet of mahogany has been delivered under this contract.

During this period mahogany has continued to be imported by private importers with the aid of the RFC.

CANADIAN ALCOHOL: A contract for 6,000,000 to 9,000,000 gallons of Canadian alcohol was negotiated and prepared by BEW. This required 7½ months, although the contract was substantially similar to contracts for the purchase of domestic alcohol which RFC has been handling for some time. In 1942, RFC bought 90,000,000 gallons of domestic alcohol and its purchases during 1943 will probably reach 350,000,000 gallons.

CHINESE BRISTLES: January, 1943, BEW started negotiations for additional Chinese bristles. Six months later, despite the urgent need for this critical material, the contract has not been made.

HORSETAIL AND MANE HAIR: From December, 1942, to June, 1943, BEW held up all new imports of dressed horsetail and mane hair, while the plan previously inaugurated by RFC was under discussion and review. In consequence, RFC must now release to the trade a substantial portion of its stockpile in order to make available sufficient supplies to the processors.

VINYL ACETATE: The negotiations by BEW of a contract with a Canadian concern for vinyl acetate, used in plastics and as an adhesive in the manufacture of shoes in place of rubber cement, took from early January to the middle of March, 1943. A final contract for this material is similar to one previously negotiated and executed by RFC, which took less than one week.

TURKISH CHROME: Long before BEW entered the field, RFC made a large contract for the purchase of Turkish chrome. Late in 1942 it became apparent that certain amendments to this contract had become necessary because of changed conditions. BEW on January 26, 1943, informed us that it would prepare such amendments. To date they have not been submitted.

MEXICAN MICA: In January, 1943, before issuance of BEW Order No. 5, which was intended to divest RFC of authority to negotiate its own contracts, RFC authorized BEW representatives in Mexico to negotiate a contract for the development of mica resources in that country. In April, 1943, a contract was submitted, which even BEW agreed was clearly not in line with authority given and, furthermore, was bad business. On June 25, BEW submitted a new proposed draft of this contract for comment, which was in more acceptable form. The contract itself, however, has not yet been submitted to RFC for execution.

PERUVIAN ANTIMONY: The basic terms of a contract for the purchase of Peruvian antimony metal were agreed upon in February, 1943. The final contract, however, was only submitted by BEW to RFC in June, 1943, although it did not substantially depart from the terms originally agreed upon.

COBALT ORE: March 5, 1943, RFC delivered to BEW a draft of a proposed contract for the purchase of cobalt ore. BEW made some minor changes in this contract and mailed it to the seller on April 19, six weeks later.

PERUVIAN OVER-ALL AGREEMENT: The over-all agreement between the Peruvian Government and RFC relative to the purchase of strategic materials from Peru expired on September 15, 1942. BEW was unwilling to leave to RFC the negotiation of a renewal of this agreement. BEW undertook to do so. They are apparently still negotiating because the renewal has not yet been signed.

CONDENSED REPORT OF THE RUBBER SURVEY COMMITTEE
SEPT. 10, 1942

James B. Conant
Karl T. Compton
Bernard M. Baruch, chairman

ADMINISTRATION

The Committee finds that a number of different Government agencies have had overlapping jurisdiction in regard to the synthetic rubber program. This has caused delay and confusion. In particular the conflict between Rubber Reserve and the Office of Petroleum Coordinator has complicated in recent months the bringing in of new facilities for the production of butadiene from oil. The Committee has been unable to determine, in spite of many inquiries, as to where the responsibility has lain for many of the decisions which have been made in the last eight months.

The failure of the Government to provide a clearly recognized group of independent experts who would make technical decisions has added greatly to the public confusion and uncertainty. The reliance on a part-time technical adviser, aided by committees drawn from industry, has, in the opinion of the Committee, been insufficient for the development of an entirely new industry involving an investment exceeding $600,000,000. The technical adviser has testified that on more than one occasion he requested the appointment of an adequate technical staff.

It would have been wise administration for the officials in charge of policy to have delegated to a competent technical staff the function of collecting information about the various processes. Such a staff should have been relied upon for supplying through regular channels the data on which all important decisions were made. Instead of such orderly methods of procedure we have found many evidences of a chaotic situation in which nontechnical men have made decisions without consultation with subordinates nominally in positions of responsibility.

There have been many adjustments and readjustments—a "stop and go" policy—in the synthetic rubber program. Some of these were inevitable; some appear to be the result of bad administration.

There is clear evidence that the situation with respect to the alcohol supply was altered between the fall of 1941 and the spring of 1942. What had once been a deficiency became an apparent surplus. As a result of this change the proportion of alcohol and petroleum-based processes in the synthetic rubber program was altered. A more adequately staffed organization might have foreseen earlier the changed situation and altered the program a few months earlier.

As another example of faulty administration we may mention the failure to obtain early in this year the detailed information concerning the Russian process for making synthetic rubber. Russia has been manufacturing synthetic rubber successfully for more than 10 years. It would seem natural to have endeavored to benefit from this experience as soon as rubber became of major concern to the United States. If the Russian offer made in February to exchange men and information had been accepted and Russian engineers with blue prints of manufacturing had been rushed to this country last winter, it is conceivable that plants for producing synthetic rubber by the Russian process might now be well on the way to completion. To date we have no detailed information as to the process and no samples of Russian tires have as yet been obtained. *Every effort ought to be made to obtain this information.*

The dissemination of full information concerning the compounding of Buna S. to all companies has become an accomplished fact only in the last few days. An agreement was entered into on July 3 of this year between the Rubber Reserve Company and the four large rubber companies. According to this agreement, Rubber Reserve alone was permitted to give out information to the other rubber companies. But in fact it did not do so for some six weeks in spite of repeated efforts of the Rubber Branch of the WPB to have the information released. In view of this situation one hardly needs to point out that there has been very imperfect cooperation between the Rubber Reserve Company and the Rubber Branch of WPB.

Because of the record briefly summarized above, we recommend:

A complete reorganization and consolidation of the governmental agencies concerned with the rubber program.

a) The War Production Board must assume full responsibility for the rubber program in all of its phases. We therefore recommend a directive from the President ordering the Rubber Reserve Company and all other Government agencies to act in all matters relative to the rubber program as directed by the Chairman of WPB.

b) To discharge adequately the responsibilities which we recommend that the Chairman of WPB explicitly assume for the entire Rubber Program, full authority must be centered in a single official. We, therefore, recommend that the Chairman of WPB appoint a Rubber Administrator and delegate to him full and complete authority in regard to the manufacture of synthetic rubber, including research, development, construction, and operation of plants.

This single official, who must be a man of unusual capacity and power, must also have full charge of all matters connected with rubber within the WPB. It should be his duty to formulate policies and administer the operation of the rubber program subject only to the Chairman of the WPB, who should divest himself of all direct concern with these matters. Good administration dictates that the Rubber Administrator use the available facilities of other Government agencies in the execution of the program, but his decisions and not theirs must control.

c) We recommend that particular care be directed to the establishment of a Technical Division, under the immediate control of the Rubber Administrator.

d) We also recommend that the Construction Division of Rubber Reserve be designated by the Rubber Administrator as the agency to supervise the construction of all plants under the rubber program.

It will be a matter of great importance to have the Technical Division adequately staffed and provided with branches in charge of all the various phases of research and development, except for the production of butadiene from petroleum which is referred to in the next recommendation.

The Rubber Administrator, acting on authority delegated by the Chairman of WPB, should have the sole responsibility for supervision of operation of all Government plants engaged in the production of rubber. In the execution of that responsibility he may utilize other agencies of the Government upon their agreement thereto, but shall not be required to do so, and he shall cancel such arrangements when satisfactory results are not obtained.

Funds must be made available at once to WPB to provide for the staff under the Rubber Administrator and to enable him to place such contracts as he may deem necessary in connection with research and development.

e) We further recommend that the Petroleum Coordinator be directed by Presidential Order to act on specific directives from the Chairman of WPB, acting through the Rubber Administrator, to explore all methods for the production of butadiene from petroleum and natural gas products and recommend new proposals to the Rubber Administrator for his consideration and action.

f) The construction of all plants and equipment concerned with the production and purification of butadiene from petroleum should be under the authority of the Rubber Administrator, who we recommend shall designate the Construction Division of Rubber Reserve to carry out this function.

This provision is necessary in order to unify control of the construction program and make certain that no delays ensue by reason of conflicting authority and personalities. The Petroleum Coordinator should have supervision of the operation of the plants for the manufacture of butadiene from petroleum and natural gas products after completion of construction but he should be directed not to modify the presently authorized construction program or the plans for operation except as approved by the Rubber Administrator.

g) We further recommend that in the Office of Petroleum Coordinator there be created a new Technical Division responsible for research and development in connection with all problems of the manufacture of butadiene from petroleum; funds for this purpose should be provided to OPC.

This specific delegation of responsibility to the Petroleum Coordinator was made in order to secure complete coordination of the butadiene program with other petroleum and natural gas requirements, especially for aviation gasoline and for toluene for explosives.

As the situation develops it may be desirable for the funds required for the entire rubber program to be put directly at the disposal of the Chairman of the WPB for the purposes of the Rubber Administrator instead of, as at present, indirectly through RFC.

The most important part of the plan is obviously the choice of the right man for the position of Rubber Administrator. He should be a thoroughly competent operating and manufacturing executive, preferably with experience in the rubber industry; the demand for speed and the vital need for this man to start with experience and knowledge of the problem make it important that the man chosen be of proven integrity and enjoy the public's confidence and that of the rubber industry as well. We cannot stress too much the importance of choosing the right man for this work, for no plan or organization can bolster up a weak man sufficiently to meet the difficult problems he must face.

One of the problems presented to this Committee has been the difficulty of determining the future needs of the war program for rubber and the components required for the manufacture of synthetic rubber and substitutes. This difficulty arises from the unpredictable character of the war operations as to location, kind of war, and equipment employed under various conditions. In spite of these and other such difficulties, there is need for determining the requirements on an authoritative basis. Every aspect of the rubber problem must be under continuous review by a man whose sole responsibility it is. The most we can do is to appraise the present situation and indicate a sound course for the future.

A program can be no better than its administration; therefore, we place special emphasis upon this series of recommendations and wish to state that *unless they are followed there can be no assurance of the successful development of the synthetic rubber program within the time required.*

September 13, 1942 *

Dear Mr. President:

I have just now had time to read the full report of the Rubber Survey Committee. The report states:

(1) "Our Committee is convinced that the Government's present program is technically sound."

(2) "It is fortunate that the program for the needed plants is generally in the hands of as competent engineers as there are in the country. Probably the most interesting and satisfying part of our study is the confidence we have acquired in the men from industry who have the plans in hand and who are satisfied they can lick the problem in the given time. Their competence and experience, their resourcefulness and ingenuity are the best guarantees we have that they can do so."

(3) "It is our firm conclusion that present processes for manufacturing synthetic rubber and the raw materials required (butadiene and styrene) must not

---

* Original letter delivered by Mr. Jones personally, Sept. 15, 1942.

at this late date be changed unless new processes can be shown beyond peradventure to have sufficient advantages over those now employed; that more rubber could be obtained in the ensuing months than would otherwise be obtained. *We have found no such processes in the course of our investigation.*"

(4) "We should like to emphasize again that it would be a major blunder to make a further change inside the program at this date by the substitution of one process for another."

(5) "Having lost to Japan 90% of our pre-war sources of natural rubber, chief reliance for new supplies of rubber must be placed on the new synthetic rubber program, but to obtain this in time, we must, within two years after Pearl Harbor, have created one of the largest industries in the country. Normally such a development would require a dozen years. To compress it into less than two years *is almost a superhuman task.*"

From the foregoing, the rubber program approaches the accomplishment of what the Survey Committee terms *almost a superhuman task. I do not agree that it is a superhuman task, but am pleased that the Survey Committee finds that we have a technically sound program which will produce rubber in large quantities. After all, that is what matters to the people of the United States.*

It is quite natural that the Survey Committee and its twenty-five or more associates and experts, who interviewed, in a short period of time, many different government and industry representatives, would get conflicting statements and opinions in a matter so intricate and so little understood as our synthetic rubber program. Some of these exist only in the minds of the individuals, and many are due to conflicting testimony given before Congressional Committees. There has also been much deliberate intervention by selfish interests designed to cause confusion, or to muscle in on the program.

I concur in the Survey Committee's recommendation for an increase in the program. I have more than once testified before Congressional Committees and made suggestions within government that the synthetic program should be increased to 1,000,000 tons.

In the early part of the year I asked Dr. Kettering, Chairman of the Patent Planning Commission and the National Inventors' Council, to explore the possibilities for materials that would provide a substitute tire of sufficient durability to meet essential civilian requirements while our rubber program is under way. He, together with technicians from the automobile, rubber and chemical industries, investigated many different possibilities, and arrived at a definite recommendation for the production of thiokol, particularly for retreading.

We immediately authorized Dow Chemical Company to engineer a plant for the production of this material. Some thiokol is now in production, and arrangements are practically complete for facilities sufficient to meet the Survey Committee's recommendation for an actual capacity of 60,000 tons. A substantial part of this will be from conversion of existing facilities, which can be brought into production within a few weeks and at little expense both in money and critical materials.

Contracts for some additional butadiene to come from refinery conversion have already been made in cooperation with OPC, and the balance, up to the Survey Committee's recommendation, can be completed as soon as it can be fitted into the existing rubber program and those for 100-octane gasoline, toluene, and other petroleum products.

All recommended increases can be easily provided for as soon as critical construction materials are available.

In the section of the Survey Committee's report devoted to administration, the statement is made that the conflict between Rubber Reserve Company and OPC has complicated the bringing of new facilities for the production of butadiene from oil.

There has been no delay in the program from this cause. Rubber Reserve and the Rubber Coordinator have cooperated with OPC wherever the proposals would fit into, and not disrupt, the existing program. The problem has been a complicated one to avoid a conflict with aviation gasoline and other petroleum products necessary to the war effort, and not because of conflict between the two agencies. It takes a little time to fit refinery conversion into the existing rubber program which the Survey Committee has found to be sound and advised against changing.

The Survey Committee states that one part-time technical adviser, aided by committees drawn from industry, has been insufficient for the development of the program. Dr. Weidlein, our chief technical adviser, who came to us from the predecessors of WPB, states that there are one hundred eighty-four technicians working together and with him in the rubber program. The Survey Committee states that technically the program is sound, and that it found no process not now in the program worthy of inclusion. Under these circumstances, the statement that a chaotic situation exists would not appear to be justified.

The Survey Committee states there have been adjustments and readjustments in the program. This is as it must be since we are building a very large industry in a field where we have had to learn as we go. Any changes have been under technical advice. We could not afford to wait on perfected plans to start the program.

The use of alcohol for making butadiene in the initial stages of the enlarged synthetic rubber program was limited because of its need for military purposes. When WPB found that more alcohol could be allocated for the production of butadiene, it was immediately fitted in.

As for the exchange with Russia of technical information for the production of synthetic rubber, our technical advisers are definitely of the opinion that our information is basically the same as theirs. They did request an exchange of specimens of the finished product for testing.

The Survey Committee makes the statement that in an agreement between Rubber Reserve Company and four large rubber companies, only Rubber Reserve was permitted to give out compounding information to other rubber companies. I advised the Survey Committee that the contract provided that Rubber Reserve Company should release any information to any rubber manufacturer interested in participating in the program and, in any event, would when requested by WPB. It has always been our purpose to include every competent manufacturer or fabricator of rubber, however small, who wants to be included.

In recommending a reorganization and consolidation of the rubber program, the Survey Committee states that the War Production Board must assume full responsibility for the rubber program in all its phases. The War Production Board has had full responsibility for the rubber program since January 16, and Mr. Donald Nelson has so stated before Congressional Committees and otherwise. Furthermore, neither Mr. Nelson nor Mr. Newhall, the Rubber Coordinator, has ever made a request of me that has not been promptly carried out.

The appointment of a rubber administrator by War Production Board as recommended by the Survey Committee represents no change in policy. Such a single official has existed in the person of Arthur B. Newhall, the Rubber Coordinator, ever since his appointment by Mr. Nelson soon after the creation of the War Production Board. Mr. Newhall was authorized to represent the Chairman of the War Production Board with respect to all aspects of the rubber problem. Rubber Reserve Company has kept in the closest possible contact with Mr. Newhall, and I with him and Mr. Nelson.

The Survey Committee's recommendation that the construction of plants be left in the hands of the construction division of Rubber Reserve Company calls for no change in existing practice. Contracts have already been made by Rubber Reserve Company for the operation of most of the plants. They are with the principal rubber, chemical and oil companies. The remaining contracts will soon be completed. The operators can account to the Rubber Administrator, Rubber Reserve Company, or anyone else that you or the War Production Board may designate. Sound business judgment would seem to dictate that the operation of the plants be in the hands of the Rubber Reserve Company, under the supervision of the Rubber Administrator.

As for the Survey Committee's statement that it may be desirable for the funds required for the entire rubber program to be put directly at the disposal of the Chairman of the War Production Board, no request or suggestion has ever come from the Chairman of the War Production Board or the Rubber Coordinator as to funds that has not been promptly complied with.

The report suggests the purchase of excess tires from private consumers for government use. Such a program has, as you know, been under development for several months. The mechanics of it have been thoroughly worked out and only the appointment of the Rubber Survey Committee postponed the campaign. The excess tire purchase program was worked out by Defense Supplies Corporation, War Production Board and OPA, on a basis of complete cooperation.

The Survey Committee's consideration of the scrap rubber program deals only in part with activities coming under my supervision. Rubber Reserve Company, in cooperation with OPA and WPB, has for some time been buying rubber scrap at $25 a ton, a figure well above the ceiling price, taking delivery anywhere in the United States, and paying all freight. It has also made contracts for the collection of scrap through normal channels.

The report recommends nationwide gasoline rationing, a national speed limit, restrictions on the use of automobiles, and several other regulatory measures which fall under the jurisdiction of the other agencies. The report also discusses priorities, agricultural rubber, and the capacity of rubber goods manufacturing, which are not under my supervision.

The Survey Committee in its digest, but not in the full report, mentions "the failure to build a greater stockpile of crude rubber." As you know, RFC was authorized to create a stockpile of crude rubber June 28, 1940. No amount was ever specified but we acquired every ton of rubber that we could purchase until the sources of natural rubber were cut off by enemy action. We contracted with the International Rubber Regulation Committee within three days after the Bill giving us the authority was signed, and continually pressed this Committee for greater production and shipment of rubber. We were able to accumulate more than 634,000 tons of rubber, by far the largest rubber stockpile ever possessed by any nation in the world. Much of this now must be exported to other fighting nations.

There has been no failure to use any source of obtaining rubber at our command with all possible dispatch.

The Survey Committee is to be commended for its untiring effort in making its study in the shortest time possible. The report should go far toward answering questions that naturally arise in the minds of people all over the country who have been confused by conflicting statements, many of which have been false, misleading and self-serving.

The principal value of the report, aside from specific recommendations, is that in spite of any such confusion which may have existed in the public mind, we have, in the opinion of the Survey Committee, a good rubber program. This, I think, is already clear to you because I have kept you fully advised since the program was begun.

I shall, of course, continue to cooperate wholeheartedly with WPB, the new administrator, and anyone else that may be designated to have a part in the rubber program.

Sincerely yours,

JESSE H. JONES

Secretary of Commerce

The President
The White House

APPENDIX II

❈

DIRECTORS OF THE RFC, 1932–1950

THE ORIGINAL BOARD, APPOINTED FEBRUARY 2, 1932

Eugene Meyer, Republican, New York, chairman. Ex-officio director, as Governor of the Federal Reserve Board. Retired July 31, 1932, with elimination of this ex-officio directorship by Act of Congress, effective Aug. 1, 1932.

Charles G. Dawes, Republican, Illinois, president. Resigned June 15, 1932.

Paul Bestor, Rep., District of Columbia. Ex-officio director, as Farm Loan Commissioner. Retired July 31, 1932, with elimination of this ex-officio directorship by Act of Congress, effective Aug. 1, 1932.

Andrew W. Mellon, Republican, Pennsylvania. Ex-officio director, as Secretary of the Treasury. Mr. Mellon had attended only two or three of the meetings of the RFC board when he resigned, Feb. 5, 1932, as Secretary of the Treasury, to become Ambassador to the Court of St. James's.

Harvey C. Couch, Democrat, Arkansas. Resigned Aug. 29, 1934.

Wilson McCarthy, Democrat, Utah. Resigned Sept. 30, 1933.

Jesse H. Jones, Democrat, Texas. Elected chairman May 5, 1933. Resigned as chairman July 15, 1939, to become Federal Loan Administrator, with general supervision over the RFC and its subsidiaries as well as various other agencies until he left government service Mar., 1945.

SUCCEEDING DIRECTORS

Ogden L. Mills, Rep., New York. Ex-officio director by appointment as Secretary of the Treasury, Feb. 5, 1932. Retired as Secretary, Mar. 4, 1933.

Gardner Cowles, Sr., Rep., Iowa. Appointed July 5, 1932. Resigned Apr. 8, 1933.

Atlee Pomerene, Dem., Ohio. Appointed Aug. 1, 1932. Not confirmed by Senate. Retired automatically Mar. 4, 1933.

Charles A. Miller, Rep., New York. Appointed Aug. 1, 1932. Not confirmed by Senate. Retired automatically Mar. 4, 1933.

William H. Woodin, Dem., New York. Ex-officio director by appointment as Secretary of the Treasury, Mar. 4, 1933. Resigned as Secretary, Jan. 1, 1934.

Carroll B. Merriam, Rep., Kansas. Appointed June 15, 1933. Died Dec. 12, 1941.

John J. Blaine, Rep., Wisconsin. Appointed June 19, 1933. Died Apr. 16, 1934.

Frederic H. Taber, Rep., Massachusetts. Appointed June 21, 1933. Retired Jan. 31, 1938.

Henry Morgenthau, Jr., Dem., New York. Ex-officio director by appointment as Secretary of the Treasury, Jan. 1, 1934. This ex-officio directorship was eliminated by Act of Congress, effective Feb., 1938.

Charles B. Henderson, Dem., Nevada. Appointed Feb. 20, 1934. Succeeded Emil Schram as chairman July 1, 1941. Relinquished chairmanship Apr. 9, 1947, and resigned from Board July 15, 1947.

Hubert D. Stephens, Dem., Mississippi. Appointed Apr. 14, 1935. Resigned Feb. 29, 1936.

Charles T. Fisher, Jr., Rep., Michigan. Appointed Apr. 25, 1935. Resigned Dec. 31, 1936.

Emil Schram, Dem., Illinois. Appointed June 22, 1936. Elected chairman July 16, 1939. Resigned from Board July 1, 1941.

Howard J. Klossner, Rep., Minnesota. Appointed Apr. 28, 1937. Resigned Aug. 1, 1945.

Sam H. Husbands, Dem., South Carolina. Appointed Aug. 2, 1939. Resigned Jan. 21, 1946.

Henry A. Mulligan, Dem., New York. Appointed July 30, 1941. Resigned Apr. 30, 1950.

Charles T. Fisher, Jr., Rep., Michigan. Appointed June 15, 1942. Resigned Jan. 21, 1946.

Harvey J. Gunderson, Rep., South Dakota. Appointed Oct. 17, 1945. Resigned Aug. 9, 1950.

Henry T. Bodman, Rep., Michigan. Appointed Feb. 14, 1946. Resigned Dec. 16, 1948.

George E. Allen, Dem., District of Columbia. Appointed Mar. 25, 1946. Resigned Jan. 15, 1947.

John D. Goodloe, Dem., Kentucky. Appointed Jan. 27, 1947. Elected chairman Apr. 9, 1947. Resigned Apr. 30, 1948.

Harvey Hise, Dem., California. Appointed July 17, 1947. Resigned Aug. 9, 1950.

William E. Willett, Dem., Maryland. Appointed June 29, 1948. Resigned Aug. 9, 1950.

Walter Lee Dunham, Rep., Michigan. Appointed Jan. 31, 1949. Retired 1951.

APPENDIX III

LOAN AGENCY MANAGERS SINCE
ESTABLISHMENT OF THE RFC

Agency	Manager	Appointed
Atlanta	A. M. Bergstrom	Feb. 20, 1932
	Erle Cocke	Jan. 1, 1934
	Scott Candler (Actg. Mgr.)	June 8, 1938
	M. E. Everett	Mar. 20, 1939
Birmingham	T. J. Cottingham	Mar. 9, 1932
	E. W. Long	Apr. 5, 1937
	Fred H. Foy	July 1, 1946
Boston	Harry A. Saunders	Feb. 8, 1932
	Edward H. Osgood	Jan. 1, 1933
	Joseph P. Carney	Nov. 26, 1934
	John J. Hagerty	Apr. 19, 1937
	M. J. McGrath	Apr. 8, 1949
Charlotte	John A. Campbell, Jr.	Mar. 1, 1932
	J. K. Wilson	Oct. 19, 1947
Chicago	Howard M. Sims	Feb. 16, 1932
	H. P. Preston	June 1, 1932
	Ira A. Moore	Apr. 1, 1933
	F. D. Gallagher	Nov. 1, 1933
	Frank M. Murchison	Aug. 5, 1939
	B. A. Mattingly	Mar. 29, 1944
	Peter I. Bukowski	Mar. 13, 1945
	M. O. Hoel	Nov. 1, 1945
Cleveland	M. J. Fleming	Feb. 16, 1932
	Sidney B. Congdon	Dec. 16, 1932
	F. S. Callander	Feb. 26, 1934
	Loring L. Gelbach	July 8, 1936
	J. A. Fraser	Sept. 1, 1938

Agency	Manager	Appointed
Dallas	Warren P. Andrews	Feb. 9, 1932
	L. B. Glidden	Feb. 24, 1937
Denver	J. E. Olsen	Mar. 1, 1932
	T. E. McClintock	May 6, 1932
	Ross L. Hudson	July 5, 1938
Detroit	Charles T. Fisher, Jr.	Feb. 16, 1932
	John C. Hicks	Oct. 11, 1932
	Charles T. Fisher, Jr.	Sept. 5, 1933
	Charles H. Hewitt	Apr. 1, 1935
	Gladding B. Coit	Feb. 16, 1937
	Raymond J. Hodgson	Apr. 11, 1938
	Arthur J. Fushman	Jan. 2, 1942
	Charles E. Williams	Oct. 15, 1946
	Henry F. Eckfeld	Oct. 13, 1947
Helena	Robert E. Towle	Feb. 14, 1932
	Stuart A. Bingham	June 16, 1933
	Leon E. Choquette	Mar. 22, 1943
Houston	R. F. Ford	Feb. 11, 1932
	Ike Ashburn	Apr. 8, 1936
	Marion McConnell	Oct. 5, 1937
	Walter I. Phillips	Jan. 1, 1943
	Charles L. South	Sept. 23, 1949
Jacksonville	Fred H. Farwell	Mar. 19, 1932
Kansas City	Roy L. Bone	Feb. 12, 1932
	Frank Hodges	Aug. 19, 1933
	Albert L. Strong	Feb. 1, 1943
	David H. Powell	May 3, 1948
Little Rock	John W. Jarrett	Feb. 18, 1932
	John J. Truemper	May 3, 1948
Los Angeles	F. C. Bold	Mar. 1, 1932
	A. B. Nordling	June 1, 1932
	A. R. LeRoy	Mar. 16, 1933
	Thomas C. Scroggs	Feb. 21, 1934
	Hector C. Haight	Feb. 24, 1937
Louisville	Frank D. Rash	Feb. 18, 1932
	J. Fort Abell	May 28, 1934
Minneapolis	Joseph Chapman	Feb. 10, 1932
	Ben C. Maynard	Oct. 1, 1934
	China R. Clarke	Mar. 4, 1940
	Arthur W. Carlson	Sept. 1, 1948

Agency	Manager	Appointed
Nashville	John F. Joyner	Mar. 11, 1932
	J. M. Gardenhire	July 15, 1933
	Thomas M. Hobbs	Oct. 5, 1947
New Orleans	W. D. Davis	Feb. 12, 1932
	A. P. Imahorn	Aug. 16, 1932
	George F. Buskie	July 1, 1934
	George W. Robertson	May 22, 1939
New York	Charles A. Miller	Feb. 8, 1932
	Stewart S. Hathaway	Aug. 16, 1932
	D. J. Mahoney	July 15, 1933
	Thomas J. Ahearn, Jr.	Mar. 1, 1936
	William J. Farthing	June 4, 1945
	Charles R. Diebold	Mar. 1, 1946
	Percy Gale, Jr.	Aug. 10, 1947
Oklahoma City	C. E. Daniel	Mar. 1, 1932
	John C. Eagen	June 16, 1932
	Carl B. Sebring	Aug. 23, 1948
Omaha	L. H. Earhart	Mar. 1, 1932
	William M. Wilson	July 1, 1932
	C. F. Mudgett	Mar. 8, 1933
	Herbert S. Daniel	Oct. 2, 1933
	Joseph V. Johnson	Aug. 1, 1947
	China R. Clarke	May 8, 1950
Philadelphia	O. Howard Wolfe	Feb. 8, 1932
	George W. Brown, Jr.	June 1, 1932
	Samuel Graham, Jr.	June 23, 1933
	Jonathan F. Kilbourn	Feb. 1, 1934
	Robert J. Kiesling	Aug. 20, 1935
	Gladding B. Coit	Apr. 11, 1938
	E. Raymond Scott	Feb. 16, 1939
	Bernard J. Kelley	Aug. 15, 1946
Portland	R. B. West	Mar. 1, 1932
	Walter Schultz	June 1, 1932
	E. F. Slade	Dec. 1, 1933
	William Kennedy	Sept. 23, 1937
Richmond	J. K. Doughton	Apr. 19, 1932
	E. R. Combe	Dec. 16, 1933
	Henry G. Gilmer	June 20, 1934
	William B. Cloe	Jan. 21, 1942
St. Louis	O. M. Attebery	Feb. 6, 1932
	John R. Longmire	Apr. 18, 1932
	James K. Vardaman, Jr.	July 7, 1933
	John W. Snyder, Jr.	Apr. 23, 1937
	B. Glenn Gulledge	Feb. 16, 1943
	Charles G. Alexander	Jan. 1, 1948

Agency	Manager	Appointed
Salt Lake City	W. L. Partner	Mar. 1, 1932
	Marion Taylor	June 1, 1932
	Elias A. Smith	Apr. 27, 1933
	Gerald L. Leaver	Mar. 23, 1942
San Antonio	Otto Meerscheidt	Feb. 11, 1932
	William T. Montgomery	Jan. 1, 1940
	L. C. Andrews	Nov. 10, 1943
	Francis M. Conlon	Mar. 7, 1948
San Francisco	W. A. Day	Mar. 1, 1932
	Allard A. Calkins	June 1, 1932
	John S. McCullough, Jr.	Jan. 22, 1940
Seattle	C. R. Shaw	Mar. 1, 1932
	C. L. Lamping	June 1, 1932
	R. L. Davis	Aug. 16, 1933
	George B. Grieve	Dec. 18, 1939
	Richard M. Price	Oct. 26, 1943
	Charles R. Johnsone	Nov. 2, 1947
Spokane	D. L. Davis	Mar. 1, 1932
	John I. Tuttle	June 1, 1932
	Walter Ferguson	Aug. 16, 1933
	Orrin M. Green	Apr. 23, 1941

APPENDIX IV

SOME RFC ALUMNI WHO HAVE DONE WELL

Alumnus	*Former RFC Position*	*Present Position*
Aberg, Walter C.	Gen'l Loan Exec. RFC Mortgage Company	Vice Pres., Greenwich Savings Bank, Broadway at 36th St., New York
Ahearn, Thomas J., Jr.	Manager, New York Loan Agency	Vice Pres., William B. Nichols & Co., 475 Fifth Ave., New York
Allman, Carroll B.	Auditor	Sec. and Treas. Canton Provision Co., Canton, O.
Barnes, Stuart K.	Exec. Dir. Office of Defense Supplies	Sec. Guaranty Trust Company of New York, 140 Broadway, New York
Bassett, Henry N.	Ass't Treas. Defense Supplies Corp.	Sec.-Treas. Pacific Molasses Co., 120 Wall St., New York
Baukhages, Frederick E.	Counsel	Gen'l Solicitor, Baltimore & Ohio R.R. Co., Baltimore
Baybutt, Richard	Dep. Dir. Office of Rubber Reserve	Ernest Jacoby & Co., 79 Milk St., Boston
Blair, Newell	Att'y, Litigation Sec. Legal Div.	Blair & Blair, 1405 K St., Washington, D.C.
Bowen, Charles C.	Ass't to Charles B. Henderson	Charles C. Bowen & Co., Russ Bldg., San Francisco
Braverman, A. Marvin	Counsel	Braverman & Ketcham, Barr Bldg., Washington, D.C.
Brownell, Eugene B.	Examiner	Ass't to Pres. Monroe Auto Equipment Co., Monroe, Mich.

Alumnus	Former RFC Position	Present Position
Bukowski, Peter I.	Mgr. Chicago Loan Agency	Pres. Cosmopolitan National Bank of Chicago
Burling, John	Member Advisory Committee	Pres. Citizens Bank, White Plains, N. Y.
Buss, Ralph	Examiner, Washington office	Managing Dir. Detroit Branch Federal Reserve Bank
Chappelear, Edgar S.	Cotton Export Corp.	Vice Pres. Bankers Trust Co., 16 Wall St., New York
Christensen, Frank A.	Exec. Vice Pres. War Damage Corporation	Pres. Continental Insurance Co., 80 Maiden Lane, New York
Close, James W.	Counsel	Wilson & McIlvaine, 120 W. Adams St., Chicago
Cocke, Erle	Mgr. Atlanta Agency	Pres. Fulton National Bank, Atlanta
Congdon, Sidney B.	Mgr. Cleveland Loan Agency; Chief Examining Div., Washington	Pres. National City Bank of Cleveland
Connerat, George H.	Chief Accountant	Treas.-Controller, Telecoin Corp., 12 E. 44th St., New York
Coombs, J. Wendell	Ass't to Sam H. Husbands	Exec. Vice Pres. Transamerica Corp., 460 Montgomery St., San Francisco
Crimmins, John M.	Counsel, Defense Plant Corp.	Ass't Counsel, Koppers Co., Pittsburgh
Crossland, Stanley T.	Exec. Vice Pres., Rubber Reserve Co.; Vice Pres., War Damage Corp.	Vice Pres. and Treas. Ethyl Corp., 405 Lexington Ave., New York
Dawes, Henry	Admin. Ass't to Engineers Adv. Board	Ass't Sec. Connecticut General Life Insurance Co., Hartford
Dorsey, Lloyd W.	Engineer, Railroad Div.	H. H. Copeland & Son, 74 Trinity Pl., New York

Alumnus	*Former RFC Position*	*Present Position*
Dreibelbis, J. Paschal	Counsel	Vice Pres., Bankers Trust Co., New York
Farthing, William J.	Mgr. New York Loan Agency	Pres. Madison Operating Corp., 10 E. 40th St., New York
Foley, E. H., Jr.	Attorney Legal Div.	Ass't Sec. of the Treasury
Fountain, Eugene J.	Examiner	Stroud & Co., 120 Broadway, New York
Friedman, Sidney	Counsel	Alley, Cole, Grimes & Friedman, 30 Broad St., New York
Fushman, Arthur J.	Mgr. Detroit Loan Agency	Vice Pres., Manufacturers National Bank of Detroit
Gelbach, Loring L.	Mgr. Cleveland Loan Agency	Pres. Central National Bank of Cleveland
Giddings, William C.	Examiner and Negotiator	Folger, Nolan & Co., Washington, D.C.
Grafton, Arthur W.	Agency Counsel	Wyatt & Grafton, Louisville, Ky.
Gregson, W. F.	Chicago Loan Agency	Vice Pres., City National Bank & Trust Co., Chicago
Hanrahan, Frank R.	Asst. Chief Examiner	Dir. of Finance, City of Cleveland
Hathaway, Stewart S.	Manager New York Loan Agency	Chairman Buda Co., Harvey, Ill.
Hersh, Robert W.	Examiner, New York Agency	Hersh Motor Car Co., Elizabeth, N. J.
Herson, James F.	Administrative Assistant	Vice President, Hudson County National Bank, Jersey City, N. J.
Hobbs, William J.	Counsel	Pres., Coca-Cola Co., Atlanta
Hodgson, Raymond J.	Mgr. Detroit Loan Agency	Vice Pres., National Bank of Detroit
Homire, James L.	Chief Railroad Counsel	General Solicitor, St. Louis-San Francisco Ry. Co., St. Louis

Alumnus	*Former RFC Position*	*Present Position*
Hovey, Scott W.	Counsel	Counsel, Armour & Co., Chicago
Johnson, Ben	Special Ass't to Board of Directors	Chairman, Pickering Lumber Corp., Standard, Calif.
Johnson, Wilford J.	Ass't Chief Examiner	Retired, 7927 S.E. 29th Ave., Portland, Ore.
Kelly, Frank R., Jr.	Examiner	Meinhard Greeff & Co., 51 Madison Ave., New York
Kiesling, Robert J.	Mgr. Philadelphia Loan Agency	Pres., Camden Trust Co., Camden, N.J.
Klagsbrunn, Hans A.	Exec. Vice Pres. and Gen'l Coun., Defense Plant Corp.	Attorney, Ring Bldg., Washington, D.C.
Langhammer, John F.	Examiner	Vice Pres., American Credit Corp., 10 Washington Pl., Newark, N.J.
Lapsley, John W.	Counsel	Gamble & Lapsley, Selma, Ala.
Lauter, Kurt C.	Examiner	Vice Pres., Grace National Bank, Hanover Sq., New York
Lawrence, Donald E.	Director, RFC Mortgage Company	Treasurer Robin Line, 39 Cortlandt St., New York
LeRoy, Allen R.	Examiner	Vice Pres., Merchandise National Bank, 222 W. North Bank Dr., Chicago
Lindquist, R. J.	Chief Auditor	Vice Pres., Standard Oil Co. of Indiana, 910 S. Michigan Ave., Chicago
Lyford, Frederic E.	Examiner	Partner in Lyford & Eberle, 36 E. 36th St., New York
McCarthy, William G.	Ass't Sec.	New York Telephone Co., 140 West St., New York
MacLennan, C.	Outside Auditor	R. G. Rankin & Co., 30 Broad St., New York

Alumnus	Former RFC Position	Present Position
Mahoney, Daniel J.	Mgr. New York Loan Agency	Pres., Bronx County Trust Co., 2804 Third Ave., New York
Miley, William H.	Counsel	Seagram Distillers Corp., 405 Lexington Ave., New York
Milford, W. R.	Chief Examining Div.	Managing Dir., Baltimore Branch of Federal Reserve Bank of Richmond, Baltimore, Md.
Miller, David	Counsel	Engel, Judge, Miller & Sterling, 52 Vanderbilt Ave., New York
Miller, Joseph F.	Counsel New York Agency	Attorney, 37 Wall St., New York
Moore, Ira A.	Mgr. Chicago Loan Agency	Pres., People's National Bank, Grand Rapids, Mich.
Moroney, J. C.	Counsel	Counsel, Standard Oil Co. of New Jersey, 30 Rockefeller Plaza, New York
Mulligan, Minot C.	Ass't Sec.	Sec., Civil Aeronautics Board, Washington, D.C.
Norton, John E.	Chief Mining Section	Engineer, Anaconda Copper Mining Co., New York
O'Hara, Francis J., Jr.	Exec. Dir.	Summers & O'Hara, 1625 K St., N.W., Washington, D.C.
Patterson, Robert C.	Chief Administrative Office	Ass't Vice Pres., Bankers Trust Co., New York
Persons, Henry Z.	Examiner	Pres., Brattleboro Trust Co., Brattleboro, Vt.
Preston, Howard P.	Manager Chicago Agency	Pres., Hamilton National Bank, Knoxville, Tenn.
Rainier, J. A.	Admin. Ass't to Dirs.	J. A. Rainier & Co., 19 W. 44th St., New York

Alumnus	*Former RFC Position*	*Present Position*
Ravlin, James N.	Counsel	American Airlines, 100 E. 42nd St., New York
Reese, Lemuel V.	Chief Engineering Sec.	Exec. Vice Pres. Arnold Brithart, Ltd.
Robinson, Stephen P., Jr.	Examiner New York Loan Agency	Pres., Savings, Investment & Trust Co., East Orange, N.J.
Sandford, Clarence R.	Chief Examiner	Pres., Elizabethport Banking Co., Elizabeth, N.J.
Shanks, Carrol M.	Legal Department	Pres., Prudential Life Insurance Co., 763 Broad St., Newark, N.J.
Sheehan, William F.	Asst. Examiner	Vice Pres., Franklin Washington Trust Co., Newark, N.J.
Slacks, John W.	President RFC Mortgage Company	E. Leitz, Inc., 304 Hudson St., New York
Smith, Frederick P.	Counsel	Sec. and Dir., Central New York Power Corp., 300 Erie Blvd., W., Syracuse, N.Y.
Snodgrass, R. L.	Ass't Gen. Counsel	Vice Pres., Baltimore & Ohio RR. Co., Baltimore, Md.
Snyder, William H.	Ass't Chief Examining Div.	Vice Pres., Federal Reserve Bank of Chicago
Stephenson, Hugh R.	Admin. Ass't	Vice President, Bowes & Company, Inc., 55 Liberty Street, New York
Stoddard, Howard J.	Examiner	Pres., Michigan National Bank, Lansing
Summers, George C.	Counsel	Attorney, 1625 K St., N.W., Washington, D.C.
Tatlow, Richard H. III	Ass't to Engineer's Advisory Board	Pres., Abbott, Merkt & Co., 10 E. 40th St., New York
Taylor, William	Chicago Agency, RFC	Pres., First Wisconsin National Bank, Milwaukee

Alumnus	*Former RFC Position*	*Present Position*
Telsey, Leon G.	Counsel	Telsey, Lowenthal & Telsey, 55 Liberty St., New York
Throop, Allen E.	Counsel	Shearman & Sterling & Wright, 20 Exchange Pl., New York
Truitt, Max O'Rell	Solicitor	Cummings, Stanley, Truitt, & Cross, 1625 K St., N.W., Washington, D.C.
Tucker, William I.	Examiner	Exec. Vice Pres., New Rochelle Trust Co., New Rochelle, N.Y.
Warner, Paul A.	Examiner	Exec. Vice Pres., Knox County Savings Bank, Mt. Vernon, O.
Weaver, William A.	Treas., Elec. Home and Farm Authority	Pres. and Treas., Arabol Manufacturing Co., 110 E. 42nd St., New York
Weinstein, Walter H.	Special Ass't	Executive Vice Pres., Russeks Fifth Avenue, Inc., New York
Williams, Yates S.	Auditor	Ass't Comptroller, Standard Oil Co. of Indiana, 910 S. Michigan Ave., Chicago
Wilson, J. G.	Asst. Chief Examiner	Pres., First Bank & Trust Co., Perth Amboy, N.J.
Yeager, William B.	Industrial Loan Examiner	Pres. and chairman, Metropolitan Commercial Corp., 545 Fifth Ave., New York
Young, R. D.	Vice Pres., Rubber Reserve Co.	Pres., Rubber Trade Association of New York, 15 William St., New York
Zevely, John G.	Counsel	Gen'l Attorney, American Airlines, 100 E. 42nd St., New York

APPENDIX V

LIST OF SYNTHETIC RUBBER PLANTS

LIST OF DEFENSE HOMES CORPORATION PROPERTIES

RFC DISBURSEMENTS TO BANKS AND TRUST COMPANIES,
1932–1949

SOME BOOM, BUST, AND REVIVAL STOCK PRICES,
1929–1938

RUBBER RESERVE COMPANY

GOVERNMENT-OWNED PLANTS OPERATED IN THE SYNTHETIC RUBBER PROGRAM

Operator	Plant	Product	Approximate Investment June 30, 1945	Operations Commenced
RUBBER PLANTS:				
Goodyear Synthetic Rubber Corp.	Akron, Ohio	GR-S	$ 7,100,000	May 18, 1942
Goodyear Synthetic Rubber Corp.	Houston, Tex.	GR-S	12,800,000	Oct. 26, 1943
Goodyear Synthetic Rubber Corp.	Los Angeles	GR-S	15,000,000	June 15, 1943
United States Rubber Co.	Los Angeles	GR-S		Oct. 13, 1943
United States Rubber Co.	Naugatuck, Conn.	GR-S	7,700,000	Sept. 4, 1942
United States Rubber Co.	Institute, W.Va.	GR-S	17,800,000	Mar. 31, 1943
B. F. Goodrich Co.	Louisville, Ky.	GR-S	10,800,000	Nov. 27, 1943
B. F. Goodrich Co.	Borger, Tex.	GR-S	8,500,000	July 27, 1943
B. F. Goodrich Co.	Port Neches, Tex.	GR-S	30,800,000	Aug. 22, 1943
Firestone Tire & Rubber Co.	Port Neches, Tex.	GR-S		Nov. 28, 1943
Firestone Tire & Rubber Co.	Akron, Ohio	GR-S	6,700,000	Apr. 26, 1942
Firestone Tire & Rubber Co.	Lake Charles, La.	GR-S	12,500,000	Sept. 1, 1943
Copolymer Corp. (1)	Baton Rouge, La.	GR-S	6,800,000	Mar. 31, 1943
General Tire & Rubber Co.	Baytown, Tex.	GR-S	7,700,000	July 21, 1943
National Synthetic Rubber Co. (2)	Louisville, Ky.	GR-S	6,500,000	Sept. 30, 1943
E. I. du Pont de Nemours & Co.	Louisville, Ky.	GR-M (neoprene)	38,400,000	Oct. 1, 1942
Standard Oil Co. of New Jersey	Baton Rouge, La.	GR-I (butyl)	24,900,000	Mar. 6, 1943
Humble Oil & Refining Co.	Baytown, Tex.	GR-I (butyl)	25,600,000	Sept. 10, 1944
E. I. du Pont de Nemours & Co.	Deepwater, N.J.	GR-P (thiokol)	100,000	Nov. 11, 1942
			$239,700,000	
BUTADIENE PLANTS:				
Alcohol base:				
Carbide & Carbon Chemical Corp.	Institute, W.Va.	Butadiene	37,300,000	Jan. 29, 1943
Carbide & Carbon Chemical Corp.	Louisville, Ky.	Butadiene	34,000,000	July 30, 1943
Koppers Co., Inc.	Kabuta, Pa.	Butadiene	60,300,000	June 30, 1943
			$131,600,000	
Petroleum base:				
Phillips Petroleum Co.	Borger, Texas	Butadiene	35,400,000	Sept. 12, 1943
Humble Oil & Refining Co.	Baytown, Texas	Butadiene	18,100,000	Aug. 15, 1943
Humble Oil & Refining Co.	Ingleside, Texas	Butadiene	4,000,000	Oct. 18, 1943
Standard Oil Co. of New Jersey	Baton Rouge, La.	Butadiene	2,800,000	May 22, 1943

RUBBER RESERVE COMPANY PLANTS (Continued)

Operator	Plant	Product	Approximate Investment June 30, 1945	Operations Commenced
Standard Oil Co. of New Jersey	Baton Rouge, La.	Butadiene	$ 1,900,000	Mar. 27, 1943
Cities Service Refining Co.	Lake Charles, La.	Butadiene	16,600,000	July 30, 1943
Neches Butane Products Co. (3)	Port Neches, Texas	Butadiene	54,300,000	Feb. 25, 1944
Shell Union Oil Co.	Torrance, Calif.	Butadiene	19,500,000	July 27, 1943
Sinclair Rubber, Inc.	Houston, Texas	Butadiene	30,000,000	Apr. 23, 1944
Southern California Gas Co.	Los Angeles, Calif.	Butadiene	12,400,000	June 18, 1943
Sun Oil Co.	Toledo, Ohio	Butadiene	7,400,000	June 30, 1943
Lion Oil & Refining Co.	El Dorado, Ark.	Butadiene	2,100,000	Sept. 29, 1943
Taylor Refining Co.	Corpus Christi, Texas	Butadiene	1,900,000	Apr. 4, 1944
Standard Oil Co. of California	El Segundo, Calif.	Butadiene	7,700,000	Jan. 9, 1944
Eastern States Petroleum Co.	Houston, Texas	Butadiene	3,600,000	May 21, 1943
			$223,700,000	
STYRENE PLANTS:				
Carbide & Carbon Chemical Corp.	Institute, W. Va.	Styrene	9,500,000	May 12, 1943
Koppers Co., Inc.	Kabuta, Pa.	Styrene	(see Butadiene plant)	Aug. 22, 1943
Dow Chemical Co.	Los Angeles, Calif.	Styrene	13,800,000	June 14, 1943
Dow Chemical Co.	Velasco, Texas	Styrene	18,100,000	Sept. 14, 1943
Monsanto Chemical Co.	Texas City, Texas	Styrene	18,600,000	Mar. 19, 1943
			$ 60,000,000	
CHEMICAL PLANTS:				
Standard Oil Co. of New Jersey	Baton Rouge, La.	Catalyst	700,000	Dec. 28, 1943
United States Rubber Co.	Naugatuck, Conn.	Catalyst	400,000	Apr. 18, 1943
E. I. du Pont de Nemours & Co.	Newark, N. J.	Silica gel	1,300,000	Jan. 29, 1943
National Carbide Corp.	Ashtabula, Ohio	Calcium carbide	3,100,000	Sept. 1, 1943
National Carbide Corp.	Louisville, Ky.	Acetylene and nitrogen	900,000	Aug. 23, 1943
Q.O. Chemical Co.	Memphis, Tenn.	Furfural	4,300,000	July 17, 1943
Filtros, Inc.	Rochester, N. Y.	Catalyst support (filtres)	200,000	Nov. 16, 1942
Westvaco Chlorine Products Co.	Newark, Calif.	1707 Catalyst	900,000	Oct. 1, 1942
Davison Chemical Corp.	Baltimore, Md.	Silica gel	2,100,000	Dec. 1, 1942
			$ 13,900,000	

MISCELLANEOUS:

Tank cars, pilot plants, canceled and miscellaneous projects 6,100,000

TOTAL APPROXIMATE INVESTMENT, JUNE 30, 1945 .... $677,000,000

DEFENSE HOMES CORPORATION PROPERTIES

Project	Units	Development Cost	Government Investment *	Sale Price *	Gross Profit * from Operation and Sale (— Designates Loss)
Sheffield, Ala.: York Terrace	160 houses	$ 874,650	$ 695,960	$ 831,640	$ 135,680
Jacksonville, Fla.: Riverdale Gardens	164 houses	728,760	665,744	839,698	173,954
Joliet, Ill.: Marquette Gardens	150 houses	1,036,390	815,247	911,527	96,280
Boulder City, Nev.:	{ 60 houses / 26 apts.	409,650	297,164	347,300	50,136
Portsmouth, N.H.: Pannaway Manor	159 houses	772,450	716,880	779,060	62,180
Niagara Falls, N.Y.: Hennepin Manor	150 houses	1,180,735	954,490	983,785	29,295
Massillon, Ohio: Crescent Gardens	200 houses	1,786,830	1,433,925	1,341,070	—92,855
Columbus, Ohio: Colonial Hills & Dales	200 houses	1,365,600	1,272,450	1,298,450	26,000
North Charleston, S.C.: Palmetto Gardens / Eliza Lucas Hall	251 houses / 161 rooms	1,122,950 / 131,250	933,947 / 10,795	1,260,740 / 17,500	326,793 / 6,705
Nashville, Tenn.: Berry Hill Gardens	200 houses	865,860	757,769	881,550	123,781
Corpus Christi, Texas Pineda Park	200 houses	961,790	870,854	1,063,910	193,056
Orange, Texas: Sunset Park	149 houses	$ 601,570	$ 502,271	$ 606,340	$ 104,069

DEFENSE HOMES CORPORATION PROPERTIES (*Continued*)

Project	Units	Development Cost	Government Investment *	Sale Price *	Gross Profit * from Operation and Sale (— Designates Loss)
Newport News, Va.: Stuart Gardens	{479 houses / 501 apts.	3,941,830	3,458,266	3,625,000	166,734
Portsmouth, Va.: Simmonsdale Gardens	150 houses	502,890	328,253	496,310	168,057
Radford, Va.: Monroe Terrace	93 houses	343,180	251,215	311,470	60,255
Falls Church, Va.: Fairfax County	12 houses	90,700	73,812	48,000	—25,812
Bremerton, Wash.: Bremerton Gardens	182 apts.	950,420	585,108	731,020	145,912
Morgantown, W.Va.: Suncrest Park	95 houses	769,210	633,693	598,120	—35,573
Washington, D.C.: Meridian Hill Hotel	637 rooms	1,824,970	893,160	2,775,000	1,881,840
Naylor Gardens	757 apts.	6,607,400	5,546,208	5,125,000	—421,208
McLean Gardens	724 apts.				
Residence Halls	1,185 rooms				
Fairlington	3,439 apts.	46,637,070	37,740,156	42,254,900	4,514,744
Lucy Diggs Slowe Hall	299 rooms	847,500	1,413,961	1,450,000†	39,119
Geo. Washington Carver Hall	181 rooms	602,500	....	....	—3,080
9 tracts of unused land	499 acres	669,300	669,299	625,080	—44,219
TOTALS		$75,625,455	$61,520,627	$69,202,470	$7,681,843
Gross profit from operations and sales					7,681,843
Less Central Office overhead and interest on borrowed money					5,581,843
TOTAL NET PROFIT					$2,100,000

[613]

* Approximate.
† Book value of Lucy Diggs Slowe Hall and George Washington Carver Hall, which were transferred to Howard University on June 30, 1948, by authorization of Public Law 796, signed by President Truman on June 28, 1948.

RECONSTRUCTION FINANCE CORPORATION
DISBURSEMENTS TO BANKS AND TRUST COMPANIES
FEBRUARY 2, 1932, TO DECEMBER 31, 1949

	Loans to Aid in the Reorganization or Liquidation of Closed Banks	Loans to Open Banks	Investment in Preferred Stock, Capital Notes, and Debentures	Total Open Banks	Grand Total
Alabama	$ 3,195,442.37	$ 6,905,558.62	$ 16,203,575.00	$ 23,109,133.62	$ 26,304,575.99
Arizona	279,701.73	1,594,550.00	2,430,000.00	4,024,550.00	4,304,251.73
Arkansas	7,012,263.07	14,959,064.89	4,465,000.00	19,424,064.89	26,436,327.96
California	14,167,039.16	105,712,260.00	96,029,225.00	201,741,485.00	215,908,524.16
Colorado	1,497,478.87	2,883,137.82	4,893,500.00	7,776,637.82	9,274,116.69
Connecticut	2,655,765.52	14,772,748.66	7,192,126.00	21,964,874.66	24,620,640.18
Delaware		249,000.00	567,300.00	816,300.00	816,300.00
Florida	3,078,559.97	1,942,655.08	2,201,200.00	4,143,855.08	7,222,415.05
Georgia	2,952,127.06	7,336,472.56	4,835,500.00	12,171,972.56	15,124,099.62
Idaho	3,264,193.27	1,993,929.60	2,130,000.00	4,123,929.60	7,388,122.87
Illinois	47,526,362.71	138,557,267.59	92,121,114.17	230,678,381.76	278,204,744.47
Indiana	20,325,674.54	18,085,280.59	16,966,250.00	35,051,530.59	55,377,205.13
Iowa	15,388,970.18	39,085,936.08	10,263,000.00	49,348,936.08	64,737,906.26
Kansas	2,502,412.56	4,493,533.24	5,272,750.00	9,766,283.24	12,268,695.80
Kentucky	7,309,814.84	10,019,574.45	9,079,850.00	19,099,424.45	26,409,239.29
Louisiana	45,877,607.81	50,266,816.19	15,547,000.00	65,813,816.19	111,691,424.00
Maine	39,507,925.34	14,438,954.47	9,125,500.00	23,564,454.47	63,072,379.81
Maryland	11,438,298.47	45,677,362.37	9,348,170.00	55,025,532.37	66,463,830.84
Massachusetts	30,634,737.78	29,049,257.19	16,674,200.00	45,723,457.19	76,358,194.97
Michigan	315,013,435.49	80,645,969.73	40,850,261.00	121,496,230.73	436,509,666.22
Minnesota	2,826,687.41	7,507,256.31	17,668,525.00	25,175,781.31	28,002,468.72
Mississippi	5,964,957.99	9,882,673.18	14,720,630.00	24,603,303.18	30,568,261.17
Missouri	13,229,021.83	27,623,562.74	21,034,925.00	48,658,487.74	61,887,509.57
Montana	908,579.23	1,806,534.24	4,035,500.00	5,842,034.24	6,750,613.47
Nebraska	2,858,658.07	3,720,856.33	8,693,550.00	12,414,406.33	15,273,064.40

	Loans to Aid in the Reorganization or Liquidation of Closed Banks	Loans to Open Banks	Investment in Preferred Stock, Capital Notes, and Debentures	Total Open Banks	Grand Total
Nevada	2,471,965.58	4,923,667.17	205,000.00	5,128,667.17	7,600,632.75
New Hampshire	460,402.31	977,457.77	786,635.00	1,764,092.77	2,224,495.08
New Jersey	21,054,567.17	52,816,972.35	96,711,516.07	149,528,488.42	170,583,055.59
New Mexico	739,319.92	675,677.36	715,000.00	1,390,677.36	2,129,997.28
New York	47,644,752.62	52,731,140.61	338,502,654.16	391,233,794.77	438,878,547.39
North Carolina	8,777,494.53	20,244,302.07	7,488,500.00	27,732,802.07	36,510,296.60
North Dakota	1,709,348.18	5,423,851.85	4,044,500.00	9,468,351.85	11,177,700.03
Ohio	188,691,806.51	99,569,370.13	94,007,237.00	193,576,607.13	382,268,413.64
Oklahoma	1,600,352.42	2,017,519.30	10,944,000.00	12,961,519.30	14,561,871.72
Oregon	3,281,029.86	5,019,070.34	1,950,000.00	6,969,070.34	10,250,100.20
Pennsylvania	85,190,986.30	81,676,160.94	46,029,226.50	127,705,387.44	212,896,373.74
Rhode Island	1,156,070.50	495,625.00	898,500.00	1,394,125.00	2,550,195.50
South Carolina	7,988,924.22	12,865,230.99	2,911,800.00	15,777,030.99	23,765,955.21
South Dakota	1,443,515.21	2,830,955.59	4,438,100.00	7,269,055.59	8,712,570.80
Tennessee	16,656,805.90	50,003,978.93	12,559,050.00	62,563,028.93	79,219,834.83
Texas	11,084,957.67	20,978,372.15	31,424,125.00	52,402,497.15	63,487,454.82
Utah	2,264,173.37	4,589,281.69	4,045,000.00	8,634,281.69	10,898,455.06
Vermont	1,064,999.29	8,030,807.57	17,295,000.00	25,325,807.57	26,390,806.86
Virginia	6,195,981.79	10,773,837.20	10,944,650.00	21,718,487.20	27,914,468.99
Washington	19,758,179.51	9,910,379.99	6,514,500.00	16,424,879.99	36,183,059.50
West Virginia	9,910,379.51	11,493,975.76	6,461,066.66	17,955,042.42	27,865,421.93
Wisconsin	7,468,420.89	23,940,964.50	33,660,600.00	57,601,564.50	65,069,985.39
Wyoming	....	1,196,532.89	1,367,500.00	2,564,032.89	2,564,032.89
Alaska	....	100,000.00	37,500.00	137,500.00	137,500.00
District of Columbia	14,127,392.96	14,075,072.44	2,900,000.00	16,975,072.44	31,102,465.40
Hawaii	....	835,897.00	....	835,897.00	835,897.00
Puerto Rico	....	845,305.75	1,250,000.00	2,095,305.75	2,095,305.75
Virgin Islands	....	....	125,000.00	125,000.00	125,000.00
TOTAL	$1,060,157,541.49	$1,138,251,619.27	$1,170,565,311.56	$2,308,816,930.83	$3,368,974,472.32

SOME BOOM, BUST, AND REVIVAL STOCK PRICES

	1929		1930		1931		1932		1933	
	High	*Low*	*High*	*Low*	*High*	*Low*	*High*	*Low*	*High*	*Low*
American Telephone & Telegraph	310¼	193¼	274¼	170⅜	201¾	112⅛	137⅜	70¼	134¾	86½
New York Central R.R.	256½	160	192¾	105⅛	132¼	24⅞	36⅝	8¾	58½	14
Pennsylvania R.R.	110	72½	86⅝	53	64	16¼	23⅜	6½	42¼	13¾
Missouri Pacific R.R.	101⅜	46	98½	20⅜	42¾	6⅝	11	1½	10¼	1⅛
Chicago, Rock Island & Pacific R.R.	143½	101	125⅛	45¼	65½	7⅞	16⅜	1½	10⅛	2
St. Louis-San Francisco Ry.	133¾	101	118⅞	39¾	62¾	3	6⅝	⅝	9	⅞
General Motors	91¾	33½	54¼	31½	48	21⅜	24⅝	7⅝	35¾	10
Baltimore & Ohio R.R.	145⅛	105	122⅜	55⅜	87⅞	14	21⅜	3¾	37⅞	8¼
Illinois Central R.R.	153½	116	136¾	65¾	89	9⅛	24⅞	4¾	50¾	8½
Erie R.R.	93½	41½	63¾	22½	39¾	5	11¾	2	25¾	3¾
Southern Pacific R.R.	157½	105	127	88	109½	26½	37⅝	6½	38¾	11⅛
Southern Ry. Co.	162⅛	109	134¾	46½	65⅞	6⅜	18½	2½	36	4⅛
Great Northern Ry.	128¼	85¼	102	51	69¼	15⅝	25	5½	33¾	4⅝
Colorado & Southern Ry.	135	86¼	95	40⅛	48	7½	29½	4½	51	15¼
Chase National Bank (N.Y.)	285	135	180	15⅛	110	24¾	48	19	38⅞	15¾
National City Bank (N.Y.)	[a] 585	[a] 180	260	79	108	46⅛	64½	23¼	46⅛	16⅜
Manufacturers Trust Co. (N.Y.)	* 360	92	* 152	25	* 54	27¼	† 36¼	15⅛	† 31½	10½
Continental Illinois Bk. & Tr.	1040	635	778	360	416	115	147	55	97½	18¾
First National Bank (Chicago)	1290	640	830	460	541	215	254	129	176	52

[a] Represented by $20 par stock. Previous years, $100 par stock.
[b] Before stock dividend paid in that year.
[c] After stock dividend paid in that year.
* $25 par.
† $20 par.

SOME BOOM, BUST, AND REVIVAL STOCK PRICES (*Continued*)

	1934		1935		1936		1937		1938	
	High	*Low*	*High*	*Low*	*High*	*Low*	*High*	*Low*	*High*	*Low*
American Telephone & Telegraph	125¼	100⅛	160⅛	98⅞	190⅛	149½	187	140	150¼	111
New York Central R.R.	45¼	18⅜	29¾	12¼	49⅝	27¾	55¼	15⅛	21¾	10
Pennsylvania R.R.	37⅞	20⅛	32½	17¼	45	28¼	50¼	20	24½	14⅛
Missouri Pacific R.R.	6	1½	3	1	4	2⅛	6¼	1¼	2⅜	½
Chicago, Rock Island & Pacific R.R.	6¼	1⅜	2⅝	¾	3	1½	3⅝	¾	1¼	¼
St. Louis-San Francisco Ry.	4⅝	1½	2	¾	3⅝	1½	4¾	1	1⅜	⅜
General Motors	42	24⅝	59⅜	26⅝	77	53⅞	70½	28⅝	53⅞	25½
Baltimore & Ohio R.R.	34½	12¾	18	7½	26½	15⅞	40½	8⅛	11	4
Illinois Central R.R.	38⅞	13⅝	22¼	9⅛	29½	18⅝	38	8	20⅞	6⅛
Erie R.R.	24⅞	9⅜	14	7⅛	18¼	11	23⅝	4¼	6¼	1½
Southern Pacific R.R.	33¾	14⅞	25½	12¾	47⅞	23½	65⅜	17	22⅛	9¼
Southern Ry. Co.	36½	11½	16½	5½	26½	12¾	43⅜	9	23⅜	5½
Great Northern Ry.	32½	11⅝	35⅓	9⅝	46⅜	32¼	56¾	20½	30⅝	12⅜
Colorado & Southern Ry.	40⅜	16⅝	22½	10¾	36¼	19	27¼	5	8¾	3¼
Chase National Bank (N.Y.)	32⅜	19¼	42	20¼	50	34	63½	28¾	34½	24¼
National City Bank (N.Y.)	32	19	39	18¼	45	31	59½	24½	28½	19½
Manufacturers Trust Co. (N.Y.)	† 23½	14¾	† 46½	19	† 54	42½	† 69	31½	† 40½	27¼
Continental Illinois Bk. & Tr.	60	24	133	35	{ c 201½ { b 181	127 119½	c 187 b 224	60 193	c 90 b 114	47 86
First National Bank (Chicago)	135	78	220	77½	309	216½	393	172	236	148

[a] Represented by $20 par stock. Previous years, $100 par stock.
[b] Before stock dividend paid in that year.
[c] After stock dividend paid in that year.
* $25 par.
† $20 par.

INDEX

---- ☼ ----

17837